OURSELVES AMONG OTHERS

---

*Cross-Cultural Readings
for Writers*

Second Edition

BY

Carol J. Verburg

Bedford Books *of* St. Martin's Press · Boston

Dedicated to the memory of my parents,
Robert M. and Jane H. Verburg

For Bedford Books
Publisher: Charles H. Christensen
Associate Publisher: Joan E. Feinberg
Managing Editor: Elizabeth M. Schaaf
Developmental Editor: Karen S. Henry
Production Editor: Deborah Liehs
Copyeditor: Susan M. S. Brown
Text Design: Anna Post-George
Cover Design: Hannus Design Associates
Cover Art: Jacob Lawrence, *University*, 1977. Collection of Gabrielle and Herbert Kayden.
Cover Photograph: Paul Macapia, Seattle Art Museum. Through the courtesy of Francine Seders Gallery.
Map Design: Richard D. Pusey

Manufactured in the United States of America.
5   4   3   2   1   0
f   e   d   c   b   a

For information, write: St. Martin's Press, Inc.
175 Fifth Avenue, New York, NY 10010

Editorial Offices: Bedford Books *of* St. Martin's Press
29 Winchester Street, Boston, MA 02116

ISBN: 0–312–03468–7

ACKNOWLEDGMENTS

David Abram, "Making Magic," *Parabola*, August 1982. Reprinted by permission of the author.
Chinua Achebe, "Civil Peace" from *Girls at War and Other Stories* by Chinua Achebe, copyright © 1972, 1973 by Chinua Achebe. Used by permission of Doubleday, a division of Bantam Doubleday Dell Publishing Group, Inc.

Acknowledgments and copyrights are continued at the back of the book on pages 692–696, which constitute an extension of the copyright page.

PREFACE

Every year, the case for a cross-cultural composition reader becomes more compelling. Daily papers and nightly newscasts remind us how interdependent we in the United States are with our worldwide neighbors. Look at recent upheavals in Europe, the Soviet Union, the Persian Gulf, South Africa, or Central America and you see urgent reasons for encouraging college students to become better informed about our "global village." The aims of *Ourselves Among Others* include giving readers in this country information to use in writing about the larger world and introducing them to the craft, imagination, and social consciousness of the best current foreign writers. Yet even to say "foreign" is to remind oneself that many students have roots, experience, or both outside the United States. For them, *Ourselves Among Others* offers recognition, a chance to utilize knowledge that is too often undervalued or ignored.

As you'll see from the table of contents, *Ourselves Among Others* consists of seven thematic parts comprising essays from all rhetorical categories, a few interviews and news reports, and over a dozen short stories. (For an overview of each part's theme and components, see the introduction on its opening page.) Unlike most books featuring international writers, this one emphasizes insider accounts: pieces that depict a culture from within rather than from the "objective" viewpoint of a Western visitor. The authors are of both literary and political importance: Václav Havel, Nadine Gordimer, Nelson Mandela, Benazir Bhutto, Mikhail Gorbachev, Simone de Beauvoir, Gabriel García Márquez. Each part also includes at least one selection from and about the United States, by writers representing a range of subcultures: Ishmael Reed, Leslie Marmon Silko, Amy Tan, John Updike. These full-length pieces augment each unit's opening section, *Looking at Ourselves*, a collection of shorter observations on the unit's topic by U.S. writers.

The second edition has three significant changes from the first. First are the full-length pieces representing "ourselves" in each part of the book. Second are the thirty-three new selections in this edition, many of them highlighting recent political events around the world: the liberation of Eastern Europe, the reorganization of the Soviet Union, apartheid and tribal warfare in South Africa, the drug trade in Colombia, the Palestinian uprising, the Tiananmen Square massacre and its aftermath, the Troubles in Northern Ireland. The third innovation is a new opening unit, "The West and the World," in which writers from around the globe comment on the nature and the phenomenally powerful worldwide influence of U.S. and Western culture.

To help students and instructors place each selection in context, extensive headnotes provide geographic, political, and historical background, as well as a biographical introduction to the author. A world map inside the book's back cover provides additional visual assistance. Three types of questions follow each piece: *Explorations*, which focus on content and craft; *Connections*, which link this essay or story to others in the book; and *Elaborations*, which guide students' writing in response to the selection. A note on translations (p. xv) compares three renderings from Farsi into English of the opening paragraph of Gholam-Hossein Sa'edi's story "The Game Is Over," demonstrating some of the obstacles to cross-cultural comprehension. An appendix (p. 690) provides supplementary information on the European Community, NATO, and the Warsaw Pact.

The comprehensive instructor's manual, prepared by two veteran composition instructors and users of the first edition of *Ourselves Among Others*, is now bound with the book in an Instructor's Edition. My thanks to Kathleen Shine Cain of Merrimack College and Marilyn Rye of Rutgers University for their excellent work. *Resources for Teaching Ourselves Among Others* offers practical advice on launching the course, sample syllabi, suggestions for teaching each selection, suggested answers for the Explorations and Connections questions in the text, a rhetorical index to the selections, a chart listing rhetorical writing assignments, an index to headnote information, and a list of audiovisual resources.

Acknowledgments

My thanks to the following instructors, who answered a detailed questionnaire about the first edition of the book, for their help in shaping this second edition: Curtis J. Adler, University of North Carolina, Chapel Hill; Helen Aron, Union County College; Rebecca Bennet, Broome Community College; John Benvenuto, Westfield State College; Keith Beyer, Northwest Community College; Daniel J. Brooks, State University of New York, Binghamton; Mary Casper, West Valley College; Sylvia Charshoodian, Boston University; Cheryl Christian, University of Texas, Austin; Juan Delgado, California State University, San Bernardino; Steven Dolgin, Oakton Community College; Ann Fields, University of North Carolina, Chapel Hill; Cheryl Fish, Hunter College; Peggy J. Hailey, Rutgers University, Newark; Marcia Peoples Halio, University of Delaware, Newark; Jan A. Geesaman, College of DuPage; Nancy Gerber, Rutgers University, Newark; Ramola S. Gereben, University of San Francisco; Angela Ingram, Southwest Texas State University; Madelyn Jablon, Clarion University; Valerie Kent, Eckerd College; Gloria Lustig, The City College; Sheng-mei Ma, Indiana University, Bloomington; Sara W. McAulay, California State University, Hayward; Gary Mitchner, Sinclair Community College; A. Pecastaings, Tufts University; Kathleen Pfeiffer, Brandeis University; Diane Quantic, Wichita State University; Sally Raines, West Virginia University; Timothy Roufs; University of Minnesota; Sara Schuyler, University of Washington; Joan G. Silberman, Rockland Community College; Dorothy Stephens, University of California, Berkeley; Carole Stone, Montclair State College; Mary Ann Trevathan, California Polytechnic State University; Lynn Tullis, University of Oregon; Karen Welch, University of Wisconsin, Eau Claire; John O. White, California State University, Fullerton; and Sandra R. Woods, West Virginia University.

Essential to the creation of *Ourselves Among Others*, Second Edition, were the staff of Bedford Books. Publisher Chuck Christensen continues to be a strong supporter of useful and innovative textbooks. My editor, Karen S. Henry, also a writer, supplied endless patience and imagination to the revision. Beth Castrodale utilized her talents as a journalist to track down information for headnotes. Ellen Kuhl assisted with research and manuscript preparation. Kim Chabot helped to pull together the instructor's manual and to keep the book on track. Thanks also to Deborah Liehs, production editor, Susan M. S. Brown, copyeditor, and Maria Maimone, permissions editor. Freelance writer Shirley Taggart also helped me with headnote research.

Thanks most of all to the worldwide writers represented in *Ourselves Among Others*, many of whom make their creative contributions under harsher conditions than most of us in the United States can appreciate.

CONTENTS

5. WORK: *We Are What We Do* 395

A NOTE
ON TRANSLATIONS

The three excerpts that follow come from different English translations of the same Iranian short story, originally written in Farsi. As you compare them, keep an eye out for differences and also for unexpected similarities. What do you learn from these passages about the choices a translator must make?

1

Hasani himself told me. He said, "Let's go over to my place tonight." I'd never been to their place, nor had he to mine; that is, I'd always been too afraid of what my father would do to ask him over, and he, he too, feared his father. But that night being unlike other nights, I couldn't get out of it; Hasani was mad at me, he imagined I no longer liked him, I wasn't his friend — so I went; it was the first time I had set foot in his place. We always ran into each other outdoors; mornings I would go by his little shanty and would whistle loud like a bulbul,[1] with a pretty bulbul's whistle that he himself had taught me. And so, it was as if I had whistled, "Come on, Hasani, it's time to get going." Hasani would pick up a can and come out. Instead of saying Hi, we would box with each other a bit, with firm, respectable punches that hurt. So had we arranged — whenever we would see each other, whenever we would part, we would box. Unless we were angry with one another, or we had cheated each other.

> – "The Game Is Over"
> Gholamhosein Saedi
> Translated by Robert A. Campbell (1978)

---

[1]A Persian songbird, probably a nightingale, frequently mentioned in poetry. — ED.

2

Hasani himself asked me. He asked me to go to their hut that evening. I had never gone to their hut. He had never come to ours. I'd never asked him to, because I was scared of my pa. He was scared of his pa, too — a lot more than I was of mine. But that evening was different. I had to go. Hasani would feel hurt and get angry at me if I didn't. He would think I didn't like him anymore and wasn't his friend. That's why I went. That was the first time I set foot in their hut. We always met outside. Our huts were in a cluster of squatters' huts. I'd stop by their hut in the morning and whistle — a pretty whistle he had taught me. This was our signal. It was like saying, "Come Hasani! Time to go to work." Hasani would pick up his bucket and come out of the hut. Instead of saying hello, we would fistfight for a spell — nice, hard blows that hurt really good. We fistfought when we met, and we fistfought when we parted — except when we were mad at each other for some reason.

> – "The Game Is Up"
> Ghulamhusayn Sa'idi
> Translated by Minoo S. Southgate (1980)

3

Hasani said it to me himself: "Let's go over to my place tonight." I'd never been to their place. He'd never been to mine. What I'm getting at is, we were always too afraid of our fathers. He was a lot more afraid than I was. But that night it was different: Hasani was mad at me. He imagined that I didn't like him anymore, that I wasn't his friend. So we went. Usually we just met each other outside. In the morning I would go to their little shack and give a long-drawn-out whistle that Hasani had taught me. When I whistled, Hasani would grab a can and come out. Instead of saying "Hi," we would fight a little. We would hit each other hard so it hurt. That's how we'd decided to behave, and whenever we met, or whenever we left each other, we would fight like that — unless we were either angry or had tricked each other.

> – "The Game Is Over"
> Gholam-Hossein Sa'edi
> Translated by Robert Campbell (1981)

What structural differences do you notice in these three translations?

What contrasts in emphasis can you identify? What ideas are condensed in one version and spelled out in another?

Which passages in each one do you think are more successful than in the other two? Which translation do you like best and why?

PART ONE

THE WEST
AND THE WORLD

"OH, EAST IS EAST, AND WEST IS WEST, AND NEVER THE TWAIN SHALL meet," wrote Rudyard Kipling in 1889. *East* for Kipling and his fellow Britons meant colonies such as India, Egypt, and Hong Kong. *West* was home — Europe, England, the hub of civilization.

Now, most European colonies are independent nations. Indeed, one former colony — the United States — epitomizes the West. As expanding political, economic, technological, and even recreational networks shrink the globe, Westerners can no longer cling to the old fantasy that we define civilization. Instead, we are discovering that every culture has something to teach us. Yet our first response to foreign customs and ideas may not be appreciation but alienation. Like us, the people we meet take their superiority for granted. To most of the world's inhabitants, we, not they, are the foreigners.

Part One looks at the West in general and the United States in particular, first from the inside and then from various viewpoints around the globe. In "What's American about America?" Ishmael Reed holds up a mirror: Is the United States a melting pot, where diverse traditions blend into one, or a "cultural bouillabaisse," in which each ingredient contributes a distinct flavor? Octavio Paz turns flavor into a political metaphor, casting an ironic eye northward from Mexico in "Hygiene and Repression." Raymonde Carroll's "Money and Seduction" outlines an equally fascinating contrast between her native country — France and the United States. In "Proxemics in the Arab World," Edward T. Hall explains why Arabs and Americans consider each other pushy. The South African writer Ezekiel Mphahlele looks inward at the tension created by contrasting cultural pressures in "Tradition and the African Writer." An overall assessment of the West's impact on other countries is offered by Paul Harrison in "The Westernization of the World." V. S. Naipaul, a native of Trinidad, watches the balance tilt between the Ivory Coast's African heritage and its French colonial legacy in "Entering the New World." James Fallows takes a different slant in "A Few Pointers," suggesting that today's Westerners ought to study the recent economic progress of such Eastern nations as Japan and Korea. A noteworthy Eastern perspective comes from Soviet President Mikhail Gorbachev, whose "The US and the USSR" explores the mistrust and mutual dependence between these two superpowers. Finally, in "Meeting the Gorbachevs," Joyce Carol Oates gives a personal, often humorous account of a Soviet reception for American intellectuals and artists. ◈

ISHMAEL REED

What's American about America?

The black American novelist, poet, editor, and essayist Ishmael Reed (who also uses the pseudonym Emmett Coleman) was born in 1938 in Chattanooga, Tennessee. Known for his satiric wit, Reed abolishes time and rearranges history in his novels to create and revive a special kind of black folklore that includes magic and voodoo. With the aesthetic he calls "Neo-HooDoo" he has parodied genre fiction such as westerns (*Yellow Back Radio Broke Down*, 1969) and mysteries (*Mumbo Jumbo*, 1972 and *The Last Days of Louisiana Red*, 1974). *Flight to Canada* (1976) is a farcical treatment of slavery. Besides publishing several volumes of poetry and essays on black culture, Reed has produced a video soap opera and founded a publishing company devoted to the work of unknown ethnic artists. Reed is currently a senior lecturer at the University of California, Berkeley. "What's American about America?" is reprinted from the March-April 1989 Utne Reader. A longer version originally appeared in Reed's *Writin' Is Fightin'* (1983).

As Reed suggests in this essay, the United States is not the WASP (white Anglo-Saxon Protestant) society of Norman Rockwell paintings. Indeed, white Americans may become a minority in the twenty-first century. Census statistics show that already one out of four Americans is nonwhite or Hispanic. Immigration and birth rates indicate that by the year 2000, the collective population of Hispanics, Asians, and blacks will have doubled, while the white population will have increased by only a few percent. In some parts of the country — California schools, for example — a nonwhite majority is already a reality. As more and more Americans recognize the diversity of our population and heritage, questions such as What language do we speak? What holidays do we observe? and Who are our heroes? challenge the Anglo-Saxon bias in our culture.

An item from the *New York Times*, June 23, 1983: "At the annual Lower East Side Jewish Festival yesterday, a Chinese woman ate a pizza slice in front of Ty Thuan Duc's Vietnamese grocery store. Beside her a Spanish-speaking family patronized a cart with two signs: 'Italian Ices' and 'Kosher by Rabbi Alper.' And after the pastrami ran out, everybody ate knishes."

On the day before Memorial Day, 1983, a poet called me to describe a city he had just visited. He said that one section included mosques, built by the Islamic people who dwelled there. Attending his reading, he said, were large numbers of Hispanic people, 40,000 of whom lived in the same city. He was not talking about a fabled city located in some mysterous region of the world. The city he'd visited was Detroit.

A few months before, as I was visiting Texas, I heard the taped voice used to guide passengers to their connections at the Dallas Airport announcing items in both Spanish and English. This trend is likely to continue; after all, for some southwestern states like Texas, where the largest minority is now Mexican-American, Spanish was the first written language and the Spanish style lives on in the western way of live.

Shortly after my Texas trip, I sat in a campus auditorium at the   4
University of Wisconsin at Milwaukee as a Yale professor — whose original work on the influence of African cultures upon those of the Americas has led to his ostracism from some intellectual circles — walked up and down the aisle like an old-time Southern evangelist, dancing and drumming the top of the lectern, illustrating his points before some Afro-American intellectuals and artists who cheered and applauded his performance. The professor was "white." After his lecture, he conversed with a group of Milwaukeeans — all who spoke Yoruban, though only the professor had ever traveled to Africa.

One of the artists there told me that his paintings, which included African and Afro-American mythological symbols and imagery, were hanging in the local McDonald's restaurant. The next day I went to McDonald's and snapped pictures of smiling youngsters eating hamburgers below paintings that could grace the walls of any of the country's leading museums. The manager of the local McDonald's said, "I don't know what you boys are doing, but I like it," as he commissioned the local painters to exhibit in his restaurant.

Such blurring of cultural styles occurs in everyday life in the United States to a greater extent than anyone can imagine. The result is what the above-mentioned Yale professor, Robert Thompson, referred to as a cultural bouillabaisse. Yet members of the nation's present educational and cultural elect still cling to the notion that the United States belongs to some vaguely defined entity they refer to as "Western civilization," by which they mean, presumably, a civilization created by people of Europe, as if Europe can even be viewed in monolithic terms. Is Beethoven's Ninth Symphony, which includes Turkish marches, a part of Western

civilization? Or the late-nineteenth- and twentieth-century French paintings, whose creators were influenced by Japanese art? And what of the
cubists, through whom the influence of African art changed modern
painting? Or the surrealists, who were so impressed with the art of the
Pacific Northwest Indians that, in their map of North America, Alaska
dwarfs the lower forty-eight states in size?

Are the Russians, who are often criticized for their adoption of "Western" ways by Tsarist dissidents in exile, members of Western civilization?
And what of the millions of Europeans who have black African and Asian
ancestry, black Africans having occupied several European countries for
hundreds of years? Are these "Europeans" a part of Western civilization?
Or the Hungarians, who originated across the Urals in a place called
Greater Hungary? Or the Irish, who came from the Iberian Peninsula?

Even the notion that North America is part of Western civilization   8
because our "system of government" is derived from Europe is being
challenged by Native American historians who say that the founding
fathers, Benjamin Franklin especially, were actually influenced by the
system of government that had been adopted by the Iroquois hundreds
of years prior to the arrival of Europeans.

Western civilization, then, becomes another confusing category —
like Third World, or Judeo-Christian culture — as humanity attempts to
impose its small-screen view of political and cultural reality upon a
complex world. Our most publicized novelist recently said that Western
civilization was the greatest achievement of mankind — an attitude that
flourishes on the street level as scribbles in public restrooms: "White
Power," "Niggers and Spics Suck," or "Hitler was a prophet." Where did
such an attitude, which has caused so much misery and depression in
our national life, which has tainted even our noblest achievements,
begin? An attitude that caused the incarceration of Japanese-American
citizens during World War II, the persecution of Chicanos and Chinese
Americans, the near-extermination of the Indians, and the murder and
lynchings of thousands of Afro-Americans.

The Puritans of New England are idealized in our schoolbooks as the
first Americans, "a hardy band" of no-nonsense patriarchs whose discipline razed the forest and brought order to the New World (a term that
annoys Native American historians). Industrious, responsible, it was their
"Yankee ingenuity" and practicality that created the work ethic.

The Puritans, however, had a mean streak. They hated the theater
and banned Christmas. They punished people in a cruel and inhuman
manner. They killed children who disobeyed their parents. They exter-

minated the Indians, who had taught them how to survive in a world unknown to them. And their encounter with calypso culture, in the form of a servant from Barbados working in a Salem minister's household, resulted in the witchcraft hysteria.

The Puritan legacy of hard work and meticulous accounting led to the   12 establishment of a great industrial society, but there was the other side — the strange and paranoid attitudes of that society toward those different from the elect.

The cultural attitudes of that early elect continue to be voiced in everyday life in the United States; the president of a distinguished university, writing a letter to the *Times*, belittling the study of African civilizations; the television network that promoted its show on the Vatican art with the boast that this art represented "the finest achievements of the human spirit."

When I heard a schoolteacher warn the other night about the invasion of the American educational system by foreign curricula, I wanted to yell at the television set, "Lady, they're already here." It has already begun because the world is here. The world has been arriving at these shores for at least 10,000 years from Europe, Africa, and Asia. In the late nineteenth and early twentieth centuries, large numbers of Europeans arrived, adding their cultures to those of the European, African, and Asian settlers who were already here, and recently millions have been entering the country from South American and the Caribbean, making Robert Thompson's bouillabaisse richer and thicker.

North America deserves a more exciting destiny than as a repository of "Western civilization." We can become a place where the cultures of the world crisscross. This is possible because the United States and Canada are unique in the world: The world is here.

EXPLORATIONS

1. What is a "cultural bouillabaisse" (para. 6)? How does this image of the United States differ from the frequently cited "melting pot"?

2. How many continents are represented in Reed's essay? Which ones include countries that are generally considered part of Western civilization? Which of the world's continents are generally considered non-Western?

3. What is the thesis of this essay? What recommendations does Reed make, and to whom?

CONNECTIONS

1. Look at Paul Harrison's "The Westernization of the World" (p. 40). Harrison describes Western culture spreading around the world as overwhelming traditional local customs and values. What cause and effect relationship, if any, exists between the westernization of the world and the "cultural bouillabaisse" Ishmael Reed describes in the United States? How do you think the world's growing uniformity and the United States' diversity are likely to affect each other in the future?

2. Ishmael Reed is optimistic about the United States' future as "a place where the cultures of the world crisscross" (para. 15). In "A Few Pointers" (p. 52), James Fallows voices concerns about the United States losing its competitive edge in the world to Asian countries that are less culturally diverse. Given the concerns Fallows mentions, what do you think are the advantages and dangers to the United States of becoming a cultural crossroads?

ELABORATIONS

1. Write a comparison-contrast essay explaining these two concepts of the United States: a melting pot and a cultural bouillabaisse. What are the key differences between these concepts? Which one do you think we as Americans should work to make a reality, and why?

2. Paragraphs 6 and 7 of Reed's essay consist mainly of questions. Starting with a thesis similar (or contrary) to Reed's, write a classification essay in which you answer each of these questions and explain the reasons for your answer.

OCTAVIO PAZ

Hygiene and Repression

Although Octavio Paz is represented here by an essay, he is also known for his fiction and most of all for his poetry. "Poetic activity is revolutionary by nature," he has written, "a means of interior liberation." Paz was born in Mexico City in 1914. Educated at a Roman Catholic school and the National University of Mexico, he published his first book of poems at nineteen. Four years later he went to Europe, where he supported the Republican side in the Spanish Civil War, established himself as a writer with another book of poems, and met prominent Surrealist poets in Paris. Back in Mexico he founded and edited several literary reviews and produced his famous study of Mexican character and culture, "The Labyrinth of Solitude" (1950). After working for the Mexican embassy in Japan, Paz served as Mexico's ambassador to India from 1962 to 1968, resigning over Mexico's brutal treatment of student radicals. He has also lived in England, France, and the United States, where he taught at Harvard University and at the University of Texas. "Hygiene and Repression" comes from "At Table and in Bed," which he wrote at Harvard in 1971. Translated from the Spanish by Helen R. Lane, the essay appears in Paz's 1987 collection *Convergences: Essays on Art and Literature.* In 1990 Paz won the Nobel Prize for literature.

The United States' neighbor to the south has been populated since around 21,000 B.C. The great Olmec, Toltec, Mayan, and Aztec civilizations arose between A.D. 100 and A.D. 900. When Hernán Cortés and other explorers arrived from Spain in the 1500s, they conquered the ruling Aztecs and made Mexico a heavily exploited colony until a series of rebellions achieved independence in 1823. While democracy has persisted, reform has progressed haltingly. After an oil boom in the 1970s, Mexico's economy declined; most of the rural and much of the urban population remains poor, so many workers seek jobs across the northern border. Recently Mexico's economy has been improving, after years of stagnation, as wages, job opportunities, and exports increase. Meanwhile, both folk art and fine art have burgeoned: Writers such as Paz and Carlos Fuentes are internationally regarded, as are a number of Mexican painters, composers, and other artists.

Traditional American cooking is a cuisine without mystery: simple, nourishing, scantily seasoned foods. No tricks: a carrot is a homely, honest carrot, a potato is not ashamed of its humble condition, and a steak is a big, bloody hunk of meat. This is a transubstantiation of the democratic virtues of the Founding Fathers: a plain meal, one dish following another like the sensible, unaffected sentences of a virtuous discourse. Like the conversation among those at table, the relation between substances and flavors is direct: sauces that mask tastes, garnishes that entice the eye, condiments that confuse the taste buds are taboo. The separation of one food from another is analogous to the reserve that characterizes the relations between sexes, races, and classes. In our countries food is communion, not only between those together at table but between ingredients; Yankee food, impregnated with Puritanism, is based on exclusions. The maniacal preoccupation with the purity and origin of food products has its counterpart in racism and exclusivism. The American contradiction — a democratic universalism based on ethnic, cultural, religious, and sexual exclusions — is reflected in its cuisine. In this culinary tradition our fondness for dark, passionate stews such as moles, for thick and sumptuous red, green, and yellow sauces, would be scandalous, as would be the choice place at our table of *huitlacoche,* which not only is made from diseased young maize but is black in color. Likewise our love for hot peppers, ranging from parakeet green to ecclesiastical purple, and for ears of Indian corn, their grains varying from golden yellow to midnight blue. Colors as violent as their tastes. Americans adore fresh, delicate colors and flavors. Their cuisine is like watercolor painting or pastels.

American cooking shuns spices as it shuns the devil, but it wallows in slews of cream and butter. Orgies of sugar. Complementary opposites: the almost apostolic simplicity and soberness of lunch, in stark contrast to the suspiciously innocent, pregenital pleasures of ice cream and milkshakes. Two poles: the glass of milk and the glass of whiskey. The first affirms the primacy of home and mother. The virtues of the glass of milk are twofold: it is a wholesome food and it takes us back to childhood. . . . As for whiskey and gin, they are drinks for loners and introverts. For Fourier,[1] Gastrosophy was the science of combining not only foods but guests at table: matching the variety of dishes is the variety of persons sharing the meal. Wines, spirits, and liqueurs are the complement of a meal, hence their object is to stimulate the relations and unions consolidated round a table. Unlike wine, pulque, champagne, beer, and vodka,

---

[1]Charles Fourier (1772–1837), French philosopher and social theorist. — ED.

neither whiskey nor gin accompanies meals. Nor are they apéritifs or digestifs.[2] They are drinks that accentuate uncommunicativeness and unsociability. In a gastrosophic age they would not enjoy much of a reputation. The universal favor accorded them reveals the situation of our societies, ever wavering between promiscuous association and solitude.

Ambiguity and ambivalence are resources unknown to American cooking. Here, as in so many other things, it is the diametrical opposite of the extremely delicate French cuisine, based on nuances, variations, and modulations — transitions from one substance to another, from one flavor to another. In a sort of profane Eucharist, even a glass of water is transfigured into an erotic chalice:

> Ta lèvre contre le cristal
> Gorgée à gorgée y compose
> Le souvenir pourpre et vital
> De la moins éphémère rose.[3]

It is the contrary as well of Mexican and Hindu cuisine, whose secret is the shock of tastes: cool and piquant, salt and sweet, hot and tart, pungent and delicate. Desire is the active agent, the secret producer of changes, whether it be the transition from one flavor to another or the contrast between several. In gastronomy as in the erotic, it's desire that sets substances, bodies, and sensations in motion; this is the power that rules their conjunction, commingling, and transmutation. A reasonable cuisine, in which each substance is what it is and in which both variations and contrasts are avoided, is a cuisine that has excluded desire.

Pleasure is a notion (a sensation) absent from traditional Yankee cuisine. Not pleasure but health, not correspondence between savors but the satisfaction of a need — these are its two values. One is physical and the other moral; both are associated with the idea of the body as work. Work in turn is a concept at once economic and spiritual: production and redemption. We are condemned to labor, and food restores the body after the pain and punishment of work. It is a real *reparation*, in both the physical and the moral sense. Through work the body pays its debt; by earning its physical sustenance, it also earns its spiritual recompense. Work redeems us and the sign of this redemption is food. An active sign

4

---

[2]Drinks served before or after a meal to whet the appetite or to aid digestion. — ED.

[3]Your lip against the crystal / Sip by sip forms therein / The vital deep crimson memory / Of the least ephemeral rose. — Stéphane Mallarmé, "Verre d'eau." (My translation — TRANS.)

in the spiritual economy of humanity, food restores the health of body and soul. If what we eat gives us physical and spiritual health, the exclusion of spices for moral and hygienic reasons is justified: They are the signs of desire, and they are difficult to digest.

Health is the condition of two activities of the body, work and sports. In the first, the body is an agent that produces and at the same time redeems; in the second, the sign changes: Sports are a wasteful expenditure of energy. This is a contradiction in appearance only, since what we have here is reality is a system of communicating vessels. Sports are a physical expenditure that is precisely the contrary of what happens in sexual pleasure, since sports in the end become productive — an expenditure that produces health. Work in turn is an expenditure of energy that produces goods and thereby transforms biological life into social, economic, and moral life. There is, moreover, another connection between work and sports: Both take place within a context of rivalry; both are competition and emulation. . . . Sports possess the rigor and gravity of work, and work possesses the gratuity and levity of sports. The play element of work is one of the few features of American society that might have earned Fourier's praise, though doubtless he would have been horrified at the commercialization of sports. The preeminence of work and sports, activities necessarily excluding sexual pleasure, has the same significance as the exclusion of spices in cuisine. If gastronomy and eroticism are unions and conjunctions of substances and tastes or of bodies and sensations, it is evident that neither has been a central preoccupation of American society — as ideas and social values, I repeat, not as more or less secret realities. In the American tradition the body is not a source of pleasure but of health and work, in the material and the moral sense.

The cult of health manifests itself as an "ethic of hygiene." I use the word *ethic* because its prescriptions are at once physiological and moral. A despotic ethic: sexuality, work, sports, and even cuisine are its domains. Again, there is a dual concept: Hygiene governs both the corporeal and the moral life. Following the precepts of hygiene means obeying not only rules concerning physiology but also ethical principles: temperance, moderation, reserve. The morality of separation gives rise to the rules of hygiene, just as the aesthetics of fusion inspires the combinations of gastronomy and erotics. In India I frequently witnessed the obsession of Americans with hygiene. Their dread of contagion seemed to know no bounds; anything and everything might be laden with germs: food, drink,

objects, people, the very air. These preoccupations are the precise counterpart of the ritual preoccupations of Brahmans fearing contact with
certain foods and impure things, not to mention people belonging to a
caste different from their own. Many will say that the concerns of the
American are justified, whereas those of the Brahman are superstitions.
Everything depends on the point of view: For the Brahman the bacteria
that the American fears are illusory, while the moral stains produced by
contact with alien people are real. These stains are stigmas that isolate
him: No member of his caste would dare touch him until he had
performed long and complicated rites of purification. The fear of social
isolation is no less intense than that of illness. The hygienic taboo of the
American and the ritual taboo of the Brahman have a common basis:
the concern for purity. This basis is religious even though, in the case of
hygiene, it is masked by the authority of science.

In the last analysis, the cult of hygiene is merely another expression
of the principle underlying attitudes toward sports, work, cuisine, sex,
and races. The other name of purity is separation. Although hygiene is
a social morality based explicitly on science, its unconscious root is
religious. Nonetheless, the form in which it expresses itself, and the
justifications for it, are rational. In American society, unlike in ours,
science from the very beginning has occupied a privileged place in the
system of beliefs and values. The quarrel between faith and reason never
took on the intensity that it assumed among Hispanic peoples. Ever since
their birth as a nation, Americans have been modern; for them it is
natural to believe in science, whereas for us this belief implies a negation
of our past. The prestige of science in American public opinion is such
that even political disputes frequently take on the form of scientific
polemics, just as in the Soviet Union they assume the guise of quarrels
about Marxist orthodoxy. Two recent examples are the racial question
and the feminist movement: Are intellectual differences between races
and sexes genetic in origin or a historico-cultural phenomenon?

The universality of science (or what passes for science) justifies the   8
development and imposition of collective patterns of normality. Obviating
the necessity for direct coercion, the overlapping of science and Puritan
morality permits the imposition of rules that condemn peculiarities,
exceptions, and deviations in a manner no less categorical and implacable
than religious anathemas. Against the excommunications of science, the
individual has neither the religious recourse of abjuration nor the legal
one of *habeas corpus*. Although they masquerade as hygiene and science,

these patterns of normality have the same function in the realm of eroticism as "healthful" cuisine in the sphere of gastronomy: the extirpation or the separation of what is alien, different, ambiguous, impure. One and the same condemnation applies to blacks, Chicanos, sodomites, and spices.

EXPLORATIONS

1. What does Paz mean by *hygiene*? Reread paragraphs 5–7. What examples can you give, besides those noted here, of "the obsession of Americans with hygiene"?
2. Does Paz regard the United States as a melting pot or a "cultural bouillabaisse"? What is his opinion of American cooking and culture? What specific words, similes, and metaphors reveal this opinion?
3. What terms with religious connotations does Paz use in this essay? What is the impact of his use of such terms?
4. Do you think Paz's assessment of American culture is fair? exaggerated? meant to be taken seriously? At what points does he use humor, and with what effect? Which of his tactics aim at his readers' emotions rather than their reason?

CONNECTIONS

1. What statements by Ishmael Reed in "What's American about America?" contradict Paz's observations about American food? about American culture?
2. What words and statements in "Hygiene and Repression" and in Reed's "What's American about America?" paint a similar portrait of the early European settlers in the United States?

ELABORATIONS

1. Choose two groups of Americans who, in your opinion, approach food differently: women and men, children and adults, or athletes and couch potatoes, for instance. Write an essay comparing and contrasting their treatment of food. As Paz does here, use metaphors and similes within paragraphs to emphasize your overall comparison.

2. Does American (U.S.) cooking indeed hint at hygiene and repression, or is the diversity of our culture reflected by our cuisine? Write an essay classifying, defining, or describing the foods that you or your family eat, or that your school cafeteria or local restaurants serve, identifying the national origins of various dishes or ingredients.

RAYMONDE CARROLL

Money and Seduction

"When I meet someone from another culture, I behave in the way
that is natural to me, while the other behaves in the way that is natural
to him or her," writes Raymonde Carroll. "The only problem is that our
natural ways do not coincide." Born in Tunisia, Carroll was educated in
France and the United States. Her work as an anthropologist has taken
her, among other places, to the Pacific atoll of Nukuoro, where she lived
for three years and published *Nukuoro Stories* (1980). On her return,
Carroll interviewed a wide variety of subjects in France and the United
States for her book *Évidences Invisibles* (1987). "Money and Seduction,"
translated from the French by Carol Volk, comes from the conclusion of
the American edition of this book, *Cultural Misunderstandings: The
French-American Experience* (1988). Carroll currently teaches at Oberlin
College in Ohio, where she lives with her American husband.

Although France was settled by the Parisii in the third century B.C.,
the French celebrated their bicentennial in 1989. Bastille Day, July 14,
marks the date in 1789 when outraged citizens stormed Paris's notorious
Bastille prison and launched the Revolution, which ended nearly a thousand years of monarchy. King Louis XVI was beheaded by the guillotine
in 1793, followed by his queen, the extravagant and unpopular Marie
Antoinette. After a two-year orgy of executions and a short-lived republic,
Napoleon Bonaparte ruled as emperor from 1804 to 1815. After him
came a series of republics and the brief Second Empire, culminating in
the Fifth Republic, which holds power today. During World War II,
France was occupied by Germany. Having accumulated worldwide colonies during the centuries of European expansion, France withdrew in
the 1950s from Indochina, Morocco, and Tunisia, and subsequently from
most of its other African territories. France also withdrew most of its
troops in 1966 from the North Atlantic Treaty Organization (NATO). A
founding member of the European Community (see Appendix, p. 690),
France continues to play a significant political, economic, and cultural
role in Europe and the world.

Money. For a French person, the face of an American could easily
be replaced by a dollar sign. A sign of "incurable materialism," of arrogance, of power, of "vulgar," unrefined pleasure . . . the list goes on. I
have never read a book about Americans, including those written with

sympathy, which did not speak of the "almighty dollar"; I have never had or heard a conversation about Americans which did not mention money.

Foreigners often discover with "horror" or "repulsion" that "everything in the United States is a matter of money." Indeed, one need only read the newspapers to find constant references to the price of things. Thus, a fire is not a news item but an entity (natural or criminal), the dimensions of which are calculated by what it has destroyed — for example, ". . . a house worth two hundred *thousand* dollars . . ." In fact, if it is at all possible to attach a price to something, as approximate as it may be, that price will surely be mentioned. Thus, a French woman became indignant toward her American brother-in-law: "He showed us the engagement ring he had just bought, and he just had to give us all the details about the deal he got in buying the diamond. . . . Talk about romantic!" I cannot even count the number of informants who had similar stories to tell ("I was admiring the magnificent antique pieces in his living room, and do you know what he did? He gave me the price of each piece, with all kinds of details I hadn't asked for. I felt truly uncomfortable . . . really . . ."). Many French informants claimed to be shocked by the "constant showing off," the "lack of taste typical of nouveaux riches" and added, some not in so many words, "As for me, you know, I am truly repulsed by money."

On the other side, many Americans expressed surprise at the frequency with which French people spoke about money, only to say that "they weren't interested in it" ("so why talk about it?"), or at the frequency with which they say "it's too expensive" about all types of things. Some find the French to be "cheap" ("They always let you pay") or "hypocritical" ("Why, then, do the French sell arms to just anyone?"), too respectful of money to trifle with it, or too petty to take risks. The list of adjectives hurled from either side on this topic seems particularly long.

Yet a brief examination of certain ethnographic details left me puzzled.   4 For instance, what is the American article, about the forest fire that destroyed the row of two-hundred-thousand-dollar homes in California, really saying? Living in the United States, I know that a house worth two-hundred-thousand dollars in California is far from a palace; on the contrary. Thus, if I took the price quoted literally, I would misinterpret the article as meaning that the fire had destroyed a row of quite ordinary houses — in which case the mention of the "price" is uninformative, uninteresting, and useless. Therefore, what this article conveys, by talking about hundreds of thousands of dollars, is the fact that the fire destroyed very valuable homes. This meaning is also conveyed by the use of the word "homes," which connotes individuality and uniqueness, rather than "houses," which suggests plain buildings. The mention of the price, therefore, carries meaning of a different nature: I think that this "price" serves only as a common point of reference; it does not represent the true monetary values but a symbolic value which can be grasped immediately by anyone reading this article. A French equivalent would be a reference to the period ("from the seventeenth century") with no mention of the state of the building.

Similarly, it is difficult to take the example of the engagement ring literally ("I'm a tightwad"; "I'm not romantic"); it is more comprehensible if we interpret it as a message with a different meaning. For the American in question, having obtained a discount in no way altered the true value of the diamond or the symbolic value of the gesture; this "feat" probably made the gesture even more significant because of the time and attention devoted to it (the worst gift is the one that demands no effort) and probably earned him the admiration and appreciation of his fiancée.

The study of cases in which money is mentioned would require an entire book. . . . I will content myself merely with raising the question here and will indicate the general orientation of my interpretation.

The striking thing is that money is charged with a multiplicity of meanings in American culture, that it has attained a level of abstraction difficult to imagine elsewhere. Money represents both good and bad, dependence and independence, idealism and materialism, and the list of opposites can go on indefinitely, depending on whom one speaks to. It is power, it is weakness, seduction, oppression, liberation, a pure gamble, a high-risk sport; a sign of intelligence, a sign of love, a sign of scorn; able to be tamed, more dangerous than fire; it brings people together, it separates them, it is constructive, it is destructive; it is reassuring, it is anxiety-producing; it is enchanting, dazzling, frightening; it accumulates slowly or comes in a windfall; it is displayed, it is invisible; it is solid, it evaporates. It is everything and nothing, it is sheer magic, it exists and does not exist at the same time; it is a mystery. The subject provokes hatred, scorn, or impassioned defense from Americans themselves, who are constantly questioning themselves on the topic.

I believe that one association remains incontestable, no matter how 8 much resentment it provokes. Money symbolizes success. It is not enough to have money to be admired, but quite the contrary; there is no excuse for the playboy who squanders an inherited fortune. To earn money, a lot of money, and to spend it, is to give the most concrete, the most visible sign that one has been able to realize one's potential, that one has not wasted the "opportunities" offered by one's parents or by society, and that one always seeks to move on, not to stagnate, to take up the challenge presented in the premises shaping the education of children. . . .

As a result, money has become a common denominator. It is supposed to be accessible to all, independent of one's origins. And if it creates classes, it also allows free access to those classes to whoever wants to enter. (Let's not forget that we are talking here about "local verities," about cultural premises, and not about social realities.) Money is therefore the great equalizer, in the sense that the highest social class is, in principle, open to everyone, and that while those who are born into this social class have definite advantages, they must nonetheless deserve to remain there, must "prove themselves." And the newspapers are filled with enough stories of poor people turned millionaires to reinforce this conviction.

From this perspective, it is understandable that one does not hide one's success but displays it, shows it off. By making my humble origins known, by displaying my success, I am not trying to humiliate others (although it is possible that I, personally, am a real "stinker"), but I am showing others that it is possible, I am encouraging emulation through example, I am reaffirming a cultural truth: "if I can do it, you can do it." Hence the constant copresence of dreams and success, that is to say, the constant reaffirmation that the impossible is possible, and that attaining the dream depends solely on me. The logical, and ironic, conclusion to all this is the essentially idealistic significance of money in American culture, which does not exclude its "materialistic" utilization.

I do not believe that the misunderstanding between the French and Americans concerning money can be resolved by performing a parallel analysis of the meaning of money in French culture, not because money is not a concern for the French, but because I believe that what Americans express through money is expressed by the French in another domain.

From this brief analysis, I will reiterate three points. The first is that money in America serves as a common point of reference, a shortcut for communication, a means of defining a context that is recognizable by all and comprehensible no matter what one's financial situation may be. The second is that it is not in bad taste to recount one's triumphs, one's success in this domain, whether it is a matter of having obtained a half-price diamond or of having accumulated a veritable fortune, insofar as this in no way implies that I wish to put down others, that I am conceited, and so on, characteristics which depend not on money but on my personality. And the third is that money is accessible to all, makes possible upward mobility, that is to say, access to any class.

To the extent that these three points I just made are not "true" for French culture — and that they might in fact provoke "real repulsion" — one must look in a realm other than that of money for what carries the same message. . . .

The repulsion with which many French people react to the "bad taste" of Americans who "brag about their wealth," "show off their money," and so on closely resembles the disgust with which many Americans speak of the "bad taste," the "vulgarity" of French people who "brag about their sexual exploits," "are proud of their sexual successes," which is a subject reserved by Americans for the "uncivilized" world of locker rooms, for the special and forced intimacy of these dressing rooms for athletes. (Although the expression "locker-room talk" traditionally evokes male conversation, it is just as applicable today to female locker-room talk.) The repugnance on the part of "tasteful" Americans to speak in public about their successes with men or women or their sexual "conquests" is interpreted, among the French, as additional proof of American "puritanism," whereas the French "modesty" concerning public conversations about money would tend to be interpreted by Americans as a type of French "puritanism."

This reciprocal accusation of "bad taste" led me to wonder if what was true for financial successes and conquests in American culture was not true for seduction, for amorous conquests, for sexual successes in French culture.

While it is not looked on favorably, in France, to show off one's money or titles, one may speak of one's amorous conquests without shocking anyone (unless one does it to belittle others with one's superiority, to insult them, etc., in which case it is not the subject that is important but the manner in which a particular person makes use of it). We have, in France, a great deal of indulgence and admiration for the "irresistible" man or woman, for "charmers" large and small of both cases. Seduction is an art which is learned and perfected.

Like money for Americans, amorous seduction is charged with a multiplicity of contradictory meanings for the French, depending on the person to whom one is speaking and the moment one raises the topic. Nonetheless, if a (French) newspaper article defines a particular person as *séduisante*, the term does not refer to indisputable characteristics but to a category recognizable by all, to a common point of reference, to a comprehensible descriptive shortcut. (It is interesting to note that the American translation of *séduisante* would be "attractive," a word which, as opposed to the French, evokes identifiable and predictable characteristics. The word *seductive* — not an adequate translation — evokes manipulation and the negative connotations attached to taking advantage of naiveté.)

Seduction, as I have said, is an art for the French. It is not enough to be handsome or beautiful to seduce; a certain intelligence and expertise are necessary, which can only be acquired through a long apprenticeship, even if this apprenticeship begins in the most tender infancy. (Thus, an ad for baby clothing, a double spread in the French version of the magazine *Parents,* shows the perfect outfit for the "heartbreak girl" and for the "playboy"; this is an indication of the extent to which this quality is desirable, since I assume the ad is geared toward the parents who provide for and teach these babies, and not toward the babies themselves.) It is therefore "normal" for me to be proud of my successes, for me to continually take up the challenge of new conquests, for me never to rest on my laurels, for me not to waste my talent. It is therefore not in "bad taste" to talk about it (bad taste and seduction are, in a sense, mutually exclusive in French). What is more, I can "freely" share my secrets and my "reflections" on the subject of men or women — a topic I have thoroughly mastered.

Like money for Americans, seduction for the French may be the only true class equalizer. In fact, one of the greatest powers of amorous seduction is precisely the fact that it permits the transgression of class divisions. The French myths of the "kept woman," of the attractiveness of the *midinette* (a big-city shopgirl or office clerk, who is supposed to be very sentimental), of the seductive powers of "P'tit Louis" (a "hunk," a good dancer, from the working class), and the innumerable seducers of both sexes in French novels, songs, and films are sufficient proof.

The interest of a parallel such as the one I have just established is that it shows how astonishingly similar meanings can be expressed in areas which seem to be completely unrelated. Yet the greatest attraction of cultural analysis, for me, is the possibility of replacing a dull exchange of invectives with an exploration that is, at the very least, fascinating — a true feast to which I hereby invite you.

EXPLORATIONS

1. Does Carroll regard the United States as a melting pot or a "cultural bouil-labaisse"? How can you tell?

2. What is the thesis of Carroll's essay? What are her main sources of information on American attitudes toward money? on French attitudes toward seduction?

3. In her last paragraph, what course of action or change of attitude or both is Carroll recommending? What is the effect of her phrasing her recommendations as an invitation?

4. Carroll uses the word *playboy* in paragraphs 8 and 18. What kind of person is the American playboy? the French playboy? On the basis of Carroll's essay, what would you expect a French and an American playboy to think of each other?

CONNECTIONS

1. What references does Carroll make to puritanism in American culture? What similarities can you find between the French attitude toward Americans described here and the Latin attitude toward Americans expressed by Octavio Paz in "Hygiene and Repression"?

2. What direct and indirect references does Carroll make to cultural diversity in the United States? Does her concept of Americans seem closer to Paz's in "Hygiene and Repression" or to Ishmael Reed's in "What's American about America?"? On what evidence do you base your answer?

ELABORATIONS

1. Carroll notes in paragraph 9 that her comments on money as "the great equalizer" refer to "cultural premises, and not . . . social realities." What does she mean by this? Write an essay defining or classifying the social role(s) of money in the United States. You may focus on the equalizing role that our culture wishes for money to play (its ideal role), or the limits on money's equalizing power (its real role), or both.

2. Having read Paz's "Hygiene and Repression" and Carroll's "Money and Seduction," write an essay comparing and contrasting the social functions in American culture of money, sex, and food.

EDWARD T. HALL

Proxemics in the Arab World

Edward T. Hall was born in Webster Groves, Missouri, in 1914. His affinity for travel began early: His education took him from Pomona College to Columbia University, and he has taught at institutions from the University of Denver to Harvard Business School as well as worked for the U.S. State Department. Hall's special interest is proxemics, the study of people's responses to spatial relationships. He has done anthropological fieldwork in Micronesia, the southwestern United States, and Europe. His books include *The Handbook for Proxemic Research* (written with Mildred Reed Hall, 1974) and *Hidden Differences: Doing Business with the Japanese* (1987). "Proxemics in the Arab World" comes from his book *The Hidden Dimension* (1966).

The term *Arab* generally refers to any of the Semitic peoples living in Arabia, the peninsula between Africa and the Asian continent, or in northern Africa (see p. 348). The Arab League, formed in 1945, overlaps these geographic boundaries: Egypt, Iraq, Jordan, Lebanon, Saudi Arabia, and Syria were founding members, and Algeria, Kuwait, Libya, Morocco, Sudan, Tunisia, and Yemen have joined since. (Yemen, currently divided into the northern Yemen Arab Republic and the southern People's Democratic Republic of Yemen, signed a league-sponsored unification agreement in 1979.) Although all the Arab countries are predominantly Islamic, not all Islamic countries are Arab; noteworthy exceptions include Turkey (see p. 371), Pakistan (see pp. 280 and 359), and Iran (see p. 164). Hall's opening reference to two thousand years of contact applies to only half the Arab population: Most Islamic women seldom leave their homes and have no contact with men outside their own families (see Minai, "Women in Early Islam," p. 348).

In spite of over two thousand years of contact, Westerners and Arabs still do not understand each other. Proxemic research reveals some insights into this difficulty. Americans in the Middle East are immediately struck by two conflicting sensations. In public they are compressed and overwhelmed by smells, crowding, and high noise levels; in Arab homes Americans are apt to rattle around, feeling exposed and often somewhat inadequate because of too much space! (The Arab houses and apartments of the middle and upper classes which Americans stationed abroad commonly occupy are much larger than the dwellings such Americans usually inhabit.) Both the high sensory stimulation which is experienced in public places and the basic insecurity which comes from being in a dwelling that is too large provide Americans with an introduction to the sensory world of the Arab.

Pushing and shoving in public places is characteristic of Middle Eastern culture. Yet it is not entirely what Americans think it is (being pushy and rude) but stems from a different set of assumptions concerning not only the relations between people but how one experiences the body as well. Paradoxically, Arabs consider northern Europeans and Americans pushy, too. This was very puzzling to me when I started investigating these two views. How could Americans who stand aside and avoid touching be considered pushy? I used to ask Arabs to explain this paradox. None of my subjects was able to tell me specifically what particulars of American behavior were responsible, yet they all agreed that the impression was widespread among Arabs. After repeated unsuccessful attempts to gain insight into the cognitive world of the Arab on this particular point, I filed it away as a question that only time would answer. When the answer came, it was because of a seemingly inconsequential annoyance.

While waiting for a friend in a Washington, D.C., hotel lobby and wanting to be both visible and alone, I had seated myself in a solitary chair outside the normal stream of traffic. In such a setting most Americans follow a rule, which is all the more binding because we seldom think about it, that can be stated as follows: As soon as a person stops or is seated in a public place, there balloons around him a small sphere of privacy which is considered inviolate. The size of the sphere varies with the degree of crowding, the age, sex, and the importance of the person, as well as the general surroundings. Anyone who enters this zone and stays there is intruding. In fact, a stranger who intrudes, even for a specific purpose, acknowledges the fact that he has intruded by beginning his request with "Pardon me, but can you tell me . . . ?"

To continue, as I waited in the deserted lobby, a stranger walked up   4 to where I was sitting and stood close enough so that not only could I easily touch him but I could even hear him breathing. In addition, the dark mass of his body filled the peripheral field of vision on my left side. If the lobby had been crowded with people, I would have understood his behavior, but in an empty lobby his presence made me exceedingly uncomfortable. Feeling annoyed by this intrusion, I moved my body in such a way as to communicate annoyance. Strangely enough, instead of moving away, my actions seemed only to encourage him, because he moved even closer. In spite of the temptation to escape the annoyance, I put aside thoughts of abandoning my post, thinking, "To hell with it. Why should I move? I was here first and I'm not going to let this fellow drive me out even if he is a boor." Fortunately, a group of people soon arrived whom my tormentor immediately joined. Their mannerisms explained his behavior, for I knew from both speech and gestures that they were Arabs. I had not been able to make this crucial identification by looking at my subject when he was alone because he wasn't talking and he was wearing American clothes.

In describing the scene later to an Arab colleague, two contrasting patterns emerged. My concept and my feelings about my own circle of privacy in a "public" place immediately struck my Arab friend as strange and puzzling. He said, "After all, it's a public place, isn't it?" Pursuing this line of inquiry, I found that in Arab thought I had no rights whatsoever by virtue of occupying a given spot; neither my place nor my body was inviolate! For the Arab, there is no such thing as an intrusion in public. Public means public. With this insight, a great range of Arab behavior that had been puzzling, annoying, and sometimes even frightening began to make sense. I learned, for example, that if A is standing on a street corner and B wants his spot, B is within his rights if he does what he can to make A uncomfortable enough to move. In Beirut only the hardy sit in the last row in a movie theater, because there are usually standees who want seats and who push and shove and make such a nuisance that most people give up and leave. Seen in this light, the Arab who "intruded" on my space in the hotel lobby had apparently selected it for the very reason I had: It was a good place to watch two doors and the elevator. My show of annoyance, instead of driving him away, had only encouraged him. He thought he was about to get me to move.

Another silent source of friction between Americans and Arabs is in an area that Americans treat very informally — the manners and rights of the road. In general, in the United States we tend to defer to the vehicle that is bigger, more powerful, faster, and heavily laden. While a pedestrian walking along a road may feel annoyed he will not think it unusual to step aside for a fast-moving automobile. He knows that because he is moving he does not have the right to the space around him that he has when he is standing still (as I was in the hotel lobby). It appears that the reverse is true with the Arabs who apparently *take on rights to space as they move*. For someone else to move into a space an Arab is also moving into is a violation of his rights. It is infuriating to an Arab to have someone else cut in front of him on the highway. It is the American's cavalier treatment of moving space that makes the Arab call him aggressive and pushy.

The experience described above and many others suggested to me that Arabs might actually have a wholly contrasting set of assumptions concerning the body and the rights associated with it. Certainly the Arab tendency to shove and push each other in public and to feel and pinch women in public conveyances would not be tolerated by Westerners. It appeared to me that they must not have any concept of a private zone outside the body. This proved to be precisely the case.

In the Western world, the person is synonymous with an individual inside a skin. And in northern Europe generally, the skin and even the clothes may be inviolate. You need permission to touch either if you are a stranger. This rule applies in some parts of France where the mere touching of another person during an argument used to be legally defined as assault. For the Arab the location of the person in relation to the body is quite different. The person exists somewhere down inside the body. The ego is not completely hidden, however, because it can be reached very easily with an insult. It is protected from touch but not from words. The dissociation of the body and the ego may explain why the public amputation of a thief's hand is tolerated as standard punishment in Saudi Arabia. It also sheds light on why an Arab employer living in a modern apartment can provide his servant with a room that is a boxlike cubicle approximately 5 by 10 by 4 feet in size that is not only hung from the ceiling to conserve floor space but has an opening so that the servant can be spied on.

As one might suspect, deep orientations toward the self such as the one just described are also reflected in the language. This was brought to my attention one afternoon when an Arab colleague who is the author of an Arab-English dictionary arrived in my office and threw himself into a chair in a state of obvious exhaustion. When I asked him what had been going on, he said: "I have spent the entire afternoon trying to find the Arab equivalent of the English word 'rape.' There is no such word in Arabic. All my sources, both written and spoken, can come up with no more than an approximation, such as 'He took her against her will.' There is nothing in Arabic approaching your meaning as it is expressed in that one word."

Differing concepts of the placement of the ego in relation to the body are not easily grasped. Once an idea like this is accepted, however, it is possible to understand many other facets of Arab life that would otherwise be difficult to explain. One of these is the high population density of Arab cities like Cairo, Beirut, and Damascus. . . . While it is probable that Arabs are suffering from population pressures, it is also just as possible that continued pressure from the desert has resulted in a cultural adaptation to high density which takes the form described above. Tucking the ego down inside the body shell not only would permit higher population densities but would explain why it is that Arab communications are stepped up as much as they are when compared to northern European communication patterns. Not only is the sheer noise level much higher, but the piercing look of the eyes, the touch of the hands, and the mutual bathing in the warm moist breath during conversation represent stepped-up sensory inputs to a level which many Europeans find unbearably intense.

The Arab dream is for lots of space in the home, which unfortunately many Arabs cannot afford. Yet when he has space, it is very different from what one finds in most American homes. Arab spaces inside their upper-middle-class homes are tremendous by our standards. They avoid partitions because Arabs *do not like to be alone*. The form of the home is such as to hold the family together inside a single protective shell, because Arabs are deeply involved with each other. Their personalities are intermingled and take nourishment from each other like the roots and soil. If one is not with people and actively involved in some way, one is deprived of life. An old Arab saying reflects this value: "Paradise without people should not be entered because it is Hell." Therefore, Arabs in the United States often feel socially and sensorially deprived and long to be back where there is human warmth and contact.

Since there is no physical privacy as we know it in the Arab family, 12 not even a word for privacy, one could expect that the Arabs might use some other means to be alone. Their way to be alone is to stop talking. Like the English, an Arab who shuts himself off in this way is not indicating that anything is wrong or that he is withdrawing, only that he wants to be alone with his own thoughts or does not want to be intruded upon. One subject said that her father would come and go for days at a time without saying a word, and no one in the family thought anything of it. Yet for this very reason, an Arab exchange student visiting a Kansas farm failed to pick up the cue that his American hosts were mad at him when they gave him the "silent treatment." He only discovered something was wrong when they took him to town and tried forcibly to put him on a bus to Washington, D.C., the headquarters of the exchange program responsible for his presence in the United States.

Like everyone else in the world, Arabs are unable to formulate specific rules for their informal behavior patterns. In fact, they often deny that there are any rules, and they are made anxious by suggestions that such is the case. Therefore, in order to determine how the Arab sets distances, I investigated the use of each sense separately. Gradually, definite and distinctive behavioral patterns began to emerge.

Olfaction occupies a prominent place in the Arab life. Not only is it one of the distance-setting mechanisms, but it is a vital part of a complex system of behavior. Arabs consistently breathe on people when they talk. However, this habit is more than a matter of different manners. To the Arab good smells are pleasing and a way of being involved with each other. To smell one's friend is not only nice but desirable, for to deny him your breath is to act ashamed. Americans, on the other hand, trained as they are not to breathe in people's faces, automatically communicate shame in trying to be polite. Who would expect that when our highest diplomats are putting on their best manners they are also communicating shame? Yet this is what occurs constantly, because diplomacy is not only "eyeball to eyeball" but breath to breath.

By stressing olfaction, Arabs do not try to eliminate all the body's odors, only to enhance them and use them in building human relationships. Nor are they self-conscious about telling others when they don't like the way they smell. A man leaving his house in the morning may be told by his uncle, "Habib, your stomach is sour and your breath doesn't smell too good. Better not talk too close to people today." Smell is even considered in the choice of a mate. When couples are being matched for marriage, the man's go-between will sometimes ask to smell the girl, who may be turned down if she doesn't "smell nice." Arabs recognize that smell and disposition may be linked.

In a word, the olfactory boundary performs two roles in Arab life. It [16] enfolds those who want to relate and separates those who don't. The Arab finds it essential to stay inside the olfactory zone as a means of keeping tab on changes in emotion. What is more, he may feel crowded as soon as he smells something unpleasant. While not much is known about "olfactory crowding," this may prove to be as significant as any other variable in the crowding complex because it is tied directly to the body chemistry and hence to the state of health and emotions. . . . It is not surprising, therefore, that the olfactory boundary constitutes for the Arabs an informal distance-setting mechanism in contrast to the visual mechanisms of the Westerner.

One of my earliest discoveries in the field of intercultural communication was that the position of the bodies of people in conversation varies with the culture. Even so, it used to puzzle me that a special Arab friend seemed unable to walk and talk at the same time. After years in the United States, he could not bring himself to stroll along, facing forward while talking. Our progress would be arrested while he edged ahead, cutting slightly in front of me and turning sideways so we could see each other. Once in this position, he would stop. His behavior was explained when I learned that for the Arabs, to view the other person peripherally is regarded as impolite, and to sit or stand back-to-back is considered very rude. You must be involved when interacting with Arabs who are friends.

One mistaken American notion is that Arabs conduct all conversations at close distances. This is not the case at all. On social occasions, they may sit on opposite sides of the room and talk across the room to each other. They are, however, apt to take offense when Americans use what are to them ambiguous distances, such as the four- to seven-foot social-consultative distance. They frequently complain that Americans are cold or aloof or "don't care." This was what an elderly Arab diplomat in an American hospital thought when the American nurses used "professional" distance. He had the feeling that he was being ignored, that they might not take good care of him. Another Arab subject remarked, referring to American behavior, "What's the matter? Do I smell bad? Or are they afraid of me?"

Arabs who interact with Americans report experiencing a certain flatness traceable in part to a very different use of the eyes in private and in public as well as between friends and strangers. Even though it is rude for a guest to walk around the Arab home eying things, Arabs look at each other in ways which seem hostile or challenging to the American. One Arab informant said that he was in constant hot water with Americans because of the way he looked at them without the slightest intention of offending. In fact, he had on several occasions barely avoided fights with American men who apparently thought their masculinity was being challenged because of the way he was looking at them. . . . Arabs look each other in the eye when talking with an intensity that makes most Americans highly uncomfortable.

As the reader must gather by now, Arabs are involved with each other   20 on many different levels simultaneously. Privacy in a public place is foreign to them. Business transactions in the bazaar, for example, are not just between buyer and seller, but are participated in by everyone. Anyone who is standing around may join in. If a grownup sees a boy breaking a window, he must stop him even if he doesn't know him. Involvement and participation are expressed in other ways as well. If two men are fighting, the crowd must intervene. On the political level, *to fail to intervene* when trouble is brewing is to take sides, which is what our State Department always seems to be doing. Given the fact that few people in the world today are even remotely aware of the cultural mold that forms their thoughts it is normal for Arabs to view *our* behavior as though it stemmed from *their* own hidden set of assumptions.

In the course of my interviews with Arabs the term *tomb* kept cropping up in conjunction with enclosed space. In a word, Arabs don't mind being crowded by people but hate to be hemmed in by walls. They show a much greater overt sensitivity to architectural crowding than we do. Enclosed space must meet at least three requirements that I know of if it is to satisfy the Arabs: There must be plenty of unobstructed space in which to move around (possibly as much as a thousand square feet); very high ceilings — so high in fact that they do not normally impinge on the visual field; and, in addition, there must be an unobstructed view. It was spaces such as these in which the Americans referred to earlier felt so uncomfortable. One sees the Arab's need for a view expressed in many ways, even negatively, for to cut off a neighbor's view is one of the most effective ways of spiting him. In Beirut one can see what is known locally as the "spite house." It is nothing more than a thick, four-story wall, built at the end of a long fight between neighbors, on a narrow strip of land for the express purpose of denying a view of the Mediterranean to any house built on the land behind. According to one of my informants, there is also a house on a small plot of land between Beirut and Damascus which is completely surrounded by a neighbor's wall built high enough to cut off the view from all windows!

Proxemic patterns tell us other things about Arab culture. For example, the whole concept of the boundary as an abstraction is almost impossible to pin down. In one sense, there are no boundaries. "Edges" of towns, yes, but permanent boundaries out in the country (hidden lines), no. In the course of my work with Arab subjects I had a difficult time translating our concept of a boundary into terms which could be equated with theirs. In order to clarify the distinctions between the two very different definitions, I thought it might be helpful to pinpoint acts which constituted trespass. To date, I have been unable to discover anything even remotely resembling our own legal concept of trespass.

Arab behavior in regard to their own real estate is apparently an extension of, and therefore consistent with, their approach to the body. My subjects simply failed to respond whenever trespass was mentioned. They didn't seem to understand what I meant by this term. This may be explained by the fact that they organize relationships with each other according to closed social systems rather than spatially. For thousands of years Moslems, Marinites, Druses, and Jews have lived in their own villages, each with strong kin affiliations. Their hierarchy of loyalties is: first to one's self, then to kinsman, townsman, or tribesman, coreligionist and/or countryman. Anyone not in these categories is a stranger. Strangers and enemies are very closely linked, if not synonymous, in Arab thought. Trespass in this context is a matter of who you are, rather than a piece of land or a space with a boundary that can be denied to anyone and everyone, friend and foe alike.

In summary, proxemic patterns differ. By examining them it is possible   24
to reveal hidden cultural frames that determine the structure of a given people's perceptual world. Perceiving the world differently leads to differential definitions of what constitutes crowded living, different interpersonal relations, and a different approach to both local and international politics. There are in addition wide discrepancies in the degree to which culture structures involvement, which means that planners should begin to think in terms of different kinds of cities, cities which are consistent with the proxemic patterns of the peoples who live in them.

EXPLORATIONS

1. According to Hall, why do Arabs seem pushy to Americans? Why do Americans seem pushy to Arabs? What contrasting concept of the person underlies this mutual misunderstanding?

2. What kinds of data does Hall use as the basis for his conclusions about Arab versus Western concepts of personal space? How would the credibility of his findings change (if at all) if Hall depended on statistical data instead of the types of information he draws on here?

3. Who is Hall's apparent intended audience? What clues in his essay enable you to tell? To publish "Proxemics in the Arab World" in an Arab magazine, what changes in presentation would Hall need to make?

4. Does Hall regard the United States as a melting pot or a "cultural bouilla-baisse"? At what points does he treat northern Europeans and Americans together as more or less identical Westerners? At what points, if any, does he draw conclusions about one group from data relating to the other?

CONNECTIONS

1. What generalizations does Hall make about French attitudes toward personal space (para. 8), in contrast to Arab attitudes? Having read Hall's essay and Raymonde Carroll's "Money and Seduction," how would you describe the connection between a culture's rules about personal space and its rules about openly expressed sensuality?

2. What comments does Hall make about his own responses to his findings? What comments does Carroll make about her response to her findings? How do these comments affect each essay's impact?

3. In what ways is the structure of Hall's essay similar to that of Octavio Paz's "Hygiene and Repression"? How do these essays differ in their tactics? in the nature of their appeal to the reader?

4. What account does Hall take, if any, of cultural diversity in the United States? Look back at paragraph 4 of Ishmael Reed's "What's American about America?" What is the role of proxemics in this scene?

ELABORATIONS

1. Hall's essay is filled with examples of misunderstandings between Arabs and Westerners based on contrasting ideas about personal space. At the official level such misunderstandings can be dangerous to international relations. Based on Hall's observations, write a process essay recommending step-by-step guidelines for men and women representing the U.S. government or a U.S. business in the Middle East.

2. Hall touches on Western concepts of public and private space mainly as a standard of comparison for his investigation of contrasting Arab concepts. Write an essay in which you classify and examine various attitudes toward personal space in the United States. Use examples from your own experience, and from Hall's essay if you wish, as illustrations.

EZEKIEL MPHAHLELE

Tradition and the African Writer

Born in South Africa in 1919, Ezekiel Mphahlele grew up in the capital city of Pretoria and became a writer in exile in 1957. He received his Ph.D. from the University of Denver in 1968 and taught in the English department there; he also lived in Kenya, Nigeria, and France. He returned to South Africa in 1978. Even though his books were banned under apartheid, he taught and was head of African Literature at the University of Witwatersrand. He currently lives in Johannesburg. Mphahlele has published three story collections, several works of criticism, and an autobiography; his essays have appeared in numerous journals. His novel *The Wanderers* was designated Best African Novel of 1968–69. "Tradition and the African Writer" comes from his essay "African Literature: What Tradition?" which originally appeared in the *Denver Quarterly.*

Covering Africa's southern tip, the Republic of South Africa is about twice the size of Texas. Bantus (blacks) are a majority of the population, which also includes Afrikaners (whites of Dutch descent), Asians (mostly Indians), and Coloureds (those of mixed Khoisan and white descent). The region's Khoisan tribes — formerly known as Bushmen and Hottentots — had been joined by Bantus from the north by the time Dutch settlers arrived in the seventeenth century. Many of Mphahlele's works are concerned, directly or indirectly, with the racial and political conflicts in his homeland, which began when the British seized the Cape of Good Hope in 1806. At that time many Dutch moved north and founded two new republics, the Transvaal and the Orange Free State, displacing native Khoisan and Bantu tribes. They and their white compatriots kept political control by means of apartheid, a policy of racial separation that severely limits blacks' access to jobs, housing, income, and influence. Conflict intensified when diamonds and gold were discovered in the late 1800s. The ensuing Anglo-Boer (British versus Dutch) War was won by the British, who created the Union of South Africa in 1910. In 1948 apartheid became official, legally enforcing racially separate development and residential areas. In 1961, with only whites allowed to vote, South African voters withdrew their nation from the British Commonwealth. In the late 1980s, Asians and Coloureds received the right to vote (with restrictions), and laws banning interracial marriage were repealed. Today, South Africa, like Eastern Europe (see pp. 502, 517), is reversing long-standing repressive policies. (For more information on South Africa, see p. 578.)

It all started when Africa was shanghaied into the history of the West in the late nineteenth century. What were we coming into? — a long line of continuity going back some 9000 years since the civilizations of the great river valleys of the Nile, the Tigris and Euphrates, the Indus, and the Hwang-ho had launched man on a long intellectual quest. We had been discovered by an aggressive Western culture which was never going to let us be. Nor could we cease following the neon lights — or has it been a will o' the wisp? Time will tell. Perhaps Hegelian historical determinism will have it that it is as it should be: How could Africa be left out of it all indefinitely?

And so here I am, an ambivalent character. But I'm nothing of the oversimplified and sensationalized Hollywood version of a man of two worlds. It is not as if I were pinned on a rock, my legs stretched in opposite directions. Education sets up conflicts but also reconciles them in degrees that depend on the subject's innate personality equipment. It seems to me a writer in an African setting must possess this equipment and must strive toward some workable reconciliation inside himself. It is an agonizing journey. It can also be humiliating to feel that one has continually to be reassessing oneself with reference to the long line of tradition he has entered — the tradition of the West. How else? I have assimilated the only education the West had to offer me. I was brought up on European history and literature and religion and made to identify with European heroes while African heroes were being discredited, except those that became Christians or signed away their land and freedom, and African gods were being smoked out. I later rejected Christianity. And yet I could not return to ancestral worship in any overt way. But this does not invalidate my ancestors for me. Deep down there inside my agnostic self, I feel a reverence for them.

The majority of writers in Africa, I venture to say, are attached in a detached manner to one indigenous religion or another. They are not involved in its ritual, but they look at it with reverence. When, in their full consciousness, they have found themselves Christian — which can often just mean baptized — they have not adopted churchianity. Because our whole education system in Africa has been mission-ridden right from the beginning, and the white minister was supposed by the government or commercial or school-board employer to know the "native," you had always to produce a testimonial signed by a white church minister when you were applying for a job. Not even black ministers could speak for you. If you wanted to go out for further studies, you knew where to find

St. Peter. The black minister himself required testimonials from one of his white brethren, never from another black minister. So we called ourselves Christians; we entered "Christian" on the line against an item that asked for it on all the multiplicity of forms, just in order to save ourselves the trouble of explaining and therefore failing to go through the gates. In independent Africa, we are luckily able to trust fellow blacks who vouch for us and others. And you can almost see the Christian veneer peeling off because it has nothing to do with conscience. . . .

By far the larger part of Africa is still traditionally minded in varying   4
degrees. The whole dialogue around tradition is an intellectual one. The parents of people of my generation, although they may be urbanized, are still close to tradition. They worry a great deal about the way in which we break loose at one point and ignore some elements of tradition. Each time an African mother sends a child to high school, it is like giving birth to him all over again. She knows she is yielding something. Dialogue between her and the child decreases and eventually stays on the level of basic essentials: our needs, our family relations, family life, which must continue more or less normally, whatever else around us may progressively be reduced to abstractions or gadgets. It is no less excruciating for the young man who stands in this kind of relationship with his parents. But he can reconcile himself to it — the very educational process that wrenches him from his moorings helps him to arrange a harmonization within himself.

The parent will often moan and complain to him about the awkward distance he has reached away from tradition. But it is never a reprimand; it is an indulgent complaint. Because, I think, the parents are always aware that this whole business of education does not of itself engage you in an activity that expressly subverts the morals of the family, the clan, or of the tribe. They are aware of the many situations around them that require an education to cope with them. The benefits of tradition are abstract, and the parents' own thinking has not been stagnant while the whole landscape around them has been changing, while the white man's government has been impinging on their way of life over several decades. And the benefits of a modern education are tangible, real.

I have always asked myself what it is in one's formal education that leads to the rupture, to the ever widening gulf between one and one's parents and one's community. You recognize the alphabet, then words, and then you can extract meaning from many sentences in a row. With that shock of recognition, words leap into life in front of you. They set your mind on fire; longings and desires you would never have known are released and seem to whirl around in currents that explode into other currents: something like what you see in a glass flask of water that you have on a naked flame to observe the movement of heat in liquid. From then on, one must not stop. Yet it is not something one can take for granted in an African context, because to start at all is not inevitable: education is not compulsory, and the financial cost of it is immense.

In your higher education, you assimilate patterns of thought, argument, and so on from an alien culture in an alien language; they become your own. Of course you cannot help using your African setting as your field of reference; you cannot help going out of the queue of Western orientation now and again to consult those of your people who are not physically in it. You try to express their philosophy in a European language whose allegory, metaphor, and so on are alien to the spirit of that philosophy: something that can best be understood in terms of allegory and metaphor that are centered heavily on human relationships and external nature. All the same, you are in the queue, and you belong not only to an African community but also to a worldwide intellectual or worldwide economic community, or both. This is why communication becomes difficult, sometimes impossible between your people who are still not tuned into Western intellectual systems and yourself. Your mind operates in a foreign language, even while you are actually talking your mother tongue, at the moment you are engaged in your profession. You try hard to find correspondences and you realize there are only a few superficial ones: you have to try to *make* most of them. In the pure sciences, which are universally applicable, the correspondences are numerous; there is no problem.

Indigenous languages that have only recently become literary, that is, only since the church missions established presses in Africa, seem to have relied more and more heavily on the spoken word, so that gesture, facial expression, inflection of voice became vital equipment in communication. Language became almost a ritual in itself, and metaphor and symbol became a matter of art and device. Metaphor became a sacred thing if it had descended from usage in earlier times; when an elder, in a traditional court case, prefaced a proverb or aphorism or metaphor by saying, "Our elders say . . ." his audience listened with profound reverence. Notice the present tense in "our elders *say*. . . ." Because his elders would be the ancestors, who are still present with us in spirit. You can imagine what confusion prevails in a modern law court

8

when a witness or the accused operate in metaphor and glory in the sensuousness of the spoken word quite irrelevant to the argument at hand. Ask any magistrate or prosecutor or lawyer in a differentiated Western-type society whether they find a court trial a sensuous activity, and hear what they say. Even the rhetoric that a lawyer may indulge in is primarily a thing of the brain rather than of the heart. In African languages, activities overlap a great deal, and there are no sharp dividing lines between various functions.

All that I have said so far has been an attempt to indicate the relative distances between tradition and the present — some shifting, others freezing, some thawing, others again presenting formidable barriers. And we are living in a situation in which the past and the present live side by side, because the past is not just a segment in time to think *back* upon: we can see it in living communities. We need to appreciate these distances if we are to understand what the African writer is about. He is part of the whole pattern.

EXPLORATIONS

1. As an African writer, to what "two worlds" does Mphahlele belong? What choices does his dual heritage force him to make?

2. Why does Mphahlele perceive education as so crucial an issue for African writers? What price do they pay for it? What happens if they refuse to pay that price?

3. "The whole dialogue around tradition is an intellectual one," writes Mphahlele (para. 4). Cite three or four passages that show him to be part of the Western intellectual tradition. What passages show that he also belongs to the African tradition, in which speakers "operate in metaphor and glory in the sensuousness of the spoken word" (para. 8)?

4. How would you summarize the thesis of Mphahlele's essay? What are his main sources of information?

CONNECTIONS

1. How does Mphahlele's approach to his subject in this essay differ from Edward T. Hall's in "Proxemics in the Arab World"? What kind of appeal is each author making to his readers? How does the impact of these two essays differ?

2. In paragraphs 22–23 of "Proxemics in the Arab World," Hall comments on Arab legal concepts. Does Arab legal tradition seem closer to the African elders' tactics or to the "modern law courts" described by Mphahlele in paragraph 8? What clues in Hall's essay are the basis for your answer?

3. "Africa was shanghaied into the history of the West," Mphahlele writes in his opening paragraph. In what respects is this also true of Latin America? Look back at Octavio Paz's "Hygiene and Repression." What qualities does Mphahlele value in African tradition which Paz also values in Latin American culture?

ELABORATIONS

1. "I have always asked myself," writes Mphahlele, "what it is in one's formal education that leads to the rupture, to the ever widening gulf between one and one's parents and one's community" (para. 6). Write a cause-and-effect essay that addresses this question, using "Tradition and the African Writer" and your own experience as sources.

2. "The benefits of tradition are abstract," writes Mphahlele. "The benefits of a modern education are tangible, real" (para. 5). What does he mean? Looking at your own role in the world as an adult, what have you gained (or do you hope to gain) from your education? from the tradition(s) in which you grew up? Write an essay classifying the abstract and tangible benefits to you of your education and heritage.

PAUL HARRISON

The Westernization of the World

Paul Harrison is a free-lance writer and journalist based in London. He has traveled widely in Asia, Africa, and Latin America, visiting twenty-eight developing countries. He has contributed frequently to the *Guardian, New Society,* and *New Scientist,* and to publications of major United Nations agencies, such as the World Health Organization, the Food and Agriculture Organization, UNICEF, and the International Labor Organization. He is a contributor to *Encyclopaedia Britannica.* Harrison attended Manchester Grammar School and took master's degrees at Cambridge University and the London School of Economics. His interest in the Third World began in 1968 when he was lecturing in French at the University of Ife, Nigeria. Among his recent books are *Inside the Inner City: Life under the Cutting Edge* (rev. ed. 1985) and *The Greening of Africa* (1987).

"The Westernization of the World" comes from the second edition of Harrison's 1981 book *Inside the Third World,* as do these biographical notes. Harrison based his book on research and travel between 1975 and 1980, visiting Sri Lanka, Upper Volta and the Ivory Coast, Colombia and Peru, Brazil, Indonesia and Singapore, India, Bangladesh, and Kenya. His book was reprinted with a revised postscript in 1987. "In some ways it was a mad enterprise to attempt to cover so much ground," he admits. However, "The underdevelopment of countries and of human beings cannot be compartmentalized if it is to be fully grasped. It is a total situation, in which every element plays a part."

Like many commentators, Harrison refers to underdeveloped countries and their citizens collectively as the *Third World.* The term has more than one definition: nations in Africa, Asia, and Latin America that are not heavily industrialized and have a low standard of living; nations that are not aligned with either the Communist or the non-Communist bloc. Shiva Naipaul (see p. 405) writes: "Whatever the confusions, we do, I believe, have a picture of the exemplary Third World denizen: He lives a hand-to-mouth existence, he is indifferent to the power struggles of the mighty ones, and he is dark-skinned." Naipaul adds, "To blandly subsume, say, Ethiopia, India, and Brazil under the one banner of Third Worldhood is as absurd and as denigrating as the old assertion that all Chinese look alike." Still, keeping in mind the dangers noted by Simone de Beauvoir of dividing humanity into "us" and "them" (see p. 333), we can use the concept of the Third World to examine, as Harrison does, certain tendencies shared by nations that are otherwise dissimilar.

> The bourgeoisie has, through its exploitation of the world
> market, given a cosmopolitan character to production and
> consumption in every country.
>
> –Karl Marx

In Singapore, Peking opera still lives, in the back streets. On Boat
Quay, where great barges moor to unload rice from Thailand, raw rubber
from Malaysia, or timber from Sumatra, I watched a troupe of traveling
actors throw up a canvas-and-wood booth stage, paint on their white
faces and lozenge eyes, and don their resplendent vermilion, ultramarine,
and gold robes. Then, to raptured audiences of bent old women and
little children with perfect circle faces, they enacted tales of feudal princes
and magic birds and wars and tragic love affairs, sweeping their sleeves
and singing in strange metallic voices.

The performance had been paid for by a local cultural society as part
of a religious festival. A purple cloth temple had been erected on the
quayside, painted papier-mâché sculptures were burning down like giant
joss sticks, and middle-aged men were sharing out gifts to be distributed
among members' families: red buckets, roast ducks, candies, and moon
cakes. The son of the organizer, a fashionable young man in Italian shirt
and gold-rimmed glasses, was looking on with amused benevolence. I
asked him why only old people and children were watching the show.

"Young people don't like these operas," he said. "They are too old-
fashioned. We would prefer to see a high-quality Western variety show,
something like that."

He spoke for a whole generation. Go to almost any village in the 4
Third World and you will find youths who scorn traditional dress and
sport denims and T-shirts. Go into any bank and the tellers will be
dressed as would their European counterparts; at night the manager will
climb into his car and go home to watch TV in a home that would not
stick out on a European or North American estate. Every capital city in
the world is getting to look like every other; it is Marshall McLuhan's
global village, but the style is exclusively Western. And not just in
consumer fashions: the mimicry extends to architecture, industrial technology, approaches to health care, education, and housing.

To the ethnocentric Westerner or the Westernized local, that may
seem the most natural thing in the world. That is modern life, they
might think. That is the way it will all be one day. That is what development and economic growth are all about.

Yet the dispassionate observer can only be puzzled by this growing world uniformity. Surely one should expect more diversity, more indigenous styles and models of development? Why is almost everyone following virtually the same European road? The Third World's obsession with the Western way of life has perverted development and is rapidly destroying good and bad in traditional cultures, flinging the baby out with the bathwater. It is the most totally pervasive example of what historians call cultural diffusion in the history of mankind.

Its origins, of course, lie in the colonial experience. European rule was something quite different from the general run of conquests. Previous invaders more often than not settled down in their new territories, interbred, and assimilated a good deal of local culture. Not so the Europeans. Some, like the Iberians or the Dutch, were not averse to cohabitation with native women: unlike the British, they seemed free of purely racial prejudice. But all the Europeans suffered from the same cultural arrogance. Perhaps it is the peculiar self-righteousness of Pauline Christianity that accounts for this trait. Whatever the cause, never a doubt entered their minds that native cultures could be in any way, materially, morally, or spiritually, superior to their own, and that the supposedly benighted inhabitants of the darker continents needed enlightening.

And so there grew up, alongside political and economic imperialism, that more insidious form of control — cultural imperialism. It conquered not just the bodies, but the souls of its victims, turning them into willing accomplices.   8

Cultural imperialism began its conquest of the Third World with the indoctrination of an elite of local collaborators. The missionary schools sought to produce converts to Christianity who would go out and proselytize among their own people, helping to eradicate traditional culture. Later the government schools aimed to turn out a class of junior bureaucrats and lower military officers who would help to exploit and repress their own people. The British were subtle about this, since they wanted the natives, even the Anglicized among them, to keep their distance. The French, and the Portuguese in Africa, explicitly aimed at the "assimilation" of gifted natives, by which was meant their metamorphosis into model Frenchmen and Lusitanians, distinguishable only by the tint of their skin.

The second channel of transmission was more indirect and voluntary. It worked by what sociologists call reference-group behavior, found when someone copies the habits and life-style of a social group he wishes to belong to, or to be classed with, and abandons those of his own group.

This happened in the West when the new rich of early commerce and industry aped the nobility they secretly aspired to join. Not surprisingly the social climbers in the colonies started to mimic their conquerors. The returned slaves who carried the first wave of Westernization in West Africa wore black woolen suits and starched collars in the heat of the dry season. The new officer corps of India were molded into what the Indian writer Nirad Chaudhuri has called "imitation, polo-playing English sub-alterns," complete with waxed mustaches and peacock chests. The elite of Indians, adding their own caste-consciousness to the class-consciousness of their rulers, became more British than the British (and still are).

There was another psychological motive for adopting Western ways, deriving from the arrogance and haughtiness of the colonialists. As the Martiniquan political philosopher, Frantz Fanon, remarked, colonial rule was an experience in racial humiliation. Practically every leader of a newly independent state could recall some experience such as being turned out of a club or manhandled on the street by whites, often of low status. The local elite were made to feel ashamed of their color and of their culture. "I begin to suffer from not being a white man," Fanon wrote, "to the degree that the white man imposes discrimination on me, makes me a colonized native, robs me of all worth, all individuality. . . . Then I will quite simply try to make myself white: that is, I will compel the white man to acknowledge that I am human." To this complex Fanon attributes the colonized natives' constant preoccupation with attracting the attention of the white man, becoming powerful like the white man, proving at all costs that blacks too can be civilized. Given the racism and culturism of the whites, this could only be done by succeeding in their terms, and by adopting their ways.

This desire to prove equality surely helps to explain why Ghana's 12 Nkrumah built the huge stadium and triumphal arch of Black Star Square in Accra. Why the tiny native village of Ivory Coast president Houphouët-Boigny has been graced with a four-lane motorway starting and ending nowhere, a five-star hotel and ultramodern conference center. Why Sukarno transformed Indonesia's capital, Jakarta, into an exercise in gigantism, scarred with six-lane highways and neofascist monuments in the most hideous taste. The aim was not only to show the old imperialists, but to impress other Third World leaders in the only way everyone would recognize: the Western way.

The influence of Western life-styles spread even to those few nations who escaped the colonial yoke. By the end of the nineteenth century, the elites of the entire non-Western world were taking Europe as their reference group. The progress of the virus can be followed visibly in a room of Topkapi, the Ottoman palace in Istanbul, where a sequence of showcases display the costumes worn by each successive sultan. They begin with kaftans and turbans. Slowly elements of Western military uniform creep in, until the last sultans are decked out in brocade, epaulettes, and cocked hats.

The root of the problem with nations that were never colonized, like Turkey, China, and Japan, was probably their consciousness of Western military superiority. The beating of these three powerful nations at the hands of the West was a humiliating, traumatic experience. For China and Japan, the encounter with the advanced military technology of the industrialized nations was as terrifying as an invasion of extraterrestrials. Europe's earlier discovery of the rest of the world had delivered a mild culture shock to her ethnocentric attitudes. The Orient's contact with Europe shook nations to the foundations, calling into question the roots of their civilizations and all the assumptions and institutions on which their lives were based.

In all three nations groups of Young Turks grew up, believing that their countries could successfully take on the West only if they adopted Western culture, institutions, and even clothing, for all these ingredients were somehow involved in the production of Western technology. As early as the 1840s, Chinese intellectuals were beginning to modify the ancient view that China was in all respects the greatest civilization in the world. The administrator Wei Yüan urged his countrymen to "learn the superior technology of the barbarians in order to control them." But the required changes could not be confined to the technical realm. Effectiveness in technology is the outcome of an entire social system. "Since we were knocked out by cannon balls," wrote M. Chiang, "naturally we became interested in them, thinking that by learning to make them we could strike back. From studying cannon balls we came to mechanical inventions which in turn led to political reforms, which led us again to the political philosophies of the West." The republican revolution of 1911 attempted to modernize China, but her subjection to the West continued until another Young Turk, Mao Tse-tung, applied that alternative brand of Westernization: communism, though in a unique adaptation.

The Japanese were forced to open their border to Western goods in 16 1853, after a couple of centuries of total isolation. They had to rethink fast in order to survive. From 1867, the Meiji rulers Westernized Japan with astonishing speed, adopting Western science, technology, and even manners: short haircuts became the rule, ballroom dancing caught on, and *moningku* with *haikara* (morning coats and high collars) were worn. The transformation was so successful that by the 1970s the Japanese were trouncing the West at its own game. But they had won their economic independence at the cost of losing their cultural autonomy.

Turkey, defeated in the First World War, her immense empire in fragments, set about transforming herself under that compulsive and ruthless Westernizer, Kemal Atatürk. The Arabic script was abolished and replaced with the Roman alphabet. Kemal's strange exploits as a hatter will probably stand as the symbol of Westernization carried to absurd lengths. His biographer, Lord Kinross, relates that while traveling in the West as a young man, the future president had smarted under Western insults and condescension about the Turkish national hat, the fez. Later, he made the wearing of the fez a criminal offense. "The people of the Turkish republic," he said in a speech launching the new policy, "must prove that they are civilized and advanced persons in their outward respect also. . . . A civilized, international dress is worthy and appropriate for our nation and we will wear it. Boots or shoes on our feet, trousers on our legs, shirt and tie, jacket and waistcoat — and, of course, to complete these, a cover with a brim on our heads. I want to make this clear. This head covering is called a hat."

EXPLORATIONS

1. What general cause, and what three specific channels, does Harrison cite as responsible for the Third World's Westernization? What differences between Western newcomers and Third World natives seem to have most strongly affected relations between them?

2. "By the end of the nineteenth century," writes Harrison, "the elites of the entire non-Western world were taking Europe as their reference group" (para 13). How does he explain the initial westward tilt of countries that were never colonized? What explanation does he give, or hint at, for their present continuing interest in Western ways?

3. Early in his essay Harrison asks the central question: "Why is almost everyone following virtually the same European road?" (para. 6). What are the characteristics of this "European road"? What are the origins of the specific examples the author cites?

4. What types of evidence does Harrison present for his assumptions about

Western homogeneity? Do you think his evidence justifies his conclusions? Why or why not?

CONNECTIONS

1. In paragraph 9 Harrison mentions Christian missionary schools as one means by which "cultural imperialism began its conquest of the Third World." What specific steps or tactics in this process does Ezekiel Mphahlele mention in "Tradition and the African Writer"?

2. What does Harrison say in paragraph 7 about the policy of the Iberian (Spanish and Portuguese) colonizers toward the native peoples they met in the New World? Look back at Octavio Paz's "Hygiene and Repression." How do Latin American food and attitudes toward food reflect that colonial Spanish policy?

3. In paragraph 10 Harrison discusses "reference-group behavior." What examples of this behavior can you find in Raymonde Carroll's "Money and Seduction"?

ELABORATIONS

1. Harrison focuses on Westernization in non-Western countries. What explanation (if any) does he offer for the spread of a single cultural trend all over Europe and North America? On the basis of Harrison's theories, plus evidence from other selections you have read, write an essay identifying causes and effects behind the West's homogeneity.

2. It has become fairly common for childless couples and individuals in the United States to adopt babies from Third World countries. In what ways does cross-cultural adoption benefit the child, the original and adoptive parents, and the child's original and adoptive homeland? What are the drawbacks of this practice? Write an argumentative essay defending or opposing cross-cultural adoption, or a process analysis essay advising the would-be parent(s) on how to protect the interests of all involved.

V. S. NAIPAUL

Entering the New World

V. S. Naipaul, like his brother Shiva (see p. 405), was born in Trinidad of Indian descent but has lived most of his life in England. Feeling stifled on his small native island, which lies off the coast of Venezuela and constitutes half the Republic of Trinidad and Tobago, Naipaul vowed to escape. In 1950, at the age of eighteen, he left for Oxford University on a government scholarship. At twenty-one he became a broadcaster for the Caribbean Service of the British Broadcasting Company (BBC). He wrote three novels, two of which were in print by the time he was twenty-six. At twenty-nine he published what is widely considered his masterpiece, *A House for Mr. Biswas*. Since then Naipaul has lived in India, Africa, South America, and the Middle East as well as England. He has written twenty-two books, the majority nonfiction, including *The Enigma of Arrival* (1987) and *A Turn in the South* (1989). Naipaul has won both critical praise and a number of literary awards, including England's prestigious Booker Prize. He currently lives with his wife, Patricia Hale, whom he met at Oxford, and writes alone in a Wiltshire cottage. "Entering the New World" comes from "The Crocodiles of Yamoussoukro," a narrative about his travels in the Ivory Coast, published as part of his 1984 book *Finding the Center.*

The Ivory Coast (République de la Côte d'Ivoire) lies almost directly across the Atlantic Ocean from Trinidad, between Liberia and Ghana on Africa's Gulf of Guinea. A former French colony, it gained independence in 1960. Economic (particularly agricultural) diversification, foreign investment, and close ties to France have helped make the Ivory Coast the most prosperous of tropical African nations. However, a drop in cocoa and coffee prices in the world market, and an aging president's austere solutions, which include a 25 to 40 percent income tax to pay off foreign debt, have recently led to an economic slump and political dissent. Naipaul's meeting with Ebony takes place in the Ivory Coast's capital city — then Abidjan, now Yamoussoukro.

"Volta" is Upper Volta, which also became independent of France in 1960; its name was changed to Burkina Faso in 1984. Landlocked in the southwest African savannah north of the Ivory Coast, Burkina Faso has a largely agricultural economy but only 10 percent arable land; several hundred thousand of its farm workers migrate every year to the Ivory Coast and Ghana. Benin — another French colony until 1960 — lies east of the Ivory Coast beyond Ghana and Togo.

In the morning I was telephoned from the hotel lobby by a man called Ebony. He said he had heard from Busby that a writer was in Abidjan, and he had come to meet this writer. He, Ebony, was himself a poet.

I went down to see him. He was a cheerful young man of regal appearance, with the face of a Benin bronze, and he was regally attired, with a brightly patterned skullcap and a rich African tunic. He said the skullcap and tunic were from Volta. His family employed laborers from Volta and he had always, even as a child, liked their clothes.

He had been a journalist, he said, but he had given it up, because in the Ivory Coast journalism was like smoking: It could damage your health. He liked the joke; he made it twice. But he was vague about the journalism he had done. He said he was now a government servant, in the department of the environment. He had written a paper on things that might be done environmentally in the Ivory Coast. But after twelve months he had heard nothing about his paper. So now he just went to the office and from time to time he wrote poetry.

He said, "I have a theory about African administrations. But it is   4 difficult and will take too long to tell you."

He had come to see me — and the hotel was a good way out of the town — because he was sociable; because he wanted to practice his English; and because, as a poet and intellectual, he wanted to try out his ideas.

I offered coffee. He offered me a cola nut, the African token of friendship. I nibbled at my grubby, purple-skinned nut: bitter. He chewed his zestfully, giving little dry spits of chewed husk to his left and right, and then at the end of his chew taking out the remainder of the husk with his fingers and placing it on the ashtray.

He asked why I had come to the Ivory Coast. I said because it was successful and French.

He said, "Charlemagne wasn't my ancestor."   8

I felt it had been said before, and not only by Ebony. He ran on to another idea. "The French run countries like pigsties. They believe that the sole purpose of men is to eat, to go to the toilet, and to sleep." So the French colonialists created bourgeois people. Bourgeois? "The bourgeois want peace, order. The bourgeois can fit into any political system, once they have peace. On the other hand, the British colonialists created entrepreneurs." Entrepreneurs? "Entrepreneurs want to change things." Entrepreneurs were revolutionaries.

Antithesis, balance: the beauty rather than the validity of a thought: I thought I could detect his French training. I began to examine his ideas of the bourgeois and the entrepreneur, but he didn't encourage me. He said, playfully, it was only an idea.

Starting on another cola nut — he had a handful in his tunic pocket — he said, "Africans live at peace with nature. Europeans want to conquer or dominate nature."

That was familiar to me. I had heard similar words from young Muslim fundamentalists in Malaysia: ecological, Western romance bouncing back like a corroborating radio signal from remote, inactive worlds. But that again was an idea Ebony didn't want to stay with.

Ebony said, "I saw white men for the first time when I was fourteen or fifteen, when I went to school. That was the first time I discovered the idea of racial superiority. African children are trained not to look elders in the eye. It is disrespectful. At school the French teachers took this to be a sign of African hypocrisy."

What was the point of this story?

Ebony said, "So I thought my French teachers inferior."

I felt this racial story, with its triumphant twist, had previously had a sympathetic foreign listener. And it turned out that there was a Scandinavian woman journalist who had made a great hit with Ebony. She was now in Spain and Ebony earnestly asked me — two or three times — to look her up and pass on his regards.

Ebony said, "When my father sent me to the school, do you know what he said? He said, 'Remember. I am not sending you to the school to be a white man or a Frenchman. I am sending you to enter the new world, that's all.'"

I felt that in his own eyes Ebony had done that. . . . Ebony said he had no money, no car. The salary he got from the government was less than the rent he paid. He had come to the hotel on his bicycle. But I thought he was relaxed, a whole man. He knew where he was, how he had got there, and he liked the novelty of what he saw. There was no true anxiety behind his scattered ideas. At any rate he was less anxious than a romantic or concerned outsider might have wished him to be. Ideas about Africa, words, poetry, meeting foreigners — all this was part of his relishing of life, part of his French-inspired role as intellectual, part of the new world he had happily entered.

He went away on his bicycle, and I took a taxi later to a beach restaurant at the other end of the city, beyond the industrial and port area. The lunch there, and the French style of the place, were usually worth the fare and the journey in the midday heat through the traffic and the crowds. But today it wasn't so.

It was more than a matter of an off day. The waiters, impeccable the
day before, were casual, vacant. There were long delays, mistakes, some
of the portions were absurdly small; the bill, when it came, was wrong.
Someone was missing, perhaps the French or European manager. And
with him more than good service had gone: The whole restaurant idea
had vanished. An elaborate organization had collapsed. The waiters —
Ivorian: These jobs were lucrative — seemed to have forgotten, from one
day to the next, why they were doing what they did. And their faces
seemed to have altered as well. They were not waiters now, in spite of
their flowered tunics. Their faces and manners radiated various degrees
of tribal authority. I saw them as men of weight in the village: witch
doctors, herbalists, men who perhaps put on masks and did the sacred
dances. The true life was there, in the mysteries of the village. The
restaurant, with its false, arbitrary ritual, was the charade: I half began
to see it so.

Ebony had been told by his father: "I am not sending you to the school
to become a white man. I am sending you to enter the new world."

The new world existed in the minds of other men. Remove those
men, and their ideas — which after all had no finality — would disappear.
Skills could be taught. What was fragile — to men whose complete, real
life lay in another realm of the spirit — was faith in the new world.

EXPLORATIONS

1. "The new world existed in the minds of other men," writes Naipaul in his
   closing paragraph. "Remove those men, and their ideas — which after all
   had no finality — would disappear." What incidents during the author's lunch
   at a "French" restaurant trigger this conclusion? What assumption does Naipaul make about the restaurant to explain the incidents? On what evidence
   does he base that assumption?

2. What opinion does Ebony express of the European colonial influence in
   Africa? What statements reveal his opinion? What are the apparent sources
   of his views?

3. What statements by Naipaul encourage us as readers to focus on the style
   rather than the content of Ebony's remarks? What impression of Ebony does
   Naipaul give us in the first half of his essay? How do you think he means our
   impression to change in the second half?

CONNECTIONS

1. What statements by Paul Harrison in "The Westernization of the World" are echoed by Naipaul and Ebony? How does Naipaul's assessment of Western influence on the Third World differ from Harrison's?

2. How would you summarize Ebony's view of the difference between French and British colonizers? How would you summarize Paul Harrison's view of this difference? In what respects do these two commentators agree and disagree?

3. Like Ezekiel Mphahlele in "Tradition and the African Writer," Naipaul investigates the impact of a dual heritage on an African writer. What evidence in "Entering the New World" suggests that Ebony has faced the same conflict between native and European influences as Mphahlele? How does Naipaul suggest that Ebony has (or has not) resolved his dilemma?

ELABORATIONS

1. What does Naipaul's opinion of Ebony seem to be? Does he like Ebony? Does he respect his views? How can you tell? List the comments Naipaul makes that reveal his personal response to Ebony. Then write an essay analyzing the techniques Naipaul uses to depict Ebony sympathetically or unsympathetically without directly stating his opinion.

2. Have you ever eaten in a restaurant, or patronized a store, where you unexpectedly became aware of the "real" life of someone waiting on you? Have you ever held a job, attended a class, or participated in a social function where an unplanned event shattered the group's customary identity? Write an essay using your experience to illustrate Naipaul's comments about the fragility of worlds that exist mainly in someone's mind.

JAMES FALLOWS

A Few Pointers

Born in Philadelphia in 1949, James Fallows graduated from Harvard University in 1970. Studying in England as a Rhodes Scholar, he earned a diploma in economic development from Queen's College, Oxford. Fallows served as an editor for the *Washington Monthly* and the *Texas Monthly* before becoming President Jimmy Carter's chief speech writer, a position he held for two years. He has written two books, including *More Like Us: Making America Great Again* (1989), and co-edited two others. In *The Water Lords* (1971), Fallows used the findings of a consumer advocacy group in Georgia to unveil a corporation's passion for profit at the expense of the environment. More often wielding a lively wit, Fallows is currently a contributing editor of the *Washington Monthly* and the Washington editor of *The Atlantic Monthly.* He has lived and traveled extensively in Asia. "A Few Pointers" appeared in the *Atlantic* in November 1989.

Asia, the world's largest continent, is also its most geographically and culturally diverse. Dominating Asia are contrasting giants: the Soviet Union, China, Japan, India. Christianity, Buddhism, Confucianism, Taoism, Shintoism, and Hinduism are just a few of the region's religions. West of India, the Islamic countries of Iran, Afghanistan, and Pakistan are Asian, as is most of Turkey (see p. 371). A traveler flying east from India might pass over Nepal, Tibet, Bhutan, Bangladesh, Sri Lanka, Burma, Thailand, and Malaysia, as well as the smaller Indochinese nations of Laos, Cambodia, and Vietnam. Asia's thousands of islands include Borneo, Sumatra, Java, the Philippines, and Taiwan. The Korean peninsula off China, west of Japan, has been divided into Communist North Korea and democratic South Korea since World War II — just one of the many Asian battlegrounds where larger nations have vied for power. Still a source of cheap labor for Western businesses, Asia in the last quarter century has become a source of capital as well, as Japan in particular has moved into a dominant world economic role.

Living in a foreign culture is, most of the time, exhilarating and liberating. You don't have to feel responsible for the foibles of your temporary home; you can forget about the foibles of your real home for a while. Your life seems longer, because each day is dense with new and surprising experiences. I can remember distinctly almost every week of the past three and a half years. The preceding half dozen years more or less run together in a blur.

But there is also distress in foreign living, particularly in living in Asia at this time in its history. It comes not from daily exasperations, which after all build character, but from the unsettling thoughts that living in Asia introduces. As I head for home, let me mention the thought that disturbs me most.

It concerns the nature of freedom: whether free societies are fit to compete, in a Darwinian sense. Until the repression in China last summer [1989], many Westerners assumed that the world had entered an era of overall progress. True, environmental problems were getting worse rather than better, and many African and Latin American societies were still in bad shape. But in Asia it seemed possible to believe that people had learned how to make their societies both richer and freer year by year. As countries in Asia became more advanced and prosperous, they loosened their political controls — and as the controls came off, economic progress speeded up. This was the moral of the Korean and Taiwanese success stories, as those countries evolved toward the ideal set by stable, prosperous Japan. Even China, before the summer [of 1989], seemed to be loosening up, both economically and politically. China's crackdown made the spread of democracy and capitalism seem less certain than it had seemed before, but even this step backward confirmed the idea that political freedoms and economic progress were naturally connected. Everyone assumes that as China makes its political system more repressive, its economy will stagnate.

I draw a darker conclusion from the rise of the Asian economies. The economic success stories of Asia do not prove that political freedom and material progress go hand in hand. On the contrary: the Asian societies are, in different ways, fundamentally more repressive than America is, and their repression is a key to their economic success. Japan, Korea, Taiwan, and Singapore allow their citizens much less latitude than America does, and in so doing they make the whole society, including the business sector, function more efficiently than ours does. The lesson of the Soviet economic collapse would seem to be that a completely controlled economy cannot survive. The lesson of the rising Asian system is that economies with some degree of control can not only survive but prevail.

The crucial concepts here are "excessive" choice and "destructive" competition. Classical free-market economic theory says that these are impossibilities; a person can never have too much choice, and there can never be too much competition in a market. Asian societies approach this issue from a fundamentally different perspective. They were built on neither an Enlightenment concept of individual rights nor a capitalist concept of free and open markets, and they demonstrate in countless ways that less choice for individuals can mean more freedom and success for the social whole.

The examples of economic efficiency are the most familiar. Japanese businessmen have almost no freedom to move to another company, even if they're dissatisfied with conditions where they're working. (Of course, they're technically free to quit, but very few reputable big companies will hire someone who has left another big firm.) This may be frustrating for the businessmen, but so far it has been efficient for the companies. For instance, they can invest in employee training programs without fear that newly skilled workers will use their skills somewhere else. Singaporeans have been forced to put much of their income into a national retirement fund; Koreans have been discouraged from squandering their money overseas on tourism (until this year, only people planning business trips and those in a few other narrow categories were granted passports); Japanese consumers are forced to pay inflated prices for everything they buy. All these measures have been bad for individuals but efficient for the collective. In different ways they have transferred money from people to large institutions, which then invest it for future productivity. To illustrate the point the opposite way: Korea has in the past two years become a more successful democracy and a less successful export economy. Precisely because workers have been going on strike and consumers demanding a higher standard of living, Korean companies have temporarily lost their edge against competitors in Taiwan and Japan.

Yu-Shan Wu, of The Brookings Institution, has suggested a useful way to think about this combination of economic freedom and political control. In communist economies, he says, property is owned by the state, and investment decisions are made by the state. The result is a disaster. The style of capitalism practiced in the United States takes the opposite approach: Private owners control most property, and private groups make most investment decisions. The result over the past century has been a big success, but now some inefficiencies are showing up. Japan, Wu says, has pioneered a new approach: private ownership of property, plus public guidance of investment decisions. The big industrial combines of Japan are as private and profit-oriented as those of the United States, and therefore at least as efficiency-minded (unlike state enterprises in Russia or China). But in Japan's brand of capitalism some of the largest decisions are made by the state, not the "invisible hand." This private-public approach, Wu concludes, reduces the freedom of people and single companies, but it has certain long-term advantages over the private-private system.

Last year two U.S. companies made supercomputers, the Cray corporation and a subsidiary of Control Data. This year only one does. Control Data abandoned the business, finding it unprofitable. The same circumstances have applied in Japan — difficult but important technology, lean or nonexistent profits for the foreseeable future — but the results have been different, because the state occasionally overrules the invisible hand. It is inconceivable that the Japanese government would have let one of only two participants abandon an area of obvious future technical importance. If Japan left decisions to the invisible hand, there would be no aircraft engineers at work in the country, because Mitsubishi and Kawasaki cannot hope to earn a profit competing against Boeing. But the big Japanese companies keep their aerospace-engineering departments active, in part because of government-directed incentives to do so. (These range from explicit subsidies, like the FSX fighter-plane contracts, to a system of industrial organization that makes it possible for companies to subsidize unprofitable divisions for years.) Eventually, Japanese planners believe, the aerospace expertise will pay off.

Americans should not be surprised by what the private-public system can accomplish. It's essentially the way our economy worked during the Second World War. People were forced to save, through Liberty Bonds, and forced not to consume, through rationing. Big companies were privately owned and run, but overall goals were set by the state. Under this system the output of the U.S. economy rose faster than ever before or since. (Part of the reason for the rapid rise, of course, was that wartime production finally brought America out of the Great Depression.) For the United States this managed economy was a wartime exception. For the Japanese-style economic systems of Asia it has been the postwar rule. This is not to say that we need a wartime mentality again but, rather, to show that the connection between individual freedom and collective prosperity is more complicated than we usually think. We may not like the way the Japanese-style economic system operates, but we'd be foolish not to recognize that it does work, and in many ways works better than ours.

Here's an even harder truth to face: The most successful Asian economies employ a division of labor between men and women that we may find retrograde but that has big practical advantages for them. Despite some signs of change — for instance, the rising influence of Takako Doi at the head of the Socialist Party in Japan — the difference between a man's role and a woman's is much more cut and dried in Asia than in the United States. It is tempting to conclude that a time lag is all that separates Asian practices from American, and that Japanese and Korean women will soon be demanding the rights that American women have won during the past generation. But from everything I've seen, such an assumption is as naive as imagining that Japan is about to be swept by an American-style consumer-rights movement.

There is a lot to dislike in this strict assignment of sex roles. It's unfair in an obvious way to women, because 99 percent of them can never really compete for business, political, academic, or other opportunities and success. I think it's ultimately just as bad for men, because most of them are cut off from the very idea of dealing with women as equals, and have what we would consider emotionally barren family lives. The average Japanese salaryman takes more emotional satisfaction in his work-place life than the average American does, but less in his relations with wife and children. Nonetheless, this system has one tremendous practical advantage. By making it difficult for women to do anything except care for their families, the traditional Asian system concentrates a larger share of social energy on the preparation of the young.

The best-educated American children are a match for the best in Asia,   12 but the average student in Japan, Korea, Singapore, or Taiwan does better in school than the average American. The fundamental reason, I think, is that average students in these countries come from families with two parents, one of whom concentrates most of her time and effort on helping her children through school. Limits on individual satisfaction undergird this educational achievement in two ways: The mother is discouraged from pursuing a career outside the house, and she and the father are discouraged from even thinking about divorce. The typical Asian marriage is not very romantic. In most countries arranged marriages are still common, and while extramarital affairs are at least as frequent as they are in the United States, they seem to cause less guilt. But because most husbands and wives expect less emotional fulfillment from marriage, very few marriages end in divorce. Individual satisfaction from marriage may be lower, but the society enjoys the advantages of having families that are intact.

The Asian approach to the division of labor is not one that Americans want to emulate, or can. Except in emergencies we have believed in satisfying individual desires rather than suppressing them. But, to come back to the central point, we shouldn't fool ourselves about the sheer effectiveness of the system that the Asian societies have devised. Their approach to child-rearing, as to economic development, is worse for many individuals but better for the collective welfare than ours seems to be. The Asian model is not going to collapse of its own weight, unlike the Soviet communist system. So the puzzle for us is to find ways to evoke similar behavior — moderation of individual greed, adequate attention to society's long-term interests, commitment to raising children — within our own values of individualism and free choice.

I hope somebody has figured out the answer to this while I've been away.

EXPLORATIONS

1. What is Fallows's thesis in this essay? Where does he state it?

2. What qualities does Fallows seem to admire in the Asian approach to economic competition? What qualities does he seems not to admire?

3. Does Fallows treat the United States as a melting pot or a "cultural bouillabaisse"? What comments does he make about the role in this country's economy of differences between groups?

4. In paragraph 12 Fallows notes that "the average student in Japan, Korea, Singapore, or Taiwan does better in school than the average American." What reason does he suggest for the difference? Do you agree? What other factors might play a role?

CONNECTIONS

1. What does V. S. Naipaul have to say in "Entering the New World" about the balance between the economic efficiency of business organizations and the personal priorities of their employees? How do you think Naipaul would reply to Fallows?

2. Does Fallows share the views expressed by Paul Harrison in "The Westernization of the World"? What Western concepts appear in Fallows's essay? Go through "A Few Pointers" and write down every phenomenon that appears to have come to Asia from the West.

3. Look back at Raymonde Carroll's "Money and Seduction." What three func-

tions does she believe are served by Americans' talk about money? What national values do these functions reflect? What attitudes toward these values are held by the Asian cultures Fallows discusses?

ELABORATIONS

1. What attributes of American society would make it very difficult or impossible for the United States to adopt the Asian competitive strategies Fallows describes? Write a cause-and-effect essay explaining how goals, values, and traditions in the United States prevent this country from following the Asian model.

2. How does Harrison describe the United States' position in the world? How does Fallows describe it? Who do you think is right, and why? Write your own argumentative essay about the United States' position in the world, drawing on these two writers (and others in this book) for support and illustrations.

MIKHAIL GORBACHEV

The US and the USSR

Mikhail S. Gorbachev was born in Privolnoye, Krasnogvadeisky District, in 1931. He graduated from the Faculty of Law, Moscow State University, in 1955, and from the Stavropol Agricultural Institute in 1967. An active Party member and organizer, he held several positions in Stavropol before becoming a member of the Central Communist Party Soviet Union in 1971 and the Politburo in 1980. He was elected general secretary of the Soviet Communist Party in 1985. Foreign Minister Andrei Gromyko recommended him to the Central Committee, commenting that he "has a nice smile . . . but iron teeth." In 1987 Gorbachev published *Perestroika: New Thinking for Our Country and the World* (from which this piece is taken).

Perestroika, or restructuring, is one of two pivotal Gorbachev policies for bringing the Soviet Union into full partnership with the West and the world. It involves rethinking and reorganizing the Soviet Union's inefficient state-run economy (see Smith, *"Skoro Budet*: It'll Be Here Soon," p. 461). Gorbachev's other key policy is glasnost, or openness. Glasnost has led to new arms-control proposals, the release of political dissidents and loosening of immigration policy, less censorship and more international exchange in the arts and sciences, broader media coverage of events inside the Soviet Union, and greater freedom of movement for foreign visitors. The combination of glasnost and perestroika also has helped to free Eastern Europe from Soviet domination.

Politically, Gorbachev has laid the foundation for pluralism and a parliamentary democracy in the Soviet Union. (The first direct election by popular vote is scheduled for 1994.) In March 1990, the Soviet Parliament voted Gorbachev executive president, transferring control to him from the Politburo, and ended the Communist Party's seventy-two-year political monopoly. Among Gorbachev's top priorities as president is domestic economic reform: improving food and housing, and raising the quality of Soviet industries' products and operations. Nevertheless, he also seems to be a strong supporter of the KGB, the Soviet secret police. Gorbachev's contributions to world harmony have earned him several awards, including The Order of Lenin, the Indira Gandhi Award, and the 1990 Nobel Peace Prize. He has a daughter, Irina, and lives with his wife, Raisa, in the Kremlin in Moscow.

The Union of Soviet Socialist Republics is the largest country in the world, covering a sixth of the earth's land area and featuring every climate but tropical. Its nearly 300 million people live in fifteen republics and belong to more than a hundred different nationalities and religions. The largest republic and headquarters of the central government is Russia. Some of the smaller republics, such as the Baltic states, were freed by the Bolshevik Revolution of 1917 and reconquered by the Red Army. Long-suppressed grievances and internal strife between ethnic groups are emerging in the current glasnost climate. Confronting the question of independence, the republics must consider economic issues. Russia, rich in resources, supplies more than half the Soviet Union's electricity and almost all its oil while subsidizing faltering industries in the republics. However, change is hard to implement in the heavily centralized Soviet system, a problem that has encouraged quasi-capitalist experimentation similar to China's.

(For more information on the Soviet Union, see pp. 109, 301, and 507.)

While still a student at Moscow University, I took an interest in the history of the United States, I read several books by American authors and traced the history of our relations. There were abrupt ups and downs in these relations: from the wartime alliance to the Cold War of the forties and fifties; from the *détente* of the seventies to a drastic deterioration at the turn of the eighties.

The interval between the April 1985 Plenary Meeting, which was a turning point for us, and the publication of this book saw a great many events, including some directly connected with the development of Soviet-American relations. Now we keep up a dialogue with the United States and U.S. President and I periodically write to each other. Our negotiators discuss really important problems.

There has been a slight thaw in such areas as scientific and cultural cooperation in the last year or two. Currently, the Soviet Union and the United States are discussing, at various levels, issues that were once subjects for mutual recrimination. Outlines of contact have begun to emerge, even in the field of information activity, which must be rid of the propaganda of violence and enmity, and of interference in each other's internal affairs.

Well, has the ice been broken, and is our relationship entering a   4
quieter and more constructive phase? One would like this process to continue, but to claim that some notable headway has been made would be to sin against the truth. If we care about a real improvement in Soviet-American relations, we must appraise their state honestly. The change for the better, if any, has been extremely slow. Now and again the former

inconsistent modes of approach prevail over the imperative need to re-vitalize Soviet-American relations.

The progress of high technology and informatics have now brought people closer together. These processes can be used to promote greater mutual understanding. They can also be used to divide people. There have been immense losses on that account already. But now the world has reached a point where we — I mean both the United States and the USSR — have to think of how we are going to continue. If we change nothing, it is difficult to foresee where we shall be ten, fifteen, twenty years from now. It seems to me that concern for our countries and for the future of all civilization is increasing. It is growing within the Soviet as well as within the American nation.

I will never accept the claim — whatever anyone might tell me — that the American people are aggressive toward the Soviet Union. I cannot believe that. There are, perhaps, some individuals who are pleased that there is tension, confrontation, or intense rivalry between our countries. Perhaps some people do gain something from it. But such a state of things does not meet the larger interests of our peoples.

We are thinking, after all, of what must be done for our relations to improve. And they do need to. For not only have we failed to advance in this sense since the mid-seventies, but much of what was then created and done has been destroyed. We have not been moving forward, rather the other way round. We say that the Americans are to blame. The Americans say the Soviet Union is to blame. Perhaps, we should seek out the reasons behind what happened, because we must draw lessons from the past, including the past record of our relations. That is a science, a serious and responsible science, if one sticks to the truth, of course. And yet today what we must think of most is how we are going to live together in this world and how we are going to cooperate.

I have had a lot of meetings with American politicians and public 8 figures. Sometimes it creates quite a crowded schedule for me, but on each occasion I try to find the time for such meetings. My mission is, as I see it, not only to get across an understanding of our policy and our vision of the world, but to understand and appreciate more fully the American frame of mind, to learn better what the American problems are, and, in particular, the specific political processes in the United States. One cannot do otherwise. A scientific policy must be built on a strict assessment of reality. It is impossible to move toward more harmonious relations between the United States and the USSR while being mesmer-ized by ideological myths.

We don't communicate enough with one another, we don't understand one another well enough, and we don't even respect one another enough. Certain forces have done a great deal to bring about such a state of affairs. Many misconceptions have built up to hamper cooperation and stand in the way of its development.

The history of Soviet-American relations in the postwar period is not the subject of this book. But recalling in one's mind's eye even the events of the recent past one can see the disservice done by prejudice and rejection of new ideas. When I met former U.S. President Jimmy Carter early in the summer of 1987, I told him frankly that we did not by any means consider everything that occurred during his presidency to have been negative. There were some positive things, too. I refer, in particular, to the SALT-II Treaty which, even though never ratified, does play a useful part in spite of the present line of the U.S. Administration. The spirit of this treaty is alive. But at the same time, one cannot fail to see that many opportunities have been missed. We believed, and still believe, that, as the eighties loomed up, major accords were just a stone's throw away for such areas as anti-satellite weapons, the arms trade, reductions in military activity in the Indian Ocean, and the Middle Eastern settlement issues. Ten years ago! How much time and how many resources have been wasted on the arms race, and how many human lives have been lost!

When I responded to *Time* magazine late in August 1985 I said: "Our countries simply cannot afford to allow matters to reach a confrontation. Herein lies the genuine interest of both the Soviet and American people. And this must be expressed in the language of practical politics. It is necessary to stop the arms race, to tackle disarmament, to normalize Soviet-American relations. Honestly, it is time to make these relations between the two great peoples worthy of their historic role. For the destiny of the world, the destiny of world civilization really depend on our relations. We are prepared to work in this direction."

We must learn to live in a real world, a world which takes into account 12 the interests of the Soviet Union and the United States, of Britain and France and the Federal Republic of Germany. But there are also the interests of China and India, Australia and Pakistan, Tanzania and Angola, Argentina and other nations; the interests of Poland, Vietnam, Cuba, and other socialist countries. Not to recognize them would be to deny those people the freedom of choice and the right to a social set-up that suits them. Even if they err in their choice, they must themselves find a way out. That is their right.

I have spoken about this with many Americans, including Mr. George Shultz, who was in Moscow in the spring of 1987. We had a wide-ranging conversation, but I kept bringing him round to the same idea: Let us try and live in a real world, let us take the interests of both nations into account. And that is impossible without taking into account the interests of other members of the world community. We shall not have proper international relations if we proceed from the interests of the USSR and the United States alone. There has to be a balance.

This matter takes on a new aspect at each stage of history. Interests change, so does the balance. That implies new modes of approach. I repeat it would be dangerous and damaging to build politics at the end of the twentieth century on the approach that inspired Churchill's Fulton speech[1] and the Truman Doctrine.[2] An earnest effort to reshape Soviet-American relations is long overdue. Once that is admitted, the habit to command will have to be dropped. Neither the Soviet Union, nor the United States, nor any other country can regard the world or any part of it as an object for exploitation, not even under a cloak of "national interest."

Attempts to build relations on dictatorial practices, violence, and command hardly succeed even at this point. They soon won't succeed at all. The process of grasping the new realities is not a simple one. It requires everybody's time and effort. But once started, that process will go on. We must learn to listen to one another, and to understnd one another. We are in favor, I told Mr. Shultz, of cooperating with the United States, and I mean cooperating constructively, for nobody else will take on the responsibility that the USSR and the United States have to bear.

I recall my conversation with the former President of the United States 16 of America, Mr. Richard Nixon. He quoted Winston Churchill's words, not prophetic, I hope, that the bright wings of science might bring the Stone Age back to Earth, and he stressed that I, as General Secretary, and President Reagan and his successors, would have to make the historic choice in favor of a peaceful future. I told Mr. Nixon then that I had once seen a film about a journey made by some American tourists down the Volga. There were shots of our citizens alongside Americans. And it was not easy to tell an American from a Russian. People were talking

---

[1]British Prime Minister Winston Churchill gave this famous speech on March 5, 1946, about the need for his country and the United States to join as guardians of peace against Soviet communism, which had lowered an "Iron Curtain" across Europe. — ED.

[2]After World War II, the U.S. President Harry S Truman pledged 400 million dollars in emergency aid to the governments of Greece and Turkey to keep them from falling under Soviet influence. — ED.

away and one felt they were talking like friends, understanding each other: that is just what politicians fail to do well enough.

It is good that it is not only politicians who speak to each other, but that grass-root representatives of the people do so also. That is very important. I would welcome that. Let Soviet people and Americans meet more often, and let them form their own impression of each other. Communication, direct communication of people is a great thing. Without it, without full-scale communication and mutual understanding between peoples, politics can do little.

I pointed out to Mr. Nixon that the fact that it was our two countries that were in possession of a colossal military, including nuclear, arsenal was the most serious reality in today's world. I told him that if we built our policies with respect to each other and with respect to the rest of the world on erroneous premises, things could reach an extreme point of confrontation fraught with the most tragic consequences for the USSR, the United States, and the whole world.

And today I am ready to repeat what I said in that conversation: There is the firm intention in Soviet society, not only in the leadership, to look for ways toward normalizing Soviet-American relations, to find and enlarge the areas of common ground so as to arrive at a friendly relationship in the long run. Perhaps, this might seem too much to hope for at this juncture. Yet we are convinced that this is the choice to make, for otherwise it is impossible to imagine what we would arrive at.

For better or worse, there is no subjunctive mood in politics. History 20 is made without rehearsals. It cannot be replayed. That makes it all the more important to perceive its course and its lessons.

EXPLORATIONS

1. What does Gorbachev cite as the main reasons for the tension between the United States and the Soviet Union?

2. What general recommendations does Gorbachev make for improving U.S.-Soviet relations? What specific steps does he recommend, if any? What useful steps does he note have already been taken?

3. What comments in Gorbachev's essay foreshadow his loosening, since 1989, of the Soviet Union's tight control over its Eastern Bloc satellites? Cite at least three such statements.

4. In paragraph 16 Gorbachev recalls former President Richard Nixon quoting

Winston Churchill's warning "that the bright wings of science might bring the Stone Age back to Earth." What specific disaster does this warning refer to? In his reply to Nixon, what course was Gorbachev recommending to avoid this disaster?

CONNECTIONS

1. In "A Few Pointers," James Fallows cites Asians' willingness to give group interests a higher priority than individual interests. In what form(s) does this idea appear in Gorbachev's essay?

2. Gorbachev and Fallows both stress the importance of learning to live in the real world. What does Fallows mean by this? What does Gorbachev mean?

3. In paragraphs 12 and 13 Gorbachev stresses "taking into account the interests of other members of the world community." Having read Paul Harrison's "The Westernization of the World," what do you think Gorbachev means by this? What specific actions or changes in attitude might he recommend to the United States and its Western allies?

4. What observations by Ishmael Reed in "What's American about America?" offer encouragement to Gorbachev's hope for better understanding between peoples? What observations by Reed suggest that achieving this goal will not be easy?

ELABORATIONS

1. In paragraphs 15 and 18 Gorbachev writes of the enormous responsibility that the United States and the Soviet Union share. Do you agree with his assessment? How may the U.S.-Soviet role in the world be affected by the Asian economic prosperity Fallows describes? by the development of nuclear weapons in other countries? by the reunification of Germany and strengthening of the European Community (see the Appendix, p. 690)? Choose a world trend that interests you and write a cause-and-effect or process analysis essay explaining its potential impact on U.S. and Soviet dominance.

2. Elsewhere in the book from which this selection is taken, Gorbachev criticizes the arms race as futile (either side can destroy the other many times over) and wasteful (it diverts economic resources that could be used for more constructive purposes). Is he right? Write an argumentative essay defending your own viewpoint on disarmament.

JOYCE CAROL OATES

Meeting the Gorbachevs

In contrast to the turbulent, tormented characters in her fiction, Joyce Carol Oates has lived quietly. Born in 1938 in Lockport, New York, she escaped flat farmland and a one-room schoolhouse by writing down daydreams. At twelve she discovered the typewriter. By fifteen she had completed her first novel. At twenty-one, while attending Syracuse University, she entered and won *Mademoiselle* magazine's college fiction prize. After graduating from Syracuse as class valedictorian and earning an M.A. from the University of Wisconsin, Oates became one of the most prominent writers in the United States. She is the author of more than twenty novels, many volumes of short stories, volumes of poetry and literary criticism, plays, and many reviews and articles. One of her plays was produced Off Broadway, and several of her stories have been adapted to the screen and televised. She has won many awards, including the O. Henry Award for Continuing Achievement three times. Best known for her social analysis and vivid psychological portraits, Oates also has experimented with genre fiction, such as gothic and mystery novels. Still, she admits an affinity for depicting the rural and city life she knew as a child in upstate New York and as a young adult in Detroit. Fascinated by Detroit, she has set many novels and stories there; one, *them* (1969), won the National Book Award. Oates taught at Princeton University for many years and lives in New Jersey with her husband. "Meeting the Gorbachevs" appeared in the *New York Times Magazine* on January 3, 1988.

A great man? All I see is the actor creating his own ideal image.

—Nietzsche[1]

Listening to Mikhail Gorbachev's impassioned address in the rococo white-and-gold ballroom of the Soviet embassy on Sixteenth Street in Washington, D.C., on the late afternoon of 8 December 1987, in a heterogeneous gathering of some fifty fellow American "intellectuals" and "artists," I recalled these cryptic words of Nietzsche's, but wondered if

---

[1]Friedrich Nietzsche (1844–1900), German philosopher. — ED.

my habitual skepticism, particularly regarding politics in its most public, theatrical mode, might be irrelevant here; unjustified. Simply because one of the world's most powerful men, indeed, the world's supreme Communist leader, the General Secretary of the Central Committee of the Communist Party of the Soviet Union, Mikhail Gorbachev, was speaking to us in warmly seductive tones, employing words reminiscent of the social mysticism of the sixties — *interrelatedness, integral, global peace, democratization* — and assuring us of matters that sounded almost literally too good to be true, as if our deepest, most desperate wishes were being uttered in an exotically foreign language and translated into our own, did it mean that these matters could not be true? — or even probable? Though the grim lessons of history suggest otherwise, and idealism's trajectory usually sinks rapidly downward, man is of all creatures the hopeful animal; and it is a hard task to resist believing in the very things (above all an end to the fanatic arms race of past decades: the suicidal stockpiling of nuclear weapons) that we have been talking about for so long. Shaking Mikhail Gorbachev's hand, looking the man in the eye — he is famed for making "eye contact" and is clearly happiest in such quasi-intimate public situations — one comes away with the visceral certitude that this is a person of surpassing integrity; a man of the utmost sincerity; somewhat larger than life, perhaps. And so brimming with energy! And a sense of his own historic worth! Yet one recalls too, more soberly, that the political enthusiasms of past eras (for "Uncle Joe" Stalin, for the bearded revolutionary Castro, for the ascetic Ayatollah Khomeni, among others) can look rather bleakly ironic in retrospect. History is the only true philosophy.

It was with the evident intention of circumnavigating, perhaps frustrating, conventional political and media channels, and speaking directly to a presumed intelligentsia, with a presumed power of its own to shape public opinion, that Gorbachev chose to arrange a special meeting at the Soviet embassy, on his own territory, so to speak, with American "intellectuals" and "artists" in the midst of his heroically crammed three-day schedule. Here, in an elegantly Old World sort of setting, with enormous crystal chandeliers hanging from the ceiling, and vases of white tulips on our tables, the already heated air given an added incandescence by ubiquitous television cameras, Gorbachev spoke with disarming candor of domestic Soviet problems, economic and moral; of the political necessities that brought *glasnost* into being; of his many-times-reiterated hope for world disarmament and peace; of his sense of the world's nations as "contradictory" yet "integral." Such words and noble concepts are hardly new but their utterance, by a Soviet leader of proven shrewdness and prescience, is certainly new; even rather astonishing. From where, within the repressive Soviet system, did such a man come? And how, and why? In Gorbachev, the personal anecdote has the weight of a political parable, conversationally, even confidentially, delivered: He told us of vacationing in Italy some years ago, with his wife, Raisa, and attending an evening entertainment in their hotel in which actors playing national types greeted one another and behaved in comically characteristic ways, and when the "American" and the "Russian" met each man looked stonily away without acknowledging the other. The Italian audience laughed at such idiotic behavior, Gorbachev said, and he was struck by the irony that two "such great nations" were at an impasse, and that the rest of the world should laugh. "I thought, why can't something be done to change our mutual attitudes? Why should the world find Americans and Russians so laughable?"

Though by this time Gorbachev had been speaking for perhaps a half hour without pause, only now and then glancing down, unobtrusively, at his notes, he is so practiced and charming a speaker that those of us who are usually stupefied by speeches remained attentive, even rapt, throughout. Yes, really, why can't something be done? The question hung in the air, eminently answerable. Though Paul Newman would afterward comment that Gorbachev is a gifted performer in whom you don't see the "machinery" of his technique, does it necessarily follow that histrionic gifts exclude sincerity? Must surface and substance be at odds?

I asked Henry Kissinger, seated beside me at our table, whether Mr.   4
Gorbachev was radically different from other Soviet leaders he had known, and Kissinger paused, thought, and said, "This one is more skillful."

When, at about 10 P.M. on 30 November, the wholly unexpected telephone call came from the cultural attaché of the Soviet embassy in Washington, inviting me to meet Mr. Gorbachev and the USSR ambassador to the United States, Yuri Dubinin, at a reception for artists, writers, and intellectuals the following week, I must confess that my first instinct was to decline: Thank you for the honor, I said, but I'm afraid I am too busy. (Such is the introvert's habitual response: did not William Faulkner laconically decline an invitation to dine at the White House, with the remark that it was too far to go for dinner?) But my husband was appalled and insisted I rethink my decision. It was a "historic" occasion, he said.

And so it was, and so I did, telephoning back the next morning to accept. And were spouses included in the invitation? I asked. Sorry, spouses were not.

(For two days following the call from the Soviet embassy our telephone line was disturbed by loud nervous clicks of a kind we had never heard before. Wiretapping? Could it be? A friend whose telephone conversations were monitored when he traveled in Korea told me yes, he recognized the sounds; another friend, a Princeton colleague who recently taught a seminar on American intelligence operations, assured me that it was nothing to be upset about. Probably, no one was listening; conversations were just being taped. "These things are perhaps done routinely for security purposes," he said. Meaning Gorbachev's security.)

When we arrived in Washington for the 4:30 to 6:00 P.M. reception   8
we discovered that the block containing the Soviet embassy at 1125 Sixteenth Street N.W. was officially cordoned off; the area was alarmingly aswarm with officers, both uniformed and plainclothes, and one could not help but imagine marksmen hidden in upstairs windows, regarding targets thoughtfully through telescopic lenses. It did not escape my attention that the large, prosperous-looking national headquarters for the National Rifle Association was a stone's throw, so to speak, from the heavily guarded Soviet embassy; nor that, of the streams of people entering the embassy building, not another woman was within sight. (In all, I would see perhaps four or five women at the reception, amid a crowd of as many as one hundred men.) Guests to the reception were required to proceed through three checkpoints, the first on the street, where an unidentified man (Soviet? American?) examined my gilt-embossed invitation, checked my name on his list, and allowed me through. My husband, who had accompanied me, stood behind watching the activity in the sealed-off zone — with virtually hundreds of police milling about, he thought, something was sure to happen — but simply by standing there, outside the barrier and gazing in, he aroused the suspicion of a Washington city policeman, who advanced upon him belligerently. "He's just watching his wife walk away," the man with the checklist explained. But by this time my husband had become discouraged at the prospect of participating in the historic event.

Guests went through a second, less formal checkpoint in front of the heavy wrought-iron gates of the embassy, and, inside, just beyond the mirrored foyer, we were asked to walk through a metal-detector frame. Handbags and attaché cases were carefully examined, with apologies — "We are very sorry to do this," an embassy official said. I said, "I understand." I didn't want any violence at the reception either.

At the crowded buzzing reception I gravitated toward Bill Styron, the only familiar face. Invitations to the meeting had gone out so mysteriously, with no American involvement, we were at a loss as to which of our friends and colleagues might be there. Norman Mailer had been mentioned, but we hadn't yet sighted him. And who else? Anyone else? "Look over there," I said, pointing to a far corner of the room, "that man in profile: Isn't he Paul Newman?" Styron considered, but shook his head. "Too young," he said.

A few minutes later we were introduced to Paul Newman, whose left arm was in a sling, and who was a member of our very small "cultural" contingent. Most of the invitations to the reception had gone to American scientists, academicians, and men of the stature of Henry Kissinger, John Kenneth Galbraith, George Kennan, and Cyrus R. Vance; the "artists" consisted of William Styron, Norman Mailer, Paul Newman, Sidney Pollock, John Denver, Yoko Ono, Bel Kaufmann (whose *Up the Down Staircase* was enormously popular in the Soviet Union), one or two others, and me. Amid the crowd Paul Newman, slender, almost slight, with his eerily lapidary features, stood out dramatically: introduced, he had the guarded expression of a man who has been told too frequently that his eyes are blue. "Why are you here?" someone asked. "I was invited," he said.

And then there was a murmur of excitement, and the Gorbachevs 12 were entering the room, and it was as if royalty had appeared in our midst; or media celebrities whose actual faces — youthful, high-colored, smiling, assured — were considerably more attractive than their reproductions. In newspaper photographs Gorbachev has looked jowly, heavyset, and stolid; in person, he fairly radiates energy and vigor, the warmth of a naturally charismatic leader who knows his worth and delights in its reflection in others' eyes. The first thing one sees about him is the cranberry-red birthmark, descending on the right side of his head, with a look of a hieratic (or demonic) sign out of Dostoyevski. To shake hands with Gorbachev — that is, to have one's hand shaken vigorously by Gorbachev — is to feel the grand conviction, no less powerful because it is absurd, that the man has hurried to you for this purpose alone; that, for a blurred moment, *you* are indeed the center of *his* universe. By way of his interpreter the General Secretary seemed to be telling me that he was an admirer of my work — or was it, yet more unexpectedly, "I am a great admirer of your work, Mrs. Oates"? To this I could say only, "I am honored to meet you, Mr. Gorbachev," or some such banality, for to my shame I had not read the Gorbachev *Perestroika*, and at this great moment the inappropriate thought had entered my mind that the real Mrs. Oates, my mother, was in upstate New York.

Then I was shaking hands with Raisa Gorbachev, yet more warmly, and through the interpreter we managed to talk, to a degree, for as it turned out Mrs. Gorbachev too declared herself a "great admirer" of my work, and had read two novels, *A Garden of Earthly Delights* and *Angel of Light*, the latter published in 1987 in Russia. Mrs. Gorbachev, petite, stylish, a beautiful woman only slightly past the bloom of her beauty, held my hand in both of hers and told me that my books are "much read" and "much admired" in her homeland: "You write of women well? And of politics?" The Gorbachevs moved on, meeting my fellow Americans, artists, writers, intellectuals, scientists, shaking hands happily, not at all as if it were a duty, or even a gesture of *noblesse oblige*; there were television cameras and flashbulbs everywhere; and suddenly everyone was craning to see a photo opportunity of some significance — the several-times-posed handshake of Mikhail Gorbachev and Henry Kissinger. As Bill Styron observed, "It *is* a historic occasion; it's hard to stay away from things like this."

The reception ended punctually at 5 P.M. and the guests were ushered into another, even larger and grander ballroom, and seated at numbered tables; fifteen little round tables, six people at each, mainly Americans, with a scattering of Soviets. The color scheme was white and gold, or white and gilt; white tulips, an unexpected choice for December, but beautiful, and fragile, beginning to wilt in the over-warm atmosphere; bottles of mineral water, that Eastern European staple, on each of the tables. I saw to my mild alarm that I was seated beside Henry Kissinger, about whom I had written, briefly, though perhaps critically, in my Washington-set novel *Angel of Light*; but surely, I thought, he had not read those paragraphs? Surely he had never read a word I'd written? When we introduced ourselves Mr. Kissinger said, unsmiling, "Of course I know who you are."

Like an expert leading a university seminar Gorbachev addressed the gathering, telling us much, I suppose, that was familiar, yet speaking with surprising candor. On the subject of the new era in Soviet politics, *glasnost, perestroika*, "openness," "restructuring," he said: "Why are we moved to this? Because we have no choice. The people have lost their tolerance." If socialism seems to have failed it is because it has not been imaginatively utilized; its potential has been thwarted. "But this is our problem, not yours." As Gorbachev spoke he looked out at his audience steadily, and smiled almost steadily, like a popular and aggressive professor who needs to establish rapport with his charges as a way of suggesting not camaraderie but control; thus, sighting John Kenneth Galbraith, he made reference to Galbraith's books, which, he said, he had studied; sighting Henry Kissinger he made a humorous remark to him, as if inviting complicity. Kindred souls; Alpha males.[2] He also recognized John Denver by sight — as few of the intellectuals and academicians would have.

Part of Gorbachev's now legendary charm for Americans is that he tells us things we desperately want to hear, as religious and political leaders have always told their listeners what is most desperately wanted. That Gorbachev comes from the far side of the world, as through a murky looking-glass, only intensifies the drama of the situation: Recall the hugely popular quasi-mystical films of recent years, *2001*, *Close Encounters of the Third Kind*, *E.T.*, the latter two rather juvenile retellings of wisdom/savior myths; sitcom variants of the archetype in the human psyche that craves an other-worldly confirmation of our hopes for salvation, redemption, unique and individual worth. So it is not surprising that the leader of the most powerful Communist nation on earth, the United States's shadow-figure, or dreaded twin, should prove so charismatic to Americans. What is surprising is the historic phenomenon of Mikhail Gorbachev himself: that the man should have such ideas, such revolutionary courage, one might say such amazing faith in the possibility of a radical transformation of his long-repressed and calcified society, in a context of power politics. For after all Gorbachev is not royalty — Raisa is not "the little empress" — but both are subject to censure by the Politburo.

The question-and-answer part of the session was less rewarding than Gorbachev's presentation, perhaps because, in such contexts, the more thoughtful tend to remain silent while others plunge forward to speak. In fact there were few questions, but rather mini-speeches of varying degrees of coherence and plausibility. "Who the hell is that?" and "Who the hell is *that*?" Henry Kissinger several times murmured in my ear, as well-intentioned but possibly rather naïve ideas were aired. One unidentified man, speaking almost rhapsodically, suggested that instead of organizing exchange programs between our two countries involving small numbers of students and professionals, tens of thousands of citizens should be exchanged, not unlike hostages — "taxi drivers, farmers, factory

16

---

[2]Scientific term for the dominant males in animal groups. — ED.

workers"; a woman involved in a worldwide children's fund made an impassioned plea, throwing her arms wide to Gorbachev, while saying in a voice that seemed close to tears, "We throw our arms wide to you!" There were proposals for joint U.S.-USSR research into AIDS, and travel to Mars; a suggestion that the arms manufacturers in the United States begin to produce automobiles, computers, and other domestic machines, to be donated to the USSR. One histrionic gentleman spoke of a multinational production of a Shakespearean play, in different languages. "Who is *that*?" Henry Kissinger asked several of us. But no one knew.

And so it went, until, near the end of the session, Gorbachev called upon a Russian Orthodox priest (incongruous in our midst, fiercely bearded, and wearing sacerdotal robes) to tell the gathering about Soviet freedom of worship, which, in rather vague rhetorical terms, the priest did. "And tell us, what are the statistics? How many marriages each year in the churches? How many baptisms?" Gorbachev smilingly inquired; but the priest backed down, faltering, or missing his cue entirely, saying only vaguely that religion in Russia was a "mass movement" and that "we don't keep records." There was an awkward pause. Had something gone wrong? Was Gorbachev disappointed in his countryman's performance? But the General Secretary's affable calm was not rippled, not once, in our presence.

Punctually at 6 P.M. the session ended, and Mr. and Mrs. Gorbachev were hurried away to their next appointment, at the White House. The protracted formality of a state dinner awaited; one could not envy them, much. I was thinking how anachronistic the tragic sense of life had come to seem, suddenly — at least in this cordoned-off ballroom in the Soviet embassy, with dozens of security men — KGB? Secret Service? — stationed obtrusively against the walls; and Gorbachev's measured, reasonable, persuasive words, everything electronically recorded for posterity. I was thinking, It is all too good to be true but does it logically follow, then, that it is not true; or that some of it, some day, might become true? We want so badly to believe.

In parting, Henry Kissinger shook my hand and said, with an unread- 20
able expression, "I am a great admirer of your work." I was so taken by surprise I had not the wit to call after him, as of course I should have done, "And I'm a great admirer of your work too."

EXPLORATIONS

1. What pair of somewhat contradictory conclusions does Oates draw from her encounter with Mikhail Gorbachev? Which conclusion does she seem to think she ought to believe? Which one does she want to believe?

2. What is the effect of Oates's opening her essay as she does, rather than telling her story in chronological order? How would you summarize the thesis of her introductory section (paras. 1–4)?

3. What is Oates's initial reaction to the embassy's invitation? How does her response to the reception change once she arrives, and why?

4. How would the impact of Oates's essay be different without Henry Kissinger? without Paul Newman?

CONNECTIONS

1. What reasons does Mikhail Gorbachev give in "The US and the USSR" for holding the reception to which Oates and other American artists, writers, and intellectuals were invited? How does his summary of his reasons differ from Oates's?

2. Oates writes, "Part of Gorbachev's now legendary charm for Americans is that he tells us things we desperately want to hear" (para. 16). What comments by Gorbachev in "The US and the USSR" support this statement? What comments by Gorbachev do not reflect what Americans want to hear?

3. Oates reports an anecdote Gorbachev told about the rest of the world laughing at Americans and Russians. According to Raymonde Carroll in "Money and Seduction," what American qualities do the French find laughable, and why? According to Octavio Paz in "Hygiene and Repression," what U.S. qualities do Latin Americans find laughable, and why? Do you think the rest of the world enjoys laughing at the United States and the Soviet Union more than at less powerful nations? Why or why not?

ELABORATIONS

1. Have you ever been present at a historic occasion? If not, think of a historic event you followed in the media as it took place. Write a narrative essay about such an event in which you combine, as Oates does, the ideas that made it important and the sensory details that gave it a personal reality for you.

2. On the basis of the selections in this unit and your own opinion, write an essay predicting what the United States's role in the world will be in the twenty-first century.

PART TWO

THE FAMILY

Cornerstone of Culture

LOOKING AT OURSELVES

Michael Novak, Carol Kleiman, Jean Seligman, Arlie Hochschild
with Anne Machung, Claudia Wallis, Ellen Goodman

Bruno Bettelheim, *Why Kibbutzim?* (ISRAEL)

Liang Heng and Judith Shapiro, *Chairman Mao's Good
Little Boy* (CHINA)

Carola Hansson and Karin Lidén, *Liza and Family*
(SOVIET UNION)

John Updike, *The Lovely Troubled Daughters of Our Old Crowd*
(UNITED STATES)

Margaret Atwood, *Scenes from Two Childhoods* (CANADA)

John David Morley, *Acquiring a Japanese Family* (JAPAN)

Gyanranjan, *Our Side of the Fence and Theirs* (INDIA)

Wole Soyinka, *Nigerian Childhood* (NIGERIA)

Gholam-Hossein Sa'edi, *The Game Is Over* (IRAN)

ALL OVER THE WORLD, FAMILIES ARE THE MEANS BY WHICH NEW MEM-
bers of a society start learning its rules. From this introduction come the
child's earliest ideas about what is "normal" and what is "strange." Human
beings are astonishingly adaptable. Thus, as we scan different societies,
we see children — and their parents — playing a wide variety of roles.

Just as the family's structure and dynamics change from one society
to another, so does the writer's focus. What is significant about families?
unusual? amusing? inspiring? tragic? We open with *Looking at Ourselves*
passages: Michael Novak on capitalism's impact on the American family;
Carol Kleiman's frustrations as a divorced mother; Jean Seligman on the
changing definition of family; Arlie Hochschild and Anne Machung on
the division of labor in families with two working parents; Claudia Wallis
on our national preoccupation with day care; and Ellen Goodman as-
sessing the family as "social glue."

As we see how writers of different nationalities approach this universal
institution, we look into the heart of culture. Bruno Bettelheim examines
the Israeli communal strategy of child rearing in "Why Kibbutzim?" In
"Chairman Mao's Good Little Boy," Liang Heng and Judith Shapiro
recount the anguish of a Chinese family torn apart by state-controlled
parenthood. Communism has a different impact on families in the Soviet
Union, as Carola Hansson and Karin Lidén reveal in their portrait of a
harried Moscow mother, "Liza and Family." Liza's wistfulness is shared
by the narrator of John Updike's short story "The Lovely Troubled Daughters of Our Old Crowd," but here it is a father who wonders how family
life in his comfortable New England suburb ever became so difficult.
Across the border, "Scenes from Two Childhoods" compares Margaret
Atwood's memories of growing up in Canada with her mother's.

Identification between self, home, and family infuses John David
Morley's "Acquiring a Japanese Family": In Japan, the word for "home"
can also mean "myself." In Gyanranjan's short story "Our Side of the
Fence and Theirs," an Indian family watches their new neighbors for
breaches of the social code. Wole Soyinka's "Nigerian Childhood" depicts
an Anglican household where British propriety is cheerfully mixed with
African magic. Finally, in Gholam-Hossein Sa'edi's chilling story "The
Game Is Over," poverty and parental abuse spur two Iranian boys to an
act that staggers their whole village.   ◈

LOOKING AT OURSELVES

1

Choosing to have a family used to be uninteresting. It is, today, an act of intelligence and courage. To love family life, to see in family life the most potent moral, intellectual, and political cell in the body politic is to be marked today as a heretic.

Orthodoxy is usually enforced by an economic system. Our own system, postindustrial capitalism, plays an ambivalent role with respect to the family. On the one hand, capitalism demands hard work, competition, sacrifice, saving, and rational decision-making. On the other, it stresses liberty and encourages hedonism.

Now the great corporations (as well as the universities, the political professions, the foundations, the great newspapers and publishing empires, and the film industry) diminish the moral and economic importance of the family. They demand travel and frequent change of residence. Teasing the heart with glittering entertainment and gratifying the demands of ambition, they dissolve attachments and loyalties. Husbands and wives live in isolation from each other. Children of the upwardly mobile are almost as abandoned, emotionally, as the children of the ghetto. The lives of husbands, wives, and children do not mesh, are not engaged, seem merely thrown together. There is enough money. There is too much emotional space. It is easier to leave town than to pretend that one's lives truly matter to each other. (I remember the tenth anniversary party of a foreign office of a major newsmagazine; none of its members was married to his spouse of ten years before.) At an advanced stage capitalism imparts enormous centrifugal forces to the souls of those who have most internalized its values, and these forces shear marriages and families apart. . . .

An economic order that would make the family the basic unit of social policy would touch every citizen at the nerve center of daily life. The family is the primary teacher of moral development. In the struggles and conflicts of marital life, husbands and wives learn the realism and adult practicalities of love. Through the love, stability, discipline, and laughter of parents and siblings, children learn that reality accepts them, welcomes them, invites their willingness to take risks. The family nourishes "basic trust." From this spring creativity, psychic energy, social dynamism. If infants are injured here, not all the institutions of society can put them back together.

> – Michael Novak
> "The Family Out of Favor"
> *Harper's*

2

One summer day, my son Robert, then five years old, took me by the hand and asked me to go outside with him.

Holding on tightly, he carefully walked around the house with me, looking at doors and windows and shaking his head. There was something he didn't understand.

"Mommy," he finally asked, pressing my hand with his warm, chubby fingers, "is our home broken?"

His words shot through my body, alerting every protective instinct, activating my private defense system, the one I hold in reserve to ward off attacks against women and children.

"Oh, Robbie," I answered, hugging him, "did someone tell you that we have a broken home?"

"Yes," he said sweetly. "But it doesn't *look* broken!"

"It's not," I assured him. "Our house is not broken and neither are we."

I explained that "broken" is some people's way of describing a home with only one parent, usually the mother. Sometimes there was only one parent because of divorce, like us. "There are still lots of homes like ours. And they're still homes."

Robbie looked relieved and went to play with his friends. I stood there, shaking with anger.

What a way to put down a little kid and me, too, I thought. I supported my three children, fed and clothed them. I was there for them emotionally and physically. I managed to keep up payments on the house. Although we struggled financially, we were happy and loving. What was "broken" about us?

> – Carol Kleiman
> "My Home Is Not Broken, It Works"
> *Ms.*

3

What's in a family? A mommy, a daddy, a couple of kids, and maybe a grandma, right? Well, yes, but that's not the whole picture anymore. The family tree of American society is sending forth a variety of new and fast-growing branches. Gay and lesbian couples (with or without children) and unmarried heterosexual couples are now commonplace. What's surprising is not so much that these offshoots of the main trunk are flourishing but that the public seems more and more willing to recognize them as families. [In 1990] the Massachusetts Mutual Life Insurance Co. asked 1,200 randomly selected adults to define the word *"family."* Only 22 percent picked the legalistic definition. "A group of people related by blood, marriage, or adoption." Almost three quarters instead chose a much broader and more emotional description: "A group of people who love and care for each other." As usual, the American people are changing old perceptions much faster than the courts are. But in many parts of the country lawmakers are now finally catching up and validating the legitimacy of the nontraditional family.

– Jean Seligman
"Variations on a Theme"
Newsweek

4

As masses of women have moved into the economy, families have been hit by a "speedup" in work and family life. There is no more time in the day than there was when wives stayed home, but there is twice as much to get done. It is mainly women who absorb this speedup. Twenty percent of the men in my study shared housework equally. Seventy percent did a substantial amount (less than half of it, but more than a third), and 10 percent did less than a third.

Even when couples share more equitably in the work at home, women do two thirds of the daily jobs at home. such as cooking and cleaning up — jobs that fix them into a rigid routine. Most women cook dinner, and most men change the oil in the family car. But, as one mother pointed out, dinner needs to be prepared every evening around six o'clock, whereas the car oil needs to be changed every six months, any day around that time, any time that day. Women do more child care then men, and men repair more household appliances. A child needs to be tended daily, whereas the repair of household appliances can often wait "until I have time." Men thus have more control over when they make their contributions than women do. They may be very busy with family chores, but, like the executive who tells his secretary to "hold my calls," the man has more control over his time. The job of the working mother, like that of the secretary, is usually to "take the calls."

Another reason why women may feel more strained than men is that women more often do two things at once — for example, write checks and return phone calls, vacuum and keep an eye on a three-year-old, fold laundry and think out the shopping list. Men more often cook dinner *or* take a child to the park. Indeed, women more often juggle three spheres — job, children, and housework — while most men juggle two — job and children. For women, two activities compete with their time with children, not just one.

Beyond doing more at home, women also devote proportionately more of their time at home to housework and proportionately less of it to child care. Of all the time men spend working at home, a growing amount of it goes to child care. That is, working wives spend relatively more time mothering the house; husbands spend more time mothering the children. Since most parents prefer to tend to their children than to clean house, men do more of what they'd rather do. More men than women take their children on "fun" outings to the park, the zoo, the movies. Women spend more time on maintenance, such as feeding and bathing children — enjoyable activities, to be sure, but often less leisurely or "special" than going to the zoo. Men also do fewer of the most undesirable household chores: Fewer men than women wash toilets and scrub the bathroom.

As a result, women tend to talk more intently about being overtired, sick, and emotionally drained. Many women I could not tear away from the topic of sleep. They talked about how much they could "get by on": six and a half, seven, seven and a half, less, more. They talked about who they knew who needed more or less. Some apologized for how much sleep they needed — "I'm afraid I need eight hours of sleep" — as if eight was "too much." They talked about the effect of a change in baby sitter, the birth of a second child, or a business trip on their child's pattern of sleep. They talked about how to avoid fully waking up when a child called them at night, and how to get back to sleep. These women talked about sleep the way a hungry person talks about food.

All in all, if, in this period of American history, the two-job family is suffering from a speedup of work and family life, working mothers are its primary victims.

– Arlie Hochschild
with Anne Machung
"Second Shift"
New Age Journal

5

With both Mom and Dad away at the office or store or factory, the child-care crunch has become the most wrenching personal problem facing millions of American families. In 1986, 9 million preschoolers spent their days in the hands of someone other than their mother. Millions of older children participate in programs providing after-school supervision. As American women continue to pour into the work force, the trend will accelerate. "We are in the midst of an explosion," says Elinor Guggenheimer, president of the Manhattan-based Child Care Action Campaign. In ten years, she predicts, the number of children under six who will need daytime supervision will grow more than 50 percent. Says Jay Belsky, a professor of human development at Pennsylvania State University: "We are as much a society dependent on female labor, and thus in need of a child-care system, as we are a society dependent on the automobile, and thus in need of roads."

At the moment, though, the American child-care system — to the extent that there is one — is riddled with potholes. Throughout the country, working parents are faced with a triple quandary: Day care is hard to find, difficult to afford, and often of distressingly poor quality. Waiting lists at good facilities are so long that parents apply for a spot months before their children are born. Or even earlier. The Empire State center in Farmingdale, N.Y., received an application from a woman attorney a week after she became engaged to marry. Apparently she hoped to time her pregnancy for an anticipated opening. The Jeanne Simon center in Burlington, Vt., has a folder of applications labeled "preconception." . . .

Fretting about the effects of day care on children has become a national preoccupation. What troubles lie ahead for a generation reared by strangers? What kind of adults will they become? "It is scaring everybody that a whole generation of children is being raised in a way that has never happened before," says Edward Zigler, professor of psychology at Yale and an authority on child care. At least one major survey of current research, by Penn State's Belsky, suggests that extensive day care in the first year of life raises the risk of emotional problems, a conclusion that has mortified already guilty working parents. With high-quality supervision costing upwards of $100 a week, many families are placing their children in the hands of untrained, overworked personnel. "In some places, that means one woman taking care of nine babies," says Zigler. "Nobody doing that can give them the stimulation they need. We encounter some real horror stories out there, with babies being tied into cribs."

The U.S. is the only Western industrialized nation that does not guarantee a working mother the right to a leave of absence after she has a child. Although the Supreme Court ruled last January [1987] that states may require businesses to provide maternity leaves with job security, only 40 percent of working women receive such protection through their companies. Even for these, the leaves are generally brief and unpaid. This forces many women to return to work sooner than they would like and creates a huge demand for infant care, the most expensive and difficult child-care service to supply. The premature separation takes a personal toll as well, observes Harvard pediatrician T. Berry Brazelton, heir apparent to Benjamin Spock as the country's preeminent guru on child rearing. "Many parents return to the workplace grieving."

– Claudia Wallis
"The Child-Care Dilemma"
Time

6

They are going home for Thanksgiving, traveling through the clogged arteries of airports and highways, bearing bridge chairs and serving plates, Port-a-Cribs and pies. They are going home to rooms that resound with old arguments and interruptions, to piano benches filled with small cousins, to dining-room tables stretched out to the last leaf.

They no longer migrate over the river and through the woods straight into that Norman Rockwell poster: Freedom from Want. No, Thanksgiving isn't just a feast, but a reunion. It's no longer a celebration of food (which is plentiful in America) but of family (which is scarce).

Now families are so dispersed that it's easier to bring in the crops than the cousins. Now it's not so remarkable that we have a turkey to feed the family. It's more remarkable that there's enough family around to warrant a turkey.

For most of the year, we are a nation of individuals, all wrapped in separate cellophane packages like lamb chops in the meat department of a city supermarket. Increasingly we live with decreasing numbers. We create a new category like Single Householder, and fill it to the top of the Census Bureau reports.

For most of the year, we are segregated along generation lines into retirement villages and singles complexes, young married subdivisions and college dormitories, all exclusive clubs whose membership is defined by age. . . .

The family — as extended as that dining-room table — may be the one social glue strong enough to withstand the centrifuge of special interests which sends us spinning away from each other. There, in the family, the Elderly Rights are also grandparents and the Children Rights are also nieces and nephews. There, the old are our parents and the young are our children. There, we care about each others' lives. There, self-interest includes concern for the future of the next generation. Because they are ours.

Our families are not just the people (if I may massacre Robert Frost) who, "when you have to go there, they have to let you in." They are the people who maintain an unreasonable interest in each other. They are the natural peacemakers in the generation war.

"Home" is the only place in society where we now connect along the ages, like discs along the spine of society. The only place where we remember that we're all related. And that's not a bad idea to go home to.

> – Ellen Goodman
> "Family: The One Social Glue"
> *Close to Home*

BRUNO BETTELHEIM

Why Kibbutzim?

Bruno Bettelheim, born in Vienna in 1903, is known for his pioneering work on children's emotional development and disorders. He received his Ph.D. from the University of Vienna in 1938, the same year the Nazis invaded Austria. Bettelheim was sent to the concentration camps at Dachau and Buchenwald. Released the next year, he emigrated to the United States and became a naturalized citizen. In addition to serving as a professor of education, psychology, and psychiatry at the University of Chicago, he headed the university's Sonia Shankman Orthogenic School from 1944 until 1973. He wrote numerous books, articles, and essays, as well as a long-running monthly column for the *Ladies' Home Journal,* and he coproduced a motion picture, *The Kibbutz.* Bettelheim continued to write into his eighties and published his last book, *A Good Enough Parent,* in 1987. In March 1990 — six years after his wife died, three years after a stroke impaired his mental acuity, and several weeks after he moved to a Maryland nursing home — he committed suicide at the age of eighty-six.

"Why Kibbutzim?" comes from Bettelheim's 1969 book *The Children of the Dream,* which he wrote after spending seven weeks studying communal child rearing in the Israeli kibbutz. These collective farms (singular *kibbutz,* plural *kibbutzim*) were first established by Palestinian Jews even before the United Nations officially created the state of Israel in 1948. Jews fleeing discrimination and persecution all over the world had been migrating to this strip of land on the eastern Mediterranean coast, seeking to reestablish the ancient Jewish homeland. After World War II more than a million refugees flocked here. Creating kibbutzim was one concrete way of helping to build a new and better future. In a country of 7,992 square miles which includes the Dead Sea and the Negev Desert, and only a fifth of which is arable, kibbutzim have been practically as well as politically crucial. Today they remain a way of life for a significant minority of Israelis, and a cornerstone of Israeli culture.

(For more background on Israel, see p. 618.)

From its very inception the purpose of the kibbutz movement, for both sexes, was first and foremost to create a new way of life in a very old and hostile land. True, the raising of a new generation to this new way of life was soon of crucial importance, but of necessity it took second place. Because unless the first generation created the society, how could it shelter any new generations? It was this older generation that subjected itself to great hardships and dangers, that first reclaimed the land, wresting harvests from a barren soil, and later fought the war that gained them statehood.

Today, apart from the still pervasive problem of making fast their new statehood, there is still the war for social ideals to be waged. But those ideals are harder to maintain when the problem is no longer one of creating a homeland, but of maintaining themselves as a splinter group in a land swept up in a booming economy. Such ideals are specially hard to preserve when the surrounding population is by now so largely concerned with acquiring the more convenient life that goes with a higher standard of living. The kibbutz parent, in his devotion to ideals, may be likened to our own early Puritans; except that these latter-day Puritans are not surrounded by a wilderness but by modern city life, which makes things a lot harder.

Kibbutzniks have never been more than a tiny minority in Israel. Nevertheless they have played a critical role there, both as idea and reality, out of all proportion to their numbers. For example, in 1944 Henrik Infield, in his book *Co-operative Living in Palestine,* places the total membership of all kibbutzim at about sixteen thousand. Twenty years later their numbers had grown to about eighty thousand, living in about 250 kibbutzim, but they were still only about 4 percent of the population of Israel. Yet this 4 percent accounted for some 15 percent of all members of the Knesset (Israeli parliament).

Even if the kibbutz stood for no more than a small sect, living by its   4 esoteric convictions and trying to raise its children by these lights, their devotion to lofty ideals would command respect. But for Israel they do much more than that, since they still provide much of the national ethos, and the best part of it. As many thoughtful Israelis told me: Were it not for the kibbutz dream of a better society, there would be nothing unique left about Israel. Having created a refuge where Jews can live free of persecution, Israel would be nothing more now than just a tiny new nation.

(Though written before the 1967 war, I see no reason to change this statement. The Arab-Israeli conflict is no longer a matter of the majority group persecuting a minority of its own citizens, but of two or more nation-states at odds over territorial rights. That one is smaller than the others does not make war and persecution the same thing, which they are not.)

It is also a nation with only one tenuous claim to the land: namely, that some two thousand years ago it was occupied by the spiritual ancestors of those who again hold possession now. This is not much of a claim compared to the uniqueness Jews felt, and which kept the Jews going during the two thousand years they were homeless.

All this has, in fact, led to many contradictions from which kibbutz life still suffers: In reclaiming the land, as in creating the state of Israel, kibbutzniks displaced Arab neighbors and fought them though violence was contrary to their socialist convictions. Kibbutz founders wanted Israel to be an ideal state, free of all exploitation, where life would proceed in peace close to the biblical land. But the realities of the Middle East force Israel to be a garrison nation geared to defense, if not a war; a capitalist nation with many of the unpleasant features of a new nation trying to industrialize in a hurry.

I know that they also suffer from another contradiction, because they are keenly aware of it: Since they are atheists, they cannot base their claim to the land on the biblical promise that gave it to the Jews. The Jews needed a homestead. How desperately they needed it was made clear first by Hitler, and then by the plight of the Jews in Arab countries. But no other land was acceptable to the religious group, and no other land offered asylum to areligious Jews. So it had to be Israel, whether for political or emotional reasons.

In the face of all this contradiction and conflict, then, is where the kibbutz ethos makes a difference. It stands for utter devotion to the idea that once again Jews in Israel must not only create a new model of the good and just life, but actually live it — when need be at the cost of great personal hardship — or die for it if they must. Certainly the six-day war vindicated kibbutz child-rearing methods and made it once again a symbol of all that is best in Israel. Not only did the kibbutz provide an inordinate percentage of the officer corps, it also suffered staggering losses. Some 4 percent of the Israeli population lives in the kibbutz, and kibbutzniks thus accounted for some 4 percent of the fighting force. But while about eight hundred soldiers fell in the war, two hundred of them came from the kibbutz (most of them born and raised there). Thus the 4 percent kibbutz segment of the Israeli army suffered 25 percent of all casualties. This was the true measure of their heroism, courage, and devotion to duty. Once more, as in the settling of the land and the war of liberation, the kibbutz ethos gives special meaning to the lives of Israelis today.

It is in this context of self-elected mission that the entire phenomenon of the kibbutz must be understood, and flowing from it, what the parents do or do not do in raising their children. . . .

How did the kibbutz way of raising children come about? First, it seems that kibbutz founders did not trust themselves to raise their own children in such a way as to become the carriers of a new society. To quote [Stanley] Diamond:

> The collective method of child rearing represents a rejection of the family, with particular reference to the parental roles. . . . It was felt that the family itself has to be banished, in order to rear the "new Jew." . . . [Kibbutz founders] were moved by the desire to create a new generation that would be "normal," "free," and "manly," unsullied by the exile. . . . They did not think themselves worthy of rearing such children within the confines of their own nuclear families, and they dared not trust themselves to the task.[1]

Thus the realization of their larger dream depended on this new and uniquely brought up generation. But the new generation, and the unique way of bringing them up, were an afterthought, an accident. The kibbutz — a society that devotes its all to the future, and hence to its children, that has turned upside down all traditional modes of child rearing to realize its goals — started out as a society that had no interest in children whatsoever and no room for children in its life. 12

While this in no way invalidates the educational method, it accounts for many contradictions that cannot be understood except from its unplanned inception. We are faced with the anomaly that what started as a nuisance, because it stood in the way of the founders' main purposes — to execute an idea — has become a central feature on which the idea's survival now depends.

As Joseph Baratz (1954) tells the story of Degania, the first kibbutz, the original kibbutzniks (of whom he was one) wanted no children in their community. Most of the settlers did not even want to marry, because "they were afraid that children would detach the family from the group, that . . . comradeship would be less steadfast." Therefore it was seriously proposed that all members should oblige themselves not to marry for at least five years after joining the kibbutz, because "living as we do . . . how can we have children?"

---

[1]In *Social Problems* 5. 2 (1957), and *Dissent* 4 (1957). — ED.

When the first child was born in the kibbutz "nobody knew what to do with him. Our women didn't know how to look after babies." But eventually "we saw it couldn't go on like this. . . . By the time there were four children in the settlement we decided something must be done. It was a difficult problem. How were the women both to work and look after their children? Should each mother look after her own family and do nothing else?" The men did not seem to feel strongly either way.

> But the women wouldn't hear of giving up their share of the communal work and life. . . . Somebody proposed that the kibbutz should hire a nurse . . . we didn't hire a nurse, but we chose one girl to look after the lot of them and we put aside a house where they could spend the day while the mothers were at work. And so this system developed and was afterwards adopted in all the kibbutzim, with the difference that in most of them the children sleep in the children's house, but with us [at Degania] they stay at night in their parents' quarters. . . . Only recently have we built a hostel for children over twelve where our own children live.[2]

This is how the famous communal education of children began.   16

I myself questioned the founding generation: I wondered why the original group, so intent on creating a new way of life, had given no thought to their own continuity by planning for the next generation. The answer was always the same as the one given in published accounts by the earliest settlers: "Founding the settlements, cultivating the land was so arduous, so much a grown-ups' task, that we could not think about children." I cannot help feeling that part of the original attraction of a thus-defined task might have been that it left no place for children. Because if one does not think of having children, it is because one has no wish for them at the time, and not because the task at hand is so arduous.

If my speculation is valid, one might carry it a step further and say that the founding generation knew they had no wish to replicate the family as they knew it, and of this they were entirely conscious. But despite their rejection they could not think of how else to raise children. Hence to them, the decision not to form families meant not to have children. If so, then kibbutz life was attractive to those who for this or other reasons did not wish to have children. My assumption seems

---

[2]In *A Village by the Jordan* (London: Harville Press). — ED.

supported by the incredibly low birthrate in the early days of kibbutz history, which contrasts sharply with other settings in which a people live in hardship and danger and nevertheless produce many children.

It would seem, then, that chance and a desire for quite other things dictated the child-caring arrangements made hastily, piecemeal, and with little plan or thought; arrangements that were later formalized into dogma, as is probably the origin of most dogmas.

EXPLORATIONS

1. Bettelheim writes, "The kibbutz parent, in his devotion to ideals, may be likened to our own early Puritans" (para. 2). What similarities is he referring to? In what ways do you think "modern city life . . . makes things a lot harder" for the kibbutz parent than for the Puritans?

2. Most of Bettelheim's paragraphs open with a topic sentence which is followed by supporting evidence. Look at four or five paragraphs in "Why Kibbutzim?" What different types of evidence does Bettelheim use? Which type(s) do you find most persuasive?

3. Bettelheim speaks of "the kibbutz dream of a better society" (para. 4). Based on his description of how kibbutzim came to exist and how they operate, what kind of "better society" does "the kibbutz dream" seem to represent? What are its ideals and goals as a culture and for individual members of the culture?

CONNECTIONS

1. According to Bettelheim, the kibbutz policy of communal child rearing was created because early kibbutzniks placed other priorities before parenthood. Reread *Looking at Ourselves*. Which passages show Americans creating non-traditional approaches to child rearing in order to accommodate priorities besides parenthood? What are these other priorities?

2. Look at the quotation in Bettelheim's paragraph 15. How does child care on the kibbutz, as described here, compare with day care in the United States, as discussed by Claudia Wallis in *Looking at Ourselves*? What advantages does each system have over the other? Which system would you expect to produce healthier, happier children, and why?

3. What statements by Michael Novak in *Looking at Ourselves* suggest that some

contemporary Americans share the qualms about having families which Bettelheim attributes to the Israeli kibbutzniks? According to Novak and Bettelheim, how are Americans' and Israelis' reasons for avoiding this commitment similar and different?

ELABORATIONS

1. Bettelheim quotes Stanley Diamond: "The collective method of child rearing represents a rejection of the family" (para. 11). What specific aspects of the traditional nuclear family do you think the early kibbutzniks rejected, and why? Based on "Why Kibbutzim?" and *Looking at Ourselves*, as well as your own knowledge of life in nuclear families, write an essay about the practical and psychological conflicts between work (or political activism, or any other time-consuming commitment) and traditional parenthood.

2. According to Bettelheim, the kibbutz's communal approach to child rearing derived from the potential parents' wish for their children to be better, stronger, and happier than they were. Do you think American parents share this wish? If so, what strategies do they pursue to fulfill it, and how well do they succeed? If not, what are their goals for their children? Drawing on Bettelheim's analysis and *Looking at Ourselves*, write an essay on the aims and dreams of American parents (or some specific segment thereof) and their impact on American children.

LIANG HENG and
JUDITH SHAPIRO

Chairman Mao's Good Little Boy

Liang Heng was born in 1954 in Changsha, the Central Chinese city where Mao Zedong went to high school. Liang's childhood coincided with a period of violent pendulum swings in Communist Party policy. For about eight years after establishing the People's Republic of China in 1949, Chairman Mao and his cohorts enjoyed wide popular support for unifying the government and improving economic and social conditions. In the mid-1950s, however, the Party's moves to encourage criticism boomeranged into an "Anti-Rightist" campaign against the critics. "Chairman Mao's Good Little Boy" comes from the first chapter of Liang's autobiography, *Son of the Revolution* (1983), which describes the chaos and fear of those early years.

His family's victimization hardly dampened Liang's revolutionary loyalty. After the events he narrates here, Liang became one of Mao's Red Guards (working-class students on an ideological warpath against the "bourgeoisie" and intellectuals). The takeover of China by Mao and his Communist cohorts marked the climax of a long push to modernize an ancient empire. While Mao's government achieved much progress and won wide popular support, its methods included periodic crackdowns on ideological foes — real or imagined. One such violent wave of oppression was the Cultural Revolution launched in 1966. Swept up in Mao's Confucian philosophy of saving the Chinese spirit by rejecting Western culture, politics, and technology, Liang went on a quixotic "New Long March" during which he nearly starved and froze. He traveled to Beijing to see Mao, plunged into the "black society" of teenage dropouts scrounging for a living on the streets of Changsha, and worked as a peasant on a commune. His escape route was basketball, which took him to a city job and eventually to college.

Judith Shapiro was born in 1953. She met Liang at Hunan Teachers' College, where she was teaching American literature. Their secret romance culminated in marriage in 1980. In addition to *Son of the Revolution,* they coauthored two more books on China after Chairman Mao before they divorced. Liang, who received a master's degree in literature from Columbia University, now lives in New York, where he edits *The Chinese Intellectual,* a Chinese-language quarterly for visiting scholars and students from the People's Republic. Shapiro is a resident scholar at the Foreign Policy Research Institute in Philadelphia and an adjunct lecturer in sociology at the University of Pennsylvania. Her most recent book, written with her mother, Joan Hatch Lennox, is *Lifechanges: How Women Can Make Courageous Choices* (1990).

(For more background on China, see pp. 583 and 656.)

Once when I was nearly four, I decided to escape from the child-care center. The idea of waiting through another Saturday afternoon was unbearable. I would stand with the other children in the office doorway, yelling out the names of those whose relatives we spotted coming to rescue them. I would become frantic and miserable as the possibility that I had been forgotten seemed more and more real. Then at last the frail figure of my beloved Waipo, my maternal grandmother, would appear to take me away. But this week I wouldn't have to wait. I had just discovered a doorway leading from the kitchen directly onto the Changsha streets, left ajar, perhaps, by the cooks now that the bitter winter weather had passed. So, during after-lunch nap, I crawled over the green bars of my crib and stole softly out, past the sleeping rows of my fellow inmates, past Nurse Nie dozing in her chair. I crept into the coal-dark kitchen with its silent black works. Then I exploded out the door into the dazzling light of freedom.

The child-care center was hateful. You couldn't eat sweets when you wanted to, and you had to fold your hands behind your back and sing a song before the nurses would let you eat your meals. Then, if you ate too fast, they hit you over the head with a fly swatter. The songs and dances — like "Sweeping the Floor," "Working in the Factory," and "Planting Trees in the Countryside" — were fun, but I was constantly in trouble for wanting to dance the army dance when it was time for the hoeing dance or for refusing to take the part of the landlord, the wolf, or the lazybones. I also had problems with the interminable rest periods. We weren't allowed to get up even if we weren't tired, so I had nothing to do but stare at a small mole on my leg for hours at a time.

At the time, such early education was a privilege for which only the children of cadres were eligible. Although neither of my parents' ranks was high, my father's position as reporter, editor, and founding member of the Party newspaper the *Hunan Daily*, and my mother's as a promising cadre in the Changsha Public Security Bureau were enough to qualify me. My parents were deeply involved in all the excitement of working to transform China into a great Socialist country, eager to sacrifice themselves for others. They dreamed passionately of the day when they would be deemed pure and devoted enough to be accepted into the Party. It was only natural that the family come second; Father's duties at the newspaper often kept him away for several months at a time, and my mother came home only on Sundays, if at all, for she had a room in her own unit and stayed there to attend evening meetings. So at the age of three I was sent off to the child-care center for early training in Socialist thought through collective living, far from the potentially corrupting influence of family life. My departure may have been harder for my two grandmothers, of course. They had had the major responsibility for raising the three of us children; I was the last child to go and they would miss me very much.

I had lived first with my paternal grandmother, my Nai Nai, a tall,   4 stern, bony woman who always wore traditional black. She lived in the apartment the *Hunan Daily* had allotted to Father, two rooms on the second floor of a cadres' dormitory, spacious enough but with a shared kitchen and an outhouse some distance away. She was a pious Buddhist and a vegetarian, strict with herself and everyone else but her own grandchildren.

At ten pounds, I had been the biggest baby ever recorded at Changsha's No. 1 Hospital, and Nai Nai had hired a series of seven wet nurses before she found one who could satisfy my appetite. She was a nineteen-year-old peasant girl from a town beyond the city whose own baby had died. Nai Nai told me later that she was the only one who had enough milk so that I could suck her breasts dry without throwing a tantrum immediately afterwards; I have always given credit to her for my unusual height — I am 6'1". Then after she left because she had no Changsha city residence card, Nai Nai sent me to live with my maternal grandmother, my Waipo, who lived off a winding little alleyway not far away.

It was much more crowded there, since Waipo, my Uncle Yan, and his wife and their small children made three generations in a single dark room. But I liked the place for its liveliness and because I was Waipo's favorite. She gave me candies and took me everywhere with her, even to the free market to buy from the peasants who had carried in their vegetables from the suburbs. Waipo was a tiny woman with big twisted teeth and little wrinkled hands, talkative and lively and very different from Nai Nai. Her husband had died when she was young, after only two children, whereas Nai Nai's husband had given her nine before he slipped and fell on the icy road in front of the old City Gate. In the old society, a woman couldn't remarry and remain respectable, so Waipo had supported herself and her children by making shoe soles at home. She continued to do this even after Mother and Uncle Yan were grown and had jobs, and the cloth patches she used were among my first toys.

Another reason I liked living with Waipo was that Mother often preferred to go there on Sundays rather than to our own home, where Nai Nai was, because she didn't get along well with her mother-in-law. Nai Nai sometimes carried her concern for others so far that she became a busybody. She was always the first to sweep the public stairwell or volunteer to lead neighborhood hygiene movements, and she was constantly scolding Mother for not dressing us warmly enough or not buying us more milk to drink. She was so tall that she must have been imposing for Mother to deal with, and tradition demanded that Mother obey her. So although Mother was a feisty woman, she was supposed to look on silently as Nai Nai spoiled us with candy and, in later years, did my second sister's homework for her. Father was no help, because he was bound by the same filial laws as she.

In any case, Mother's ties to her new home could not have been strong ones, for she had hardly known Father before they married. Someone had introduced them as prospective mates; they had exchanged a few letters (Father was working in Guilin at the time) and decided the question soon after on the basis of their common political enthusiasm. Father was far more intellectual than she, for he had been trained by the Party as a reporter, had a wide range of literary interests, and was an accomplished poet as well as an amateur composer and conductor. Mother was capable too, of course, a strong-willed person who liked to express her opinions, and a loving mother when she had the time. Still, as I thought back on it in later years, I realized my parents were so rarely together that it was almost a marriage of convenience.

So it was Waipo's home that was my early emotional center, and it was there that I went on the fresh spring day of my flight. I had to cross a large street, but fortunately I made it from one side to the other without mishap, and ran the remaining few hundred yards to the narrow room off the little gray alley.

To my utter dismay, Waipo didn't look at all glad to see me. "Little Fatso, what are you doing here?" she cried, and with scarcely a pause grabbed my hand and pulled me the few blocks to Nai Nai's home in *Hunan Daily* compound. From there the two old ladies half lifted, half dragged me back to my confinement, ignoring my screams and tears.

The nurses had discovered my absence. Without any show of the politeness they usually maintained before their charges' relatives, they cursed and scolded me as if they would never stop. When my grandmothers had left, they locked me up in a room with two other offenders, saying, "You are not Chairman Mao's good little boy; you haven't upheld Revolutionary discipline. You can stay in there until you think things over."

My fellow captives were as miserable as I. One had stolen some candy, 12 and the other, having graduated proudly from wearing slit pants, had promptly soiled his new ones. Although it was certainly convenient to be able to squat down anywhere and do one's business, among us children the slit was an embarrassing symbol of immaturity. It had another drawback too: Nai Nai's blows still stung on my bottom. I looked at the unlucky boy with pity. He would now be doomed to at least another year of babyhood and easy spankings.

The nurses' words had another kind of sting for me, since I had been taught Chairman Mao was like the sun itself. At home, "Mao" had been my first word after "Mama," "Baba," and "Nai Nai," for I had been held up to the large framed picture Father had hung over the doorway and instructed in the sound. Later I had learned how to say "I love Chairman Mao" and "Long Live Chairman Mao." But it wasn't until I got to the child-care center that I really began to understand. He presided over our rest and play like a benevolent god, and I believed that apples, grapes, everything had been given to us because he loved us. When the nurses told me the next day that Chairman Mao had forgiven me, I was the happiest child in the world.

During the next year, my second at the child-care center, I learned how to write my first characters. The first word was made up of the four strokes in the Chairman's name. Next I learned to write the characters in my own name, and I discovered that I was not called "Little Fatso," as Waipo had proudly nicknamed me, but something quite different, with a political story behind it:

On the morning of May 2, 1954, the Vietnamese won a decisive victory over the French at Dien Bien Phu. That very afternoon my mother gave birth to me, a ten-pound baby boy, the distant sounds of drums and cymbals an accompaniment to her labors. My father, reporting the Vietnam story for the *Hunan Daily*, thought it only natural to name me Liang Dian-jie, "Liang Good News from Dien Bien Phu." He was flushed with a double victory, for at last he had a son to carry on the family line.

It wasn't the first time he had chosen a significant name for a child.   16
My eldest sister was born in 1949, so she joined the ranks of thousands
of children named for the birth of New China with the name Liang
Fang, "Liang Liberation." My second sister, born in 1952 when the
Chinese armies were marching across the Yalu River to defend Korea
against the Americans, was called Liang Wei-ping, "Liang Defender of
Peace." As we grew up we discovered that you could often guess someone's age by his name, and that at times, if someone had been named
at the height of some movement that was later discredited, a name could
become an embarrassment, a burden, or even a reason for being attacked.
My parents' own names reflected an earlier, less politicized time; my
mother Yan Zhi-de was "Yan the Moral," and my father Liang Ying-qiu
was "Liang Whose Requests Will Be Answered," although he usually
went by his literary name, Liang Shan.

I came gradually to recognize all of these characters and more, for
during the third year and final fourth year at the child-care center we
began our study properly, writing "Chairman Mao is our Great Saving
Star," "We are all Chairman Mao's good little children," "The Communist Party is like the sun," "When I am big I will be a worker" (or
peasant or soldier). We also learned simple arithmetic, paper folding and
paper cutting, and were given small responsibilities like watering the
plants or cleaning the classroom.

Meanwhile, whenever I went home to Waipo's, I hoped Mother would
be there, for I loved her very much despite our limited time together.
But when I was about four, I began to sense there was something wrong.
She would come home looking worried and she never played with me,
just talked on and on with Uncle Yan in a hushed Liuyang County
dialect which I couldn't understand. Finally, one Saturday afternoon it
was Nai Nai who came to get me, and I was told Mother had gone away
and I shouldn't go to Waipo's house anymore.

Only years later was I old enough to understand what had happened,
and more than twenty years passed before anyone, including Mother
herself, got the full picture. In early 1957 the "Hundred Flowers Movement" had been launched. Its official purpose was to give the Party a
chance to correct its shortcomings by listening to the masses' criticisms.
Father was away in the countryside reporting on something, but in the
Changsha Public Security Building, meetings were held and everyone
was urged to express his or her opinions freely.

Mother didn't know what to do. She really loved the Party and didn't   20
have any criticisms to make; the Party had given her a job and saved her

from the most abject poverty. Still, her leaders said that everyone should participate actively in the movement, especially those who hoped some-day to join the Party. Mother was already in favor; she had been given the important job of validating arrest warrants for the whole city. So, regarding it her duty to come up with something, she finally thought of three points she could make. She said that her Section Head sometimes used crude language and liked to criticize people, that he should give his housekeeper a bed to sleep on instead of making her sleep on the floor, and that sometimes when it came time to give raises, the leaders didn't listen to the masses' opinions.

But then, with utterly confusing rapidity, the "Hundred Flowers Move-ment" changed into the "Anti-Rightist Movement." Perhaps the Party was caught off guard by the amount of opposition and felt compelled to crack down. Or maybe, as I've heard said, the "Hundred Flowers Move-ment" had been a trap designed from the beginning to uncover Rightist elements. Anyway, every unit was given a quota of Rightists, and Mother's name was among those at the Public Security Bureau.

It was disastrous. When she was allowed to see her file in 1978, she found out that she had been given a Rightist's "cap" solely because of those three criticisms she had made. Perhaps her Section Head was angry at her; perhaps her unit was having trouble filling its quota. At the time she had no idea what the verdict was based on, she only knew that a terrible wrong had been done. But there was no court of appeal. Mother was sent away to the suburb of Yuan Jia Ling for labor reform. She lost her cadre's rank and her salary was cut from fifty-five to fifteen *yuan* a month. (A *yuan* is one hundred Chinese cents. . . .) My naive and trusting mother went to work as a peasant.

Just as his wife was being declared an enemy of the Party, Father was actively participating in the Anti-Rightist Movement in his own unit. Father believed in the Party with his whole heart, believed that the Party could never make a mistake or hand down a wrong verdict. It was a tortuous dilemma; Father's traditional Confucian sense of family obli-gation told him to support Mother while his political allegiance told him to condemn her. In the end, his commitment to the Party won out, and he denounced her. He believed that was the only course that could save the family from ruin.

I still remember the first time Mother came home for a visit. It was a 24 rainy Sunday in late autumn, and Father and Nai Nai were both out.

There were footsteps on the stairs and in the corridor, but it was almost a minute before the knock came, timidly. Liang Fang opened the door.

Mother was almost unrecognizable. She was in patched blue peasant clothing, muddy up to the knees. The skin on her kind round face looked thick, leathery, and not too clean, and someone had chopped her hair off short and uneven. There was something both broader and thinner about her. "Mama!" cried Liang Fang.

Liang Wei-ping and I ran up to her too, and she was hugging us all at once, weeping, forgetting to put down her oilpaper umbrella. Then as my sisters rushed to pour tea and bring a basin of hot water for her to wash her face, she sat on the bed and held me tightly for a long time. After she had rested, she busied herself with all the housework Nai Nai couldn't do alone, sweeping, dusting, and sharpening our pencils for us, scrubbing our clothes, and cleaning the windows. She wouldn't speak of where she'd been, just asked us about our schoolwork, our health, Father's health. We were so happy. We thought Mother had come home.

She was tying bows on Liang Fang's braids when Father came back. He was astounded to see her, and not very warm. "What are you doing here?" he demanded. "Did you ask for leave?"

Mother lowered her head at his harshness. "Of course I asked for   28
leave," she said defensively. "I can come home once a month."

This silenced Father for a few minutes, and he paced meditatively around the room, his tall thin frame overpowering hers as Nai Nai's used to do. Then he poured out a stream of words, political words — on the meaning of the Anti-Rightist Movement, on her obligation to recognize her faults and reform herself. It was as if he had turned into a propaganda machine. I suppose he thought it was his duty to help reeducate her.

For a while she listened in silence, her head bowed, but at last she protested. "All right, I'm a Rightist, it's all my fault. You don't have to say anything else, my head is bursting. I hear this kind of thing all day long, write self-criticisms every week, and now I come home and I have to hear it all over again."

"I don't think you recognize what you've done. You're just wasting your labor reform," he said.

"What makes you so sure?" Mother's face was white and defiant.   32

Father exploded: "Rightist element! Have some thought for your influence on the children."

It was Mother's turn to lose control. "What did I ever do wrong? The Party asked me to make suggestions, so I did. You give me one example — " But Mother stopped midsentence, for Father had struck her a ringing blow across the face.

She fell back on the bed, weeping; Father strode into the other room and slammed the door. Then slowly, painfully, she picked up her dirty jacket and umbrella as we sobbed miserably. When she was halfway out the door, Father emerged and shouted after her, "Don't come back until you've reformed yourself. The children in this house need a Revolutionary mother, not a Rightist mother." When she paused and turned her tear-streaked face to him, his voice became gentler. "It doesn't matter what you say here, I won't tell anyone. But please watch what you say at the labor camp."

Despite Father's cruelty, Mother came back every month to see us.   36 She must have missed us very much to endure Father's lectures and the inevitable fights. Sometimes she slept in Father's bed and I slept with them; she never lay still and her pillow was always wet in the morning. On other occasions the quarrel was so fierce that she left again almost as soon as she arrived. Father often warned us against her, and if we defended her he became furious, calling us ignorant children who understood nothing.

We didn't know that Father had already raised the question of divorce. He must have reasoned that all of us were doomed unless he broke off with Mother completely, for the custom in such instances was that the whole family would be considered as guilty as the single member who had committed the crime. If there were no legal separation, Father would never be allowed to join the Party, and the files that would be opened on us when we came of age for middle school would say that we came from a Rightist background. We would be branded forever as people with "questions," and it would be difficult for us to go to middle school and college, get decent jobs, or find husbands and wives. Mother's misfortune might mean the end of all of Father's dreams for himself and for his children; he must have hated her for what she had done.

Mother was a proud woman. She believed so deeply she had been wrongly accused that she told him she would divorce him only after her Rightist label was removed. Her stubbornness enraged Father, particularly because there was a secondary movement to criticize those with Rightist tendencies, and with his Rightist wife, Father was a natural target. He had to criticize Mother publicly, write reports confessing his innermost thoughts. And the pressure became even greater after what happened to Uncle Yan.

When Mother first came under attack, her older brother had been as outraged as she. He went to the Public Security Bureau to argue in her defense, and spoke for her at his own unit, the No. 1 Hospital, where he worked with the Communist Youth League. He even came to our house to urge Father to try to help her, although Father thought he was crazy to stick out his neck like that. Sure enough, Uncle Yan was punished for his family loyalties and given a Rightist "cap" of his own to wear, bringing a second black cloud to rest over Waipo's home. His experience proved that Father's sad choice had been a practical one in view of the harsh political realities; when we were old enough to understand, we could hardly blame Father for what he had done.

Nai Nai was frightened to see how easily the Rightist label could   40
spread from one member of the family to another. She had been an enthusiastic supporter of the "Get Rid of the Four Evils" hygiene movement, but where cartoons had once shown housewives sweeping away rats, flies, mosquitoes, and fleas, now they had added a fifth evil, Rightists. Nai Nai could no longer face lecturing lazy neighbors on the dangers of letting water stagnate; she could imagine what they might be saying behind her back about how she ought to get rid of that evil in her own house. When, with traditional filial deference, Father asked for her opinion on the divorce question, she agreed with relief. The family burden was too heavy for her.

Meanwhile, Mother was working hard to rid herself of her "cap." The calluses on her hands were thicker and sharper every time she came home, and her shoulders were rough where the shoulder pole rested. Her skin toasted to a rich yellow-brown. It was a hard life for a young woman who had lived between the protection of her mother's home and her Public Security Bureau office.

The Rightists at Yuan Jia Ling were all trying to prove to the political officials in charge that they had reformed themselves and were ready to leave. There were all types of people, intellectuals, high-ranking cadres, and ordinary workers, but friendships were impossible because the best strategy for gaining the officials' confidence was to report on others. Thus everyone was always watching everyone else, and a grain of rice dropped on the floor could mean an afternoon of criticism for disrespecting the labors of the peasants. Everything was fair game, even what people said in their sleep.

The second essential strategy was to write constant Thought Reports about oneself. Few of the people in the camp felt they were really Rightists, but the only thing to do was to confess one's crimes penitently, record one's lapses, and invent things to repent. Writing these reports eventually became a kind of habit, and Mother almost believed what she was saying about herself.

The last important route to freedom was hard work. One had to add deliberately to one's misery in small ways, like going without a hat under the hot summer sun or continuing to work in the rain after everyone else had quit. Generally the Rightists did ordinary peasants' work, like digging fish-breeding ponds and planting fruit trees, but sometimes they were taken in trucks to special laboring areas to break and carry stones. Then they were put together with ordinary thieves, hoodlums, and Kuomintang (KMT)[1] spies. The people whose arrest warrants Mother had once been in charge of validating were now her equals; it was almost more than she could bear. Still, bear it she did, and all the rest of it, and after three long years, when she could carry more than a hundred pounds of rocks on her back with ease, a bored-looking official summoned her and told her she was no longer a Rightist. She could go home.

She came to the house late at night, looking like a beggar traveling with her ragged belongings. But when she spoke, her voice was clear and proud. "Old Liang," she announced to Father, "I'm a person again." She told us she had been assigned to the headlight-manufacturing plant on May First Road as an ordinary worker. Her salary would be much lower than it had been at the Public Security Bureau and the loss of her cadre status would be permanent, but she was free, a normal member of society. My sisters and I thought all the trouble was over, but that night as I lay in bed with them I heard talk not of the beginning of a new family life but of how to institute divorce proceedings.

The difficulty lay in what to do with us. We were fought over like basketballs that winter, for Mother insisted that she wanted at least one of us, preferably Liang Fang, who was already eleven and understood life better than Liang Wei-ping and I. Mother was staying at Waipo's, but she came every day to the house. When I got home from the *Hunan Daily*'s Attached Primary School, she was always there, waiting.

One bitterly cold Sunday she took the three of us out to the Martyr's Park so we could talk alone. No one else was out in that weather; they were all at home huddled under their blankets or warming themselves

---

[1]Non-Communist political party. — ED.

by coal burners. We were bundled up in everything we had, and I felt as though I could have been rolled down a hill, but I was still cold. The park was desolate and beautiful, the huge monument to the dead martyrs a lonely pinnacle over the city, the pavilions gray and defenseless against the wind. We walked to the large manmade lake, the park's main attraction, and sat by the water, usually filled with rowboats but now covered with a thin layer of ice. I crawled between Mother's knees and Liang Fang and Liang Wei-ping pressed up on each side of her. She spoke to us with great emotion and tenderness.

"Your mother is an unlucky woman. When you're older, you'll under-   48
stand how I've wept for all of us these three years. Now I won't be able to come see you anymore, but you can visit me at Waipo's house. Liang Fang will live with me, but I don't have enough money for all of you. . . ."

Liang Wei-ping and I were in tears, saying that we wanted to go with her too. Soon everyone was crying. Mother held us so tightly that I could hardly believe it was true that she would go away.

We stayed in the park for a long time, but when Mother noticed that my cheeks were chapped red, she took us home. She brought us to the stairwell and refused to come up. Her parting words were "Remember, Liang Fang, you'll come with me."

That evening Father called us into the inner room. "Children, you're still small and there are many things you don't understand," he said sadly. "If you went with your mother, your life with her would be unhappy. Look at the way your father has to criticize himself because of her. Stay here with me and Nai Nai and we'll take care of you."

Liang Fang wouldn't listen. "Mama isn't a Rightist anymore," she   52
said. "What difference does it make who I go with? Isn't it glorious to be a worker?"

"Your mother's political life is over," said Father with annoyance. "Her file will always have a black mark, and the Party will never trust her again. Don't you know that if you want to go to middle school you'll be asked if your parents have made any political mistakes? If you stay with me, you won't even have to mention your mother, because there will be a legal separation. But if you go with her, you might not even get to go to middle school, to say nothing of joining the Communist Youth League or the Party. And you," he said angrily, turning to me and Liang Wei-ping. "Can't you guess why you haven't been allowed to join the Young Pioneers? Isn't it because of your mother?"

Nai Nai rushed into the room to urge him to control his temper, then she turned to us. "Children, your father is good to you, he understands the situation. Don't I wish I had a good daughter-in-law? Don't I know you need a good mother? But Fate is inevitable. Stay with us, children. It's the only way."

Ultimately, the question was decided in court. Father came home one afternoon looking exhausted and said, "It's settled, you'll all stay with me. Mother is coming in a little while to say good-bye."

We had dinner with her that night, and even Nai Nai's eyes were wet. 56 No one said anything, and no one had any appetite for the fish or the tofu soup. As Nai Nai took the dishes away and washed up, Mother went through her possessions, leaving almost everything for us. Father sat smoking furiously, as he did whenever he was upset. Finally she stood up to leave.

Then the three of us broke out of our numbness and ran to her, begging her not to go, pulling her back, wrapping ourselves around her legs so she couldn't walk. Father didn't interfere; he just let her embrace us again and again and at last shake us off and close the door firmly behind herself. We ran to the balcony and called after her until her broad square figure turned the corner and she was gone.

In fact, Father had been much too optimistic, and the divorce did nothing to rid us of having a Rightist in the family. He even forbade our having the slightest contact with Mother, thinking that if we drew a clear line of separation, things might be better. But there wasn't the slightest change in our status: In the eyes of the Party, my sisters and I were the children of a Rightist and Father had a Rightist wife. Liang Fang still had to say she had a Rightist mother on her application to go to middle school, Liang Wei-ping still found "Rightist child" written on her desk in chalk when she went to class, and I was still turned down when I asked to be allowed to join the Young Pioneers.

When I first went to the Attached Primary School in the *Hunan Daily* compound at age six, my classmates had often teased me about Mother. I had always shrugged off their taunts because I did well and achieved more than enough recognition to offset a few minor slights. I remember how pleased Father was when I started to take prizes for my paintings; my drawing of a morning glory was first in the whole primary school.

But as I got older, more and more stress was placed on the three stages 60 of Revolutionary glory: the Young Pioneers, the Communist Youth League, and the Party itself. It became clear to me that success in the political arena was a prerequisite for success in anything else, and if I had the slightest ambitions for myself I had to achieve these basic signs of social recognition. Those students who had the right to wear the Pioneer's triangular red scarf received much more praise than those who didn't, no matter what their grades; and at home Father and Nai Nai were constantly asking me if my application had been approved. But it was no use. I was rejected year after year, until I found myself in a tiny minority of outsiders whose "political performances" were the very worst in the class.

One day I was given a clue to the trouble when our teacher gave us a lecture. "We all have to join forces to oppose Capitalist thought," Teacher Luo said. "Some students want to eat well and dress well from the time they are small. This is Capitalist thought. Some students are from good worker or Revolutionary cadre backgrounds; they should be careful not to be proud of themselves. And those students from families with questions — they must be more careful to draw a clear line of separation." He looked meaningfully at me and at the other boy with a Rightist in his family. And all the other students in the classroom turned to stare at us too.

In fact, after the divorce I had continued to go secretly to see my mother despite Father's warnings that doing so would harm my future. She was always overjoyed to see me, and, even during China's hard years, just after the breakup, she always found a way to give me a few *fen* (a *fen* is a Chinese cent . . .) or a roasted sweet potato. But after Teacher Luo's lecture, it really began to bother me when other students mocked me as a Rightist's son. And they became bolder in their mockery, as well. They would slap me, or kick me when I wasn't looking, and then pretend not to have done anything. Sometimes I would get into real fights, and then there were reprimands from Father and the teachers. The other Rightist's son was as lonely as I, but we never spoke much, for that might have made things even worse.

So perhaps inevitably, over the years, I came to resent my mother for making my life so miserable. I began to believe that she really had done something wrong. My father and teachers said so, and my classmates hated me for her supposed crimes. At last I no longer wished to visit her despite my loneliness, and when I saw her at a distance I didn't even call out to her. I cut her out of my life just as I had been told to do, and became solitary and self-reliant. But that was when I was much older, and many things happened before then.

EXPLORATIONS

1. What appears to be the standard Party definition of a Rightist? of a Revolutionary? What definition of each term was in use when Liang's mother was discredited?

2. Where did the various members of Liang's family live when he was a small child? Who would have been affected, and how, if Liang's father as well as his mother had been removed from his job and sent away for rehabilitation? In what other ways did the Party use housing, work, and family ties to control behavior?

3. Look at Liang's first paragraph, particularly the last sentence. How do he and his coauthor, Shapiro, notify their readers of the point of view they intend to take? Through whose eyes is Liang's childhood depicted? Through what kind of consciousness is it interpreted? What is the significance of the paragraph's last sentence?

CONNECTIONS

1. How does the child-care center described by Liang and Shapiro compare in purpose and function with the Israeli communal system described by Bruno Bettelheim in "Why Kibbutzim?"? How does it compare with American day care (see Claudia Wallis's comments in *Looking at Ourselves*)? What are the main differences among these three approaches to child care?

2. In *Looking at Ourselves*, Michael Novak cites problems that the United State's capitalist economic system creates for the family. Which of these problems are also created by the Chinese Communist system? On balance, which economic system establishes a better climate for families, and how does it do so?

3. Look at Ellen Goodman's observations in *Looking at Ourselves*. How does the Chinese family, as Liang and Shapiro depict it, serve as "social glue" among generations?

ELABORATIONS

1. Liang and Shapiro scatter information about Liang's child-care center through the first seventeen paragraphs of this essay. List all the relevant details in those paragraphs. Then write a descriptive essay about the child-care center: For

instance, where is it? What rooms and furnishings does it have? What do the children do there? What roles do adults at the center play?

2. Do parents in the United States name their children after military victories? Do they divorce each other to avoid government and public censure? Write a comparison-contrast essay about public influence on personal decisions in Mao's China and in the United States today.

CAROLA HANSSON
and KARIN LIDÉN

Liza and Family

Carola Hansson and Karin Lidén are natives of Sweden. Living on the northeastern edge of the Soviet Union, they have been moved by their interest in women's position there to visit the USSR many times. In addition to *Moscow Women* (1983), in which the following interview appears, they have translated material by exiled Leningrad feminists for a book published in Sweden in 1981. At present Hansson works for Swedish television and lives with her husband and children in Uppsala. Lidén works as a writer and consultant for Swedish radio and lives with her husband and child in Paris. "Liza and Family" was translated from the Swedish by Gerry Bothmer, George Blecher, and Lone Blecher.

The Union of Soviet Socialist Republics came into being after the Bolshevik Revolution of 1917 toppled the hereditary czar (a title derived from the Roman *caesar*). Although Western ideas and modernization had begun spreading across Russia in the nineteenth century, the political system had remained feudal. The czars' downfall was triggered by losses in Russia's 1904 war with Japan, and climaxed when workers' strikes in 1917 escalated into revolution. Vladimir Ilyich Lenin took over at the end of the year, imposing a central Communist government which controlled not only Russia but the fourteen other "republics" of the Soviet Union. Religion was suppressed; St. Petersburg, recalling both the church and the 400-year-old dynasty of Czar Peter the Great, was renamed Leningrad. Communism's central idea that the people rather than a ruling elite should own all means of production (such as farms and factories) has not worked well in practice. Although nearly all legal economic enterprises are state owned, for example, a huge illegal black market flourishes, and imported goods are prized. Traditional values persist, but in new forms. "Liza and Family" illustrates the daily contradictions faced by one young Soviet worker-mother.

Hansson and Lidén interviewed Liza in her Moscow apartment. She is twenty-eight, an editor for a publishing house. "She doesn't walk into the room; she makes an entrance," write the authors. "She seems delighted to see us and to play the role of hostess. . . . She is wearing a long, tight, ruffled dress with a turn-of-the-century look and platform sandals. She invites us to sit down in her kitchen, one of the most impractically arranged we have ever seen. The stove is in one corner, the small sink in the other, and in the middle, with hardly any space to move around, is a small table. A few watercolors depicting beautiful Russian summer landscapes are tacked up on the walls, a reminder of what exists outside this bleak high-rise kitchen."

(For more background on the Soviet Union, see pp. 59, 435, and 461.)

Tell us something about yourself.

I'm twenty-eight. I have a degree in literature and work for a publishing house. I have a son, Emil. I had a husband, who was an artist, but now he's gone. We got married in 1970 and divorced in 1975, I think.

I own my apartment, which my father bought for me, since it's so difficult to get an apartment here; for someone my age it's totally impossible. I lived here with my husband, and now I live here alone.

What is your daily routine like? Can you tell us what you did yesterday, for instance?

4

I got up at seven o'clock and went to work. Mostly I have to travel during rush hours; the streetcar was so crowded that I was almost knocked down . . . horrible.

Oh no! Yesterday was Monday! I woke at six, pulled my child out of bed, packed a bag full of stuff for the whole week, and then he and I took off for the subway. The *two* of us were practically knocked down. A woman was sitting and reading and wouldn't give up her seat, even though my son was squashed against the doors. He almost fell on her, and I tightened my grip to keep him from falling and getting hurt. I told him, "Emil, a child could die in front of that woman while she sat there reading. Don't you ever be like that." It took us fifty minutes to get to the day-care center.

I took him inside and undressed him and then I had to rush off to work. He cried, "Mama, I don't want to stay here. I want to go home." I said, "Emil, sweetheart, please stay in the day-care center now. I'll come and get you soon. I'll pick you up on Friday." And yesterday was Monday. It was terrible, but I had to hurry off to work.

I left him crying. The teachers took him by the arm and brought him over to the group because I couldn't stay to comfort him. I picked up my things and put my shawl over my head. Outside it was still rush hour. And I was going to the opposite end of Moscow. It was another hour's trip, and I was already late for work. When I dashed out of the subway I was planning to transfer to a bus, and I felt as if I were about

8

to have a minor heart attack. But the bus was just pulling away, so I had to run instead, knowing I'd be in trouble because I was late. I was trying to work out a scheme. If only there were an open window at my office so that I could throw my stuff in and crawl in after it! That way no one would know I was late.

However, the windows were closed, and I quickly ran in. There was a lot of work on my desk. First on the agenda was a weekly report. There was also a lot of mail, proofreading, and editing. Then I had to race around to various departments, pick up files, etc. After lunch I became terribly drowsy because I had hardly slept all night long. I was absent-minded and couldn't seem to pull myself together. Later when I felt I couldn't stand it any longer we sent someone for a bottle of wine. Sometimes we do that where I work. Yesterday, toward the end of the day, we drank a big glass of port to clear our heads.

Then, exhausted, I dropped by my parents' since I hadn't prepared any food at home. I knew they would have something for me. Afterwards I watched television — one of those series. I was too tired to think or read, although I had a book that had been hard to get my hands on. It had been such a difficult day. So that's what my day was like yesterday, a typical Monday.

So Emil's at the day-care center all week. Is he there at night as well?

Yes, it's called weekly boarding school. I could pick him up on   12
Wednesdays, but it doesn't seem to work out. If I fetch him after work we don't get home until eight. He goes to bed at nine, and then I have to get up at six to get him back to the day-care center. The rush again, the mobs. That isn't good for him. He might catch influenza since he wears his little fur coat in the subway, although it's terribly hot and he's soaked with perspiration when we get into the street to walk to the center. As a result he has a cold almost the whole winter.

Does he like the boarding school?

It's O.K. By Friday when I pick him up he's happy. He's been playing with his friends and it's hard to tear him away. He's gotten used to it. But on Monday it's the same story all over again.

Doesn't his father spend time with him?

No, he rarely sees his father. The situation is complicated. When the   16
baby was born I gave him my surname. I decided that since I had had to carry the whole burden and I suffered the most, I wanted to give him

my name. His father was very upset that the boy didn't have his name. They almost never see each other, although Emil is the image of his father. He never gets anything from him, but I do get alimony, 35 rubles a month.[1]

How do you spend your free time?

Saturdays and Sundays are mostly devoted to my child. When he sleeps I have some time to read, but a lot of my energy goes into him. Free time? Yes, on weekdays after work. Of course I'm tired, but at least I can do as I please. Sometimes when I have a few moments I try to write; I couldn't imagine not writing. I'll probably write all my life — how regularly I don't know, since I don't have the time. But when I have a free evening I write poetry.

How much time do you spend on your household? Shopping, for instance.

I have an easier time than most because of my parents. When I can't   20 bear to do the shopping — because as sure as anything I'll start arguing with someone, complain to the manager, or hit somebody; that's just the way I am — and when I can't stand the mass of people, the crowd, the confusion, and I need to be alone, I go to my parents' and my mother feeds me.

My relationship with my parents is very good. Of course we argue, but we argue with an understanding of each other, because I'm like them in my way of thinking. We always enjoy each other's company. I share my most intimate thoughts with them — especially with my father. When we talk I don't feel that he's older than I am — we're the same age in our souls.

When I was a child that feeling was even stronger — one of us could tell what the other was thinking, even if we were apart. It's said that Blok[2] had a similar relationship with his mother; for me it's with my father.

I remember that when I was about five, he was going through a difficult time. I was in a country day-care center; I was restless and couldn't sleep — I sensed that Papa was having a hard time. Then we went to Moscow and I asked him why. Something had happened. I remember the incident

---

[1]One ruble (divided into 100 kopeks) is currently equivalent to around $1.64.
[2]Alexander Blok (1880–1921) was a Russian Symbolist poet.

so clearly. A poet — he's dead now — had written an article criticizing him. I didn't understand any of this, since I couldn't read, but I sensed that Papa was in trouble. We had always been able to communicate — even better before I was married. Then we used to travel together. He is a poet and often makes public appearances. I appeared on the stage with him and read his poems.

In this country when children leave their family they seldom think about their parents; children and parents usually don't understand each other. The children take off when they're about seventeen and get married. When children and parents have to live together they live as neighbors in a joint or communal apartment.[3] But the children have to obey their parents. There's a saying in our country: If you spit on old people you spit on your country; if you spit on your ancestors you spit in your own face.

Were you born in Moscow?

Yes. Six of us lived in a room twenty square meters in size, which was part of a communal apartment. It was Mama's room. Papa wasn't born in Moscow; he came from . . . the frontier you could say, from the country. He married my mother and settled down in that room. There was also Mama's sister, Grandmother, and I, and then my brother, Alyosha, was born. As a young girl Mama had lived in a whole apartment. Then in 1937 her father was put in prison. If my grandmother had divorced him she could have avoided going with him and could have stayed with her three children. But she didn't think it was right to divorce him after he was jailed, so she went to prison for eight years as a family member of an enemy of the people. When the children were left alone they were forced to leave their apartment, which consisted only of two rooms — small ones at that — even though her husband had had an important position in the government. They were kicked out, and my mother, who was sixteen at the time, was left with two small children. Her youngest sister was three, and the authorities wanted to put her in an orphanage, but the family pleaded with them, and finally she was allowed to stay. She had a very interesting life, my aunt, but you came to talk about me. . . .

---

[3]Because of the continued shortage of housing in Moscow and other large cities, it is still common for several families to share an apartment with a communal kitchen and bathroom but separate living/sleeping quarters.

Can you envisage a life without children?

Definitely not. If a couple already in their forties haven't heard the 28
sound of children's voices in their home, life is meaningless, period. Of
course it's obvious that the woman suffers the most. Formerly, among
the peasants, divorce was granted on these grounds, and I think that was
right. One should have children, no matter how difficult the situation.
Also, because of the low birthrate, Russia is wasting away . . . although
I myself don't intend to give birth to a second, third, fourth.

Would you like to have more children?

Yes, but I don't have a husband. If I did, I'd have a second and a
third. I would want a girl because they're so much closer to their mother.

How would you find the time?

I would leave the children in one of the weekly boarding schools. 32
What else can you do? Tsvetayeva[4] had three children, but she kept on
writing.

*You just said that the birthrate was low in the Soviet Union. What
could be done to raise it?*

To raise the birthrate one has to raise wages. They're so low now that
women can't afford the luxury of two or three children.

What is a good mother?

Naturally, a good mother has to take care of her baby, take it out for 36
walks and make sure it develops physically. But she should also give the
child moral guidance — a feeling that life has a spiritual dimension. A
mother who is concerned only with the child's health and safety is not a
good mother. Of course she has to be a social being as well — she has
to suffer the sorrows of her people. Then her child will turn out well.
I'm quite convinced of that.

And how would you define a good father?

A good father? I know only one example of a good father, and that's
mine. In the Soviet Union the father usually loves the wife above the
children, but a good father ought to put his children first. When I was

---

[4]Marina Tsvetayeva (1892–1941) was a Russian poet — ED.

a baby my father always used to carry me in his arms at night. He didn't worry about his time, although he wrote a lot — carrying me on his arm. A father should spend as much time with his child as possible, and not only treat it as a child, but as an adult. Perhaps my husband would have made a good father, but after six months he was conscripted. He was twenty-seven, and it was his last call of duty. He was gone for a year, and I was allotted 15 rubles per month. When he returned, the child was a year and a half old already, and he was like a stranger to the child. Things just kept on getting worse and worse between us until we divorced.

I was much closer to my father than my mother, but I feel that for a son a father is absolutely necessary. I can't imagine my own childhood without my father, and I don't know what I would have done without him. I have a feeling that he gave me everything.

Do you consider yourself a good mother? 40

No, I'm a disgusting mother! I bring up my son on the run. I get tired of trying to keep him amused and give him a pencil so that he can keep himself busy drawing.

However, I do try to teach him the love of work. That's the most important thing one can teach a child — aside from spiritual and ethical values, of course. But I don't see these qualities in my son, and therefore I consider myself a bad mother. I should have taught him better.

Do you think one ought to give boys and girls a different upbringing?

No. I believe that girls ought to be taught to cook, clean, and do 44 housework, but so should boys. People ought to be free and independent, but not arrogant. There's not really much difference between a boy and girl, except that boys have to develop more physically, and that of course is the father's job.

Do you have contraceptives in the Soviet Union?

We have the IUD, although it isn't used very much. Women who want one have to stand in line a long time. We try not to use the pill because of the possible danger to a future fetus. Some also use aspirin, but that's also considered to be dangerous.

But above all we have many abortions. They're horrible, absolutely horrible. But what's the answer? Our contraceptives aren't any good. There are condoms, but they're so repulsive and bad that we would rather go through an abortion. . . . The first Christians copulated only in order to procreate. In my opinion abortions are punishments for our sins.

Have you ever had an abortion?   48

Yes, many — seven. It's hard both physically and psychologically. Now that it's done with drugs there's no pain, but it's hard on the psyche.

How are women affected?

There are painful repercussions. There's no way of thinking about anything else when you're pregnant and you have to wait two months for an abortion. Then the aftermath is difficult. It affects not only your sex life, but also life in general. Sometimes I fear that I may be pregnant again; then I can't think about anything else, can't write, can't read, can't do anything.

People say that when a woman gives birth to a child she gets younger,   52
and when she has an abortion she gets twice as old. So I have become seven times as old! . . . The only concern doctors seem to have is to make abortions relatively painless. Previously no drugs were given. But the dread of pregnancy still remains stronger than anything else.

How did you react when you discovered that you were pregnant the first time?

I was hysterical. It was totally unexpected, since I didn't believe . . . I couldn't imagine that children were conceived that quickly. No one had told me anything. I got together with my husband, and I got pregnant immediately. It was so strange and unexpected that I had an abortion, though naturally I should have had that first baby. I went through with the second pregnancy and mostly felt fine, but I developed toxemia. The delivery was very difficult. They don't use any drugs, gas, anything. None of the women around me wanted them either. I begged for a cesarean, howled like an animal, couldn't stand the pain any longer. I screamed so much that they finally had to give me something to induce labor, and I had terrible contractions and kept on screaming until there was blood in my mouth.

A friend had a baby two months later and told me that an old lady who had taken a three months' course told her how to prepare for each contraction. She gave no drugs, but only explained in what position my friend should lie. They also give massage, but that doesn't help. One feels like an animal.

My baby was born in a special clinic, but still. . . . During the delivery   56
I was badly torn, but they didn't even sew me up. Recently I went to a gynecologist who asked me whether I had given birth in the country — but in fact I gave birth at a special clinic in the capital.

Did you feel that the pains you suffered affected your relationship to the child?

No, I felt it was quite normal. I knew that it would hurt. I was so happy to see him that I forgot it all.

EXPLORATIONS

1. Commenting on the Soviet women they met, Hansson and Lidén note that all of them "had very definite opinions . . . [but] these opinions were riddled with contradictions." What contradictions do you notice in Liza's opinions about motherhood and fatherhood? parent-child relationships? the functions of the family?

2. Liza mentions some Soviet views and customs that seem conservative by American standards and others that seem radical. Choose three practices or attitudes in "Liza and Family" that clash with your values. What practical aspects of life in Moscow appear to have caused or encouraged each one?

3. An interviewer's skill lies in her or his ability to ask questions that elicit interesting information. Look at the questions asked by Hansson and Lidén. Which ones seem designed to bring out general facts about Soviet life? Which ones seem to come from the authors' on-the-spot curiosity? What other factors can you discern behind the questions in this interview?

CONNECTIONS

1. What similar political events appear in the family backgrounds of Liza in "Liza and Family" and Liang Heng in Liang Heng and Judith Shapiro's "Chairman Mao's Good Little Boy"? How do Liza's and Liang's attitudes toward those events differ? What factors do you think are responsible for the difference?

2. According to Bruno Bettelheim in "Why Kibbutzim?" the early Israeli kibbutzniks entrusted their children to a communal system of care because parenthood conflicted with their other goals. What evidence in "Liza and Family" suggests that parenthood conflicts with Liza's other goals? What are those goals? How does Liza's attitude toward parenthood differ from that of the kibbutzniks?

3. How do Liza's problems as a working mother compare with those of the Americans described by Claudia Wallis in *Looking at Ourselves*? How do the available solutions appear to be different in these two cultures? How are parents' priorities different?

ELABORATIONS

1. In *Looking at Ourselves*, Arlie Hochschild and Anne Machung describe some of the problems faced by working mothers in the United States. Which of these problems does Liza also face as a working mother in the Soviet Union? Write a cause-and-effect essay using Hochschild and Machung's data to explain Liza's difficulties, or a comparison-contrast essay on working mothers in the United States and the Soviet Union.

2. What is a good mother? A good father? Liza states her opinions on these questions in paragraphs 36–44. Do you agree with her? Write a definition essay giving your own answers to these two questions.

JOHN UPDIKE

The Lovely Troubled Daughters of Our Old Crowd

John Updike credits his mother for encouraging him early to write. Today he is one of the most prolific and respected authors in the United States, having published more than a dozen each of novels, short story collections, and volumes of poetry, as well as several plays and children's books. Also a noted critic, Updike has won most of this country's major literary prizes, including the National Book Award, American Book Award, and Pulitzer Prize. He was born in Shillington, Pennsylvania, in 1932. After graduating summa cum laude from Harvard University, he studied in Oxford, England, at the Ruskin School of Drawing and Fine Arts. Among Updike's best-known works are *Rabbit, Run* (1960), the first of four novels about a small-town Pennsylvania car salesman; *Couples* (1968), a chronicle of suburban infidelities; and *The Witches of Eastwick* (1984), which became the basis for a motion picture. Updike is highly regarded for, among other things, his sharp observation of manners and mores, his vivid descriptions, and his grapplings with the Christian dilemmas of faith, passion, and evil. A member of the American Academy, he lives with his wife Martha north of Boston. "The Lovely Troubled Daughters of Our Old Crowd" originally appeared in *The New Yorker* and was collected in *Trust Me* (1987).

Why don't they get married? You see them around town, getting older, little spinsters already, pedaling bicycles to their local jobs or walking up the hill by the rocks with books in their arms. Annie Langhorne, Betsey Clay, Damaris Wilcombe, Mary Jo Addison: we've known them all since they were two or three, and now they've reached their mid-twenties, back from college, back from Year Abroad, grown women but not going anywhere, not New York or San Francisco or even Boston, just hanging around here in this little town letting the seasons wash over them, walking the same streets where they grew up, hanging in the shadows of their safe old homes.

On the edge of a Wilcombe lawn party, their pale brushed heads like candles burning in the summer sunlight, a ribbon or a plastic barrette attached for the occasion — I can see them still, their sweet pastel party dresses and their feet bare in the grass, those slender little-girl feet, with bony tan toes, that you feel would leave rabbit tracks in the dew. Damaris and Annie, best friends then and now, had been coaxed into carrying hors d'oeuvres around; they carried the tray cockeyed, their wrists were so weak, the deviled eggs slipping, their big eyes with their pale-blue whites staring upward so solemnly at your grinning grown-up face as you took your deviled egg and smiled to be encouraging. We were in our late twenties then, young at being old — the best of times. The summer smells of bug spray on the lawn and fresh mint in the gin; the young wives healthy and brown in their sundresses, their skin glowing warm through the cotton; the children still small and making a flock in the uncut grass beyond the lawn, running and tumbling, their pastel dresses getting stained with green, their noise coming and going in the field as a kind of higher-pitched echo of ours, creating their own world underfoot as the liquor and the sunlight soaked in and the sky filled with love.

I can still see Betsey and my own daughter the night we first met the Clays. They had just moved to town. A cousin of Maureen's had gone to school with my wife and sent us a note. We dropped by to give them the name of our dentist and doctor and happened to hit it off. April, it must have been, or May. Cocktails dragged on into dark and Maureen brought a pickup dinner out to the patio table. The two baby girls that had never met before — not much more than two years old, they must have been — were put to sleep in the same bed. Down they came into the dark, down into the cool air outdoors, hand in hand out of this house strange to the two of them, Betsey a white ghost in her nightie, her voice so eerie and thin but distinct. "See moon?" she said. Unable to sleep, they had seen the moon from the bed. The Clays had moved from the city, where maybe the moon was not so noticeable. "See moon?": her voice thin and distinct as a distant owl's call. And of course they were right, there the moon was, lopsided and sad-faced above the trees just beginning to blur into leaf. Time (at last) to go home.

Now Betsey works at the paint-and-linoleum store on Second Street 4 and gives guitar lessons on the side. She fell in love with her elderly married music teacher at Smith and went about as far as she could go with classical guitar, even to Spain for a year. When the Episcopal church sponsored a refugee Cuban family last winter, they called in Betsey for her Spanish. She lives with her mother, in that same house where she saw the moon, a gloomy place now that Maureen has closed off half the rooms to save on heat. The Clays broke up it must be all of ten years ago. There were some lovely times had on that patio.

Betsey sings in the Congregational choir alongside Mary Jo Addison, who after that bad spell of anorexia in her teens has gotten quite plump again. She has those dark eyebrows of her mother's, strange in a freckled fair face — shaped flat across and almost meeting in the middle. Both the Addisons have remarried and left town, but Mary Jo rents two rooms above the Rites of Passage travel agency and collects antiques and reads books of history, mostly medieval. My daughter invited her over for Christmas dinner but she said no, she'd rather just sit cozy by her own fire, surrounded by her things. "Her nice old things," was how it was reported.

Evelyn Addison liked nice things, too, but in her case they had to be modern — D.R.[1] sofas covered in Haitian cotton, Danish end tables with rounded edges, butterfly chairs. Where are they, I wonder, all those heavy iron frames for the worn-out canvas slings of those butterfly chairs we used to sit on? A man could straddle one of the corners, but a woman just had to dump herself in, backside first, and hope that when the time came to go her husband would be around to pull her out. They had an authentic 1690 house, the Addisons, on Salem Street, and curiously enough their modern furniture fit right into those plain old rooms with the exposed beams and the walk-in fireplaces with the big wrought-iron spits and dark brick nooks the Puritans used to bake bread in. It may be that's what Mary Jo is trying to get back to with her antiques. She dresses that way, too: dusty-looking and prim, her hair pulled into a tight roll held by a tortoiseshell pin. Her mother's auburn hair but without the spark rinsed into it. None of these girls, the daughters of our old crowd, seem to wear makeup.

The New Year's right after Fred had moved out, I remember walking Evelyn home from the Langhornes' up Salem Street just before morning, an inch of new snow on the sidewalk and everything silent except for her voice, going on and on about Fred. There had been Stingers, and she could hardly walk, and I wasn't much better. The housefronts along Salem calm as ghosts, and the new snow like mica reflecting the street-lights. We climbed her porch steps, and that living room, with its wide floorboards, her tree still up, and a pine wreath hung on an oak peg in the fireplace lintel, hit me as if we had walked smack into an old-fashioned children's book. The smell of a pine indoors or a certain glaze on wrapping paper will do that to me, or frost in the corner of a win-dowpane: spell Christmas. We sat together on the scratchy D.R. sofa so

---

[1]D.R.: Design Research, a trendy New England furniture retailer. — ED.

she could finish her tale about Fred and I could warm up for the long walk back. Day was breaking and suddenly Evelyn looked haggard; I was led to try to comfort her and right then, with Evelyn's long hair all over our faces, and her strong eyebrows right under my eyes, we heard from on high Mary Jo beginning to cough. We froze, the big old fireplace full of cold ashes sending out a little draft on our ankles and, from above, this coughing and coughing, scoopy and dry. Mary Jo, about fifteen she must have been then, and weakened by the anorexia, had caught a cold that had turned into walking pneumonia. Evelyn blamed Fred's leaving her for that, too — the pneumonia. Coughing and coughing, the child, and her mother in my arms smelling of brandy and tears and Christmas. She blamed Fred but I would have blamed him less than the environment; those old wooden houses are drafty.

Thinking of upstairs and downstairs, I think of Betsey Clay at the head   8
of her stairs, no longer in a white nightie seeing the moon but in frilly lemon-colored pajamas, looking down at some party too loud for her to sleep through. We had come in from the patio and put on some old Twist records and there was no quiet way to play them. I was sitting on the floor somehow, with somebody, so the angle of my vision was low, and like a lesson in perspective the steps diminished up to her naked feet, too big to leave rabbit tracks now. For what seemed the longest time we looked at each other — she had her mother's hollow-eyed fragile look — until the woman I was with, and I don't think it was Maureen, felt my distraction and herself turned to look up the stairs, and Betsey scampered back toward her room.

Her room would have been like my daughter's in those years: Beatles posters, or maybe of the Monkees, and prize ribbons for horsemanship in local shows. And dolls and Steiff animals that hadn't been put away yet sharing the shelves with Signet editions of Melville and *Hard Times* and Camus assigned at day school.[2] We were all so young, parents and children, learning it all together — how to grow up, how to deal with time — is what you realize now.

Those were the days when Harry Langhorne had got himself a motorcycle and would roar around and around the green on a Saturday night until the police came and stopped him, more or less politely. And the Wilcombes had put a hot tub on their second-story porch and had

---

[2]Herman Melville (1819–1891), American author of *Moby Dick* and other novels. *Hard Times*, English novel (1854) by Charles Dickens. Albert Camus (1913–1960), French writer and philosopher. — Ed.

to run a steel column up for support lest we all go tumbling down naked some summer night. In winter, there was a lot of weekend skiing for the sake of the kids, and we would take over a whole lodge in New Hampshire: heaps of snowy boots and wet parkas in the corner under the moose head, over past the beat-up player piano, and rosy cheeks at dinner at the long tables, where ham with raisin sauce was always the main dish. Suddenly the girls, long-legged in their stretch pants, hair whipping around their faces as they skimmed to a stop at the lift lines, were women. At night, after the boys had crumped out or settled to Ping-Pong in the basement, the girls stayed up with us, playing Crazy Eights or Spit with the tattered decks the lodge kept on hand, taking sips from our cans of beer, until at last the weight of all that day's fresh air toppled everyone up toward bed, in reluctant bunches. The little rooms had dotted-swiss curtains and thick frost ferns on the windowpanes. The radiators dripped and sang. There was a dormitory feeling through the thin partitions, and shuffling and giggling in the hall on the way to the bathrooms, one for girls and one for boys. One big family. It was the children, really, growing unenthusiastic and resistant, who stopped the trips. That, and the divorces as they began to add up. Margaret and I are about the last marriage left; she says maybe we missed the boat, but can't mean it.

The beach picnics, and touch football, and the softball games in that big field the Wilcombes had. Such a lot of good times, and the kids growing up through them like weeds in sunshine; and now, when the daughters of people we hardly knew at all are married to stockbrokers or off in Oregon being nurses or in Mexico teaching agronomy, our daughters haunt the town as if searching for something they missed, taking classes in macramé or aerobic dancing, living with their mothers, wearing no makeup, walking up beside the rocks with books in their arms like a race of little nuns.

You can see their mothers in them — beautiful women, full of life. I saw Annie Langhorne at the train station the other morning and we had to talk for some minutes, mostly about the antique store Mary Jo wants to open up with Betsey, and apropos of the hopelessness of this venture she gave me a smile exactly like her mother's one of the times Louise and I said goodbye or faced the fact that we just weren't going to make it, she and I — pushing up the lower lip so her chin crinkled, that nice wide mouth of hers humorous but downturned at the corners as if to buckle back tears. Lou's exact same smile on little Annie, and it was like being in love again, when all the world is a hunt and the sight of the woman's car parked at a gas station or in the Stop & Shop lot makes your Saturday, makes your blood race and your palms go numb, the heart touching base.

But these girls. What are they hanging back for? What are they afraid of?

EXPLORATIONS

1. Updike ends his story with two questions. What do you think are the answers to those questions?

2. At what points does the narrator refer (directly or indirectly) to infidelity? to divorce? What is his attitude toward each? How can you tell?

3. At what points are alcoholic drinks mentioned? What roles does drinking play in this story?

4. Updike's story is filled with visual images, presented from the narrator's viewpoint. What do these images reveal about the narrator's emotional response to the people, places, and events in the story? about his character?

CONNECTIONS

1. In Carola Hansson and Karin Lidén's "Liza and Family," Liza says she would like a daughter "because they're so much closer to their mother." What evidence in "The Lovely Troubled Daughters of Our Old Crowd" supports this statement? What are the disadvantages to the daughters in Updike's story of being close to their mothers?

2. Reread the passage by Michael Novak in *Looking at Ourselves*. What statements in it are illustrated by actions on the part of Updike's characters? This story comes from a collection entitled *Trust Me*. What comment does Novak make about family life and trust which may relate to Updike's reasons for choosing that title?

3. Recall Raymonde Carroll's "Money and Seduction" (p. 16). In what ways does Updike's story support Carroll's theories? In what ways does it contradict them? What social variables are not considered in Carroll's analysis that might account for the contradictions?

ELABORATIONS

1. Updike tosses off information about his characters as if he expects the reader to know these people. Go through his story and figure out which characters are in which family. Then write a chronological narration of each family's life history up to the present: marriages, divorces, affairs, and current status, particularly of the daughters.

2. Updike tells his story in such a way that the reader sees and understands more than the narrator does. What specific techniques does he use to accomplish this? Study the ways Updike depicts his narrator as ignorant even while he (the narrator) is giving valuable information to the reader. Then write an argumentative essay in which you make your case by posing as someone more ignorant about its merits than the reader is.

MARGARET ATWOOD

Scenes from Two Childhoods

Margaret Atwood is one of Canada's most distinguished novelists, poets, and critics. Born in Ottawa, Ontario, in 1939, she was educated at Victoria College, the University of Toronto, Radcliffe College, and Harvard University. She has taught at colleges and universities in Canada and the United States and has received more than a dozen literary awards and fellowships. In her earliest poems and her first novel, *The Edible Woman* (1969), Atwood introduced themes of distance and defenses, which have continued through her work. Her poignant characterizations, particularly of women, are supported by a virtuosity with language that ranges from wildly passionate (*Surfacing,* 1972) to coldly controlled (*Life Before Man,* 1979). Her ironic futuristic novel *The Handmaid's Tale* (1986) was made into a motion picture. The author of several volumes of short stories, as well as occasional plays and children's books, Atwood currently lives in Ontario. "Scenes from Two Childhoods" comes from her 1983 collection *Bluebeard's Egg.*

Canada, the world's second largest country (after the Soviet Union), extends from the Atlantic to the Pacific Ocean and from the North Pole to the U.S. border. Nova Scotia, where Atwood's mother grew up, juts into the Atlantic Ocean east of Maine. This small province was settled in the 1600s by the French, who called it Acadia. When the British took it over in 1717, many of the evicted French speakers migrated south to Louisiana, where "Acadians" became slurred to "Cajuns." Various British colonies united in 1867 as the Dominion of Canada, which stayed subject to British rule until 1982. Although today Canada's head of government is an elected prime minister, its head of state is still the British monarch. Ottawa, the nation's capital, lies in a narrow section of Ontario between New York State and Quebec, a province where French remains the predominant language. Tension continues between Canada's English and French heritages, with Quebec periodically threatening to secede.

My mother's family lived in a large white house near an apple orchard, in Nova Scotia. There was a barn and a carriage-house, in the kitchen there was a pantry. My mother can remember the days before commercial bakeries, when flour came in barrels and all the bread was made at home. She can remember the first radio broadcast she ever heard, which was a singing commercial about socks.

In this house there were many rooms. Although I have been there, although I have seen the house with my own eyes, I still don't know how many. Parts of it were closed off, or so it seemed; there were back staircases. Passages led elsewhere. Five children lived in it, two parents, a hired man and a hired girl, whose names and faces kept changing. The structure of the house was hierarchical, with my grandfather at the top, but its secret life — the life of pie crusts, clean sheets, the box of rags in the linen closet, the loaves in the oven — was female. The house, and all the objects in it, crackled with static electricity; undertows washed through it, the air was heavy with things that were known but not spoken. Like a hollow log, a drum, a church, it amplified, so that conversations whispered in it sixty years ago can be half-heard even today.

In this house you had to stay at the table until you had eaten everything on your plate. "'Think of the starving Armenians,' mother used to say," says my mother. "I didn't see how eating my bread crusts was going to help them out one jot."

It was in this house that I first saw a stalk of oats in a vase, each oat   4 wrapped in the precious silver paper which had been carefully saved from a chocolate box. I thought it was the most wonderful thing I had ever seen, and began saving silver paper myself. But I never got around to wrapping the oats, and in any case I didn't know how. Like many other art forms of vanished civilizations, the techniques for this one have been lost and cannot quite be duplicated.

"We had oranges at Christmas," says my mother. "They came all the way from Florida; they were very expensive. That was the big treat: to find an orange in the toe of your stocking. It's funny to remember how good they tasted, now."

When she was sixteen, my mother had hair so long she could sit on it. Women were bobbing their hair by then; it was getting to be the twenties. My mother's hair was giving her headaches, she says, but my grandfather, who was very strict, forbade her to cut it. She waited until one Saturday when she knew he had an appointment with the dentist.

"In those days there was no freezing," says my mother. "The drill was worked with a foot pedal, and it went *grind, grind, grind*. The dentist himself had brown teeth: he chewed tobacco, and he would spit the tobacco juice into a spittoon while he was working on your teeth."

Here my mother, who is good mimic, imitates the sounds of the drill   8 and the tobacco juice: "*Rrrrr! Rrrrr! Rrrrr! Phtt! Rrrrr! Rrrrr! Rrrrr! Phtt!*

It was always sheer agony. It was a heaven-sent salvation when gas came in."

My mother went into the dentist's office, where my grandfather was sitting in the chair, white with pain. She asked him if she could have her hair cut. He said she could do anything in tarnation as long as she would get out of there and stop pestering him.

"So I went out straight away and had it all chopped off," says my mother jauntily. "He was furious afterwards, but what could he do? He'd given his word."

My own hair reposes in a cardboard box in a steamer trunk in my mother's cellar, where I picture it becoming duller and more brittle with each passing year, and possibly moth-eaten; by now it will look like the faded wreaths of hair in Victorian funeral jewelry. Or it may have developed a dry mildew; inside its tissue-paper wrappings it glows faintly, in the darkness of the trunk. I suspect my mother has forgotten it's in there. It was cut off, much to my relief, when I was twelve and my sister was born. Before that it was in long curls: "Otherwise," says my mother, "it would have been just one big snarl." My mother combed it by winding it around her index finger every morning, but when she was in the hospital my father couldn't cope. "He couldn't get it around his stubby fingers," says my mother. My father looks down at his fingers. They are indeed broad compared with my mother's long elegant ones, which she calls bony. He smiles a pussy-cat smile.

So it was that my hair was sheared off. I sat in the chair in my first beauty parlor and watched it falling, like handfuls of cobwebs, down over my shoulders. From within it my head began to emerge, smaller, denser, my face more angular. I aged five years in fifteen minutes. I knew I could go home now and try out lipstick.

"Your father was upset about it," says my mother, with an air of collusion. She doesn't say this when my father is present. We smile, over the odd reactions of men to hair.

"You had such an acute sense of smell when you were younger," says my mother.

Now we are on more dangerous ground: my mother's childhood is one thing, my own quite another. This is the moment at which I start rattling the silverware, or ask for another cup of tea. "You used to march into houses that were strange to you, and you would say in a loud voice, 'What's that funny smell?' " If there are guests present, they shift a little away from me, conscious of their own emanations, trying not to look at my nose.

"I used to be so embarrassed," says my mother absentmindedly. Then   16
she shifts gears. "You were such an easy child. You used to get up at six in the morning and play by yourself in the playroom, singing away. . . ." There is a pause. A distant voice, mine, high and silvery, drifts over the space between us. "You used to talk a blue streak. Chatter, chatter, chatter, from morning to night." My mother sighs imperceptibly, as if wondering why I have become so silent, and gets up to poke the fire.

Hoping to change the subject, I ask whether or not the crocuses have come up yet, but she is not to be diverted. "I never had to spank you," she says. "A harsh word, and you would be completely reduced." She looks at me sideways; she isn't sure what I have turned into, or how. "There were just one or two times. Once, when I had to go out and I left your father in charge." (This may be the real point of the story: the inability of men to second-guess small children.) "I came back along the street, and there were you and your brother, throwing mud balls at an old man out of the upstairs window."

We both know whose idea this was. For my mother, the proper construction to be put on this event is that my brother was a hell-raiser and I was his shadow, "easily influenced," as my mother puts it. "You were just putty in his hands."

"Of course, I had to punish both of you equally," she says. Of course. I smile a forgiving smile. The real truth is that I was sneakier than my brother, and got caught less often. No front-line charges into enemy machine-gun nests for me, if they could be at all avoided. My own solitary acts of wickedness were devious and well concealed; it was only in partnership with my brother that I would throw caution to the winds.

"He could wind you around his little finger," says my mother. "Your   20
father made each of you a toy box, and the rule was — " (my mother is good at the devising of rules) " — the rule was that neither of you could take the toys out of the other one's toy box without permission. Otherwise he would have got all your toys away from you. But he got them anyway, mind you. He used to talk you into playing house, and he would pretend to be the baby. Then he would pretend to cry, and when you asked what he wanted, he'd demand whatever it was out of your toy box that he wanted to play with at the moment. You always gave it to him."

I don't remember this, though I do remember staging World War Two on the living-room floor, with armies of stuffed bears and rabbits, but surely some primal patterns were laid down. Have these early toy-box experiences — and "toy box" itself, as a concept, reeks with implications — have they made me suspicious of men who wish to be mothered, yet susceptible to them at the same time? Have I been conditioned to believe that if I am not solicitous, if I am not forthcoming, if I am not a never-ending cornucopia of entertaining delights, they will take their collections of milk-bottle tops and their mangy one-eared teddy bears and go away into the woods by themselves to play snipers? Probably. What my mother thinks was merely cute may have been lethal.

But this is not her only story about my suckiness and gullibility. She follows up with the *coup de grâce*, the tale of the bunny-rabbit cookies.

"It was in Ottawa. I was invited to a government tea," says my mother, and this fact alone should signal an element of horror: My mother hated official functions, to which however she was obliged to go because she was the wife of a civil servant. "I had to drag you kids along; we couldn't afford a lot of babysitters in those days." The hostess had made a whole plateful of decorated cookies for whatever children might be present, and my mother proceeds to describe these: wonderful cookies shaped like bunny rabbits, with faces and clothes of colored icing, little skirts for the little girl bunny rabbits, little pants for the little boy bunny rabbits.

"You chose one," says my mother. "You went off to a corner with it, by yourself. Mrs. X noticed you and went over. 'Aren't you going to eat your cookie?' she said. 'Oh, no,' you said. 'I'll just sit here and talk to it.' And there you sat, as happy as a clam. But someone had made the mistake of leaving the plate near your brother. When they looked again, there wasn't a single cookie left. He'd eaten every one. He was very sick that night, I can tell you." 24

Some of my mother's stories defy analysis. What is the moral of this one? That I was a simp is clear enough, but on the other hand it was my brother who got the stomach ache. Is it better to eat your food, in a straightforward materialistic way, and as much of it as possible, or go off into the corner and talk to it? This used to be a favorite of my mother's before I was married, when I would bring what my father referred to as "swains" home for dinner. Along with the dessert, out would come the bunny-rabbit cookie story, and I would cringe and twiddle my spoon while my mother forged blithely on with it. What were the swains supposed to make of it? Were my kindliness and essential femininity being trotted out for their inspection? Were they being told in a round-about way that I was harmless, that they could expect to be talked to by me, but not devoured? Or was she, in some way, warning them off? Because there is something faintly crazed about my behavior, some tinge of the kind of person who might be expected to leap up suddenly from the dinner table and shout, "Don't eat that! It's alive!"

There is, however, a difference between symbolism and anecdote. Listening to my mother, I sometimes remember this.

"In my next incarnation," my mother said once, "I'm going to be an archaeologist and go around digging things up." We were sitting on the bed that had once been my brother's, then mine, then my sister's; we were sorting out things from one of the trunks, deciding what could now be given away or thrown out. My mother believes that what you save from the past is mostly a matter of choice.

At that time something wasn't right in the family; someone wasn't   28
happy. My mother was angry: her good cheer was not paying off.

This statement of hers startled me. It was the first time I'd ever heard my mother say that she might have wanted to be something other than what she was. I must have been thirty-five at the time, but it was still shocking and slightly offensive to me to learn that my mother might not have been totally contented fulfilling the role in which fate had cast her: that of being my mother. What thumb-suckers we all are, I thought, when it comes to mothers.

Shortly after this I became a mother myself, and this moment altered for me.

While she was combing my next-to-impossible hair, winding it around her long index finger, yanking out the snarls, my mother used to read me stories. Most of them are still in the house somewhere, but one has vanished. It may have been a library book. It was about a little girl who was so poor she had only one potato left for her supper, and while she was roasting it the potato got up and ran away. There was the usual chase, but I can't remember the ending: a significant lapse.

"That story was one of your favorites," says my mother. She is probably   32
still under the impression that I identified with the little girl, with her hunger and her sense of loss; whereas in reality I identified with the potato.

Early influences are important. It took that one a while to come out; probably until after I went to university and started wearing black stockings and pulling my hair back into a bun, and having pretensions. Gloom set in. Our next-door neighbor, who was interested in wardrobes, tackled my mother: "'If she would only *do* something about herself,'" my mother quotes, "'she could be *quite attractive*.'"

"You always kept yourself busy," my mother says charitably, referring to this time. "You always had something cooking. Some project or other."

It is part of my mother's mythology that I am as cheerful and productive as she is, though she admits that these qualities may be occasionally and temporarily concealed. I wasn't allowed much angst[1] around the house. I had to indulge it in the cellar, where my mother wouldn't come upon me brooding and suggest I should go out for a walk, to improve my circulation. This was her answer to any sign, however slight, of creeping despondency. There wasn't a lot that a brisk sprint through dead leaves, howling winds, or sleet couldn't cure.

It was, I knew, the *zeitgeist*[2] that was afflicting me, and against it such   36 simple remedies were powerless. Like smog I wafted through her days, dankness spreading out from around me. I read modern poetry and histories of Nazi atrocities, and took to drinking coffee. Off in the distance, my mother vacuumed around my feet while I sat in chairs, studying, with car rugs tucked around me, for suddenly I was always cold.

My mother has few stories to tell about these times. What I remember from them is the odd look I would sometimes catch in her eyes. It struck me, for the first time in my life, that my mother might be afraid of me. I could not even reassure her, because I was only dimly aware of the nature of her distress, but there must have been something going on in me that was beyond her: At any time I might open my mouth and out would come a language she had never heard before. I had become a visitant from outer space, a time-traveler come back from the future, bearing news of a great disaster.

EXPLORATIONS

1. Who are the main characters in "Scenes from Two Childhoods"? How would the essay's effect change if Atwood referred to them by name instead of title?

2. What are the main time periods that appear in this essay? How does Atwood differentiate them? What tactics does she use to make every period in her essay seem immediate?

---

[1]Angst: anxious dread. — Ed.
[2]Zeitgeist: The philosophical and cultural spirit of the times. — Ed.

3. Not all Atwood's statements are factual. Find at least three images that are not literally true (for example, "What thumb-suckers we all are . . . when it comes to mothers" in para. 29) and explain what is meant by each one.

CONNECTIONS

1. Compare Atwood's factual reminiscences with John Updike's fictional ones. What ethnic and socioeconomic group do the characters in each selection belong to? What similar images appear in both selections? What details show Updike's and Atwood's characters to have different values and priorities?

2. What does Atwood regard as the best things about family life? What changes in her life seem to have caused her nostalgia for them? What does Updike's narrator regard as the best things about family life? What changes in his life seem to have caused his nostalgia for them?

3. How does the closeness among generations in Atwood's family compare with that in Liza's family in Carola Hansson and Karin Lidén's "Liza and Family"? Liang Heng's family in Liang Heng and Judith Shapiro's "Chairman Mao's Good Little Boy"? How does physical closeness — that is, amount of space in the house — compare in these three families?

4. In *Looking at Ourselves*, Ellen Goodman describes family in the United States as "social glue" between generations and between individuals. At what points, and in what ways, does Atwood show that sharing stories from their family's history strengthens bonds between Canadian generations and individuals?

ELABORATIONS

1. Hansson and Lidén use the interview format in "Liza and Family" to present their subject directly to their readers. In contrast, Atwood turns interview material into a layered, intricate narrative. To get a sense of how she accomplishes this, reverse the process: Rewrite "Scenes from Two Childhoods" as an interview between Atwood and her mother. As do Hansson and Lidén, keep the interviewer's questions brief and direct; omit Atwood's interpretations and speculations.

2. Look back at Liza's definition of a good mother in paragraph 36 of "Liza and Family." Write a definition or illustration essay using "Scenes from Two Childhoods" to show how a real woman (Margaret Atwood's mother) implements the various elements of Liza's definition.

JOHN DAVID MORLEY

Acquiring a Japanese Family

"John David Morley was born in Singapore in 1948 and was educated at Merton College, Oxford. His first job was in Mexico, as tutor to the children of Elizabeth Taylor and Richard Burton. Then he went to Germany to work in the theater, and by the age of twenty-four had begun to develop an interest in the drama — and later the general culture — of Japan, and to teach himself the language. He went to Japan on a Japanese government scholarship, to study at the Language Research Institute of Waseda University, Tokyo. Since then he has made his home in West Germany, where he works for Japanese television as a liaison officer and interpreter, researching TV documentaries. He has translated some thirty Japanese scripts into English and German." Morley's recent books include *In the Labyrinth* (1986), and *The Case of Thomas N.* (1987). "Acquiring a Japanese Family" comes from Morley's semiauto-biographical novel *Pictures from the Water Trade: Adventures of a Westerner in Japan* (1985), as does most of this paragraph.

Japan has intrigued Westerners since its self-imposed isolation was ended in 1854 by U.S. Commodore Matthew C. Perry, who forced the opening of trade. At that point this 2,360-mile archipelago off Asia's east coast was ruled by the shoguns, a succession of military governors who had dominated Japan since 1192. Before the shogunate came the empire, which supposedly began in 660 B.C., and which reestablished itself in 1868. Today Emperor Akihito is Japan's head of state, in a parliamentary democracy led by a prime minister. Japan consists of 4 main islands and over 3,000 smaller ones; almost three-fourths of the country is hills and mountains, many of them dormant or active volcanoes. While Japan remains ethnically homogeneous, contact with the West has spurred enough cultural and economic change to give this nation the highest growth rate in the industrialized world.

(For more background on Japan, see p. 52.)

Boon did not like the Foreign Students Hall where it had been arranged for him to live, and on the same evening he moved in he decided he would move out. . . . But the decision that he did not want to live there was one thing, finding somewhere else to stay was quite another, and this in turn would have been impossible or at least very difficult if he had not happened to meet Sugama a few days after arriving in the country.

The introduction was arranged through a mutual acquaintance, Yo-shida, at the private university where Boon was taking language courses and where Sugama was employed on the administrative staff. They met one afternoon in the office of their acquaintance and inspected each other warily for ten minutes.

"Nice weather," said Boon facetiously as he shook hands with Sugama. Outside it was pouring with rain.

"Nice weather?" repeated Sugama doubtfully, glancing out of the   4
window. "But it's raining."

It was not a good start.

Sugama had just moved into a new apartment. It was large enough for two, he said, and he was looking for someone to share the expenses. This straightforward information arrived laboriously, in bits and pieces, sandwiched between snippets of Sugama's personal history and vague professions of friendship, irritating to Boon, because at the time he felt they sounded merely sententious. All this passed back and forth between Sugama and Boon through the mouth of their mutual friend, as Boon understood almost no Japanese and Sugama's English, though well-intentioned, was for the most part impenetrable.

It made no odds to Boon where he lived or with whom. All he wanted was a Japanese-speaking environment in order to absorb the language as quickly as possible. He had asked for a family, but none was available.

One windy afternoon in mid-October the three of them met outside   8
the gates of the university and set off to have a look at Sugama's new apartment. It was explained to Boon that cheap apartments in Tokyo were very hard to come by, the only reasonable accommodation available being confined to housing estates subsidized by the government. Boon wondered how a relatively prosperous bachelor like Sugama managed to qualify for government-subsidized housing. Sugama admitted that this was in fact only possible because his grandfather would also be living there. It was the first Boon had heard of the matter and he was rather taken aback.

It turned out, however, that the grandfather would "very seldom" be there — in fact, that he wouldn't live there at all. He would only be there on paper, he and his grandson constituting a "family." That was the point. "You must *say* he is there," said Sugama emphatically.

The grandfather lived a couple of hundred miles away, and although he never once during the next two years set foot in the apartment he still managed to be the bane of Boon's life. A constant stream of representatives from charities, government agencies, and old people's clubs, on average one or two a month, came knocking on the door, asking to speak to grandfather. At first grandfather was simply "not in" or had "gone for a walk," but as time passed and the flow of visitors never faltered, Boon found himself having to resort to more drastic measures. Grandfather began to make long visits to his home in the country; he had not yet returned because he didn't feel up to making the journey; his health gradually deteriorated. Finally Boon decided to have him invalided, and for a long time his condition remained "grave." On grandfather's behalf Boon received the condolences of all these visitors, and occasionally even presents.

Two years later grandfather did in fact die. Boon was thus exonerated, but in the meantime he had got to know grandfather well and had become rather fond of him. He attended his funeral with mixed feelings.

Sugama had acquired tenure of his government-subsidized apartment by a stroke of luck. He had won a ticket in a lottery. These apartments were much sought after, and in true Japanese style their distribution among hundreds of thousands of applicants was discreetly left to fate. The typical tenant was a young couple with one or two children, who would occupy the apartment for ten or fifteen years, often under conditions of bleak frugality, in order to save money to buy a house. Although the rent was not immoderate, prices generally in Tokyo were high, and it was a mystery to Boon how such people managed to live at all. Among the lottery winners there were inevitably also those people for whom the acquisition of an apartment was just a prize, an unexpected bonus, to be exploited as a financial investment. It was no problem for these nominal tenants to sublet their apartments at prices well above the going rate.

Boon had never lived on a housing estate and his first view of the tall concrete compound where over fifty thousand people lived did little to reassure him. Thousands of winner families were accommodated in about a dozen rectangular blocks, each between ten and fifteen stories high, apparently in no way different (which disappointed Boon most of all) from similar housing compounds in Birmingham or Berlin. He had naively expected Japanese concrete to be different, to have a different color, perhaps, or a more exotic shape.

But when Sugama let them into the apartment and Boon saw the interior he immediately took heart: this was unmistakably Japanese. Taking off their shoes in the tiny boxlike hall, the three of them padded reverently through the kitchen into the *tatami* rooms.

"Smell of fresh *tatami*," pronounced Sugama, wrinkling his nose.

Boon was ecstatic. Over the close-woven pale gold straw matting lay   16
a very faint greenish shimmer, sometimes perceptible and sometimes not,
apparently in response to infinitesimal shifts in the texture of the falling
light. The *tatami* was quite unlike a carpet or any other form of floor
covering he had ever seen. It seemed to be alive, humming with colors
he could sense rather than see, like a greening tree in the brief interval
between winter and spring. He stepped on to it and felt the fibers recoil,
sinking under the weight of his feet, slowly and softly.

"You can see green?" asked Sugama, squatting down.

"Yes indeed."

"Fresh *tatami*. Smell of grass, green color. But not for long, few weeks
only."

"What exactly is it?"   20

"Yes."

Boon turned to Yoshida and repeated the question, who in turn asked
Sugama and conferred with him at great length.

"*Tatami* comes from *oritatamu*, which means to fold up. So it's a
kind of matting you can fold up."

"Made of straw."   24

"Yes."

"How long does it last?"

Long consultation.

"He says this is not so good quality. Last maybe four, five years."   28

"And then what?"

"New *tatami*. Quite expensive, you see. But very practical."

The three *tatami* rooms were divided by a series of *fusuma*, sliding
screens made of paper and light wood. These screens were decorated at
the base with simple grass and flower motifs; a natural extension, it
occurred to Boon, of the grasslike *tatami* laid out in between. Sugama
explained that the *fusuma* were usually kept closed in winter, and in
summer, in order to have "nice breeze," they could be removed altogether. He also showed Boon the *shoji*, a type of sliding screen similar
to the *fusuma* but more simple: an open wooden grid covered on one
side with semitransparent paper, primitive but rather beautiful. There
was only one small section of *shoji* in the whole apartment; almost as a
token, thought Boon, and he wondered why.

With the exception of a few one- and two-room apartments every   32
house that Boon ever visited in Japan was designed to incorporate these
three common elements: *tatami*, *fusuma*, and *shoji*. In the houses of

rich people the *tatami* might last longer, the *fusuma* decorations might be more costly, but the basic concept was the same. The interior design of all houses being much the same, it was not surprising to find certain similarities in the behavior and attitudes of the people who lived in them.

The most striking feature of the Japanese house was lack of privacy; the lack of individual, inviolable space. In winter, when the *fusuma* were kept closed, any sound above a whisper was clearly audible on the other side, and of course in summer they were usually removed altogether. It is impossible to live under such conditions for very long without a common household identity emerging which naturally takes precedence over individual wishes. This enforced family unity was still held up to Boon as an ideal, but in practice it was ambivalent, as much a yoke as a bond.

There was no such thing as the individual's private room, no bedroom, dining- or sitting-room as such, since in the traditional Japanese house there was no furniture determining that a room should be reserved for any particular function. A person slept in a room, for example, without thinking of it as a bedroom or as his room. In the morning his bedding would be rolled up and stored away in a cupboard; a small table known as the *kotatsu*, which could also be plugged into the mains to provide heating, was moved back into the center of the room and here the family ate, drank, worked, and relaxed for the rest of the day. Although it was becoming standard practice in modern Japan for children to have their own rooms, many middle-aged and nearly all older Japanese still lived in this way. They regarded themselves as "one flesh," their property as common to all; the *uchi* (household, home) was constituted according to a principle of indivisibility. The system of movable screens meant that the rooms could be used by all the family and for all purposes: walls were built round the *uchi*, not inside it.

Boon later discovered analogies between this concept of house and the Japanese concept of self. The Japanese carried his house around in his mouth and produced it in everyday conversation, using the word *uchi* to mean "I," the representative of my house in the world outside. His self-awareness was naturally expressed as corporate individuality, hazy about quite what that included, very clear about what it did not. . . .

The almost wearying sameness about all the homes which Boon vis- 36
ited, despite differences in the wealth and status of their owners, prompted a rather unexpected conclusion: the classlessness of the Japanese house. The widespread use of traditional materials, the preservation of traditional structures, even if in such contracted forms as to have become merely

symbolic, suggested a consensus about the basic requirements of daily life which was very remarkable, and which presumably held implications for Japanese society as a whole. Boon's insight into that society was acquired very slowly, after he had spent a great deal of time sitting on the *tatami* mats and looking through the sliding *fusuma* doors which had struck him as no more than pleasing curiosities on his first visit to a Japanese-style home.

Sugama, Yoshida, and Boon celebrated the new partnership at a restaurant in Shinjuku, and a week later Boon moved in.

The moment he entered the apartment a woman who was unexpectedly standing in the kitchen dropped down on her knees and prostrated herself in a deep bow, her forehead almost touching the floorboards, introducing herself with the words "*Irrashaimase. Sugama de gozaimasu . . .*"

Boon was extremely startled. He wondered whether he should do the same thing and decided not, compromising with a halfhearted bow which unfortunately the woman couldn't even see, because she had her face to the ground. She explained that she was *o-kaasan*, Sugama's mother.

Sugama had a way of springing surprises — or rather, he indicated his 40 intentions so obtusely that Boon usually failed to realize what would happen until it was already in progress — and so for quite a while Boon assumed that there must have been a change in plan, that the mother had perhaps joined the household as a stand-in for the grandfather. He greeted her in fluent Japanese (he had been studying introductions for the past week) and promptly fell into unbroken silence, mitigated by the occasional appreciative nod. Boon for his part hardly understood a word of what Sugama's mother was saying but she, encouraged by the intelligible sounds he had initially produced, talked constantly for the best part of an hour, and by the time Sugama eventually arrived Boon had become resigned to the idea that his talkative mother was going to be a permanent resident.

The misunderstanding was swiftly ironed out. No, *o-kaasan* had only come up to Tokyo for a few days (from whatever angle of the compass one approached Tokyo the journey to the capital was described as an elevation) in order to help with the move.

Sugama's mother was a small, wiry woman in her late fifties. Her teeth protruded slightly; like most Japanese women, even those who had very good teeth, she covered her mouth with her hand whenever she laughed. She was a vivacious woman and laughed frequently, so one way and another, with all the cooking, cleaning, and sewing she also did during the next four days, her hands were kept continually busy. She was of slight build but very sound in lung, with the effect that when she laughed it resounded throughout her whole body, as if the laugh were more than the body could accommodate. Perhaps this laughter drew Boon's attention to a girlish quality she had about her, despite her age and a rather plain appearance. He often watched her working, and in the spare, effortless movements of a woman who has performed the same tasks so many times that not even the tiniest gesture is superfluous there was also something unexpectedly graceful.

On the far side of the *fusuma* Boon often heard them talking late into the night. Night after night she sawed away at him with her flinty, abrasive voice. In the mornings Sugama was moody, the atmosphere in the house increasingly tense. Boon was left guessing. Gradually, in the course of weeks and months, Sugama began to take him into his confidence, and in retrospect he learned what must have been the subject of those nightly conversations.

O-kaasan's most pressing concern was that her son, at the advanced age of twenty-eight, was still unmarried. Boon couldn't see what the fuss was about, but Sugama was slowly coming round to his mother's view, who was quite sure it was a disaster. "The wind blows hard," he announced mysteriously, apparently by way of explanation — Boon himself had to blow pretty hard to keep up with conversations on this level. He said it was up to Sugama to decide when and whether he wanted to get married. It wasn't anybody else's business. Sugama would clearly have liked to be able to agree with this facile advice and just as clearly he could not, entangled in a web of sentiment and duty of which Boon was wholly ignorant. 44

The promptings of filial duty which caused Sugama such heartache and which to Boon were so alien demanded of Sugama a second, even more painful decision. He was the *chonan*, the eldest son, thereby inheriting the obligation not merely to provide for his aging parents but to live with them in the same house. There were two alternatives open to him. He could either bring his parents to live with him in Tokyo or he could return home to his province in the north. A house in Tokyo large enough to provide room for grandfather, parents, Sugama, and — sooner or later — a fourth generation family was out of the question; on his present salary he would have to work for several lifetimes in order to pay for it. A one-way ticket home came a great deal cheaper, which was just as well, since the only job awaiting him at the other end would be poorly

paid and with even poorer prospects. Such was the path of righteous-
ness. . . .

O-kaasan had only just packed her bags and gone home when — as
usual without any forewarning — Sugama turned up late one evening
accompanied by an old man, his wife, and an enormous cardboard box.
Boon was sitting in his pajamas eating noodles out of a saucepan when
these unexpected visitors arrived. Consternation. The old lady caught
sight of him and dropped her bag (very probably she had not been
forewarned either), immediately prostrating herself on the floor in the
deepest of deep bows, old-style obeisance with the added advantage of
concealing momentary shock and embarrassment. The old man was no
slouch either. Palms on the floor and fingers turned inwards he bobbed
his head up and down several times in Boon's direction, apologizing
profusely every time he came up for air. All this happened so quickly
that the astonished Boon didn't even have the presence of mind to put
down the saucepan he was holding, and he sat there in his pajamas
uneasily aware that he was the most unworthy object of the visitors'
attentions.

Sugama came forward rather sheepishly, stepping in cavalier fashion
between the prone bodies on the kitchen floor, and explained who they
were.

"My grandfather's brother — younger brother — and wife."   48

"Not your grandfather?" asked Boon doubtfully, always alert to the
possibility of misunderstandings when Sugama ventured into English.

"No, no *not* my grandfather."

"Your *great*-uncle, then."

"Ah! Great-uncle? *Great* uncle?"   52

Sugama paused to digest this new word, mustering his ancient relative
with pursed lips. It was clear what was passing through his mind.

Boon was still not reassured. He kept an eye on the ominous cardboard
box, quite large enough to accommodate a third, perhaps enfeebled
relative, and wondered what else was in store for him.

"What are they doing here?"

"Earthquake," said Sugama simply. Boon fetched his dictionary and   56
Sugama, reverting to Japanese, sat down to explain the situation.

At about nine o'clock that evening his great-uncle had called him in
his office (Sugama worked a late shift) with the startling news that a
major earthquake was imminent. How did he know? His wife had told
him so. How did she know? A fortune-teller she regularly visited and in
whom she placed absolute confidence had seen it in his cards and crystal

ball. She was terrified, and having personally experienced the Great Kanto Earthquake of 1923 in which over a hundred thousand people had died she was not taking any chances. Her fortune-teller couldn't predict exactly when the earthquake would occur, but it might be at any time within the next three days; the greatest likelihood of its occurrence was forecast for midnight on the following day. The two old people ran a little shop in the downtown area of Tokyo where many of the houses were flimsy wooden structures which tended to slump and collapse very easily, even without the encouragement of an earthquake. But their great-nephew, they heard, had just moved into a marvelous modern building that was supposed to be *earthquake-proof*. Could they come and stay for a few days? Of course, said Sugama. So without more ado they bundled their worldly goods into the largest available box and Sugama brought them over in a neighbor's truck.

As a matter of fact there had been a slight tremor the previous evening. It was Boon's first. He had been standing in the kitchen helping himself to another glass of whiskey when the floor unaccountably began to sway and a set of irreproachable stainless steel ladles, which until then had given him no cause for complaint, started rattling menacingly on the kitchen wall. Boon had replaced the whiskey and made himself a cup of tea instead.

Great-uncle and his wife knelt on the *tatami* listening to Sugama's recital, wagging their heads and smiling from time to time, as if allowing that there was something rather droll about the situation, but also wanting to be taken absolutely seriously. However, with every moment they spent in the apartment this became increasingly hard to do, for the eccentric old couple seemed to be guided by a mischievous genius — they belonged to nature's blunderers, everything they touched turned to farce. Their great-nephew had just finished his dramatic account when there was a shrill call of *ohayo!* (Good morning) from the kitchen, and all eyes turned to the neglected cardboard box.

"Oh dear! The poor thing!" crowed the old lady, getting up at once 60
and pattering over to the box. She pulled open the flap and gently lifted out a bright yellow parrot. The indignant bird rapped her knuckles a couple of times with the side of his beak and settled frostily on the tip of her finger.

Sugama, Boon, the elderly couple, and the yellow parrot housed together for the next three days. Once he had provided his relatives with a roof over their heads Sugama took no further interest in them and was unaccountably busy for as long as they stayed there, leaving the house earlier and returning later than usual. His prodigiously long working hours impressed great-uncle and worried his wife, who took to preparing nutritious cold snacks for the laboring hero before retiring for the night. Sugama did justice to these snacks with the same appetite he applied himself to his work, warding off their anxieties with careless equanimity.

"You've got to hand it to him — he certainly works hard," said great-uncle at breakfast one morning, just after Sugama had left the house.

"Ah," replied Boon noncommittally. He knew perfectly well that Sugama's overtime was not spent at the office but at mah-jongg parlors in Nakano and Takadanobaba.

In the meantime Boon was left to study the evacuees and the evacuees 64 Boon with mutual curiosity. On the whole he had the impression that they were rather disappointed in him. At first they looked at him as if he had descended from another planet, but when it became obvious that he was not going to live up to these expectations their interest declined into an attitude of gently reproachful familiarity. For Boon did not sleep on a bed, he dispensed with bacon and egg, he knew nothing about baseball, ate rice and drank green tea with relish, and was unpardonably fond of dried cuttlefish and raw squid, foods which foreigners were commonly supposed to regard with horror and loathing. Altogether Boon was not as Boon should be, and they were rather disconcerted.

This attitude — a national prejudice, really — that foreigners and the Japanese way of life must almost as a matter of principle be wholly incompatible was something Boon encountered time and again. Under the cover of courtesy, of polite considerations for differences in tastes and customs, many Japanese would gleefully reveal their own select cabinet of horrors, confronting their guest with fermented bean curd or prawns drowned in sake not as something he might care to sample but as a kind of ethnological litmus test: If he found it indigestible and swiftly turned green this would be taken by them as confirmation of their own cultural and racial singularity. With barely concealed triumph the host would commiserate with his victim, invariably remarking *Yappari, nihonjin ja nai to* . . . (Ah well, unless one is Japanese . . .). . . .

On the fateful morning great-uncle took cover under the *kotatsu* earlier than usual and sat tight for the rest of the day. His wife went about her household tasks as briskly as ever, but when there was nothing left for her to do and at last she knelt down beside great-uncle at the little table it became evident how restless she really was. From time to time she laid down her sewing, listened intently, sighed, and picked it up again. As the evening wore on and the tension began to mount, Boon couldn't resist cracking a few jokes, which great-uncle good-humoredly deflected at his wife. It was only to set her mind at rest that they had come to stay, he assured Boon. Women couldn't resist fortune-tellers, but it was just a lot of nonsense after all; and for good measure he made a few jokes himself at her expense. Boon was not deceived. Throughout the evening great-uncle helped himself to the bottle of fine old malt whiskey, originally intended as Sugama's present, much more liberally than he otherwise did and by midnight he was in true fighting spirit, his face shining with such particular splendor that his wife's attention was diverted from the impending destruction of Tokyo to the threat of great-uncle's imminent collapse.

There was no earthquake that night, but the old lady couldn't quite believe this and for two more days she sat it out in her nephew's apartment waiting for the dust to clear. Sugama was dispatched, like a kind of dove from Noah's Ark, to report on the state of the world, and it was only after he had personally confirmed that the house in downtown Tokyo was still in perfect order that she consented to their departure. Boon particularly regretted the loss of the parrot, which spoke few words of Japanese but those very frequently, thus improving his pronunciation of the language.

EXPLORATIONS

1. According to Morley's account, what is the attitude of Japanese adults to the older members of their family? to the younger members? How are Sugama's obligations as a family member different from those of a typical twenty-eight-year-old American?

2. Morley tells his story from the point of view of Boon, a fictional English visitor to Japan. At what points in the narrative does Boon act and react like a stranger in a strange land? At what points does he behave (or try to behave) like a Japanese native? In what respects was it probably easier for Morley to write this narrative in the third person than the first person? — that is, to depict Japan through Boon's eyes instead of his own?

3. Morley has interwoven information about Japanese customs with the story of Boon, Sugama, and his family. How would the impact of "Acquiring a Japanese Family" change if the factual sidelights (for example, on interior decoration) were omitted? What information in this narrative do you as a reader find most striking and memorable?

CONNECTIONS

1. As the central figure in Morley's essay (the figure through whom we see the events), is Boon more like John Updike's narrator in "The Lovely Troubled Daughters of Our Old Crowd" or the narrator in Margaret Atwood's "Scenes from Two Childhoods"? Support your answer with specific evidence and a summary of Boon's and the narrators' functions.

2. Scarcity of space is a major influence on life in both Japanese and Chinese cities. In what ways do the Communist Chinese described in Liang Heng and Judith Shapiro's "Chairman Mao's Good Little Boy" approach this issue differently from the capitalist Japanese? What attitudes and tactics do the two cultures share? How does the family's function as "social glue" appear to differ in Japan and China?

3. What concepts of how the family functions (or should function) appear in both "Acquiring a Japanese Family" and Michael Novak's passage in *Looking at Ourselves?* Which of these concepts are depicted by Novak as endangered in the United States and by Morley as thriving in Japan? What factors can you identify as having influenced the family's divergence in these two cultures?

ELABORATIONS

1. Much of the information Morley gives his readers about the Japanese family is indirect: for example, his discussion of the interior of Japanese homes and the concept of *uchi.* After carefully rereading "Acquiring a Japanese Family," write an essay describing Japanese attitudes toward the family: its social role, its influence on the individual, and the responsibilities and privileges of family members.

2. Morley writes: "The most striking feature of the Japanese house was lack of privacy; the lack of individual, inviolable space. . . . It is impossible to live under such conditions for very long without a common household identity emerging which naturally takes precedence over individual wishes. This enforced family unity was still held up to Boon as an ideal, but in practice it was ambivalent, as much a yoke as a bond" (para. 33). Choose one of the other essays in this unit, such as Carola Hansson and Karin Lidén's "Liza and Family" or Bruno Bettelheim's "Why Kibbutzim?," and write an illustrative essay showing how Morley's statements apply in another culture.

GYANRANJAN

Our Side of the Fence and Theirs

The son of a renowned writer, Gyanranjan was born in 1936 in Allahabad, India, where he received his M.A. from Allahabad University. Although he began his literary career as a poet, he published his first short story in 1960 and was soon hailed as representing the new writing of the sixties. "Our Side of the Fence and Theirs" is the title story from his first collection, published in 1968 and translated from the Hindi by Gordon C. Roadarmel. A second collection followed in 1971. Today Gyanranjan continues to work mainly in the story form.

With a third of the area of the United States, India has three times its population. The Indian civilization is one of the world's oldest, dating back more than five thousand years. European traders discovered this South Asian peninsula in the sixteenth century; by the mid-1800s the British had wrested control from the native rajas. After World War I, Mohandas "Mahatma" Gandhi led his people in nonviolent resistance and civil disobedience. From independence in 1947 until 1989, India's central family was that of its first prime minister, Jawaharlal Nehru, whose daughter Indira Gandhi (no relation to Mohandas) succeeded him and was in turn succeeded by her son Rajiv. The Nehru-Gandhi dynasty ended when Rajiv Gandhi lost the November 1989 election. His successor, V. P. Singh, faces an electorate that is more assertive and more impatient, a new divergence between state and society, and ongoing tensions between India and its neighbors, particularly Pakistan. The 1990 clash over Kashmir, which left many dead at the hands of guerrillas from the Jammu-Kashmir Liberation Front (JKLF), is only the latest incident in a long-standing conflict (see page 280). Less than a year after Britain established India and Pakistan as separate states, Pakistan invaded India's Muslim-dominated Kashmir. The United Nations intervened and negotiated a cease-fire, but the struggle, which escalated into war in 1965 and 1971, continues.

(For more background on India, see pp. 262 and 419.)

Mukherji has been transferred and no longer lives in our neighborhood. The new people who moved in have no contact with us. They appear to be Punjabis, but maybe not. It's hard to know anything about them.

Ever since they arrived, I've been strangely anxious to find out about them. For some reason I can't stand staying detached. Even on journeys I have to get acquainted with the other travelers. Perhaps it's just my nature. But no one at our house is indifferent to those people. We're respectable, honorable people. Having young women in the home, we're forced to understand everything and to be constantly aware. We're full of curiosity, and keep forming impressions based on the activities of our new neighbors.

I'd like to invite the whole family over to our house and be able to come and go at their place. But probably they're completely unaware of my feelings. Their life is an unusual one. They spend a good part of the day sitting around on chairs set on the firm ground near the veranda of their house. Those chairs remain outside all the time, even at night. They're very careless, but the chairs have never been stolen.

On one side of our house, there's a government office and a high brick wall. Behind us is the back of a two-story apartment building and, in front, the main street. As a result, we have no real proximity with any other family. The new neighbors seem like certain people found in big cities who establish no connection with others and keep strictly to themselves. Both this city and the neighborhood are quiet and peaceful. People come and go at a leisurely pace and stroll around casually, since life has no great urgency. That's why we find our neighbors strange.

I went outside. Those people were having morning tea, at the late hour of nine. Besides the husband and wife, there's one girl who must be their daughter. One always sees these same three people, never a fourth. The daughter may not be pretty, but she's a well-mannered young woman. If she used the right makeup, she might even look pretty. I've noticed that she laughs a lot — and frequently. Her mother and father laugh also. They always look happy. What sorts of things do they talk about, and why are they always laughing? Are their lives so full of delightful circumstances which keep them laughing? Or are they insensitive to the harsh, realistic circumstances of life? Amazed, I compare my family with the neighbors.

They startle me by suddenly bursting into laughter. I'd been concentrating on the rose beds, but now my trowel stopped. Their laughter seemed unable to stop. The girl rose from the chair and stood up, handing her teacup to her mother for fear of spilling it. Instead of standing straight, she was doubled over. Something funny in the conversation, perhaps a joke, must have set off the explosion of laughter. The girl, helpless with laughter, was unaware that her dupatta[1] had slipped off one shoulder. The movement of her bosom was visible — free and unrestrained. This was too much! Her mother should have scolded her for that carelessness. What kind of person was she not to mind? But maybe, unlike me, none of them had even looked in that direction.

Daily a kind of mild compulsion grips me, and my helpless fascination about the new neighbors grows. I'm not the only one. Puppi is very curious too, and keeps praising the material of that girl's kurtas.[2] My brother's wife also glances periodically from the kitchen toward their house, and Granny even knows when the neighbors have bought water chestnuts or squash and when the stove has been lit. Nevertheless, those people don't show a scrap of interest in us.

The girl never looks in our direction, nor do her parents. It doesn't even seem intentional. So the thought of them conversing with us is remote and unimaginable. Perhaps they don't need us in their world. Maybe they consider us inferior. Or maybe they fear trouble because of our proximity. I don't know to what extent that could be true, however, since the sight of a young man in the vicinity doesn't seem to fill her parents with the fear which my father feels for Puppi at the sight of my friends.

We never hear a radio at their place, while ours blares constantly. There's bare ground in front of their house, with not even a blade of grass. Our house has a lawn, along with a vegetable garden and beds of strong-smelling flowers. Why doesn't that girl make friends with my sister and my sister-in-law? Why don't her parents mix with mine? Why don't they notice us drinking tea out of cups prettier than theirs? What they ought to do is add us to their list of acquaintances. They should be interested in everything of ours. Next to the fence, on our side, there's a big tall tamarind tree with fruit six inches long hanging from it. Girls are crazy about tamarind fruit, and yet this neighbor girl never even looks over longingly. She's never given me the satisfaction of breaking a piece of fruit off the tree.

I keep waiting. . . .

Our neighbors evidently have no problem that might make them want to seek our help. Perhaps the little internal problems that exist in our home and others don't exist in theirs, which is astonishing. None of the three ever appears worried. The girl's father must frown occasionally, and

8

---

[1]A long, thin scarf worn over the shoulders. — ED.
[2]Long, loose shirts. — ED.

at times her mother must get upset, but nothing can be seen or heard from our place. Possibly the girl has some secret and private corner in her heart — some complication or emotional conflict. Maybe so, maybe not. Nothing definite can be known.

A light usually burns at night in their middle room, where Mukherji 12 and his whole family used to sleep. Apparently even indoors they sit together and talk. They must have an endless supply of stories and material for conversation. A sigh slips from my lips. In our house the talk deals only with the weather, mosquitoes, the birth of children, the new wives of relatives, kitchen matters, and ancient divine heroes who obliterate the present.

The fence between our houses is a barrier only in name. It's only a foot-high ridge of dirt with some berry bushes, a long stretch of dry twisted wild cactus, and some unknown shrubs with white ants clustered around the roots. In between, the ridge is broken in several places. Paths have formed, used by the fruit and vegetable sellers as well as the sweeper woman and the newspaper vendor. The postman and milkman have been using these paths for years. Despite the damage from dogs and cats coming and going and from animals grazing on the plants, the fence remains much the same as ever. Until a short time ago, Mukherji's daughter Shaila used to take this route bringing books over to me. It's such a convenient and simple fence that we can easily ride bicycles through the gaps from one side to the other without dismounting. And previously we used to pass through that way, but no longer, because our neighbors interpret a fence as something uncrossable.

They've been living here for three months. . . .

I often move my desk outdoors for study. At this time of year the outside air is lovely, like ice water in an intense summer thirst. But studying there is difficult. My eyes leap the fence and my mind hovers around the neighbors' house. A young and unattached girl. Cheerful and fearless parents. If only I'd been born in that home! That's the way my mind wanders.

At times the neighbor girl sits outside all alone, doing some work or 16 doing nothing. Occasionally she strolls over to the wall on the other side of her house. Elbows propped on the wall, she watches the street. Then she returns. Loafers from other neighborhoods come into our area a lot. Not that there's any lack of them in our neighborhood too. But she always seems innocent and free, walking with small swaying steps.

At our place, in contrast, my sister-in-law takes Puppi along even when she goes outside to get flowers for worship. She's scared outside the house and in it too. She's kept scared. A sharp eye is kept on Puppi also. One time the neighbor girl's father put his hand on his wife's shoulder in the course of conversation, and Puppi was immediately called into the house on some pretext. That scene produced an uproar at our place. Such shamelessness! Gradually people in our house have begun considering the neighbors quite dangerous.

With the passing of time, the attraction toward the neighbors has changed into dislike, though they might as well be nonexistent as far as we're concerned. In time, however, our family has made the neighbors a focal point for all the evils in the world. Our eyes cross the fence thousands of times in what has become a part of our daily routine. A new distress has crept into our minds, added to our other worries. I, too, waste a lot of time, but not a glance from there ever falls this way.

Somewhere nearby a diesel engine, finding no signal to proceed, stands shrieking. The novelty of the sound is startling. For a while all of us will talk about nothing but the diesel engine.

Yesterday those neighbors had not been home since noon. A few guests were staying at their place, but there was no hustle and bustle — just the usual carefree atmosphere. I rose and went inside. Sister-in-law was drying her hair. Then, I don't know why, she teased me slyly, connecting me with the neighbor girl. Smiling to myself, I went outdoors. Just then the girl and her mother returned, probably from the bazaar, carrying some packages. The father must have remained behind. 20

Both that evening and this morning people kept coming and going there. But it couldn't be considered a large number of people. Their house has the atmosphere of some ordinary festival celebration — just faintly. We were all astonished when the milkman reported that the daughter's marriage took place last night. It was some man from the other side of town. She'd had an Arya Samaj[3] wedding. My sister-in-law threw me a teasing look of sympathy, and I started laughing. I laughed openly and freely, thinking what dreamers we all are.

Now and then three or four people would arrive at their house. They'd go inside, then come out a little later and go away. They were mostly serious and restrained people. At times children gathered, shouting and running around, but otherwise there was no commotion — as though everything were taking place easily and smoothly. There was no way to know just what was happening, nor how.

---

[3]A reform sect of Hinduism that stresses a return to the principles and practices found in the Vedic scriptures. — ED.

At our house this has been a day of great uneasiness. After several hours, the girl emerged. She was wearing a sari, maybe for the first time. She stepped out on the veranda straightening her sari and carrying a coconut. Her swaying walk was restricted considerably by the sari and she moved forward with an eye on each step. She hadn't veiled herself in any way, nor, even with her husband walking so close to her, did she show any of the embarrassment and coquettishness of a traditional bride. Her husband looked like some friend of mine. No one was weeping and wailing. Several times the girl's mother kissed her warmly on both cheeks. The father patted her head. The girl's eyes could no longer conceal a shimmer of tears reflecting her excitement over the new life ahead.

Squirrels were darting across the fence from one corner to the other. Mother expressed amazement to me over the girl's failure to cry. According to her, the girl had become hardened by her education and had no real love or attachment for her mother and father. "They're all like that these days . . . with not one tear for those who struggled and sacrificed to raise them."

I was not interested in listening to such things. I observed that Mother was enjoying the sun, shifting her position to stay in the patches of sunshine. Then Father made a pronouncement — "In the old days, girls would cry all the way to the edge of the village. Anyone who didn't was beaten and forced to cry. Otherwise her life at her husband's home could never be happy." Father feels very distressed that things are no longer like that. "The old days are passing and men's hearts have become machines, just machines!" At such times his voice grows sharp, and the wreckage of Kali Yug, this Age of Darkness, dances before his eyes.

A few small isolated fragments of cloud have appeared in the sky over our home and then passed on. The parents and relatives reached the gate and were waiting to give the girl a last farewell. The boy's party had brought a Herald car for the groom which looked like a colorful room. That colorful room glided slowly away and was gone.

Granny was the most astounded of all and kept muttering to herself. This marriage made no sense at all to her. "No fanfare, no uproar, no feasting. What's the point of such stinginess! And besides, not even asking the neighbors on such an occasion. What's happening to mankind? Good god!"

Having said good-bye to the girl, the people walked back to the house. Each carried out a chair and sat down outdoors. Ever since the girl's departure, her mother had been a little sad and subdued. A few people kept her company, probably trying to cheer her up. My friend Radhu swore that he could prove the girl was a woman of the world. I felt only the sadness of an intense loss. A sort of strange emptiness — an emptiness at being left behind and an emptiness produced by Radhu's loose talk about the girl. Absolutely unfounded! Maybe talking about a girl's misconduct provides a kind of depraved satisfaction. But perhaps in one corner of my mind, I, too, like my family, can't tolerate the behavior of the neighbors.

Night is sloughing off the cover of evening. The people who were seated around a table across the fence have risen and dispersed. As usual, a light is burning in the middle room of the neighbors' house. Their night has become peaceful and quiet as usual, and there's no way to know how they're feeling about the absence of one member of the family. At our house, though, the bazaar of neighbor-criticism is doing a heated business.

EXPLORATIONS

1. What are the social functions of the Indian family as Gyanranjan depicts it? Based on "Our Side of the Fence and Theirs," how would you describe Indian parents' responsibilities to their children, and children's obligations to their parents?

2. Gyanranjan's narrator gives only fragmentary information about himself and his family members in terms of such standard characteristics as name, gender, age, relationship, and appearance. What can you deduce about the narrator and the other members of his household from clues in the story? What aspects of people does the narrator seem to think are more interesting and important than these "standard" characteristics?

3. How would you describe the narrator's attitude toward the family next door? Looking back through "Our Side of the Fence and Theirs," note each place where the narrator judges the other family's behavior. What sense do these judgments give you of what kind of people the next-door neighbors are? What sense do they give you of the narrator and his family in comparison?

4. The only dialogue in "Our Side of the Fence and Theirs" comes near the end of the story. Technically, *dialogue* means speech between two or more characters, such as a conversation or argument. How do the quoted speeches in this story diverge from that definition? What role do these speeches play in the story? How would the story's impact change if Gyanranjan used true dialogue throughout?

CONNECTIONS

1. How does the relationship of Gyanranjan's narrator to his housemates resemble that of Boon in John David Morley's "Acquiring a Japanese Family"? What similarities in personality do you notice between these two characters? How are their functions as point-of-view characters (that is, characters through whose eyes we view events) alike and different?

2. How do Gyanranjan here and John Updike in "The Lovely Troubled Daughters of Our Old Crowd" use their narrators in similar ways? What similar effects are created in both stories? What contrast exists in these two characters' moral stances, and how does that contrast affect the stories' impact?

3. How does Gyanranjan use social rituals to reveal the emotional truth about his narrator's family? How does Updike use social rituals to reveal the emotional truth about his narrator's family?

4. What views expressed in *Looking at Ourselves* about the family's functions and values are echoed by the narrator's family in "Our Side of the Fence and Theirs"? What views are expressed in *Looking at Ourselves* are embodied by the family on the other side of the fence?

ELABORATIONS

1. "We're respectable, honorable people," declares Gyanranjan's narrator in the second paragraph. On the basis of "Our Side of the Fence and Theirs," write a definition essay describing the values, habits, attitudes, and relationships that the narrator's family apparently believes define a "respectable, honorable" Indian family.

2. With his first sentence, Gyanranjan lets us know that this is the story of someone who believes his life is shaped by events outside his control. We learn by paragraph 2 that the narrator wishes he could get to know the family next door but feels powerless to do so. Most of us have had similar experiences. Write a narrative essay about a situation in which you wanted to become better acquainted with someone but felt prevented from doing so by family or social pressure.

WOLE SOYINKA

Nigerian Childhood

Playwright, poet, novelist, and critic Wole Soyinka won the 1986
Nobel Prize for literature. He was born Akinwande Oluwole Soyinka near
Abeokuta, Nigeria, in 1934. Educated in Ibadan, Nigeria, and at Leeds
University in England, he studied theater in London and had a number
of plays produced there. Returning to Ibadan, Soyinka became co-editor
of the literary journal *Black Orpheus* and was instrumental in the development of a Nigerian theater. His career was interrupted by two years in
prison for allegedly supporting Biafra's secession from Nigeria (see p.
684). Soyinka has taught drama and comparative literature at the universities of Ibadan, Lagos, and Ife in Nigeria; he holds an honorary
doctorate of letters from Yale University and has been accorded major
literary prizes in England, including the prestigious John Whiting Drama
Prize. His plays have appeared in theaters around the world, including
Ife, London, Stratford, New York, and Chicago. "Nigerian Childhood"
comes from his 1981 autobiography *Ake: The Years of Childhood.* His
recent works include the play *Requiem for a Futurologist* (1985) and the
autobiographical *Isara: A Voyage around Essay* (1988).

A pluralistic nation of many tribes (Soyinka is a Yoruba), Nigeria lies
in the large curve of Africa's western coast. Its early cultures date back
to at least 700 B.C. Portuguese and British slavers began arriving in the
fifteenth century. In 1861 Britain seized the capital city of Lagos during
an antislavery campaign and gradually extended its control over the
country. Nigeria regained its independence a century later and is now a
republic within the British Commonwealth. British influence remains
strong; the nation's official language is English. For most of the thirty
years since independence, Nigeria's governments have been military.
President Ibrahim Babangida, who took control in a 1985 coup, pledged
to return the country to civilian rule in 1992. His campaign for national
self-reliance has included democratic reforms, stiff measures for economic
recovery (including less dependence on imports and more support of
private enterprise), preservation of the nation's multifaceted culture, and
a more liberal role for women.

"Nigerian Childhood" takes place about twenty years before the end
of British rule. At that time Soyinka lived with his father, Essay, the
headmaster of the Anglican Girls' School in the town of Aké; his mother,
nicknamed Wild Christian; and his sister Tinu. "Bishop Ajayi Crowther"
is Samuel Adjai Crowther. Enslaved in 1821, freed and educated by the
British, he became the first black African bishop of the Anglican church.

If I lay across the lawn before our house, face upwards to the sky, my head towards BishopsCourt, each spread-out leg would point to the inner compounds of Lower Parsonage. Half of the Anglican Girls' School occupied one of these lower spaces, the other half had taken over BishopsCourt. The lower area contained the school's junior classrooms, a dormitory, a small fruit garden of pawpaws, guava, some bamboo, and wild undergrowth. There were always snails to be found in the rainy season. In the other lower compound was the mission bookseller, a shriveled man with a serene wife on whose ample back we all, at one time or the other slept, or reviewed the world. His compound became a short cut to the road that led to Ibarà, Lafenwá, or Igbèin and its Grammar School over which Ransome-Kuti presided and lived with his family. The bookseller's compound contained the only well in the parsonage; in the dry season, his place was never empty. And his soil appeared to produce the only coconut trees.

BishopsCourt, of Upper Parsonage, is no more. Bishop Ajayi Crowther would sometimes emerge from the cluster of hydrangea and bougainvillea, a gnomic face with popping eyes whose formal photograph had first stared at us from the frontispiece of his life history. He had lived, the teacher said, in BishopsCourt and from that moment, he peered out from among the creeping plants whenever I passed by the house on an errand to our Great Aunt, Mrs. Lijadu. BishopsCourt had become a boarding house for the girls' school and an extra playground for us during the holidays. The Bishop sat, silently, on the bench beneath the wooden porch over the entrance, his robes twined through and through with the lengthening tendrils of the bougainvillea. I moved closer when his eyes turned to sockets. My mind wandered then to another photograph in which he wore a clerical suit with waistcoat and I wondered what he really kept at the end of the silver chain that vanished into the pocket. He grinned and said, Come nearer, I'll show you. As I moved towards the porch he drew on the chain until he had lifted out a wholly round pocket watch that gleamed of solid silver. He pressed a button and the lid opened, revealing, not the glass and the face dial but a deep cloud-filled space. Then, he winked one eye, and it fell from his face into the bowl of the watch. He snapped back the lid, nodded again and his head went bald, his teeth disappeared, and the skin pulled backward till the whitened cheekbones were exposed. Then he stood up and, tucking the watch back into the waistcoat pocket, moved a step towards me. I fled homewards.

BishopsCourt appeared sometimes to want to rival the Canon's house.

It looked a houseboat despite its guard of whitewashed stones and luxuriant flowers, its wooden fretwork frontage almost wholly immersed in bougainvillea. And it was shadowed also by those omnipresent rocks from whose clefts tall, stout-boled trees miraculously grew. Clouds gathered and the rocks merged into their accustomed gray turbulence, then the trees were carried to and fro until they stayed suspended over BishopsCourt. This happened only in heavy storms. BishopsCourt, unlike the Canon's house, did not actually border the rocks or the woods. The girls' playing fields separated them and we knew that this buffer had always been there. Obviously bishops were not inclined to challenge the spirits. Only the vicars could. That Bishop Ajayi Crowther frightened me out of that compound by his strange transformations only confirmed that the Bishops, once they were dead, joined the world of spirits and ghosts. I could not see the Canon decaying like that in front of my eyes, nor the Rev. J. J. who had once occupied that house, many years before, when my mother was still like us. J. J. Ransome-Kuti had actually ordered back several ghommids[1] in his lifetime; my mother confirmed it. She was his grandniece and, before she came to live at our house, she had lived in the Rev. J. J.'s household. Her brother Sanya also lived there and he was acknowledged by all to be an òrò,[2] which made him at home in the woods, even at night. On one occasion, however, he must have gone too far.

"They had visited us before," she said, "to complain. Mind you, they   4
wouldn't actually come into the compound, they stood far off at the edge, where the woods ended. Their leader, the one who spoke, emitted wild sparks from a head that seemed to be an entire ball of embers — no, I'm mixing up two occasions — that was the second time when he chased us home. The first time, they had merely sent an emissary. He was quite dark, short and swarthy. He came right to the backyard and stood there while he ordered us to call the Reverend.

"It was as if Uncle had been expecting the visit. He came out of the house and asked him what he wanted. We all huddled in the kitchen, peeping out."

"What was his voice like? Did he speak like an *egúngún*?"[3]

"I'm coming to it. This man, well, I suppose one should call him a man. He wasn't quite human, we could see that. Much too large a head,

---

[1]Wood spirits. — ED.
[2]A kind of tree demon.
[3]Spirit of a dead ancestor. — ED.

and he kept his eyes on the ground. So, he said he had come to report us. They didn't mind our coming to the woods, even at night, but we were to stay off any area beyond the rocks and that clump of bamboo by the stream."

"Well, what did Uncle say? And you haven't said what his voice was like."   8

Tinu turned her elder sister's eye on me. "Let Mama finish the story."

"You want to know everything. All right, he spoke just like your father. Are you satisfied?"

I did not believe that but I let it pass. "Go on. What did Grand Uncle do?"

"He called everyone together and wanted us to keep away from the place."   12

"And yet you went back!"

"Well, you know your Uncle Sanya. He was angry. For one thing the best snails are on the other side of that stream. So he continued to complain that those *òrò* were just being selfish, and he was going to show them who he was. Well, he did. About a week later he led us back. And he was right you know. We gathered a full basket and a half of the biggest snails you ever saw. Well, by this time we had all forgotten about the warning, there was plenty of moonlight and anyway, I've told you Sanya is an *òrò* himself. . . ."

"But why? He looks normal like you and us."

"You won't understand yet. Anyway, he is *òrò*. So with him we felt   16 quite safe. Until suddenly this sort of light, like a ball of fire began to glow in the distance. Even while it was still far we kept hearing voices, as if a lot of people around us were grumbling the same words together. They were saying something like, 'You stubborn, stiff-necked children, we've warned you and warned you but you just won't listen. . . .'"

Wild Christian looked above our heads, frowning to recollect the better. "One can't even say, 'they.' It was only this figure of fire that I saw and he was still very distant. Yet I heard him distinctly, as if he had many mouths which were pressed against my ears. Every moment, the fireball loomed larger and larger."

"What did Uncle Sanya do? Did he fight him?"

"*Sanya wo ni yen?* He was the first to break and run. *Bo o ló o yǎ mi, o di kítìpà kítìpà!*[4] No one remembered all those fat snails. That *iwin*[5]

---

[4] If you aren't moving, get out of my way!
[5] A ghommid; a wood sprite which is also believed to live in the ground.

followed us all the way to the house. Our screams had arrived long before us and the whole household was — well, you can imagine the turmoil. Uncle had already dashed down the stairs and was in the backyard. We ran past him while he went out to meet the creature. This time that *iwin* actually passed the line of the woods, he continued as if he meant to chase us right into the house, you know, he wasn't running, just pursuing us steadily." We waited. This was it! Wild Christian mused while we remained in suspense. Then she breathed deeply and shook her head with a strange sadness.

"The period of faith is gone. There was faith among our early chris-   20
tians, real faith, not just church-going and hymn-singing. Faith. *Igbàgbó*. And it is out of that faith that real power comes. Uncle stood there like a rock, he held out his Bible and ordered, 'Go back! Go back to that forest which is your home. Back I said, in the name of God.' Hm. And that was it. The creature simply turned and fled, those sparks falling off faster and faster until there was just a faint glow receding into the woods." She sighed. "Of course, after prayers that evening, there was the price to be paid. Six of the best on every one's back. Sanya got twelve. And we all cut grass every day for the next week."

I could not help feeling that the fright should have sufficed as punish-ment. Her eyes gazing in the direction of the square house, Wild Chris-tian nonetheless appeared to sense what was going on in my mind. She added, "Faith and — Discipline. That is what made those early believers. Psheeaw! God doesn't make them like that any more. When I think of that one who now occupies that house . . ."

Then she appeared to recall herself to our presence. "What are you both still sitting here for? Isn't it time for your evening bath? Lawanle!" "Auntie" Lawanle replied "Ma" from a distant part of the house. Before she appeared I reminded Wild Christian, "But you haven't told us why Uncle Sanya is *òrò*."

She shrugged, "He is. I saw it with my own eyes."

We both clamored, "When? When?"   24

She smiled, "You won't understand. But I'll tell you about it some other time. Or let him tell you himself next time he is here."

"You mean you saw him turn into an *òrò*?"

Lawanle came in just then and she prepared to hand us over, "Isn't it time for these children's bath?"

I pleaded, "No, wait Auntie Lawanle," knowing it was a waste of time.   28
She had already gripped us both, one arm each. I shouted back, "Was Bishop Crowther an *òrò*?"

Wild Christian laughed. "What next are you going to ask? Oh I see. They have taught you about him in Sunday school have they?"

"I saw him." I pulled back at the door, forcing Lawanle to stop. "I see him all the time. He comes and sits under the porch of the Girls' School. I've seen him when crossing the compound to Auntie Mrs. Lijadu."

"All right," sighed Wild Christian. "Go and have your bath."

"He hides among the bougainvillea. . . ." Lawanle dragged me out of hearing. 32

Later that evening, she told us the rest of the story. On that occasion, Rev. J. J. was away on one of his many mission tours. He traveled a lot, on foot and on bicycle, keeping in touch with all the branches of his diocese and spreading the Word of God. There was frequent opposition but nothing deterred him. One frightening experience occurred in one of the villages in Ijebu. He had been warned not to preach on a particular day, which was the day for an *egúngún* outing, but he persisted and held a service. The *egúngún* procession passed while the service was in progress and, using his ancestral voice, called on the preacher to stop at once, disperse his people, and come out to pay obeisance. Rev. J. J. ignored him. The *egúngún* then left, taking his followers with him but, on passing the main door, he tapped on it with his wand, three times. Hardly had the last member of his procession left the church premises than the building collapsed. The walls simply fell down and the roof disintegrated. Miraculously however, the walls fell outwards while the roof supports fell among the aisles or flew outwards — anywhere but on the congregation itself. Rev. J. J. calmed the worshippers, paused in his preaching to render a thanksgiving prayer, then continued his sermon.

Perhaps this was what Wild Christian meant by Faith. And this tended to confuse things because, after all, the *egúngún* did make the church building collapse. Wild Christian made no attempt to explain how that happened, so the feat tended to be of the same order of Faith which moved mountains or enabled Wild Christian to pour ground-nut oil from a broad-rimmed bowl into an empty bottle without spilling a drop. She had the strange habit of sighing with a kind of rapture, crediting her steadiness of hand to Faith and thanking God. If however the basin slipped and she lost a drop or two, she murmured that her sins had become heavy and that she needed to pray more.

If Rev. J. J. had Faith, however, he also appeared to have Stubbornness in common with our Uncle Sanya. Stubbornness was one of the earliest sins we easily recognized, and no matter how much Wild Christian tried to explain the Rev. J. J. preaching on the *egúngún*'s outing day, despite warnings, it sounded much like stubbornness. As for Uncle Sanya there was no doubt about his own case; hardly did the Rev. J. J. pedal out of sight on his pastoral duties than he was off into the woods on one pretext or the other, and making for the very areas which the òrò had declared out of bounds. Mushrooms and snails were the real goals, with the gathering of firewood used as the dutiful excuse.

Even Sanya had however stopped venturing into the woods at night,   36 accepting the fact that it was far too risky; daytime and early dusk carried little danger as most wood spirits only came out at night. Mother told us that on this occasion she and Sanya had been picking mushrooms, separated by only a few clumps of bushes. She could hear his movements quite clearly, indeed, they took the precaution of staying very close together.

Suddenly, she said, she heard Sanya's voice talking animatedly with someone. After listening for some time she called out his name but he did not respond. There was no voice apart from his, yet he appeared to be chatting in friendly, excited tones with some other person. So she peeped through the bushes and there was Uncle Sanya seated on the ground chattering away to no one that she could see. She tried to penetrate the surrounding bushes with her gaze but the woods remained empty except for the two of them. And then her eyes came to rest on his basket.

It was something she had observed before, she said. It was the same, no matter how many of the children in the household went to gather snails, berries, or whatever, Sanya would spend most of the time playing and climbing rocks and trees. He would wander off by himself, leaving his basket anywhere. And yet, whenever they prepared to return home, his basket was always fuller than the others'. This time was no different. She came closer, startling our Uncle, who snapped off his chatter and pretended to be hunting snails in the undergrowth.

Mother said that she was frightened. The basket was filled to the brim, impossibly bursting. She was also discouraged, so she picked up her near empty basket and insisted that they return home at once. She led the way but after some distance, when she looked back, Sanya appeared to be trying to follow her but was being prevented, as if he was being pulled back by invisible hands. From time to time he would snatch forward his arm and snap,

"Leave me alone. Can't you see I have to go home? I said I have to   40 go."

She broke into a run and Sanya did the same. They ran all the way home.

That evening, Sanya took ill. He broke into a sweat, tossed on his mat all night, and muttered to himself. By the following day the household was thoroughly frightened. His forehead was burning to the touch and no one could get a coherent word out of him. Finally, an elderly woman, one of J. J.'s converts, turned up at the house on a routine visit. When she learnt of Sanya's condition, she nodded wisely and acted like one who knew exactly what to do. Having first found out what things he last did before his illness, she summoned my mother and questioned her. She told her everything while the old woman kept on nodding with understanding. Then she gave instructions:

"I want a basket of *àgìdi*, containing fifty wraps. Then prepare some *èkuru* in a large bowl. Make sure the *èkuru* stew is prepared with plenty of locust bean and crayfish. It must smell as appetizing as possible."

The children were dispersed in various directions, some to the market 44 to obtain the *àgìdi*, others to begin grinding the beans for the amount of *èkuru* which was needed to accompany fifty wraps of *àgìdi*. The children's mouths watered, assuming at once that this was to be an appeasement feast, a *sàarà*[6] for some offended spirits.

When all was prepared, however, the old woman took everything to Sanya's sickroom, plus a pot of cold water and cups, locked the door on him, and ordered everybody away.

"Just go about your normal business and don't go anywhere near the room. If you want your brother to recover, do as I say. Don't attempt to speak to him and don't peep through the keyhole."

She locked the windows too and went herself to a distant end of the courtyard where she could monitor the movements of the children. She dozed off soon after, however, so that mother and the other children were able to glue their ears to the door and windows, even if they could not see the invalid himself. Uncle Sanya sounded as if he was no longer alone. They heard him saying things like:

"Behave yourself, there is enough for everybody. All right you take 48 this, have an extra wrap . . . Open your mouth . . . here . . . you don't have to fight over that bit, here's another piece of crayfish . . . behave, I said . . ."

---

[6]An offering, food shared out as offering.

And they would hear what sounded like the slapping of wrists, a scrape of dishes on the ground, or water slopping into a cup.

When the woman judged it was time, which was well after dusk, nearly six hours after Sanya was first locked up, she went and opened the door. There was Sanya fast asleep but, this time, very peacefully. She touched his forehead and appeared to be satisfied by the change. The household who had crowded in with her had no interest in Sanya however. All they could see, with astonished faces, were the scattered leaves of fifty wraps of *àgìdi*, with the contents gone, a large empty dish which was earlier filled with *èkuru*, and a water pot nearly empty.

No, there was no question about it, our Uncle Sanya was an *òrò*; Wild Christian had seen and heard proofs of it many times over. His companions were obviously the more benevolent type or he would have come to serious harm on more than one occasion, J. J.'s protecting Faith notwithstanding.

EXPLORATIONS

1. What is the relationship in Soyinka's family between Anglican religious beliefs and traditional African magic? At what points in "Nigerian Childhood" do parents use each of these belief systems to control or teach children? At what points do the children's beliefs guide them toward "good" behavior?

2. "Stubbornness was one of the earliest sins we easily recognized," writes Soyinka in paragraph 35. What other virtues, failings, and rules of behavior have these children evidently been taught? Cite specific evidence for your conclusions.

3. What aspects of Soyinka's narrative make it clear that he was an adult when he wrote "Nigerian Childhood"? What passages indicate that he is telling his story from a child's rather than an adult's point of view?

CONNECTIONS

1. What physical barriers separate Soyinka's family from dangerous outside influences? What physical barriers separate the family of Gyanranjan's narrator from dangerous outside influences in "Our Side of the Fence and Theirs"? What ritualistic barriers does each family use to protect itself from the rest of the world?

2. When Carola Hansson and Karin Lidén in "Liza and Family" asked "What

is a good mother?" Liza answered that, in addition to providing physical care, "she should also give the child moral guidance — a feeling that life has a spiritual dimension. . . . She has to be a social being as well — she has to suffer the sorrows of her people." What actions and statements by Wild Christian fit this definition? What actions and statements by Soyinka suggest whether he believes Wild Christian is a good mother?

3. What do Soyinka's reminiscences have in common with Margaret Atwood's in "Scenes from Two Childhoods"? Atwood speaks of identifying the moral of a story her mother told (para. 25). What are the morals of Wild Christian's stories?

4. In "Entering the New World" (p. 47), V. S. Naipaul describes the fragility of European rituals among Africans "whose complete, real life lay in another realm of the spirit." Reread the last few paragraphs of Naipaul's essay. Which of his ideas about the old and new worlds does "Nigerian Childhood" support, and which does it contradict?

ELABORATIONS

1. In "Tradition and the African Writer" (p. 34), Ezekiel Mphahlele talks of embodying two distinct cultural histories. How has Soyinka made use of a similar dual heritage? Is Soyinka writing as "an ambivalent character . . . a man of two worlds" (Mphahlele's self-description) or as someone who has reconciled his histories? Write a comparison-contrast essay using Mphahlele and Soyinka as examples of Mphahlele's theses.

2. When you were a child, were you afraid of imaginary monsters? Have you or a friend ever had an encounter with a ghost? Write a narrative essay about an experience that most American adults would respond to with skepticism, depicting it (as Soyinka does) as a real event.

GHOLAM-HOSSEIN SA'EDI

The Game Is Over

Widely considered the leading Iranian writer of his time, Gholam-Hossein Sa'edi was born in Tabriz in 1935. He became involved in political activities while studying medicine; as a physician specializing in psychiatry, he served the poorest section of Tehran. A satirical author of plays, novels, and short stories attacking social injustice, Sa'edi was imprisoned and tortured by the shah's regime. Many of his writings were banned. He was eventually released and allowed to come to the United States but insisted on returning home. Sa'edi is one of the founders of Iran's modern drama and theater; *The Cow*, a film adapted from one of his novels, was shown at international film festivals, such as the prestigious Edinburgh Film Festival. When the Ayatollah Khomeini replaced the shah, Sa'edi was forced underground and into exile in Paris, where he died in 1985. "The Game Is Over" (*Bazi tamam shud*) first appeared in the Tehran publication *Alifba* in 1973. The following translation from the Farsi, by Robert Campbell, was done for Sa'edi's American story collection *Dandil* (1981). (For samples from two other translations, see p. xv.)

Sa'edi's homeland, the Islamic Republic of Iran, lies south of the Soviet Union and northeast of Saudi Arabia. Iran is an expanse of large salt deserts and mountains dotted with oases and forest areas. Long known as Persia, it was conquered repeatedly over its 4,000-year history. The British and Russian empires vied for influence there in the nineteenth century; Afghanistan was severed from Iran by the British in 1857. The notorious dynasty of the shahs began in 1925 with military leader Reza Khan. He abdicated in 1941 in favor of his son. Shah Mohammad Reza Pahlavi — a U.S. ally — instituted economic and social reforms, but he also arrested thousands and executed hundreds of political opponents. Conservative Muslim protests erupted into violence in 1978. In 1979 the shah fled to Egypt, where he died the following year. Meanwhile, the exiled religious leader Ayatollah Ruhollah Khomeini returned to Iran and became head of the government. Political turmoil, arrests, and executions continued, while mounting religious fanaticism isolated Iran from most of the rest of the world. In 1989 Khomeini sparked international riots and protests by calling on Muslims everywhere to kill the "blasphemous" British novelist Salman Rushdie, a death sentence that remained in effect even after the Ayatollah's death several months later.

I

Hasani said it to me himself: "Let's go over to my place tonight." I'd never been to their place. He'd never been to mine. What I'm getting at is, we were always too afraid of our fathers. He was a lot more afraid than I was. But that night it was different: Hasani was mad at me. He imagined that I didn't like him any more, that I wasn't his friend. So we went. Usually we just met each other outside. In the morning I would go to their little shack and give a long-drawn-out whistle that Hasani had taught me. When I whistled, Hasani would grab a can and come out. Instead of saying "Hi," we would fight a little. We would hit each other hard so it hurt. That's how we'd decided to behave, and whenever we met, or whenever we left each other, we would fight like that — unless we were either angry or had tricked each other.

After that we'd go running between all the little shacks and drop into Body Washer's Hollow. The city garbage trucks dumped their trash there. We'd root around in the trash. One day I might pick up some tin, and Hasani might find some glass. Now and then we'd get our hands on something better, like an empty salad oil can, a baby's bottle, a broken doll, a useful shoe, a perfectly good sugar bowl with a handle broken off, or maybe a plastic pitcher. Once I found a gold charm with a verse from the Koran on it. Like from a baby's necklace. Hasani had found a full pack of foreign cigarettes. When we got tired, we'd go to the side of the hollow where there's a big flat place: Hājji Timur's Kiln's at the far side of the terrace. They didn't use it any more. It was ruined.

There were all these big wells on the terrace — not just two or three, but well after well after well. Once I got the idea of counting them two by two. After we counted fifty, we got tired of it and quit. Every time we went to the wells we played these games that were fun. We would lie down and crawl up to where our chests were over the wells, and then we'd make funny noises. The noises would echo in the wells and come out again. Every well was different and would answer us with a special sound. Mostly we'd just laugh into the well, and instead of laughs, we'd hear cries coming back out. We'd get scared, and we'd laugh some more, louder, but the crying just got louder too. Hasani and I would be alone, mostly. Other kids hardly ever came to the hollow. Their mamas wouldn't let them. They were scared they'd fall in a well or get hurt some other way. But Hasani and me, it wasn't just that we'd gotten bigger, or that we always came home with sackfuls of stuff. Our mamas didn't mess with us any more. They never said anything.

That afternoon, the one before the night I went to Hasani's place,   4
Hasani came out, and he was really low. He was wrinkling his forehead. You could see he'd been crying a lot. He didn't feel like doing anything. His heart wasn't in it. When we went to the hollow, he just wandered around, poking at the trash with his stick. He swore at his dad some. I knew what had happened. His dad had come home from work at noon and been really mad. He had argued with his boss and been fired, and when he got home he had jumped Hasani and beat him like there was no tomorrow.

We'd heard Hasani yelling. My ma had sworn at Hasani's dad. She said, "Why are you beating an innocent child?" I saw the marks the belt had left on his shoulders, and a place under one eye that had gotten swollen and turned black and blue. Every night when Hasani's dad came home, before he changed clothes or washed, he would beat Hasani. He would beat him with his fists. He'd kick him. He'd use a club, or a rope, or a belt. He swore at Hasani and beat him till he cried bloody murder; you could hear him scream all over the place.

The neighbors would go running up. They'd swear, "May I die and you die," and make him let him go. Hasani's dad would beat him every night, but my dad would only beat Ahmad and me once or twice a week. Like when he was feeling bad, or things at the shop hadn't gone well, he would take it out on us. He'd beat us till suppertime. My ma would take to crying and carrying on and saying, "You bastard! Why are you killing my children! Why are you crippling them!" My dad would turn around and start taking it out on her. She'd yell, "Children, get out, get out!" By the time we'd got out, my dad would have calmed down. He'd just sit real quiet in a corner and chew on his mustache, and he'd say, "Call the children and let's guzzle down something."

But Hasani's dad didn't bother the other kids. He just beat on Hasani, and his ma would never say, "Get out!" Because Hasani's dad would always block the door and lay into him just like that. He would hit and kick him all over. He'd grab his head and pound it on the wall.

That was the first day he'd taken it out on Hasani around noon. Hasani   8
was really down, so I tried to cheer him up. I said to him, "Let's go up there." We got out of the hollow and went to the flat place where the wells are. We sat down beside one. No matter what I tried, he didn't say anything. He just stayed gloomy. I even lay down by the well and stuck my head in, and I made noises like a cow and a puppy, and I laughed

and cried and did everything I knew how to do. But would you believe it? Hasani just sat there frowning. He kept hitting his toes with his stick. At last I whistled to him in our private code, "Hasani, what's with you?" Hasani didn't answer. I called again, "Hasani, Hasani." He turned around and said, "What?" I said, "What are you being so cross for?"

"Why should it be for anything?"

"By God, stop your frowning. What are you frowning for?"

"I didn't make myself start frowning. How can I quit?"

I got up and said, "Come on, get up and let's do something so you'll cheer up." 12

Hasani, who was still hitting his toes with his stick, said, "Like what?"

I thought a bit, but couldn't come up with anything to bring him around. I said, "Let's go to the road and watch the cars."

"What for?"

"Let's go and count the hearses like we did the other day. Let's see how many go by in an hour." 16

"As many as go by, go by. So what?"

"You want to go on top of Hājji Timur's Kiln and throw rocks?"

He said listlessly, "I don't feel like it. If you want, go by yourself and throw rocks."

I sat down on a heap of garbage. No way was he going to listen to what I was saying. I said, "Better yet, get up, let's go to the square. There's lots to see." 20

"What's there to see?"

"We'll look at movie posters, then we'll go back of Stone Cutter's Square, and watch Sagdast the Dervish do magic tricks."

"By the time we get to the square it'll be dark."

"So we'll take a bus." 24

"With what money?"

"I've got twelve *riāls*."

"Keep it for yourself."

"Let's go get something to eat, OK?" 28

"There's no point in eating anything."

I was at my wits' end. I went on looking around, and my eyes fell on Shokrāi's garden. I said, "Hey, Hasani, do you want to go steal walnuts?"

"Yeah, since I haven't been beaten enough today, let's go get caught by the gardener."

A while went by. Neither of us said anything. Two men showed up from behind the kilns. They stood around and watched us for a while, 32 and then they headed for the garden and jumped over the wall. First there were yells. Then we could hear some men in there laughing. I said to Hasani, "Why are you mad at me?"

He said, "I'm not mad at you."

We shut up again. Hasani went on hitting his toes. I said, "Cut that out. Are you going crazy?"

He said, "All right. But it doesn't hurt."

"Now you say something."   36

"I don't know anything to say."

Angrily, I shouted, "You're getting pretty sickening. Get up, let's go."

We both got up and got going. While we were walking along between the wells, I said, "Hasani!"

"What?"   40

"Out with it. Whatever you want, whatever's on your mind, spit it out."

"I want to beat the crap out of that father of mine."

"Great. Well, go beat the crap out of him."

"I can't do it all by myself."   44

"Of course you can't."

He stopped all of a sudden and asked me, "Will you come with me so we can give him what's coming to him?"

I thought a bit. Hasani's dad hated children. You couldn't so much as look at him. He'd never say hello back to you. He'd just go by glaring. My dad would say that this bastard's crazy, a bit cracked, unsound of mind, you might say. Now how was I going to jump him? And if I didn't do it, Hasani would be mad at me. I didn't want Hasani mad at me. I was turning this over in my mind when Hasani said, "Don't you want to help me?"

"Why not? I want to. I want to a lot."   48

"Then why don't you answer me?"

"So how are we going to jump him?"

"You come over to our place tonight. We each hide in a corner. When he comes after me, all of a sudden we attack and grab his legs and knock him down and wipe him out!"

"And then what?"   52

"And then nothing. Just he'll know what it feels like to be beaten. I'll be happy."

"OK."

So that's how we wound up at his place. It was just about sunset, the time when the sky is turning gray. Hasani's dad hadn't shown up yet. Hasani's ma told us to go bring water for them. We went and got the water, and then we just waited, shifting from foot to foot. Finally we saw Hasani's dad way off. He was bent over, with a bag across his shoulder. Hasani said, "Here comes the son of a bitch." We went running off. We took a short cut and got to his shack. Hasani's ma was sitting outside cooking tomatoes over the primus. Hasani's little brother was sitting with his ma's arm around him. He was bawling. We went in the yard and set the pitcher of water by the window, then walked into the house. Hasani's ma yelled from outside, "Hey, Hasani, light the lamp."

Hasani lit the lamp. His little sister had gone to sleep in a corner of   56
the room. I said, "What do we do now?"

"Nothing. Just sit there by the door and don't do nothing."

I sat and waited. Hasani sat on the other side of the room. There was no sign of his dad yet.

Hasani said, "Don't forget, just grab his leg."

"What are you going to do?"   60

"First I'll punch him in the jaw, then I'll jump him and beat him into the ground."

Fear grabbed hold of me. I didn't know how things were going to end up. I was waiting like that when we heard his dad yelling outside. He started shouting, "You filthy slut, I hadn't come yet. What are you cooking dinner for?"

Hasani's ma said, "What the hell am I supposed to do? You always want to wolf something down when it gets dark."

Hasani's dad shouted, "Are you and your whelps eating too, you slut?"   64

Hasani's ma cried out, "Help, people! Help! Would to God you get crippled and your legs broken at the roots."

Hasani said, "You hear?"

"Hear what?"

"He's kicking my ma. The crazy pig!"   68

We heard Hasani's dad start yelling, "What's this little bastard doing hanging around here?"

"So where's he supposed to hang around?"

"How should I know, somewhere else, some other corner."

He came into the yard and set his bag and junk beside the door. He   72
started coughing and spitting up phlegm. He cursed under his breath, then picked up the water jug, sloshed some water around his mouth, gulped some down and came toward the room. He took off his shoes.

My heart had stopped beating. As his dad came in, Hasani looked just like a cat that's scared, half-crouching and inching back. His dad gnashed his teeth and snarled. Hasani, who was pinned up against the wall, said, "What are you going to do?" His dad said, "Nothing. What can one do with you, you snot-nosed little brat?" All of a sudden he noticed me. He looked me over from head to foot and twirled his mustache. I was terrified. I began edging back without getting up. "Glory be, what's this fat baboon doing here?" he sneered.

"He's my friend, Abdul Āghā's son."

"I don't care what piece of shit's son he is. What's he doing in my house?"

"I told him he could come."

"You mean the wretches don't have a hole of their own to crawl in?"   76

"Sure they have a house, a much nicer one, too."

"So how did he wind up here?"

He turned on me and yelled, "Get up, beat it, go crawl in your own shack."

Full of fear, I was getting up, when he said, "Move it!"   80

Hasani said from the back of the room, "He's not going. He stays here."

Hasani's dad turned around and clenched his fists. He headed for Hasani. "You fruit of adultery, you've become so brazen you're standing up to your father?"

Hasani's little sister woke up with a start and ran in panic out of the room. Hasani's dad was moving in and raising his fists, when suddenly Hasani shouted, "Come on!" I charged in. As Hasani's dad brought his fists down, Hasani jumped to one side. His fists hit the wall. I lunged and grabbed his leg. Hasani got loose from his dad and grabbed the other leg. We both yanked, and Hasani's dad fell on us shouting. First a fist connected with my head, and then another fist got Hasani's. Then he hit both our heads at the same time. The two of us wriggled out from under him. Hassani, swearing under his breath, kicked his dad in the side, and we both lit out the door. The guy kept yelling, "Now I'm really going to get you bastards. You couldn't take it, so you're going after your hit man to finish me off?"

He took after us. Hasani's ma stood by the lantern wailing. She didn't   84
know what to do. We went right past her and flew like the wind up a back path to the hollow. We heard Hasani's dad shouting, "Catch them! Catch them!"

He ran a few steps behind us, and then he stood still, swearing and wailing. It had gotten dark. Nobody came after us, and nobody seemed to feel like catching us. We jumped into the hollow, panting. We took each other's hands and waited to see if Hasani's dad or anyone else would show up and grab us. I said to Hasani, "We better get out of the hollow."

"Yeah. Or you'll see the bastard coming along with a club in his hand. Then we've had it."

We climbed up out of the hollow and sat down on a little rise. While we were catching our breath, I said to Hasani, "We did a good job of getting away from him."

"It's a shame we couldn't really work him over."   88

"When do you want to go home?"

"Go home? The hell I want to go back home! God, he's just waiting for me to go back so he can get his hands on me and really tear me to pieces."

"So what do you want to do?"

"Nothing."   92

"Where will you stay the night?"

"Nowhere. I've got nowhere to go."

"Come on over to our place."

"Right, fall into *your* dad's clutches. Those bastards are all alike.   96 There's not a shred of mercy in them."

"If you don't go back tonight, what will you do tomorrow? What will you do day after tomorrow? Finally you'll have to go back."

"I'm not so sure. One of these days you'll look and see I've up and gone somewhere else."

"Like where?"

"Wherever."   100

"To do what?"

"How should I know what I'll end up doing? I'll become an apprentice. I'll run errands. I'll be a porter."

"You're just a kid. Nobody will hire you."

"Why not!"   104

"Because you don't know how to do anything."

"So I don't know a trade. I can wash and sweep in front of stores."

"Anyway you'd have to be bigger for them to hire you."

"I could still collect trash and sell it."   108

"Where'd you sleep nights?"

"In the ruins."

"It's no good. A day, two days, OK. Finally you'll die of hunger or something will happen to you."

"Never! I won't die. I'll go and beg and survive."   112

"Right. So keep on dreaming. They'll take you and put you in the poor-house. Have you forgotten about the kids at Asadul and Ābji-ye Rezā?"

"So what should I do?"

"I don't know. It seems to me you should go back home."

We both shut up. The moon had come out, and most everywhere was   116
brightly lit, except for the dark holes of the wells that nothing could light
up. You could see lanterns here and there among the shacks. Hasani
looked at them and said, "There's no going back home now. He'd peel
the skin off my head."

We were quiet again and listened to the crickets. Hasani all of a
sudden jumped up and said, "Listen, I've got a plan. You get up now
and run like hell to the houses and start crying and carrying on and
yelling and start a commotion and say Hasani's fallen in a well."

I jumped up with my heart in my throat. I cried, "You mean you
want to throw yourself in a well?"

"You think I'm such a jackass that I'd go throwing myself in a well?
You just say I've fallen, and then you'll see my dad pass out cold. Then
you'll see him get his."

"And then?"   120

"And then nothing. I'll go and settle down somewhere."

"Then they'll go search the wells."

"They can't search all the wells. So what if they look in one or two?
Finally they'll get tired and guess that I've died. Then they'll get together
and cry for me, and read out of the Koran. My ma and dad will beat
their heads and say nice things about me."

"Hasani, this isn't a good thing to do."   124

"Why isn't it?"

"If your dad just wastes away, or your ma dies of grief, then what will
you do?"

"You're imagining things. It's not like that at all. I know them better
than that. They won't waste away and they won't die of grief. When
they've finally made mincemeat of themselves and beaten their heads
and chests, you come quietly and let me know. I'll go running home.
When they see I'm alive and I haven't fallen in the well, you don't know
how happy they'll be. I think my dad will make peace and not beat me
any more."

"Well . . ."   128

"Well what?"

"Well, I'm afraid of your dad. I'm afraid that after I say this stuff, he'll get me and kill me."

"What do you have to do with my dad? When you get to the houses, start yelling and beating your head and say, 'Hasani's fallen in the well! Hasani's fallen in the well!'"

"Then I'll have to cry. What if I can't?"   132

Hasani looked me up and down and said, "You're such a jackass! In the dark who'll know if you're crying or not?"

"OK. Then what will you do?"

"I'll go sit in some cranny of the kiln."

"And when you die of hunger?"   136

He asked me, with his voice full of surprise, "You mean you won't bring me water and bread? Huh? You really won't come?"

"Sure I'll come."

"Fine, so get going."

I was starting off when Hasani said something else. "What is it?" I   140
asked.

"Don't forget I'm hungry. Bring me some bread and water in the morning."

"OK. I'll come for sure."

"Good. So go!"

I still hadn't made my mind up to go or not. Hasani grabbed my hand   144
and said, "First come here. I'll show you where I'll be."

We were on our way to Hājji Timur's Kiln when some dogs came at us. We took care of them with rocks. Then we went around the wells and went into the last oven. Its roof had fallen in, and nobody would have believed anyone could possibly be staying in there. Hasani said to me, "I'll stay right here. OK?"

"OK."

He said, "Don't wait around. Get going. Don't forget to really really yell."

"Right. OK."   148

I walked around the kiln and went between the wells. Then I dropped into the hollow. A bunch of dogs were running around. They ran away when they saw me. My throat was clogged with dust. I drank a little water from the tap. I remembered that I had to run harder and to yell bloody murder.

I jumped up and rushed screaming toward the shacks. There was a crowd around our place. I didn't know what was going on. You would

have thought from hearing me that Hasani had really and truly fallen in
a well, I raised such hell and wailed so loud. The crowd milled in my
direction. I saw my dad and Hasani's dad. They seemed to lunge at me
at the same time. I wailed in a tear-choked voice, "Hasani! Hasani!"
Hasani's dad, standing there with a club in his hand, asked, "What
happened to Hasani? Huh? What happened?"

"He fell," I wailed, "He fell! He fell!"

I started crying in earnest, tears pouring down my face.   152

Hasani's dad shouted, "Where did he fall? Tell me, where did Hasani
fall?" I yelled, "In the well, he fell in the well!" For a minute everyone
was silent, and then a strange murmuring rose up. A jumble of voices
near and far shouted, "Hasani's fallen in the well! Hasani's fallen in the
well!"

People lost their heads and didn't know what to do. Those who were
in their houses came pouring out. Some brought lanterns. Everyone set
out running toward the upper part of the hollow. I was stretched out on
the ground wailing when my dad bent over me and took my hand to
pull me to my feet. He said, "Get up. Come on, let's see, which well
did he fall in?" We had just started running when several men surrounded
me. They ran right along with my dad and me, asking over and over,
"Which well? Which one did he fall in?"

We passed the hollow and got to the wells. The moon had risen
higher, and the holes of the wells had gotten darker and deeper. Everyone
was standing around. Hasani's father swayed like a willow. He grabbed
my arms and shook me, saying, "Which one? Which one?"

Before I could answer, he threw himself onto the trash heap and began   156
wailing loudly. Two or three men went up to him. Abbās Charkhi kept
trying to comfort him, saying, "Don't worry a bit. We'll have him out of
there in no time. Nothing's the matter. Don't cry. Take it easy, we'll find
him soon."

By the time Hasani's father had calmed down, another commotion
had begun. The women came weeping. Hasani's mother was in front of
them all, beating her head and clawing at her face, moaning from the
bottom of her heart, "My Hasani! My Hasani! My Hasani!"

She said other things you couldn't make out. Abbās Charkhi came
closer and said to me, "Listen, child. Tell us which one he fell into."

"I don't know."

Hasani's father rushed me, shouting, "Bastard! Say what really hap-   160
pened to my child!" Āghā Ghāder held him back and told him, "Get a

hold of yourself. Let him say what happened." I swallowed my sobs and
said, "Hasani's dad caught us and he was going to beat us up."

Hasani's father broke in: "Just tell us where he fell!"

"Hurry up and tell us!" yelled my dad.

Abbās Charkhi said, "Let him have his say, man. How did it happen?"

"We got away and came here. Hasani was way in front of me. We   164
were both running. Hasani was afraid his dad would catch up and grab
us, so he ran faster than me. I turned around and looked in back of me
and saw he wasn't coming. Nobody was coming. I yelled, 'Wait, Hasani!'
But he didn't wait. Just then all of a sudden he screamed and fell."

Hasani's dad said, "Where did he fall!"

I said, "I thought the earth had swallowed him up. I called and called,
but he didn't answer. However much I looked, I couldn't find him."

Hasani's dad just shouted again, "Which one did he fall in!"

Abbās Charkhi said in a mean voice, "How should he know which   168
one he fell in? Let's go find him ourselves."

Then he turned to the men and said, "Get moving. Come ahead. Be
careful!"

As they set out, they stopped talking. No one cried. No one shouted.
Only Hasani's mother moaned softly, while the other women kept telling her, "Be calm, sister, don't fuss, they'll find him now and get him
out."

Some people kept going, "Shhh." You'd think Hasani was sleeping
and might wake up. They went up to several wells, and then Hasani's
dad lowed like a cow, "Hasani, Hasani." He was so mean and nasty that
if maybe Hasani had really fallen in a well and could get out, he would
grab him and start hitting and kicking him again. Abbās Charkhi said,
"Calm down a bit. Cool down and let us get on with our work."

Someone said out of the dark, "We must have rope and lanterns. We   172
can't go into wells empty-handed."

Several people went running to the houses. A couple of lanterns were
brought up. Abbās Charkhi took one of them. He stretched out by one
of the wells, and held it over the hole. Everyone had made a circle
around the well. Abbās, with his head in the well, said in a muffled
voice, "I don't think he's fallen into this one."

So they went to the next well. This time it was Mosayyeb who stretched
out flat and held the lantern over the well. He said, with his drawn-out
voice like a peddler's, "Where are you, child? Where are you?"

There was no answer. They went on to the third well. Then to the fourth well. Then to the fifth well. Then to the sixth. Then they split up into two groups, then into four. They brought extra lanterns, seven or eight of them, and a lot of rope. Several people started tying knots in the ropes. The more they went on with no sign of Hasani, the madder they got, and the more they would argue. After a while they called everyone to one well, I mean Abbās Charkhi called everyone, and everyone ran up to it. Abbās had gone out of his wits. He said, "I think he's here. I heard something. It's as if someone is crying in there." Everyone fell silent. Several people stretched out and stuck their heads into the well, listened, and said, "Yeah. That is it."

Hasani's dad started raising hell. He said, "Hurry up, hurry up. Get 176
my boy out of there! Get my boy out!"

Mosayyeb said, "Who will go down?"

Ghāder said, "The well is old. It might cave in."

Hasani's father said, "By God, it won't cave in. Go on in, go in and get him out."

Everyone looked at one another. Abbās Charkhi said, "No one's man 180
enough? I'll go myself. Pass the rope and let's see."

Abbās's wife cried out from where the women were, "Not you, not you! You can't! You don't know how!"

Abbās shouted angrily, "What business is it of yours, you bitch? Shut up, I can't let the boy die in there!"

His wife shoved everyone aside, ran up and clung to Abbās, saying, "I won't let you. I won't let you. By God, I won't let you!"

Abbās slapped his wife hard and said, "Get lost, you're being impos- 184
sible."

Then he shouted firmly, "Rope!" They brought rope and tied it around Abbās's waist. Then they tested the knots one by one. Abbās said, "Be careful. Don't let go of me on the way down."

Several men said, "Don't worry. We'll be careful."

Abbās got ready. He grabbed one of the lanterns, bent over, and looked down the well. Then he handed the lantern to someone and said "*Bis-millāh*" loudly. Everyone prayed then. Hasani's dad raised his hands to the sky and said, "O most Merciful of the merciful, O Grandfather of Hosein the Oppressed, O Grandfather of Fātemeh the Pure, O Grandfather of Khadijeh the Magnificent, bring up my child alive, bring Hasani back alive!"

Abbās was hanging there in the well with his elbows resting on the 188
rim. He said, "Watch that rope closely. When I jerk on it, pull me up."

His wife started crying behind us. My ma comforted her. Then Abbās went down. Five or six of the men held the rope. They clutched it tightly and let it go handspan by handspan. They muttered things to each other. Hasani's dad was walking around in circles, saying things like, "O God! O God!" I had completely forgotten that Hasani was at the kiln. In the bottom of my heart I was saying, "Oh, if only Hasani were in there, and Abbās wouldn't come out empty-handed, and everything would be OK!" After a while, my dad, who was holding the rope with the others, said, "Haul it up. Haul it up. Haul it up."

Rahmat said, "What for?"

"The rope is shaking. Are you blind or something?"

Everyone stopped talking. They started drawing up the rope. Hasani's dad was peering over the heads of the others and waiting for Abbās to appear. Then Abbās's two hands gripped the rim of the well. He drew his elbows up the rim, hauled himself over it, and flung himself across the ground. Ghāder asked, "Wasn't he in there? Wasn't he in there?" Hasani's dad wailed and started to cry and groan. Abbās rolled over and sat up. He said, "I was suffocating."

Ghāder said, "That's all?"   192

"All there was in there was the carcass of a fat dog."

Mosayyeb said, "You're sure?"

"Imbecile, can't I tell Hasani from a dead dog?"

He got up and took the rope off his waist. Everyone got together again   196 and went to another well, then to a third, then to a fourth. They divided again, and then again. They would kneel over each well, calling Hasani. At that point I sneaked off and headed for the houses, slipping through the shadows and byways so that nobody would see me. I drank some water from the tap and then went behind the tin wall. I crept into our own place. No one was there. I scooped up a loaf of flatbread and a pitcher without a handle. I scurried out, and, when I got to the tap again, I drew some water. I passed the hollow, turned at the road, and reached Hājji Timur's Kiln just where Hasani was staying. I peeped in and called him softly. He didn't answer. I called him again. He didn't answer. I called him loudly. There was nothing. I was afraid. Then I said to myself, "God forbid he should mistake me for someone else." I started whistling and right away I heard Hasani's whistle over my head. He was stretched out on the platform and was watching me. I said, "Hey Hasani!"

He said, "Come up carefully."

I handed him the pitcher, got hold of the bricks of the wall, and climbed. We both crawled slowly forward and sat by the bottom of the kiln's chimney. I said, "Hadn't we decided that you would wait down there?"

He said, "I climbed up to see what was going on."

"You know what would happen if they saw you?"   200

"No way. No one will see me."

He began to laugh. I asked, "What are you laughing for?"

He said, "I'm laughing at my old man, at all of them. Look at them, the way they're running around."

He pointed to the terrace of the wells. Some people with lanterns in   204
their hands were going this way and that around the wells. Others seemed to be glued to one well. They weren't moving.

I said, "We've done something very bad, Hasani."

"Why?"

"Your dad's killing himself. You don't know the state he's in."

"Don't worry, he won't kill himself. What's my mother doing?"   208

"She's beating her head and chest. She keeps crying."

"Let her."

"You don't know how it is. Abbās went down a well, and instead of finding you, he found a fat dog's body down there."

"He's found his father's body."   212

We both laughed. I took out the bread, and we split it up and ate it. I wasn't thirsty, but Hasani gulped down some water. I said, "Now shouldn't we go down to them?"

He said, "For what?"

"To get the thing over with. They can't go through all those wells one by one."

"It's much too soon. Let them try."   216

"Someone might fall in a well and die."

"Don't worry. They all have dogs' lives and nothing'll happen to them."

"This is an awful thing we've done."

He turned and looked me up and down, and said, "Isn't it an awful   220
thing they do, always going around and beating us before supper?"

"For God's sake, cut it out, Hasani. Come on, let's go back."

"I can't go."

"Why not, then?"

"Supposing I go back. What will I say?"   224

"Say you'd gone to Shokrāi's garden to eat walnuts."

"Then they'd find out you were lying."

"I'll say, how would I know where you'd gone. I thought you'd fallen in the well."

"No. They'll know for sure and it'll be all over for us."

"By God, let it be. Come on."

"I'm not coming. I can't come."

"Then I'll go and say Hasani hasn't fallen in a well, that he's staying at Hājji Timur's Kiln."

He turned, looked at me angrily, and said, "Fine. Go and tell. From then on we'll have nothing to do with each other. You'll see me when you see the back of your ear."

"Then when do you want to go back to your house?"

"The day of mourning, when they read the Koran for me. All of a sudden I'll come in. That will feel so great!"

"Don't talk garbage. What'll be so great about it?"

"It's so obvious. When everyone is beating their heads and chests, I'll just quietly saunter up, walk in real nonchalant-like, and say 'Hello!' First everyone will be scared. They'll cringe. The women'll scream. The children will run away thinking I've come back from the next world. Then when they see, no, it's just me, I'm alive, I see, I laugh, I move my hands and feet, they'll all be happy. They'll leap in the air. They'll fall on the ground. They'll keep hugging me and kissing my face. You don't think that's any fun? Really?"

We went on staring at the people going around the wells with their lanterns. Now and then I would hear men or women shouting. I said, "So I guess I'll be going back."

"Go on, but don't let them know where I am."

I crawled down from the recess on all fours. I looked around and jumped to the ground. I passed by the roadside, dropped into the hollow, and climbed out again. Everyone had formed a circle around one well. I went running up to it too. I saw my mother pounding on her head and wailing. The men had a rope hanging down the well. I squeezed through and got to the brim. I saw Abbās saying to the other men, "Haul up! Haul up!"

Ghāder asked, "What for?"

"Are you blind or something? Can't you see it's shaking?"

Everyone fell silent and started hauling on the rope. Behind me Hasani's father was beating on his chest rhythmically. He was saying, "O Great Khadijeh! O Prophet Mostafā! O Stranger of Strangers! O Lord of the Martyrs!"

Then I saw my dad with his elbows on the rim of the well drawing himself up. He had turned black from head to foot and was gasping. Abbās said, "Lie down. Stretch out and catch your breath." Several men got hold of my dad under the arms and stretched him out beside the well.

II

The next morning, no one went to work. Everyone was worn out and 244 went back to their shacks. They hadn't found Hasani. Abbās Charkhi said, "It's no use. No one can search all the wells."

They had just been through the deeper wells that opened into one another and had sewage running through them. In their black depths weird things had been seen. Ustā Habib had run across some creature, about as big as a cow, with four tails and a dead man's head between its teeth, going here and there. The Sayyed had run into a bunch of naked people covered with wool clinging to the sides of the well. When they saw him, they dived into the sewage and disappeared. Mir Jalāl had seen with his own eyes huge, black wings that flew around by themselves. They said weird noises had come from the very depths, like the sounds of cats wailing, and the laughter of women you couldn't see. Several of them had even heard cymbals and trumpets, like they play on the Day of Āshurā. They'd heard wailing and crying behind them.

Abbās said it was no use, it was all over, there was no way to find Hasani. So then they went back home, tired and sleepy, and dazed. Everyone but Hasani's dad, who kept on wandering around the shacks, jerking his head right and left, forward and back, pounding his hands together and saying, "Did you see what happened? Did you see how my child has gone away? How he's died young?"

Hasani's dad wasn't wailing and crying any more. Instead he began worrying about pointless things, like the roofs of the houses, the dark openings of tombs, covered barrels lined up against the walls, stains on the gunny sacks hanging in front of the houses. Now and then he would stop and bend over to pick some stupid thing off the ground — a scrap of tin, or a broken glass, or a worn-out shoe. He would fiddle with it, and then throw it away and go after something else, muttering, "Now they're eating him. It's all over. My Hasani is finished."

I walked around him several times. It was always the same. He 248 wouldn't see me, or he would see me and not care. After a few minutes of this, I remembered that Hasani would be hungry and waiting for me.

I went to our place. Everyone was asleep. My dad had flopped over so that his muddy feet stuck out. I snitched a loaf of bread and a fistful of lump sugar that were in easy reach, and went out again. Everything was sullen and gloomy. I saw Hasani's dad standing behind a house scraping his fingernail across something on the wall. The sun was up and lighting everything. I got to the tap and drank some water. No one was around. I dropped into the hollow, and, past the upper end, I made it to Hājji Timur's Kiln. I headed for the recess, knowing Hasani was there. Hasani was sleeping. When I called him, he woke up with a start. He got scared and shouted, "Who is it? Who is it?"

"Don't worry," I said, "it's just me."

He sat up. He looked different. His eyes were sunken, and his hands shook. I said, "What's up with you? Anything happened?"

"I dreamed that I fell in a well, and whatever I tried, I couldn't get out."

"It's your own fault. You were the one who wanted to keep up this 252 game. Your dad has cracked up."

He didn't say anything. He just dragged himself outside. We both sat in the sun. I handed him the bread and the handful of sugar. He hadn't finished his water. He picked up the pitcher, gulped down some water, and splashed some over his face. As he woke up more, he asked, "How have things gone?"

"They're sure now you've died," I said.

"What did you do?"

"I didn't do anything. I didn't say anything."   256

"Now what do they want to do?"

"They haven't decided on anything."

"Aren't they going to read the Koran for me?"

"I don't know. I haven't heard anything."   260

"I think they'll do it this afternoon."

"Where do you get that?"

"Do you remember when Bibi's grandson died? They read the Koran the day after."

"If that's how it goes, this is your big day all right."   264

"Yeah. God, let it be today. I can't handle any more of this."

"God willing, this will be the day."

"You won't forget to come tell me?"

"No, why should I forget? But get yourself ready for a real beating." 268

"No way. I'll just make them happy."

"Go right on thinking that. You'll see."

"Want to bet?"

"What's the bet?"   272

"If they get sore about like why am I alive and didn't die, and they jump me and beat me up, you win, and if they're glad, I win, and you'll get a real thrashing from me."

"That's just great. I've gone through all this for you, and in return you want to beat me up?"

He laughed and said, "I'm kidding. I'll buy you an ice cream."

"OK. You're on."   276

He tore off a piece of bread and stuffed it in his mouth. He asked, "Now what do we do?"

"Nothing," I said. "You stay in this cranny, and I go to the house to see what happens."

"If the reading is tonight, you'll let me know?"

"Sure."   280

Hasani's reading was that afternoon, in front of the houses. Abbās had nailed a piece of black cloth on the end of a stick and had stuck it into the ground at the head of the square. Everyone was sitting outside, the women on one side, and the men on the other. People from other places had been told, and were coming in batches. From Yusof Shāh Hollow, from the tenements of Sarpich, the kilns of Shamsābād, the hovels of Shotor Khun and Mollā Ahmad Hollow. They were all strangers, and they were dressed in every color you can think of. As they would come into the square, the women would run up to Hasani's mother. She was sitting with her scratched and bloody face in front of their house. She wasn't crying any more. She was beating her head and sometimes pounding her chest. As the women came up to her, they would begin to cry, tearing at their own faces and saying, "Dear sister, dear sister, what has befallen you, what has befallen you?"

Hasani's dad was sitting in front of our place, not sitting exactly, but sprawled across the ground, staring ahead senseless. Whoever came and understood who the dead boy's father was, went up to him and said, "*Salām.*" Not hearing an answer, he would turn away and go sit down. Abbās, who was standing, bellowed, "Fātiheh!"

The men recited the Fātiheh, the Opening of the Koran. Ustā Habib went around the crowd with a pitcher, giving water to the thirsty. Two old men had come from Ghoribā Hollow with a pouch of tobacco. They were rapidly rolling cigarettes in newspaper and setting them on a tray. Bibi's oldest son Ramazān was passing the tray among the people. Everyone smoked, and everyone drank water, except Hasani's dad. He didn't do either. He just kept running his tongue over his lips, and sometimes he would spit on the ground.

An hour had gone by when a lot of people showed up running from 284 the road. Everybody turned and looked. Abbās shouted, "The Gypsies of the Black Tents from Elders' Hollow are coming. Let's go meet them."

Several people took off. The Gypsies, panting hard, came running. A lot of them were holding banners. There were several old men in worn-out clothing running in front of everyone. They beat their breasts and looked nervous. Among them was a thin *ākhond*[1] with a long neck and a small turban. The women came behind, all of them barefoot and dusty. As they got to the little square, the sounds of prayers rose up. The men and women separated. The women ran shrieking toward Hasani's ma, and the old men greeted his dad. He didn't answer. Then the *ākhond* went off to sit on the steps of our place. Esmāil Āghā shouted, "Make prayers! Make them loud!"

Everyone offered prayers. The *ākhond* said in a hoarse, nasal voice, "Be seated, all be seated, all be seated. Be seated so that we may weep and recite the doleful story of Ghāsem son of Hasan, how he found martyrdom at Karbalā, in remembrance of this other unfortunate youth." First he read a strange prayer, and then he started reciting the story. All at once, people started crying and wailing. Everyone cried. The men cried. The women cried. Their children cried. Even I cried. Only Hasani's dad did not cry, but kept wandering here and there, running his tongue over his parched lips. The crying got louder and louder. The Gypsies rose and bared their chests. The *ākhond* rose and bared his chest. He said in a loud voice, "Now to rejoice the Lord of the Martyrs and the dear unfortunate one, we will beat our breasts."

He began reciting songs of mourning. The Gypsies began beating their breasts. The other men stood up and bared their breasts and began beating them. The women shrieked even louder, as they stood arm in arm, wailing. Suddenly I remembered: Now is the time. Now I must go tell Hasani.

No one was paying any attention to me. No one was paying any 288 attention to anyone at all but himself or herself. I slipped away quietly. First I backed away, then I turned and ran. I wiped away my tears. When I got to the tap, I drank some water. Then I dropped into Body Washer's Hollow and climbed out. No one was around. I started running again.

---

[1]One learned in religious matters; a mullah.

Running like the wind, I went around the wells and kept on. My heart was full of dread. Sweat was pouring down my face when I reached Hājji Timur's Kiln, circled around, and made my way to Hasani's niche. Hasani was stretched out on the platform. When he saw me he stood up, stepped out, and said, "What's going on?"

"They're mourning for you," I said.

"What are they doing?"

"People have come from everywhere and they're beating their chests for you."

He stared at me for a moment and said, "What are you crying for?"   292

"For you."

"You're such a jackass! You knowing I was alive and hadn't died!"

"It's all the fault of the *ākhond* the Gypsies brought along. He made everybody cry."

He clapped his hands together in delight and said, "So it's time, right?"   296

"All right, I think it's time."

"Now we'll see who wins the bet."

"Would to God that you win."

He laughed and said, "Run, we're off!"   300

He broke into a run. And then so did I. We both charged ahead, but Hasani was flying like the wind. He ran so fast no one could have caught up with him. I kept shouting, "Hasani! Hasani!"

He called back, "Hoo! Hoo!"

Then, suddenly, I don't know what happened — how can I say what happened? Hasani hit his foot against a pile of rubbish, and — just like that — he fell. He fell right into a well. I thought — I mean I didn't think Hasani had fallen in a well — I thought the earth had swallowed him up. I ran up. There was no Hasani. Hasani had fallen in a well. In a huge well, bigger than all the rest of them. My tongue became tied in knots. I wanted to shout "Hasani!" but I couldn't. I had no voice. My mouth wouldn't open. No matter how hard I tried, I couldn't say "Hasani!" I sat on the heap of garbage and held my shoulders. I couldn't catch my breath. Three times I pounded my head on the garbage, and then I got up, not by myself, but it seemed like something picked me up and set me on my two feet. I started to run again. Faster than ever, faster than Hasani had run. I wished I had jumped and fallen in a well. All of a sudden, I found myself running down the road. When I reached the tap, I caught my breath, my tongue came untied and I said softly, "Hasani! Hasani! Hasani!"

As I came up to the square, the breast-beating had come to an end. 304
Everyone was sitting quietly facing each other. Ramazān was passing out
cigarettes among the men, and Ustā Habib was going here and there
carrying the pitcher of water. I shrieked, "Hasani! Hasani! Hasani!" I
pounded my head hard with my fists and rolled on the ground. Everyone
got up and mobbed me. Abbās, who was the first to get to me, took my
hands so I wouldn't beat myself and asked me, "What happened? What
happened?"

I shouted, "Hasani. Hasani fell in the well."

I rolled over and bit the ground. First there was a murmuring, and
then a clamor. Everyone tried to calm me down. They kept saying, "OK.
OK. May God have mercy on him. Don't hit yourself any more. Be
calm." I shouted, "Just now he fell, just now, this very minute he fell,
Hasani fell in the well!" My dad pushed the others away and came up
to me, saying, "Shut up, child. Don't make things more painful for his
father and mother."

"He fell, he fell in the well before my eyes."

"I said shut your mouth. Be silent, you little jackass."   308

He picked me up and gave me a hard slap on the ear. Esmāil Āghā
pulled my dad back and roared, "Don't hit him, you son of a bitch.
Can't you see he's out of his head?" He took me in his arms and said,
"Calm down, calm down."

Ustā Habib handed Esmāil Āghā a glass of water, and he poured it
over my face. However hard I fought to get free from the arms of Esmāil
Āghā, it was no use. Several people helped him keep me from getting
away. I was wailing loudly, "Hasani fell! He fell in the well! Hasani!
Hasani!" when Esmāil Āghā clapped a big hand over my mouth, and
they all dragged me into our own house. As I was dragged past Hasani's
dad, I looked at him and pointed at the wells with my hand. He didn't
look at me. He wasn't aware of me. He just went on staring ahead. As
we went into my house, Esmāil Āghā said, "Be still, child. Everyone
knows Hasani was your friend. You liked each other a lot. Now what
can one do? This was the will of fate."

I yelled, "He fell just now! He fell just now!"

I tried to break away and get out, but they didn't let me. My dad said, 312
"What do we do with him? Huh? What do we do with him?" Esmāil
Āghā said, "He's gone mad. It's best we bind his hands and feet." So
then they bound my hands and feet. I started to wail. My dad said,
"What do we do about his wailing?" Esmāil Āghā said, "We'll gag him."

They gagged me and tossed me into a corner. My dad rubbed his hands together and said over and over, "What will I do? My God, my God, if he stays this way, what the hell am I to do!"

Esmāil Āghā said, "Don't worry. Right now we'll go ask the *ākhond* 316 of the Gypsies to write out a talisman for him. Then he'll improve."

Ustā Habib said, "If he doesn't get better, we'll take him to the shrine at Shāh 'Abdol 'Azim."

My dad moaned a long-drawn-out moan, and began walking in circles, saying, "O Imam of the Age, O Imam of the Age, O Imam of the Age!"

Esmāil Āghā said, "Better we leave him alone. Perhaps he'll come around."

They left the house and fastened the door. The sounds of the gathering's prayers rose up again, and the *ākhond* of the Gypsies read the eulogy in his hoarse, nasal voice.

EXPLORATIONS

1. Sa'edi starts his story with a suggestion from Hasani, the significance of which becomes evident only later. What sentence in his first paragraph does the author use as a transition out of the present? Where and how does he make the transition back into the moment of Hasani's suggestion? What does Sa'edi accomplish by jumping around in time rather than telling his story in chronological order?

2. Sa'edi lets us know immediately that Hasani and the narrator have already been influenced by the violence in their families. What signs of this influence do you find in paragraph 1? Over the next few pages, what other speeches and actions by the story's characters reveal their attitudes toward physical and emotional abuse within the family?

3. What is your response to the ending of "The Game Is Over"? How would the story's impact be different if Hasani did manage to show up at his own funeral? What tactics does Sa'edi use to make his readers curious about how Hasani's parents and others will react to his miraculous return? Did these tactics succeed in diverting you from guessing the story's ending?

CONNECTIONS

1. In what ways is Sanya's adventure with the *òrò* in Wole Soyinka's "Nigerian Childhood" similar to Hasani's adventure with the wells in "The Game Is

Over"? What important differences in the causes of these two adventures are responsible for their different outcomes?

2. What role does religion play in "The Game Is Over"? in Gyanranjan's "Our Side of the Fence and Theirs"? What major advantages do Gyanranjan's characters have over Sa'edi's?

3. In *Looking at Ourselves*, Michael Novak writes: "The lives of husbands, wives, and children do not mesh, are not engaged, seem merely thrown together." What causes does Novak identify for this problem in upwardly mobile America? What causes does Sa'edi identify for this problem in the Iranian village of "The Game Is Over"?

ELABORATIONS

1. Imagine you are a journalist covering Hasani's tragic story for a magazine or newspaper. Based on "The Game Is Over," write an account of the boy's fate, its apparent causes, and its implications for other children like Hasani. (Your "article" may take either an expository or an argumentative form.)

2. Friction, as we all know, is part of family dynamics. Nearly every young person living with his or her parents or guardians feels tempted at some point to leave home because of a conflict. Write an essay about an experience which caused you to leave home either permanently or temporarily, or to seriously consider leaving. What do you think of your decision in retrospect? How did the experience affect you as an individual? as a family member?

PART THREE

COMING OF AGE

Landmarks and Turning Points

LOOKING AT OURSELVES

Gail Sheehy, Olga Silverstein, Jack Agueros,
Langston Hughes, "Racketeer"

Nik Cohn, *Delinquent in Derry* (IRELAND)

Liliana Heker, *The Stolen Party* (ARGENTINA)

Sophronia Liu, *So Tsi-fai* (HONG KONG)

Amy Tan, *Two Kinds* (UNITED STATES)

Mark Salzman, *Gong Fu* (CHINA)

Mario Vargas Llosa, *Sunday, Sunday* (PERU)

Ved Mehta, *Pom's Engagement* (INDIA)

Marjorie Shostak, *Nisa's Marriage* (BOTSWANA)

Benazir Bhutto, *The Day They Killed My Father* (PAKISTAN)

As each of us progresses from infancy toward old age, we continually encounter change — in our circumstances, and in ourselves. Sought or unsought, good or bad, all change creates stress. Particularly disruptive are shifts from one phase to another: from childhood dependence into adult self-reliance, from solitude into companionship, from intimacy into loss.

The playwright George Bernard Shaw wrote that when you learn something, it feels at first as if you've lost something. The passage from youth to maturity for most of us is a matter less of age than of moving from ignorance into awareness, from innocence into experience. Sometimes the change is marked by a ritual (formal or informal); sometimes we only notice it afterward. The passages in *Looking at Ourselves* offer a sampling of rituals and turning points in the United States: Gail Sheehy on pulling up roots, Olga Silverstein on today's women and their mothers, Jack Agueros on a Puerto Rican boy's alienation from the American dream. Langston Hughes recalls failing to hear the call of salvation; and eighteen-year-old "Racketeer" (not his real name) talks about being one of the Crips, a gang with about 20,000 members in Los Angeles.

The accounts of coming of age elsewhere in the world are arranged in roughly chronological order. "Delinquent in Derry" is Nik Cohn's recollection of becoming a convert to rock 'n' roll as a schoolboy in Northern Ireland. In Liliana's Heker's short story "The Stolen Party," an Argentine maid's bright, spunky daughter discovers class prejudice. "So Tsi-fai" shows Sophronia Liu still haunted by a rebellious classmate's suicide during sixth grade in Hong Kong. Another battle of wills takes place in Amy Tan's short story "Two Kinds," as Jing-mei Woo's Chinese-born mother pushes her to win fame and fortune in America. In "Gong Fu," Mark Salzman recalls his thrilling but painful introduction to the martial arts as an American in China.

Romance spurs many a turning point, as Mario Vargas Llosa reminds us in "Sunday, Sunday," a short story about a Peruvian teenager's dangerous plunge into rivalry with his best friend. A contrasting view of courtship is presented by Ved Mehta, who describes the Hindu rituals and the emotional shock that marked his sister's involuntary coming of age in "Pom's Engagement." Marjorie Shostak's "Nisa's Marriage" is a !Kung woman's account of being forced into social adulthood before physical puberty. Finally, Benazir Bhutto's "The Day They Killed My Father" is a wrenching account by Pakistan's first woman prime minister of trying to save her father's life after his government was toppled by a military coup.   ♦

LOOKING AT OURSELVES

1

Before eighteen, the motto is loud and clear: "I have to get away from my parents." But the words are seldom connected to action. Generally still safely part of our families, even if away at school, we feel our autonomy to be subject to erosion from moment to moment.

After eighteen, we begin Pulling Up Roots in earnest. College, military service, and short-term travels are all customary vehicles our society provides for the first round trips between family and a base of one's own. In the attempt to separate our view of the world from our family's view, despite vigorous protestations to the contrary — "I know exactly what I want!" — we cast about for any beliefs we can call our own. And in the process of testing those beliefs we are often drawn to fads, preferably those most mysterious and inaccessible to our parents.

Whatever tentative memberships we try out in the world, the fear haunts us that we are really kids who cannot take care of ourselves. We cover that fear with acts of defiance and mimicked confidence. For allies to replace our parents, we turn to our contemporaries. They become conspirators. So long as their perspective meshes with our own, they are able to substitute for the sanctuary of the family. But that doesn't last very long. And the instant they diverge from the shaky ideals of "our group," they are seen as betrayers. Rebounds to the family are common between the ages of eighteen and twenty-two.

The tasks of this passage are to locate ourselves in a peer group role, a sex role, an anticipated occupation, an ideology or worldview. As a result, we gather the impetus to leave home physically and the identity to *begin* leaving home emotionally.

Even as one part of us seeks to be an individual, another part longs to restore the safety and comfort of merging with another. Thus one of the most popular myths of this passage is: We can piggyback our development by attaching to a Stronger One. But people who marry during this time often prolong financial and emotional ties to the family and relatives that impede them from becoming self-sufficient.

A stormy passage through the Pulling Up Roots years will probably facilitate the normal progression of the adult life cycle. If one doesn't have an identity crisis at this point, it will erupt during a later transition, when the penalties may be harder to bear.

– Gail Sheehy
Passages

<><><><><>

2

If you had lived at a different time in history, your relationship with your mother would have been different. You would have done what your mother did, in an actual succession. But this generation has split off not only from what their mothers did, but from their mothers themselves. It's as if you can't love and respect your mother and still live your own life — a nonsensical idea based on current notions about autonomy. . . .

In adolescence you don't split from your mother because you want to catapult into the outside world, the father's world, in which competitiveness and ambition and making it are the big things. In adolescence you *have* to split off; otherwise, you feel too dependent, too cozy, too loved, too comfortable. It's a search for your own voice. But now the struggle extends far beyond adolescence: it's a mass rejection of a whole generation of women by a younger generation of women. The younger women are often denying the feminine voice, and yet they can't take on the masculine voice either. This has led to tremendous difficulties in marriages — trying to find a new way to be in a relationship that's not the way it was, but has not yet evolved into something different.

Things are beginning to turn around as thinking women, writing women, are asking, "What are we giving up by moving into the male place in the world?" It's such a sad and empty place. So there's the beginning of a new sort of affirmation about what's good about being a woman and what's important about relationships, about nurturing, about caring, about worrying about one another, about being closer. That brings us back to our mothers: these were important things we learned from our mothers. If we lose our relationship with our mothers, we lose a very important part of what it is to be human. . . .

We all, men and women, marry some version of our mothers. That is your primary intense relationship, the one you spend the rest of your life trying to resolve through other relationships. It's the one that we're always trying to redo, to undo. That's why it's so important to resolve it.

> – Olga Silverstein
> "The Good Mother: An Interview with
> Olga Silverstein"
> *Vogue*

◇–◇–◇–◇–◇

3

My mother kept an immaculate household. Bedspreads (chenille seemed to be very in) and lace curtains, washed at home like everything else, were hung up on huge racks with rows of tight nails. The racks were assembled in the living room, and the moisture from the wet bedspreads would fill the apartment. In a sense, that seems to be the lasting image of that period of my life. The house was clean. The neighbors were clean. The streets, with few cars, were clean. The buildings were clean and uncluttered with people on the stoops. The park was clean. The visitors to my house were clean, and the relationships that my family had with other Puerto Rican families, and the Italian families that my father had met through baseball and my mother through the garment center, were clean. Second Avenue was clean and most of the apartment windows had awnings. There was always music, there seemed to be no rain, and snow did not become slush. School was fun, we wrote essays about how grand America was, we put up hunchbacked cats at Halloween, we believed Santa Claus visited everyone. I believed everyone was Catholic. I grew up with dogs, nightingales, my godmother's guitar, rocking chair, cat, guppies, my father's occasional roosters, kept in a cage on the fire escape. Laundry delivered and collected by horse and wagon, fruits and vegetables sold the same way, windowsill refrigeration in winter, iceman and box in summer. The police my friends, likewise the teachers.

In short, the first seven or so years of my life were not too great a variation on Dick and Jane, the schoolbook figures who, if my memory serves me correctly, were blond Anglo-Saxons, not immigrants, not migrants like the Puerto Ricans, and not the children of either immigrants or migrants.

My family moved in 1941 to Lexington Avenue into a larger apartment where I could have my own room. It was a light, sunny, railroad flat on the top floor of a well-kept building. I transferred to a new school, and whereas before my classmates had been mostly black, the new school had few blacks. The classes were made up of Italians, Irish, Jews, and a sprinkling of Puerto Ricans. My block was populated by Jews, Italians, and Puerto Ricans.

And then a whole series of different events began. I went to junior high school. We played in the backyards, where we tore down fences to build fires to cook stolen potatoes. We tore up whole hedges, because the green tender limbs would not burn when they were peeled, and thus made perfect skewers for our stolen "mickies." We played tag in the abandoned buildings, tearing the plaster off the walls, tearing the wire lath off the wooden slats, tearing the wooden slats themselves, good for fires, for kites, for sword fighting. We ran up and down the fire escapes playing tag and over and across many rooftops. The war ended and the heavy Puerto Rican migration began. The Irish and the Jews disappeared from the neighborhood. The Italians tried to consolidate east of Third Avenue. . . .

Dick and Jane were dead, man. Education collapsed. Every classroom had ten kids who spoke no English. Black, Italian, Puerto Rican relations in the classroom were good, but we all knew we couldn't visit one another's neighborhoods. Sometimes we could not move too freely within our own blocks. On 109th, from the lamp post west, the Latin Aces, and from the lamp post east, the Senecas, the "club" I belonged to. The kids who spoke no English became known as Marine Tigers, picked up from a popular Spanish song. (The *Marine Tiger* and the *Marine Shark* were two ships that sailed from San Juan to New York and brought over many, many migrants from the island.)

The neighborhood had its boundaries. Third Avenue and east, Italian. Fifth Avenue and west, black. South, there was a hill on 103rd Street known locally as Cooney's Hill. When you got to the top of the hill, something strange happened: America began, because from the hill south was where the "Americans" lived. Dick and Jane were not dead; they were alive and well in a better neighborhood.

When, as a group of Puerto Rican kids, we decided to go swimming to Jefferson Park Pool, we knew we risked a fight and a beating from the Italians. And when we went to La Milagrosa Church in Harlem, we knew we risked a fight and a beating from the blacks. But when we went over Cooney's Hill, we risked dirty looks, disapproving looks, and questions from the police like, "What are you doing in this neighborhood?" and "Why don't you kids go back where you belong?"

Where we belonged! Man, I had written compositions about America. Didn't I belong on the Central Park tennis courts, even if I didn't know how to play? Couldn't I watch Dick play? Weren't these policemen working for me too?

> – Jack Agueros
> "Halfway to Dick and Jane"

4

I was saved from sin when I was going on thirteen. But not really saved. It happened like this. There was a big revival at my Auntie Reed's church. Every night for weeks there had been much preaching, singing, praying, and shouting, and some very hardened sinners had been brought to Christ, and the membership of the church had grown by leaps and bounds. Then just before the revival ended, they held a special meeting for children, "to bring the young lambs to the fold." My aunt spoke of it for days ahead. That night I was escorted to the front row and placed on the mourners' bench with all the other young sinners, who had not yet been brought to Jesus.

My aunt told me that when you were saved you saw a light, and something happened to you inside! And Jesus came into your life! And God was with you from then on! She said you could see and hear and feel Jesus in your soul. I believed her. I had heard a great many old people say the same thing and it seemed to me they ought to know. So I sat there calmly in the hot, crowded church, waiting for Jesus to come to me.

The preacher preached a wonderful rhythmical sermon, all moans and shouts and lonely cries and dire pictures of hell, and then he sang a song about the ninety and nine safe in the fold, but one little lamb was left out in the cold. Then he said: "Won't you come? Won't you come to Jesus? Young lambs, won't you come?" And he held out his arms to all us young sinners there on the mourners' bench. And the little girls cried. And some of them jumped up and went to Jesus right away. But most of us just sat there.

A great many old people came and knelt around us and prayed, old women with jet-black faces and braided hair, old men with work-gnarled hands. And the church sang a song about the lower lights are burning, some poor sinners to be saved. And the whole building rocked with prayer and song.

Still I kept waiting to *see* Jesus.

Finally all the young people had gone to the altar and were saved, but one boy and me. He was a rounder's son named Westley. Westley and I were surrounded by sisters and deacons praying. It was very hot in the church, and getting late now. Finally Westley said to me in a whisper: "God damn! I'm tired o' sitting here. Let's get up and be saved." So he got up and was saved.

Then I was left all alone on the mourners' bench. My aunt came and knelt at my knees and cried, while prayers and songs swirled all around me in the little church. The whole congregation prayed for me alone, in a mighty wail of moans and voices. And I kept waiting serenely for Jesus, waiting, waiting — but he didn't come. I wanted to see him, but nothing happened to me. Nothing! I wanted something to happen to me, but nothing happened.

I heard the songs and the minister saying: "Why don't you come? My dear child, why don't you come to Jesus? Jesus is waiting for you. He wants you. Why don't you come? Sister Reed, what is this child's name?"

"Langston," my aunt sobbed.

"Langston, why don't you come? Why don't you come and be saved? Oh, Lamb of God! Why don't you come?"

Now it was really getting late. I began to be ashamed of myself, holding everything up so long. I began to wonder what God thought about Westley, who certainly hadn't seen Jesus either, but who was now sitting proudly on the platform, swinging his knickerbockered legs and grinning down at me, surrounded by deacons and old women on their knees praying. God had not struck Westley dead for taking his name in vain or for lying in the temple. So I decided that maybe to save further trouble, I'd better lie, too, and say that Jesus had come, and get up and be saved.

So I got up.

Suddenly the whole room broke into a sea of shouting, as they saw me rise. Waves of rejoicing swept the place. Women leaped in the air. My aunt threw her arms around me. The minister took me by the hand and led me to the platform.

When things quieted down, in a hushed silence, punctuated by a few ecstatic "Amens," all the new young lambs were blessed in the name of God. Then joyous singing filled the room.

That night, for the last time in my life but one — for I was a big boy twelve years old — I cried. I cried, in bed alone, and couldn't stop. I buried my head under the quilts, but my aunt heard me. She woke up and told my uncle I was crying because the Holy Ghost had come into my life, and because I had seen Jesus. But I was really crying because I couldn't bear to tell her that I had lied, that I had deceived everybody in the church, that I hadn't seen Jesus, and that now I didn't believe there was a Jesus any more, since he didn't come to help me.

– Langston Hughes
"Salvation"
The Big Sea

◇–◇–◇–◇–◇

5

From an interview with "Racketeer," a Los Angeles gang member, in the May 6–12, 1988 issue of L.A. Weekly. *Racketeer (not his real street name) is an eighteen-year-old member of one of the several dozen factions — known as sets — that make up the Crips, a gang with about 20,000 members in Los Angeles. The Crips have been battling the Bloods for almost two decades. At the time of the interview, Racketeer was living at home with his family while on probation for attempted murder. The interview, which took place at the Kenyon Juvenile Justice Center, was conducted by Léon Bing.*

Why did you get into a gang?

I wasn't in it at first. I was just young, about twelve years old, and I started talking about gangbanging and all that. Then they started breaking my stuff and all that, you know, so you figure, well, what's the use, it's protection. So you thinking about it and then somebody sock you when you not looking and then you fight 'em back and you end up in their set.

What if you want to leave the set?

That's really hard. They probably kill you or catch your mother, something like that. When they think you don't want to be from their set no more they probably wind up killing you.

When I was younger I didn't even think people did that — I thought that was just on TV, like with the Mafia and all that, biggest gang in the world, and they get hit men and do that. But you ain't got no friends out in L.A. Not even in your set. You by yourself.

Do a lot of guys feel that way?

Lots of guys.

Why?

They fight against each other every time they get loaded. And that's why a lot of homeboys be getting killed, because after they fight they got a grudge against each other, you know. So then they thinking: "I'll get him — I'll *let* him get killed, I'll *let* somebody shoot him." So that person can't trust the other person no more and the other person can't trust him, there ain't no trust left and then when they get out there, they both get shot up.

What makes you feel bad?

When somebody get killed who you feel close to. That make me angry enough to go kill somebody.

How do you feel afterward?

You see, sometimes after you kill somebody, you feel like "Why did I do that? I should not have even done that, that wasn't even called for. What made me do this?" You be thinking all that, then you see someone look just like the person you killed. Then you be thinking, "I probably didn't even kill him — he probably coming back to get me."

I used to "jack" people — you know, with a gun or your hand, just catch 'em and go into their pockets — because I thought it was fun. But, you know, you get to the point where you wouldn't like nobody doing you like that when you get old, and you wouldn't like nobody just coming around you mother and just snatching her purse and lapping her, you know, so I start thinking, I can't be doing this no more, because somebody who do my mother like that make me ready to kill *anybody*. I started to be, like, sorry for things that I done, started to think that if I had stayed in school maybe I wouldn't have been into some of those things that I done. What I done in my life ain't so bad, maybe — the problem is, I done it.

Do you ever feel bad because you killed somebody who was somebody's son, somebody's brother, somebody's boyfriend, just like you are?

See, if you friend get shot, you will get somebody. You don't care who it is, you will get somebody, just to let your friend know, if he was still here, that's what you would do, you know. Like most of the times the set be down and stuff, they take off they head rags, put 'em in the casket with the bullets they killed people with — let the friend know they did this for him. Right now I'd say our set be cooled down, we ain't been killing nobody, we ain't been doing nothing but kickin' it. But that's hard because we been fighting each other.

How do you get involved in a drive-by shooting?

See, like when one of your homeboys get killed, you think you gonna go kill somebody — you gonna do it because *he* died — you gonna do it for *him*, just to let him know you really miss him.

What if somebody in the set says, "I can't do that"?

You don't. See, when a homeboy says, "Come on!" and you say, "No," that's like saying you don't want to be from the set. You ain't really down for your set if you ain't ready to *die* for the set. Then they probably kill you. You can't say no to your set.

What does your sister think about you being in a gang?

She into the Lord. That's what got me thinking. She be playing that gospel music, all that stuff, and I be sitting at home listening to it and she be telling me the Lord ain't gonna keep on letting me get away with the crimes I been doing. He ain't gonna keep on helping me out. Day before yesterday my cousin got shot in the chest in a drive-by.

Who do you think shot him?

We got so many enemies we don't know which one done it.

Who is your worst enemy?

Bounty Hunters [a Blood set].

Do you have Crip enemies?

P.Gs., 60s.

Would you kill another Crip?

Bloods kill Bloods. Crips will kill Crips. That's why I don't even know why it's Bloods and Crips, because they be killing each other.

If you didn't have Bloods or 60s or some other enemies to fight, who would you turn your anger on?

Just fight our own selves.

Do you think gangs are moving east?

Yeah — I don't know how far. I'm thinking all over the world. I think Crips will rule the world — that's what they trying to do.

If you could be anybody you wanted to be, who would you be?

Somebody rich. Somebody famous, like the rappers. You know, make a lot of money. But you know, the rappers, they got the same problems we all do: They got to think, like, they up there on the stage one day and they be saying the wrong thing and somebody just shoot 'em from the crowd.

If you could change the world, how would you do it?

I wouldn't know what to do. Because if I take all the guns away, then, you know, you can just use a knife. I would not know what to change.

Are other gangbangers starting to think about stopping the killing and shooting too?

Most of 'em. They think about it, but they try not to show it, you know. Like me — I think it, but I try not to show it.

What makes you happy?

When all my homeboys is just kickin' it, like we all just go somewhere, like a big old park — we be going to a picnic or something, and there just be a long line of cars, you know, like a funeral — only we going to a picnic and we just get up there and we just be kickin' and having fun, and then the police come and they run everybody off the place, and we come back to our 'hood and we be talking about how much fun we had, and then the next thing you know, somebody just drive by and start shooting and somebody got hit and somebody got killed, so that just spoil all the fun that we done had, and now you ready to go do the same thing, but you ain't gonna do it that night, because you know the police is gonna be out so you gonna try to find a night the police ain't gonna be out. But you ain't gonna do it when you're sober; you will get like all tipsy and you will start talking crazy, like saying, "Fuck Blood!" and all of that, and then there's gonna be another homeboy saying, "What you-all want to do? You-all wanna go get 'em?" And you will just be so drunk and all of that, you just say, "Come on!" and everybody start getting guns and stuff. And the next thing you know, we drove over and shot them up.

What do you think you'll be doing in ten years?

I don't think I be alive in ten years.

— "Racketeer"
"Reflections of a Gangbanger"
Harper's

NIK COHN

Delinquent in Derry

Nik Cohn was born in London, England, in 1946. As he notes in the
following essay, he attended secondary school in Londonderry, Northern
Ireland. His first novel, *Market,* was published in 1965. Cohn continues
to write novels, nonfiction books, and stories, many of them about
popular music, such as *A Wop Bopa Loo Bop a Lop Bam Boom: Pop
from the Beginning* (1970), *Rock Dreams* (1973), and the story that
became the film *Saturday Night Fever.* He also does free-lance writing
for newspapers and magazines in England and the United States, including *Queen, Mademoiselle,* and *Esquire.* Most recently he has lived in
Hertfordshire, England, and on Shelter Island in New York.

The United Kingdom of Great Britain and Northern Ireland comprises
England, Scotland, Wales, and — across the Irish Sea — six of the nine
Irish counties known as Ulster. The island of Ireland's division into a
smaller northern and larger southern section is religious as well as geographic and political: The independent south is 94 percent Catholic,
while the north is two-thirds Protestant. In 1921, when a treaty ended
seven centuries of Ireland's occupation by England, Northern Ireland
voted to remain part of the United Kingdom. However, the Irish Republican Army (IRA) went on fighting, to reunite the island and to protest
discrimination in Northern Ireland against the Catholic minority. The
conflict is still going on, often in the form of bombings, shootings, and
other terrorist attacks.

(For more background on Ireland, see p. 666.)

The winter I turned eleven I came upon a certain snake in the street.
This was in Londonderry, Northern Ireland, where I grew up and where
no snakes should have been.

Time has blurred the context. Exactly what led me to the snake in
question, how I even happened inside its neighborhood, I can't now
imagine. All I remember is that I was walking by myself on an empty
backstreet after dark and this street was dim and shuttered, curfew-silent,
the way that all good Protestant streets in Derry were meant to be. It
must have been a Thursday, the day we ran cross-country at school,
because my feet ached. Anyhow. At a given moment I turned a blind
corner, and I blundered on the snake.

I didn't register it right away. I was dazzled by bright lights and the enormity of where I was. My feet had brought me to the one place where no soul who hoped to be saved must ever venture — the downtown end of The Strand, hard by the docks, on the borders of the Bogside, the Papist war zone.

I had no idea what made it a plague-spot. But a plague-spot it was.   4
Tiggle, the janitor, said as much. So did McAlee, the man who did the drains. In the walled fastness of Magee, the college where my father taught French, it was freely referred to as an MKS, for Mobile Knocking Shop. And here I was, smack dab at the heart of it. After dark. By daylight, on the few furtive occasions I'd glimpsed it, it had only looked shabby, terminally depressed. But by night it had been transfigured: a style of place I hadn't dared to dream existed.

Directly across the street was a perfect neon inferno, brightly lit and self-contained like a stage-set: rock 'n' roll blasting from the open doors of coffee bars; beehive blondes with sky-blue or scarlet skirts and bright orange lipstick; sailors hunting in packs; leather boys, motorbikes, the reek of diesel.

Nothing had prepared me, not remotely. Derry, before the Provos[1] and long before Bloody Sunday,[2] was a backwater some thirty to fifty years behind the moment and proud of it. As for Magee itself, its isolation was almost monastic. Nobody owned a television, precious few a gramophone; and, although my father read the *Irish Times* each morning in the college library, my own hot news came entirely from the *Dandy* and the *Eagle*: Dan Dare had landed on Mars, Wyatt Earp was Sheriff in Tombstone, and Desperate Dan had made himself ill by devouring a box of six-inch nails, believing them to be sweet cigarettes. Once, when I was four, I'd caught a whiff of *Put Another Nickel In*, Teresa Brewer, courtesy of a passing bus, and my mother had had to drag me off the street by force. But at the moment I had stumbled on to The Strand, in 1957, the only pop singer I'd heard of was Rita Murray, and then only because she came from Belfast.

So I froze. If I'd been transported here by a time machine, I could not have been more out of place. Immediately I understood that my role was as a voyeur, a worshipper at one remove, and I snuck back inside an unlit doorway, from which, in safety, I could watch unobserved — see and not be seen.

---

[1]Provisional IRA: the Irish Republican Army, a paramilitary group; see p. 666. — ED.
[2]In January 1972, 14 demonstrators were killed by British paratroopers in Derry.

Only then did I notice the snake. From deep inside the chasm of the   8
Roseland Café a jukebox let loose with *Tutti Frutti*, Little Richard, and
on the pavement outside an impromptu jitterbug broke out. Teenagers
in fancy dress, whom I later learned were Teddy Boys, began to jive with
each other, males with males, in a craze of flashing fluorescent socks and
shocking-pink drapes, drainpipes and blue suede shoes; and as they
whirled they kept passing the snake, which I took at first to be a whip or
a length of elastic tubing, back and forth like a baton.

When the music died out, so did the dancing. But the snake remained,
dangled beneath a street lamp, framed and backlit by the Roseland's
plate-glass window. I could now see it clearly. It appeared to be about
two feet long, with a tapering greenish coil for a body and a great, black
hooded skull. Something between a cobra and a python, I guessed, and
it twirled and corkscrewed, stretched and contracted in rhythm, twined
around a blue mohair sleeve with a purple velvet cuff.

It didn't seem a discovery, exactly. Recognition was more like it. It
was as if there was something I had always known, only I'd forgotten or
misplaced it, let it escape me; and now the snake, and everything that
went with the snake, had restored it.

The something in question had no name, of course. And I did not
try to give it one. All I thought consciously was that I now possessed a
secret, and this secret made me powerful, in some way superior.

The feeling was not familiar. In my pre-Strand existence, secret power   12
was the last thing I thought to possess. On the contrary, I was consumed
by not belonging, by having no place, either in Derry or anywhere else
on Planet Earth. In this, I had support: "Unfit to fit," some kindergarten
confrère once carved into the lid of my desk, and the motion seemed to
be carried by acclamation.

Part of the problem was genetic. By birth and upbringing I was an
Anglo-Teutonic Russian Menshevik Agnostic Jew, and pretty much typical of the type. Born in London, weaned in Scotland and South Africa,
I didn't arrive in Ireland until I was five, and somehow I never fully
acclimatized. Certainly not in native eyes, at any rate. My father wrote
books about heretics, my mother had an accent, and I myself was neither
Protestant nor Catholic, not Irish but also nothing else. In the context
of Derry and, in particular, of Foyle, the moth-eaten Presbyterian shrine
in decline where I went to school, I might as well have come from Mars
— the man who fell to Earth and, abysmally, failed to bounce.

Magee completed the curse. In theory it was a training school for

Calvinist ministers; in reality, with its high stone walls and imported tutors, more like an unarmed encampment; and its isolation from the town was absolute. Dimly one was conscious of the hatred outside, with its perpetual roundelay of Catholic ambuscades and Protestant reprisals, Black masses and Orange parades. But it seemed to carry no reality. If it had not been for Tiggle, the janitor, my only link to life beyond Magee's walls, I would hardly have been aware that men, when shot, did actually bleed.

Always, the key was that I myself took no part. From my very earliest remembrance — in which my twenty-month self enticed a five-year-old gardener's daughter into climbing up a tree and getting stuck, thus allowing me to study from below the effects of light and shade on her sky-blue knickers,[3] her sweating spun-gold legs all covered with scabs, ripe and pickable as currants baked into damp bread, also the way in which her screams caused her thighs to shimmy and shudder like blancmange[4] in a gale — my intuition was that my best role was not to perform but always to watch, preferably from a distance.

There was one exception. At Magee, down by Tiggle's cottage and   16 the tennis court where he died, there was an outhouse with a long and flat cement exterior wall, and up against this wall, every rainless afternoon after school, I used to bat a tennis ball. Sometimes I would hit it with a rot-gutted racket as flaccid as a butterfly net, sometimes with a sawn-off broomstick or the flat of a cricket bat, and sometimes, when times were tough, with a cabbage-stalk soaked in brine; and as I hit, I counted.

The formula never varied. First I would attempt to execute one hundred strokes on my forehand, then another hundred backhand, then forehand again, then backhand, and so interminably on, until at last I missed, at which point I'd go back to the beginning, starting over from stroke one.

What was the use? I'm still not sure. No special target was involved, no astronomical figure whose attainment would somehow release me. There was no question of athletic prowess. On the contrary, in my passion not to flub, I kept all my shots as passive and pattycake as possible, never dared the slightest variation. Avoiding error was not the main thing, it

---

[3] British slang for girls' underpants. — ED.
[4] Vanilla pudding. — ED.

was the only thing, and so metronomic was the thud of ball on wall, I might have been marking time.

Faced with such futility, even the mildest divinity students were goaded beyond endurance. With time I acquired a regular gallery of hecklers, beseeching me, just once, to give the ball a free and hearty whack. But I never did. The very soullessness of this unending putt-puttery was its perverse pleasure. One afternoon, halfway through my 700th on the forehand, Tiggle keeled over in midimprecation, belly-up and purple-headed, with a pale pink froth about his lips that was like the lees of lemonade sherbet. There were murmurings of manslaughter, and these I took as a compliment.

For years the ceremony never varied. Then I came out into The Strand, observed the snake, and later, safe back in the sanctuary of Magee, I went down to the outhouse wall. Even though it was now pitch dark, I grabbed a trusty coal shovel, whirled it like a shillelagh. And I began to smash the balls at random. I hit out blindly, possessed. Exploding all about me like so many hand-grenades, balls ricocheted into my face and eyes, my belly; knocked me backwards, drove me to my knees. Ball the wall, indeed I did and the tarmac beneath me, and the air, and all of the darkness, too. I didn't quit till every last ball I owned had been splatted or forever lost. Then I hurled the shovel as high and as far as my mean strength could launch it, and I never played that game again.

I took to traveling, instead. Of a sudden Magee no longer seemed a refuge, only a confinement, and I invented numberless excuses to be free of it, go out scavenging. My feet, for instance. Claiming incipient droop-age of the instep, I won permission to pay a weekly visit after Friday school to one Bernard Dinty, a cobbler turned foot-healer.

Dinty's office, a bare white room above a flesher's on Shipquay Street, lay deep within the walled city, overlooking the Bogside, and it hid behind drawn blinds. There I would be marched back and forth across a narrow strip of linoleum, one full hour by the clock, practicing posture, balance, and what Dinty termed tone of gait.

This office, it was rumored, doubled as a front for a butter-smuggling ring. And it was true there was something rancid and furtive in its air, a smell of dirty little secrets. As for the healer himself, a rumpled little squit of a man, all polka dot bow-tie and stained white medico's coat, he liked to soundtrack my perambulations with lectures on the evils of masturbation and of patronizing brothels or, as he preferred, the Temples of Venus. "Fallen arches today, fallen women next Saturday," was his motto, and, each time he delivered it, he would touch my bare short-trousered leg above the knee, not so much sweating as oozing, clammily steaming, like an overheated jam pudding in meltdown.

My compensation was that, by the time I won release, it would be   24
after dark, all the streets would have changed for night, and the straightest, safest way home would lead me directly past the Roseland Café.

The snake itself, I never saw again. But the Teddy Boys, its votaries, were regulars, and they came to embody everything I sensed, everything that I still couldn't spell.

In their daytime incarnations, I understood, the Teds were only Papist scum, the delinquent flotsam and jetsam of the Bogside. As such, their life prospects were nil. Foredoomed, dispossessed, they had traded away the Free for the Welfare State, and now they had no work, no home, no hope whatever, unless the fleeting glory of an IRA martyrdom. They were, in every common sense, nonpersons. And yet, here on The Strand, in the neon night by rock 'n' roll, they were made heroic. In every flash of fluorescent sock or velvet cuff, every jive-step swagger for Chuck Berry, every leer and flaunt of their greased pompadoured ducktails, they beggared the fates, made reality irrelevant.

My enthusiasm was unshared. At Magee and Foyle, such stuff was viewed as indecency and shame. And this, of course, became its clinching attraction. Like everything else that I was equipped to love, the Roseland must be kept my own secret.

The second step was Elvis.   28

Again, I had Bernard Dinty partly to thank. Late one Friday dusk, heading for my weekly treadmill, I let myself loiter outside the fly-blown windows of McCafferty's Journals & Uncommonly Fine Books, Ltd., and there sat a copy of *Tidbits*, a weekly yellow tabloid barred by my mother as "cheap and nasty," therefore a jewel beyond price. On its cover was a head-and-shoulders glossy of the King.

In the first shock of impact I was conscious only of the mouth, in particular the upper lip. This seemed to loom disembodied, in the style of a Cheshire cat grin, only twisted and lopsided, as serpentine as any real or rubber snake, so that its smile became a sneer. And this sneer said: "Oh, yeah?"

To which echo answered: "Oh, yeah!" It seemed to me then, it seems to me still, the wisest remark ever made. In that instant, I accepted Elvis Presley to be my personal living savior and nothing has happened since to change my mind, or bruise my faith.

What I saw in him, beyond sheer physical gorgeousness, was the 32
possibility of the impossible. The upper lip, the sneer were a direct
extension of the Teddy Boys and Roseland. For Elvis, I sensed at once
and soon discovered for a fact, was derived from the same unregarded
stable. He too had started out foredoomed, dispossessed, the most hopeless
of White Trash. His ambition had been to grow up into a truck driver.
Specifically, he'd lusted after the peaked mesh caps that truckers affected;
he'd thought these made them look daring. Also, he'd envied their
freedom. But such heroics, he understood, were beyond him. In the
crunch, he was too soft-skinned, too scared, too much a mother's boy.
A true trucker he could never be. So he became a Messiah instead.

Now my pilgrimage began in earnest. But it did not prove easy going.
For Protestant Derry, home of the Apprentice Boys, rock 'n' roll was
poison. The Teddy Boys riots over *Blackboard Jungle* and Bill Haley in
England had panicked all of loyalist Ulster. This was not just a teenage
rebellion that loomed: it was as if the massed forces of Satan had been
unleashed, threatening to wipe out all sanity, all sanctity — in the words
of *The Derry Sentinel*, all "Civilization as we know it."

All rock shows, artifacts, and films were outlawed. And anyone who
challenged this suppression was in for a bumpy ride. Mary Fadden, a
comely fifth-former at Northlands, the local girls' school, was expelled
for secreting a picture of Jerry Lee Lewis in her desk; discs and posters
fueled bonfires; and Elvis himself was ceremonially torched in effigy at
the Brandywell Football Grounds, nailed to a flaming cross. Only Catholics, since idolatry was their nature, were free to devil-worship in peace.

What to do? There seemed only one solution. So my feet took a turn
for the worse. In reality, I had ceased to frequent Dinty after a session at
which, suggesting that I might benefit from being fitted with metal instep
supports, he insisted on taking my inner-thigh measurements. For public
consumption, however, I now increased my visits from weekly to almost
nightly and, with the freedom thus gained, I went exploring.

Across the river, in a Catholic enclave in the Waterside district, there 36
was a disused funeral home in which, three nights a week, at 6d[5] a shot,
contraband Teen movies could be sat through and sometimes seen,
according to the state of the projector. One drawback was that a cross-
pollination of embalming fluid and scented wax flowers still hung in the

---

[5]Sixpence. — ED.

air, an intimation of mortality sickly-sweet enough to turn the most fanatic stomach. Still, hunched in the suffocating dark, I drowned myself in *Don't Knock the Rock, The Girl Can't Help It,* and *I Was a Teenage Werewolf,* had a crush on Eddie Cochran but chose to marry Sheree North.

The Crypt, as it was aptly named, was just the start. By perching myself atop a stepladder, then balancing the family steam-wireless on a stack of Encylopaediae Britannicae, 1911, in thirty-four volumes, I could jam my left ear tight up against the sound-box, four inches below my bedroom ceiling, and so receive the faintest static-riddled crackling of Radio Luxemburg, a thousand miles away across Europe; at Thos. Mullen, Tonsorial Artist, on Ferryquay Street, back copies of *Titbits* and *Men Only* tutored me in the hit parades, also in anatomy ("Petunia, 19, is an artist's model and this is one pulchritudinous petal that any Old Master would be proud to pluck"); and at last one night at the Palace, the first cinema in town openly to dare show Elvis film, halfway through the *Teddy Bear* sequence in *Loving You,* I heard a siren shrieking above, looked up from my lair in the back stalls, and saw the balcony overhead shaking, literally buckling, from sheer humping tonnage of wet-knickered nymphs. "Earthquake!" the inevitable alarmist hollered and a minor stampede ensued, cravens of all persuasions scrabbling wholesale for the exits, like so many extras from *The Last Days of Pompeii.*

I myself failed to budge. For this, I knew well, was no earthquake or even holocaust — it was the end of the world. Or leastways, of civilization as we knew it.

EXPLORATIONS

1. What clues suggest that the snake in Cohn's essay is more than a simple reptile? What does the snake represent on an immediate level? on a symbolic level?

2. What aspects of Cohn's background do you think influenced his reaction to Elvis Presley? What are the effects of Cohn's using religious imagery to describe that reaction?

3. How did Cohn's discovery of rock 'n' roll change his response to the social rules and prejudices around him? Cite specific examples.

CONNECTIONS

1. What similar experiences appear in Cohn's essay and Jack Agueros's passage in *Looking at Ourselves*? What similar changes do both boys go through?
2. What comments by Cohn support ideas presented by Gail Sheehy in *Looking at Ourselves*? What comments by Cohn seem to contradict statements by Sheehy?

ELABORATIONS

1. "Like everything else that I was equipped to love," writes Cohn in paragraph 27, "the Roseland must be kept my own secret." In what ways does having secrets mark a step toward adulthood? Using Cohn's experience and yours as sources, answer this question in a cause-and-effect or classification essay.
2. Others besides the Protestants of Derry have decried rock 'n' roll as a medium of Satan. Why? Are they right? Write an argumentative essay about this issue, or some aspect of it.

LILIANA HEKER

The Stolen Party

Argentine writer Liliana Heker published her highly regarded first volume of short stories, *Those Who Beheld the Burning Bush,* while still in her teens. As editor in chief of the literary magazine *El Ornitorrinco* (*The Platypus*), Heker kept open a national forum for writers throughout the years of Argentina's chaotic and bloody military dictatorships. In its pages she debated with the late Julio Cortázar about the proper role of a writer in a strife-torn, oppressed society: Cortázar, living in Paris, defended his role as a writer in exile, while Heker took a position similar to Nadine Gordimer's in South Africa (see p. 564): "To be heard, we must shout from within." Heker's second novel, *Zona de Clivage,* was published in 1988 and won the Buenos Aires Municipal Prize.

Four times the size of Texas, Argentina occupies most of South America's southern tip. When the first Spanish settlers appeared in the early 1500s, nomadic Indians roamed the pampas. By the late 1800s nearly all of them had been killed, making room for the influx of Europeans who today comprise 97 percent of the population. Argentina had won independence from Spain in 1819; by the century's end it was the most prosperous, educated, and industrialized Latin American nation. Military dictatorships and coups have dominated this century, however. Aside from General Juan Perón, elected president from 1946 to 1955 and again in 1973, most regimes have been nasty, brutish, and short-lived. Argentina's failed attempt to take the Islas Malvinas (Falkland Islands) from Great Britain in 1982 led to the first general election since Perón's, which established a democratic government in this economically beleaguered nation. Despite opposition from former military officers and some of his fellow Peronists, current President Carlos Menem's aggressive economic policies have begun to slow Argentina's runaway inflation and budget deficit.

"The Stolen Party," first published in 1982, was translated from the Spanish by Alberto Manguel for his anthology *Other Fires* (1985).

As soon as she arrived she went straight to the kitchen to see if the monkey was there. It was: what a relief! She wouldn't have liked to admit that her mother had been right. *Monkeys at a birthday?* her mother had sneered. *Get away with you, believing any nonsense you're told!* She was cross, but not because of the monkey, the girl thought; it's just because of the party.

"I don't like you going," she told her. "It's a rich people's party."

"Rich people go to Heaven too," said the girl, who studied religion at school.

"Get away with Heaven," said the mother. "The problem with you,   4 young lady, is that you like to fart higher than your ass."

The girl didn't approve of the way her mother spoke. She was barely nine, and one of the best in her class.

"I'm going because I've been invited," she said. "And I've been invited because Luciana is my friend. So there."

"Ah yes, your friend," her mother grumbled. She paused. "Listen, Rosaura," she said at last. "That one's not your friend. You know what you are to them? The maid's daughter, that's what."

Rosaura blinked hard: she wasn't going to cry. Then she yelled: "Shut   8 up! You know nothing about being friends!"

Every afternoon she used to go to Luciana's house and they would both finish their homework while Rosaura's mother did the cleaning. They had their tea in the kitchen and they told each other secrets. Rosaura loved everything in the big house, and she also loved the people who lived there.

"I'm going because it will be the most lovely party in the whole world, Luciana told me it would. There will be a magician, and he will bring a monkey and everything."

The mother swung around to take a good look at her child, and pompously put her hands on her hips.

"Monkeys at a birthday?" she said. "Get away with you, believing any   12 nonsense you're told!"

Rosaura was deeply offended. She thought it unfair of her mother to accuse other people of being liars simply because they were rich. Rosaura too wanted to be rich, of course. If one day she managed to live in a beautiful palace, would her mother stop loving her? She felt very sad. She wanted to go to that party more than anything else in the world.

"I'll die if I don't go," she whispered, almost without moving her lips.

And she wasn't sure whether she had been heard, but on the morning of the party she discovered that her mother had starched her Christmas dress. And in the afternoon, after washing her hair, her mother rinsed it in apple vinegar so that it would be all nice and shiny. Before going out, Rosaura admired herself in the mirror, with her white dress and glossy hair, and thought she looked terribly pretty.

Señora Ines also seemed to notice. As soon as she saw her, she said: 16
"How lovely you look today, Rosaura."

Rosaura gave her starched skirt a slight toss with her hands and walked
into the party with a firm step. She said hello to Luciana and asked about
the monkey. Luciana put on a secretive look and whispered into Rosaura's
ear: "He's in the kitchen. But don't tell anyone, because it's a surprise."

Rosaura wanted to make sure. Carefully she entered the kitchen and
there she saw it: deep in thought, inside its cage. It looked so funny that
the girl stood there for a while, watching it, and later, every so often, she
would slip out of the party unseen and go and admire it. Rosaura was
the only one allowed into the kitchen. Señora Ines had said: "You yes,
but not the others, they're much too boisterous, they might break something." Rosaura had never broken anything. She even managed the jug
of orange juice, carrying it from the kitchen into the dining room. She
held it carefully and didn't spill a single drop. And Señora Ines had said:
"Are you sure you can manage a jug as big as that?" Of course she could
manage. She wasn't a butterfingers, like the others. Like that blonde girl
with the bow in her hair. As soon as she saw Rosaura, the girl with the
bow had said:

"And you? Who are you?"   20

"I'm a friend of Luciana," said Rosaura.

"No," said the girl with the bow, "you are not a friend of Luciana
because I'm her cousin and I know all her friends. And I don't know
you."

"So what," said Rosaura. "I come here every afternoon with my mother
and we do our homework together."

"You and your mother do your homework together?" asked the girl,   24
laughing.

"I and Luciana do our homework together," said Rosaura, very seriously.

The girl with the bow shrugged her shoulders.

"That's not being friends," she said. "Do you go to school together?"

"No."   28

"So where do you know her from?" said the girl, getting impatient.

Rosaura remembered her mother's words perfectly. She took a deep
breath.

"I'm the daughter of the employee," she said.

Her mother had said very clearly: "If someone asks, you say you're the   32
daughter of the employee; that's all." She also told her to add: "And

proud of it." But Rosaura thought that never in her life would she dare say something of the sort.

"What employee?" said the girl with the bow. "Employee in a shop?"

"No," said Rosaura angrily. "My mother doesn't sell anything in any shop, so there."

"So how come she's an employee?" said the girl with the bow.

Just then Señora Ines arrived saying *shh shh*, and asked Rosaura if she 36 wouldn't mind helping serve out the hotdogs, as she knew the house so much better than the others.

"See?" said Rosaura to the girl with the bow, and when no one was looking she kicked her in the shin.

Apart from the girl with the bow, all the others were delightful. The one she liked best was Luciana, with her golden birthday crown; and then the boys. Rosaura won the sack race, and nobody managed to catch her when they played tag. When they split into two teams to play charades, all the boys wanted her for their side. Rosaura felt she had never been so happy in all her life.

But the best was still to come. The best came after Luciana blew out the candles. First the cake. Señora Ines had asked her to help pass the cake around, and Rosaura had enjoyed the task immensely, because everyone called out to her, shouting "Me, me!" Rosaura remembered a story in which there was a queen who had the power of life or death over her subjects. She had always loved that, having the power of life or death. To Luciana and the boys she gave the largest pieces, and to the girl with the bow she gave a slice so thin one could see through it.

After the cake came the magician, tall and bony, with a fine red cape. 40 A true magician: he could untie handkerchiefs by blowing on them and make a chain with links that had no openings. He could guess what cards were pulled out from a pack, and the monkey was his assistant. He called the monkey "partner." "Let's see here, partner," he would say, "turn over a card." And, "Don't run away, partner: time to work now."

The final trick was wonderful. One of the children had to hold the monkey in his arms and the magician said he would make him disappear.

"What, the boy?" they all shouted.

"No, the monkey!" shouted back the magician.

Rosaura thought that this was truly the most amusing party in the 44 whole world.

The magician asked a small fat boy to come and help, but the small fat boy got frightened almost at once and dropped the monkey on the floor. The magician picked him up carefully, whispered something in his ear, and the monkey nodded almost as if he understood.

"You mustn't be so unmanly, my friend," the magician said to the fat boy.

"What's unmanly?" said the fat boy.

The magician turned around as if to look for spies.   48

"A sissy," said the magician. "Go sit down."

Then he stared at all the faces, one by one. Rosaura felt her heart tremble.

"You, with the Spanish eyes," said the magician. And everyone saw that he was pointing at her.

She wasn't afraid. Neither holding the monkey, nor when the magician   52 made him vanish; not even when, at the end, the magician flung his red cape over Rosaura's head and uttered a few magic words . . . and the monkey reappeared, chattering happily, in her arms. The children clapped furiously. And before Rosaura returned to her seat, the magician said:

"Thank you very much, my little countess."

She was so pleased with the compliment that a while later, when her mother came to fetch her, that was the first thing she told her.

"I helped the magician and he said to me, 'Thank you very much, my little countess.'"

It was strange because up to then Rosaura had thought that she was   56 angry with her mother. All along Rosaura had imagined that she would say to her: "See that the monkey wasn't a lie?" But instead she was so thrilled that she told her mother all about the wonderful magician.

Her mother tapped her on the head and said: "So now we're a countess!"

But one could see that she was beaming.

And now they both stood in the entrance, because a moment ago Señora Ines, smiling, had said: "Please wait here a second."

Her mother suddenly seemed worried.   60

"What is it?" she asked Rosaura.

"What is what?" said Rosaura. "It's nothing; she just wants to get the presents for those who are leaving, see?"

She pointed at the fat boy and at a girl with pigtails who were also waiting there, next to their mothers. And she explained about the presents. She knew, because she had been watching those who left before her. When one of the girls was about to leave, Señora Ines would give her a bracelet. When a boy left, Señora Ines gave him a yo-yo. Rosaura preferred the yo-yo because it sparkled, but she didn't mention that to her mother. Her mother might have said: "So why don't you ask for one, you blockhead?" That's what her mother was like. Rosaura didn't feel like explaining that she'd be horribly ashamed to be the odd one out. Instead she said:

"I was the best-behaved at the party."   64

And she said no more because Señora Ines came out into the hall with two bags, one pink and one blue.

First she went up to the fat boy, gave him a yo-yo out of the blue bag, and the fat boy left with his mother. Then she went up to the girl and gave her a bracelet out of the pink bag, and the girl with the pigtails left as well.

Finally she came up to Rosaura and her mother. She had a big smile on her face and Rosaura liked that. Señora Ines looked down at her, then looked up at her mother, and then said something that made Rosaura proud:

"What a marvelous daughter you have, Herminia."   68

For an instant, Rosaura thought that she'd give her two presents: the bracelet and the yo-yo. Señora Ines bent down as if about to look for something. Rosaura also leaned forward, stretching out her arm. But she never completed the movement.

Señora Ines didn't look in the pink bag. Nor did she look in the blue bag. Instead she rummaged in her purse. In her hand appeared two bills.

"You really and truly earned this," she said handing them over. "Thank you for all your help, my pet."

Rosaura felt her arms stiffen, stick close to her body, and then she   72 noticed her mother's hand on her shoulder. Instinctively she pressed herself against her mother's body. That was all. Except her eyes. Rosaura's eyes had a cold, clear look that fixed itself on Señora Ines's face.

Señora Ines, motionless, stood there with her hand outstretched. As if she didn't dare draw it back. As if the slightest change might shatter an infinitely delicate balance.

EXPLORATIONS

1. What central conflict does Heker establish in her opening paragraph? What conflict does she introduce in her second paragraph? How would the story's balance change if Heker started with the second paragraph, leaving the monkey question until its chronological place?

2. At the end of "The Stolen Party," what is the intended message of Señora Ines's gift to Rosaura? What message does Rosaura draw from the gift? What changes occur in the characters' perceptions of each other, and of themselves, in the story's last two paragraphs?

3. Rosaura has a number of standards for judging people — more specifically, for measuring herself against others. For example, in paragraph 5: "The girl didn't approve of the way her mother spoke. She was barely nine, and one of the best in her class." Find at least four other points in the story when Rosaura makes a comparative judgment. How well does she fare in her own estimation? What do you learn about Rosaura as a character from these judgments?

CONNECTIONS

1. Is "The Stolen Party" told from Rosaura's point of view as a child or as an adult looking back on her childhood? Cite specific evidence for your answer. Is "Delinquent in Derry" told from Nik Cohn's point of view as a child or as an adult looking back on his childhood? Cite specific evidence.

2. What comments by Olga Silverstein in *Looking at Ourselves* apply to Rosaura's relationship with her mother? Do you think Silverstein would view this relationship as a healthy one? Why or why not?

3. Look back at Jack Agueros's passage in *Looking at Ourselves*. Who represents "Dick and Jane" to Rosaura in Heker's story? How are Rosaura's circumstances different from Agueros's? Which child do you think has better prospects, and why?

ELABORATIONS

1. The characters in "The Stolen Party" — particularly the two mother-daughter pairs — all have different concepts of the extent to which they control their own destinies. Write an essay classifying these concepts: Describe each mother's and daughter's sense of herself as a social actor; identify the factors she views as conferring or limiting her power, such as age, intelligence, and social class; and cite the evidence in the story that supports your conclusions.

2. In "The Stolen Party," Cohn's "Delinquent in Derry," and Agueros's passage in *Looking at Ourselves*, the central character's innocence is an important factor. In what ways does each character's youthful ignorance of the adult world work for or against her or him? Write an essay comparing and contrasting Cohn's, Agueros's, and Heker's views of the pros and cons of innocence.

SOPHRONIA LIU

So Tsi-fai

Born in Hong Kong in 1953, Sophronia Liu came to the United States to study at the age of twenty. Some of her family are still in Hong Kong; others now live in the United States, Canada, and England. Liu received a bachelor's degree in English and French, and a master's degree in English, from the University of South Dakota. Currently a teaching assistant in composition at the University of Minnesota, she is working toward her Ph.D. in English. She returned to Hong Kong in the fall of 1990 to do research for a program she is developing for Asian-American students. Under the program, students will travel abroad to learn about their Asian roots, and they will be encouraged to do autobiographical writing, as Liu has done. Liu's dissertation is her memoir, which she hopes to publish. "So Tsi-fai" was written in response to a class assignment and originally appeared in the Minnesota feminist publication *Hurricane Alice.*

Hong Kong, where Liu attended The Little Flower's School with So Tsi-fai, is a British Crown Colony at the mouth of China's Pearl River. Its nucleus is Hong Kong Island, which Britain acquired from China in 1841. Most of the colony's 409 square miles consist of other Chinese territory held by Britain on a ninety-nine-year lease. Hong Kong's population of over five million includes fewer than 20,000 British; it absorbed more than a million Chinese refugees after Mao's Communists won the mainland in 1949. In 1985 China and Britain agreed that Hong Kong will revert to China in 1997, when the lease expires, but will be allowed to keep its capitalist system for fifty years after that. Hong Kong is currently negotiating with China to form a new constitution called Basic Law. In the meantime, Hong Kong (meaning "fragrant harbor") remains the world's busiest port.

Voices, images, scenes from the past — twenty-three years ago, when I was in sixth grade:

"Let us bow our heads in silent prayer for the soul of So Tsi-fai. Let us pray for God's forgiveness for this boy's rash taking of his own life . . ." Sister Marie (Mung Gu-liang). My sixth-grade English teacher. Missionary nun from Paris. Principal of The Little Flower's School. Disciplinarian, perfectionist, authority figure: awesome and awful in my ten-year-old eyes.

"I don't need any supper. I have drunk enough insecticide." So Tsi-fai. My fourteen-year-old classmate. Daredevil; good-for-nothing lazy-bones (according to Mung Gu-liang). Bright black eyes, disheveled hair, defiant sneer, creased and greasy uniform, dirty hands, careless walk, shuffling feet. Standing in the corner for being late, for forgetting his homework, for talking in class, for using foul language. ("Shame on you! Go wash your mouth with soap!" Mung Gu-liang's sharp command. He did, and came back with a grin.) So Tsi-fai: Sticking his tongue out behind Mung Gu-liang's back, passing secret notes to his friends, kept behind after school, sent to the Principal's office for repeated offense. So Tsi-fai: incorrigible, hopeless, and without hope.

It was a Monday in late November when we heard of his death,   4
returning to school after the weekend with our parents' signatures on our midterm reports. So Tsi-fai also showed his report to his father, we were told later. He flunked three out of the fourteen subjects: English Grammar, Arithmetic, and Chinese Dictation. He missed each one by one to three marks. That wasn't so bad. But he was a hopeless case. Overaged, stubborn, and uncooperative; a repeated offender of school rules, scourge of all teachers; who was going to give him a lenient passing grade? Besides, being a few months over the maximum age — fourteen — for sixth graders, he wasn't even allowed to sit for the Secondary School Entrance Exam.

All sixth graders in Hong Kong had to pass the SSE before they could obtain a seat in secondary school. In 1964 when I took the exam, there were more than twenty thousand candidates. About seven thousand of us passed: four thousand were sent to government and subsidized schools, the other three thousand to private and grant-in-aid schools. I came in around no. 2000; I was lucky. Without the public exam, there would be no secondary school for So Tsi-fai. His future was sealed.

Looking at the report card with three red marks on it, his father was furious. So Tsi-fai was the oldest son. There were three younger children. His father was a vegetable farmer with a few plots of land in Wong Juk-hang, by the sea. His mother worked in a local factory. So Tsi-fai helped in the fields, cooked for the family, and washed his own clothes. ("Filthy, dirty boy!" gasped Mung Gu-liang. "Grime behind the ears, black rims on the fingernails, dirty collar, crumpled shirt. Why doesn't your mother iron your shirt?") Both his parents were illiterate. So Tsi-fai was their biggest hope: He made it to the sixth grade.

Who woke him up for school every morning and had breakfast waiting for him? Nobody. ("Time for school! Get up! Eat your rice!" Ma nagged and screamed. The aroma of steamed rice and Chinese sausages spread all over the house. "Drink your tea! Eat your oranges! Wash your face! And remember to wash behind your ears!") And who helped So Tsi-fai do his homework? Nobody. Did he have older brothers like mine who knew all about the arithmetic of rowing a boat against the currents or with the currents, how to count the feet of chickens and rabbits in the same cage, the present perfect continuous tense of "to live" and the future perfect tense of "to succeed"? None. Nil. So Tsi-fai was a lost cause.

I came first in both terms that year, the star pupil. So Tsi-fai was one of the last in the class: he was lazy; he didn't care. Or did he?   8

When his father scolded him, So Tsi-fai left the house. When he showed up again, late for supper, he announced, "I don't need any supper. I have drunk enough insecticide." Just like another one of his practical jokes. The insecticide was stored in the field for his father's vegetables. He was rushed to the hospital; dead upon arrival.

"He gulped for a last breath and was gone," an uncle told us at the funeral. "But his eyes wouldn't shut. So I said in his ear, 'You go now and rest in peace.' And I smoothed my hand over his eyelids. His face was all purple."

His face was still purple when we saw him in his coffin. Eyes shut tight, nostrils dilated and white as if fire and anger might shoot out, any minute.

In class that Monday morning, Sister Marie led us in prayer. "Let us pray that God will forgive him for his sins." We said the Lord's Prayer and the Hail Mary. We bowed our heads. I sat in my chair, frozen and dazed, thinking of the deadly chill in the morgue, the smell of disinfectant, ether, and dead flesh.   12

"Bang!" went a gust of wind, forcing open a leaf of the double door leading to the back balcony. "Flap, flap, flap." The door swung in the wind. We could see the treetops by the hillside rustling to and fro against a pale blue sky. An imperceptible presence had drifted in with the wind. The same careless walk and shuffling feet, the same daredevil air — except that the eyes were lusterless, dripping blood; the tongue hanging out, gasping for air. As usual, he was late. But he had come back to claim his place.

"I died a tragic death," his voice said. "I have as much right as you to be here. This is my seat." We heard him; we knew he was back.

. . . So Tsi-fai: Standing in the corner for being late, for forgetting his homework, for talking in class, for using foul language. So Tsi-fai: palm outstretched, chest sticking out, holding his breath: "Tat. Tat. Tat." Down came the teacher's wooden ruler, twenty times on each hand. Never batting an eyelash: then back to facing the wall in the corner by the door. So Tsi-fai: grimy shirt, disheveled hair, defiant sneer. So Tsi-fai. Incorrigible, hopeless, and without hope.

The girls in front gasped and shrank back in their chairs. Mung Guliang went to the door, held the doorknob in one hand, poked her head out, and peered into the empty balcony. Then, with a determined jerk, she pulled the door shut. Quickly crossing herself, she returned to the teacher's desk. Her black cross swung upon the front of her gray habit as she hurried across the room. "Don't be silly!" she scolded the frightened girls in the front row.

What really happened? After all these years, my mind is still haunted by this scene. What happened to So Tsi-fai? What happened to me? What happened to all of us that year in sixth grade, when we were green and young and ready to fling our arms out for the world? All of a sudden, death claimed one of us and he was gone.

Who arbitrates between life and death? Who decides which life is worth preserving and prospering, and which to nip in its bud? How did it happen that I, at ten, turned out to be the star pupil, the lucky one, while my friend, a peasant's son, was shoveled under the heap and lost forever? How could it happen that this world would close off a young boy's life at fourteen just because he was poor, undisciplined, and lacked the training and support to pass his exams? What really happened?

Today, twenty-three years later, So Tsi-fai's ghost still haunts me. "I died a tragic death. I have as much right as you to be here. This is my seat." The voice I heard twenty-three years ago in my sixth-grade classroom follows me in my dreams. Is there anything I can do to lay it to rest?

EXPLORATIONS

1. How do you think Liu regarded So Tsi-fai before his death? How did her view change after his suicide? How can you tell? What other attitudes did Liu evidently reexamine and alter at that point?

2. Whom and what does Liu blame for So Tsi-fai's suicide? What preventive measures does her story suggest to protect other students from a similar fate?

Judging from Liu's narrative, what changes in Hong Kong's social and educational institutions do you think would help students like So Tsi-fai?

3. Liu's first three paragraphs consist almost entirely of incomplete sentences. How does she use these sentence fragments to establish her essay's central conflict? At what points does she use complete sentences? What is their effect?

CONNECTIONS

1. Both Liu's "So Tsi-fai" and Liliana Heker's "The Stolen Party" focus on young people who represent, to themselves or their families or both, ambitions higher than their present circumstances. What disadvantages do So Tsi-fai and Rosaura share? Why does Rosaura appear likely to succeed where So Tsi-fai fails?

2. "Education collapsed," writes Jack Agueros in *Looking at Ourselves*. How were Agueros's prospects at that point similar to So Tsi-fai's? How did each boy respond to his situation? What factors do you think steered them in different directions?

3. Look back at Wole Soyinka's "Nigerian Childhood" (p. 154). Both Soyinka and Liu describe encounters with ghosts. What role does each ghost play in the narrative? How are their dramatic functions different? What cultural similarities do they suggest between Nigeria and Hong Kong?

ELABORATIONS

1. What is the role of Mung Gu-liang/Sister Marie in "So Tsi-fai"? Do you think the nun would agree with Liu's assessment of what happened? How might her memory and interpretation of these events differ from Liu's? Write a narrative or argumentative version of So Tsi-fai's story from Mung Gu-liang's point of view.

2. When you were in elementary school, who were the outcasts in your class and why? If you recall one student in particular who was regarded as "different," write an essay describing him or her and narrating some of the incidents that set him or her apart. If your class consisted of two or more distinct groups, write an essay classifying these groups according to their special characteristics and their behavior toward each other. In either case, how has your attitude toward the "outcasts" changed?

AMY TAN

Two Kinds

Amy Tan's parents emigrated from China to Oakland, California, shortly before she was born in 1952. Like the mother in "Two Kinds," Tan's mother had to leave the daughters of her disastrous first marriage in China after the Red Army marched into Beijing in 1949. Tan recalls learning of her half sisters at fifteen, when her father died. "Two Kinds" comes from her book *The Joy Luck Club* (1989), which began as three short stories and grew into a novel told in the voices of four Chinese women and their California-born daughters. The central character, Jing-mei (June) Woo, bears the closest resemblance to her creator, whose mother expected her to be not only a concert pianist but a neurosurgeon. Tan, who closed down her technical writing business to write *The Joy Luck Club,* lives in San Francisco.

(For background about China, see pp. 93, 235, 583, and 656.)

My mother believed you could be anything you wanted to be in America. You could open a restaurant. You could work for the government and get good retirement. You could buy a house with almost no money down. You could become rich. You could become instantly famous.

"Of course you can be prodigy, too," my mother told me when I was nine. "You can be best anything. What does Auntie Lindo know? Her daughter, she is only best tricky."

America was where all my mother's hopes lay. She had come here in 1949 after losing everything in China: her mother and father, her family home, her first husband, and two daughters, twin baby girls. But she never looked back with regret. There were so many ways for things to get better.

We didn't immediately pick the right kind of prodigy. At first my 4 mother thought I could be a Chinese Shirley Temple. We'd watch Shirley's old movies on TV as though they were training films. My mother would poke my arm and say, *"Ni kan"* — You watch. And I would see Shirley tapping her feet, or singing a sailor song, or pursing her lips into a very round O while saying, "Oh my goodness."

"*Ni kan*," said my mother as Shirley's eyes flooded with tears. "You already know how. Don't need talent for crying!"

Soon after my mother got this idea about Shirley Temple, she took me to a beauty training school in the Mission district and put me in the hands of a student who could barely hold the scissors without shaking. Instead of getting big fat curls, I emerged with an uneven mass of crinkly black fuzz. My mother dragged me off to the bathroom and tried to wet down my hair.

"You look like Negro Chinese," she lamented, as if I had done this on purpose.

The instructor of the beauty training school had to lop off these soggy   8
clumps to make my hair even again. "Peter Pan is very popular these days," the instructor assured my mother. I now had hair the length of a boy's, with straight-across bangs that hung at a slant two inches above my eyebrows. I liked the haircut and it made me actually look forward to my future fame.

In fact, in the beginning, I was just as excited as my mother, maybe even more so. I pictured this prodigy part of me as many different images, trying each one on for size. I was a dainty ballerina girl standing by the curtains, waiting to hear the right music that would send me floating on my tiptoes. I was like the Christ child lifted out of the straw manger, crying with holy indignity. I was Cinderella stepping from her pumpkin carriage with sparkly cartoon music filling the air.

In all of my imaginings, I was filled with a sense that I would soon become *perfect*. My mother and father would adore me. I would be beyond reproach. I would never feel the need to sulk for anything.

But sometimes the prodigy in me became impatient. "If you don't hurry up and get me out of here, I'm disappearing for good," it warned. "And then you'll always be nothing."

Every night after dinner, my mother and I would sit at the Formica   12
kitchen table. She would present new tests, taking her examples from stories of amazing children she had read in *Ripley's Believe It or Not*, or *Good Housekeeping, Reader's Digest*, and a dozen other magazines she kept in a pile in our bathroom. My mother got these magazines from people whose houses she cleaned. And since she cleaned many houses

each week, we had a great assortment. She would look through them all, searching for stories about remarkable children.

The first night she brought out a story about a three-year-old boy who knew the capitals of all the states and even most of the European countries. A teacher was quoted as saying the little boy could also pronounce the names of the foreign cities correctly.

"What's the capital of Finland?" my mother asked me, looking at the magazine story.

All I knew was the capital of California, because Sacramento was the name of the street we lived on in Chinatown. "Nairobi!" I guessed, saying the most foreign word I could think of. She checked to see if that was possibly one way to pronounce "Helsinki" before showing me the answer.

The tests got harder — multiplying numbers in my head, finding the queen of hearts in a deck of cards, trying to stand on my head without using my hands, predicting the daily temperatures in Los Angeles, New York, and London.   16

One night I had to look at a page from the Bible for three minutes and then report everything I could remember. "Now Jehoshaphat had riches and honor in abundance and . . . that's all I remember, Ma," I said.

And after seeing my mother's disappointed face once again, something inside of me began to die. I hated the tests, the raised hopes and failed expectations. Before going to bed that night, I looked in the mirror above the bathroom sink and when I saw only my face staring back — and that it would always be this ordinary face — I began to cry. Such a sad, ugly girl! I made high-pitched noises like a crazed animal, trying to scratch out the face in the mirror.

And then I saw what seemed to be the prodigy side of me — because I had never seen that face before. I looked at my reflection, blinking so I could see more clearly. The girl staring back at me was angry, powerful. This girl and I were the same. I had new thoughts, willful thoughts, or rather thoughts filled with lots of won'ts. I won't let her change me, I promised myself. I won't be what I'm not.

So now on nights when my mother presented her tests, I performed listlessly, my head propped on one arm. I pretended to be bored. And I was. I got so bored I started counting the bellows of the foghorns out on the bay while my mother drilled me in other areas. The sound was comforting and reminded me of the cow jumping over the moon. And the next day, I played a game with myself, seeing if my mother would   20 give up on me before eight bellows. After a while I usually counted only one, maybe two bellows at most. At last she was beginning to give up hope.

Two or three months had gone by without any mention of my being a prodigy again. And then one day my mother was watching *The Ed Sullivan Show* on TV. The TV was old and the sound kept shorting out. Every time my mother got halfway up from the sofa to adjust the set, the sound would go back on and Ed would be talking. As soon as she sat down, Ed would go silent again. She got up, the TV broke into loud piano music. She sat down. Silence. Up and down, back and forth, quiet and loud. It was like a stiff embraceless dance between her and the TV set. Finally she stood by the set with her hand on the sound dial.

She seemed entranced by the music, a little frenzied piano piece with this mesmerizing quality, sort of quick passages and then teasing lilting ones before it returned to the quick playful parts.

"*Ni kan,*" my mother said, calling me over with hurried hand gestures. "Look here."

I could see why my mother was fascinated by the music. It was being   24
pounded out by a little Chinese girl, about nine years old, with a Peter Pan haircut. The girl had the sauciness of a Shirley Temple. She was proudly modest like a proper Chinese child. And she also did this fancy sweep of a curtsy, so that the fluffy skirt of her white dress cascaded slowly to the floor like the petals of a large carnation.

In spite of these warning signs, I wasn't worried. Our family had no piano and we couldn't afford to buy one, let alone reams of sheet music and piano lessons. So I could be generous in my comments when my mother bad-mouthed the little girl on TV.

"Play note right, but doesn't sound good! No singing sound," complained my mother.

"What are you picking on her for?" I said carelessly.

"She's pretty good. Maybe she's not the best, but she's trying hard." I knew almost immediately I would be sorry I said that.

"Just like you," she said. "Not the best. Because you not trying."   28
She gave a little huff as she let go of the sound dial and sat down on the sofa.

The little Chinese girl sat down also to play an encore of "Anitra's

Dance" by Grieg. I remember the song, because later on I had to learn how to play it.

Three days after watching *The Ed Sullivan Show,* my mother told me what my schedule would be for piano lessons and piano practice. She had talked to Mr. Chong, who lived on the first floor of our apartment building. Mr. Chong was a retired piano teacher and my mother had traded housecleaning services for weekly lessons and a piano for me to practice on every day, two hours a day, from four until six.

When my mother told me this, I felt as though I had been sent to hell. I whined and then kicked my foot a little when I couldn't stand it anymore.

"Why don't you like me the way I am? I'm *not* a genius! I can't play   32 the piano. And even if I could, I wouldn't go on TV if you paid me a million dollars!" I cried.

My mother slapped me. "Who ask you be genius?" she shouted. "Only ask you be your best. For you sake. You think I want you be genius? Hnnh! What for! Who ask you!"

"So ungrateful," I heard her mutter in Chinese. "If she had as much talent as she has temper, she would be famous now."

Mr. Chong, whom I secretly nicknamed Old Chong, was very strange, always tapping his fingers to the silent music of an invisible orchestra. He looked ancient in my eyes. He had lost most of the hair on top of his head and he wore thick glasses and had eyes that always looked tired and sleepy. But he must have been younger than I thought, since he lived with his mother and was not yet married.

I met Old Lady Chong once and that was enough. She had this   36 peculiar smell like a baby that had done something in its pants. And her fingers felt like a dead person's, like an old peach I once found in the back of the refrigerator; the skin just slid off the meat when I picked it up.

I soon found out why Old Chong had retired from teaching piano. He was deaf. "Like Beethoven!" he shouted to me. "We're both listening only in our head!" And he would start to conduct his frantic silent sonatas.

Our lessons went like this. He would open the book and point to different things, explaining their purpose: "Key! Treble! Bass! No sharps or flats! So this is C major! Listen now and play after me!"

And then he would play the C scale a few times, a simple chord, and then, as if inspired by an old, unreachable itch, he gradually added more notes and running trills and a pounding bass until the music was really something quite grand.

I would play after him, the simple scale, the simple chord, and then   40
I just played some nonsense that sounded like a cat running up and down on top of garbage cans. Old Chong smiled and applauded and then said, "Very good! But now you must learn to keep time!"

So that's how I discovered that Old Chong's eyes were too slow to keep up with the wrong notes I was playing. He went through the motions in half-time. To help me keep rhythm, he stood behind me, pushing down on my right shoulder for every beat. He balanced pennies on top of my wrists so I would keep them still as I slowly played scales and arpeggios. He had me curve my hand around an apple and keep that shape when playing chords. He marched stiffly to show me how to make each finger dance up and down, staccato like an obedient little soldier.

He taught me all these things, and that was how I also learned I could be lazy and get away with mistakes, lots of mistakes. If I hit the wrong notes because I hadn't practiced enough, I never corrected myself. I just kept playing in rhythm. And Old Chong kept conducting his own private reverie.

So maybe I never really gave myself a fair chance. I did pick up the basics pretty quickly, and I might have become a good pianist at that young age. But I was so determined not to try, not to be anybody different that I learned to play only the most ear-splitting preludes, the most discordant hymns.

Over the next year, I practiced like this, dutifully in my own way.   44
And then one day I heard my mother and her friend Lindo Jong both talking in a loud bragging tone of voice so others could hear. It was after church, and I was leaning against the brick wall wearing a dress with stiff white petticoats. Auntie Lindo's daughter, Waverly, who was about my age, was standing farther down the wall about five feet away. We had grown up together and shared all the closeness of two sisters squabbling over crayons and dolls. In other words, for the most part, we hated each other. I thought she was snotty. Waverly Jong had gained a certain amount of fame as "Chinatown's Littlest Chinese Chess Champion."

"She bring home too many trophy," lamented Auntie Lindo that Sunday. "All day she play chess. All day I have no time do nothing but dust off her winnings." She threw a scolding look at Waverly, who pretended not to see her.

"You lucky you don't have this problem," said Auntie Lindo with a sigh to my mother.

And my mother squared her shoulders and bragged: "Our problem worser than yours. If we ask Jing-mei wash dish, she hear nothing but music. It's like you can't stop this natural talent."

And right then, I was determined to put a stop to her foolish pride.   48

A few weeks later, Old Chong and my mother conspired to have me play in a talent show which would be held in the church hall. By then, my parents had saved up enough to buy me a secondhand piano, a black Wurlitzer spinet with a scarred bench. It was the showpiece of our living room.

For the talent show, I was to play a piece called "Pleading Child" from Schumann's *Scenes from Childhood*. It was a simple, moody piece that sounded more difficult than it was. I was supposed to memorize the whole thing, playing the repeat parts twice to make the piece sound longer. But I dawdled over it, playing a few bars and then cheating, looking up to see what notes followed, I never really listened to what I was playing. I daydreamed about being somewhere else, about being someone else.

The part I liked to practice best was the fancy curtsy: right foot out, touch the rose on the carpet with a pointed foot, sweep to the side, left leg bends, look up and smile.

My parents invited all the couples from the Joy Luck Club to witness   52 my debut. Auntie Lindo and Uncle Tin were there. Waverly and her two older brothers had also come. The first two rows were filled with children both younger and older than I was. The littlest ones got to go first. They recited simple nursery rhymes, squawked out tunes on miniature violins, twirled Hula Hoops, pranced in pink ballet tutus, and when they bowed or curtsied, the audience would sigh in unison, "Awww," and then clap enthusiastically.

When my turn came, I was very confident. I remember my childish excitement. It was as if I knew, without a doubt, that the prodigy side of me really did exist. I had no fear whatsoever, no nervousness. I remember thinking to myself, This is it! This is it! I looked out over the audience, at my mother's blank face, my father's yawn, Auntie Lindo's stiff-lipped smile, Waverly's sulky expression. I had on a white dress layered with sheets of lace, and a pink bow in my Peter Pan haircut. As I sat down I envisioned people jumping to their feet and Ed Sullivan rushing up to introduce me to everyone on TV.

And I started to play. It was so beautiful. I was so caught up in how lovely I looked that at first I didn't worry how I would sound: So it was a surprise to me when I hit the first wrong note and I realized something didn't sound quite right. And then I hit another and another followed that. A chill started at the top of my head and began to trickle down. Yet I couldn't stop playing, as though my hands were bewitched. I kept thinking my fingers would adjust themselves back, like a train switching to the right track. I played this strange jumble through two repeats, the sour notes staying with me all the way to the end.

When I stood up, I discovered my legs were shaking. Maybe I had just been nervous and the audience, like Old Chong, had seen me go through the right motions and had not heard anything wrong at all. I swept my right foot out, went down on my knee, looked up and smiled. The room was quiet, except for Old Chong, who was beaming and shouting, "Bravo! Bravo! Well done!" But then I saw my mother's face, her stricken face. The audience clapped weakly, and as I walked back to my chair, with my whole face quivering as I tried not to cry, I heard a little boy whisper loudly to his mother, "That was awful," and the mother whispered back, "Well, she certainly tried."

And now I realized how many people were in the audience, the whole   56
world it seemed. I was aware of eyes burning into my back. I felt the shame of my mother and father as they sat stiffly throughout the rest of the show.

We could have escaped during intermission. Pride and some strange sense of honor must have anchored my parents to their chairs. And so we watched it all: the eighteen-year-old boy with a fake mustache who did a magic show and juggled flaming hoops while riding a unicycle. The breasted girl with white makeup who sang from *Madama Butterfly* and got honorable mention. And the eleven-year-old boy who won first prize playing a tricky violin song that sounded like a busy bee.

After the show, the Hsus, the Jongs, and the St. Clairs from the Joy Luck Club came up to my mother and father.

"Lots of talented kids," Auntie Lindo said vaguely, smiling broadly.

"That was somethin' else," said my father, and I wondered if he was   60
referring to me in a humorous way, or whether he even remembered what I had done.

Waverly looked at me and shrugged her shoulders. "You aren't a genius like me," she said matter-of-factly. And if I hadn't felt so bad, I would have pulled her braids and punched her stomach.

But my mother's expression was what devastated me: a quiet, blank look that said she had lost everything. I felt the same way, and it seemed as if everybody were now coming up, like gawkers at the scene of an accident, to see what parts were actually missing. When we got on the bus to go home, my father was humming the busy-bee tune and my mother was silent. I kept thinking she wanted to wait until we got home before shouting at me. But when my father unlocked the door to our apartment, my mother walked in and then went to the back, into the bedroom. No accusations. No blame. And in a way, I felt disappointed. I had been waiting for her to start shouting, so I could shout back and cry and blame her for all my misery.

I assumed my talent-show fiasco meant I never had to play the piano again. But two days later, after school, my mother came out of the kitchen and saw me watching TV.

"Four clock," she reminded me as if it were any other day. I was   64 stunned, as though she were asking me to go through the talent-show torture again. I wedged myself more tightly in front of the TV.

"Turn off TV," she called from the kitchen five minutes later.

I didn't budge. And then I decided. I didn't have to do what my mother said anymore. I wasn't her slave. This wasn't China. I had listened to her before and look what happened. She was the stupid one.

She came out from the kitchen and stood in the arched entryway of the living room. "Four clock," she said once again, louder.

"I'm not going to play anymore," I said nonchalantly. "Why should   68 I? I'm not a genius."

She walked over and stood in front of the TV. I saw her chest was heaving up and down in an angry way.

"No!" I said, and I now felt stronger, as if my true self had finally emerged. So this was what had been inside me all along.

"No! I won't!" I screamed.

She yanked me by the arm, pulled me off the floor, snapped off the   72 TV. She was frighteningly strong, half pulling, half carrying me toward the piano as I kicked the throw rugs under my feet. She lifted me up and onto the hard bench. I was sobbing by now, looking at her bitterly. Her chest was heaving even more and her mouth was open, smiling crazily as if she were pleased I was crying.

"You want me to be someone that I'm not!" I sobbed. "I'll never be the kind of daughter you want me to be!"

"Only two kinds of daughters," she shouted in Chinese. "Those who are obedient and those who follow their own mind! Only one kind of daughter can live in this house. Obedient daughter!"

"Then I wish I wasn't your daughter. I wish you weren't my mother,"

I shouted. As I said these things I got scared. I felt like worms and toads and slimy things were crawling out of my chest, but it also felt good, as if this awful side of me had surfaced, at last.

"Too late change this," said my mother shrilly.   76

And I could sense her anger rising to its breaking point. I wanted to see it spill over. And that's when I remembered the babies she had lost in China, the ones we never talked about. "Then I wish I'd never been born!" I shouted. "I wish I were dead! Like them."

It was as if I had said the magic words. Alakazam! — and her face went blank, her mouth closed, her arms went slack, and she backed out of the room, stunned, as if she were blowing away like a small brown leaf, thin, brittle, lifeless.

It was not the only disappointment my mother felt in me. In the years that followed, I failed her so many times, each time asserting my own will, my right to fall short of expectations. I didn't get straight As. I didn't become class president. I didn't get into Stanford. I dropped out of college.

For unlike my mother, I did not believe I could be anything I wanted   80
to be. I could only be me.

And for all those years, we never talked about the disaster at the recital or my terrible accusations afterward at the piano bench. All that remained unchecked, like a betrayal that was now unspeakable. So I never found a way to ask her why she had hoped for something so large that failure was inevitable.

And even worse, I never asked her what frightened me the most: Why had she given up hope?

For after our struggle at the piano, she never mentioned my playing again. The lessons stopped. The lid to the piano was closed, shutting out the dust, my misery, and her dreams.

So she surprised me. A few years ago, she offered to give me the   84
piano, for my thirtieth birthday. I had not played in all those years. I saw the offer as a sign of forgiveness, a tremendous burden removed.

"Are you sure?" I asked shyly. "I mean, won't you and Dad miss it?"

"No, this your piano," she said firmly. "Always your piano. You only one can play."

"Well, I probably can't play anymore," I said. "It's been years."

"You pick up fast," said my mother, as if she knew this was certain.   88
"You have natural talent. You could been genius if you want to."

"No I couldn't."

"You just not trying," said my mother. And she was neither angry nor sad. She said it as if to announce a fact that could never be disproved. "Take it," she said.

But I didn't at first. It was enough that she had offered it to me. And after that, every time I saw it in my parents' living room, standing in front of the bay windows, it made me feel proud, as if it were a shiny trophy I had won back.

Last week I sent a tuner over to my parents' apartment and had the piano reconditioned, for purely sentimental reasons. My mother had died a few months before and I had been getting things in order for my father, a little bit at a time. I put the jewelry in special silk pouches. The sweaters she had knitted in yellow, pink, bright orange — all the colors I hated — I put those in moth-proof boxes. I found some old Chinese silk dresses, the kind with little slits up the sides. I rubbed the old silk against my skin, then wrapped them in tissue and decided to take them home with me.

After I had the piano tuned, I opened the lid and touched the keys. It sounded even richer than I remembered. Really, it was a very good piano. Inside the bench were the same exercise notes with handwritten scales, the same secondhand music books with their covers held together with yellow tape.

I opened up the Schumann book to the dark little piece I had played at the recital. It was on the left-hand side of the page, "Pleading Child." It looked more difficult than I remembered. I played a few bars, surprised at how easily the notes came back to me.

And for the first time, or so it seemed, I noticed the piece on the right-hand side. It was called "Perfectly Contented." I tried to play this one as well. It had a lighter melody but the same flowing rhythm and turned out to be quite easy. "Pleading Child" was shorter but slower; "Perfectly Contented" was longer but faster. And after I played them both a few times, I realized they were two halves of the same song.

EXPLORATIONS

1. What appears to be the top goal of the narrator's mother in "Two Kinds"? Which of her statements and actions show how important it is to her? What clues in the story's first three paragraphs suggest why she has fixed on this goal?

2. What is the top goal of the narrator at the beginning of "Two Kinds"? Why has she fixed on this goal? How does her goal change as the story progresses and why?

3. Why does the narrator say that "what frightened me the most" was her mother's giving up hope (para. 82)? Why do you think her mother's offering her the piano "made me feel proud, as if it were a shiny trophy I had won back" (para. 91)?

CONNECTIONS

1. What central dilemma does Jing-mei Woo, the narrator of "Two Kinds," share with Sophronia Liu's schoolmate So Tsi-fai? In what sense do both Jing-mei Woo and So Tsi-fai take the same way out?

2. "Two Kinds," Liu's "So Tsi-fai," and Liliana Heker's "The Stolen Party" show adults opposing children. What adult in each selection creates obstacles for the young main character? What strategy is tried by all three adults, and why does it fail?

3. How do Jing-mei Woo's struggles fit the pattern described by Gail Sheehy in *Looking at Ourselves*? Find evidence in "Two Kinds" for at least three of Sheehy's statements.

ELABORATIONS

1. In "Tradition and the African Writer" (p. 34), Ezekiel Mphahlele comments about parents: "They worry a great deal about the way in which we break loose at one point and ignore some elements of tradition." How is this true of the characters in "Two Kinds"? Reread Mphahlele's essay and Tan's story. Then write a cause-and-effect essay about the problems faced by families consisting of traditional parents and nontraditional children.

2. Why do you think Tan chose the ending she did for "Two Kinds"? Write an essay examining how the narrator's final actions and conclusions bring the story to an appropriate close.

MARK SALZMAN

Gong Fu

As Mark Salzman explains in the following essay, *gong fu* is not the Chinese name for what we call *kung fu;* rather, the term refers to the harmonious beauty expressed by this and other physical disciplines when expertly performed. The martial art itself is called *wushu.* Salzman started studying wushu and Chinese calligraphy and painting at thirteen. After graduating summa cum laude from Yale University in 1982 with a degree in Chinese language and literature, he went to the People's Republic of China, where he taught English for two years at Hunan Medical College in Changsha. His experiences there are described in his book *Iron and Silk* (1986), from which "Gong Fu" is taken. The success of Salzman's *shifu-tudi* (master-student) relationship with the legendary Pan Qingfu led to an invitation to return to China in 1985 to participate in the National Martial Arts Competition and Conference in Tianjin, where Salzman gave a public performance along with the first-place winners. A Connecticut native, he now lives and writes in New Haven.

Salzman visited China during a time of change, as Chairman Deng Xiaoping and other officials chiseled away at the rigid political, economic, and social systems created during Chairman Mao Zedong's regime (see p. 93). After Mao's death in 1976, backlash against the Cultural Revolution — masterminded partly by Mao's wife, Jiang Quing — swept Jiang and her three top comrades, the "Gang of Four," out of power and into prison. In contrast to his predecessors, Deng recognized the country's need for intellectuals as well as for workers, peasants, and soldiers. He took steps to open China to the outside world, countering Mao's dogmatic socialism with remarks like "Black cat, white cat — it's a good cat if it catches mice." Living and working conditions for students remained harsh by Western standards; Salzman recalls a Chinese friend yearning for the luxury of a full night's sleep and a good meal. Still, China's progress toward greater political freedom and a more market-driven economy gave it the reputation of a model for Communist reform until Deng and his allies cracked down on student-headed demonstrations in the spring of 1989 (see p. 656).

(For more background on China, see p. 583.)

Early one Saturday morning in March one of my doctor students knocked at my door. A cold, steady drizzle that had been falling since

January had convinced me to stay in bed as long as possible, but at ten past seven a terrific pounding and the voice of Dr. Nie calling my name woke me from a dream. I remember the dream clearly. A team of cadres from the Public Security Bureau had tied me by my feet to a giant ferris wheel, so that each time it completed a circle my head scraped along the ground. Once awake, I thought I might keep silent and pretend to be out, as I was in no mood to smile and answer grammar questions at that hour. Then I heard Old Sheep telling Dr. Nie that I hadn't gotten up yet, so he should just knock louder. When the pounding became unbearable I got up. I didn't bother putting clothes on over my several layers of woolen underwear, and tried to look as much like hell as I could manage, but this only seemed to amuse him. "Follow me," he said, and started down the stairs. My annoyance grew as he yelled from the front door for me to hurry. I told him that I had something to do. That was all right, he didn't mind, and he laughed — let's go! I said I was expecting a visitor any minute now, so I couldn't leave the house; he said it didn't matter, and laughed — let's go! I said I didn't feel well, maybe we could go out and play another day; he said we could do that, too, and laughed — hurry up! I put on some clothes, went downstairs, and pleaded with him to leave me alone, but he grabbed my arm and pulled me out of the house. "Do you have grammar questions this morning, Dr. Nie?" I asked. "Thank you," he answered, and led me out of the college gate.

I was in a poor mood as we wandered through the streets, splashing up coal dust mixed with rain, at seven-fifteen in the morning. I could only hope that this would be a half-day outing instead of the full-day English-speaking marathons our students loved so well. At least it was winter; if it had been warmer out, I would have been obliged to spend several hours in a rented rowboat at Martyrs' Park eating dried melon seeds and enjoying "free talk" with no hope of interruption or distraction. "Free talk" involved relentless, vigorous conversation of absolutely no import that drove me to near-madness. Floating helplessly in the middle of a dirty pond only made it worse. "Where are we going?" I asked. "A surprise," he answered, and I shuddered to imagine what it could be.

Twenty minutes later we came to the gate of the Provincial Sports Unit, a large complex for the Hunan athletes. Each province in China has such a unit, where the best athletes live and train. They receive their education there, too, but an abbreviated one. They are the closest thing to professional athletes China has, and they spend most of their time training.

I remembered that Dr. Nie specialized in athletic medicine and per- 4
formed surgery on the more serious cases that arose in this unit. He led
me to a large five-story cement building, which had a training space on
its uppermost floor, judging from the arrangement of its windows. We
climbed the filthy, unlit staircase and Dr. Nie paused in front of two
large wooden doors to savor the moment. He turned and smiled at me,
indicating that I should listen. I heard through the doors a cacophony of
cracks, whooshes, and thuds. Just as it began to dawn on me what might
be going on, he swung open the doors to reveal a dingy, cavernous room
with bare cement walls and a dull red carpet on the floor.

Ten or eleven young men and women in battered sweatsuits stood
around against the walls, watching silently as three of their colleagues
engaged in furious armed combat. Two of the men had six-foot wooden
poles, and were teamed up to defeat the third, who wielded a three-
section staff — three short poles connected by chains. Even in the movies,
with the assistance of trick photography and trampolines, I had never
seen anything to match this fight. I felt my stomach tighten, thinking
one of the fighters would surely be brained by the poles, which swung
by so fast I could barely see them. Suddenly, in perfect unison, the two
with the long poles froze in position, poised for the last attack. The other
athletes tensed, and all was quiet for a full second. Then several of them
shrieked, and the fighters seemed to go mad, rushing into their final
clash. The man with the three-section staff leapt into the air, rolled over
the back of one of his opponents, and took an overhead swing at them
both. They moved out of the way just in time and the weapon crashed
to the ground, inches from their feet, with such force that the whole
carpet shook and the air filled with dust. Without stopping, the three
spun and froze again in an attitude of readiness, held it, then doubled
over to breathe. The assistant trainer, a frail-looking woman in her
thirties, walked over to them and barked a few words of criticism on the
routine, then told them to get out of the way for the next group. The
three fighters, who looked more like panthers than humans, loped off to
one side. Immediately, two young women marched to the center of the
room. Theirs was to be an unarmed battle.

They stood about an arm's length from one another, staring straight
ahead. The trainer gave a yell and the two women turned their heads to
exchange a deadly glance before exploding into action. One of the women
was fairly tall, with long hair put up in a bun; the other was short, with
thick shoulder-length hair that hung loose around her face. The tall

woman began the attack, lashing out with a backfist. The short woman leaned back so that it just grazed her throat, spinning around and jumping into the air as she did so, so that her right leg swung in an arc that ended full-force on the chest of the tall woman. Both crashed to the ground and lay still. Then, as if they had springs underneath them, they bounced up into the air and continued to fight. What struck me most about these women was their power; they hit with enough force to knock a large man unconscious. The short woman, especially, fought like a demon. I found out later that she had doubled for the heroines in the fight scenes of several movies. But she was not to be the main attraction this morning. After the women finished up, Dr. Nie led me into the room. The men looked at me curiously. The women all giggled and shifted to the far corner of the room, taking turns looking quickly at me and then at the ground.

The assistant trainer came over to greet us. Dr. Nie introduced her as Little Liu, and me as the American Professor Mr. Sima Ming (my Chinese name). I had to go through this ritual at least once a day in China, where "distinguished Foreign Guests" must be introduced politely, meaning that their credentials are blown well out of proportion. I explained to her that I was not a professor, but an English teacher, and that since she was older than me, she should refer to me as Little Sima, but she and Dr. Nie agreed that since I had been educated in America, I should be a professor, and that since I had traveled far, my experience was great, so I should at least be Mr. Sima Ming.

Little Liu pointed to the athletes. "These are the members of the Hunan Provincial Wushu Troupe. Today you are our guest. Please feel free to ask any questions you like, and voice your criticisms to help us improve." "Where is he?" Dr. Nie asked her. "He'll come soon," she assured him, "but he didn't want to get here first. He wanted the professor to wait a while." Liu invited me to sit down on one of the long wooden benches that lined the walls of the room. "Now they'll practice their solo routines."

The solo routines of wushu are something like floor exercises in gymnastics; each routine is a prearranged series of moves, created by the master and student together, that best displays the student's versatility and special strengths, but within the aesthetic boundaries of that particular style of wushu. For example, a double-edged sword routine must not contain moves characteristic of saber. Each style has its own repertoire and personality, and mixing them is considered a sign of poor taste or careless training.

First, one of the young men who had been fighting earlier with a long pole performed the "Drunken Sword." In this style the fighter must stumble, weave, leap, and bob as if drunk, at the same time whipping his sword around him at full speed, all the while maintaining perfect control. Then a woman with a single braid reaching to her waist performed the double saber. The two blades flashed around her but never touched, and she finished by leaping into the air, crossing the sabers, and landing in a full split. One after the other, the athletes performed routines with spears, halberds, hooks, knives, and their bare hands. My stomach hurt by now just from the excitement of watching them; I'd never seen martial arts of this quality before, nor sat so close to such tremendous athletes as they worked. Just as the last man finished a routine with the nine-section steel whip, someone clapped once, and all the athletes rushed into a line and stood at perfect attention. I turned toward the wooden doors to see who had clapped and for the first time saw Pan.

I recognized him immediately as one of the evil characters in *Shaolin Temple,* and I knew from magazine articles about the movie that he had choreographed and directed the martial arts scenes. This movie, shot partly on location at the real Shaolin temple where Chinese boxing has been practiced for more than fifteen hundred years, featured China's most famous boxers and was produced and distributed by studios in Hong Kong. It became an immediate success in East Asia when it was released in 1981, and remains China's only blockbuster film to date. Not long after my arrival in Changsha, several people had mentioned to me that someone connected with this movie was in Hunan, but no one had actually seen him or could agree upon who he was. They did agree, however, that one would need a significant "back door" to gain an introduction, if he was really in Hunan at all. Pan had a massive reputation as a fighter from the days when scores were settled with blows rather than points. His nickname, "Iron Fist," was said to describe both his personality and his right hand, which he had developed by punching a fifty-pound iron plate nailed to a concrete wall one thousand to ten thousand times a day.

Pan walked over to where the athletes stood, looked them over, and 12 told them to relax. They formed a half-circle around him; some leaned on one leg or crossed their arms, but most remained at stiff attention. He gave them his morning address in a voice too low for me to hear, but it was clear from the expressions on his face that he was exhorting them to push harder, always harder, otherwise where will you get?

He stood about five foot eight, with a medium to slight build, a deep receding hairline, a broad, scarred nose, and upper front teeth so badly arranged that it looked as if he had two rows of them, so that if he bit you and wrecked the first set, the second would grow in to replace them. Most noticeable, though, were his eyebrows. They swept up toward his temples making him look permanently angry, as if he were wearing some sort of Peking Opera mask. At one point he gestured to one of the athletes with his right hand, and I saw that it was strangely disfigured. Dr. Nie, who must have known what I was thinking, leaned over and said, "That is the iron fist."

Pan looked fearsome, but what most distinguished him was that, when he talked, his face moved and changed expression. I had been in China for eight months, but thought this was the first time I had seen a Chinese person whose face moved. Sometimes his eyes opened wide with surprise, then narrowed with anger, or his mouth trembled with fear and everyone laughed, then he ground his teeth and looked ready to avenge a murder. His eyebrows, especially, were so mobile that I wondered if they had been knocked loose in one of his brawls. He commanded such presence that, for the duration of his address, no one seemed to breathe.

At last he finished. He clapped his hands once again and the athletes jumped back to their positions in the room, ready to continue their morning workout. He started to walk toward the far side of the room, where all the weapons lay on a wooden rack, then pretended to notice us for the first time. He looked surprised, spread his palms in a welcoming gesture, then said to Dr. Nie, "Why didn't you tell me we had a guest?"

Dr. Nie introduced me once again as Professor Mr. Sima Ming, this   16 time adding that I was a wushu expert and had performed several times in China with great success. "The professor practiced Chinese martial arts for nine years before coming to China and has performed not only for our college, but for the governor of Hunan as well." While this was true, it was not true that I was an expert, or that the success of my performances was due to the quality of my wushu. Anything a foreigner did in front of a Chinese audience received thunderous applause. "He is especially good at 'Drunken Fist.'" In fact, I knew very little Drunken Fist, but since all my performances occurred after huge banquets, where drinking contests with baijiu were required, my thrashing about was usually identified as "Drunken Fist." I would typically jump over a table, trip over a chair and throw it around, fall down a few times, punch an imaginary opponent, and leave to be sick. Before I could explain all this, though, Dr. Nie turned to our host and said, "And this is Master Pan Qingfu. There is no need to introduce him further."

Pan extended his hand for me to shake. It was not deformed, but simply decorated with several large calluses on his knuckles and finger joints that had turned black as if scorched. I put my hand in his, and to my great surprise and relief, he shook it gently. We sat down and he asked how it happened that I spoke Chinese and lived in China.

As we spoke the troupe continued to practice, even more furiously than before, now that Pan had arrived. Every few minutes he pointed to his stopwatch, shook his head, and asked some poor athlete if he was napping or practicing. He criticized one of the women so fiercely that it looked as if she were on the verge of tears. He made her repeat a move, a complicated leap ending in a crouched position, until she collapsed in a heap on the floor. "Who's next?" he shouted, and another athlete came forward, taking care not to step on the woman as she dragged herself off to the side. None of the athletes even twitched an eyebrow when receiving instructions or criticism. He ordered, and instantly they obeyed, without so much as a sigh, and they obeyed in this fashion until they could no longer stand.

After two hours or so morning practice came to an end. Pan reminded them to be on time for afternoon practice and seemed about to dismiss them when a smile came over his face. He pointed at me. "Please welcome our American friend." The athletes burst into applause, smiling with what energy they had left. "He has practiced wushu for nine years — don't you think he should do something for us?" The applause turned to cheers of delight. I felt all the blood drain from my face and thought I would faint if I stood up. As soon as I could speak I refused, but this only brought louder cheering. Dr. Nie, ever the friend in need, announced that I was just being modest, and that I was as strong as a lion and fast as a swooping pigeon, or something like that, and began to pull me from the bench. I looked at Pan; he was smiling at me the way a wolf might smile at a lame deer.

Then the blood rushed back into my face, and I nearly saw double 20 with anger. Humiliating unwitting foreigners is something of a popular sport in China, and it occurred to me that my little spectacle would soon be legendary. But he had me. If I accepted, I would go down in local history as the foreigner who made a fool of himself in front of Pan Qingfu and the Hunan Wushu Troupe; if I refused, I would be remembered as the foreigner who left the Hunan Sports Unit with his tail between his legs.

I stood up, and the applause died down. Pan sat down, continuing to smile. I explained that my wushu couldn't be compared to theirs and added, truthfully, that I had never imagined I would see such expertise as they possessed. I then said that for me to perform a Chinese routine would be a waste of time, since they did wushu so much better. I had come to learn. Better for me to do something they might not otherwise have a chance to see. I told them that in America, fighters have been exposed to a variety of Asian martial arts, Western boxing, and African dancing rhythms. Making it up as I went along, I explained that a distinctly American style has come out of all this, and is called "On the Street Boxing," I started clapping out a syncopated beat, began moving in a modified hustle, and let loose, trying to make up for what I lacked in gymnastic skill with unrestrained violence. At the time I was not in good condition, so after a few minutes, when I started to taste blood in my throat, I stopped. The athletes exploded into cheers, and Dr. Nie slapped Pan's shoulders in excitement, but Pan sat dead still, with the same smile on his face. I started to see black around the edges of my field of vision and no longer heard all the noise, but only saw Pan at the end of a darkening tunnel. He stood up and walked toward me, stopping when his face was very near my own. His smile had disappeared. In a very low voice he said, "That's not gong fu." We stared at each other for a long time, then he raised one eyebrow. "I could fix it, if you wanted." I must have nodded, because then he asked me if I could *chi ku*, eat bitter, the Chinese expression meaning to endure suffering. Lying, I said yes. Then he asked me if I was afraid of pain. Lying again, I said no. "You want?" he asked. "I want," I said, and became his student.

EXPLORATIONS

1. How does the long first paragraph of "Gong Fu" give meaning to Pan's final questions and Salzman's answers? How would the essay's impact change if it began at the Hunan Provincial Sports Unit?

2. How does Salzman let his readers know how important wushu is to him? Why do you think he chose to accept rather than reject Pan's invitation to perform for the Hunan Wushu Troupe? As things turn out, why was or wasn't this a wise choice?

3. What contrasts between Chinese and American customs does Salzman respect, or regard as valuable opportunities to learn, or both? What contrasts does he find annoying, and why?

CONNECTIONS

1. What similar experience functions as a turning point for Salzman in "Gong Fu" and for Jing-mei Woo in Amy Tan's "Two Kinds"? What advantages does Salzman have over Jing-mei Woo?

2. "Gong Fu" and Sophronia Liu's "So Tsi-fai" show Chinese teachers fiercely insisting on success from their students. How do the students respond? How do you think students in the United States would respond to this teaching strategy?

3. How is Pan Qingfu's role in "Gong Fu" similar to Elvis Presley's role in Nik Cohn's "Delinquent in Derry"? What character traits does each narrator share with his hero?

ELABORATIONS

1. In both Tan's "Two Kinds" and Salzman's "Gong Fu," a public performance becomes a turning point in the narrator's life. Why? Write a comparison-contrast essay examining each narrator's expectations before the performance, emotions during the performance, and actions after the performance.

2. Recall a point in your life when someone forced you to work your hardest at something you care about, or challenged you to do better at something than you thought you could. How did you feel? What did you do? What was the outcome? Write a narrative essay describing your experience.

MARIO VARGAS LLOSA

Sunday, Sunday

Novelist, playwright, and essayist Mario Vargas Llosa made headlines in the spring of 1990 by running for president of Peru. As an outsider he won a big lead, but he lost the election to someone even more removed from Peruvian politics — the agronomist Alberto Fujimori. Born in Arequipa in 1936, Vargas Llosa received his early education in Bolivia, where his grandfather was the Peruvian consul. Back home in Lima, Peru's capital, his family sent him to military school. His response was to use the school as the setting for his first novel, *La ciudad y los perros* ("The City and the Dogs," 1963; published in English as *Time of the Hero*, 1966). Vargas Llosa edited two literary journals and worked as a journalist and broadcaster. Since receiving his doctorate from the University of Madrid, he has lived in Paris, London, and Barcelona and has lectured and taught throughout the West. In addition to numerous novels, plays, and stories, Vargas Llosa is the author of *Gabriel García Márquez: Historia de un deicidio* (1972) and critical studies of the French writers Gustave Flaubert, Jean-Paul Sartre, and Albert Camus. His friendships with García Márquez (see p. 531) and other Latin American writers have suffered, however, as his political views have become more conservative. "Sunday, Sunday" (*"Día domingo,"* 1959) first appeared in *Los jefes;* the following translation from the Spanish is by Alastair Reid.

Peru, an arid coastal strip north of Chile along the Pacific Ocean, was the heart of South America's ancient Inca empire. Spaniards led by Francisco Pizarro conquered the region in 1532, reducing the Indians to serfdom. Peru regained its independence almost three hundred years later as part of the general liberation movement among Spain's South American colonies, led by rebels including Simón Bolívar and the Argentine José de San Martín, who took Lima in 1821. The present population is 45 percent Indian, 37 percent mestizo (mixed Spanish and Indian), 15 percent white, and the rest black and Asian. Over 90 percent of Peruvians are Roman Catholic; Spanish and Quechua are both official languages. After a succession of civilian and military governments, a constitutional republic was established in 1980. Democracy, however, did not solve Peru's problems. Vargas Llosa was propelled into politics by his country's corrupt and bloated bureaucracy, economic problems including a nearly 3,000 percent inflation rate, and political violence, mainly by the Maoist guerrilla group Sendero Luminosa ("Shining Path").

He held his breath an instant, dug his nails into the palms of his hands, and said quickly: "I'm in love with you." He saw her redden suddenly, as if someone had slapped her cheeks, which had a smooth and pale sheen to them. Terrified, he felt confusion rising and petrifying his tongue. He wanted to run off, be done with it; in the still winter morning, he felt the surge of that inner weakness which always overcame him at decisive moments. A few moments before, among the vivid, smiling throng in the Parque Central in Miraflores, Miguel was still saying to himself: "Now. When we get to Avenida Pardo. I'll take a chance. Ah, Rubén, if you knew how I hate you!" And even earlier, in church, looking for Flora, he spotted her at the foot of a column and, elbowing his way brusquely through the jostling women, he managed to get close to her and greet her in a low voice, repeating tersely to himself, as he had done that morning, stretched on his bed watching the first light: "Nothing else for it. I must do it today, this morning. Rubén, you'll pay for this." And the previous night he had wept for the first time in many years, realizing that the wretched trap lay in wait for him. The crowd had gone on into the park and the Avenida Pardo was left empty. They walked on along the avenue, under the rubber trees with their high, dense foliage. "I have to hurry," Miguel thought, "or else I'll be in trouble." He glanced sideways, round about him. There was nobody; he could try it. Slowly he moved his left hand until it touched hers. The sudden contact told her what was happening. He longed for a miracle to happen, to put an end to that humiliation. "Tell her, tell her," he thought. She stopped, withdrawing her hand, and he felt himself abandoned and foolish. All the glowing phrases prepared passionately the night before had blown away like soap bubbles.

"Flora," he stammered, "I've waited a long time for this moment. Since I've known you, I think only of you. I'm in love for the first time, truly. I've never known a girl like you."

Once again a total blankness in his mind, emptiness. The pressure was extreme. His skin was limp and rubbery and his nails dug into the bone. Even so, he went on speaking painfully, with long pauses, overcoming his stammer, trying to describe his rash, consuming passion, till he found with relief that they had reached the first oval on the Avenida Pardo, and he fell silent. Flora lived between the second and third tree after the oval. They stopped and looked at one another. Flora by now was quite agitated, which lent a bright sheen to her eyes. In despair, Miguel told himself that she had never looked so beautiful. A blue ribbon bound her hair, and he could see where her neck rose, and her ears, two small and perfect question marks.

"Please, Miguel." Her voice was smooth, musical, steady. "I can't   4
answer you now. Besides, my mother doesn't want me to go out with boys until I finish school."

"All mothers say that, Flora," Miguel insisted. "How will she know? We'll meet when you say so, even if it's only Sundays."

"I'll give you an answer, only I have to think first," Flora said, lowering her eyes. And after a moment, she added, "Forgive me, but I have to go. It's late."

Miguel experienced a deep weariness, a feeling which spread through his whole body, relaxing it.

"You're not angry with me, Flora?" he asked, feebly.   8
"Don't be an idiot," she answered brightly. "I'm not angry."

"I'll wait as long as you want," said Miguel. "But we'll go on seeing each other, won't we? We can go to the movies this afternoon, can't we?"

"I can't this afternoon," she said softly. "Martha's invited me to her house."

A warm flush swept violently through him and he felt himself lacer-   12
ated, stunned, at the reply he had expected, which now seemed to him torture. So it was true what Melanés had whispered fiercely in his ear on Saturday afternoon. Martha would leave them alone; it was the usual trick. Later, Rubén would tell the gang how he and his brother had planned the setup, the place, and the time. In payment, Martha had claimed the privilege of spying from behind the curtain. His hands were suddenly wet with anger.

"Don't Flora. We'll go to the matinee as usual. I won't speak about this. I promise."

"No, I really can't," said Flora. "I've got to go to Martha's. She came to my house yesterday to invite me. But afterwards I'll go with her to the Parque Salazar."

Not even in those final words did he feel any hope. A moment later, he was brooding on the spot where the slight blue figure had disappeared, under the majestic arch of the rubber trees of the avenue. It was possible to take on a simple adversary, but not Rubén. He remembered the names of the girls invited by Martha, one Sunday afternoon. He could do nothing now; he was beaten. Once more there arose that fantasy which always saved him in moments of frustration: against a distant background of clouds swollen with black smoke, at the head of a company of cadets from the Naval Academy, he approached a saluting base set up in the park; distinguished people in formal dress, top hats in hand, and ladies with glittering jewels, all applauded him. Thick on the sidewalks, a crowd in which the faces of his friends and enemies stood out, watched him in awe, murmuring his name. Dressed in blue, a broad cape flowing from his shoulders, Miguel marched at the head, gazing off to the horizon. He raised his sword; his head described a half circle in the air. There, in the center of the stand, was Flora, smiling. In one corner, ragged and ashamed, he noticed Rubén. He confined himself to a brief, contemptuous glance. He went on marching; he disappeared amid cheers.

Like steam wiped off a mirror, the image disappeared. He was in the   16
doorway of his house, hating the whole world, hating himself. He entered and went straight up to his room. He threw himself face down on the bed. In the half-dark under his eyelids appeared the girl's face. "I love you, Flora," he said out loud — and then came the face of Rubén, with his insolent jaw and his mocking smile. The faces were side by side, coming closer. Rubén's eyes turned to mock him while his mouth approached Flora.

He jumped up from his bed. The wardrobe mirror gave him back a face both ravaged and livid. I won't allow it, he decided. He can't do that, I won't let him pull that on me.

The Avenida Pardo was still empty. Increasing his pace, he walked on till it crossed Avenida Grau; there he hesitated. He felt the cold — he had left his jacket in his room and his shirt alone was not enough to protect him from the wind which came from the sea and which combed the dense foliage of the rubber trees in a steady swish. The dreaded image of Flora and Rubén together gave him courage and he went on walking. From the door of the bar beside the Montecarlo cinema, he saw them at their usual table, occupying the corner formed by the far and left-hand walls. Francisco, Melanés, Tobías, the Scholar, they noticed him and, after a second's surprise, they turned toward Rubén, their faces wicked and excited. He recovered himself at once — in front of men he certainly knew how to behave.

"Hello," he said, approaching. "What's new?"

"Sit." The Scholar drew up a chair. "What miracle brings you here?"   20

"It's a century since you've been this way," said Francisco.

"I was keen to see you," Miguel said warmly. "I knew you'd be here. What are you so surprised about? Or am I no longer a Buzzard?" He took a seat between Melanés and Tobías. Rubén was opposite him.

"Cuncho!" called the Scholar. "Bring another glass. Not too dirty a one." When he brought the glass and the Scholar filled it with beer, Miguel toasted "To the Buzzards!" and drank it down.

"You'd have the glass as well!" said Francisco. "What a thirst!"   24

"I bet you went to one o'clock Mass," said Melanés, winking one eye in satisfaction, as he always did when he was up to something. "Right?"

"Yes, I went," said Miguel, unperturbed. "But only to see a chick, nothing more."

He looked at Rubén with a challenge in his eyes, but Rubén paid no attention. He was drumming on the table with his fingers and, the point of his tongue between his teeth, he whistled softly "La Niña Popoff."

"Great," Melanés applauded. "Great, Don Juan. Tell us, which chick?"   28

"That's a secret."

"Among the Buzzards, there are no secrets," Tobías reminded him. "Have you forgotten? Come on, who was it?"

"What's it to you?" said Miguel.

"A lot," said Tobías. "I have to know who you go with to know who   32
you are."

"There you are!" said Melanés to Miguel. "One to zero."

"I'll bet I can guess who it is," said Francisco. "Can't you?"

"I know," said Tobías.

"Me too," said Melanés. He turned to Rubén, his eyes and voice all   36
innocence. "And you, brother, can you guess? Who is it?"

"No," said Rubén coldly. "And I couldn't care less."

"My stomach's on fire," said the Scholar. "Is nobody going to order a beer?"

Melanés drew a pathetic finger across his throat. "I have not money, darling," he said in English.

"I'll buy a bottle," Tobías announced with a grand gesture. "Who'll   40
follow me? We have to quench this moron's fire."

"Cuncho, bring a half dozen Cristals," said Miguel. Cries of enthusiasm, exclamations.

"You're a real Buzzard," Francisco affirmed.

"Crazy, crazy," added Melanés. "Yes sir, a Top Buzzard."

Cuncho brought the beers. They drank. They listened to Melanés tell   44
dirty stories, crude, exaggerated, and lushed-up, and a bitter argument on football broke out between Tobías and Francisco. The Scholar told a story. He was coming from Lima to Miraflores on a bus. The other passengers got off at the Avenida Arequipa. At the top of Javier Prado, Tomasso got on, the one they call the White Whale, that giant albino

who's still in the first grade, lives in Quebrada, get it? — pretending to be interested in the bus, he began to ask the driver questions, leaning over the seat from behind, at the same time slicing the cloth of the seat back systematically with a knife.

"He did it because I was there," the Scholar said. "He wanted to show off."

"He's a mental degenerate," said Francisco. "You do things like that when you're ten. At his age it isn't funny."

"The funny thing is what happened next," laughed the Scholar. "'Listen, driver, don't you know that that monster is destroying your bus?'"

"What's that?" said the driver, braking suddenly. Ears flaming, eyes   48
wide with fright, Tomasso the Whale forced his way out the door.

"With his knife," the Scholar said. "Imagine the state he left the seat in."

The Whale finally managed to get out of the bus. He set off at a run down the Avenida Arequipa. The driver ran after him shouting: "Grab that creep!"

"He got him?" Melanés asked.

"I don't know. I got out. And I took the ignition key as a souvenir.   52
Here it is."

He took a little silver key from his pocket and placed it on the table. The bottles were empty. Rubén looked at his watch and stood up.

"I'm off," he said. "See you."

"Don't go," said Miguel. "Today I'm rich. I invite you all to eat."

A shower of hands clapped him on the back; the Buzzards thanked   56
him noisily, cheered him.

"I can't," said Rubén. "I have things to do."

"All right then, go, my boy," Tobías said. "Say hello to Martha for me."

"We'll be thinking about you, brother," said Melanés.

"No," Miguel shot out. "I'm inviting everybody or nobody. If Rubén   60
goes, it's off."

"You hear him Buzzard Rubén?" said Francisco. "You've got to stay."

"You've got to stay," said Melanés, "no question."

"I'm going," said Rubén.

"The thing is that you're drunk," said Miguel. "You're going because   64
you're afraid of screwing up in front of us, that's all."

"How many times have I taken you home nearly passed out?" said Rubén. "How many times have I helped you up the railing so your father wouldn't catch you? I can hold ten times more than you."

"You could," said Miguel. "Now it'd be difficult. Want to try?"

"With pleasure," said Rubén. "We'll meet tonight, here?"

"No. Right now." Miguel turned to the others, arms open. "Buzzards, 68 I'm making a challenge."

Fortunately, the old formula still worked. In the midst of the noisy excitement he had provoked, he saw Rubén sit down, pale.

"Cuncho!" shouted Tobías. "The menu. And two baths of beer. A Buzzard has just made a challenge."

They ordered steaks *a la chorrillana* and a dozen beers. Tobías put three bottles in front of each of the competitors. The others had the rest. They ate, scarcely speaking. Miguel drank after each mouthful and tried to show some zest, but the fear of not being able to hold the beer grew in proportion to the acid taste in his throat. They finished the six bottles just after Cuncho had taken the plates away.

"You order," said Miguel to Rubén.   72

"Three more each."

After the first glass of the new round, Miguel felt a buzzing in his ears. His head was spinning slowly; everything was moving.

"I need to piss," he said. "I'm going to the john." The Buzzards laughed.

"Give up?" asked Rubén.   76

"I'm going to piss," shouted Miguel. "Have them bring more if you want."

In the lavatory, he vomited. Then he washed his face thoroughly, trying to remove every revealing sign. His watch said half past four. In spite of the overwhelming sick feeling, he felt happy. Rubén could do nothing. He went back to the others.

"*Salud!*" said Rubén, raising his glass.

He's furious, Miguel thought. But I've stopped him now.   80

"There's corpse smell," said Melanés. "Someone here's dying on us."

"I'm like new," affirmed Miguel, trying to overcome both his disgust and his sickness.

"*Salud!*" repeated Rubén.

When they had finished the last beer, his stomach felt leaden; the 84 voices of the others reached him as a confused mixture of sounds. A hand appeared suddenly under his eyes, white and large-fingered, took him by the chin, and forced him to raise his head. Rubén's face had grown. He was comical, all tousled and angry.

"Give up, kid?"

Miguel pulled himself together suddenly and pushed Rubén, but before the gesture could be followed up, the Scholar intervened.

"Buzzards never fight," he said, making them sit down. "They're both drunk. It's all over. Vote."

Melanés, Francisco, and Tobías agreed, grumblingly, to declare a   88 draw.

"I already had it won," said Rubén. "This one's incapable. Look at him."

Indeed, Miguel's eyes were glassy, his mouth hung open, and a thread of saliva ran from his tongue.

"Shut up," said the Scholar. "You are no champion, as we say, at beer-swilling."

"You're not beer-drinking champion," added Melanés. "You're only   92 the swimming champion, the scourge of the swimming pools."

"Better keep quiet," said Rubén. "Can't you see you're eaten up with envy?"

"Long live the Esther Williams of Miraflores," said Melanés.

"Over the hill already and you hardly know how to swim," said Rubén. "Don't you want me to give you lessons?"

"Now we know it all, champ," said the Scholar. "You've won a   96 swimming championship. And all the chicks are dying over you. The little champ."

"Champion of nothing," said Miguel with difficulty. "He's a phony."

"You're about to pass out," said Rubén. "Will I take you home, girl?"

"I'm not drunk," Miguel insisted. "And you're a phony."

"You're pissed off because I'm going to see Flora," said Rubén. "You're   100 dying of jealousy. Do you think I don't catch on to things?"

"Phony," said Miguel. "You won because your father is Federation President. Everybody knows that he pulled a fast one, just so you would win."

"And you most of all," said Rubén, "you can't even surf."

"You swim no better than anyone else," said Miguel. "Anybody could leave you silly."

"Anybody," said Melanés. "Even Miguel, who is a creep."   104

"Permit me to smile," said Rubén.

"We permit you," said Tobías. "That's all we need."

"You're getting at me because it's winter," said Rubén. "If it weren't, I'd challenge you all to go to the beach to see if you'd be so cocky in the water."

"You won the championship because of your father," said Miguel. 108 "You're a phony. When you want to take me on swimming, just let me know, that's all. On the beach, in Terrazas, where you like."

"On the beach," said Rubén. "Right now."

"You're a phony," said Miguel.

"If you win," said Rubén, "I promise I won't see Flora. And if I win, you can go sing somewhere else."

"Who do you think you are?" stammered Miguel. "Bastard, just who 112 do you think you are?"

"Buzzards," said Rubén, spreading his arms, "I'm offering a challenge."

"Miguel's not in shape now," said the Scholar. "Why don't you just toss for Flora?"

"You keep out of it," said Miguel. "I accept. Let's go to the beach."

"They're crazy," said Francisco. "I'm not going to the beach in this 116 cold. Make a different bet."

"He's accepted," said Rubén. "Let's go."

"When a Buzzard makes a challenge, everyone holds his tongue," said Melanés. "Let's go to the beach. And if they're scared to go in, we'll throw them in ourselves."

"They're both drunk," the Scholar insisted. "The challenge doesn't stand."

"Shut up, Scholar," roared Miguel. "I'm a big boy. I don't need you 120 to look after me."

"All right," said the Scholar, shrugging his shoulders. "Suit yourself, then."

They went out. Outside, a quiet grayness hung in wait for them. Miguel took deep breaths; he felt better. Francisco, Melanés, and Rubén walked ahead, Miguel and the Scholar behind. There were a few idlers on the Avenida Grau, mostly maids dressed up, out on their free day. Gray-looking men, with long lank hair, followed them and watched them greedily. They laughed, showing gold teeth. The Buzzards paid no attention. They walked with long strides, excitement slowly growing in them.

"Feeling better?" said the Scholar.

"Yes," replied Miguel. "The fresh air's done me good." 124

At the corner of Avenida Pardo, they turned. They walked, deployed like a squadron, in the same line, under the rubber trees of the walk, over the flagstones bulged from time to time by huge tree roots which occasionally broke through the surface like great hooks. Going down Diagonal, they passed two girls. Rubén bowed to them, very formally.

"Hello, Rubén," they sang out together.

Tobías imitated them, fluting his voice.

"Hello, Prince Rubén."   128

The Avenida Diagonal gave out on a short bend which forked; in one direction wound the Malecón, paved and shining; in the other, there was an incline which followed the downward slope and reached the sea. It is called the "bathers' descent" and its surface is smooth and shines from the polish of car tires and the feet of bathers from many summers.

"Let's give off some heat, champs," shouted Melanés, breaking into a run. The others followed him.

They ran against the wind and the thin fog which came up from the beach, caught up in a whirlwind of feeling. Through ears, mouth, and nostrils, the air came in, into their lungs, and a feeling of re- lief and clearheadedness spread through their bodies as the slope steepened and suddenly their feet obeyed only a mysterious force which seemed to come from deep in the earth. Arms whirling like propellers, a salty tang on their tongues, the Buzzards ran down in full cry to the circular platform over the bathing huts. The sea disappeared some fifty meters from the shore, in a thick cloud which seemed ready to charge against the cliffs, the high dark bulk of which spread all along the bay.

"Let's go back," said Francisco. "I'm frozen."   132

At the edge of the platform there was a banister stained here and there with moss. An opening in it indicated the head of the almost vertical ladder which led down to the bench. The Buzzards looked down from there at a short strip of clear water, its surface unbroken, frothing where the fog seemed to join with the foam from the waves.

"I'll leave if this one gives up," said Rubén.

"Who's talking about giving up?" retorted Miguel. "Who do you think you are?"

Rubén went down the ladder three rungs at a time, unbuttoning his 136 shirt as he did so.

"Rubén!" shouted the Scholar. "Are you crazy? Come back!"

But Miguel and the others also went down, and the Scholar followed them.

From the terrace of the long, wide building backed against the cliff, which contains the changing rooms, down to the curving edge of the sea, there is a stretch of smooth stones where, in summer, people took the sun. The small beach hummed with life then, from early morning until twilight. Now the water was well up the slope, there were no brightly colored umbrellas, no elastic girls with bronzed bodies, no melodramatic screams of children and women when a wave succeeded in splashing them before receding backward over the groaning stones and pebbles, there was not a strip of beach to be seen under the flooding current which went up as far as the dark narrow space under the columns which held up the building; and in the surge of the tide, it was difficult to make out the wooden ladders and the cement supports, hung with stalactites and seaweed.

"You can't see the surf," said Rubén. "How will we do it?"   140

They were in the left-hand gallery, the women's section; their faces were serious.

"Wait until tomorrow," said the Scholar. "At noon it will be clear. Then you can judge it."

"Now that we've come all the way, let it be now," said Melanés. "They can judge it themselves."

"All right by me," said Rubén. "You?"   144

"Fine," said Miguel.

When they had undressed, Tobías joked about the veins which spread across Miguel's smooth stomach. They went down. The wood of the steps, steadily worn for months by the water, was slippery and very smooth. Holding the iron rail so as not to fall, Miguel felt a shiver run from the soles of his feet to his brain. He figured that, in some ways, the mist and the cold were in his favor, that success would depend not so much on skill as on endurance, and Rubén's skin was already purple, risen all over in gooseflesh. One rung lower, Rubén's neat body bent forward. Tensed, he waited for the ebb and the arrival of the next wave, which came evenly, lightly, leading with a flying crest of foam. When the top of the wave was two meters from the ladder, Rubén leaped. His arms stretched like arrows, his hair streaming with the dive, his body cut the air cleanly, and fell without bending, his head not dropping, his knees straight, he entered the foam, hardly going down at all, and immediately, making use of the tide, he glided forward; his arms appeared and disappeared in a frenzy of bubbles, and his feet were leaving behind a steady, flying wake. Miguel in turn climbed down one rung and waited for the next wave. He knew that the bottom there was shallow, that he would have to dive like a board, hard and rigid, without moving, or he would scrape the stones. He closed his eyes and dived; he did not touch bottom but his body was lacerated from forehead to knees, and he stung all over as he swam with all his strength to bring back to his limbs the warmth which the water had suddenly drained away. In that stretch of sea beside the Miraflores beach, the waves and undertow meet, there are whirlpools and conflicting currents, and last summer was so far away that Miguel had forgotten how to ride the water without using force. He did not remember that you had to go limp, let go, let yourself be carried with the ebb, submitting, swimming only when a wave gets up and you are on the crest, on that shelf of water where the foam is, which runs on top of the water. He forgot that it is better to suffer with patience and a certain resistance that first contact with the sea ebbing from the beach, which tumbles the limbs and makes water stream from eyes and mouth, not to resist, to be a cork, to gulp air, nothing more, every time a wave comes in without force, or through the bottom of the wave if the breaking crest is close — to cling to a rock and wait out patiently the deafening thunder of its passing, to push out sharply and keep forging ahead, furtively, with the arms, until the next obstacle, and then to go limp, not struggling against the undertow but moving slowly and deliberately in a widening spiral and suddenly escaping, at the right moment, in a single burst. Farther out, the surface is unexpectedly calm, the movement of surf small; the water is clear and level, and at some points you can make out dark, underwater rocks.

After fighting his way through the rough water, Miguel stopped, exhausted, and gulped air. He saw Rubén not far away, looking at him. His hair fell in curls on his forehead; his teeth were bared.

"Let's go."

"Okay."

148

After swimming a few moments, Miguel felt the cold, which had momentarily gone, surge back, and he stepped up his kick, for it was in the legs, above all in the calves, where the water had most effect, numbing them first and then stiffening them. He was swimming with his face in the water, and every time his right arm came out of the water, he turned his head to get rid of his held breath and to breathe again, immediately dipping his forehead and chin, lightly, so as not to check his forward motion, and to make instead a prow which parted the water, the easier to slip through. At each stroke he would see Rubén with one eye, swimming smoothly on the surface, not exerting himself, scarcely raising a wash, with the ease and delicacy of a gliding gull. Miguel tried to forget

Rubén and the sea and the surf (which must still have been some distance away, for the water was clear, calm, and crossed only by small, spontaneous waves). He wanted to keep in mind only Flora's face, the down on her arms which on sunny days gleamed like a small forest of gold thread, but he could not prevent the girl's face from being succeeded by another image, shrouded, dominant, thunderous, which tumbled over Flora and hid her, the image of a mountain of tormented water, not exactly the surf (they had once reached the surf, two summers ago, with its thundering waves and greenish-black foam, for out there, more or less, the rocks ended and gave way to mud, which the waves brought to the surface and stirred up with clumps of seaweed, staining the water), instead a sea on its own wracked by internal storms, in which rose up enormous waves which could have lifted up a whole ship and upset it quickly and easily, scattering passengers, lifeboats, masts, sails, buoys, sailors, bull's-eyes, and flags.

He stopped swimming, his body sinking until it was vertical. He raised his head and saw Rubén drawing away. He thought of calling to him on some pretext, of shouting for example, "Why don't we rest a moment?" but he refrained. All the cold in his body seemed to be concentrated in his calves; he felt the muscles growing numb, the skin tightening, his heartbeat accelerating. He moved his legs weakly. He was in the center of a circle of dark water, enclosed by the fog. He tried to make out the beach, or at least the shadow of the cliffs, but the fog which appeared to dissolve as he penetrated it was deceptive, and not in the least transparent. He saw only a short stretch of sea surface, blackish, green, and the shrouding clouds, flush with the water. At that point he felt fear. The memory of the beer he had drunk came back and he thought "That could have weakened me, I suppose." Suddenly it seemed that his arms and legs had disappeared. He decided to go back, but after a few strokes in the direction of the beach, he turned and swam as easily as he could. "I won't make the beach alone," he thought: "Better to be close to Rubén. If I poop out I'll tell him he's won but we'll get back." Now he was swimming carelessly, his head up, swallowing water, stiff-armed, his eyes fixed on the imperturbable shape ahead of him.

The activity and the energy relaxed his legs, and his body recovered 152 some warmth. The distance between him and Rubén had lessened and that calmed him. Shortly after, he caught him up; flinging out an arm, he touched one of Rubén's feet. Immediately the other stopped. Rubén's eyes were very red, his mouth open.

"I think we've gone off course," said Miguel. "We seem to be swimming sideways on to the beach."

His teeth were chattering, but his voice was firm. Rubén looked all around him. Miguel watched him, tense.

"You can't see the beach any more," said Rubén.

"Not for some time," said Miguel. "There's a lot of fog."

"We haven't gone off," said Rubén. "Look. There's the surf."

Actually, some waves were reaching them with a fringe of foam which dissolved and suddenly formed again. They looked at them in silence.

"Then we're close to the surf," Miguel said, finally.

"Sure. We've been swimming fast."

"I've never seen so much fog."

"Are you very tired?" asked Rubén.

"Me? You're crazy. Let's go."

He immediately regretted that reply, but it was now too late. Rubén had already said, "Okay, let's go."

He had counted twenty strokes before he decided that he could not go on. He was hardly moving forward; his right leg was semiparalyzed by cold, his arms felt limp and heavy. Panting, he called out, "Rubén!" The other one kept on swimming. "Rubén, Rubén!" He turned and began to swim toward the beach, or to splash, rather, in desperation; and suddenly he was praying to God to save him, he would be good in the future, he would obey his parents, he would not miss Sunday mass, and then he remembered having confessed to the Buzzards, "I go to church only to see a chick," and he was struck by the certainty that God was going to punish him by drowning him in those troubled waters which he was desperately battling, waters beneath which a terrible death was awaiting him and, beyond that, possibly Hell itself. Into his distress there suddenly swam up a phrase used occasionally by Father Alberto in his religion class, that divine mercy knows no limits, and while he flailed at the water with his arms — his legs were hanging down like lead weights — moving his lips, he prayed to God to be good to him, he was so young, and he swore that he would become a priest if saved, but a second later he corrected that quickly and promised that instead of becoming a priest he would offer up sacrifices and other things and dispense charity, and then he realized that hesitation and bargaining at so desperate a time could prove fatal, and suddenly he heard, quite close, wild shouts coming from Rubén, and, turning his head, he saw him, some ten meters away, his face half submerged, waving an arm, pleading:

"Miguel, friend Miguel, come, I'm drowning. Don't go!"

He remained rigid a moment, puzzled, and then it was as if Rubén's desperation stifled his own, for he felt his courage and strength return, and the tightness in his legs relax.

"I have a stomach cramp," Rubén hissed out. "I can't go on, Miguel. 168 Save me, whatever you do, don't leave me, pal."

He floated toward Rubén and was about to go to him when he remembered that drowning men always manage to hang on like leeches to their rescuers, drowning them with them, and he kept his distance, but the cries frightened him and he realized that if Rubén drowned, he would not reach the beach either, and he went back. Two meters from Rubén, a white shriveled mass which sank and then rose, he shouted: "Don't move, Rubén. I'm going to pull you by the head, but don't try to hang on to me. If you hang on we'll both drown. Rubén, you're going to keep still, pal. I'm going to pull you by the head but don't touch me." He kept a safe distance, stretching out a hand until he grasped Rubén's hair. He began to swim with his free arm, doing all he could to help himself along with his legs. Progress was slow and painful. He concentrated all his efforts and scarcely heard Rubén's steady groaning, or the sudden terrible cries of "I'm going to die; save me, Miguel!" or the retching that convulsed him. He was exhausted when he stopped. He supported Rubén with one hand, making a circular sweep on the surface with the other. He breathed deeply through his mouth. Rubén's face was twisted in pain, his lips drawn back in a strange grimace.

"Friend Rubén," gasped Miguel, "there's not far to go. Have a shot at it. Answer me, Rubén. Shout. Don't stay like that."

He slapped him sharply, and Rubén opened his eyes; he moved his head weakly.

"Shout, pal," Miguel repeated. "Try to move yourself. I'm going to 172 massage your stomach. It's not far now. Don't give up."

His hands went underwater and found the tightness of Rubén's stomach muscles, spreading over his belly. He rubbed them several times, slowly at first, and then strongly, and Rubén shouted, "I don't want to die, Miguel; save me!"

He began to swim again, this time pulling Rubén by his chin. Each time a wave caught up with them, Rubén choked, and Miguel shouted at him to spit out. And he kept swimming, not resting a moment, closing his eyes at times, in good spirits because a kind of confidence had sprung up in his heart, a warm, proud, stimulating feeling which protected him against the cold and fatigue. A stone scraped one of his feet, and he shouted aloud, and hurried. A moment later he was able to stand up, and he reached out his arms to support Rubén. Holding him against himself, feeling his head leaning on one of his shoulders, he rested a long time. Then he helped Rubén to move and loosen his shoulders, and supporting him on his forearms, he made him move his knees. He massaged his stomach until the tightness began to yield. Rubén had stopped shouting and was doing all he could to get moving again, massaging himself with his own hands.

"Better?"

"Yes, pal. I'm fine. Let's go."   176

An inexpressible joy filled them as they made their way over the stones, leaning forward against the undertow, oblivious of sea urchins. Soon they caught sight of the groins of the cliffs, the bathing house, and finally, close to the water's edge by now, the Buzzards, standing in the women's gallery, looking out.

"Listen," Rubén said.

"Yes."

"Don't say anything to them. Please don't tell them I was crying for 180 help. We've always been good friends, Miguel. Don't do that to me."

"Think I'm a creep?" said Miguel. "I won't say a thing, don't worry."

They came out shivering. They sat down on the foot of the ladder, with the Buzzards buzzing around them.

"We were ready to send out condolences to your families," said Tobías.

"You've been in over an hour," said the Scholar. "Tell us, how did it 184 come out?"

Speaking steadily, drying his body with his shirt, Rubén explained: "Nothing at all. We got to the surf and then we came back. That's how the Buzzards do things. Miguel beat me. By nothing more than a hand's reach. If it had been in a pool, of course, I'd have made him look silly."

A rain of congratulatory handclaps fell on the shoulders of Miguel, who had dressed without drying himself.

"Why, you're becoming a man," Melanés said to him.

Miguel did not reply. Smiling, he thought that that very evening he 188 would go to the Parque Salazar. All Miraflores would know, thanks to Melanés's ready mouth, of the heroic trials he had come through and Flora would be waiting for him with shining eyes. Before him was opening a golden future.

EXPLORATIONS

1. In the first paragraph of "Sunday, Sunday," why does Miguel think, "Ah, Rubén, if you knew how I hate you!" and "Rubén, you'll pay for this"? What has apparently been the relationship between Miguel and Flora up until now? between Miguel and Rubén?

2. When Miguel and Rubén stagger onto the shore, why are they filled with "an inexpressible joy" (para. 177)? What has Miguel learned from his swimming contest with Rubén?

3. What are Flora's dramatic functions in "Sunday, Sunday"? What information does Vargas Llosa give us about the kind of person she is? What seem to be Miguel's and Rubén's reasons for vying for her? How much control does Flora have over her role in this drama?

CONNECTIONS

1. How does rivalry bring out immaturity in Miguel in "Sunday, Sunday"? How does it propel him toward maturity? What scenes and statements in "Gong Fu" show rivalry having a similar dual effect on Mark Salzman?

2. In *Looking at Ourselves*, the Los Angeles gang member "Racketeer" reports asking himself after killing somebody: "Why did I do that? I should not have even done that, that wasn't even called for." How does Rubén's membership in the Buzzards push him to do something he later regrets? What personal priorities do you think are behind Rubén's and Racketeer's willingness to risk their own and their friends' lives?

3. "Whatever tentative memberships we try out in the world, the fear haunts us that we are really kids who cannot take care of ourselves," writes Gail Sheehy in *Looking at Ourselves*. What statements and acts in "Sunday, Sunday" are examples of Sheehy's observations?

ELABORATIONS

1. In "Sunday, Sunday," Miguel's feelings about Flora strongly affect his feelings about Rubén, and vice versa. What do you think are the likely advantages and disadvantages of this two-way influence? Write an essay comparing and contrasting the importance of opposite-sex relationships and same-sex relationships to someone moving, like Miguel, from youth into adulthood.

2. Look closely at Vargas Llosa's long description of the swimming match between Miguel and Rubén. What passages could apply to either or both of the relationships in which Miguel is floundering? Write an essay examining the parallels between the literal sea and the sea of human drama in this story.

VED MEHTA

Pom's Engagement

Completely blind since the age of three, Ved Mehta is the author of more than a dozen books of autobiography, Indian social and political history, and interviews with international historians, philosophers, and theologians. His screenplay *Chachaji, My Poor Relation* airs periodically on public television. Mehta's family was instrumental in his success: He was sent away (briefly) to a school in Bombay when he was five and to the Arkansas State School for the Blind at age fifteen. He went on to graduate Phi Beta Kappa from Pomona College in California, received a master's degree from Harvard University, won a scholarship at Balliol College of Oxford University, and now works as a staff writer for *The New Yorker* magazine. "Pom's Engagement" comes from his 1984 autobiography *The Ledge between the Streams.*

Born in 1934, Mehta grew up in the Punjab, a large plain formed by five rivers in northwestern India and northeastern Pakistan. Here the earliest Indian civilization flourished thousands of years ago. Mussoorie is a hill station — a former British summer resort — to the east; a journey to Dehra Dun, a city in the same region, would have meant an over-500-mile round trip from the Mehta home in Lahore.

The Indian caste system is an ancient hereditary class structure that operated to preserve the status quo. The four principal castes are the Brahman (priests and scholars), the Kshatriya (warriors and rulers), the Vaisya or Bania (farmers and merchants), and the Sudra (peasants and laborers). Below all these were the now illegal caste of Untouchables or Panchamas, who performed the most menial tasks.

(For more background on India, see p. 146.)

Before we moved to Lahore, Daddyji had gone to Mussoorie, a hill station in the United Provinces, without telling us why he was going out of the Punjab. Now, several months after he made that trip, he gathered us around him in the drawing room at 11 Temple Road while Mamaji mysteriously hurried Sister Pom upstairs. He started talking as if we were all very small and he were conducting one of our "dinner-table-school" discussions. He said that by right and tradition the oldest daughter had to be given in marriage first, and that the ripe age for marriage was nineteen. He said that when a girl approached that age her parents, who had to take the initiative, made many inquiries and followed many leads. They investigated each young man and his family background, his relatives, his friends, his classmates, because it was important to know what kind of family the girl would be marrying into, what kind of company she would be expected to keep. If the girl's parents decided that a particular young man was suitable, then his people also had to make their investigations, but, however favorable their findings, their decision was unpredictable, because good, well-settled boys were in great demand and could afford to be choosy. All this took a lot of time. "That's why I said nothing to you children about why I went to Mussoorie," he concluded. "I went to see a young man for Pom. She's already nineteen."

We were stunned. We have never really faced the idea that Sister Pom might get married and suddenly leave, I thought.

"We won't lose Pom, we'll get a new family member," Daddyji said, as if reading my thoughts.

Then all of us started talking at once. We wanted to know if Sister   4
Pom had been told; if she'd agreed; whom she'd be marrying.

"Your mother has just taken Pom up to tell her," Daddyji said. "But she's a good girl. She will agree." He added, "The young man in question is twenty-eight years old. He's a dentist, and so has a profession."

"Did you get a dentist because Sister Pom has bad teeth?" Usha asked. Sister Pom had always been held up to us as an example of someone who, as a child, had spurned greens and had therefore grown up with a mouthful of poor teeth.

Daddyji laughed. "I confess I didn't think of anyone's teeth when I chose the young man in question."

"What is he like?" I asked. "What are we to call him?"   8

"He's a little bit on the short side, but he has a happy-go-lucky nature, like Nimi's. He doesn't drink, but, unfortunately, he does smoke. His father died at an early age of a heart attack, but he has a nice mother, who will not give Pom any trouble. It seems that everyone calls him Kakaji."

We all laughed. Kakaji, or "youngster," was what very small boys were called.

"That's what he must have been called when he was small, and the name stuck," Daddyji said.

In spite of myself, I pictured a boy smaller than I was and imagined   12
him taking Sister Pom away, and then I imagined her having to keep his

pocket money, to arrange his clothes in the cupboards, to comb his hair. My mouth felt dry.

"What will Kakaji call Sister Pom?" I asked.

"Pom, silly — what else?" Sister Umi said.

Mamaji and Sister Pom walked into the room. Daddyji made a place for Sister Pom next to him and said, "Now, now, now, no reason to cry. Is it to be yes?"

"Whatever you say," Sister Pom said in a small voice, between sobs.   16

"Pom, how can you say that? You've never seen him," Sister Umi said.

"Kakaji's uncle, Dr. Prakash Mehrotra, himself a dentist, has known our family from his student days in Lahore," Daddyji said. "As a student dentist, he used to be welcomed in Babuji's Shahalmi Gate house. He would come and go as he pleased. He has known for a long time what kind of people we are. He remembered seeing you, Pom, when we went to Mussoorie on holiday. He said yes immediately, and his approval seemed to be enough for Kakaji."

"You promised me you wouldn't cry again," Mamaji said to Sister Pom, patting her on the back, and then, to Daddyji, "She's agreed."

Daddyji said much else, sometimes talking just for the sake of talking,   20 sometimes laughing at us because we were sniffling, and all the time trying to make us believe that this was a happy occasion. First, Sister Umi took issue with him: parents had no business arranging marriages; if she were Pom she would run away. Then Sister Nimi: all her life she had heard him say to us children, "Think for yourself — be independent," and here he was not allowing Pom to think for herself. Brother Om took Daddyji's part: girls who didn't get married became a burden on their parents, and Daddyji had four daughters to marry off, and would be retiring in a few years. Sisters Nimi and Umi retorted: they hadn't gone to college to get married off, to have some young man following them around like a leech. Daddyji just laughed. I thought he was so wise, and right.

"Go and bless your big sister," Mamaji said, pushing me in the direction of Sister Pom.

"I don't want to," I said. "I don't know him."

"What'll happen to Sister Pom's room?" Usha asked. She and Ashok didn't have rooms of their own. They slept in Mamaji's room.

"Pom's room will remain empty, so that any time she likes she can   24 come and stay in her room with Kakaji," Daddyji said.

The thought that a man I never met would sleep in Pom's room with Sister Pom there made my heart race. A sob shook me. I ran outside.

The whole house seemed to be in an uproar. Mamaji was shouting at Gian Chand, Gian Chand was shouting at the bearer, the bearer was shouting at the sweeper. There were the sounds of the kitchen fire being stoked, of the drain being washed out, of water running in bathrooms. From behind whichever door I passed came the rustle of saris, salwars, and kemises. The house smelled of fresh flowers, but it had a ghostly chill. I would climb to the landing of Sister Pom's room and thump down the stairs two at a time. Brother Om would shout up at me, "Stop it!" Sister Umi would shout down at me, "Don't you have anything better to do?" Sister Nimi would call to me from somewhere, "You're giving Pom a headache." I wouldn't heed any of them. As soon as I had thumped down, I would clatter to the top and thump my way down again.

Daddyji went past on the back veranda. "Who's coming with Kakaji?" I asked. Kakaji was in Lahore to buy some dental equipment, and in a few minutes he was expected for tea, to meet Sister Pom and the family.

"He's coming alone," Daddyji said, over his shoulder. "He's come   28 from very far away." I had somehow imagined that Kakaji would come with at least as many people as we had in our family, because I had started thinking of the tea as a kind of cricket match — the elevens facing off.

I followed Daddyji into the drawing room. "Will he come alone for his wedding, too?"

"No. Then he'll come with the bridegroom's party."

We were joined by everyone except Mamaji and Sister Pom, who from the moment we got the news of Sister Pom's marriage had become inseparable.

Gian Chand came in, the tea things rattling on his tray.   32

Later, I couldn't remember exactly how Kakaji had arrived, but I remember noticing that his footfall was heavy, that his greeting was affectionate, and that his voice seemed to float up with laughter. I don't know what I'd expected, but I imagined that if I had been in his place I would have skulked in the *gulli*, and perhaps changed my mind and not entered at all.

"Better to have ventured and lost than never to have ventured at all," Daddyji was saying to Kakaji about life's battles.

"Yes, Daddyji, just so," he said, with a little laugh. I had never heard anybody outside our family call my father Daddyji. It sounded odd.

Sister Pom was sent for, and she came in with Mamaji. Her footsteps   36 were shy, and the rustle of her sari around her feet was slow, as if she felt too conscious of the noise she was making just in walking. Daddyji made some complimentary remark about the silver border on her sari, and told her to sit next to Kakaji. Kakaji and Sister Pom exchanged a few words about a family group photograph on the mantelpiece, and about her studies. There was the clink of china as Sister Pom served Kakaji tea.

"Won't you have some tea yourself?" Kakaji asked Sister Pom.

Sister Pom's sari rustled over her shoulder as she turned to Daddyji.

"Kakaji, none of my children have ever tasted tea or coffee," Daddyji said. "We consider both to be bad habits. My children have been brought up on hot milk, and lately Pom has been taking a little ghi in her milk at bedtime, for health reasons."

We all protested at Daddyji's broadcasting family matters.   40

Kakaji tactfully turned the conversation to a visit to Mussoorie that our family was planning.

Mamaji offered him onion, potato, and cauliflower pakoras. He accepted, remarking how hot and crisp they were.

"Where will Sister Pom live?" Usha asked.

"In the summer, my practice is in Mussoorie," Kakaji said, "but in   44 the winter it's in Dehra Dun."

It struck me for the first time that after Sister Pom got married people we didn't know, people she didn't know, would become more important to her than we were.

Kakaji had left without formally committing himself. Then, four days later, when we were all sitting in the drawing room, a servant brought a letter to Mamaji. She told us that it was from Kakaji's mother, and that it asked if Sister Pom might be engaged to Kakaji. "She even wants to know if Pom can be married in April or May," Mamaji said excitedly. "How propitious! That'll be the fifth wedding in the family in those two months." Cousins Prakash and Dev, Cousin Pushpa (Bhaji Ganga Ram's adopted daughter), and Auntie Vimla were all due to be married in Lahore then.

"You still have time to change your mind," Daddyji said to Sister Pom. "What do you really think of him?"

Sister Pom wouldn't say anything.   48

"How do you expect her to know what her mind is when all that the two talked about was a picture and her bachelor's exam in May?" Sister Umi demanded. "Could she have fallen in love already?"

"Love, Umi, means something very different from 'falling in love,'" Daddyji said. "It's not an act but a lifelong process. The best we can do as Pom's parents is to give her love every opportunity to grow."

"But doesn't your 'every opportunity' include knowing the person better than over a cup of tea, or whatever?" Sister Umi persisted.

"Yes, of course it does. But what we are discussing here is a simple   52 matter of choice — not love," Daddyji said. "To know a person, to love a person, takes years of living together."

"Do you mean, then, that knowing a person and loving a person are the same thing?" Sister Umi asked.

"Not quite, but understanding and respect are essential to love, and that cannot come from talking together, even over a period of days or months. That can come only in good time, through years of experience. It is only when Pom and Kakaji learn to consider each other's problems as one and the same that they will find love."

"But, Daddyji, look at the risk you're taking, the risk you're making Pom take," Sister Nimi said.

"We are trying to minimize the risk as much as we can by finding   56 Pom a family that is like ours," Daddyji said. "Kakaji is a dentist, I am a doctor. His life and way of thinking will be similar to mine. We are from the same caste, and Kakaji's family originally came from the Punjab. They eat meat and eggs, and they take religion in their stride, and don't pray every day and go to temples, like Brahmans. Kakaji knows how I walk into a club and how I am greeted there. The atmosphere in Pom's new home will be very much the same as the atmosphere here. Now, if I were to give Pom in marriage to a Brahman he'd expect Pom to live as he did. That would really be gambling."

"Then what you're doing is perpetuating the caste system," Sister Nimi said. She was the political rebel in the family. "You seem to presuppose that a Kshatriya should marry only a Kshatriya, that a Brahman should marry only a Brahman. I would just as soon marry a shopkeeper from the Bania caste or an Untouchable, and help to break down caste barriers."

"That day might come," Daddyji said. "But you will admit, Nimi, that by doing that you'd be increasing the odds."

"But for a cause I believe in," Sister Nimi said.

"Yes, but that's a whole other issue," Daddyji said.   60

"Daddyji, you say that understanding and respect are necessary for love," Sister Umi said. "I don't see why you would respect a person more because you lived with him and shared his problems."

"In our society, we think of understanding and respect as coming only through sacrifice," Daddyji said.

"Then you're advocating the subservience of women," Sister Nimi said, "because it's not Kakaji who will be expected to sacrifice — it's Pom. That's not fair."

"And why do you think that Pom will learn to respect Kakaji because   64 she sacrifices for him?" Sister Umi said, pressing her point.

"No, Umi, it is the other way around," Daddyji said. "It is Kakaji who will respect Pom because she sacrifices for him."

"But that doesn't mean that Pom will respect Kakaji," Sister Umi persisted.

"But if Kakaji is moved by Pom's sacrifices he will show more consideration for her. He will grow to love her. I know in my own case I was moved to the depths to see Shanti suffer so because she was so ill-prepared to be my wife. It took me long enough — too long, I believe — to reach that understanding, perhaps because I had broken away from the old traditions and had given in to Western influences."

"So you admit that Pom will have to suffer for years," Sister Umi said.   68

"Perhaps," Daddyji said. "But all that time she will be striving for ultimate happiness and love. Those are precious gifts that can only be cultivated in time."

"You haven't told us what this ultimate happiness is," Sister Umi said. "I don't really understand it."

"It is a uniting of ideals and purposes, and a merging of them. This is the tradition of our society, and it is the means we have adopted to make our marriages successful and beautiful. It works because we believe in the goodness of the individuals going into the marriage and rely on the strength of the sacred bond."

"But my ideal is to be independent," Sister Nimi said. "As you say,   72 'Think for yourself.'"

"But often you have to choose among ideals," Daddyji said. "You may have to choose between being independent and being married."

"But aren't you struck by the fact that all the suffering is going to be on Pom's part? Shouldn't Kakaji be required to sacrifice for their happiness, too?" Sister Nimi said, reverting to the old theme.

"There has to be a start," Daddyji said. "Remember, in our tradition it's her life that is joined with his; it is she who will forsake her past to build a new future with him. If both Pom and Kakaji were to be obstinate, were to compete with each other about who would sacrifice first, who would sacrifice more, what hope would there be of their ever getting on together, of their ever finding love?"

"Daddyji, you're evading the issue," Sister Nimi said. "Why shouldn't   76 he take the initiative in this business of sacrifice?"

"He would perhaps be expected to if Pom were working, too, as in the West, and, though married, leading a whole different life from his. I suppose more than this I really can't say, and there may be some injustice in our system, at that. In the West, they go in for romantic love, which is unknown among us. I'm not sure that that method works any better than our method does."

Then Daddyji said to Sister Pom, "I have done my best. Even after you marry Kakaji, my responsibility for you will not be over. I will always be there in the background if you should need me."

"I respect your judgment, Daddyji," Sister Pom said obediently. "I'll do what you say."

Mamaji consulted Shambu Pandit. He compared the horoscopes of   80 Sister Pom and Kakaji and set the date of the marriage for the eleventh of May. . . . "That's just three days after she finishes her B.A. finals!" we cried. "When will she study? You are sacrificing her education to some silly superstition."

But Shambu Pandit would not be budged from the date. "I am only going by the horoscopes of the couple," he said. "You might as well protest to the stars."

We appealed to Daddyji, but he said that he didn't want to interfere, because such matters were up to Mamaji. That was as much as to say that Shambu Pandit's date was a settled thing.

I recall that at about that time there was an engagement ceremony. We all — Daddyji, Mamaji, Sister Pom, many of our Mehta and Mehra relatives — sat cross-legged on the floor of the front veranda around Shambu Pandit. He recited the Gayatri Mantra, the simple prayer he used to tell us to say before we went to sleep, and made a thank offering of incense and ghi to a fire in a brazier, much as Mamaji did — behind Daddyji's back — when one of us was going on a trip or had recovered from a bout of illness. Servants passed around a platter heaped up with crumbly sweet balls. I heard Kakaji's sister, Billo, saying something to Sister Pom; she had just come from Dehra Dun bearing a sari, a veil, and the engagement ring for Sister Pom, after Romesh Chachaji, one of Daddyji's brothers, had gone to Dehra Dun bearing some money, a silver platter and silver bowls, and sweetmeats for Kakaji. It was the first time that I was able to think of Kakaji both as a remote and frightening dentist who was going to take Sister Pom away and as someone ordinary like us, who had his own family. At some point, Mamaji prodded me, and I scooted forward, crab fashion, to embrace Sister Pom. I felt her hand on my neck. It had something cold and metallic on it, which sent a shiver through me. I realized that she was wearing her engagement ring, and that until then Mamaji was the only one in our family who had worn a ring.

In the evening, the women relatives closeted themselves in the drawing room with Sister Pom for the engagement singsong. I crouched outside with my ear to the door. The door pulsated with the beat of a barrel drum. The pulse in my forehead throbbed in sympathy with the beat as I caught snatches of songs about bedsheets and henna, along with explosions of laughter, the songs themselves rising and falling like the cooing of the doves that nested under the eaves of the veranda. I thought that a couple of years earlier I would have been playing somewhere outside on such an occasion, without knowing what I was missing, or been in the drawing room clapping and singing, but now I was crouching by the door like a thief, and was feeling ashamed even as I was captivated.

84

EXPLORATIONS

1. When Daddyji makes his opening announcement, Mehta writes, "We were stunned. We have never really faced the idea that Sister Pom might get married and suddenly leave, I thought" (para. 2). What other evidence in Mehta's narrative indicates that Pom has been treated as a child until a husband is found for her?

2. Judging from "Pom's Engagement," how is the traditional Indian concept of coming of age different for a woman and a man? What are the responsibilities of an adult woman? an adult man?

3. At what points and in what ways does Mehta reveal his feelings about his sister's change in status? What other clues suggest that Pom's engagement marks a coming of age for all the Mehta children?

4. Reading "Pom's Engagement" it is easy to forget that the author is blind. What sensory impressions does Mehta describe where a sighted writer might focus on what he or she sees? Give at least five examples.

CONNECTIONS

1. Compare Pom's social life in "Pom's Engagement" with Miguel's in Mario Vargas Llosa's "Sunday, Sunday." How are the limits on contact between young men and women different in India and Peru? How are each country's social restrictions different for males (Kakaji and Miguel) and for females (Pom and Flora)?

2. Unlike Mehta's Sister Pom, Jing-mei Woo in Amy Tan's "Two Kinds" is not an obedient daughter. What factors appear to be responsible for these young women's different reactions to their parents' wishes?

3. In *Looking at Ourselves*, Olga Silverstein writes, "In adolescence you *have* to split off [from your mother]; otherwise, you feel too dependent, too cozy, too loved, too comfortable." How do you think Mehta would react to this statement with regard to his family? According to "Pom's Engagement," how is the mother-daughter split handled in India?

ELABORATIONS

1. Look back at Gyanranjan's "Our Side of the Fence and Theirs" (p. 146). Judging from that story and "Pom's Engagement," how do Indian assumptions about the role of marriage in a woman's (or man's) life differ from ours? Given Indian values and priorities, what are the advantages of their system of arranged marriages? What benefits might such a system have in the United States, with its high divorce rate and disintegrating nuclear family? Write an argumentative essay exploring one or more of these questions.

2. "Even as one part of us seeks to be an individual, another part longs to restore the safety and comfort of merging with another," writes Gail Sheehy of the years from age eighteen to twenty-two in *Looking at Ourselves*. "But people who marry during this time often prolong financial and emotional ties to the family and relatives that impede them from becoming self-sufficient." After reading "Pom's Engagement," how do you think Daddyji would respond to these statements? Write an essay comparing the balance between self-sufficiency and prolonged family ties in Indian and in American culture.

MARJORIE SHOSTAK

Nisa's Marriage

"Nisa's Marriage" comes from Marjorie Shostak's 1981 book *Nisa: The Life and Words of a !Kung Woman,* based on Shostak's two and a half years among the !Kung San of Botswana. (The ! indicates a clicking sound.) At the time she was a research assistant on the Harvard Kalahari Desert Project, having previously received a bachelor's degree in English literature from Brooklyn College. Shostak, born in 1945, now teaches anthropology at Emory University in Atlanta. Her most recent book, coauthored with S. Boyd Eaton and Melvin Konner, is *The Paleolithic Prescription: A Program of Diet and Exercise and a Design for Living.* In 1989 Shostak returned to Botswana and met up with Nisa, who is now sixty-eight.

In her introduction to *Nisa,* Shostak writes: "Nisa is a member of one of the last remaining traditional gatherer-hunter societies, a group calling themselves the *Zhun/twasi,* the "real people," who currently live in isolated areas of Botswana, Angola, and Namibia. . . . They are also known as the !Kung Bushmen, the !Kung San, or simply the !Kung. They are short — averaging about five feet in height — lean, muscular, and, for Africa, light-skinned. They have high cheekbones and rather Oriental-looking eyes." Population biologists call these people Khoisan, from *Khoi,* the group previously known as Hottentots, and *San,* the group known as Bushmen, who together were the original inhabitants of South Africa (see pp. 34 and 578).

Shostak describes meeting Nisa, who was then close to fifty years old: "Nisa wore an old blanket loosely draped over the remnants of a faded, flower-print dress, sizes too big. . . . [She] was all activity: constantly in motion, her face expressive, she spoke fast and was at once strong and surprisingly coquettish." In the following excerpt, the events Nisa describes took place more than thirty-five years earlier, just as she entered puberty.

The day of the wedding, everyone was there. All of Tashay's friends were sitting around, laughing and laughing. His younger brother said, "Tashay, you're too old. Get out of the way so I can marry her. Give her to me." And his nephew said, "Uncle, you're already old. Now, let *me* marry her." They were all sitting around, talking like that. They all wanted me.

I went to my mother's hut and sat there. I was wearing lots of beads and my hair was completely covered and full with ornaments.

That night there was another dance. We danced, and some people fell asleep and others kept dancing. In the early morning, Tashay and his relatives went back to their camp; we went into our huts to sleep. When morning was late in the sky, they came back. They stayed around and then his parents said, "Because we are only staying a short while — tomorrow, let's start building the marriage hut."

The next day they started. There were lots of people there — Tashay's 4 mother, my mother, and my aunt worked on the hut; everyone else sat around, talking. Late in the day, the young men went and brought Tashay to the finished hut. They set him down beside it and stayed there with him, sitting around the fire.

I was still at my mother's hut. I heard them tell two of my friends to go and bring me to the hut. I thought, "Oohh . . . I'll run away." When they came for me, they couldn't find me. They said, "Where did Nisa go? Did she run away? It's getting dark. Doesn't she know that things may bite and kill her?" My father said, "Go tell Nisa that if this is what she's going to do, I'll hit her and she won't run away again. What made her want to run away, anyway?

I was already far off in the bush. They came looking for me. I heard them calling, "Nisa . . . Nisa . . ." I sat down at the base of a tree. Then I heard Nukha, "Nisa . . . Nisao . . . my friend . . . a hyena's out there . . . things will bite and kill you . . . come back . . . Nisa . . . Nisao . . ."

When Nukha finally saw me, I started to run. She ran after me, chasing me and finally caught me. She called out to the others, "Hey! Nisa's here! Everyone, come! Help me! Take Nisa, she's here!"

They came and brought me back. Then they laid me down inside the 8 hut. I cried and cried. People told me, "A man is not something that kills you; he is someone who marries you, who becomes like your father or your older brother. He kills animals and gives you things to eat. Even tomorrow, while you are crying, Tashay may kill an animal. But when he returns, he won't give you any meat; only he will eat. Beads, too. He will get beads but he won't give them to you. Why are you so afraid of your husband and what are you crying about?"

I listened and was quiet. Later, we went to sleep. Tashay lay down beside the opening of the hut, near the fire, and I lay down inside; he thought I might try and run away again. He covered himself with a blanket and slept.

While it was dark, I woke up. I sat up. I thought, "How am I going to jump over him? How can I get out and go to mother's hut to sleep beside her?" I looked at him sleeping. Then came other thoughts, other thoughts in the middle of the night, "Eh . . . this person has just married me . . ." and I lay down again. But I kept thinking, "Why did people give me this man in marriage? The older people say he is a good person, yet . . ."

I lay there and didn't move. The rain came beating down. It fell steadily and kept falling. Finally, I slept. Much later dawn broke.

In the morning, Tashay got up and sat by the fire. I was so frightened   12
I just lay there, waiting for him to leave. When he went to urinate, I went and sat down inside my mother's hut.

That day, all his relatives came to our new hut — his mother, his father, his brothers . . . everyone! They all came. They said, "Go tell Nisa she should come and her in-laws will put the marriage oil on her. Can you see her sitting over there? Why isn't she coming so we can put the oil on her in her new hut?"

I refused to go. They kept calling for me until finally, my older brother said, "Uhn uhn. Nisa, if you act like this, I'll hit you. Now, get up and go over there. Sit over there so they can put the oil on you."

I still refused and just sat there. My older brother grabbed a switch from a nearby tree and started coming toward me. I got up. I was afraid. I followed him to where the others were sitting. Tashay's mother rubbed the oil on me and my aunt rubbed it on Tashay.

Then they left and it was just Tashay and me. . . .   16

That Zhun/twa, that Tashay, he really caused me pain.

Soon after we were married, he took me from my parents' village to live at his parents' village. At first my family came and lived with us, but then one day they left, left me with Tashay and his parents. That's when I started to cry. Tashay said, "Before your mother left, you weren't crying. Why didn't you tell me you wanted to go with them? We could have followed along." I said, "I was afraid of you. That's why I didn't tell you."

But I still wanted to be with my mother, so later that day, I ran away. I ran as fast as I could until I finally caught up with them. When my mother saw me she said, "Someday a hyena is going to kill this child in the bush. She's followed us. Here she is!" I walked with them back to their village and lived with them a while.

A long time passed. One day Tashay left and came to us. When I   20 saw him, I started to cry. He said, "Get up. We're going back." I said, "Why does this person keep following me? Do I own him that he follows me everywhere?" My father said, "You're crazy. A woman follows her husband when he comes for her. What are you just sitting here for?"

Tashay took me with him and I didn't really refuse. We continued to live at his village and then we all went and lived at another water hole. By then, I knew that I was no longer living with my mother. I had left my family to follow my husband.

We lived and lived and then, one day, my heart started to throb and my head hurt; I was very sick. My father came to visit and went into a medicinal trance to try and cure me. When I was better, he left and I stayed behind.

After Tashay and I had been living together for a long time, we started to like each other with our hearts and began living nicely together. It was really only after we had lived together for a long time that he touched my genitals. By then, my breasts were already big.

We were staying in my parents' village the night he first had sex with   24
me and I didn't really refuse. I agreed, just a little, and he lay with me. But the next morning, I was sore. I took some leaves and wound them around my waist, but I continued to feel pain. I thought, "Ooo . . . what has he done to my insides that they feel this way?"

I went over to my mother and said, "That person, last night . . . I'm only a child, but last night he had sex with me. Move over and let me eat with you. We'll eat and then we'll move away. Mother . . . mother . . ."

My mother turned to my father and said, "Get up, get a switch and hit this child. She's ruining us. Get up and find something to hit her with." I thought, "What? Did I say something wrong?"

My father went to find a switch. I got up and ran to my aunt's hut. I sat there and thought, "What was so bad? How come I talked about something yet . . . is that something so terrible?"

My father said to my aunt, "Tell Nisa to come back here so I can beat   28
her. The things this young girl talks about could crack open the insides of her ears."

My mother said, "This child, her talk is terrible. As I am now, I would stick myself with a poison arrow; but my skin itself fears and that's why I won't do it. But if she continues to talk like that, I will!"

They wanted me to like my husband and not to refuse him. My

mother told me that when a man sleeps with his wife, she doesn't tell; it's a private thing.

I got up and walked away from them. I was trembling, "Ehn . . . nn . . . nn . . ." I looked at my genitals and thought, "Oh, this person . . . yesterday he took me and now my genitals are ruined!" I took some water and washed my genitals, washed and washed.

Because, when my genitals first started to develop, I was afraid. 32 I'd look at them and cry and think something was wrong with them. But people told me, "Nothing's wrong. That's what you yourself are like."

I also thought that an older person, an adult like my husband, would tear me apart, that his penis would be so big that he would hurt me. Because I hadn't known older men. I had only played sex play with little boys. Then, when Tashay did sleep with me and it hurt, that's when I refused. That's also when I told. But people didn't yell at him, they only yelled at me, and I was ashamed.

That evening, we lay down again. But this time, before he came in, I took a leather strap, held my leather apron tightly against my legs, tied the strap around my genitals, and then tied it to the hut's frame. I was afraid he'd tear me open and I didn't want him to take me again.

The two of us lay there and after a long time, he touched me. When he touched my stomach, he felt the leather strap. He felt around to see what it was. He said, "What is this woman doing? Last night she lay with me so nicely when I came to her. Why has she tied her genitals up this way? What is she refusing to give me?"

He sat me up and said, "Nisa . . . Nisa . . . what happened? Why 36 are you doing this?" I didn't answer. He said, "What are you so afraid of that you had to tie up your genitals?" I said, "Uhn, uhn. I'm not afraid of anything." He said, "No, now tell me. In the name of what you did, I'm asking you."

Then he said, "What do you think you're doing when you do something like this? When you lie down with me, a Zhun/twa like yourself, it's not as though you were lying with another, a stranger. We are both Zhun/twasi, yet you tied yourself up!"

I said, "I refuse to lie down with anyone who wants to take my genitals. Last night you had sex with me and today my insides hurt. That's why I've tied myself up and that's why you won't take me again."

He said, "Untie the strap. Do you see me as someone who kills people? Am I going to eat you? No, I'm not going to kill you, but I have married you and want to make love to you. Do you think I married you thinking

I wouldn't make love to you? Did you think we would just live beside each other? Do you know any man who has married a woman and who just lives beside her without having sex with her?"

I said, "I don't care. I don't want sex. Today my insides hurt and I refuse." He said, "Mm, today you will just lie there, but tomorrow, I will take you. If you refuse, I'll pry your legs open and take you by force." 40

He untied the strap and said, "If this is what use you put this to, I'm going to destroy it." He took his knife and cut it into small pieces. Then he put me down beside him. He didn't touch me; he knew I was afraid. Then we went to sleep.

The next day we got up, did things, and ate things. When we returned to our hut that night, we lay down again. That's when he forced himself on me. He held my legs and I struggled against him. But I knew he would have sex with me and I thought, "This isn't helping me at all. This man, if he takes me by force, he'll really hurt me. So I'll just lie here, lie still and let him look for the food he wants. But I still don't know what kind of food I have because even if he eats he won't be full."[1]

So I stopped fighting and just lay there. He did his work and that time it didn't hurt so much. Then he lay down and slept.

After that, we just lived. I began to like him and he didn't bother me again, he didn't try to have sex with me. Many months passed — those of the rainy season, those of the winter season, and those of the hot season. He just left me alone and I grew up and started to understand about things. Because before that, I hadn't really known about men. . . . 44

We continued to live and it was as if I was already an adult. Because, beginning to menstruate makes you think about things. Only then did I bring myself to understand, only then did I begin to be a woman.

When Tashay wanted to lie with me, I no longer refused. We just had sex together, one day and then another. In the morning, I'd get up and sit beside our hut and I wouldn't tell. I'd think, "My husband is indeed my husband now. What people told me, that my husband is mine, is true."

We lived and lived, the two of us, together, and after a while I started to really like him and then, to love him. I had finally grown up and had

---

[1]Food and eating are universally used by the !Kung as metaphors for sex. However, they claim no knowledge or practice of oral-genital contact.

learned how to love. I thought, "A man has sex with you. Yes, that's what a man does. I had thought that perhaps he didn't."

We lived on and I loved him and he loved me. I loved him the way 48
a young adult knows how to love; I just *loved* him. Whenever he went away and I stayed behind, I'd miss him. I'd think, "Oh, when is my husband ever coming home? How come he's been gone so long?" I'd miss him and want him. When he'd come back my heart would be happy, "Eh, hey! My husband left and once again has come back."

We lived and when he wanted me, I didn't refuse; he just lay with me. I thought, "Why had I been so concerned about my genitals? They aren't that important, after all. So why was I refusing them?"

I thought that and gave myself to him, gave and gave. We lay with each other and my breasts were very large. I was becoming a woman.

EXPLORATIONS

1. What are Nisa's responses to her wedding? to being married? What events in her narrative play the most important role in her formal social transition from childhood to adulthood? in her personal psychological transition?

2. Judging from "Nisa's Marriage," what specific rituals are part of a Zhun/twasi wedding? What is the practical or symbolic (or both) purpose of each ritual?

3. What facts can you glean about the Zhun/twasi way of life from "Nisa's Marriage"? What appears to be the group's main food source? What dangers do they fear? What metaphoric examples can you find of these basic elements of their existence in their speech?

4. When Nisa runs home to her mother after having sex with her husband, her mother says, "As I am now, I would stick myself with a poison arrow; but my skin itself fears and that's why I won't do it. But if she continues to talk like that, I will!" (para. 29). What does she mean? How might an American mother express the same sentiments?

CONNECTIONS

1. What common rituals and related features appear in Ved Mehta's "Pom's Engagement" and in "Nisa's Marriage"? What can you deduce from these two accounts about the universal functions of marriage as a social institution?

2. What attitudes toward marriage do Pom and Nisa share? When, how, and why does each girl resist her parents' plans for her? Why do you think both Pom and Nisa ultimately yield to their parents' wishes?

3. By the end of her narrative, how does Nisa feel about moving from childhood to womanhood? What statements in Mario Vargas Llosa's "Sunday, Sunday" indicate a comparable response by Miguel? Look back at Gail Sheehy's passage in *Looking at Ourselves*. In Sheehy's terms, what do Nisa and Miguel evidently believe they have achieved?

ELABORATIONS

1. Reread Olga Silverstein's passage in *Looking at Ourselves* on the separation between mother and daughter, and Gail Sheehy's on pulling up roots. Write an essay using Silverstein's and Sheehy's ideas to identify Nisa's feelings and explain her behavior in "Nisa's Marriage."

2. Nisa resists being thrown out of the parental nest, but finally she capitulates. Write an essay in which you either classify the tactics her old and new families use to push her into adulthood, or compare the Zhun/twasi tactics with your own family's at some point when you faced a new and scary experience.

BENAZIR BHUTTO

The Day They Killed My Father

At thirty-five, Benazir Bhutto became not only Pakistan's youngest prime minister but also the first woman prime minister in the Muslim world. She was born to the job: Her family is a powerful feudal clan in Pakistan's Sind Province, and her father, Zulfikar Ali Bhutto, ruled Pakistan as president and then prime minister for six years. Known as a brilliant and ruthless leader, the elder Bhutto included his daughter both in top-level meetings and in the political maneuvering that went on behind the scenes. Benazir Bhutto graduated cum laude in comparative government from Radcliffe College in Cambridge, Massachusetts, and earned a degree in politics, philosophy, and economics at Oxford University. Her plans to enter Pakistan's foreign service were eclipsed by her father's overthrow by General Mohammad Zia ul-Haq in 1977. Enraged by the coup and Zia's trumped-up charge of murder, Benazir Bhutto devoted herself first to saving her father and then, when that failed, to avenging him. In and out of prison herself, she shared leadership of the Pakistan People's Party (PPP) with her mother. Their popularity threatened Zia, causing him repeatedly to cancel scheduled elections. In 1984 Bhutto went into exile. She returned two years later, after elections were held and parties legalized, and was again imprisoned. Her credibility among Pakistan's Muslims was bolstered by an arranged marriage in 1987, which produced a son. After Zia's death in a 1988 airplane crash, Bhutto was elected prime minister. Initially a successful democratic leader, she was ousted in August 1990 amid charges of nepotism and corruption. As we go to press, her political future is uncertain.

(For more background on Pakistan, see p. 359.)

They killed my father in the early morning hours of April 4, 1979, inside Rawalpindi District Jail. Imprisoned with my mother a few miles away in a deserted police training camp at Sihala, I felt the moment of my father's death. Despite the Valiums my mother had given me to try to get through the agonizing night, I suddenly sat bolt-upright in bed at 2 A.M. "No!" the scream burst through the knots in my throat. "No!" I couldn't breathe, didn't want to breathe. Papa! Papa! I felt cold, so cold, in spite of the heat, and couldn't stop shaking. There was nothing my mother and I could say to console each other. Somehow the hours passed

as we huddled together in the bare police quarters. We were ready at
dawn to accompany my father's body to our ancestral family graveyard.

"I am in *Iddat* and can't receive outsiders. You talk to him," my
mother said dully when the jailer arrived, as she began a widow's four
months and ten days of seclusion from strangers.

I walked into the cracked cement-floored front room that was supposed
to serve as our sitting room. It stank of mildew and rot.

"We are ready to leave with the prime minister," I told the junior   4
jailor standing nervously before me.

"They have already taken him to be buried," he said.

I felt as if he had struck me. "Without his family?" I asked bitterly.
"Even the criminals in the military regime know that it is our family's
religious obligation to accompany his body, to recite the prayers for the
dead, to see his face before burial. We applied to the jail superintendent
. . ."

"They have taken him," he interrupted.

"Taken him where?" The jailer was silent.

"It was very peaceful," he finally replied. "I have brought what was   8
left."

He handed me the pitiful items from my father's death cell one by
one: my father's *shalwar khameez,* the long shirt and loose trousers he'd
worn to the end, refusing as a political prisoner to wear the uniform of
a condemned criminal; the tiffin box for food that for the last ten days
he had refused; the roll of bedding they had allowed him only after the
broken wires of his cot had lacerated his back; his drinking cup . . .

"Where is his ring?" I managed to ask the jailer.

"Did he have a ring?" he asked.

I watched him make a great show of fishing through his bag, through   12
his pockets. Finally he handed me my father's ring, which toward the
end had regularly slipped off his emaciated fingers.

"Peaceful. It was very peaceful," he kept muttering. How could a
hanging be peaceful?

Basheer and Ibrahim, our family bearers who brought us supplies
every day because the authorities did not provide us with food, came into
the room. Basheer's face went white when he recognized my father's
clothes.

"*Ya* Allah! *Ya* Allah! They've killed Sahib! They've killed him!" he   16
screamed. Before we could stop him, Basheer grabbed a can of petrol
and doused himself with it, preparing to set himself aflame. My mother
had to rush out to prevent his self-immolation.

I stood in a daze, not believing what had happened to my father, not wanting to. It was just not possible that Zulfikar Ali Bhutto, the first prime minister of Pakistan to be elected directly by the people, was dead. Where there had been repression under the generals who had ruled Pakistan since its birth in 1947, my father had been the first to bring democracy. Where the people had lived as they had for centuries at the mercy of their tribal chiefs and landlords, he had installed Pakistan's first Constitution to guarantee legal protection and civil rights. Where the people had had to resort to violence and bloodshed to unseat the generals, he had guaranteed a parliamentary system of civilian government and elections every five years.

No. It was not possible. "*Jiye* Bhutto! Long live Bhutto!" millions had cheered when he became the first politician ever to visit the most forlorn and remote villages of Pakistan. When his Pakistan People's Party was voted into office, my father had started his modernization programs, redistributing the land held for generations by the feudal few among the many poor, educating the millions held down by ignorance, nationalizing the country's major industries, guaranteeing minimum wages and job security, and forbidding discrimination against women and minorities. The six years of his government had brought light to a country steeped in stagnant darkness — until the dawn of July 5, 1977.

Zia ul-Haq. My father's supposedly loyal army chief of staff. The general who had sent his soldiers in the middle of the night to overthrow my father and take over the country by force. Zia ul-Haq, the military dictator who had subsequently failed to crush my father's following in spite of all his guns and tear gas and Martial Law regulations, who had failed to break my father's spirit despite his isolation in a death cell. Zia ul-Haq, the desperate general who had just sent my father to his death.

I stood numbly in front of the junior jailer, holding the small bundle that was all that was left of my father. The scent of his cologne was still on his clothes, the scent of Shalimar. I hugged his *shalwar* to me, suddenly remembering Kathleen Kennedy, who had worn her father's parka at Radcliffe long after the senator had been killed. Our two families had always been compared in terms of politics. Now, we had a new and dreadful bond. That night and for many others, I, too, tried to keep my father near me by sleeping with his shirt under my pillow.

I felt completely empty, that my life had shattered. For almost two years, I had done nothing but fight the trumped-up charges brought against my father by Zia's military regime and work with the Pakistan

People's Party toward the elections Zia had promised at the time of the coup, then had canceled in the face of our impending victory. I had been arrested six times by the military regime and been repeatedly forbidden by the Martial Law authorities to set foot in Karachi and Lahore. So had my mother. As acting chairperson of the PPP during my father's imprisonment, she had been detained eight times. We had spent the last six weeks under detention is Sihala, the six months before that under detention in Rawalpindi. Yet not until yesterday had I allowed myself to believe that General Zia would actually assassinate my father.

Who would break the news to my younger brothers, who were fighting my father's death sentence from political exile in London? And who would tell my sister, Sanam, who was just finishing her final year at Harvard? I was especially worried about Sanam. She had never been political. Yet she had been dragged into the tragedy with all of us. Was she alone now? I prayed she wouldn't do anything foolish.

I felt as if my body were being torn apart. How could I go on? In spite of our efforts, we had failed to keep my father alive. I felt so alone. I just felt so alone. "What will I do without you to help me?" I had asked him in his death cell. I needed his political advice. For all that I held degrees in government from Harvard and Oxford, I was not a politician. But what could he say? He had shrugged helplessly.

I had seen my father for the last time yesterday. The pain of that meeting was close to unbearable. No one had told him he was to be executed early the next morning. No one had told the world leaders who had officially asked the military regime for clemency, among them U.S. president Jimmy Carter, British prime minister Margaret Thatcher, Leonid Brezhnev of the Soviet Union, Pope John Paul II, Indira Gandhi, and many others from the entire Muslim spectrum, Saudi Arabia, the Emirates, Syria. Certainly none of the cowards in Zia's regime had announced the date of my father's execution to the country, fearing the people's reaction to their prime minister's murder. Only my mother and I knew. And that, by accident and deduction.

I had been lying on my army cot in the early morning of April 2nd when my mother had come suddenly into the room. "Pinkie," she said, calling me by my family nickname, but in a tone that immediately made my body go rigid. "There are army officers outside saying that both of us should go to see your father today. What does that mean?"

I knew exactly what it meant. So did she. But neither of us could bear to admit it. This was my mother's visiting day, allowed her once a week.

Mine was scheduled for later in the week. That they wanted both of us to go could only mean that this was to be the last visit. Zia was about to kill my father.

My mind raced. We had to get the word out, to send a last call to the international community and to the people. Time had run out. "Tell them I'm not well," I said to my mother hastily. "Say that if it is the last meeting then, of course, I will come, but if it is not, we will go tomorrow." While my mother went to speak with the guards, I quickly broke open a message I had already wrapped to send out with Ibrahim and wrote a new one. "I think they are calling us for our last meeting," I scribbled furiously to a friend on the outside, hoping she would alert the party's leaders, who in turn would inform the diplomatic corps and mobilize the people. The people were our last hope.

"Take this immediately to Yasmin," I told Ibrahim, knowing we were   28 taking a great risk. There wasn't time for him to wait for a sympathetic or lackadaisical guard to come on duty. He could be searched and followed. He wouldn't be able to take the normal precautions. The danger was enormous, but so were the stakes. "Go, Ibrahim, go!" I urged him. "Tell the guards you're fetching medicine for me!" And off he ran.

I looked outside the window to see the Martial Law contingent consulting with each other, then transmitting the message that I was ill on their wireless set and waiting to receive information back. In the confusion, Ibrahim reached the gate. "I have to get medicine for Benazir Sahiba quickly. Quickly!" he said to the guards who had overheard the talk of my ill health. Miraculously they let Ibrahim through, barely five minutes after my mother had first come to me in the bedroom. My hands would not stop trembling. I had no idea if the message would be safely delivered.

Outside the window, the wireless sets crackled. "Because your daughter is not feeling well, then tomorrow will be fine for the visit," the authorities finally told my mother. We had gained another twenty-four hours of my father's life. But when the compound gates were sealed immediately after Ibrahim had fled, we knew something terribly ominous was about to occur.

Fight. We had to fight. But how? I felt so powerless, locked inside the stockade while the moments toward my father's death ticked by. Would the message get through? Would the people rise up in spite of the guns and bayonets they had faced since the coup? And who would lead them? Many of the leaders of the Pakistan People's Party were in jail. So were thousands of our supporters, including, for the first time in Pakistan's history, women. Countless others had been teargassed and flogged just for mentioning my father's name, the number of lashes to be administered painted on their half-naked bodies. Would the people heed this last desperate call? Would they even hear it?

At 8:15 P.M. my mother and I tuned in the BBC Asia report on our radio. Every muscle in my body was rigid. I sat expectantly forward as the BBC reported that I had sent a message from prison that tomorrow, April 3rd, was to be the last meeting with my father. The message had got through! I waited for the BBC to announce our call for the people to rise in protest. There was none. Instead, the BBC went on to report that there was no confirmation of the news from the jail superintendent. "She's panicked," it quoted one of my father's former ministers as saying. My mother and I couldn't even look at each other. Our last hope had died.

April 3, 1979. A speeding jeep. Crowds frozen in fear behind security forces, not knowing the fate of their prime minister. Prison gates hastily opened and closed. My mother and I being searched again by jail matrons, first leaving our own prison in Sihala, then again when we arrived at the jail in Rawalpindi.

"Why are you both here?" my father says from inside the inferno of his cell.

My mother doesn't answer.

"Is this the last meeting?" he asks.

My mother cannot bear to answer. "I think so," I say.

He calls for the jail superintendent who is standing nearby. They never leave us alone with Papa.

"Is this the last meeting?" my father asks him.

"Yes," comes the reply. The jail superintendent seems ashamed to be the bearer of the regime's plans.

"Has the date been fixed?"

"Tomorrow morning," the superintendent says.

"At what time?"

"At five o'clock, according to jail regulations."

"When did you receive this information?"

"Last night," he says reluctantly.

My father looks at him.

"How much time do I have with my family?"   48

"Half an hour."

"Under jail regulations, we are entitled to an hour," he says.

"Half an hour," the superintendent repeats. "Those are my orders."

"Make arrangements for me to have a bath and a shave," my father   52
tells him. "The world is beautiful and I want to leave it clean."

Half an hour. Half an hour to say goodbye to the person I love more
than any other in my life. The pain in my chest tightens into a vise. I
must not cry. I must not break down and make my father's ordeal any
more difficult.

He is sitting on the floor on a mattress, the only furniture left in his
cell. They have taken away his table and his chair. They have taken
away his cot.

"Take these," he says, handing me the magazines and books I had
brought him before. "I don't want them touching my things."

He hands me the few cigars his lawyers have brought him. "I'll keep   56
one for tonight," he says. He also keeps his bottle of Shalimar cologne.

He starts to hand me his ring, but my mother tells him to keep it on.
"I'll keep it for now, but afterwards I want it to go to Benazir," he tells
her.

"I have managed to send out a message," I whisper to him as the jail
authorities strain to hear. I outline the details and he looks satisfied. She's
almost learned the ropes of politics, his expression reads.

The light inside the death cell is dim. I cannot see him clearly. Every
other visit they have allowed us to sit together inside his cell. But not
today. My mother and I squeeze together at the bars in his cell door,
talking to him in whispers.

"Give my love to the other children," he says to my mother. "Tell   60
Mir and Sunny and Shah that I have tried to be a good father and wish
I could have said goodbye to them." She nods, but cannot speak.

"You have both suffered a lot," he says. "Now that they are going to
kill me tonight, I want to free you as well. If you want to, you can leave
Pakistan while the Constitution is suspended and Martial Law imposed.
If you want peace of mind, to pick up your lives again, then you might
want to go to Europe. I give you my permission. You can go."

Our hearts are breaking. "No, no," my mother says. "We can't go.
We'll never go. The generals must not think they have won. Zia has
scheduled elections again, though who knows if he will dare to hold
them. If we leave, there will be no one to lead the party, the party you
built."

"And you, Pinkie?" my father asks.

"I could never go," I say.   64

He smiles. "I'm so glad. You don't know how much I love you, how much I've always loved you. You are my jewel. You always have been."

"The time is up," the superintendent says. "The time is up."

I grip the bars.

"Please open up the cell," I ask him. "I want to say goodbye to my   68
father."

The superintendent refuses.

"Please," I say. "My father is the elected prime minister of Pakistan. I am his daughter. This is our last meeting. I want to hold him."

The superintendent refuses.

I try to reach my father through the bars. He is so thin, almost wasted   72
away from malaria, dysentery, starvation. But he pulls himself erect, and touches my hand.

"Tonight I will be free," he says, a glow suffusing his face. "I will be joining my mother, my father. I am going back to the land of my ancestors in Larkana to become part of its soil, its scent, its air. There will be songs about me. I will become part of its legend." He smiles. "But it is very hot in Larkana."

"I'll build a shade." I manage to say.

The jail authorities move in.

"Goodbye, Papa," I call to my father as my mother reaches through   76
the bars to touch him. We both move down the dusty courtyard. I want to look back, but I can't. I know I can't control myself.

"Until we meet again," I hear him call.

Somehow my legs move. I cannot feel them. I have turned to stone. But still I move. The jail authorities lead us back though the jail ward, the courtyard filled with army tents. I move in a trance, conscious only of my head. High. I must keep it high. They are all watching.

The car is waiting inside the locked gates so the crowds outside won't see us. My body is so heavy I have difficulty getting in. The car speeds forward through the gate. At its sight the crowds surge toward us but are shoved back roughly by the security forces. I suddenly glimpse my friend Yasmin at the edge of the crowd, waiting to deliver my father's food. "Yasmin! They are going to kill him tonight!" I try and shout from the window. Did she hear me? Did I make any sound at all?

Five o'clock came and went. Six o'clock. Each breath I took reminded   80
me of the last breaths of my father. "God, let there be a miracle," my

mother and I prayed together. "Let something happen." Even my little cat, Chun-Chun, whom I had smuggled into detention with me, felt the tension. She had abandoned her kittens. We couldn't find them anywhere. Yet we clung to hope.

The Supreme Court had unanimously recommended that my father's death sentence be commuted to life imprisonment. Moreover, by Pakistani law, the date of any execution must be announced at least a week before its implementation. There had been no such announcement.

PPP leaders on the outside had also sent word that Zia had promised Saudi Arabia, the Emirates, and others in confidence that he would commute the death sentence against my father to life. But Zia's record was filled with broken promises and disregard for the law. In the face of our persistent fears that my father would be executed, the foreign minister of Saudi Arabia and the prime minister of Libya had promised to fly in should a date for execution be announced. Had they heard my message on the BBC? Was there time for them to fly in now?

A Chinese delegation was in Islamabad. My father had pioneered Pakistan's friendship with China. Would they sway Zia on his behalf?

My mother and I sat motionless in the white heat at Sihala, unable   84 to speak. Zia had also let it be known that he would entertain a plea for clemency only from my father, or us, his immediate family. My father had forbidden it.

How do such moments pass in the countdown toward death? My mother and I just sat. Sometimes we cried. When we lost the strength to sit up, we fell onto the pillows on the bed. They'll snuff out his life, I kept thinking. They'll just snuff out his life. How alone he must be feeling in that cell, with no one near him. He didn't keep any books. He didn't keep anything. He has just that one cigar. My throat tightened until I wanted to rip it open. But I didn't want the guards who were always laughing and talking right outside our window to have the pleasure of hearing me scream. "I can't bear it, Mummy, I can't," I finally broke down at 1:30. She brought me some Valium. "Try to sleep," she said.

A half hour later, in the early hours of April 4, I shot up in bed, feeling my father's noose around my neck.

EXPLORATIONS

1. In what ways was her father's death a turning point for Benazir Bhutto?

2. As a woman running for prime minister in an Islamic country, Bhutto's greatest asset was her father. What statements in this essay show her utilizing this asset, and in what ways?

3. Where and how does Bhutto emphasize her own credentials to rule Pakistan, independent of her father's legacy? Which credentials would impress an international audience? Which ones would impress her fellow Muslims?

4. How does Bhutto show her devastation at her father's death without undermining her image as someone able to steer a nation through difficult times?

CONNECTIONS

1. What steps does Bhutto take to avert a brutal turning point in her life? What steps does Nisa take in Marjorie Shostak's "Nisa's Marriage" to avert a turning point she perceives as brutal? What emotions drive both women to act as they do?

2. "I must keep [my head] high," declares Bhutto. "They are all watching" (para. 78). What other clues in her essay indicate that the social rules in her culture are different for showing emotion in public and in private? What clues in Ved Mehta's "Pom's Engagement" and in Mario Vargas Llosa's "Sunday, Sunday" indicate a similar contrast in social rules? Do we in the United States follow the same rules?

3. In "Two Kinds," Amy Tan's mother says there are only two kinds of daughters. What are they? What kind is Pom in Mehta's "Pom's Engagement"? What kind is Bhutto? How can you tell?

ELABORATIONS

1. Through her narrative Bhutto weaves an argument for her father and against Zia ul-Haq. What is her thesis? How does she support it? Identify the elements of Bhutto's argument in "The Day They Killed My Father," and write an expository essay stating and defending her position.

2. What has been the main turning point in your life so far? Write a narrative essay about it. What prompted it? What were your fears and hopes? How did you handle it? How has it changed you?

PART FOUR

WOMEN AND MEN

Images of the Opposite Sex

LOOKING AT OURSELVES
Gayle Early, Susan Brownmiller, Joe Kane, Gloria Steinem,
Rose Weitz, Scott Russell Sanders, Amy Gross, Anne Roiphe

Francine du Plessix Gray, *Sex Roles in the Soviet Union*
(SOVIET UNION)

Clara Piriz, *Marriage by Pros and Cons* (URUGUAY)

Richard Rodriguez, *You Are a Man* (UNITED STATES/MEXICO)

Leslie Marmon Silko, *Yellow Woman* (UNITED STATES)

Simone de Beauvoir, *Woman as Other* (FRANCE)

Alberto Moravia, *The Chase* (ITALY)

Naila Minai, *Women in Early Islam* (ARABIA)

Cherry Lindholm and Charles Lindholm, *Life Behind the Veil*
(PAKISTAN)

Yashar Kemal, *A Dirty Story* (TURKEY)

ESSENTIAL TO THE SURVIVAL OF HUMANITY IS THE BOND BETWEEN A woman and a man. Recognizing its importance, nearly every culture creates a social structure of rules, expectations, ideals, and rituals around this central relationship. Yet perhaps in no other aspect of existence is the contrast between cultures so striking. We differ not only in our courtship and marriage customs but in our basic assumptions about what love is, what constitutes a good reason for two (or more) people to marry or divorce, and even how women and men are fundamentally different.

It is this last subject — the variety of ways men and women perceive each other — on which we focus here. In *Looking at Ourselves*, Gayle Early outlines the John Wayne image of masculinity and Susan Brownmiller describes traditional femininity. Joe Kane comments on gender rivalry over power; Gloria Steinem notes the illogic of oppression; Rose Weitz talks about both genders' fears of homosexuality. Scott Russell Sanders pays homage to the force field of sex, Amy Gross appreciates androgynous men, and Anne Roiphe confesses female chauvinism.

Moving abroad, "Sex Roles in the Soviet Union" is Francine du Plessix Gray's report on the battle of the sexes in the USSR. Clara Piriz's letter to her imprisoned Uruguayan husband, "Marriage by Pros and Cons," depicts a relationship battered by politics. Richard Rodriguez tells of young men sneaking across the U.S. border and older men sending money home to Mexico in "You Are a Man." Leslie Marmon Silko's short story "Yellow Woman" shows a Laguna Pueblo woman entranced by a lover sprung from the old tribal legends.

To French feminist Simone de Beauvoir, conflict between the sexes arises from man's age-old habit of viewing woman as alien and therefore threatening. Alberto Moravia shows that male tendency in a different light with his short story "The Chase," in which an Italian husband gains a new appreciation for his wife's unpredictability.

The gender gap widens in the Islamic Middle East. Naila Minai's "Women in Early Islam" explains how Muhammad created a religion meant to safeguard women. Cherry Lindholm and Charles Lindholm, visiting Pakistan's Swat Valley in "Life Behind the Veil," find evidence that Muhammad's plan has gone awry: women are viewed as too potent and treacherous to leave their homes or even show their faces without male permission. Sexual prejudice turns violent in Yashar Kemal's "A Dirty Story," where the citizens of a fictional Turkish village turn a victim into a villain. ◇

LOOKING AT OURSELVES

1

It used to be that males could model themselves after that all-American hero, John Wayne. He was tough, rugged, and plenty adventurous. Problems were solved in a gunslinging match or a fistfight, whichever came first.

But in today's society the John Wayne image is being shot down. Important categories of traditional male work like the cowboy or lawman are being ambushed by the advent of automated equipment and the emergence of women in traditionally male jobs.

Warren Farrell, author of *The Liberated Man*, calls John Wayne the "Moses of Masculinity," and pictures him complete with a tablet on which are written the "Ten Commandments" of traditional maledom:

1. Thou shalt not cry or expose other feelings of emotion, fear, weakness, sympathy, empathy, or involvement before thy neighbor.
2. Thou shalt not be vulnerable, but honor and respect the "logical," "practical," or "intellectual" — as thou definest them.
3. Thou shalt not listen except to find fault.
4. Thou shalt condescend to women in the smallest and biggest of ways.
5. Thou shalt control thy wife's body.
6. Thou shalt have no other egos before thee.
7. Thou shalt have no other breadwinners before thee.
8. Thou shalt not be responsible for housework — before anybody.
9. Thou shalt honor and obey the straight-and-narrow pathway to success: job specialization.
10. Thou shalt have an answer to all problems at all times.

But the problems associated with "old male" socialization are reflected in men's health statistics:

men live, on the average, almost 10 years less than women;
males commit suicide 300 percent more often;
all the major diseases leading to death show significantly higher rates for males;

men have higher murder, assault, and battery rates; and
men show a significantly higher rate of drug and alcohol abuse.

– Gayle Early
"The Hazards of Being Male"
Chico News & Review

2

The world smiles favorably on the feminine woman: It extends little courtesies and minor privilege. Yet the nature of this competitive edge is ironic, at best, for one works at femininity by accepting restrictions, by limiting one's sights, by choosing an indirect route, by scattering concentration and not giving one's all as a man would to his own, certifiably masculine, interests. It does not require a great leap of imagination for a woman to understand the feminine principle as a grand collection of compromises, large and small, that she simply must make in order to render herself a successful woman. If she has difficulty in satisfying femininity's demands, if its illusions go against her grain, or if she is criticized for her shortcomings and imperfections, the more she will see femininity as a desperate strategy of appeasement, a strategy she may not have the wish or the courage to abandon, for failure looms in either direction. . . .

Femininity pleases men because it makes them appear more masculine by contrast; and, in truth, conferring an extra portion of unearned gender distinction on men, an unchallenged space in which to breathe freely and feel stronger, wiser, more competent, is femininity's special gift. One could say that masculinity is often an effort to please women, but masculinity is known to please by displays of mastery and competence while femininity pleases by suggesting that these concerns, except in small matters, are beyond its intent. Whimsy, unpredictability, and patterns of thinking and behavior that are dominated by emotion, such as tearful expressions of sentiment and fear, are thought to be feminine precisely because they lie outside the established route to success. . . .

Femininity serves to reassure men that women need them and care about them enormously. By incorporating the decorative and the frivolous into its definition of style, femininity functions as an effective antidote to the unrelieved seriousness, the pressure of making one's way in a harsh, difficult world. In its mandate to avoid direct confrontation and to smooth over the fissures of conflict, femininity operates as a value system of niceness, a code of thoughtfulness and sensitivity that in modern society is sadly in short supply.

> – Susan Brownmiller
> *Femininity*

3

For all the supposed enlightenment of the last decade, there is still no accepted place in our culture for the man whose mate is a more powerful figure than he is.

Women have begun to ascend — *have* ascended — into roles of power and prestige once reserved for men. No corresponding change in acceptable roles has occurred for men. . . .

Come on, admit it: When you meet an ambitious, successful woman, and the man in her life is not an achiever of equal note, you figure him for a wimp, don't you? And your judgment of him is far more severe than your judgment of her would be if the situation were reversed. If there is no new role for men in a world where women are rising, men will just be that much more reluctant to give up the roles they already have.

> – Joe Kane
> "Star Wars: How Men Are Coping with Female Success"
> *Ms.*

4

Living in India made me understand that a white minority of the world has spent centuries conning us into thinking a white skin makes people superior, even though the only thing it really does is make them more subject to ultraviolet rays and wrinkles.

Reading Freud made me just as skeptical about penis envy. The power of giving birth makes "womb envy" more logical, and an organ as external and unprotected as the penis makes men very vulnerable indeed.

But listening recently to a woman describe the unexpected arrival of her menstrual period (a red stain had spread on her dress as she argued heatedly on the public stage) still made me cringe with embarrassment. That is, until she explained that, when finally informed in whispers of the obvious event, she had said to the all-male audience, "and you should be *proud* to have a menstruating woman on your stage. It's probably the first real thing that's happened to this group in years!"

Laughter. Relief. She had turned a negative into a positive. Somehow her story merged with India and Freud to make me finally understand the power of positive thinking. Whatever a "superior" group has will be used to justify its superiority, and whatever an "inferior" group has will be used to justify its plight. Black men were given poorly paid jobs because they were said to be "stronger" than white men, while all women were relegated to poorly paid jobs because they were said to be "weaker." As the little boy said when asked if he wanted to be a lawyer like his mother, "Oh no, that's women's work." Logic has nothing to do with oppression.

> – Gloria Steinem
> *Outrageous Acts and Everyday Rebellions*

◇–◇–◇–◇–◇

5

Western culture teaches that women are the weaker sex, that they cannot flourish — or perhaps even survive — without the protection of men. Women are taught that they cannot live happy and fulfilled lives without a Prince Charming, who is superior to them in all ways. In the struggle to find and keep their men, women learn to view each other as untrustworthy competitors. They subordinate the development of their own psychological, physical, and professional strengths to the task of finding male protectors who will make up for their shortcomings. In this way, Western culture keeps women from developing bonds with each other, while it maintains their dependence on men.

Lesbians throw a large wrench into the works of this cultural system. In a society that denigrates women, lesbians value women enough to spend their lives with women rather than with men. Lesbians therefore do not and cannot rely on the protection of men. Knowing that they will not have that protection, lesbians are forced to develop their own resources. The very survival of lesbians therefore suggests the potential strength of all women and their ability to transcend their traditional roles. At the same time, since lesbians do not have even the illusion of male protection that marriage provides, and since they are likely to see their fate as tied to other women rather than to individual men, lesbians may be more likely than heterosexual women to believe in the necessity of fighting for women's rights; the heavy involvement of lesbians in the feminist movement seems to support this thesis.

Lesbians also threaten the dominant cultural system by presenting, or at least appearing to present, an alternative to the typical inequality of heterosexual relationships. Partners attempting to equalize power in a heterosexual relationship must first neutralize deeply ingrained traditional sex roles. Since lesbian relationships generally contain no built-in assumption of the superiority of one partner, developing an egalitarian relationship may be easier. Lesbian relationships suggest both that a love between equals is possible and that an alternative way of obtaining such a love may exist. Regardless of the actual likelihood of achieving equality in a lesbian relationship, the threat to the system remains, as long as lesbian relationships are believed to be more egalitarian. This threat increases significantly when, as in the past few years, lesbians express pride in and satisfaction with their life-style. . . .

The sanctions against male homosexuality appear even stronger than those against lesbianism. Why might this be so? First, I would argue that anything women do is considered relatively trivial—be it housework, mothering, or lesbianism. Second, whereas lesbians threaten the status quo by refusing to accept their inferior position as women, gay males may threaten it even more by appearing to reject their privileged status as men. Prevailing cultural mythology holds that lesbians want to be males. In a paradoxical way, therefore, lesbians may be perceived as upholding "male" values. Male homosexuality, on the other hand, is regarded as a rejection of masculine values; gay males are regarded as feminized "sissies" and "queens." Thus male homosexuality, with its implied rejection of male privilege, may seem even more incomprehensible and threatening than lesbianism. Finally, research indicates that people in general are more fearful and intolerant of homosexuals of their own sex than of homosexuals to the opposite sex. The greater stigmatization of male than female homosexuality may therefore simply reflect the greater ability of males to enforce their prejudices.

– Rose Weitz
"What Price Independence?"
Women: A Feminist Perspective

◇–◇–◇–◇–◇

6

The distance a man stares across at a woman, or a woman at a man, is a gulf in the soul, out of which a voice cries, *Leap, leap.* One day all men may cease to look on themselves as prototypically human and on women as lesser miracles; women may cease to feel themselves the targets for desire; men and women both may come to realize that we are all mere flickerings in the universal fire; and then none of us, male or female, need give up humanity in order to become the Other.

Ever since I gawked at the girl in pink shorts, I have dwelt knowingly in the force-field of sex. Knowingly or not, it is where we all dwell. Like the masses of planets and stars, our bodies curve the space around us. We radiate signals constantly, radio sources that never go off the air. We cannot help being centers of attraction and repulsion for one another. That is not all we are by a long shot, nor all we are capable of feeling, and yet, even after our much-needed revolution in sexual consciousness, the power of eros will still turn our heads and hearts. In a world without beauty pageants, there will still be beauty, however its definition may have changed. As long as men have eyes, they will gaze with yearning and confusion at women.

> – Scott Russell Sanders
> "Looking at Women"
> *The Georgia Review*

7

James Dean was my first androgynous man. I figured I could talk to him. He was anguished and I was twelve, so we had a lot in common. With only a few exceptions, all the men I have liked or loved have been a certain kind of man: a kind who doesn't play football or watch the games on Sunday, who doesn't tell dirty jokes featuring broads or chicks, who is not contemptuous of conversations that are philosophically speculative, introspective, or otherwise foolish according to the other kind of man. He is more self-amused, less inflated, more quirky, vulnerable, and responsive than the other sort (the other sort, I'm visualizing as the guys on TV who advertise deodorant in the locker room). He is more like me than the other sort. He is what social scientists and feminists would call androgynous: having the characteristics of both male and female.

Now the first thing I want you to know about the androgynous man is that he is neither effeminate nor hermaphroditic. All his primary and secondary sexual characteristics are in order and I would say he's all-man, but that is just what he is not. He is more than all-man.

The merely all-man man, for one thing, never walks to the grocery store unless the little woman is away visiting her mother with the kids, or is in the hospital having a kid, or there is no little woman. All-men men don't know how to shop in a grocery store unless it is to buy a six-pack and some pretzels. Their ideas of nutrition expand beyond a six-pack and pretzels only to take in steak, potatoes, scotch or rye whiskey, and maybe a wad of cake or apple pie. All-men men have absolutely no taste in food, art, books, movies, theater, dance, how to live, what are good questions, what is funny, or anything else I care about. . . .

Male chauvinism is an irritation, but the real problem I have with the all-man man is that it's hard for me to talk to him. He's alien to me, and for this I'm at least half to blame. As his interests have not carried him into the sissy, mine have never taken me very far into the typically masculine terrains of sports, business and finance, politics, cars, boats, and machines. But blame or no blame, the reality is that it is almost as difficult for me to connect with him as it would be to link up with an Arab shepherd or Bolivian sandalmaker. There's a similar culture gap.

> – Amy Gross
> "The Appeal of the Androgynous Man"
> *Mademoiselle*

8

The women's movement cannot remake consciousness, or reshape the future, without acknowledging and shedding all the unnecessary and ugly baggage of the past. It's easy enough now to see where men have kept us out of clubs, baseball games, graduate schools; it's easy enough to recognize the hidden directions that limit Sis to cake baking and Junior to bridge building; it's now possible for even Miss America herself to identify what *they* have done to us, and, of course, *they* have and *they* did and *they* are. . . . But along the way we also developed our own hidden prejudices, class assumptions, and an antimale humor and collection of expectations that gave us, like all oppressed groups, a secret sense of superiority (coexisting with a poor self-image — it's not news that people can believe two contradictory things at once). . . .

Why are there laws insisting on alimony and child support? Well, everyone knows that men don't have an instinct to protect their young and, given half a chance, with the moon in the right phase, they will run off and disappear. Everyone assumes a mother will not let her child starve, yet it is necessary to legislate that a father must not do so. We are taught to accept the idea that men are less than decent; their charms may be manifold but their characters are riddled with faults. To this day I never blink if I hear that a man has gone to find his fortune in South America, having left his pregnant wife, his blind mother, and taken the family car. I still gasp in horror when I hear of a woman leaving her asthmatic infant for a rock group in Taos because I can't seem to avoid the assumption that men are naturally heels and women the ordained carriers of what little is moral in our dubious civilization. . . .

I remember shivering in the cold vestibule of a famous men's athletic club. Women and girls are not permitted inside the club's door. What are they doing in there, I asked? They're naked, said my mother, they're sweating, jumping up and down a lot, telling each other dirty jokes, and bragging about their stock market exploits. Why can't we go in? I asked. Well, my mother told me, they're afraid we'd laugh at them.

The prejudices of childhood are hard to outgrow. I confess that every time my business takes me past that club, I shudder. Images of large bellies resting on massage tables and flaccid penises rising and falling with the Dow Jones average flash through my head. There it is, chauvinism waving its cancerous tentacles from the depths of my psyche.

Minorities automatically feel superior to the oppressor because, after all, they are not hurting anybody. In fact, they feel morally better. The old canard that women need love, men need sex — believed for too long by both sexes — attributes moral and spiritual superiority to women and makes of men beasts whose urges send them prowling into the night. This false division of good and bad, placing deforming pressures on everyone, doesn't have to contaminate the future. We know that the assumptions we make about each other become a part of the cultural air we breathe and, in fact, become social truths. Women who want equality must be prepared to give it and to believe in it, and in order to do that it is not enough to state that you are as good as any man, but also it must be stated that he is as good as you and both will be humans together. If we want men to share in the care of the family in a new way, we must assume them as capable of consistent loving tenderness as we.

> – Anne Roiphe
> "Confessions of a Female Chauvinist Sow"
> *New York*

FRANCINE ᴅᴜ PLESSIX GRAY

Sex Roles in the Soviet Union

Born in 1930 in France, Francine du Plessix Gray emigrated to the
United States with her Russian mother at age eleven after her father died.
They left behind an international jet-set, high-fashion world in which
Gray had always felt a misfit. Talented at both painting and writing, she
ultimately opted to be a writer but marry a painter. After graduating from
Barnard College, Gray became a reporter for United Press International.
She returned to Paris for two years as a fashion reporter — an experience
which, she says, drove her to a Swiss sanatorium to recover. She joined
The New Yorker as a staff writer in 1968. Since then she has taught at
City College of the City University of New York and at Yale and Colum-
bia universities. Author of nonfiction books on Catholic radicalism and
Hawaii, Gray published her first novel — the semiautobiographical *Lovers
and Tyrants* — at the age of forty-six. In 1979 she attended the Soviet-
American Writers' Workshop in Batumi, USSR — her third trip to the
Soviet Union. Gray currently writes articles, stories, and reviews for
periodicals, including *The New Yorker,* where "Sex Roles in the Soviet
Union" appeared in February 1990. The essay is an excerpt from her
book *Soviet Women: Walking the Tightrope,* which she conceived at the
1987 Moscow Book Fair.

The Soviet Union's policy of *glasnost* (see p. 59) allowed Gray to
conduct candid, far-ranging interviews in that formerly closed country.
The combination of feminine dependence and self-sufficiency she discovered dates back at least to A.D. 945, when Russia's ruling Prince Igor
was killed. His widow, Olga, took over and ruled in his stead for nineteen
years. Before converting to Christianity and being canonized as the first
Russian saint, Olga avenged her husband's death by burying alive and
setting fire to envoys from his killers who proposed that she marry one of
their princes. In 1774 the empress Catherine the Great defeated both
the Turks and the Poles, annexing huge territories. In 1917, following
the Bolshevik Revolution, the Soviets were the first to include women's
rights in their constitution. Female power in the USSR today is a mixed
blessing: 92 percent of women work outside the home, and 50 percent
work at backbreaking manual jobs, in addition to bearing the burdens of
motherhood and all household chores.

One of the first questions I ask any Soviet woman aims at deciphering her views of *us* — American women. What central differences does she detect between her community of women and ours?

Among the many traits that Soviet women admire in their American peers is our lack of inhibitions, our boldness and daring.

"How I envy your inner freedom," a restaurant waitress in Moscow told me. "My generation was bred in a reign of terror — terror of jails, of reprisals, of authorities, of standing out in a crowd, of speaking our minds. . . . American women have so much more joy than we do. Our lives are so much more timid, formal, constrained."

The athleticism of American women was the trait most admired by a team of seven factory workers in Siberia. Only two of them knew how to swim; they had just learned in the past year, at one of the health clubs currently being founded in work collectives, and were now striving for "a more streamlined, American kind of silhouette" by doing thirty-lap sessions on weekends. "We hear that American women spend much of their free time *on themselves*, improving their bodies," one of the Siberians said. "That's an amazing notion to us."

There are, inevitably, some negative comparisons, and those tend to center on Americans' "sad overindividualism."

"Our sense of community is fast declining, but you're still far more solitary and lonely than we are," said the actress Sofiko Chiaureli, one of the Soviet Union's most beloved stars, who has attended film festivals in the United States. "Over here, if you fell sick in the street you'd be immediately taken into someone's house. Over there, no one would know the difference if you died. And you're so much less domestic! We always spread the table at home for a foreign guest. It's unthinkable to take a visitor to a restaurant. American women seem to *live* in restaurants."

Another recurring pattern in the impression that Soviet women have of their American peers is the youthful, daring behavior of older citizens. My Soviet acquaintances kept looking with wistful admiration at any traveling American woman over fifty years of age. One of my friends, a thirty-eight-year-old Muscovite, was particularly awed by a group of Chicago sexagenarians in white shorts, encountered in a hotel lobby, who were traveling through the Soviet Union to engage in tennis matches with Soviet players of their age group. "How admirable that you remain so adventurous," she reflected. "It would be unthinkable for us to make this kind of trip at that age. Here we become old at thirty-five. I am old already."

But there is one aspect of American women's lives that Soviet women   8
admire and envy above all others — American men. Throughout my
months of travel in the Soviet Union, I shared few conversations with
women in which I did not hear lavish praise of American men's amazing
"gentlemanliness" and "casual elegance," their talent as "good providers,"
and simultaneous invectives against the "passivity" and "boorishness" of
Soviet males.

The Leningrad fashion designer Aleksandra Sokolova, for instance,
once visited Cincinnati as a delegate to a women's congress, and her
descriptions of the United States center on our men's "nobility of manner." "Their constant smile, their gallantry — that was the most amazing
and impressive part of my trip," she said. "In the streets, in their homes,
as soon as they feel you mightn't like something, they say 'Excuse me.'
In comparison, our men's manners are constantly, uncouthly rude."

Even in the ultra-patriotic city of Tashkent, a group of women journalists concurred. "American men are so much more *gallant* in their
behavior, and take so much better care of their appearance," one of them
said. "If a Soviet man isn't taught by his wife how to dress, how to
behave, he tends to remain just boorish."

Soviet women throughout the nation are obsessed, these days, with
the decline in national courtesy. There is much self-searching and a lot
of talk about root causes: Stalin's extermination of both the pre-revolutionary and the Bolshevik intelligentsia, which had been traditional bearers of civility; the cynicism, the lessening of compassion, the spiraling
growth of black-market corruption and racketeering, the general lowering
of morals that spread through the society during the Brezhnev era, now
known as *zastoi*, "the stagnancy"; the sense of individual helplessness that
grew during those years, leading citizens to boss and shove one another
more rudely than ever before, as their only way of self-assertion.

So finding a spouse or a companion who is a decorous American-type   12
dzhentlmen (one of many words that have become part of Sovenglish)
has become an obsession among Soviet women. It leads to this irony:
our male citizenry, which for two centuries has been derided by Europeans for its uncouthness, its raw frontier manner, is now looked on by
Soviet women as the paragon of chivalry and aristocratic courtesy. Although British, French, Italian, and German tourists are more numerous
than Americans in the Soviet Union, one never hears any praise of the
deportment of these men. Only the American model will do.

Among the intelligentsia, many Soviet males are trying with touching
ardor to redeem their image. There is a growing fashion among them to

say "Madame" and to kiss women's hands in greeting. "I drink to your
aristocratic eyes" (or "aristocratic hands," or "aristocratic bearing") is one
of the most popular toasts at dinner gatherings. Soviet men's earnest
efforts to open doors, to help women in and out of coats and cars, to
carry their smallest parcels, transport one to prewar Europe, and make
the most polished American fellows seem quite rustic. And this fixation
on manners must be seen in the context of a far wider nostalgia for "the
cultivated person" of pre-revolutionary culture. It is a nostalgia that has
to do also with the current search for a more clearly defined national
identity and the renewed interest in Russian history and religion, which
are among the most striking aspects of the *glasnost* era.

"The tragedies of the past decades have created generations of males
who are a totally different species from those of forty years ago," Aleksandra Sokolova says. "As late as the mid-nineteen-forties, it would have
been unthinkable in this city for a man not to stand up for a woman in
a bus, or for an adolescent to shove his way through a tram without
being reprimanded by dozens of his elders. No courses, no book manuals
can restructure them. Even our contemporary youth may be lost to us
— Russian men's traditional generosity, nobility of character are gone.
We are left just dreaming, merely dreaming of such creatures. Now there
are only a few exceptions left who are bearable to live with." . . .

Throughout my stays in the Soviet Union, I kept remembering . . .
early glimpses of male passivity and disillusionment, of female power and
self-esteem, while talking to the few scholars who are beginning to research patterns of sex differences in Soviet society. Because of the distaste
for such analysis that prevails in any Marxist state, it is an area of
psychology that has been virtually untouched in the Soviet Union until
recently.

Olga Voronina, my philosopher friend in Moscow who is one of the   16
even smaller group of scholars who consider themselves "feminists" (she
estimates that no more than twenty women in Moscow would accept that
label), views the situation this way: Soviet girls are favored by teachers
from the earliest preschool days, because, having stronger role models,
they are more obedient than boys and do far better in school. "Even in
such patriarchal organizations as Pioneer groups, until the age of fourteen
or so the girls were always far more active — I say 'were' because the
popularity of such Party organizations has much decreased lately," she
said. "Look at their role models: mother often alone at home ruling the
roost, an all-female cast of teachers, and, all around them, women

handling the double shift of career and home. The girls absorb this female energy and are more active on every level throughout their school years. But as they reach adolescence they tend consciously to slow down, and curb themselves; they think an overactive woman is less appealing. Well, God only knows how aggressive we'd be if we *didn't* curb ourselves a little bit!"

"I know that a majority of public-school teachers in the U.S.A. are also women," my friend Elvira Novikova, another feminist scholar, said. "But it's a Soviet phenomenon for teachers to favor girls as much as we do. That creates a pattern of antisocial behavior among boys. It leads them to feel that it's not 'cool' to get good grades, and it reinforces their resentment of women. A boy's ego is further undermined because he spends most of his time at home with his mother; his father — if he has one — is often too passive or too macho or not sensitive enough to deal with a child's problems and become a proper role model."

"Our young men have gone out into the world with the attitude that they're little boys, still under the wings of their mommies," said Monika Zile, the magazine editor. "When they've had to take a responsibility or make a decision, a woman has always stepped in to take over."

Mariya Osorina, a Leningrad psychologist, offered more complex historical reasons for what one could call "the Powerful Woman Syndrome" in Russian society. She sees a breaking point in nineteenth-century history, in the Decembrist rebellion of 1825: when that first wave of political dissent was brutally crushed by the czar, Russia's male intelligentsia lost much of its self-esteem, began to feel marginal and helpless before an immutable authoritarian regime. She also believes that the deepest traditions of Russian culture — the high value on inner emotional life, the life of the spirit — are far more feminine than those of most other nations. "Compare our traditional values, for instance, with the very masculine, pragmatic, utilitarian German ethos," she said. "For some eight centuries, we praised and upheld all that was connected with *dukhovnye tsennosty* — 'spiritual values' — and we were taught to disdain most practical aspects of existence. This reverence for values associated with the female principle gave women an immense psychic power, even through the feudalism and repression that lasted until the late nineteenth century, even before they were allowed to have schooling and careers. Ironically, the union of feminine and national values has continued right into postrevolutionary times. Teachers have favored girls because their behavior is more closely modeled on the Soviet system of social values — on communitarian obedience, orderliness, altruism, dutifulness."

On all levels of Soviet society, one is constantly impressed by women's   20
keen sense of their greater patience, diligence, optimism, endurance,
shrewdness, and self-esteem — a self-esteem apparently heightened by
the very arduousness of their everyday duties, their incessant foraging for
basic necessities of food and clothing. This sense of female superiority is
summed up with eerie precision by a Russian proverb: "Women can do
everything; men can do the rest."

What are some other reasons that make it easier for women than for
men to grow into powerful, responsible citizens with superior work habits?
When answering that question today, in the *glasnost* era, most Soviet
citizens feel free to put the blame on their nation's history: Through
centuries of serfdom and seven decades of dictatorship, men have never
had a chance to develop their initiative.

In a culture in which men have never felt themselves to be masters
of their fates, never felt any real worth in their work, "how could they
ever become responsible?" Monika Zile asks. "Women, on the other
hand, kept right on ruling over their little domestic kingdoms, and never
suffered an equal sense of helplessness. And at the time of the revolution,
when only some 10 percent of our women were literate, they had to take
such huge leaps that somehow they just keep leaping on and on, bypassing
the men in many ways — in levels of education, of steadfastness, and,
particularly, of diligence."

Soviet women's remarkable self-assurance (not to say their superiority
complex) leads to an often derisive view of men that might make the
most committed American feminist uncomfortable. I felt it painfully
during a discussion with a group of women who were television producers
in Riga. They had expressed the recurring complaint of *peregruzhennost*,
"overburdening," and one member of the group had cited some striking
figures that are often mentioned in women's conversations: Soviet husbands have some thirty hours more free time a week than their wives,
enjoying a total of nearly two "stolen days"; women, because of their
chores, enjoy one hour less sleep at night than men; and women have
an average of only twelve minutes a day to spend on their children's
education.

I asked my Riga acquaintances what the average man might be doing   24
with that free time.

The group burst into raucous laughter.

"He takes out the dog," one said. (Much giggling.)

"He looks at television and occasionally remembers to play with the
children," a second one said. ("Yes, yes!" and hoots of derision.)

"He mostly takes out the dog," a third one repeated. (More laughter.)   28
"He tinkers with the car." (Further hilarity.)

"He tinkers with the car to *pretend* he's doing something." (More approving laughter.)

Analyzing the mysterious force of Russian females and the relative passivity of Russian men, some of the more thoughtful women I talked to put the blame on their own sex. "Russian women have a need to control that verges on the tyrannical, the sadistic," said Elvira Osipova, a professor of British and American literature at Leningrad State University, and a wise observer of national habits. "If our men can't manage to curb the aggressive, sadistic element in their spouses' characters, women will always end up tyrannizing over them, like no other women I can think of in history."

After dozens of evenings spent with distraught, henpecked men and   32
with a dismaying abundance of superwomen, I reached the conclusion that the Soviet Union might be as much in need of a men's movement as of a women's movement. I tried out the idea on some of my female acquaintances, and found it very well received.

"The principal function of a women's movement in this country would be to quiet our women down, make them more capable of reassuring their men," Mariya Osorina said. "A good feminist movement would make our women more gentle, restore the sexes to that fine balance they had in Pushkin's time. . . . Look at the Decembrist men — powerful, positive heroes, with heroic, strong, but gentle wives."

"With emancipation, we not only freed ourselves but created a generation in which too many women tried to be the heads of families," I was told by a Riga marriage counselor named Anna Livmane. "Excuse the rudeness, but I shall put it this way: Man should always be the Minister of Exterior Affairs, the woman should be the Minister of Interior Affairs. Now women try too often to be both kinds of minister, and men, who are lazier by nature, withdraw."

Thus one of the important benefits of *perestroika*, many Soviet citizens would agree, is that by freeing women from some part of their historic double burden it may allow them to step back and relax. "*Perestroika* is about waking up the *lichnost* — 'individualism' — in our men, so that they cease feeling superfluous," Monika Zile said. "It is about creating a society of less aggressive females, who can at last regain their womanliness."

EXPLORATIONS

1. What comparisons does Gray establish in paragraphs 1–7 of her essay? in paragraphs 8–14? What additional comparison does she begin to establish in paragraph 15?

2. What role do quotations play in Gray's essay? How would the essay's impact change if she used no direct quotations?

3. Find at least three different paragraphs in which Gray writes in the first-person plural — *we, us, our.* To what group is she referring? What do you think Gray hopes to achieve by identifying herself in this way?

CONNECTIONS

1. Do Soviet and American women share the same image of American men? Look at the ways American men are portrayed in *Looking at Ourselves,* particularly in the passages by Gayle Early, Joe Kane, and Amy Gross. What points of agreement can you find between Soviet and American women about American men, and what points of disagreement?

2. Look back at Carola Hansson and Karin Lidén's "Liza and Family" (p. 109). What points about male and female roles in the Soviet Union are made in both that essay and Gray's? Cite specific evidence.

3. Look back at Joyce Carol Oates's "Meeting the Gorbachevs" (p. 66). What does Oates tell us about her relationship with her husband? What does she tell us about the relationship between Mikhail and Raisa Gorbachev? What characteristics does each of these marriages appear to share with the Soviet marriages Gray describes?

ELABORATIONS

1. In paragraphs 16–31, Gray cites several possible explanations for "the Powerful Woman Syndrome" in the Soviet Union. Her interviewees mention *qualities* (what Soviet men are like) and *processes* (how they got that way). Based on Gray's essay, *Looking at Ourselves,* and your own experience, write a comparison-contrast essay telling how Soviet and American men differ (qualities) and giving some possible reasons why they do (processes).

2. Referring to Hansson and Lidén's "Liza and Family" (p. 109) and Gray's "Sex Roles in the Soviet Union," write a classification essay on female and male stereotypes in the USSR.

CLARA PIRIZ

Marriage by Pros and Cons

Clara Piriz's letter to her husband in prison, translated from the Spanish by Regina M. Kreger, comes from Alicia Partnoy's 1988 book *You Can't Drown the Fire: Latin American Women Writing in Exile.* Partnoy supplies the following information: "Back in Uruguay after many years of exile in Holland, Clara Piriz has recently worked in the organization of the 'Uruguayan Women's Plenary.' The letter she shares with us was her first uncensored communication with her husband, who had been a political prisoner in Uruguay for twelve years."

The Oriental Republic of Uruguay, as it is formally called, is a country of rolling, grassy hills, about the size of Washington State, in southern South America. Spanish settlers began replacing the native Charua Indians in the early 1600s, followed by Portuguese from Brazil. Spain annexed Uruguay in the 1700s; rebels started fighting colonial rule in 1810 and declared an independent republic in 1825. The nation prospered until economic problems, floods, and drought struck in the late 1960s. The Tupamaros, leftist guerrillas drawn from the upper classes, increased their terrorist actions. A military insurrection in 1973 took control of the government from President Juan Maria Bordaberry, who was officially ousted three years later.

Under military rule, Uruguay had the highest percentage of political prisoners and some of the worst prison conditions in the world, according to the human rights organization Amnesty International. Half a million people fled the country (Uruguay's total population is under 3 million). In 1985 the government returned to civilian control, and in 1989 Luis Alberto Lacalle was elected president. Backed by Uruguayan farmers and other conservative factions, he campaigned on a program of economic reform and increased opportunity for private enterprise.

Abcoude, Holland,
May 12, 1984

Dear Kiddo,

I'm writing this letter with no margins, without counting lines, or pages, without measuring my words a damn bit. Our first communication uncensored and uncut.

The big question is if I will manage to write without self-censorship . . . internalized censorship. Fear. My fear of causing you pain, of

showing myself as I am, of confusing you in my confusion . . . My fear
of losing what I've gained and gaining what I've lost . . .

A while ago I wrote you that it would be good for you to try to get
out with a passport that would allow you to come and go. Let me explain
why. At bottom it just has to do with another fear: the fear of ruining
your life . . . even more.

Living in exile is a bitch. "Sure," you say, "it can't be worse than   4
prison." True, prison is much worse. But, there is one fundamental
difference: In prison you have to use all your energy to survive in a
situation that doesn't depend on you and that you can't change. To
survive in exile you have to use all your energy to change a situation of
terrible inertia, and, if it changes, it will be only because of your personal
effort.

You arrive here with nothing, no friends, no job, no house, no family.
You don't understand the system in which you've somehow got to function. The place assigned to you is marginal, socially, economically,
politically, culturally, emotionally. No one gives a damn about you. You
have no history. Or rather, the history you have, no one cares about.
Although suddenly it occurs to some reporter to use you as material for
an article. A monkey in the zoo. And you accept, of course, because it's
part of the political work: call attention to Uruguay, get political pressure.
But if you achieve anything, no one cares. There are too many people.
Most of all there are too many foreigners. Discrimination exists, and it
is rough. It sucks to feel looked down on, it sucks to have to do twice as
much to get credit for half. It sucks when you say something and they
look at you: *"and where did you crawl out . . ."* Not to mention worse
things, like insults and violence.

But not all of it comes from outside of us; a lot we bring on ourselves.
Most of the exiles resist adapting. They don't want to be here; they didn't
choose to come to this country; everything is going wrong for them. The
Dutch "smell bad"; *"you know how they are."* The exiles don't want to
learn this fucking language, they refuse to give two and be counted for
one. *"What for, anyway, if I'm going to leave . . . "* Result: Many of
them have ended up completely screwed. Ten years of doing nothing of
any worth, always running around, drinking beer and Geneva gin. Some
of them read a lot, they remind me of your brother, a vagabond with
books under his arm. Others have made a way for themselves, working
like mules. Some have had the advantage of having studied, others of
being stubborn workers with the "nasty habit of earning their living."
This small group has one other problem: We are isolated because there's

not enough time and energy to work, learn the language, etc. . . . and still maintain friendships scattered all around the country.

A while ago I was talking with two Chileans and an Argentine woman I see regularly (a recently found remedy for the isolation). They said that even though they work, speak Dutch and have Dutch friends, communication with them had a limit they couldn't cross. I've heard that from other people. I must confess that is not the case with me. I have good friends who are Dutch, with whom my communication is excellent.

Well, as you see I'm not painting you a very pleasant picture. I can imagine that after twelve years in jail all this seems banal, but experience shows that once you are here the twelve years of jail don't help you think, *"What a terrific time I'm having."* On the contrary, those years are one more problem. 8

In your case, there might be some points in your favor. Supposing our relationship works out (another subject altogether), I have made a way that can make your adjustment easier.

You might ask yourself if I am telling you this to try to discourage you. No. What it means is that I know what you'll have to face if you come here. And I don't want to have it on my conscience that I lured you with a siren song.

Our situation is not very encouraging either: two years of living together in very abnormal conditions. Twelve years without seeing each other: you in jail, which has certainly changed you. Neither one of us knows what problems are going to crop up from that. Certainly, within normal limits, you've changed a great deal. But it's also logical to expect less normal changes. There is no superman who can come unscathed out of one of those places. I don't believe those people — and there are some — who come out saying, *"Prison? A great experience, it's nothing."* I also have lived through very hard experiences; I also am very much marked.

Besides, as a couple we're going to face a very strange situation. I have matured in this country, I have carried out a whole process of learning, of critical integration, of getting situated here, which you, one way or another, will have to carry out. This puts you in a position of dependence of me, which does not contribute to a healthy adult emotional relationship. 12

I'm finishing this letter today, June 24. Happy birthday! After yesterday's phone conversation I have such anxiety to see you, to talk to you, to touch you, that I can't imagine how I'm going to live from now until we see each other.

Yet there's so much we will have to discuss and go through!

And don't get all romantic on me and tell me that love, or the will to love, can overcome everything. No. It can overcome a lot, it is an essential condition, but not enough. I've seen so many who could not withstand the pressures of the change.

From a very young age, I have been bothered by rules without reasons, by *just because* or *because I said so* or *because that's the way it has to be*. It has bothered me as much in my social as in my private life. And systematically I have created a new set of rules based on my own experiences, on their analysis and synthesis and also on the reading and studies of the ideas of other (wiser) people. This attitude toward life is not new for me. Just think, if not, Carolina would not exist. Carolina was not an impulse, a mistake, a transgression. For me she was a conscious moral act which I have never regretted.

It was not always so easy: For years I struggled inside myself. Because sincerity is one of my values, at times I had to choose between the risk of destroying you or lying in the gentle way, by keeping quiet. Sometimes I kept quiet, sometimes I didn't. Finally I arrived at a formula: I'd try to let you know as best as possible how I felt about a lot of things and avoid the details that could be painful for you.

But my evolution is not only in that area. Most important to me is my maturity and my independence. That's why I made that comment on the phone yesterday: "You are going to have a hard time with me." I don't like to be ordered around, or told what to do. I reaffirm my right to my own decisions, your right to your own decisions, our right to be and think differently.

When I stayed alone with the girls I had to perform all of the roles; I was their mother and their father and their pet dog, too. I got used to it and from there I chose what I liked best to do, and that's not necessarily the womanly duties. Therefore (referring to a fantasy you wrote me about that frightened me): If you want homemade ravioli, make them yourself. I'll help you eat them. And I'll drink the wine. As a housekeeper I am consciously a disaster. My work is much more important to me, and my personal and professional development more than anything. For years my possibilities were limited by the urgency of moment to moment life, and by the girls' ages. Nevertheless, I got started with a brave effort. Now they are grown, they have their own independence, they're not attached to me, and I have found a phenomenal job. You can imagine that I'm grabbing onto that with all my strength. At my age it's my last chance and I can't and don't want to miss it.

We don't know what each of us means by a "primary relationship." 20
You said it very blithely, as if there was a universally accepted formula.
But I am certain that it's not that way. When I was twenty years old, I
believed it, but not now, and that is not disillusionment, not at all, it's
wisdom.

For instance, you asked me if I had a boyfriend. You didn't know how
to deal with my answer. You said that could surely be the biggest stumbling block, and I answer you that the stumbling block is not that he
exists . . . but the fact that *I* am capable of having a boyfriend.

I hold that I have been relentlessly faithful. Perhaps not in the way
that you mean, but I'd bet if we talked about it, you'd see my way is
much better.

Why do I want to see you? Because I do. Because I also allow myself
the right to be (every once in a while) compulsive. I'm doing fine, I have
a good job, a good social life, a serene and comforting relationship, the
girls are growing up with no problems. Then why create problems for
myself? Why not leave things as they are? Because I want to see you.
Because I would feel terribly frustrated not to see you, because it would
be a lack of respect for you, for me, for what we were, for what we are,
and perhaps for what we might become . . . Because I want a second
chance. Because only you and I can decide if it'll work or not. That
decision is not for time, or distance, much less for the military to take.
It's ours.

On the phone I found it hard to say I love you, for fear you misun- 24
derstood what I felt. So, I'll say: In my own way I love you. We'll have
to see if my way and yours will meet — and grow.

Bye,
Clara

EXPLORATIONS

1. What are the possible meanings of Piriz's title, "Marriage by Pros and Cons"?

2. What direct statements does Piriz make about her feelings? What comments
   in her letter give the reader indirect information about her emotions regarding
   her husband? her life in exile? the political problems in Uruguay? What
   statements early in her letter suggest why so many of her comments are
   indirect?

3. What appear to be Piriz's greatest hopes and her greatest fears about a reunion with her husband? How can you tell?

CONNECTIONS

1. What qualities does Piriz share with the women described in Francine du Plessix Gray's "Sex Roles in the Soviet Union"? What specific statements in her letter reveal these qualities?

2. In *Looking at Ourselves*, Susan Brownmiller describes a shift back to a traditional concept of femininity. What remarks in Piriz's letter show her attitude toward that female role? What features of Piriz's situation make the trend described by Brownmiller relevant or irrelevant to her?

3. Look back at Benazir Bhutto's "The Day They Killed My Father" (p. 280). What statements does Bhutto make about her father's imprisonment, particularly the ways she and her father adapted to prison conditions, that are echoed by Piriz?

ELABORATIONS

1. Imagine you are a marriage counselor asked to advise Clara Piriz and her husband on resuming their marriage in exile after the husband's release from prison. Should they try to pick up where they left off? Why or why not? If not, what should they do instead? Using the information in Piriz's letter, write an argumentative essay explaining and defending your position. You may also draw on Bhutto's "The Day They Killed My Father" (p. 280), Liang Heng and Judith Shapiro's "Chairman Mao's Good Little Boy" (p. 93), and Shelley Saywell's "Women Warriors of El Salvador" (p. 636).

2. Piriz is concerned that her husband will be dependent on her in Holland, "which does not contribute to a healthy adult emotional relationship" (para. 12). Does your experience confirm this statement? Write a classification essay on the ways that partners in a couple can be dependent on each other, indicating which ways are healthy and which ones are harmful.

RICHARD RODRIGUEZ

You Are a Man

Unlike the boy whose border crossing opens "You Are a Man," Richard Rodriguez was born in 1944 in San Francisco. His parents worked hard to give him the support he needed to become part of the dominant culture, sending him to private Catholic schools and speaking English with him at home (see p. 397). After receiving his bachelor's degree from Stanford University and his master's from Columbia, Rodriguez did further graduate study at the University of California, Berkeley, and at the Warburg Institute in London. His success was marred by awareness that he owed some of it to his minority status, which opened the door for affirmative action benefits, and that most other Mexican-Americans were not so lucky. Rodriguez turned down several university-level teaching jobs, stung by the irony of being welcomed as a minority-group member after striving all his life for assimilation into the majority. He spent the next six years writing *Hunger of Memory: The Education of Richard Rodriguez* (1982). He is currently a full-time writer in San Francisco, with one foot in journalism and the other in literature. "You Are a Man" comes from an excerpt in the April 1989 *Harper's* of "Proofs," an introduction to Ken Light's collection of photographs *To the Promised Land*. (For background on Mexico, see p. 9.)

You stand around. You smoke. You spit. You are wearing your two shirts, two pants, two underpants. Jesús says if they chase you, throw that bag down. Your plastic bag is your mama, all you have left: the yellow cheese she wrapped has formed a translucent rind; the laminated scapular of the Sacred Heart nestles flame in its cleft. Put it in your pocket. Inside. Put it in your underneath pants' pocket. The last hour of Mexico is twilight, the shuffling of feet. Jesús says they are able to see in the dark. They have X rays and helicopters and searchlights. Jesús says wait, just wait, till he says. Though most of the men have started to move. You feel the hand of Jesús clamp your shoulder, fingers cold as ice. *Venga, corre.*[1] You run. All the rest happens without words. Your feet are tearing

---

[1]Come, run. — ED.

dry grass, your heart is lashed like a mare. You trip, you fall. You are now in the United States of America. You are a boy from a Mexican village. You have come into the country on your knees with your head down. You are a man.

Papa, what was it like?

I am his second son, his favorite child, his confidant. After we have polished the De Soto, we sit in the car and talk. I am sixteen years old. I fiddle with the knobs of the radio. He is fifty.

He will never say. He was an orphan there. He had no mother, he   4
remembered none. He lived in a village by the ocean. He wanted books and he had none.

You are lucky, boy.

In the Fifties, Mexican men were contracted to work in America as *braceros*, farm workers. I saw them downtown in Sacramento. I saw men my age drunk in Plaza Park on Sundays, on their backs on the grass. I was a boy at sixteen, but I was an American. At sixteen, I wrote a gossip column, "The Watchful Eye," for my school paper.

Or they would come into town on Monday nights for the wrestling matches or on Tuesdays for boxing. They worked over in Yolo County. They were men without women. They were Mexicans without Mexico.

On Saturdays, they came into town to the Western Union office where   8
they sent money — money turned into humming wire and then turned back into money — all the way down into Mexico. They were husbands, fathers, sons. They kept themselves poor for Mexico.

Much that I would come to think, the best I would think about male Mexico, came as much from those chaste, lonely men as from my own father who made false teeth and who — after thirty years in America — owned a yellow stucco house on the east side of town.

The male is responsible. The male is serious. A man remembers.

Fidel, the janitor at church, lived over the garage at the rectory. Fidel spoke Spanish and was Mexican. He had a wife down there, people said; some said he had grown children. But too many years had passed and he didn't go back. Fidel had to do for himself. Fidel had a clean piece of linoleum on the floor, he had an iron bed, he had a table and a chair. He had a coffeepot and a frying pan and a knife and a fork and a spoon, I guess. And everything else Fidel sent back to Mexico. Sometimes, on summer nights, I would see his head through the bars of the little window over the garage at the rectory.

The migration of Mexico is not only international, south to north. 12 The epic migration of Mexico, and throughout Latin America, is from the village to the city. And throughout Latin America, the city has ripened, swollen with the century. Lima, Caracas, Mexico City. So the journey to Los Angeles is much more than a journey from Spanish to English. It is the journey from *tú* — the familiar, the erotic, the intimate pronoun — to the repellent *usted* of strangers' eyes.

It is 1986 and I am a journalist. I am asking questions of a Mexican woman in her East L.A. house. She is watchful and pretty, in her thirties, she wears an apron. Her two boys — Roy and Danny — are playing next door. Her husband is a tailor. He is sewing in a bright bedroom at the back of the house. His feet work the humming treadle of an old Singer machine as he croons Mexican love songs by an open window.
I will send for you or I will come home rich.

Mexico is poor. But my mama says there are no love songs like the love songs of Mexico. She hums a song she can't remember. The ice cream there is creamier than here. Someday we will see. The people are kinder — poor, but kinder to each other.
My mother's favorite record is "*Mariachis de Mexico y Pepe Villa con* 16 *Orquesta.*"
Men sing in Mexico. Men are strong and silent. But in song the Mexican male is granted license he is otherwise denied. The male can admit longing, pain, desire.
HAIII — EEEE — a cry like a comet rises over the song. A cry like mock weeping tickles the refrain of Mexican love songs. The cry is meant to encourage the balladeer — it is the raw edge of his sentiment. HAIII-EEEE. It is the man's sound. A ticklish arching of semen, a node wrung up a guitar string, until it bursts in a descending cascade of mockery. HAI. HAI. HAI. HAI. The cry of a jackal under the moon, the whistle of the phallus, the maniacal song of the skull.

Mexico is on the phone — long distance.
A crow alights upon a humming wire, bobs up and down, needles the 20

lice within his vest, surveys with clicking eyes the field, the cloud of mites, then dips into the air and flies away.

Juanito killed! My mother shrieks, drops the phone in the dark. She cries for my father. For light.

The earth quakes. The peso flies like chaff in the wind. The police chief purchases his mistress a mansion on the hill.

The doorbell rings. I split the blinds to see three nuns standing on our front porch.

Mama. Mama.   24

Monsignor Lyons has sent three Mexican nuns over to meet my parents. The nuns have come to Sacramento to beg for Mexico at the eleven o'clock Mass. We are the one family in the parish that speaks Spanish. As they file into our living room, the nuns smell pure, not sweet, pure like candles or like laundry.

The nun with a black mustache sighs at the end of each story the other two tell. Orphan. Leper. Crutch. Dry land. One eye. Casket.

¡Que lástima![2]
Tell me, Papa.   28
What?
About Mexico.

I lived with the family of my uncle. I was the orphan in the village. I used to ring the church bells in the morning, many steps up in the dark. When I'd get up to the tower I could see the ocean.

The village, Papa, the houses too . . .   32

The ocean. He studies the polished hood of our beautiful blue De Soto.

Relatives invited relatives. Entire Mexican villages got re-created in three stories of a single house. In the fall, after the harvest in the Valley, families of Mexican adults and their American children would load up their cars and head back to Mexico in caravans, for weeks, for months. The schoolteacher said to my mother what a shame it was the Mexicans did that — took their children out of school.

---

[2]What a pity! — Ed.

Like Wandering Jews. They carried their home with them, back and forth; they had no true home but the tabernacle of memory.

Each year the American kitchen takes on a new appliance.   36
The children are fed and grow tall. They go off to school with children from Vietnam, from Kansas, from Hong Kong. They get into fights. They come home and they say dirty words.

The city will win. The city will give the children all the village could not — VCRs, hairstyles, drumbeat. The city sings mean songs, dirty songs. But the city will sing the children a great Protestant hymn.

You can be anything you want to be.

Your coming of age. It is early. From your bed you watch your mama   40
moving back and forth under the light. The bells of the church ring in the dark. Mama crosses herself. From your bed you watch her back as she wraps the things you will take.

You are sixteen. Your father has sent for you. That's what it means: He has sent an address in Nevada. He is there with your uncle. You remember your uncle remembering snow with his beer.

You dress in the shadows. You move toward the table, the circle of light. You sit down. You force youself to eat. Mama stands over you to make the sign of the cross on your forehead with her thumb. You are a man. You smile. She puts the bag of food in your hands. She says she has told *La Virgen*.³

Then you are gone. It is gray. You hear a little breeze. It is the rustle of your old black Dueña,⁴ the dog, taking her shortcuts through the weeds, crazy Dueña, her pads on the dust. She is following you.

You pass the houses of the village, each window is a proper name.   44
You pass the store. The bar. The lighted window of the clinic where the pale medical student from Monterrey lives alone and reads his book full of sores late into the night.

You want to be a man. You have the directions in your pocket: an address in Tijuana and a map with a yellow line that leads from the highway to an X on a street in Reno. You are afraid, but you have never seen snow.

You are just beyond the cemetery. The breeze has died. You turn and

---

³The Virgin Mary. — Ed.
⁴A *dueña* is an older woman acting as a chaperone of a young lady. — Ed.

throw a rock back at La Dueña, where you know she is — where you will always know where she is. She will not go past the cemetery. She will turn in circles like a *loca*[5] and bite herself.

The dust takes on gravel, the path becomes a rutted road which leads to the highway. You walk north. The sky has turned white overhead. Insects click in the fields. In time, there will be a bus.

I will send for you or I will come home rich.   48

EXPLORATIONS

1. What is happening in the first paragraph of Rodriguez's essay? Who is "you"? Who are "they"? What is the effect of the other character's being called Jesús?

2. In which paragraphs does Rodriquez write mainly in the first person? the second person? the third person? How does his choice of person relate to the kind of information he is conveying?

3. Which characters in his essay does Rodriguez quote directly? How do these speeches differ from conventional dialogue? What are the effects of the differences?

CONNECTIONS

1. What common problems are faced by the Mexican emigrants described by Rodriguez and the Uruguayan emigrants described by Clara Piriz in "Marriage by Pros and Cons"? What qualities in Piriz and in the Mexican men seem to be a reaction to exile rather than part of a gender role?

2. What characteristics do the Mexican men in Rodriguez's essay share with the John Wayne image described by Gayle Early in *Looking at Ourselves*? What characteristics do these men share with the androgynous image described by Amy Gross in *Looking at Ourselves*?

3. What is the occupational and socioeconomic status of Rodriguez's characters? How can you tell? Look back at Octavio Paz's "Hygiene and Repression" (p. 9). Is Paz writing about the same socioeconomic group as Rodriguez? How can you tell?

---

[5]Crazy woman. — Ed.

ELABORATIONS

1. In his first and last paragraphs, Rodriguez writes about leaving home. What familiar objects and sensations help to convey a sense of sadness and loss? What foreign objects and sensations help to convey fear? Think of a time when you left a place or person or family you loved, and write a narrative essay about that experience. Utilize some of the techniques Rodriguez uses to evoke the emotions you felt.

2. In paragraph 12 Rodriguez speaks of migration "from the village to the city," from being surrounded by friends and family to living among strangers. What other differences strike someone who moves from a small, well-known place to a large, anonymous one, or vice versa? Write an essay comparing and contrasting two different places to be — a village and a city, a neighborhood elementary school and a regional high school, or any other shift between big and small, friendly and strange.

LESLIE MARMON SILKO

Yellow Woman

Leslie Marmon Silko was born in Albuquerque, New Mexico, in 1948. Part Laguna Pueblo, part Mexican, and part Anglo, she grew up on the Laguna Pueblo Reservation where she now lives with her husband and two children. To the northwest stands Mt. Taylor, legendary home of the ka'tsina spirits that appear in Pueblo and Hopi mythology. Silko graduated from the University of New Mexico in 1969. After teaching at Navajo Community College in Arizona, she moved to Ketchikan, Alaska, where she would later set the title story for her collection *Storyteller* (1981). Returning to the Southwest, she taught at the University of New Mexico and at the University of Arizona, Tucson. The most widely praised of Silko's poetry and prose is her 1977 novel *Ceremony* — the first novel published by a Native American woman and a landmark in American fiction. Silko's stories have appeared in a variety of magazines and collections. She is the recipient of a five-year MacArthur Foundation Grant.

I

My thigh clung to his with dampness, and I watched the sun rising up through the tamaracks and willows. The small brown water birds came to the river and hopped across the mud, leaving brown scratches in the alkali-white crust. They bathed in the river silently. I could hear the water, almost at our feet where the narrow fast channel bubbled and washed green ragged moss and fern leaves. I looked at him beside me, rolled in the red blanket on the white river sand. I cleaned the sand out of the cracks between my toes, squinting because the sun was above the willow trees. I looked at him for the last time, sleeping on the white river sand.

I felt hungry and followed the river south the way we had come the afternoon before, following our footprints that were already blurred by lizard tracks and bug trails. The horses were still lying down, and the black one whinnied when he saw me but he did not get up — maybe it was because the corral was made out of thick cedar branches and the horses had not yet felt the sun like I had. I tried to look beyond the pale red mesas to the pueblo. I knew it was there, even if I could not see it, on the sand rock hill above the river, the same river that moved past me now and had reflected the moon last night.

The horse felt warm underneath me. He shook his head and pawed the sand. The bay whinnied and leaned against the gate trying to follow, and I remembered him asleep on the red blanket beside the river. I slid off the horse and tied him close to the other horse. I walked north with the river again, and the white sand broke loose in footprints over footprints.

"Wake up." 4

He moved in the blanket and turned his face to me with his eyes still closed. I knelt down to touch him.

"I'm leaving."

He smiled now, eyes still closed. "You are coming with me, remember?" He sat up now with his bare dark chest and belly in the sun.

"Where?" 8

"To my place."

"And will I come back?"

He pulled his pants on. I walked away from him, feeling him behind me and smelling the willows.

"Yellow Woman," he said. 12

I turned to face him. "Who are you?" I asked.

He laughed and knelt on the low, sandy bank, washing his face in the river. "Last night you guessed my name, and you knew why I had come."

I stared past him at the shallow moving water and tried to remember the night, but I could only see the moon in the water and remember his warmth around me.

"But I only said that you were him and that I was Yellow Woman — 16 I'm not really her — I have my own name and I come from the pueblo on the other side of the mesa. Your name is Silva and you are a stranger I met by the river yesterday afternoon."

He laughed softly. "What happened yesterday has nothing to do with what you will do today, Yellow Woman."

"I know — that's what I'm saying — the old stories about the ka'tsina spirit and Yellow Woman can't mean us."

My old grandpa liked to tell those stories best. There is one about Badger and Coyote who went hunting and were gone all day, and when the sun was going down they found a house. There was a girl living there alone, and she had light hair and eyes and she told them that they could sleep with her. Coyote wanted to be with her all night so he sent Badger into a prairie-dog hole, telling him he thought he saw something in it. As soon as Badger crawled in, Coyote blocked up the entrance with rocks and hurried back to Yellow Woman.

"Come here," he said gently.   20

He touched my neck and I moved close to him to feel his breathing and to hear his heart. I was wondering if Yellow Woman had known who she was — if she knew that she would become part of the stories. Maybe she'd had another name that her husband and relatives called her so that only the ka'tsina from the north and the storytellers would know her as Yellow Woman. But I didn't go on; I felt him all around me, pushing me down into the white river sand.

Yellow Woman went away with the spirit from the north and lived with him and his relatives. She was gone for a long time, but then one day she came back and she brought twin boys.

"Do you know the story?"

"What story?" He smiled and pulled me close to him as he said this.   24
I was afraid lying there on the red blanket. All I could know was the way he felt, warm, damp, his body beside me. This is the way it happens in the stories, I was thinking, with no thought beyond the moment she meets the ka'tsina spirit and they go.

"I don't have to go. What they tell in stories was real only then, back in time immemorial, like they say."

He stood up and pointed at my clothes tangled in the blanket. "Let's go," he said.

I walked beside him, breathing hard because he walked fast, his hand around my wrist. I had stopped trying to pull away from him, because his hand felt cool and the sun was high, drying the river bed into alkali. I will see someone, eventually I will see someone, and then I will be certain that he is only a man — some man from nearby — and I will be sure that I am not Yellow Woman. Because she is from out of time past and I live now and I've been to school and there are highways and pickup trucks that Yellow Woman never saw.

It was an easy ride north on horseback. I watched the change from   28
the cottonwood trees along the river to the junipers that brushed past us in the foothills, and finally there were only piñons, and when I looked up at the rim of the mountain plateau I could see pine trees growing on the edge. Once I stopped to look down, but the pale sandstone had disappeared and the river was gone and the dark lava hills were all around. He touched my hand, not speaking, but always singing softly a mountain song and looking into my eyes.

I felt hungry and wondered what they were doing at home now —
my mother, my grandmother, my husband, and the baby. Cooking breakfast, saying, "Where did she go? — maybe kidnapped," and Al going to
the tribal police with the details: "She went walking along the river."

The house was made with black lava rock and red mud. It was high
above the spreading miles of arroyos and long mesas. I smelled a mountain smell of pitch and buck brush. I stood there beside the black horse,
looking down on the small, dim country we had passed, and I shivered.

"Yellow Woman, come inside where it's warm."

II

He lit a fire in the stove. It was an old stove with a round belly and   32
an enamel coffeepot on top. There was only the stove, some faded Navajo
blankets, and a bedroll and cardboard box. The floor was made of smooth
adobe plaster, and there was one small window facing east. He pointed
at the box.

"There's some potatoes and the frying pan." He sat on the floor with
his arms around his knees pulling them close to his chest and he watched
me fry the potatoes. I didn't mind him watching me because he was
always watching me — he had been watching me since I came upon
him sitting on the river bank trimming leaves from a willow twig with
his knife. We ate from the pan and he wiped the grease from his fingers
on his Levi's.

"Have you brought women here before?" He smiled and kept chewing,
so I said, "Do you always use the same tricks?"

"What tricks?" He looked at me like he didn't understand.

"The story about being a ka'tsina from the mountains. The story about   36
Yellow Woman."

Silva was silent; his face was calm.

"I don't believe it. Those stories couldn't happen now," I said.

He shook his head and said softly, "But someday they will talk about
us, and they will say, 'Those two lived long ago when things like that
happened.'"

He stood up and went out. I ate the rest of the potatoes and thought   40
about things — about the noise the stove was making and the sound of
the mountain wind outside. I remembered yesterday and the day before,
and then I went outside.

I walked past the corral to the edge where the narrow trail cut through the black rim rock. I was standing in the sky with nothing around me but the wind that came down from the blue mountain peak behind me. I could see faint mountain images in the distance miles across the vast spread of mesas and valleys and plains. I wondered who was over there to feel the mountain wind on those sheer blue edges — who walks on the pine needles in those blue mountains.

"Can you see the pueblo?" Silva was standing behind me.

I shook my head. "We're too far away."

"From here I can see the world." He stepped out on the edge. "The   44
Navajo reservation begins over there." He pointed to the east. "The Pueblo boundaries are over here." He looked below us to the south, where the narrow trail seemed to come from. "The Texans have their ranches over there, starting with that valley, the Concho Valley. The Mexicans run some cattle over there too."

"Do you ever work for them?"

"I steal from them," Silva answered. The sun was dropping behind us and shadows were filling the land below. I turned away from the edge that dropped forever into the valleys below.

"I'm cold," I said; "I'm going inside." I started wondering about this man who could speak the Pueblo language so well but who lived on a mountain and rustled cattle. I decided that this man Silva must be Navajo, because Pueblo men didn't do things like that.

"You must be a Navajo."   48

Silva shook his head gently. "Little Yellow Woman," he said, "you never give up, do you? I have told you who I am. The Navajo people know me, too." He knelt down and unrolled the bedroll and spread the extra blankets out on a piece of canvas. The sun was down, and the only light in the house came from outside — the dim orange light from sundown.

I stood there and waited for him to crawl under the blankets.

"What are you waiting for?" he said, and I lay down beside him. He undressed me slowly like the night before beside the river — kissing my face gently and running his hands up and down my belly and legs. He took off my pants and then he laughed.

"Why are you laughing?"   52

"You are breathing so hard."

I pulled away from him and turned my back to him.

He pulled me around and pinned me down with his arms and chest. "You don't understand, do you, little Yellow Woman? You will do what I want."

And again he was all around me with his skin slippery against mine, 56
and I was afraid because I understood that his strength could hurt me. I
lay underneath him and I knew that he could destroy me. But later,
while he slept beside me, I touched his face and I had a feeling — the
kind of feeling for him that overcame me that morning along the river.
I kissed him on the forehead and he reached out for me.

When I woke up in the morning he was gone. It gave me a strange
feeling because for a long time I sat there on the blankets and looked
around the little house for some object of his — some proof that he had
been there or maybe that he was coming back. Only the blankets and
the cardboard box remained. The .30–30 that had been leaning in the
corner was gone, and so was the knife I had used the night before. He
was gone, and I had my chance to go now. But first I had to eat, because
I knew it would be a long walk home.

I found some dried apricots in the cardboard box, and I sat down on
a rock at the edge of the plateau rim. There was no wind and the sun
warmed me. I was surrounded by silence. I drowsed with apricots in my
mouth, and I didn't believe that there were highways or railroads or cattle
to steal.

When I woke up, I stared down at my feet in the black mountain dirt.
Little black ants were swarming over the pine needles around my foot.
They must have smelled the apricots. I thought about my family far
below me. They would be wondering about me, because this had never
happened to me before. The tribal police would file a report. But if old
Grandpa weren't dead he would tell them what happened — he would
laugh and say, "Stolen by a ka'tsina, a mountain spirit. She'll come home
— they usually do." There are enough of them to handle things. My
mother and grandmother will raise the baby like they raised me. Al will
find someone else, and they will go on like before, except that there will
be a story about the day I disappeared while I was walking along the
river. Silva had come for me; he said he had. I did not decide to go. I
just went. Moonflowers blossom in the sand hills before dawn, just as I
followed him. That's what I was thinking as I wandered along the trail
through the pine trees.

It was noon when I got back. When I saw the stone house I remem- 60
bered that I had meant to go home. But that didn't seem important any
more, maybe because there were little blue flowers growing in the
meadow behind the stone house and the gray squirrels were playing in
the pines next to the house. The horses were standing in the corral, and
there was a beef carcass hanging on the shady side of a big pine in front

of the house. Flies buzzed around the clotted blood that hung from the carcass. Silva was washing his hands in a bucket full of water. He must have heard me coming because he spoke to me without turning to face me.

"I've been waiting for you."

"I went walking in the big pine trees."

I looked into the bucket full of bloody water with brown-and-white animal hairs floating in it. Silva stood there letting his hand drip, examining me intently.

"Are you coming with me?"   64

"Where?" I asked him.

"To sell the meat in Marquez."

"If you're sure it's O.K."

"I wouldn't ask you if it wasn't," he answered.

He sloshed the water around in the bucket before he dumped it out   68
and set the bucket upside down near the door. I followed him to the corral and watched him saddle the horses. Even beside the horses he looked tall, and I asked him again if he wasn't Navajo. He didn't say anything; he just shook his head and kept cinching up the saddle.

"But Navajos are tall."

"Get on the horse," he said, "and let's go."

The last thing he did before we started down the steep trail was to grab   72
the .30–30 from the corner. He slid the rifle into the scabbard that hung from his saddle.

"Do they ever try to catch you?" I asked.

"They don't know who I am."

"Then why did you bring the rifle?"

"Because we are going to Marquez where the Mexicans live."   76

III

The trail leveled out on a narrow ridge that was steep on both sides like an animal spine. On one side I could see where the trail went around the rocky gray hills and disappeared into the southeast where the pale sandrock mesas stood in the distance near my home. On the other side was a trail that went west, and as I looked far into the distance I thought I saw the little town. But Silva said no, that I was looking in the wrong place, that I just thought I saw houses. After that I quit looking off into the distance; it was hot and the wildflowers were closing up their deep-yellow petals. Only the waxy cactus flowers bloomed in the bright sun, and I saw every color that a cactus blossom can be; the white ones and the red ones were still buds, but the purple and the yellow were blossoms, open full and the most beautiful of all.

Silva saw him before I did. The white man was riding a big gray horse, coming up the trail toward us. He was traveling fast and the gray horse's feet sent rocks rolling off the trail into the dry tumbleweeds. Silva motioned for me to stop and we watched the white man. He didn't see us right away, but finally his horse whinnied at our horses and he stopped. He looked at us briefly before he loped the gray horse across the three hundred yards that separated us. He stopped his horse in front of Silva, and his young fat face was shadowed by the brim of his hat. He didn't look mad, but his small, pale eyes moved from the blood-soaked gunny sacks hanging from my saddle to Silva's face and then back to my face.

"Where did you get the fresh meat?" the white man asked.

"I've been hunting," Silva said, and when he shifted his weight in the   80
saddle the leather creaked.

"The hell you have, Indian. You've been rustling cattle. We've been looking for the thief for a long time."

The rancher was fat, and sweat began to soak through his white cowboy shirt and the wet cloth stuck to the thick rolls of belly fat. He almost seemed to be panting from the exertion of talking, and he smelled rancid, maybe because Silva scared him.

Silva turned to me and smiled. "Go back up the mountain, Yellow Woman."

The white man got angry when he heard Silva speak in a language he   84
couldn't understand. "Don't try anything, Indian. Just keep riding to Marquez. We'll call the state police from there."

The rancher must have been unarmed because he was very frightened and if he had a gun he would have pulled it out then. I turned my horse around and the rancher yelled, "Stop!" I looked at Silva for an instant and there was something ancient and dark — something I could feel in my stomach — in his eyes, and when I glanced at his hand I saw his finger on the trigger of .30–30 that was still in the saddle scabbard. I slapped my horse across the flank and the sacks of raw meat swung against my knees as the horse leaped up the trail. It was hard to keep my balance, and once I thought I felt the saddle slipping backward; it was because of this that I could not look back.

I didn't stop until I reached the ridge where the trail forked. The horse was breathing deep gasps and there was a dark film of sweat on its neck.

I looked down in the direction I had come from, but I couldn't see the place. I waited. The wind came up and pushed warm air past me. I looked up at the sky, pale blue and full of thin clouds and fading vapor trails left by jets.

I think four shots were fired — I remember hearing four hollow explosions that reminded me of deer hunting. There could have been more shots after that, but I couldn't have heard them because my horse was running again and the loose rocks were making too much noise as they scattered around his feet.

Horses have a hard time running downhill, but I went that way instead   88
of uphill to the mountain because I thought it was safer. I felt better with the horse running southeast past the round gray hills that were covered with cedar trees and black lava rock. When I got to the plain in the distance I could see the dark green patches of tamaracks that grew along the river; and beyond the river I could see the beginning of the pale sandrock mesas. I stopped the horse and looked back to see if anyone was coming; then I got off the horse and turned the horse around, wondering if it would go back to its corral under the pines on the mountain. It looked back at me for a moment and then plucked a mouthful of green tumbleweeds before it trotted back up the trail with its ears pointed forward, carrying its head daintily to one side to avoid stepping on the dragging reins. When the horse disappeared over the last hill, the gunny sacks full of meat were still swinging and bouncing.

IV

I walked toward the river on a wood-hauler's road that I knew would eventually lead to the paved road. I was thinking about waiting beside the road for someone to drive by, but by the time I got to the pavement I had decided it wasn't very far to walk if I followed the river back the way Silva and I had come.

The river water tasted good, and I sat in the shade under a cluster of silvery willows. I thought about Silva, and I felt sad at leaving him; still, there was something strange about him, and I tried to figure it out all the way back home.

I came back to the place on the river bank where he had been sitting the first time I saw him. The green willow leaves that he had trimmed from the branch were still lying there, wilted in the sand. I saw the leaves and I wanted to go back to him — to kiss him and to touch him — but the mountains were too far away now. And I told myself, because I believe it, he will come back sometime and be waiting again by the river.

I followed the path up from the river into the village. The sun was 92 getting low, and I could smell supper cooking when I got to the screen door of my house. I could hear their voices inside — my mother was telling my grandmother how to fix the Jell-O and my husband, Al, was playing with the baby. I decided to tell them that some Navajo had kidnaped me, but I was sorry that old Grandpa wasn't alive to hear my story because it was the Yellow Woman stories he liked to tell best.

EXPLORATIONS

1. Why does the narrator leave her home and family to go off with Silva? Why does she return at the end of the story?

2. From whose viewpoint do we get to know Silva? What are his outstanding qualities? How is our image of him different from the image expressed by the white man who appears in paragraph 78?

3. At what points in the story does the narrator state her feelings directly? In what other ways are her feelings revealed?

4. Does the narrator believe that she and Silva really are the ka'tsina and Yellow Woman? How can you tell? What are her reasons for wanting to believe this?

CONNECTIONS

1. "Yellow Woman," like Richard Rodriguez's "You Are a Man," takes place near the U.S.-Mexican border. What role do white Americans play in these two selections? How do the other men in each selection respond to them, and why?

2. What qualities does Silva share with the masculine stereotype described by Gayle Early in *Looking at Ourselves*? What qualities does the narrator share with the feminine stereotype described by Susan Brownmiller in *Looking at Ourselves*? How do these qualities affect the characters' initial attraction to each other? their ability to sustain a relationship?

3. What similar attitudes toward mythical beings appear in "Yellow Woman" and Wole Soyinka's "Nigerian Childhood" (p. 154)? How do characters in these two selections react differently to spirits and magic? What factors do you think are responsible for the differences?

ELABORATIONS

1. What is the role of magic in American culture? Write a definition or classification essay indicating what forms magic takes in our society, whom it
   affects, and how significant an influence it is.

2. What clues in "Yellow Woman" suggest that Silva may have given the narrator
   an excuse to make a break she had been considering for some time? Write a
   narrative essay about a dramatic change made by you or someone you know.
   Identify both the event(s) that triggered the change and the long-standing
   circumstances that paved the way for it.

SIMONE DE BEAUVOIR

Woman as Other

Simone de Beauvoir, born in Paris in 1908, was best known for her feminist fiction and nonfiction and for her lifelong relationship with the existentialist philosopher and writer Jean-Paul Sartre. Beauvoir was twenty when she met Sartre while studying at the Sorbonne. The two never married, lived together, or viewed their liaison as exclusive, but they worked closely together and kept apartments in the same building until Sartre's death in 1980. Beauvoir's several memoirs chronicle her social and political development; her novels examine existentialist ideas and sometimes their proponents as well. *The Mandarins* (1954), based on her affair with American novelist Nelson Algren, won the prestigious Prix Goncourt. Beauvoir's most famous work is the international best-seller *The Second Sex* (1952; *Le Deuxième Sexe,* 1949), translated from the French by H. M. Parshley, from which "Woman as Other" is taken. A vigorous champion of antiestablishment causes, Beauvoir died in Paris in 1986.

(For background on France, see p. 16.)

What is a woman?

To state the question is, to me, to suggest, at once, a preliminary answer. The fact that I ask it is in itself significant. A man would never get the notion of writing a book on the peculiar situation of the human male. But if I wish to define myself, I must first of all say: "I am a woman"; on this truth must be based all further discussion. A man never begins by presenting himself as an individual of a certain sex; it goes without saying that he is a man. The terms *masculine* and *feminine* are used symmetrically only as a matter of form, as on legal papers. In actuality the relation of the two sexes is not quite like that of two electrical poles, for man represents both the positive and the neutral, as is indicated by the common use of *man* to designate human beings in general; whereas woman represents only the negative, defined by limiting criteria, without reciprocity. In the midst of an abstract discussion it is vexing to hear a man say: "You think thus and so because you are a woman"; but I know that my only defense is to reply: "I think thus and so because it is true," thereby removing my subjective self from the argument. It would be out of the question to reply: "And you think the contrary because you are a man," for it is understood that the fact of being a man is no peculiarity. A man is in the right in being a man; it is the woman who is in the wrong. It amounts to this: just as for the ancients there was an absolute vertical with reference to which the oblique was defined, so there is an absolute human type, the masculine. Woman has ovaries, a uterus; these peculiarities imprison her in her subjectivity, circumscribe her within the limits of her own nature. It is often said that she thinks with her glands. Man superbly ignores the fact that his anatomy also includes glands, such as the testicles, and that they secrete hormones. He thinks of his body as a direct and normal connection with the world, which he believes he apprehends objectively, whereas he regards the body of woman as a hindrance, a prison, weighed down by everything peculiar to it. "The female is a female by virtue of a certain *lack* of qualities," said Aristotle; "we should regard the female nature as afflicted with a natural defectiveness." And St. Thomas for his part pronounced women to be an "imperfect man," an "incidental" being. This is symbolized in Genesis where Eve is depicted as made from what Bossuet called "a supernumerary bone" of Adam.

Thus humanity is male and man defines woman not in herself but as relative to him; she is not regarded as an autonomous being. Michelet writes: "Woman, the relative being. . . ." And Benda is most positive in his *Rapport d'Uriel*: "The body of man makes sense in itself quite apart from that of woman, whereas the latter seems wanting in significance by itself. . . . Man can think of himself without woman. She cannot think of herself without man." And she is simply what man decrees; thus she is called "the sex," by which is meant that she appears essentially to the male as a sexual being. For him she is sex — absolute sex, no less. She is defined and differentiated with reference to man and not he with reference to her; she is the incidental, the inessential as opposed to the essential. He is the Subject, he is the Absolute — she is the Other.

The category of the *Other* is as primordial as consciousness itself. In the most primitive societies, in the most ancient mythologies, one finds the expression of a duality — that of the Self and the Other. This duality was not originally attached to the division of the sexes; it was not dependent upon any empirical facts. It is revealed in such works as that of Granet on Chinese thought and those of Dumézil on the East Indies and Rome. The feminine element was at first no more involved in such pairs as Varuna-Mitra, Uranus-Zeus, Sun-Moon, and Day-Night than it was in the contrasts between Good and Evil, lucky and unlucky auspices, right and left, God and Lucifer. Otherness is a fundamental category of human thought.

Thus it is that no group ever sets itself up as the One without at once setting up the Other over against itself. If three travelers chance to occupy the same compartment, that is enough to make vaguely hostile "others" out of all the rest of the passengers on the train. In small-town eyes all persons not belonging to the village are "strangers" and suspect; to the native of a country all who inhabit other countries are "foreigners"; Jews are "different" for the anti-Semite, Negroes are "inferior" for American racists, aborigines are "natives" for colonists, proletarians are the "lower class" for the privileged.

Lévi-Strauss, at the end of a profound work on the various forms of primitive societies, reaches the following conclusion: "Passage from the state of Nature to the state of Culture is marked by man's ability to view biological relations as a series of contrasts; duality, alternation, opposition, and symmetry, whether under definite or vague forms, constitute not so much phenomena to be explained as fundamental and immediately given data of social reality." These phenomena would be incomprehensible if in fact human society were simply a *Mitsein* or fellowship based on solidarity and friendliness. Things become clear, on the contrary, if, following Hegel, we find in consciousness itself a fundamental hostility toward every other consciousness; the subject can be posed only in being opposed — he sets himself up as the essential, as opposed to the other, the inessential, the object.

But the other consciousness, the other ego, sets up a reciprocal claim. The native traveling abroad is shocked to find himself in turn regarded as a "stranger" by the natives of neighboring countries. As a matter of fact, wars, festivals, trading, treaties, and contests among tribes, nations, and classes tend to deprive the concept *Other* of its absolute sense and to make manifest its relativity; willy-nilly, individuals and groups are forced to realize the reciprocity of their relations. How is it, then, that this reciprocity has not been recognized between the sexes, that one of the contrasting terms is set up as the sole essential, denying any relativity in regard to its correlative and defining the latter as pure otherness? Why is it that women do not dispute male sovereignty? No subject will readily volunteer to become the object, the inessential; it is not the Other who, in defining himself as the Other, establishes the One. The Other is posed as such by the One in defining himself as the One. But if the Other is not to regain the status of being the One, he must be submissive enough to accept this alien point of view. Whence comes this submission in the case of woman?

There are, to be sure, other cases in which a certain category has been   8 able to dominate another completely for a time. Very often this privilege depends upon inequality of numbers — the majority imposes its rule upon the minority or persecutes it. But women are not a minority, like the American Negroes or the Jews; there are as many women as men on earth. Again, the two groups concerned have often been originally independent; they may have been formerly unaware of each other's existence, or perhaps they recognized each other's autonomy. But a historical event has resulted in the subjugation of the weaker by the stronger. The scattering of the Jews, the introduction of slavery into America, the conquests of imperialism are examples in point. In these cases the oppressed retained at least the memory of former days; they possessed in common a past, a tradition, sometimes a religion or a culture.

The parallel drawn by Bebel between women and the proletariat is valid in that neither ever formed a minority or a separate collective unit of mankind. And instead of a single historical event it is in both cases a historical development that explains their status as a class and accounts for the membership of *particular individuals* in that class. But proletarians have not always existed, whereas there have always been women. They are women in virtue of their anatomy and physiology. Throughout history they have always been subordinated to men, and hence their dependency is not the result of a historical event or a social change — it was not something that *occurred*. The reason why otherness in this case seems to be an absolute is in part that it lacks the contingent or incidental nature of historical facts. A condition brought about at a certain time can be abolished at some other time, as the Negroes of Haiti and others have proved; but it might seem that a natural condition is beyond the possibility of change. In truth, however, the nature of things is no more immutably given, once for all, than is historical reality. If woman seems to be the inessential which never becomes the essential, it is because she herself fails to bring about this change. Proletarians say "We"; Negroes also. Regarding themselves as subjects, they transform the bourgeois, the whites, into "others." But women do not say "We," except at some congress of feminists or similar formal demonstration; men say "women," and women use the same word in referring to themselves. They do not authentically assume a subjective attitude. The proletarians have accomplished the revolution in Russia, the Negroes in Haiti, the Indochinese are battling for it in Indochina; but the women's effort has never been anything more than a symbolic agitation. They have gained only what men have been willing to grant; they have taken nothing, they have only received.

The reason for this is that women lack concrete means for organizing themselves into a unit which can stand face to face with the correlative unit. They have no past, no history, no religion of their own; and they have no such solidarity of work and interest as that of the proletariat. They are not even promiscuously herded together in the way that creates community feeling among the American Negroes, the ghetto Jews, the workers of Saint-Denis, or the factory hands of Renault. They live dispersed among the males, attached through residence, housework, economic condition, and social standing to certain men — fathers or husbands — more firmly than they are to other women. If they belong to the bourgeoisie, they feel solidarity with men of that class, not with proletarian women; if they are white, their allegiance is to white men, not to Negro women. The proletariat can propose to massacre the ruling class, and a sufficiently fanatical Jew or Negro might dream of getting sole possession of the atomic bomb and making humanity wholly Jewish or black; but woman cannot even dream of exterminating the males. The bond that unites her to her oppressors is not comparable to any other. The division of the sexes is a biological fact, not an event in human history. Male and female stand opposed within a primordial *Mitsein*, and woman has not broken it. The couple is a fundamental unity with its two halves riveted together, and the cleavage of society along the line of sex is impossible. Here is to be found the basic trait of woman: she is the Other in a totality of which the two components are necessary to one another.

One could suppose that this reciprocity might have facilitated the liberation of woman. When Hercules sat at the feet of Omphale and helped with her spinning, his desire for her held him captive; but why did she fail to gain a lasting power? To revenge herself on Jason, Medea killed their children; and this grim legend would seem to suggest that she might have obtained a formidable influence over him through his love for his offspring. In *Lysistrata* Aristophanes gaily depicts a band of women who joined forces to gain social ends through the sexual needs of their men; but this is only a play. In the legend of the Sabine women, the latter soon abandoned their plan of remaining sterile to punish their ravishers. In truth woman has not been socially emancipated through man's need — sexual desire and the desire for offspring — which makes the male dependent for satisfaction upon the female.

Master and slave, also, are united by a reciprocal need, in this case   12
economic, which does not liberate the slave. In the relation of master to
slave the master does not make a point of the need that he has for the
other; he has in his grasp the power of satisfying this need through his
own action; whereas the slave, in his dependent condition, his hope and
fear, is quite conscious of the need he has for his master. Even if the
need is at bottom equally urgent for both, it always works in favor of the
oppressor and against the oppressed. That is why the liberation of the
working class, for example, has been slow.

Now, woman has always been man's dependent, if not his slave; the
two sexes have never shared the world in equality. And even today woman
is heavily handicapped, though her situation is beginning to change.
Almost nowhere is her legal status the same as man's, and frequently it
is much to her disadvantage. Even when her rights are legally recognized
in the abstract, long-standing custom prevents their full expression in the
mores. In the economic sphere men and women can almost be said to
make up two castes; other things being equal, the former hold the better
jobs, get higher wages, and have more opportunity for success than their
new competitors. In industry and politics men have a great many more
positions and they monopolize the most important posts. In addition to
all this, they enjoy a traditional prestige that the education of children
tends in every way to support, for the present enshrines the past — and
in the past all history has been made by men. At the present time, when
women are beginning to take part in the affairs of the world, it is still a
world that belongs to men — they have no doubt of it at all and women
have scarcely any. To decline to be the Other, to refuse to be a party to
the deal — this would be for women to renounce all the advantages
conferred upon them by their alliance with the superior caste. Man-the-
sovereign will provide woman-the-liege with material protection and will
undertake the moral justification of her existence; thus she can evade at
once both economic risk and the metaphysical risk of a liberty in which
ends and aims must be contrived without assistance. Indeed, along with
the ethical urge of each individual to affirm his subjective existence,
there is also the temptation to forgo liberty and become a thing. This is
an inauspicious road, for he who takes it — passive, lost, ruined —
becomes henceforth the creature of another's will, frustrated in his transcendence and deprived of every value. But it is an easy road; on it one
avoids the strain involved in undertaking an authentic existence. When
man makes of woman the *Other*, he may, then, expect her to manifest
deep-seated tendencies toward complicity. Thus, woman may fail to lay

claim to the status of subject because she lacks definite resources, because she feels the necessary bond that ties her to man regardless of reciprocity, and because she is often very well pleased with her role as the *Other*.

EXPLORATIONS

1. "Woman as Other" was originally published as part of *The Second Sex* in 1949. Which, if any, of Beauvoir's observations about women's status have been invalidated since then by political and social changes? Which of the problems she mentions are live issues in our society today?

2. What emotionally loaded words, phrases, and sentences indicate that Beauvoir is presenting an argument in "Woman as Other"? Who is her intended audience? To what extent, and for what reasons, do you think she expects part or all of her audience to resist the case she is making?

3. What types of sources does Beauvoir cite? In what ways would her essay gain or lose impact if she included quotations from interviews with individual women and men? In what ways would it gain or lose impact if she cut all references to outside sources?

CONNECTIONS

1. What evidence in Leslie Marmon Silko's "Yellow Woman" shows the narrator perceiving herself as defined by or dependent on men, in the way Beauvoir describes? What evidence shows Silko's narrator holding views that contradict Beauvoir's?

2. Which of the passages in *Looking at Ourselves* show men viewing women as "Other"? Which ones show women viewing men as "Other"? What recommendations do the American authors make about overcoming the problems Beauvoir describes?

3. In paragraph 10, Beauvoir writes of women and men as "a totality of which the two components are necessary to one another." What does she see as the implications of this mutual dependence? Compare Rose Weitz's comments in *Looking at Ourselves* on homosexual men and women. How would you expect Weitz to disagree with Beauvoir? How would you expect her to agree?

ELABORATIONS

1. Beauvoir notes that male glands affect men's thinking as much as female glands affect women's thinking. How do the writers in *Looking at Ourselves* apply this idea? On the basis of their observations and Beauvoir's, write a cause-and-effect essay about the relationship (or absence of a relationship) between gender and attitudes.

2. "What is a woman?" asks Beauvoir in her opening paragraph. She goes on: "If I wish to define myself, I must first of all say: 'I am a woman.'" Already she is letting her readers know that her choice of *definition* as the form for her inquiry has a political as well as a rhetorical basis. That is, she is not simply defining woman, as her opening question implies; she is examining a definition of woman imposed by men. The same tactic can be applied to any issue in which a preexisting definition is crucial to the argument. Choose such an issue that interests you — for instance, What is a drug? or What is the Strategic Defense Initiative? Write a definition essay exploring the issue by examining the tacit definitions that underlie it.

ALBERTO MORAVIA

The Chase

Alberto Moravia has been called the first existential novelist in Italy
— a forerunner of Jean-Paul Sartre and Albert Camus in France. Moravia
is best known in the United States for the films that have been based on
his work: Michelangelo Antonioni's *L'Avventura* (1961), Jean-Luc
Godard's *Le Mépris* (*Contempt,* 1965), and Bernardo Bertolucci's *The
Conformist* (1970). The film of *Conjugal Love* (1949) was directed by
Moravia's wife, Dacia Maraini. Born Alberto Pincherle in Rome in 1907,
Moravia had little formal schooling but was taught to read English,
French, and German by governesses and earned a high-school diploma.
He began his first novel at age sixteen while in a sanatorium for the
tuberculosis he had contracted when he was nine; he considered his long
illness a major influence on his career. Moravia's novels, stories, and
scripts are too numerous to list. Many of them, including his 1987 novel
The Voyeur, are available in English. "The Chase," translated from the
Italian in 1969 by Angus Davidson, is from the story collection *Command, and I Will Obey You.* Moravia died in 1990.

Italy, Moravia's homeland and the setting of this story, is a boot-
shaped European peninsula across the Mediterranean Sea from Libya.
Occupied since the Stone Age, it had its political heyday during the
Roman Empire, which by A.D. 180 ruled from Britain to Africa to Persia
(now Iran). The Roman civilization fell to barbarian invaders in the
fourth and fifth centuries but left as a legacy its alphabet, roads, laws,
and arts. The United Nations Educational, Scientific, and Cultural
Organization (UNESCO) estimates that half of the world's cultural
heritage has come from Italy, which still houses a high proportion
of the finest architecture, sculpture, painting, and other visual art in
Europe.

Italy remained politically fragmented until the 1860s, when it united
under a parliament and king. In 1922 Fascist dictator Benito Mussolini
took over the government, proclaiming Victor Emmanuel III emperor
and subsequently joining Germany in World War II. After Fascism was
overthrown in 1943, Italy declared war on Germany and Japan. Mussolini
was killed in 1946, and the king was voted out the next year. Postwar governments have tended to be short-lived. However, Italy was recently rated the world's fourth most politically stable nation and fourth
largest market economy. Meanwhile, the country's birth, abortion,
and divorce rates are falling, and the traditional large Italian family is

shrinking: As of 1987, only one in thirty families numbered six or more.

(For more background on Italy, see p. 491.)

I have never been a sportsman — or, rather, I have been a sportsman only once, and that was the first and last time. I was a child, and one day, for some reason or other, I found myself together with my father, who was holding a gun in his hand, behind a bush, watching a bird that had perched on a branch not very far away. It was a large, gray bird — or perhaps it was brown — with a long — or perhaps a short — beak; I don't remember. I only remember what I felt at that moment as I looked at it. It was like watching an animal whose vitality was rendered more intense by the very fact of my watching it and of the animal's not knowing that I was watching it.

At that moment, I say, the notion of wildness entered my mind, never again to leave it: everything is wild which is autonomous and unpredictable and does not depend upon us. Then all of a sudden there was an explosion; I could no longer see the bird and I thought it had flown away. But my father was leading the way, walking in front of me through the undergrowth. Finally he stooped down, picked up something, and put it in my hand. I was aware of something warm and soft and I lowered my eyes: there was the bird in the palm of my hand, its dangling, shattered head crowned with a plume of already-thickening blood. I burst into tears and dropped the corpse on the ground, and that was the end of my shooting experience.

I thought again of this remote episode in my life this very day after watching my wife, for the first and also the last time, as she was walking through the streets of the city. But let us take things in order.

What had my wife been like; what was she like now? She once had   4
been, to put it briefly, "wild" — that is, entirely autonomous and unpredictable; latterly she had become "tame" — that is, predictable and
dependent. For a long time she had been like the bird that, on that far-
off morning in my childhood, I had seen perching on the bough; latterly,
I am sorry to say, she had become like a hen about which one knows
everything in advance — how it moves, how it eats, how it lays eggs,
how it sleeps, and so on.

Nevertheless I would not wish anyone to think that my wife's wildness
consisted of an uncouth, rough, rebellious character. Apart from being
extremely beautiful, she is the gentlest, politest, most discreet person in

the world. Rather her wildness consisted of the air of charming unpredictability, of independence in her way of living, with which during the
first years of our marriage she acted in my presence, both at home and
abroad. Wildness signified intimacy, privacy, secrecy. Yes, my wife as
she sat in front of her dressing table, her eyes fixed on the looking glass,
passing the hairbrush with a repeated motion over her long, loose hair,
was just as wild as the solitary quail hopping forward along a sun-filled
furrow or the furtive fox coming out into a clearing and stopping to look
around before running on. She was wild because I, as I looked at her,
could never manage to foresee when she would give a last stroke with
the hairbrush and rise and come toward me; wild to such a degree that
sometimes when I went into our bedroom the smell of her, floating in
the air, would have something of the acrid quality of a wild beast's lair.

Gradually she became less wild, tamer. I had had a fox, a quail, in
the house, as I have said; then one day I realized that I had a hen. What
effect does a hen have on someone who watches it? It has the effect of
being, so to speak, an automaton in the form of a bird; automatic are
the brief, rapid steps with which it moves about; automatic its hard, terse
pecking; automatic the glance of the round eyes in its head that nods
and turns; automatic its ready crouching down under the cock; automatic
the dropping of the egg wherever it may be and the cry with which it
announces that the egg has been laid. Good-by to the fox; good-by to
the quail. And her smell — this no longer brought to my mind, in any
way, the innocent odor of a wild animal; rather I detected in it the
chemical suavity of some ordinary French perfume.

Our flat is on the first floor of a big building in a modern quarter of
the town; our windows look out on a square in which there is a small
public garden, the haunt of nurses and children and dogs. One day I
was standing at the window, looking in a melancholy way at the garden.
My wife, shortly before, had dressed to go out; and once again, watching
her, I had noticed the irrevocable and, so to speak, invisible character of
her gestures and personality: something which gave one the feeling of a
thing already seen and already done and which therefore evaded even
the most determined observation. And now, as I stood looking at the
garden and at the same time wondering why the adorable wildness of
former times had so completely disappeared, suddenly my wife came into
my range of vision as she walked quickly across the garden in the direction
of the bus stop. I watched her and then I almost jumped for joy; in a
movement she was making to pull down a fold of her narrow skirt and

smooth it over her thigh with the tips of her long, sharp nails, in this movement I recognized the wildness that in the past had made me love her. It was only an instant, but in that instant I said to myself: She's become wild again because she's convinced that I am not there and am not watching her. Then I left the window and rushed out.

But I did not join her at the bus stop; I felt that I must not allow   8
myself to be seen. Instead I hurried to my car, which was standing nearby, got in, and waited. A bus came and she got in together with some other people; the bus started off again and I began following it. Then there came back to me the memory of that one shooting expedition in which I had taken part as a child, and I saw that the bus was the undergrowth with its bushes and trees, my wife the bird perching on the bough while I, unseen, watched it living before my eyes. And the whole town, during this pursuit, became, as though by magic, a fact of nature like the countryside: the houses were hills, the streets valleys, the vehicles hedges and woods, and even the passersby on the pavements had something unpredictable and autonomous — that is, wild — about them. And in my mouth, behind my clenched teeth, there was the acrid, metallic taste of gunfire; and my eyes, usually listless and wandering, had become sharp, watchful, attentive.

These eyes were fixed intently upon the exit door when the bus came to the end of its run. A number of people got out, and then I saw my wife getting out. Once again I recognized, in the manner in which she broke free of the crowd and started off toward a neighboring street, the wildness that pleased me so much. I jumped out of the car and started following her.

She was walking in front of me, ignorant of my presence, a tall woman with an elegant figure, long-legged, narrow-hipped, broad-backed, her brown hair falling on her shoulders.

Men turned around as she went past; perhaps they were aware of what I myself was now sensing with an intensity that quickened the beating of my heart and took my breath away: the unrestricted, steadily increasing, irresistible character of her mysterious wildness.

She walked hurriedly, having evidently some purpose in view, and   12
even the fact that she had a purpose of which I was ignorant added to her wildness; I did not know where she was going, just as on that far-off morning I had not known what the bird perching on the bough was about to do. Moreover I thought the gradual, steady increase in this quality of wildness came partly from the fact that as she drew nearer to the object of this mysterious walk there was an increase in her — how

shall I express it? — of biological tension, of existential excitement, of vital effervescence. Then, unexpectedly, with the suddenness of a film, her purpose was revealed.

A fair-haired young man in a leather jacket and a pair of corduroy trousers was leaning against the wall of a house in that ancient, narrow street. He was idly smoking as he looked in front of him. But as my wife passed close to him, he threw away his cigarette with a decisive gesture, took a step forward, and seized her arm. I was expecting her to rebuff him, to move away from him, but nothing happened: evidently obeying the rules of some kind of erotic ritual, she went on walking beside the young man. Then after a few steps, with a movement that confirmed her own complicity, she put her arm around her companion's waist and he put his around her.

I understood then that this unknown man who took such liberties with my wife was also attracted by wildness. And so, instead of making a conventional appointment with her, instead of meeting in a café with a handshake, a falsely friendly and respectful welcome, he had preferred, by agreement with her, to take her by surprise — or, rather, to pretend to do so — while she was apparently taking a walk on her own account. All this I perceived by intuition, noticing that at the very moment when he stepped forward and took her arm her wildness had, so to speak, given an upward bound. It was years since I had seen my wife so alive, but alas, the source of this life could not be traced to me.

They walked on thus entwined and then, without any preliminaries, just like two wild animals, they did an unexpected thing: they went into one of the dark doorways in order to kiss. I stopped and watched them from a distance, peering into the darkness of the entrance. My wife was turned away from me and was bending back with the pressure of his body, her hair hanging free. I looked at that long, thick mane of brown hair, which as she leaned back fell free of her shoulders, and I felt at that moment her vitality reached its diapason, just as happens with wild animals when they couple and their customary wildness is redoubled by the violence of love. I watched for a long time and then, since the kiss went on and on and in fact seemed to be prolonged beyond the limits of my power of endurance, I saw that I would have to intervene.

I would have to go forward, seize my wife by the arm — or actually 16 by that hair, which hung down and conveyed so well the feeling of feminine passivity — then hurl myself with clenched fists upon the blond young man. After this encounter I would carry off my wife, weeping, mortified, ashamed, while I was raging and brokenhearted, upbraiding her and pouring scorn upon her.

But what else would this intervention amount to but the shot my father fired at that free, unknowing bird as it perched on the bough? The disorder and confusion, the mortification, the shame, that would follow would irreparably destroy the rare and precious moment of wildness that I was witnessing inside the dark doorway. It was true that this wildness was directed against me; but I had to remember that wildness, always and everywhere, is directed against everything and everybody. After the scene of my intervention it might be possible for me to regain control of my wife, but I should find her shattered and lifeless in my arms like the bird that my father placed in my hand so that I might throw it into the shooting bag.

The kiss went on and on: well, it was a kiss of passion — that could not be denied. I waited until they finished, until they came out of the doorway, until they walked on again still linked together. Then I turned back.

EXPLORATIONS

1. What are the functions of the long opening section of "The Chase"? What role does the narrator assign himself here in relation to the adult male world? How would the story's impact change without this section?

2. At what point(s) in "The Chase" does the narrator recall his childhood hunting incident again? How is his role different now from the first time he mentioned the incident? How does the narrator vacillate between roles at the end of the story, and what role does he finally choose for himself?

3. Reread Moravia's last sentence; then look back at his third paragraph. What do you conclude that the narrator has done, and intends to do, after the point when the story ends? In what way is he himself adopting qualities he prizes in his wife? What effects does he apparently expect this behavior to have on his marriage?

CONNECTIONS

1. What evidence in "The Chase" confirms Simone de Beauvoir's contention that men perceive women as Other? How does Moravia's narrator feel about

his wife's "otherness"? What can you deduce from the story about his wife's view of their situation?

2. Like "The Chase," Leslie Marmon Silko's "Yellow Woman" is a first-person story about a woman who temporarily leaves her husband for another man. Which of these marriages is more likely to continue successfully after the wife returns home, and why?

3. What qualities does Moravia's narrator share with the traditional macho male described by Gayle Early in *Looking at Ourselves*? What qualities does he share with the androgynous male described by Amy Gross in *Looking at Ourselves*? By the story's end, what kind of man does the narrator evidently want to be, and why?

ELABORATIONS

1. Moravia's narrator might be said to have the opposite problem from Clara Piriz and her husband in "Marriage by Pros and Cons": With few obstacles to conquer, the romantic spark fades. Write a process essay recommending ways for a prosperous couple in a democratic society to keep their marriage alive and well.

2. In the first section of "The Chase," Moravia's narrator speaks as if he knows his wife as completely as a farmer knows his hens. In the second section, he discovers that he does not know her so well after all. Think of a situation in which you based your expectations about another person on an image — perhaps an idealized social role, such as mother, grandfather, friend, or fiancé. How did you come to realize that the person was not as predictable as you thought? Write a narrative essay about the incident(s) that changed your attitude.

NAILA MINAI

Women in Early Islam

Naila Minai was born in Japan and grew up in Turkey and many other countries of the Middle East. "My Turkish-Tatar grandmother was tutored at home, married a polygamous man, and has never discarded her head veil," she writes. "My mother never wore the veil, studied in schools close to home, and settled down as a housewife in a monogamous marriage. I left my family as a teenager to study in the United States and Europe, where I hitchhiked from country to country . . . eventually making a solo trip across the Sahara." Minai's flight took her to the Sorbonne in Paris and the University of California, Berkeley, where she received her degree in literature and biology. She has worked as a United Nations correspondent and has continued to travel widely as a free-lance journalist. She currently divides her time between the United States and her extended family in the Middle and Far East.

The city of Mecca, where Islam originated, lies near the Red Sea in what is now Saudi Arabia; Medina is north of Mecca. Arabia — the peninsula divided from Africa by the Red Sea and from Iran by the Persian Gulf — currently comprises Saudi Arabia, Yemen, South Yemen, Oman, the United Arab Emirates, Qatar, Kuwait, Bahrain, and several neutral zones. North of the Arabian peninsula, and among the members of the Arab League, are the Islamic nations of Jordan, Syria, Lebanon, and Iraq. Iran to the east and Turkey to the north are also Islamic by religion but have ethnically distinct populations from Arabia (see pp. 164 and 371). Egypt, Sudan, Libya, Tunisia, Algeria, and Morocco in northern Africa belong to the Arab League as well, are predominantly Islamic, and generally are counted as Arab nations (see p. 23). Israel, surrounded by Islamic Arabs, is a Jewish nation (see p. 552).

Khadija, an attractive forty-year-old Arabian widow, ran a flourishing caravan business in Mecca in the seventh century A.D., and was courted by the most eligible men of her society. But she had eyes only for an intelligent and hardworking twenty-five-year-old in her employ named Muhammad. "What does she see in a penniless ex-shepherd?" her scandalized aristocratic family whispered among themselves. Accustomed to having her way, however, Khadija proposed to Muhammad and married him. Until her death some twenty-five years later, her marriage was much more than the conventional Cinderella story in reverse, for Khadija not only bore six children while comanaging her business with her husband, but also advised and financed him in his struggle to found Islam, which grew to be one of the major religions of the world.

It was a religion that concerned itself heavily with women's rights, in a surprisingly contemporary manner. A woman was to be educated and allowed to earn and manage her income. She was to be recognized as legal heir to her father's property along with her brother. Her rights in marriage were also clearly spelled out: she was entitled to sexual satisfaction as well as economic support. Nor was divorce to consist any longer of merely throwing the wife out of the house without paying her financial compensation.

This feminist bill of rights filled an urgent need. Meccans in the seventh century were in transition from a tribal to an urban way of life. As their town grew into a cosmopolitan center of trade, kinship solidarity had deteriorated, but municipal laws had not yet been fully established to protect the citizens. Women were particularly vulnerable, their rights closely linked with the tribal way of life their people had known before renouncing nomadism to settle in Mecca around A.D. 400. In nomadic communities of the desert a woman was not equal to a man. During famine a female could be killed at birth to increase her brother's food supply. However, if she managed to reach adulthood she had a better status in the desert than in the city, largely because her labors were indispensable to her clan's survival in the harsh environment. While the men protected the encampment and engaged in trade, she looked after the herds and produced the items to be traded — meat, wool, yogurt, and cheese, all of which bought weapons and grains as well as other essentials. As a breadwinner the tribal woman enjoyed considerable political clout. Even if she did not always participate in council meetings, she made her views known. Only a fool refused to heed his womenfolk and risked antagonizing a good half of his tribe, with whom he had to live in the close confines of the camp and caravan.

If tribal discord was uncomfortable in the best of circumstances, it was catastrophic during the battles that broke out frequently among the clans over pasture and watering rights or to avenge heroes slain by the enemy. With the battlefront so close to home, a woman was needed as a nurse, cheerleader, and even soldier. She was sometimes captured and ransomed or sold into slavery. If her tribesmen could not pay her captors the required number of camels in ransom, they valiantly stormed the enemy's camp to rescue her. These were men brought up on recitations of epic poems about brave warriors who rescued fair damsels in distress. Poets and

4

poetesses of the tribe kept chivalry alive, constantly singing praises of heroism among their people and condemning cowardliness and disloyalty. No one who wanted a respectable place in his tribe could afford to ignore the ubiquitous "Greek chorus," for life without honor was worse than death to a nomad, who could not survive as an outcast in the desert.

Marriage customs varied from tribe to tribe, but the most popular were those that tended to maintain the woman's independence, if only incidentally, by having her remain within her family circle after marriage. If the husband was a close relative, the couple set up a conjugal tent near both of their parents. A husband who was not kin merely visited her at her home. In some clans women could be married to several visiting husbands at the same time. When the wife bore a child, she simply summoned her husbands and announced which of them she believed to be the child's father. Her decision was law. Actually, it did not matter greatly who the biological father was, since children of such unions belonged to the matrilineal family and were supported by communal property administered by her brothers or maternal uncles.

Life in the desert was so hard and precarious that some of the most impoverished tribes renounced nomadism to submit to a less independent existence in towns. Muhammad's ancestors, a segment of the Kinanah tribe, were among them. They settled down at the crossroads of important caravan routes in the place which is now Mecca, and prospered as middlemen under the new name of Quraysh. Their great wealth and power undoubtedly helped their deities extend their spiritual influence far beyond Mecca's boundaries and make Kaaba, their sanctuary, the most important shrine in central Arabia. As keepers of the shrine the leading Quraysh families grew immeasurably rich, but the wealth was not equitably distributed. As survival no longer depended on communal sharing and on women's contributing equally to the family budget, Meccans became more interested in lucrative business connections than in kinship ties. Glaring socioeconomic differences — unknown among nomads — emerged. Women lost their rights and their security.

If brothers went their separate ways, their sister who continued to live with them after marriage lost her home unless one of them took her and her children under his protection. A woman could not automatically count on her brothers to assume this duty, for with the rise of individualism the patrilineal form of marriage, which had coexisted with other marital arrangements in seventh-century Mecca, was gaining popularity. A self-made man tended to prefer leaving his property to his own sons, which sharpened his interest in ensuring that his wife bore only his children. The best ways to guarantee this was to have her live under close supervision in his house. The woman thus lost her personal freedom, but the security she gained from the marital arrangement was precarious at best in the absence of protective state laws. Not only did she have to live at her in-laws' mercy, she could be thrown out of the house on her husband's whim. Khadija escaped such a fate because she was independently wealthy and belonged to one of the most powerful families of the Quraysh — a fact that must have helped her significantly to multiply her fortune.

It was against such a backdrop of urban problems that Islam was born. 8
Even though Muhammad lived happily and comfortably with his rich wife, he continued to identify with the poor and the dispossessed of Mecca, pondering the conditions that spawned them. He himself had been orphaned in early childhood and passed on from one relative to another. Since his guardians were from the poor and neglected branch of the Quraysh, Muhammad earned his keep as a shepherd from a very early age. But he was luckier than other orphans, for he at least had a place in loving homes and eventually got a good job with Khadija's caravan, which allowed him to travel widely in the Middle East.

These journeys had a direct bearing on his spiritual growth and gave focus to his social concerns by exposing him to Christian monks and well-educated Jewish merchants. They intrigued him, for they seemed to have put into practice a monotheistic faith which a few Meccans of the educated circles were beginning to discuss. How did the Christian God inspire such diverse nationalities to worship Him alone? How did the Judaic God manage to unite widely dispersed Semitic groups under one set of laws which provided for the protection of women and children even in large cities? The astral deities that Muhammad's people inherited from their nomadic ancestors demanded offerings but gave nothing in return. After discussions with people of various faiths, Muhammad sought the ultimate solution to his community's problems in the solitude of a cave on Mount Hiraa overlooking Mecca, where he often retreated in his spare moments, with Khadija or by himself.

While meditating alone one day in the cave, Muhammad heard a voice which he believed to be the angel Gabriel's. "Proclaim in the name of thy Lord and Cherisher who created, created man out of a clot of congealed blood" (Quran, surah [chapter] 96, verses 1–2), it said, pointing out that there was only one God and that man must serve Him alone. When Muhammad recovered from his ecstasy, he ran back, shaken, and described his experience to his wife. Having shared his spiritual struggles,

Khadija understood that her husband had received a call to serve the one God whom the Christians and the Jews also worshiped. Bewildered and confused, Muhammad went on with his daily work in the city and occasional meditations on Mount Hiraa. Again the voice commanded him to tell his people about the one omnipotent God, who would welcome believers into heaven and cast wicked people into hell. With Khadija's repeated encouragement, Muhammad finally accepted his prophetic call and devoted the rest of his life to preaching God's word as the new religion of Islam (which means *submission* [*to the will of God*]). Converts to it were called Muslims (*those who submit*). They were not to be called Muhammadans, because they did not worship Muhammad, who was merely a human messenger for the one God. Though invisible and immortal, this God was named Allah after the Zeus of the old Meccan pantheon.

Numerous revelations that Muhammad received from Allah throughout his life were compiled shortly after his death into the Muslim bible, named the Quran, which formed the basis for the Shariah, or Islamic law. A supplement to it was provided by the Hadith, or Muhammad's words, which were recorded over many years as his survivors and their descendants remembered them. Despite the exotic Arabic words in which it is couched, Islam's message is similar in its essentials to the one promulgated by Judaism and Christianity, and can be summed up by the Ten Commandments. *Allah*, after all, is but the Arabic name for the God worshiped by both Jews and Christians. But the rituals differed. Muhammad required his followers to obey the commandments through the practice of five specific rituals, called the pillars of Islam. A Muslim must (1) profess faith in one God; (2) pray to Him; (3) give alms to the poor; (4) fast during Ramadan, the month in the lunar calendar during which Muhammad received his first revelation; and (5) go on a pilgrimage to Mecca at least once in his lifetime (if he can afford to do so) to pay respects to the birthplace of Islam and reinforce the spirit of fellowship with Muslims from all over the world. Although these laws preached fairness and charity among all mankind, God — through Muhammad — preferred to establish specific guidelines to protect the interests of women.

Once he had united enough people under Allah to make a viable   12
community, Muhammad devoted an impressive number of his sermons to women's rights. In doing so, however, he did not attempt to fight the irreversible tide of urbanization. Nor did he condemn the trend toward patrimonial families, although they often abused women. Too shrewd a

politician to antagonize Mecca's powerful patriarchs, he introduced a bill of rights for women which would not only ensure their protection under patriarchy but also reinforce the system itself so that it would stand as a minitribe against the rest of the world.

He did this mainly by providing for women's economic rights in marriage in such a way that they had a financial stake in the system which constantly threatened to erode their independence. Upon marriage a man had to pay his bride a dowry, which was to be her nest egg against divorce or widowhood. While married to him, she could manage the dowry and all other personal income in any way that she pleased, exclusively for her own benefit, and will them to her children and husband upon her death. In her lifetime she did not have to spend her money on herself, or her children for that matter, since only the man was responsible for supporting his family. If the woman stayed married to her husband until his death, she also inherited part of his property. While her share was less than her children's, she was assured of being supported by her sons in widowhood. By the same line of reasoning, her inheritance from her father was half that of her brother's: her husband supported her, whereas her brother had to support his wife. The daughter's right to inherit tended to divide the patriarch's wealth, but the problem was customarily solved by having her marry a paternal first cousin. Failing that, the inheritance became a part of yet another Muslim family in the same tribe of Islam, united through faith rather than kinship. In either case, a Muslim woman with neither a paid occupation nor an inheritance enjoyed a modicum of financial independence, at the price of her submission to a patriarchal form of marriage.

But she was to be allowed to choose her own spouse, according to the Hadith: "None, not even the father or the sovereign, can lawfully contract in marriage an adult woman of sound mind without her permission, whether she be a virgin or not." This freedom was to be assured by a law that required the dowry to be paid to the bride herself. Since the parents were not to pocket it, as they often did before Islam, they were presumably above being "bought." But the brides' freedom remained largely theoretical, since most of them were barely ten years old when engaged to be married for the first time. Aysha, whom Muhammad married after Khadija's death, was only about six or seven years old when she was betrothed and about ten when she moved into her husband's house with her toys. Muhammad was not playing legal tricks on women, however. He did revoke the parents' choice of mate when their daughters complained to him about it. Although parents were to be honored and obeyed, he made it clear that the grown-up daughter was to be respected as an individual — so much so that the marriage contract could be tailored to her specific needs: the bride could impose conditions on her contract. A cooperative wife, he pointed out, was the best foundation for a stable marriage.

Though Muhammad repeatedly preached compassion and love as the most important bonds of marriage, he also gave men financial enticements to keep the family together. The husband was allowed to pay only a part of the dowry upon marriage, with the balance payable upon divorce. If the dowry was large enough, the arrangement deterred the husband from throwing out his wife without substantial cause. In fact, under Islam he could no longer just throw her out. He had to pay her not only the balance of the dowry but also "maintenance on a reasonable scale" (Quran 2:241). He was also to support her through the ensuing *idda*, the three months of chastity which the Shariah asked her to observe in order to determine whether she was carrying his child. If pregnant, she was to be helped until she delivered and had nursed the infant to the point where he could be cared for by the husband's family. All of her children remained under the paternal roof. In a patriarchal society where men were not eager to support others' children or to provide employment for women, the child custody law assured children a decent home and enabled the divorcée to remarry more easily, but even an independently wealthy woman was forbidden to walk out of her husband's home with her children.

Any sexual behavior that would weaken the patriarchal system was strongly discouraged or made illegal. If the custom of taking a visiting husband was frowned upon, her taking more than one at a time was condemned as adultery, which was punishable by whipping. Although men were also forbidden to sow wild oats, they could marry up to four wives and have as many concubines as they could afford. This law may have been partly a concession by Muhammad to the widely accepted custom among wealthy urban men, but he also saw it as a way to attach surplus women to the men's households for their own protection as well as to maintain social order. Due to frequent intertribal warfare and attacks on the merchants' caravans, women always outnumbered men. The conflict became increasingly serious as Muhammad's following grew large enough to threaten the purse and the prestige of the families who amassed fortunes from pilgrims to the Kaaba. So vicious were the attacks that in A.D. 622, after Khadija died, Muhammad moved his budding Muslim community to Medina, an agricultural community without important shrines that would be threatened by Allah. Moreover, the perpetually

quarreling clans of Medina welcomed Muhammad because of his reputation as a just man and a skillful arbitrator.

Muhammad succeeded brilliantly in settling the clans' differences and
won a prominent place in Medina. This made Meccans even more
determined to destroy him before he built up an alliance against them.
Violent battles between the Muslims and the Meccans followed. Alliances
and betrayals by various tribal factions during each battle engendered
more battles, which decimated the Muslim community. The number of
widows mounted to such catastrophic proportions after the battle fought
at Uhud, near Medina, that God sent a message officially condoning
polygamy: "Marry women of your choice, two, or three, or four." But
He added, "If you fear that you cannot treat them equitably, marry only
one" (3:3). A polygamous husband was required to distribute not only
material goods but also sexual attention equally among his wives, for
sexual satisfaction, according to Muhammad, was every woman's conjugal right. Besides, a sexually unsatisfied wife was believed to be a threat
to her family's stability, as she was likely to seek satisfaction elsewhere.

Unmarried men and women also posed a threat to Muhammad's
scheme of social order, which may be one reason why he frowned upon
monasticism. Sexual instincts were natural, he reasoned, and therefore
would eventually seek fulfillment in adultery[1] unless channeled into
legitimate marriage. Wives and husbands were thus necessary for each
other's spiritual salvation. "The curse of God be upon those women who
remain unwed and say they will never marry," he said, "and a man who
does not marry is none of mine."

Though the Quran abolished the ancient custom of stoning adulter-
esses to death and called instead for public whipping — a hundred lashes
administered to male and female offenders alike — Muhammad knew
that the sexual double standard would single out women as targets of
slander. After a bitter personal experience, he hastened to build safety
features into his antiadultery and antifornication laws.

One day Aysha was left behind inadvertently by Muhammad's caravan   20
when she stepped away to look for a necklace that she had lost. She was
brought back to the caravan the following morning by a man many years
younger than her middle-aged husband, which set tongues wagging. Even
Ali, Muhammad's trusted cousin and son-in-law, cast doubt on her
reputation. The Prophet's faith in his wife was severely shaken. Aysha

---

[1]Here *adultery* refers to premarital as well as extramarital sex.

was finally saved when her husband fell into a trance, which indicated that he was receiving a message from God. Relief spread over his face. God had vouched for her innocence. The "affair of the slander," as it came to be known, was closed. Four witnesses were henceforth required to condemn women of adultery, as against only two for business transactions and murder cases. Moreover, false witnesses were to be whipped publicly.

Other than false witnesses, violators of women's rights were not punished on this earth. The law would catch up with them in the next world, where they would be cast into the fire (an idea borrowed from the Christians). The good, on the other hand, would reside forever in a heavenly oasis with cool springs in shady palm groves where their every whim would be served by lovely dark-eyed houris. Like the Christian preachers who promised believers a heaven with pearly gates and haloed creatures floating about on white clouds, Muhammad merely presented images that would spell bliss to the common man. Though he did not specify who was going to serve the deserving women, probably for fear of offending their husbands, Muhammad guaranteed a place for them in paradise. Women had the same religious duties as men, and their souls were absolutely equal in God's eyes, with not even the responsibility for original sin weighing upon them. Islam rejects the idea of original sin altogether, claiming that every child is born pure. Nor does the Quran single out Eve as the cause of man's fall (though folklore in various parts of the Middle East does condemn her). According to the Quran, Allah tells both Adam and Eve not to eat the apple. "Then did Satan make them slip from the Garden" (2:36). Allah scolds them both equally, but promises mercy and guidance when they repent.

Muhammad's decision to rely on each man's conscience to fulfill his Islamic obligation toward women reflected a realistic approach to legislation. He seems to have recognized how far he could carry his reforms without losing his constituents' support. In a city where woman had neither economic nor political weight, men would take only so much earthly punishment for disregarding her rights. By the same token, they would not entirely give up their old prerogative of divorcing their wives for any cause without answering to a third party, or pay them more than comfortably affordable compensation. Muhammad therefore struck a compromise in his laws, but repeatedly emphasized the spirit of kindness and respect for women which was implied in them. . . .

The unspecified rights that women had enjoyed during Muhammad's time were chipped away gradually. But the meticulously detailed laws on marital and financial rights were too specific to be ignored entirely, and gave women a modicum of security and independence in the patriarchal family, which survived as a minitribe in the sprawling empire. Within the family circle women exerted considerable influence, not only on their men but also on the blossoming of Arab culture in the Middle Ages. An exceptional few followed Aysha's example and ruled the caliphs and their empire, which spread Islam to lands and peoples far beyond the Arabian peninsula.

EXPLORATIONS

1. According to Minai, what were the main responsibilities, privileges, and dangers of being female in a nomadic tribe?
2. Why did Khadija's and Muhammad's Quraysh ancestors gain by giving up their nomadic existence? In what ways did the urbanization of Mecca pave the way for a monotheistic religion? for a social code ensuring protection for women?
3. How did Muhammad's marriage to Khadija contribute to the founding of Islam? How did his marriage to Aysha contribute to the religion's rules?
4. What is the effect of Minai's opening her essay with a romantic anecdote? What elements in this first paragraph were presumably added by the author rather than drawn from source documents? How would you evaluate the balance she has struck between human interest and historical accuracy?

CONNECTIONS

1. Alberto Moravia's "The Chase" defines marital success in terms of attraction between the partners. According to Minai's summary, did the Islamic code treat sexual attraction as valuable or dangerous to a marriage? Cite evidence for your answer.
2. Susan Brownmiller describes stereotypical femininity in *Looking at Ourselves*. Which of these feminine qualities were present in the tribal Arab society of Muhammad's day? What factors encouraged women to develop these qualities?
3. Look back at Ved Mehta's "Pom's Engagement" (p. 262). In what ways do the Hindu concepts of male and female rights and responsibilities resemble those of Islam? What aspects of both cultures' definition of sex roles illustrate points made by Simone de Beauvoir in "Woman as Other"?

ELABORATIONS

1. Minai undertook a delicate task in deciding to write about a religion and its founder. What different viewpoints toward Islam do you think she anticipated among her audience? What concessions, if any, does her writing show to Muslims? to members of other religions? Having looked at Minai's tactics for handling a sensitive subject, write an essay about the history of a social phenomenon with which you are familiar. For example, you might compare attitudes toward marriage in your parents' generation, your grandparents' generation, and your own; or you might describe changes in your church that have resulted from social developments in the past decade. Shape your essay, as Minai does, for a potentially diverse audience.

2. When Muhammad went home after hearing God's message from the angel Gabriel, writes Minai, "Khadija understood that her husband had received a call to serve the one God" (para. 10). In our culture people who report receiving messages from God are seldom believed. Why is this true, given the centrality of such messages in our Judeo-Christian religions? Write an essay classifying or defining the role(s) of divine intervention in our history and in our contemporary culture.

CHERRY LINDHOLM and
CHARLES LINDHOLM

Life Behind the Veil

Cherry Lindholm was born in 1942 in Hull, England. After graduating with a degree in fine art from Durham University in England, she received a master's in counseling psychology from Columbia University. Her current main pursuit is painting. Charles Lindholm was born in 1946 in Minnesota and holds a doctorate in anthropology from Columbia University. Currently at Boston University, he recently published *Charisma* (1990), a study of charismatic social movements and their leaders, including Adolf Hitler and Jim Jones. "Life Behind the Veil" originally appeared in *Science Digest* in 1980, preceding the book *Generosity and Jealousy: The Swat Pakhtun of Northern Pakistan* (1982). The authors' purpose, says Charles Lindholm, was to "look beneath the things that seem to us to be exotic, strange, alienating, and try to understand the milieu that makes those things sensible. We're trying to break through the veil of custom to touch the people beneath, to achieve some empathy with those people."

Pakistan came into existence the year after Charles Lindholm was born. Conflict between Hindus and Muslims spurred the British (who then controlled the region) to divide Islamic Pakistan from Hindu India. Both countries remained British protectorates. Pakistan — consisting of two separate sections on opposite sides of India — became an independent republic within the British Commonwealth in 1956. In 1971 East Pakistan split from West Pakistan, taking the name Bangladesh. The Swat Valley visited by Cherry and Charles Lindholm lies in northern Pakistan, near the Afghanistan border.

The bazaar teems with activity. Pedestrians throng the narrow streets, wending past donkey carts, cyclists, and overloaded vehicles. Vendors haggle in the dark doorways of their shops. Pitiful beggars shuffle among the crowds, while bearded religious mendicants wander about, their eyes fixed on a distant world.

Drifting among the mobs of men are, here and there, anonymous figures hidden beneath voluminous folds of material, who float along like ships in full sail, graceful, mysterious, faceless, instilling in the observer a sense both of awe and of curiosity. These are the Moslem women of the Middle East. Their dress is the customary *chador,* which they wear when obliged to leave the privacy of their homes. The *chador* is but one means by which women maintain their *purdah,* the institution of female seclusion, which requires that women should remain unseen by men who are not close relatives and strikes Westerners as so totally foreign and incomprehensible.

Sometimes the alien aspect is tempered with a touch of Western familiarity. A pair of plastic sunglasses may gleam from behind the lace that covers the eyes, or a platform shoe might peep forth from beneath the hem of the flowing *chador.* Nevertheless, the overall presence remains one of inscrutability and is perhaps the most striking image of Middle Eastern societies.

We spent nine months in one of the most strict of all the *purdah*   4 societies, the Yusufzai Pakhtun of the Swat Valley in the North-West Frontier Province of Pakistan. ("Pakhtun" is the designation preferred by the tribesmen, who were generally called Pathans in the days of the British *raj.*)

We had come to the Swat Valley after a hair-raising ride on a rickety bus from Peshawar over the 10,280-foot Malakand Pass. Winston Churchill came this way as a young war correspondent attached to the Malakand Field Force in 1897. As we came into the valley, about half the size of Connecticut, we passed a sign that said WELCOME TO SWAT. We were fortunate to have entrée into the community through a Swati friend we had made eight years before. In Swat, women are secluded inside the domestic compound except for family rituals, such as marriage, circumcision, and funerals, or visits to saints' tombs. A woman must always be in the protective company of other women and is never allowed out alone. It tells a great deal about the community that the word for husband in Pakhto, the language of the Pakhtun, is *khawund,* which also means God.

However, as everywhere, rules are sometimes broken or, more frequently, cleverly manipulated. Our Pakhtun host's stepmother, Bibi, an intelligent and forceful woman, was renowned for her tactics. Once, when all the females of the household had been forbidden to leave the compound to receive cholera inoculations at the temporary clinic next door, Bibi respectfully bowed her head and assured the men they could visit the mosque with easy minds. Once the men had gone, she promptly climbed the ladder to the flat roof and summoned the doctor to the door of her compound. One by one, the women extended their bare arms through the doorway and received their shots. Later, Bibi could honestly swear that no woman had set foot outside the compound walls.

Despite such circumventions, *purdah* is of paramount importance in Swat. As one Pakhtun proverb succinctly states: "The woman's place is in the home or the grave." Years ago in Swat, if a woman broke her *purdah*, her husband might kill her or cut off her nose as punishment and as a means of cleansing his honor. If a woman is caught alone with an unrelated man, it will always be assumed that the liaison is sexual, and public opinion will oblige her husband to shoot her, even if he does not desire her death; to go unavenged is to be known henceforth as *begherata*, or man without honor. As such, he would no longer have the right to call himself Pakhtun.

A shameless woman is a threat to the whole society. Our host remem- 8 bered witnessing, thirty years ago when he was a child, the entire village stoning an adulteress. This punishment is prescribed by Islamic law, though the law requires there be four witnesses to the sexual act itself to establish guilt. Nowadays, punishments for wifely misdemeanors have become less harsh, though adulterous wives are still killed.

In the rural areas, poorer families generally cannot maintain *purdah* as rigorously as their wealthier neighbors, for often the wife must help her husband in the fields or become a servant. Nevertheless, she is required to keep her hair covered at all times and to interact with men to a minimum. Here again, the rules are sometimes flouted, and a poor woman might entice a man with her eyes or even, according to village men who claimed personal experiences, become more aggressive in her seductive attempts and actually seize a man in a deserted alleyway and lure him into her house. Often, the man is persuaded. Such a woman will accept money from her lover, who is usually a man from a wealthy family. Her husband is then a *begherata*, but some men acquiesce to the situation because of the money the wife is earning or because of fear of the wife's socially superior and more powerful lover. But most poor men, and certainly all of the elite, keep their women under strict control.

In the Islamic Middle East, women are viewed as powerful and dangerous beings, highly sexual and lacking in personal discipline and discrimination. In Middle Eastern thought, sexual intercourse itself, though polluting, lacks the same negative connotations it has in the West. It has always been believed that women have sexual climaxes, and there is no notion of female frigidity. Male impotence, however, is well-documented, and some middle-aged and even young men admitted to us that they had lost their interest in women. Sometimes, though rarely, a young bride-groom will find himself incapable of consummating his marriage, either because he finds his bride unattractive or because he has been previously enchanted by a male lover and has become impotent in a heterosexual relationship. Homosexuality has never been seen as aberrant in the Middle East. As a famous Afghan saying humorously declares: "A woman is for bearing children, a boy is for pleasure, but ecstasy is a ripe watermelon!" However, with Western influence, homosexuality in the Middle East is now less overt. But even when it was common and open, the man was still expected to marry and produce children.

Men must marry, though women are regarded as a chaotic and anarchic force. They are believed to possess many times the sexual desire of men and constitute a potential threat to the family and the family's honor, which is based in large measure on the possession and control of women and their excessive and dangerous sexuality.

Among the Pakhtun of Swat, where the male-female relation is one 12 of the most hostile in the Middle East, the man avoids showing affection to his wife, for fear she will become too self-confident and will begin to assert herself in ways that insult his position and honor. She may start by leaving the compound without his permission and, if unchecked, may end by bringing outside men into the house for sexual encounters, secure in the knowledge that her husband, weakened by his affection for her, will not take action. This course of events is considered inevitable by men and women alike and was illustrated by a few actual cases in the village where we lived.

Women are therefore much feared, despite the pronouncements of male supremacy. They must be controlled, in order to prevent their alarming basic natures from coming to the fore and causing dishonor to their own lineages. *Purdah* is generally described as a system that serves to protect the woman, but implicitly it protects the men and society in general from the potentially disruptive actions of the powerful female sex.

Changes are occurring, however, particularly in the modern urban centers. The educated urban woman often dispenses with the *chador*, replacing it with a simple length of veiling draped over the head or across the shoulders; she may even decide to adopt modest Western dress. The extent of this transformation will depend partly upon the attitude of the community in which she lives.

In the urban centers of the stricter *purdah* regions the public display of *purdah* is scrupulous, sometimes even more striking than that of the tribal village. Behind the scenes, though, the city-dwelling woman does

have more freedom than she would have in the village. She will be able
to visit not only relatives but friends without specific permission from her
husband, who is out at work all day. She may, suitably veiled, go shopping
in the bazaar, a chore her husband would have undertaken in the village.
On the whole, the city woman will have a great deal more independence,
and city men sometimes lament this weakening of traditional male domination.

The urbanized male may speak of the custom-bound tribesmen (such　16
as the Swat Pakhtun, the Bedouin nomads of Saudi Arabia, or the
Qashqai herdsmen of Iran) as country bumpkins, yet he still considers
their central values, their sense of personal pride, honor, and autonomy,
as cultural ideals and views the tribesmen, in a very real way, as exemplars
of the proper mode of life. Elite families in the cities proudly emphasize
their tribal heritage and sometimes send their sons to live for a year or
so with distant tribal cousins, in order to expose them to the tribesman's
integrity and moral code. The tribesman, on the other hand, views his
urbanized relatives as weak and womanly, especially with reference to
the slackening of *purdah* in the cities. Though the *purdah* female, both
in the cities and in the tribal areas, rarely personifies the ideal virtues of
silence, submission, and obedience, the concept of *purdah* and male
supremacy remains central to the male identity and to the ideology of
the culture as a whole.

The dynamic beneath the notion of male supremacy, the institution
of *purdah*, and the ideology of women's sexual power becomes apparent
when one takes an overall view of the social structure. The family in the
Middle East, particularly in the tribal regions, is not an isolated element;
kinship and marriage are the underlying principles that structure action
and thought. Individuals interact not so much according to personal
preference as according to kinship.

The Middle Eastern kinship system is known to anthropologists as a
segmentary-lineage organization; the basic idea is that kinship is traced
through one line only. In the Middle East, the system is patrilineal,
which means that the male line is followed, and all the links through
women are ignored. An individual can therefore trace his relationship to
any other individual in the society and know the exact genealogical
distance between them; i.e., the distance that must be traced to reach a
common male ancestor. The system obliges men to defend their patrilineal relatives if they are attacked, but if there is no external force threatening the lineage, then men struggle against one another according to
the principle of genealogical distance. This principle is nicely stated in a

famous Middle Eastern proverb: "I against my brothers; my brothers and I against my cousins; my cousins, my brothers, and I against the world." The cousins in question are of course patrilineal.

Within this system, women appear to have no role, though they are the units of reproduction, the mothers of the sons who will carry on the patriline. Strange as it may seem, this is the core contradiction of the society: The "pure" patriline itself is actually descended from a woman. This helps explain the exaggerated fear of women's promiscuity and supposedly voracious sexuality. In order to protect the patriline, women must be isolated and guarded. Their sexuality, which threatens the integrity of the patriline, must be made the exclusive property of their husbands. Women, while being absolutely necessary for the perpetuation of the social order, are simultaneously the greatest threat to it.

The persistent denigration of women is explained by this core contra-   20
diction. Moslem society considers women naturally inferior in intelligence and ability — childlike, incapable of discernment, incompetent to testify in court, prey to whims and fancies. In tribal areas, women are prohibited from inheritance, despite a Koranic injunction, and in marriage they are purchased from their fathers like a commodity. Were woman not feared, these denials of her personhood would be unnecessary.

Another unique element of Middle Eastern culture is the prevalence of marriage with the father's brother's daughter. In many areas, in fact, this marriage is so favored that a boy must give explicit permission to allow his patrilineal female cousin to marry elsewhere. This peculiar marriage form, which is found nowhere else in the world, also serves to negate the woman by merging her lineage with that of her husband, since both are members of the same patriline (indeed, are the offspring of brothers). No new blood enters, and the sanctity of the patriline is steadily maintained.

However, this ploy gives rise to other problems: Cousin marriage often divides the brothers rather than uniting them. Although the bride-price is usually reduced in such marriages, it is always demanded, thus turning the brothers into opponents in a business negotiation. Furthermore, giving a woman in Swat carries an implication of inferiority; historically, victors in war took women from the vanquished. Cousin marriage thus renders the brothers' equality questionable. Finally, the young couple's fights will further alienate the brothers, especially since such marriages are notoriously contentious. This is because patrilineal male cousins are rivals for the common grandfather's inheritance (in fact, the Swati term for father's brother's son is *tarbur*, which also means enemy), and a man who marries his patrilineal cousin is marrying the sister of his lifelong opponent. Her loyalty is with her brother, and this is bound to cause frequent disputes.

Though the girl is treated like goods, she does not see herself as such. The fundamental premise of tribal life is the equality of the various landed families. There are very few hierarchies in these societies, and even the leaders are often no more than first among equals. Within this system, which has been described as a nearly perfect democracy, each *khan* (which means landowner and literally translates as king) family sees itself as superior to all others. The girls of the household feel the same pride in their lineage as their brothers and cannot help but regard their husbands' families through jaundiced eyes. The new bride is prepared to defend the honor of her family, even though they have partially repudiated her by negotiating the marriage. Her identity, like that of a man, rests on her lineage pride, which she will fight to uphold. The husband, meanwhile, is determined to demonstrate his domination and mastery, since control of women is the nexus of a man's sense of self-respect.

Hostility is thus built into marriage by the very structure of the society, 24 which pits every lineage against every other in a never-ending contest to maintain an equilibrium of power within this markedly egalitarian culture. The hostility of the marriage bond is evident from its beginnings. The reluctant bride is torn from her cot in her family's house and ensconced on a palanquin that strongly resembles a bier. The war drums that announce the marriage procession indicate the nature of the tie, as does the stoning of the palanquin by the small boys of the village as it is carried through the dusty streets. When the bride arrives at her new husband's house, his family triumphantly fires their rifles into the air. They have taken a woman! The young wife cowers in her veils as she is prodded and poked curiously by the females of the husband's house who try to persuade her to show her face. The groom himself is nowhere to be seen, having retreated to the men's house in shame. In three days, he will creep to her room and consummate the marriage. Taking the virginity of the bride is a highly charged symbolic act, and in some areas of the Middle East the display of the bloody nuptial sheet to the public is a vital part of the wedding rite. Breaking the hymen demonstrates the husband's possession of his wife's sexuality. She then becomes the most junior adult in the household, subordinate to everyone, but, most especially, under the heavy thumb of her mother-in-law.

The household the bride enters will be that of her husband's father, since the system, as well as being patrilineal, is also patrilocal. She will be surrounded by his relatives and will be alone with her husband only at night. During the day he will pay no attention to her, for it is considered shameful for a man to take note of his wife in front of others, particularly his father and mother. Within the compound walls, which shield the household from the rest of the world, she is at the mercy of her new family.

Life within the compound is hardly peaceful. Wives squabble among themselves, and wives who have built a power base by having sons even quarrel with the old matriarch, their mother-in-law. This is usually a prelude to a couple moving out of the house into their own compound, and husbands always blame their wives for the breakup of the extended family, even though they, too, will be glad to become the masters of their own homes and households.

But the worst fights among women are the fights between women married to the same man. Islam permits polygamous marriage, and legally a man may have four wives. Not all men are financially able to take more than one wife, but most men dream of marrying again, despite the Swati proverb that says, "I may be a fool, but not so much of a fool as the man with two wives." Men who can afford it often do take a second wife. The reason is not sexual desire, for wives do not mind if their husbands have liaisons with prostitutes or promiscuous poor women. Rather, the second wife is brought in to humiliate an overly assertive first wife. Bringing in a second wife is a terrible insult; it is an expression of contempt for the first wife and her entire lineage. The insult is especially cutting in Swat, where divorce is prohibited (though it is permitted in the Koran) and where a disliked wife must either endure her lot or retreat to her family's house and a life of celibacy. Small wonder then that households with two wives are pits of intrigue, vituperation, and magical incantation, as each wife seeks to expel the other. The Koran says a man should only practice polygamy if he is sure he can treat each wife equally; the only man we met who was able to approximate this ideal was a man who never went home. He spent his time in the men's house, talking with his cronies and having his meals sent to him.

The men's house is the best-built structure in any village, along with   28
the mosque, which is also prohibited to women. It is a meeting place for the clan, the center for hospitality and refuge, and the arena for political manipulation. This is where the visitor will be received, surrounded by men who gossip, doze, or clean their rifles. Here, the guest might well

imagine that women do not even exist. Only the tea and food that is sent over from the compound nearby tell him of the women working behind the walls.

Formerly, in Swat, most men slept in the men's house, visiting their wives secretly late at night and returning before daybreak. But now only a few elders and some ne'er-do-well youths live permanently in the elegant, aging buildings. Sometimes, however, a man may be obliged to move to the men's house for a few days if his wife makes his home too uncomfortable, for women too have their own weapons in the household battles. Arguments may flare up over almost anything: the husband buying a rotten piece of meat or forgetting to bring home a length of material, the wife ruining some curd or gossiping too much with a neighbor. The wife may then angrily refuse to cook, obliging the husband to retreat to the men's house for food. The man's weapon in fights is violence, while the woman can withdraw domestic services at will.

In the early days of a marriage, when the bride is new to the household and surrounded by her husband's people, she may be fairly meek. But when her status has improved as a result of producing sons, she will become more aggressive. Her lacerating tongue is renowned, and she will also begin to fight back physically as well as verbally. Finally, her exasperated husband may silence her with a blow from a heavy stick he keeps for that purpose. No shame is attached to beating one's wife, and men laugh about beatings they have administered. The women themselves, though they decry their men's brutality, proudly display their scars and bruises, characterizing a neighbor who is relatively gentle to his wife as "a man with no penis."

The older a woman gets, the more powerful and fearless she becomes. She is aided by her sons who, though respecting their father, regard him as an obstacle to their gaining rights in land. The old man, who gains his stature from his landholding, is always reluctant to allot shares to his grown sons. Furthermore, the sons' ties of affection are much stronger with the mother. The elderly father, who is generally ten or fifteen years older than his wife, is thus surrounded by animosity in his own house. The situation of the earlier years has reversed itself, and the wife, who began alone and friendless, gains allies in her old age, while the husband becomes isolated. Ghani Khan, a modern Pakhtun writer, has described the situation well: "The Pakhtun thinks he is as good as anyone else and his father rolled into one and is fool enough to try this even with his wife. She pays for it in her youth, and he in his old age."

But many women do not live to see their triumph. In northern Swat, 32 for every 100 women over the age of sixty there are 149 men, compared to the more equal 100 to 108 ratio below sixty. The women are worn out by continual childbearing, breast feeding, and a lack of protein. Though fertile in places, the Swat valley is heavily overpopulated with an estimated 1 million people, and survival is always difficult. The diet consists chiefly of bread, rice, seasonal vegetables, and some dairy products. Meat is a rarity and goes to the men and boys as a matter of course. They perpetuate the patrilineal clan and must survive, while women can always be replaced. The lives of men are hard, but the lives of women are harder, as witnessed by their early deaths.

In this environment, people must learn to be tough, just as they must learn to fit the structure of the patrilineal system. Child rearing serves both functions.

The birth of a boy in Swat is greeted by rejoicing, while the birth of a girl is an occasion for gloom. But the first few years for both sexes are virtually identical. Like most Middle Easterners, the Swatis practice swaddling, binding the baby tightly so that it is immobilized. Ostensibly, this is to help the baby sleep and prevent it from blinding itself with its flailing hands, but anthropologists have hypothesized that swaddling actually serves to develop a certain character type: a type which can withstand great restraint but which also tends to uncontrolled bursts of temper. This hypothesis fits Swat, where privation and the exigencies of the social structure demand stoicism, but where violent temper is also useful. We often saw Swati children of all ages lose themselves in tantrums to coerce their parents, and such coercion was usually successful. Grown men and women as well are prone to fits of temper, and this dangerous aspect makes their enemies leery of pressing them too hard.

Both sexes are indoctrinated in the virtues of their family and its lineage. In marital fights this training is obvious, as both partners heatedly assert, "Your ancestor was nothing, and mine was great!" At a man's death his sister, not his wife, is his chief mourner. And if a woman is killed it is her brother, not her husband, who avenges her.

Child training in Swat produces strong characters. When they give 36 affection, they give it wholeheartedly, and when they hate, they hate bitterly. The conditions under which they live are cruel and cramped, and they respond with cruelty and rigidity in order to survive. But at the same time, the people are able to bear their hard lives with pride and dignity.

EXPLORATIONS

1. On what types of evidence do the Lindholms base their generalizations about Swat? What information in their essay, if any, appears to have come from outside sources rather than from their visit to the valley?

2. What use do the Lindholms make of direct quotation? How would the essay's effect change if the authors quoted local people more extensively?

3. What statements in "Life Behind the Veil" reflect value judgments by the Lindholms? What emotionally weighted words and phrases (for example, "The *reluctant* bride is *torn from* her cot," para. 24) show the authors' feelings about the customs they describe? What is the positive or negative impact (or both) of the authors' revealing their reactions to the Pakhtun?

CONNECTIONS

1. According to Naila Minai in "Women in Early Islam," what concept did seventh-century Meccans hold of female sexuality? How did the prevailing customs of betrothal and marriage create a balance between women's right to sexual satisfaction and men's desire to support only their own children? What concept of female sexuality dominates the Swat Pakhtun today?

2. Look again at Minai's "Women in Early Islam": How do the Pakhtun customs of betrothal, marriage, and divorce coincide and conflict with those outlined by Muhammad? Why do you think Muhammad's ideas, as described by Minai, have not been more strictly followed in this Islamic culture?

3. What beliefs and practices among the Pakhtun confirm Simone de Beauvoir's contention that men perceive women as Other? How do Pakhtun customs bear out Beauvoir's explanation of why men hold this perception, and why women cooperate with it? What considerations not mentioned by Beauvoir have evidently influenced Pakhtun sex roles?

4. What aspects of the Pakhtun Islamic view of women coincide with the feminine stereotype described by Susan Brownmiller in *Looking at Ourselves?* What motives do the Pakhtun women share with the Americans?

ELABORATIONS

1. Minai's "Women in Early Islam" shows how Islam came into being; "Life Behind the Veil" shows how it affects one culture today. Which of Muham-

mad's hopes for his religion, as described by Minai, are fulfilled in modern Swat? What Islamic principles cited by Minai are violated by the Swat Pakhtun? What rules aimed at protecting women (according to Minai) have been twisted over time by the Pakhtun (according to the Lindholms) into means of oppression? Write an essay comparing and contrasting Islam 1,400 years ago in Arabia with Islam today in the Swat Valley, based on Minai's and the Lindholms' accounts.

2. According to the Lindholms, a Pakhtun wife's place in her home changes dramatically from her wedding day to her old age; so does her husband's. In what ways does the role of a wife or husband in the United States change over time? Based on your family's experience, interviews you conduct, or both, write an essay defining the different parts played by an American man or woman from courtship through retirement.

YASHAR KEMAL

A Dirty Story

Yashar Kemal, a Nobel Prize candidate, is widely considered Turkey's greatest living writer. Born in 1923 as Yashar Kemal Gokceli, he grew up among the desperately poor Anatolian peasants, whose plight became a central theme of his writing and his life. At the age of five he saw his father murdered in a mosque; after three years of secondary school he went to work in the Turkish cotton fields and factories. Kemal held a variety of jobs before his arrest in 1950 for alleged Communist propaganda (he was later acquitted). Moving to Istanbul, he dropped his surname, became a journalist, and rose to the post of Anatolian bureau chief of the daily paper *Cumhuriyet*. His 1955 novel *Ince Memed,* translated into more than fifteen languages, reached the English-speaking world in two parts: *Memed, My Hawk* (1961) and *They Burn the Thistles* (1977). Other fiction, nonfiction, and plays have followed. "A Dirty Story" comes from *Anatolian Tales (Butun hikayeler,* 1967) and was translated from the Turkish by the author's wife, Thilda Kemal. Kemal was a member of the Central Committee of the Turkish Workers' Party (now banned), which he considers the most compassionate and sensible political movement in Turkey. His recent works include *The Sea-Crossed Fisherman* (1985) and *The Birds Have Also Gone* (1987). He now lives in Istanbul.

The Islamic nation of Turkey consists of a European section and an Asian section separated by water. European Turkey borders Greece and Bulgaria. Asian Turkey, or Anatolia, is many times larger; it borders Syria, Iraq, Iran, and the Soviet Union and includes the capital city of Ankara. Human habitation there dates back to the Stone Age, at least 7000 B.C. Istanbul, perhaps the most strategically sited city in the world, stands mostly in Europe with suburbs in Asia. Founded by Greeks as Byzantium in the seventh century B.C., it was captured after a thousand years by the Roman emperor Constantine, who made it his capital and renamed it Constantinople. In 1453 the Ottoman Sultan Mehmed II swept westward from Anatolia and took the city. The Ottoman Empire, which in the sixteenth century ruled much of Europe, the Middle East, and North Africa, lasted through World War I. The Young Turk movement started a revolt in 1908, which culminated in Turkey's becoming a republic under President Kemal Ataturk in 1923. As Yashar Kemal's story suggests, however, the economy remains agrarian, and many of the Turkish people must eke out a living under unfavorable conditions.

The three of them were sitting on the damp earth, their backs against the dung-daubed brush wall and their knees drawn up to their chests, when another man walked up and crouched beside them.

"Have you heard?" said one of them excitedly. "Broken-Nose Jabbar's done it again! You know Jabbar, the fellow who brings all those women from the mountain villages and sells them in the plain? Well, this time he's come down with a couple of real beauties. The lads of Misdik have got together and bought one of them on the spot, and now they're having fun and making her dance and all that . . . It's unbelievable! Where does the fellow find so many women? How does he get them to come with him? He's the devil's own son, he is . . ."

"Well, that's how he makes a living," commented one of the men. "Ever since I can remember, this Jabbar's been peddling women for the villagers of the Chukurova plain. Allah provides for all and sundry . . ."

"He's still got the other one," said the newcomer, "and he's ready to give her away for a hundred liras."   4

"He'll find a customer soon enough," put in another man whose head was hunched between his shoulders. "A good woman's worth more than a team of oxen, at least, in the Chukurova plain she is. You can always put her to the plow and, come summer, she'll bind and carry the sheaves, hoe, do anything. What's a hundred liras? Why, a woman brings in that much in one single summer. In the fields, at home, in bed. There's nothing like a woman. What's a hundred liras?"

Just then, Hollow Osman came up mumbling to himself and flopped down beside them without a word of greeting. He was a tall, broad-shouldered man with a rather shapeless potbellied body. His lips drooped foolishly and his eyes had an odd squintlike gaze.

"Hey, Osman," the man who had been talking addressed him. "Broken-Nose Jabbar's got a woman for sale again. Only a hundred liras. Tell Mistress Huru to buy her for you and have done with living alone and sleeping in barns like a dog."

Osman shrugged his shoulders doubtfully.   8

"Look here, man," pursued the other, "this is a chance in a million. What's a hundred liras? You've been slaving for that Huru since you dropped out of your mother's womb and she's never paid you a lira. She owes you this. And anyway she'll get back her money's worth in just one summer. A woman's good for everything, in the house, in the fields, in bed . . ."

Osman rose abruptly.

"I'll ask the Mistress," he said. "How should I know? . . ."

A couple of days later, a short, broad-hipped girl with blue beads
strung into her plaited hair was seen at the door of Huru's barn in which
Hollow Osman always slept. She was staring out with huge wondering
eyes.

A month passed. Two months . . . And passersby grew familiar with
the sight of the strange wide-eyed girl at the barn door.

One day, a small dark boy with a face the size of a hand was seen
pelting through the village. He rushed up to his mother where she sat
on the threshold of her hut gossiping with Seedy Doneh.

"Mother," he screeched, "I've seen them! It's the truth, I swear it is.
Uncle Osman's wife with . . . May my eyes drop out right here if I'm
telling a lie."

Seedy Doneh turned to him sharply.

"What?" she cried. "Say it again. What's that about Fadik?"

"She was with the Agha's son. I saw them with my own eyes. He went
into the barn with her. They couldn't see me where I was hiding. Then
he took off his boots, you know the shiny yellow boots he wears . . . And
then they lay down and . . . Let my two eyes drop out if . . ."

"I knew it!" crowed Seedy Doneh. "I knew it would turn out this way."

"Hollow Osman never had any manhood in him anyway," said the
child's mother. "Always under that viper-tongued Huru's petticoats . . ."

"Didn't I tell you, Ansha, the very first day she came here that this
would happen?" said Doneh. "I said this girl's ready to play around.
Pretending she was too bashful to speak to anyone. Ah, still waters run
deep . . ."

She rose quickly and hurried off to spread the news.

"Have you heard? Just as I foretold . . . Still waters . . . The Agha's
son . . . Fadik . . ."

In a trice all the neighboring women had crowded at Ansha's door,
trying to squeeze the last drop of information out of the child.

"Come on, tell us," urged one of the women for perhaps the hundredth
time. "How did you see them?"

"Let my two eyes drop out right here if I'm lying," the child repeated
again and again with unabated excitement. "The Agha's son came in,
and then they lay down, both of them, and did things . . . I was watching
through a chink in the wall. Uncle Osman's wife, you know, was crying.

I can't do it, she was saying, and she was sobbing away all the time.
Then the Agha's son pulled off those shiny yellow boots of his . . . Then
I ran right here to tell Mother."

The news spread through the village like wildfire. People could talk
about nothing else. Seedy Doneh, for one, seemed to have made it her
job to leave no man or woman uninformed. As she scoured the village
for new listeners, she chanced upon Osman himself.

"Haven't you heard what's come upon you?" she said, drawing him   28
aside behind the wall of a hut. "You're disgraced, you jackass. The Agha's
son has got his fingers up your wife's skirt. Try and clear your good name
now if you can!"

Osman did not seem to understand.

"I don't know . . ." he murmured, shrugging his shoulders. "I'll have
to ask the Mistress. What would the Agha's son want with my wife?"

Doneh was incensed.

"What would he want with her, blockhead?" she screamed. "Damn   32
you, your wife's become a whore, that's what! She's turned your home
into a brothel. Anyone can come in and have her." She flounced off still
screaming. "I spit on you! I spit on your manhood . . ."

Osman was upset.

"What are you shouting for, woman?" he called after her. "People will
think something's wrong. I have to ask the Mistress. She knows everything. How should I know?"

He started walking home, his long arms dangling at his sides as though
they had been hitched to his shoulders as an afterthought, his fingers
sticking out wide apart as was his habit. This time he was waylaid by
their next-door neighbor, Zeynep, who planted herself before him and
tackled him at the top of her voice.

"Ah Osman! You'd be better off dead! Why don't you go and bury   36
yourself? The whole village knows about it. Your wife . . . The Agha's
son . . . Ah Osman, how could you have brought such a woman into
your home? Where's your honor now? Disgraced . . . Ah Osman!"

He stared at her in bewilderment.

"How should I know?" he stammered, his huge hands opening out like
pitchforks. "The Mistress knows all about such things. I'll go and ask her."

Zeynep turned her back on him in exasperation, her large skirt bal-
looning about her legs.

"Go bury yourself, Osman! I hope I see you dead after this."   40

A group of children were playing tipcat nearby. Suddenly one of them
broke into a chant.

"Go bury yourself, Osman . . . See you dead, Osman . . ."

The other children joined in mechanically without interrupting their game.

Osman stared at them and turned away. 44

"How should I know?" he muttered. "I must go to the Mistress."

He found Huru sitting at her spinning wheel. Fadik was there too, squatting near the hearth and listlessly chewing mastic gum.

"Mistress," said Osman, "have you heard what Seedy Doneh's saying? She's saying I'm disgraced . . ."

Huru stepped on the pedal forcefully and brought the wheel to a stop. 48

"What's that?" she said. "What about Seedy Doneh?"

"I don't know . . . She said Fadik . . ."

"Look here," said Huru, "you mustn't believe those lying bitches. You've got a good wife. Where would you find such a woman?"

"I don't know. Go bury yourself, they said. The children too . . ." 52

"Shut up," cried Huru, annoyed. "People always gossip about a beautiful woman. They go looking for the mote in their neighbor's eye without seeing the beam in their own. They'd better hold their peace because I've got a tongue in my head too . . ."

Osman smiled with relief.

"How could I know?" he said.

Down in the villages of the Chukurova plain, a sure sign of oncoming 56 spring is when the women are seen with their heads on one another's lap, picking the lice out of one another's hair. So it was, on one of the first warm days of the year. A balmy sun shone caressingly down on the fields and village, and not a leaf stirred. A group of women were sitting before their huts on the dusty ground, busy with the lice and wagging their tongues for all they were worth. An acrid odor of sweat hung about the group. Seedy Doneh was rummaging in the hair of a large woman who was stretched full length on the ground. She decided that she had been silent long enough.

"No," she declared suddenly, "it's not as you say, sister! He didn't force her or any such thing. She simply fell for him the minute she saw those shiny yellow boots. If you're going to believe Huru! . . . She's got to deny it, of course."

"That Huru was born with a silver spoon in her mouth," said white-haired, toothless old Zala, wiping her bloodstained fingers on her ragged skirt. "Hollow Osman's been slaving for her like twenty men ever since she took him in, a kid the size of your hand! And all for a mere pittance of food. And now there's the woman too. Tell me, what's there left for Huru to do?"

"Ah," sighed another woman, "fortune has smiled on Huru, she has indeed! She's got two people serving her now."

"And both for nothing," old Zala reminded her.   60

"What it amounts to," said Seedy Doneh spitefully, "is that Huru used to have one wife and now she's got two. Osman was always a woman, and as for Fadik she's a real woman. He-he!"

"That she is, a real woman!" the others agreed.

"Huru says the Agha's son took her by force," pursued Doneh. "All right, but what about the others? What about those lining up at her door all through the night, eh? She never says no to any one of them, does she? She takes in everyone, young and old."

"The Lady Bountiful, that's what she is," said Elif. "And do you know   64
something? Now that Fadik's here, the young men are leaving Omarja's yellow bitch in peace . . ."

"They've got somewhere better to go!" cackled the others.

Omarja's dumpy wife jumped up from where she was sitting on the edge of the group.

"Now look here, Elif!" she cried. "What's all this about our yellow dog? Stop blackening people's characters, will you?"

"Well, it's no lie, is it?" Doneh challenged her. "When was that bitch   68
ever at your door where she should be all night? No, instead, there she came trotting up a-mornings with a rope dangling from her neck!"

"Don't go slandering our dog," protested Omarja's wife. "Why, if Omarja hears this, he'll kill the poor creature. Upon my word he will!"

"Go on!" said Doneh derisively. "Don't you come telling me that Omarja doesn't know his yellow bitch is the paramour of all the village youths! What about that time when Stumpy Veli caught some of them down by the river, all taking it in turns over her? Is there anyone in this village who didn't hear of that? It's no use trying to whitewash your bitch to us!"

Omarja's wife was alarmed.

"Don't, sister," she pleaded. "Omarja'll shoot the dog, that's sure . . ."   72

"Well, I'm not to blame for that, sister," retorted Doneh tartly. "Anyway, the bitch'll be all right now that Fadik's around. And so will Kurdish Velo's donkey . . ."

Kurdish Velo's wife began to fidget nervously.

"Not our fault," she blurted out in her broken Turkish. "We lock our donkey in, but they come and break the door! Velo furious. Velo say people round here savage. He say, with an animal deadly sin! He say he kill someone. Then he complain to the Headman. Velo going sell this donkey."

"You know what I think?" interposed Seedy Doneh. "They're going to   76 make it hot for her in this village. Yes, they'll do what they did to Esheh."

"Poor Esheh," sighed old Zala. "What a woman she was before her man got thrown into prison! She would never have come to that, but she had no one to protect her. May they rot in hell, those that forced her into it! But she is dead and gone, poor thing."

"Eh!" said Doneh. "How could she be otherwise after the youths of five villages had done with her?" She straightened up. "Look here, sister," she said to the woman whose head was on her lap, "I couldn't get through your lice in days! They say the Government's invented some medicine for lice which they call Dee-Dee. Ah, if only we had a spoonful of that . . . Do you know, women, that Huru keeps watch over Fadik at night? She tells the youths when to come in and then drives them out with a stick. Ha-ha, and she wants us to believe in Fadik's virtue . . ."

"That's because it suits her. Where will she find people who'll work for nothing like those two?"

"Well, the lads are well provided for this year," snickered Doneh.   80 "Who knows but that Huru may hop in and help Fadik out!"

Just then, Huru loomed up from behind a hut. She was a large woman with a sharp chin and a wrinkled face. Her graying hair was always carefully dyed with henna.

"Whores!" she shouted at the top of her voice, as she bore down upon them with arms akimbo. "City trollops! You get hold of a poor fellow's wife and let your tongues go wagging away. Tell me, are you any better than she? What do you want of this harmless mountain girl?" She pounced on Doneh who cringed back. "As for you, you filthy shitty-assed bitch, you'll shut your mouth or I'll start telling the truth about you and that husband of yours who pretends he's a man. You know me, don't you?"

Doneh blenched.

"Me, sister?" she stammered. "Me? I never . . . Other people's good   84 name . . ."

The women were dispersing hastily. Only Kurdish Velo's wife, unaware of what was going on, continued picking lice out of her companion's hair.

"Velo says in our country women like this burnt alive. He says there no virtue in this Chukurova. No honor . . ."

The eastern sky had only just begun to pale as, with a great hullabaloo and calls and cries, the women and children drove the cattle out to pasture. Before their houses, red-aproned matrons were busy at the churns beating yogurt. The damp air smelled of spring.

Osman had long ago yoked the oxen and was waiting at Huru's door.   88
She appeared in the doorway.

"Osman, my lion," she said, "you're not to come back until you've plowed through the whole field. The girl Aysheh will look after your food and get you some bedding. Mind you do the sowing properly, my child. Husneh's hard pressed this year. And there's your wife to feed too now . . ."

Husneh was Huru's only child, whom in a moment of aberration she had given in marriage to Ali Efendi, a low-salaried tax collector. All the product of her land, everything Huru had, was for this daughter.

Osman did not move or say a word. He stood there in the half-light,   92
a large black shadow near the yoked oxen whose tails were flapping their legs in slow rhythm.

Huru stepped up to him.

"What's the matter with you, Osman, my child," she said anxiously. "Is anything wrong?"

"Mistress," whispered Osman, "it's what Seedy Doneh's saying. And Zeynep too . . . That my house . . . I don't know . . ."

Huru flared up.   96

"Shut up, you spineless dolt," she cried. "Don't you come babbling to me about the filthy inventions of those city trollops. I paid that broken-nosed thief a hundred good bank notes for the girl, didn't I? Did I ask you for as much as a lira? You listen to me. You can find fault with pure gold, but not with Fadik. Don't let me hear such nonsense from you again!"

Osman hesitated.

"I don't know . . ." he murmured, as he turned at last and drove the oxen off before him.

It was midmorning. A bright sun glowed over the sparkling fields.   100
Osman was struggling with the lean, emaciated oxen, which after plowing through only one acre had stretched themselves on the ground and simply refused to budge. Flushed and breathless, he let himself drop

onto a mound and took his head in his hands. After a while, he rose and tried pulling the animals up by the tail.

"Accursed beasts," he muttered. "The Mistress says Husneh's in need this year. Get up this minute, accursed beasts!"

He pushed and heaved, but to no avail. Suddenly in a burst of fury, he flung himself on the black ox, dug his teeth into its nose, and shook it with all his might. Then he straightened up and looked about him sheepishly.

"If anyone saw me . . ." He swore as he spat out blood. "What can I do? Husneh's in need and there's Fadik to feed too. And now these heathen beasts . . . I don't know."

It was in this state of perplexity that Stumpy Veli found him when he strolled over from a neighboring field.

"So the team's collapsed, eh?" he commented. "Well, it was to be expected. Look at how their ribs are sticking out. You won't be able to get anything out of them."

"I don't know," muttered Osman faintly. "Husneh's in a bad way and I got married . . ."

"And a fine mess that's landed you in," burst out Veli angrily. "You'd have been better off dead!"

"I don't know," said Osman. "The Mistress paid a hundred liras for her . . ."

Stumpy Veli took hold of his arm and made him sit down.

"Look, Osman," he said, "the villagers told me to talk to you. They say you're giving the village a bad name. Ever since the Agha's son took up with your wife, all the other youths have followed suit and your house is just like a brothel now. The villagers say you've got to repudiate her. If you don't, they'll drive you both out. The honor of the whole village is at stake, and you know honor doesn't grow on trees . . ."

Osman, his head hanging down, was as still as a statue. A stray ant had caught his eye.

What's this ant doing around here at this time of day, he wondered to himself. Where can its nest be?

Veli nudged him sharply.

"Damn you, man!" he cried. "Think what'll happen if the police get wind of this. She hasn't got any papers. Why, if the gendarmes once lay their hands on her, you know how it'll be. They'll play around with her for months, poor creature."

Osman started as though an electric current had been sent through his large frame.

"I haven't got any papers either," he whispered.

Veli drew nearer. Their shoulders touched. Osman's were trembling fitfully.

"Papers are the business of the Government," Veli said. "You and me, we can't understand such things. If we did, then what would we need a Government for? Now, listen to me. If the gendarmes get hold of her, we'll be the laughingstock of villages for miles around. We'll never be able to hold up our heads again in the Chukurova. You mustn't trifle with the honor of the whole village. Get rid of her before she drags you into more trouble."

"But where will I be without her?" protested Osman. "I'll die, that's 120 all. Who'll do my washing? Who'll cook bulgur pilaf for me? I'll starve to death if I have to eat gruel again every day. I just can't do without her."

"The villagers will buy you another woman," said Veli. "We'll collect the money among us. A better woman, an honorable one, and beautiful too . . . I'll go up into the mountain villages and pick one for you myself. Just you pack this one off quickly . . ."

"I don't know," said Osman. "It's the Mistress knows about these things."

Veli was exasperated.

"Damn the Mistress!" he shouted. "It's up to you, you idiot!"   124

Then he softened. He tried persuasion again. He talked and talked. He talked himself hoarse, but Osman sat there immovable as a rock, his mouth clamped tight. Finally Veli spat in his face and stalked off.

It was well on in the afternoon when it occurred to Osman to unyoke the team. He had not stirred since Veli's departure. As for the oxen, they had just lain there placidly chewing the cud. He managed to get them to their feet and let them wander about the field, while he walked back to the village. He made straight for the Agha's house and waited in the yard, not speaking to anyone, until he saw the Agha's son riding in, the bridle of his horse lathered with sweat.

The Agha's son was taken aback. He dismounted quickly, but Osman waylaid him.

"Listen," he pleaded, "you're the son of our all-powerful Agha. What 128 do you want with my wife?"

The Agha's son became the color of his famous boots. He hastily pulled a five-lira note out of his pocket and thrust it into Osman's hand.

"Take this," he mumbled and hurried away.

"But you're a great big Agha's son!" cried Osman after him. "Why do you want to drive her away? What harm has she done you? You're a great big . . ."

He was crushed. He stumbled away towards Huru's house, the five- 132
lira note still in his hand.

At the sight of Osman, Huru blew her top.

"What are you doing here, you feebleminded ass?" she shouted. "Didn't I tell you not to come back until you'd finished all the plowing? Do you want to ruin me, you idiot?"

"Wait, Mistress," stammered Osman. "Listen . . ."

"Listen, he says! Damn the fool!" 136

"Mistress," he pleaded, "let me explain . . ."

Huru glared at him.

"Mistress, you haven't heard. You don't know what the villagers are going to do to me. They're going to throw me out of this village. Stumpy Veli said so. He said the police . . . He said papers . . . We haven't got any papers. Fadik hasn't and I haven't either. He said the gendarmes would carry Fadik away and do things to her. He said I must repudiate her because my house is a brothel. That's what he said. I said the Mistress knows these things . . . She paid the hundred liras . . ."

Huru was dancing with fury. She rushed out into the village square 140
and began howling at the top of her voice.

"Bastards! So she's a thorn in your flesh, this poor fellow's wife! If you want to drive whores out of this village why don't you start with your own wives and daughters? You'd better look for whores in your own homes, pimps that you are, all of you! And tell your sons to leave poor folks' women alone . . ."

Then she turned to Osman and gave him a push.

"Off you go! To the fields! No one's going to do anything to your wife. Not while I'm alive."

The villagers had gathered in the square and had heard Huru out in 144
profound silence. As soon as she was gone, though, they started muttering among themselves.

"Who does that bitch think she is, abusing the whole village like that? . . ."

The Agha, Wolf Mahmut, had heard her too.

"You just wait, Huru," he said grinding his teeth. "If you think you're going to get away with this . . ."

The night was dark, a thick damp darkness that seemed to cling to the 148
face and hands. Huru had been waiting for some time now, concealed

in the blackest shadow of the barn, when suddenly she perceived a stirring in the darkness, and a voice was calling softly at the door.

"Fadik! Open up, girl. It's me . . ."

The door creaked open and a shadow glided in. An uncontrollable trembling seized Huru. She gripped her stick and flung herself on the door. It was unbolted and went crashing back against the wall. As she stood there trying to pierce the darkness, a few vague figures hustled by and made their escape. Taken by surprise, she hurled out a vitriolic oath and started groping about until she discovered Fadik crouching in a corner. She seized her by the hair and began to beat her with the stick.

"Bitch!" she hissed. "To think I was standing up for you . . ."

Fadik did not utter a sound as the blows rained down on her. At last 152 Huru, exhausted, let go of her.

"Get up," she ordered, "and light some kindling."

Fadik raked out the dying embers and with much puffing and blowing managed to light a stick of torchwood. A pale honeyed light fell dimly over the stacked hay. There was an old pallet in one corner and a few kitchen utensils, but nothing else to show that the place was lived in.

Huru took Fadik's hand and looked at her sternly.

"Didn't you promise me, girl, that you'd never do it again?"   156

Fadik's head hung low.

"Do you know, you bitch," continued Huru, "what the villagers are going to do? They're going to kick you out of the village. Do you hear me?"

Fadik stirred a little. "Mistress, I swear I didn't go after them! They just came in spite of everything."

"Listen to me, girl," said Huru. "Do you know what happened to 160 Esheh? That's what you'll come to if you're not careful. They're like ravening wolves, these men. If you fall into their clutches, they'll tear you to shreds. To shreds, I tell you!"

"But Mistress, I swear I never did anything to — "

"You must bolt your door because they'll be after you whether you do anything or not, and their pimps of fathers will put the blame on me. It's my hundred liras they can't swallow. They're dying to see it go to pot . . . Just like Esheh you'll be. They had no one in the world, she and her man, and when Ali was thrown into jail she was left all alone. He'd lifted a sheep from the Agha's flock and bought clothes and shoes for their son. A lovely child he was, three years old . . . Ali doted on him. But there he was in jail, and that yellow-booted good-for-nothing was soon after Esheh like the plague. She kept him at arm's length for as long as she could, poor Esheh, but he got what he wanted in the end. Then he turned her over to those ravening wolves . . . They dragged her about from village to village, from mountain to mountain. Twenty, thirty good-for-nothings . . . Her child was left among strangers, the little boy she had loved so. He died . . . Those who saw her said she was like a consumptive, thin and gray, but still they wouldn't let her go, those scoundrels. Then one day the village dogs came in all smeared with blood, and an eagle was circling over the plain. So the men went to look, and they found Esheh, her body half devoured by the dogs . . . They'd made her dance naked for them . . . They'd done all sorts of things to her. Yes, they as good as killed her. That's what the police said when they came up from the town. And when Ali heard of it, he died of grief in jail. Yes, my girl, you've got Esheh's fate before you. It isn't my hundred liras that I care for, it's you. As for Osman, I can always find another woman for him. Now I've warned you. Just call me if they come again. Esheh was all alone in the world. You've got me, at least. Do you swear to do as I'm telling you?"

"I swear it, Mistress," said Fadik.

Huru was suddenly very tired.   164

"Well, I'm going. You'll call me, won't you?"

As soon as she was gone, the youths crept out of the darkness and sneaked into the barn again.

"Hey, Fadik," they whispered. "Huru was lying to you, girl. Esheh just killed herself . . ."

There was a stretch of grass in front of the Agha's house, and on one   168 side of it dung had been heaped to the size of a small hillock. The dung steamed in the early morning sun and not a breath stirred the warm air. A cock climbed to the top of the heap. It scraped the dung, stretched its neck, and crowed triumphantly, flapping its wings.

The group of villagers squatting about on the grass silently eyed the angry Agha. Wolf Mahmut was a huge man whose shadow when he was sitting was as large as that of an average man standing up. He was never seen without a frayed, checked overcoat, the only one in the village, that he had been wearing for years now.

He was toying irritably with his metal-framed glasses when Stumpy Veli, who had been sent for a while ago, made his appearance. The Agha glared at him.

"Is this the way you get things done, you fraud?" he expostulated. "So you'd have Hollow Osman eating out of your hand in no time, eh?"

Stumpy Veli seemed to shrink to half his size.   172

"Agha," he said, "I tried everything. I talked and talked. I told him the villagers would drive them both out. I warned him of the gendarmes. All right, he said, I'll send her away. And then he didn't . . . If you ask me, Huru's at the bottom of it all."

The others stirred. "That she is!" they agreed.

Mahmut Agha jumped up. "I'll get even with her," he growled.

"That, you will, Agha," they assented. "But . . ."   176

"We've put up with that old whore long enough," continued the Agha, sitting down again.

"Yes, Agha," said Stumpy Veli, "but, you see, she relies on her son-in-law Ali, the tax collector. They'd better stop treading on my toes, she said, or I'll have Ali strip this village bare . . ."

"He can't do anything," said the Agha. "I don't owe the Government a bean."

"But we do, Agha," interposed one of the men. "He can come here   180 and take away our blankets and rugs, whatever we have . . ."

"It's because of Huru that he hasn't fleeced this village up to now," said another. "We owe a lot of money, Agha."

"Well, what are we to do then?" cried Mahmut Agha angrily. "All our youths have left the plow and the fields and are after the woman night and day like rutting bulls. At this rate, the whole village'll starve this year."

An old man spoke up in a tremulous voice. "I'm dead, for one," he wailed. "That woman's ruined my hearth. High morning it is already. Go to the plow, my son, I beg the boy. We'll starve if you don't plow. But he won't listen. He's always after that woman. I've lost my son because of that whore. I'm too old to plow any more. I'll starve this year. I'll go and throw myself at Huru's feet. There's nothing else to do . . ."

The Agha rose abruptly. "That Huru!" He gritted his teeth. "I'll settle   184 her account."

He strode away.

The villagers looked up hopefully. "Mahmut Agha'll settle her account," they muttered. "He'll find a way . . ."

The Agha heard them and swelled with pride. "Yes, Mahmut Agha'll settle her account," he repeated grimly to himself.

He stopped before a hut and called out.

"Hatije Woman! Hatije!"

A middle-aged woman rushed out wiping her hands on her apron.

"Mahmut Agha!" she cried. "Welcome to our home. You never visit us these days." Then she whirled back. "Get up, you damned lazybones," she shouted angrily. "It's high morning, and look who's here."

Mahmut Agha followed her inside.   192

"Look, Agha," she complained, pointing to her son, "it's high morning and Halil still abed!"

Startled at the sight of the Agha, Halil sprang up and drew on his black *shalvar* trousers shamefacedly, while his mother continued with her lamentations.

"Ah, Mahmut Agha, you don't know what's befallen us! You don't know, may I kiss your feet, my Agha, or you wouldn't have us on your land any longer . . . Ah, Mahmut Agha! This accursed son of mine . . . I would have seen him dead and buried, yes, buried in this black earth before . . ."

"What are you cursing the lad for?" Mahmut Agha interrupted her. 196 "Wait, just tell me first."

"Ah, Agha, if you knew! It was full day when he came home this night. And it's the same every night, the same ever since Hollow Osman's woman came to the village. He lies abed all through the livelong day. Who'll do the plowing, I ask you? We'll starve this year. Ah, Mahmut Agha, do something! Please do something . . ."

"You go outside a little, will you, Hatije," said the Agha. Then he turned to Halil, stretching out his long, wrinkled neck which had become as red as a turkey's. "Listen to me, my boy, this has got to end. You must get this whore out of our village and give her to the youths of another village, any village. She's got to go and you'll do it. It's an order. Do you hear me?"

"Why, Agha!" Halil said ingratiatingly. "Is that what's worrying you? I'll get hold of her this very night and turn her over to Jelil from Ortakli village. You can count on me."

The Agha's spirits rose.   200

"Hatije," he called out, "come in here. See how I'm getting you out of this mess? And all the village too . . . Let that Huru know who she's dealing with in the future. They call me Wolf Mahmut and I know how to put her nose out of joint."

Long before dawn, piercing shrieks startled the echoes in the village.

"Bastards! Pimps!" Huru was howling. "You won't get away with this, not on your life you won't. My hundred liras were too much for you to swallow, eh, you fiends? You were jealous of this poor fellow's wife, eh?

But you just wait and see, Wolf Mahmut! I'll set the tax collector after you all in no time. I'll get even with you if I have to spend my last penny! I'll bribe the Mudir, the Kaymakam, all the officials. I'll send telegrams to Ankara, to Ismet Pasha, to the head of the Democrats. I'll have you all dragged into court, rotting away in police stations. I'll get my own back on you for Fadik's sake."

She paused to get her breath and was off again even louder than 204 before.

Fadik had disappeared, that was the long and the short of it. Huru soon found out that someone else was missing too. Huseyin's half-witted son, The Tick.

"Impossible," she said. "The Tick ravishing women? Not to save his life, he couldn't! This is just another trick of those good-for-nothings . . ."

"But really, Huru," the villagers tried to persuade her, "he was after her all the time. Don't you know he gathered white snails in the hills, threaded them into a necklace, and offered it to Fadik, and she hung it up on her wall as a keepsake? That's the plain truth, Huru."

"I don't believe it," Huru said stubbornly. "I wouldn't even if I saw 208 them together with my own eyes . . ."

The next day it started raining, that sheer, plumb-line torrent which sets in over the Chukurova for days. The minute the bad news had reached him, Osman had abandoned his plow and had rushed back to the village. He was standing now motionless at Huru's door, the peak of his cap drooping over his eyes. His wet clothes clung to his flesh, glistening darkly, and his rawhide boots were clogged with mud.

"Come in out of the rain, Osman, do!" Huru kept urging him.

"I can't. I don't know . . ." was all he could say.

"Now, look here, Osman," said Huru. "She's gone, so what? Let them 212 have that bitch. I'll find you a good woman, my Osman. Never mind the money. I'll spend twice as much on a new wife for you. Just you come in out of the rain."

Osman never moved.

"Listen, Osman. I've sent word to Ali. Come and levy the taxes at once, I said. Have no mercy on these ungrateful wretches. If you don't fleece them to their last rag, I said, you needn't count on me as a mother again. You'll see what I'm going to do to them, my Osman. You just come inside . . ."

The rain poured down straight and thick as the warp in a loom, and Osman still stood there, his chin resting on his staff, like a thick tree whose branches have been lopped off.

Huru appealed to the neighbors. Two men came and pulled and 216 pushed, but he seemed nailed to the ground. It was well in the afternoon when he stirred and began to pace the village from one end to the other, his head sunk between his shoulders and the rain streaming down his body.

"Poor fellow, he's gone mad," opined the villagers.

A few strong men finally carried him home. They undressed him and put him to bed.

Huru sat down beside him. "Look, Osman, I'll get you a new woman even if it costs me a thousand liras. You mustn't distress yourself so. Just for a woman . . ."

The next morning he was more his normal self, but no amount of 220 reasoning or pleading from Huru could induce him to go back to the field. He left the house and resumed his pacing up and down.

The villagers had really begun to feel sorry for him now.

"Alas, poor Osman!" they murmured as he passed between the huts.

Osman heard them and heaved deep, heartrending sighs. And still he roamed aimlessly round and round.

Wolf Mahmut should have known better. Why, the whole village saw 224 with half an eye what a rascal Halil was! How could he be trusted to give up a woman once he had got her into his hands? He had indeed got Fadik out of the way, but what he had done was to shut her up in one of the empty sheep pens in the hills beyond the village, and there he had posted The Tick to guard her.

"Play around with her if you like," he had told him contemptuously. "But if you let her give you the slip — " and he had seized The Tick's wrist and squeezed it until it hurt — "you're as good as dead."

Though twenty years old, The Tick was so scraggy and undersized that at first glance people would take him to be only ten. His arms and legs were as thin as matchsticks and he walked sideways like a crab. He had always had a way of clinging tenaciously to people or objects he took a fancy to, which even as a child had earned him his nickname. No one had ever called him by his real name and it looked as though his own mother had forgotten it too . . .

Halil would come every evening bringing food for Fadik and The Tick, and he would leave again just before dawn. But it was not three days before the village youths found out what was going on. After that there was a long queue every night outside the sheep pen. They would take it in turns, heedless of Fadik's tears and howls, and at daybreak, singing and firing their guns as though in a wedding procession, they would make their way back to the village.

Night was falling and Fadik began to tremble like a leaf. They would 228
not be long now. They would come again and torture her. She was weak with fear and exhaustion. For the past two days, her gorge had risen at the very sight of food, and she lay there on the dirt floor, hardly able to move, her whole body covered with bruises and wounds.

The Tick was dozing away near the door of the pen.

Fadik tried to plead with him. "Let me go, brother," she begged. "I'll die if I have to bear another night of this."

The Tick half-opened his eyes. "I can't," he replied.

"But if I die, it'll be your fault. Before God it will . . . Please let me 232
go."

"Why should it be my fault?" said The Tick. "I didn't bring you here, did I?"

"They'll never know. You'll say you fell asleep. I'll go off and hide somewhere. I'll go back to my mother . . ."

"I can't," said The Tick. "Halil would kill me if I let you go."

"But I want to go to my mother," she cried desperately. "You must let 236
me go. Please let me go . . ."

It was dark now and the sound of singing drifted up from the village.

Fadik was seized with a violent fit of trembling. "They're coming," she said. "Let me get away now, brother. Save me! If you save me, I'll be your woman. I'll do anything . . ."

But The Tick had not been nicknamed for nothing.

"They'd kill me," he said. "Why should I die because of you? And 240
Halil's promised to buy me a pair of shoes, too. I'm not going to go without shoes because of you."

Fadik broke into wild sobbing. There was no hope now.

"Oh, God," she wept, "what shall I do now? Oh, Mother, why was I ever born?"

They lined up as usual at the entrance to the pen. The first one went in and a nerve-racking scream rose from Fadik, a scream that would have moved the most hardened of hearts. But the youths were deaf to everything. In they went, one after the other, and soon Fadik's screams died down. Not even a moan came out of her.

There were traces of blood on the ground at the back of the sheep 244 pen. Halil and the Agha's son had had a fight the night before and the Agha's son had split open Halil's head.

"The woman's mine," Halil had insisted. "I've a right to go in first."

"No, you haven't," the Agha's son had contended. "I'm going to be the first."

The other youths had taken sides and joined the fray which had lasted most of the night, and it was a bedraggled band that wended back to the village that night.

Bowed down with grief, Hatije Woman came weeping to the Muhtar. 248

"My son is dying," she cried. "He's at his last gasp, my poor Halil, and it's the Agha's son who did it, all because of that whore of Huru's. Ah, Muhtar, if my son dies what's to become of me? There he lies struggling for life, the only hope of my hearth. But I won't let the Agha get away with this. I'll go to the Government. An old woman's only prop, I'll say . . ."

The Muhtar had great difficulty in talking Hatije out of her purpose.

"You go back home, Hatije Woman," he said when she had calmed down a little, "and don't worry. I'll deal with this business."

He summoned the Agha and the elders, and a long discussion ensued. 252 It would not do to hand over the woman to the police station. These rapacious gendarmes! . . . The honor of the whole village was at stake. And if they passed her on to the youths of another village, Huru was sure to find out and bring her back. She would not rest until she did.

After long deliberation, they came to a decision at last. The woman would be returned to Osman, but on one condition. He would take himself off with her to some distant place and never appear in the village again. They had no doubt that Osman, grateful to have Fadik back to himself, would accept. And that would cook Huru's goose too. She would lose both the woman and Osman. It would teach her to insult a whole village!

A couple of men went to find Osman and brought him back with them to the Muhtar's house.

"Sit down," they urged him, but he just stood there grasping his staff, staring about him with bloodshot eyes. His clothes hung down torn and crumpled and stained yellow from his lying all wet on the hay. His hair was a tangled, clotted mass and bits of straw clung to the stubble on his chin.

Wolf Mahmut took off his glasses and fidgeted with them.   256

"Osman, my lad," he remonstrated, "what's this state you're in? And all for a woman! Does a man let himself break down like this just for a woman? You'll die if you go on like this . . ."

"I don't know," said Osman. "I'll die . . ."

"See here, Osman," said the Agha. "We're here to help you. We'll get your woman back for you from out of those rascals' hands. Then you'll take her and go. You'll both get away from here, as far as possible. But you're not to tell Huru. She mustn't know where you are."

"You see, Osman," said Stumpy Veli, "how good the Agha's being to   260 you. Your own father wouldn't have done more."

"But you're not to tell Huru," the Agha insisted. "If you do, she'll never let you go away. And then the youths will come and take your woman away from you again. And how will you ever get yourself another woman?"

"And who'll wash your clothes then?" added Stumpy Veli. "Who'll cook your bulgur pilaf for you? You mustn't breathe a word to Huru. Just take Fadik and go off to the villages around Antep. Once there, you'll be sure to get a job on a farm. You'll be much better off than you ever were with Huru, and you'll have your woman with you too . . ."

"But how can I do that?" protested Osman. "The Mistress paid a hundred liras for Fadik."

"We'll collect that much among us," the Agha assured him. "Don't   264 you worry about that. We'll see that Huru gets her money back. You just take the woman and go."

"I don't know," said Osman. His eyes filled with tears and he swallowed. "The Mistress has always been so good to me . . . How can I . . . Just for a woman . . ."

"If you tell Huru, you're lost," said the Agha. "Is Huru the only mistress in the world? Aren't there other villages in this country? Take the woman and go. You'll never find another woman like Fadik. Listen, Veli'll tell you where she is and tomorrow you'll take her and go."

Osman bowed his head. He thought for a long time. Then he looked up at them.

"I won't tell her," he said at last. "Why should I want to stay here? 268
There are other villages . . ."

Before dawn the next day, he set out for the sheep pen which Stumpy
Veli had indicated.

"I don't know . . ." he hesitated at the door. "I don't know . . ." Then
he called out softly, "Fadik? Fadik, girl . . ."

There was no answer. Trembling with hope and fear, he stepped in,
then stopped aghast. Fadik was lying there on the dirt floor with only a
few tatters left to cover her naked body. Her huge eyes were fixed vacantly
on the branches that roofed the pen.

He stood frozen, his eyes filling with tears. Then he bent his large 272
body over her.

"Fadik," he whispered, "are you all right?"

Her answering moan shook him to the core. He slipped off his shirt
and helped her into it. Then he noticed The Tick who had shrunk back
into a corner, trying to make himself invisible. Osman moved on him
threateningly.

"Uncle Osman," cried The Tick shaking with fear, "I didn't do it. It
was Halil. He said he'd buy me a pair of shoes . . . And Fadik would
have died if I hadn't been here . . ."

Osman turned away, heaved Fadik onto his back swiftly, and threw 276
himself out of the pen.

The mountain peaks were pale and the sun was about to rise. A few
white clouds floated in the sky and a cool breeze caressed his face. The
earth was wet with dew.

The Tick was scurrying off towards the village.

"Brother," Osman called after him, "go to the Mistress and tell her I
thank her for all she's done for me, but I have to go. Tell her to forgive
me . . ."

He set out in the opposite direction with Fadik on his back. He walked 280
without a break until the sun was up the height of two minarets. Then
he lowered Fadik to the ground and sat down opposite her. They looked
at each other for a long while without speaking.

"Tell me," said Osman. "Where shall we go now? I don't know . . ."

Fadik moaned.

The air smelled of spring and the earth steamed under the sun.

EXPLORATIONS

1. In what ways is "A Dirty Story" an appropriate title for Kemal's narrative? What people or factors does Kemal blame for Fadik's fate? What remedies, if any, does he recommend?

2. Reread the opening scene of "A Dirty Story" (paras. 1–11). What concept of women's role is presented here? Who holds this concept? How do we as readers learn it? How would the story's impact change if Kemal had written this scene as an expository paragraph from the author's point of view?

3. According to Kemal, by what qualities are men in this culture judged as successful or unsuccessful by other men? by women? How does women's concept of their own social role differ from men's concept?

4. The third scene in "A Dirty Story" (paras. 56–86) takes place among the village women. How do they interpret the situation between Fadik, Huru, and the local youths? How do their comments about Omarja's dog and Velo's donkey suggest that the situation is not really as the women depict it? What do you think is actually going on between Fadik, the youths, Osman, and Huru at this point in the story? What other clues in this scene help you to guess what is happening?

CONNECTIONS

1. Like Cherry Lindholm and Charles Lindholm's "Life Behind the Veil," Kemal's "A Dirty Story" examines sex roles and stereotypes in a poor rural Eastern culture. How are women's and men's social roles in the Swat Valley of Pakistan similar to those in the fictional Turkish village of Chukurova? What views do men in both cultures share of women, and what views do women share of men, which the opposite sex would dispute?

2. Look again at the Lindholms' "Life Behind the Veil." What role is played in that essay and in Kemal's short story by government? by religion? What is the Lindholms' view, as visiting scientists, of the Islamic custom of purdah for women? How do you think Kemal, writing as an insider, would agree and disagree with their view?

3. In "Woman as Other" Simone de Beauvoir gives several reasons why women collaborate with men's perception and treatment of them as Other. What evidence of those reasons can you find in "A Dirty Story"? Why do you think the women of Chukurova show so little inclination to protect or even stand up for Fadik?

4. In *Looking at Ourselves*, Gayle Early describes "the John Wayne image" of manhood. What qualities do the men of Chukurova share with this American

image? Which of Early's "problems associated with 'old male' socialization" do they appear to share as well? After reading these and other selections, what possible cause-and-effect links can you propose between the image and the problems?

ELABORATIONS

1. Kemal avoids editorializing in "A Dirty Story"; he follows the time-honored writers' rule of *"show* rather than *tell."* For example, woven into his narrative is a vivid description of his native Anatolia. Go through "A Dirty Story" and pick out passages about its setting. Then write an imaginary travel article for a magazine in which you describe this region of Turkey as it would appear to a Western visitor.

2. Kemal also applies a strategy of "show rather than tell" to his characters' weaknesses. How would the story's impact change if he stated their faults and mistakes explicitly? Think of a dramatic incident in your experience in which one person or group caused harm to another without acknowledging that they were behaving badly. An example might be schoolmates bullying a weakling, an older sibling teasing a younger, or an employer or landlord discriminating on the basis of race or sex. Write a narrative essay about the incident in which you let the characters' actions speak for them, as Kemal does.

3. Does economics affect — or determine — sex roles? Naila Minai in "Women in Early Islam," the Lindholms, and Kemal all describe Islamic attitudes toward male and female roles. All also focus on the poverty, lack of technology, and subsistence-farming economy that many Islamic communities have in common. On the basis of these three selections, write an essay examining the relation between male-female roles and nontechnological agrarian economies.

PART FIVE

WORK

We Are What We Do

LOOKING AT OURSELVES

Mario Puzo, Richard Rodriguez, Elliot Liebow, Russell Baker,
Fred Moody, American
Entrepreneurs' Association, Marge Piercy,
Alice Walker, Vladimir Nabokov, Studs Terkel

Shiva Naipaul, *The Palmers* (KENYA)

Maya Angelou, *Mary* (UNITED STATES)

R. K. Narayan, *Trail of the Green Blazer* (INDIA)

David Abram, *Making Magic* (BALI)

Jill Gay, *Patriotic Prostitutes*
(THAILAND, SOUTH KOREA, PHILIPPINES)

Geoffrey Matthews, *"Good Sons" Who Kill* (COLOMBIA)

Satoshi Kamata, *Six Months at Toyota* (JAPAN)

Hedrick Smith, Skoro Budet — *It'll Be Here Soon*
(SOVIET UNION)

Rosario Ferré, *Out of the Frying Pan* (PUERTO RICO)

Pablo Neruda, *The Word* (CHILE)

WE IDENTIFY OURSELVES AND RECOGNIZE EACH OTHER BY WHAT WE do. People's work varies from plowing fields to judging disputes, from teaching children to leading armies, from feeding chickens to programming computers. For some of us, work is a burden; for some, a pleasure; and for some, a source of pride. How we feel about our work both affects and is affected by how we feel about ourselves.

Looking at Ourselves starts with Mario Puzo, author of *The Godfather*, recalling his mother's modest career goals for him. Richard Rodriguez (see p. 397) notes the irony of escaping from his parents' sphere with their help. Elliot Liebow compares insider and outsider views of unskilled workers; Russell Baker sympathizes with modern children who can't understand what Daddy does. Fred Moody remarks on Americans' obsessiveness about work, a compulsion partly explained by the credo of the American Entrepreneurs' Association. Marge Piercy scrutinizes "professionalism." Alice Walker depicts her work — writing — as a source of healing. For Vladimir Nabokov, "the real writer [is] the fellow who sends planets spinning." Finally, Studs Terkel presents an organizer's views on his work with and for other workers.

An ocean away, Shiva Naipaul in "The Palmers" observes work on a Kenyan tea plantation from both ends of the social and professional scale. Maya Angelou finds the same scale in the American South, where "Mary" recounts a young black girl's adventures in a white woman's kitchen. Around the world in India, R. K. Narayan follows a pickpocket's fortunes in his short story "Trail of the Green Blazer." David Abram's "Making Magic" tells of an American magician's successful struggle to find a niche on the Indonesian island of Bali.

For poor women in Thailand, South Korea, and the Philippines, reports Jill Gay in "Patriotic Prostitutes," sometimes the only job option is selling sex — with the government's encouragement. In Colombia, Geoffrey Matthews describes the short and rocky career path of "'Good Sons' Who Kill." Shifting to Japan's famous auto factories, we follow Satoshi Kamata through a grueling "Six Months at Toyota." Factory workers in the Soviet Union tell Hedrick Smith about their monthly custom of storming in "*Skoro Budet* — It'll Be Here Soon." Back in the United States, the Puerto Rican writer Rosario Ferré describes her fight to recreate herself as an artist in "Out of the Frying Pan." Finally, from Chile comes a brief paean to the joys of writing in Pablo Neruda's "The Word." ❖

LOOKING AT OURSELVES

1

As a child I had the usual dreams. I wanted to be handsome, specifically as cowboy stars in movies were handsome. I wanted to be a killer hero in a worldwide war. Or if no wars came along (our teachers told us another was impossible), I wanted at the very least to be a footloose adventurer. Then I branched out and thought of being a great artist, and then, getting ever more sophisticated, a great criminal.

My mother, however, wanted me to be a railroad clerk. And that was her *highest* ambition; she would have settled for less. At the age of sixteen when I let everybody know that I was going to be a great writer, my friends and family took the news quite calmly, my mother included. She did not become angry. She quite simply assumed that I had gone off my nut. She was illiterate and her peasant life in Italy made her believe that only a son of the nobility could possibly be a writer. Artistic beauty after all could spring only from the seedbed of fine clothes, fine food, luxurious living. So then how was it possible for a son of hers to be an artist? She was not too convinced she was wrong even after my first two books were published many years later. It was only after the commercial success of my third novel that she gave me the title of poet.

> – Mario Puzo
> "Choosing a Dream:
> Italians in Hell's Kitchen"

2

"Your parents must be very proud of you." People began to say that to me about the time I was in sixth grade. To answer affirmatively, I'd smile. Shyly I'd smile, never betraying my sense of the irony: I was not proud of my mother and father. I was embarrassed by their lack of education. It was not that I ever thought they were stupid, though stupidly I took for granted their enormous native intelligence. Simply, what mattered to me was that they were not like my teachers. . . .

Tightening the irony into a knot was the knowledge that my parents were always behind me. They made success possible. They evened the path. They sent their children to parochial schools because the nuns "teach better." They paid a tuition they couldn't afford. They spoke English to us.

For their children my parents wanted chances they never had — an easier way. It saddened my mother to learn that some relatives forced their children to start working right after high school. To *her* children she would say, "Get all the education you can." In schooling she recognized the key to job advancement. . . .

When I was in high school, I admitted to my mother that I planned to become a teacher someday. That seemed to please her. But I never tried to explain that it was not the occupation of teaching I yearned for as much as it was something more elusive: I wanted to *be* like my teachers, to possess their knowledge, to assume their authority, their confidence, even to assume a teacher's persona.

– Richard Rodriguez
Hunger of Memory

3

Menial jobs are not, by and large, the starting point of a track system which leads to even better jobs for those who are able and willing to do them. The busboy or dishwasher in a restaurant is not on a job track which, if negotiated skillfully, leads to chef or manager of the restaurant. The busboy or dishwasher who works hard becomes, simply, a hardworking busboy or dishwasher. Neither hard work nor perseverance can conceivably carry the janitor to a sit-down job in the office building he cleans up. And it is the apprentice who becomes the journeyman electrician, plumber, steamfitter, or bricklayer, not the common unskilled Negro laborer.

Thus, the job is not a stepping-stone to something better. It is a dead end. It promises to deliver no more tomorrow, next month, or next year than it does today.

Delivering little, and promising no more, the job is "no big thing." The man appears to treat the job in a cavalier fashion, working and not working as the spirit moves him, as if all that matters is the immediate satisfaction of his present appetites, the surrender to present moods, and the indulgence of whims with no thought for the cost, the consequences, the future. To the middle-class observer, this behavior reflects a "present-time orientation" — an "inability to defer gratification." It is this "present-time" orientation — as against the "future orientation" of the middle-class person — that "explains" to the outsider why Leroy chooses to spend the day at the Carry-out rather than report to work; why Richard, who was paid Friday, was drunk Saturday and Sunday and penniless Monday; why Sweets quit his job today because the boss looked at him "funny" yesterday.

But from the inside looking out, what appears as a "present-time" orientation to the outside observer is, to the man experiencing it, as much a future orientation as that of his middle-class counterpart. The difference between the two men lies not so much in their different orientations to time as in their different orientations to future time or, more specifically, to their different futures.

– Elliot Liebow
Tally's Corner: A Study of
Negro Streetcorner Men

4

It is not surprising that modern children tend to look blank and dispirited when informed that they will someday have to "go to work and make a living." The problem is that they cannot visualize what work is in corporate America.

Not so long ago, when a parent said he was off to work, the child knew very well what was about to happen. His parent was going to make something or fix something. The parent could take his offspring to his place of business and let him watch while he repaired a buggy or built a table.

When a child asked, "What kind of work do you do, Daddy?" his father could answer in terms that a child could come to grips with. "I fix steam engines." "I make horse collars."

Well, a few fathers still fix engines and build things, but most do not. Nowadays, most fathers sit in glass buildings performing tasks that are absolutely incomprehensible to children. The answers they give when asked, "What kind of work do you do, Daddy?" are likely to be utterly mystifying to a child.

"I sell space." "I do market research." "I am a data processor." "I am in public relations." "I am a systems analyst." Such explanations must seem nonsense to a child. How can he possibly envision anyone analyzing a system or researching a market?

– Russell Baker
Poor Russell's Almanac

5

Work now pervades our nonworking lives in unprecedented, widely accepted ways: cellular phones, answering machines, personal and portable computers. The career, for many people, has taken precedence over such time-honored human endeavors as building a strong family or seeking spiritual and philosophical truths. The person who works right up to the point of self-destruction is often accorded far more esteem than the person who seeks to lead a balanced life. Overworking is an American trait, much commented on by European observers; and it has become the hallmark of strenuous yuppies, whose chief complaint about life is "I don't have enough time."

> – Fred Moody
> "When Work Becomes an Obsession"
> *Baltimore City Paper*

6

I do not choose to be a common person. It is my right to be uncommon — if I can. I seek opportunity — not security. I do not wish to be a kept citizen, humbled and dulled by having the state look after me.

I want to take the calculated risk, to dream and to build, to fail and to succeed.

I refuse to barter incentive for a dole; I prefer the challenges of life to the guaranteed existence; the thrill of fulfillment to the stale calm of Utopia.

I will not trade my freedom for beneficence nor my dignity for a handout. I will never cower before any master nor bend to any threat.

It is my heritage to stand erect, proud and unafraid; to think and act for myself, to enjoy the benefit of my creations, and to face the world boldly and say:

This, with God's help, I have done. All this is what it means to be an Entrepreneur.

> – Credo of the American Entrepreneurs'
> Association
> *Harper's Magazine*

7

One trouble: To be a professional anything in the United States is to think of oneself as an expert and one's ideas as semisacred, and to treat others in a certain way — professionally.

> – Marge Piercy
> "The Grand Coolie Damn"

8

I think writing really helps you heal yourself. . . . I think if you write long enough, you will be a healthy person. That is, if you write what you need to write, as opposed to what will make money, or what will make fame.

> – Alice Walker
> "Telling the Black Woman's Story"
> *New York Times Magazine*

<><><><><>

9

To minor authors is left the ornamentation of the commonplace: These do not bother about any reinventing of the world; they merely try to squeeze the best they can out of a given order of things, out of traditional patterns of fiction. The various combinations these minor authors are able to produce within these set limits may be quite amusing in a mild ephemeral way because minor readers like to recognize their own ideas in a pleasing disguise. But the real writer, the fellow who sends planets spinning and models a man asleep and eagerly tampers with the sleeper's rib, that kind of author has no given values at his disposal: He must create them himself. The art of writing is a very futile business if it does not imply first of all the art of seeing the world as the potentiality of fiction. The material of this world may be real enough (as far as reality goes) but does not exist at all as an accepted entirety: It is chaos, and to this chaos the author says "go!" allowing the world to flicker and to fuse. It is now recombined in its very atoms, not merely in its visible and superficial parts. The writer is the first man to map it and to name the natural objects it contains. Those berries there are edible. That speckled creature that bolted across my path might be tamed. That lake between those trees will be called Lake Opal or, more artistically, Dishwater Lake. That mist is a mountain — and that mountain must be conquered. Up a trackless slope climbs the master artist, and at the top, on a windy ridge, whom do you think he meets? The panting and happy reader, and there they spontaneously embrace and are linked forever if the book lasts forever.

> – Vladimir Nabokov
> "Good Writers and Good Readers"
> *Lectures on Literature*

<><><><><>

10

My work is trying to change this country. This is the job I've chosen. When people ask me, "Why are you doing this?" it's like asking what kind of sickness you got. I don't feel sick. I think this country is sick. The daily injustices just gnaw on me a little harder than they do on other people.

I try to bring people together who are being put down by the system, left out. You try to build an organization that will give them power to make the changes. Everybody's at the bottom of the barrel at this point. Ten years ago one could say the poor people suffered and the middle class got by. That's not true any more. . . .

I put together a fairly solid organization of Appalachian people in Pike County [Kentucky]. It's a single industry area, coal. You either work for the coal company or you don't work. Sixty percent of its people live on incomes lower than the government's guidelines for rural areas.

I was brought in to teach other organizers how to do it. I spent my first three months at it. I decided these middle-class kids from Harvard and Columbia were too busy telling everybody else what they should be doing. The only thing to do was to organize the local people. . . .

The word *organizer* has been romanticized. You get the vision of a mystical being doing magical things. An organizer is a guy who brings in new members. I don't feel I've had a good day unless I've talked with at least one new person. We have a meeting, make space for new people to come in. The organizer sits next to the new guy, so everybody has to take the new guy as an equal. You do that a couple of times and the guy's got strength enough to become part of the group.

You must listen to them and tell them again and again they are important, that they have the stuff to do the job. They don't have to shuck themselves about not being good enough, not worthy. Most people were raised to think they are not worthy. School is a process of taking beautiful kids who are filled with life and beating them into happy slavery. That's as true of a twenty-five-thousand-dollar-a-year executive as it is for the poorest.

You don't find allies on the basis of the brotherhood of man. People are tied into their immediate problems. They have a difficult time worrying about other people's. Our society is so structured that everybody is supposed to be selfish as hell and screw the other guy. Christian brotherhood is enlightened self-interest. Most sins committed on poor people are by people who've come to help them.

I came as a stranger but I came with credentials. There are people who know and trust me, who say so to the others. So what I'm saying is verifiable. It's possible to win, to take an outfit like Bethlehem Steel and lick 'em. Most people in their guts don't really believe it. Gee, it's great when all of a sudden they realize it's possible. They become alive.

Nobody believed PCCA [Pike County Citizens' Association] could stop Bethlehem from strip mining. Ten miles away was a hillside being stripped. Ten miles away is like ten million light years away. What they wanted was a park, a place for their kids. Bethlehem said, "Go to hell. You're just a bunch of crummy Appalachians. We're not gonna give you a damn thing." If I could get that park for them, they would believe it's possible to do other things.

They really needed a victory. They had lost over and over again, day after day. So I got together twenty, thirty people I saw as leaders. I said, "Let's get that park." They said, "We can't." I said, "We can. If we let all the big wheels around the country know — the National Council of Churches and everybody start calling up, writing, and hounding Bethlehem, they'll have to give us the park." That's exactly what happened. Bethlehem thought: This is getting to be a pain in the ass. We'll give 'em the park and they'll shut up about strip mining. We haven't shut up on strip mining, but we got the park. Four thousand people from Pike County drove up and watched those bulldozers grading down that park. It was an incredible victory.

Twenty or thirty people realized we could win. Four thousand people understood there was a victory. They didn't know how it happened, but a few of 'em got curious. The twenty or thirty are now in their own communities trying to turn people on. . . .

I work all the way from two in the morning until two the next morning seven days a week. (Laughs.) I'm not a martyr. I'm one of the few people I know who was lucky in life to find out what he really wanted to do. I'm just havin' a ball, the time of my life. I feel sorry for all these people I run across all the time who aren't doing what they want to do. Their lives are hell. I think everybody ought to quit their job and do what they want to do. You've got one life. You've got, say, sixty-five years. How on earth can you blow forty-five years of that doing something you hate?

I have a wife and three children. I've managed to support them for six years doing this kind of work. We don't live fat. I have enough money to buy books and records. The kids have as good an education as anybody in this country. Their range of friends runs from millionaires in San

Francisco to black prostitutes in Lexington. They're comfortable with all these people. My kids know the name of the game: living your life up to the end.

All human recorded history is about five thousand years old. How many people in all that time have made an overwhelming difference? Twenty? Thirty? Most of us spend our lives trying to achieve some things. But we're not going to make an overwhelming difference. We do the best we can. That's enough.

The problem with history is that it's written by college professors about great men. That's not what history is. History's a hell of a lot of little people getting together and deciding they want a better life for themselves and their kids.

I have a goal. I want to end my life in a home for the aged that's run by the state — organizing people to fight 'em because they're not running it right. (Laughs.)

– Bill Talcott
Studs Terkel's *Working*

SHIVA NAIPAUL

The Palmers

Shiva Naipaul was born in 1945 in Port of Spain, Trinidad. He attended college in Trinidad, then won a scholarship to Oxford University, where he studied Chinese. His first novel, *Fireflies* (1970), won four literary prizes; his second novel, *The Chip-Chip Gatherers* (1973), won the Whitbread Award. Though less well known than his brother, novelist V. S. Naipaul (see "Entering the New World," p. 47), Shiva Naipaul was highly regarded for his fiction, journalism, and travel writing, which often probed social problems of the Third World. He was living in London with his wife and son when he died of a heart attack in 1985.

"The Palmers" comes from *North of South: An African Journey* (1979). Naipaul met the Palmers in Kenya, which — as his book title implies — is north of southern Africa, on the east coast of the continent between Somalia and Tanzania. The first Europeans to appear there were German missionaries in the early nineteenth century. At that time the dominant inhabitants were the Kikuyu and Masai tribes. First the Germans and then the British took political control, making Kenya a British protectorate in 1890 and a Crown colony in 1920. In the 1950s the Kikuyus rose up in the so-called Mau Mau Rebellion, prompting the British to declare a state of emergency which lasted until the early 1960s. In 1963 Kenya became independent. Its first president was Jomo Kenyatta, who served until his death in 1978. Today the Republic of Kenya comprises about seventy different ethnic groups; the official languages are English and Swahili. Many Westerners know Kenya as the home of an elephant population that dropped from 165,000 to 16,000 over twenty years, as ivory hunters killed the animals for their tusks — a practice that is now illegal. Around four-fifths of Kenya's work force is employed in agricultural enterprises like the Palmers' tea plantation.

The ridges of the Kikuyu country stretched away on all sides, wave upon wave sweeping toward the horizon. Where the land was cut away to accommodate the passage of the road, its red heart was startlingly exposed to view. Looking at that bloody redness one sensed not only the richness of the land but — more disturbingly — its visceral appeal. It seemed to symbolize the Kikuyu's fierce attachment to it, the unity of soil and tribe. In *Facing Mount Kenya* (first published in 1938), [Jomo] Kenyatta expressed his tribe's attitude toward the land they considered peculiarly theirs. "The Gikuyu," he wrote, "consider the earth as the 'mother' of the tribe. It is the soil that feeds the child through lifetime; and again after death it is the soil that nurses the spirits of the dead for eternity. Thus the earth is the most sacred thing above all that dwell in or on it . . . an everlasting oath is to swear by the earth." Those oaths were to surface, in a more murderous form, during the Mau Mau insurrection.

The road, which to begin with had been wide enough for two cars, narrowed to a single lane. We left behind the forest reserve through which we had been traveling and entered the coffee belt, the leaves of the neatly staked-out shrubs glistening in the soupy sunlight. "Kenya is lucky," my companion said, gesturing at the plantations on either side of us. "The Brazilian crop has been hit by frost this year."

We passed through a straggling township replete with the usual beer parlors and "ration" shops and unsightly hoardings advertising detergents, refrigerators, and vacuum cleaners. The air was noisy with jukebox music. A roadside market was in progress. Long strips of colorfully dyed cloth were spread out on the ground. Young boys danced out in front of the car flourishing fruit and vegetables. Beyond the township was typical *shamba* country: small plots planted with corn; foraging goats and cows and pigs and chickens. This, even in colonial days, had been a "native" area, and it clung tenaciously to its traditional character. The coffee plantations reappeared. A veil of pearly mist obscured the more distant reaches of the open, undulating landscape. Its "English" character was emphasized by the scattered condensations of color created by stands of trees set amid the acres of coffee. The tarmac ended. Clouds of red dust billowed in our wake. We were climbing now, and after a time, the coffee country gave way to tea country. The tea gardens, emerald green, even-topped, forming an unbroken wave of cultivation, were like a scaly sheath thrown over the land.

It was almost noon when we reached the Palmers' farm. Mrs. Palmer,   4
jovial and red-faced, her hair bunched in a scarf, greeted us amiably. It was cool enough for a sweater. The day was autumnal. Gray cloud hid the sun, and there was a vapor of blue mist in the shallow valleys. A chill, clammy wind blew. The Palmers' house — a modest-sized brick bungalow — was finely situated on a rising piece of ground. We stood for a while on the well-kept lawn surrounding it, admiring the extensive views. "In good weather," our hostess said, "you can see Kilimanjaro." We gazed in the direction she indicated, paying the invisible mountain ritual homage. Then we went inside.

A fire was going in the brick fireplace; an Alsatian was stretched out on the rug in front of it. Two high-backed armchairs with chintz coverings were drawn up in front of the fireplace. Ancestral photographs lined the walls. A piano, piled with papers, occupied a corner. Next to it was a large, brass-studded chest. Agricultural journals, old copies of *The Times*, and some back numbers of the *Illustrated London News* were distributed in neat piles on a low table in the center of the room. A complete set of *Chambers' Encyclopedia* filled a small bookshelf. I noticed no other books apart from those. The wooden floor gleamed. There was not a speck of dust to be seen. It was a forbiddingly hygienic room. I felt that nothing new had happened here for a long time — just endless dusting, cleaning, preserving.

"I hear it's been a lovely summer in England," Mrs. Palmer said. "We've been reading all about it." She nodded at the pile of newspapers. "Now here you are on the Equator — and sitting in front of a fire. It must seem strange."

She rang a bell. A barefooted "boy" appeared. She ordered him to bring ice and glasses. "And Simon . . ." Simon, who had started to leave, paused but did not turn around. Mrs. Palmer smiled. " . . . when you put the ice in the glasses, do please remember to use the tongs and not your fingers. That's what the tongs are *for*. Now off you go."

Simon disappeared into the kitchen.

Mrs. Palmer was still smiling when she turned to face us. "Simon seems to have a block about using those tongs. I can't understand it. I've told him so many times. Still, Simon has one great virtue. He hasn't been *spoiled*. Not as yet, anyway. I'm keeping my fingers crossed. It's amazing how quickly they do get spoiled, though. There used to be an old saying in this country: put a native in shoes and that's the end of him. Nowadays, of course, they've all got shoes and we aren't even allowed to call them natives." Mrs. Palmer sighed, staring out the window toward invisible Kilimanjaro. Taking a key from the pocket of her dress, she unlocked the liquor cabinet. "I'm sorry to seem so jailerlike," she said, "but pilfering, I'm afraid, is a big problem. I have to keep everything under lock and key. They take the oddest things sometimes, things they can't possibly have any use for. The other day my shower cap disappeared." She peered at the ranks of bottles. "I close my eyes to the sugar and flour they take from the larder — but I *do* draw the line at our precious Scotch. Simon is still fairly trustworthy. But you can never be sure. Leaving bottles of Scotch hanging about the place is more than a temptation. It's an invitation. And once they get a taste for alcohol, that's the end."

"Worse even than putting them into shoes," my companion said.

"*Much* worse," Mrs. Palmer replied, not catching the irony. "In the old days people used to say that to give a native alcohol was like putting a loaded gun in the hands of a child. In my opinion that's still true. But . . ." She sighed again.

She extracted bottles of whiskey, gin, and sherry.   12

Simon came in carrying a bowl of ice in one hand and three glasses in the other.

"Simon . . . Simon . . ." Mrs. Palmer wagged her head.

Simon looked at her expressionlessly.

"Why didn't you use the tray, Simon?" Mrs. Palmer relieved him of   16 his burdens. "You can carry several things at once on a tray. That's what a tray is *for.*"

My eyes strayed to Simon's bare, uncorrupted feet.

"You see what I mean," Mrs. Palmer said when Simon had left the room. "The tray is another of his peculiar blocks." She poured generous measures of whiskey into our glasses.

The Alsatian sprang up, barking loudly: Mr. Palmer had arrived. He came in chattering apologies for his late arrival. He was dressed in khaki — short-sleeved khaki shirt tucked into short khaki trousers, matching knee-high socks and thick-soled brown shoes; a lean, wiry man of medium height, probably in his midfifties. He fondled and pummeled the fawning dog.

"Awfully sorry about the weather," he said. "Wish we could have put   20 on a better show for you. On a fine day you can see Kili."

The tea gardens — the Palmers had about three hundred acres under tea — began not many yards beyond the lawn surrounding the house. The day's work was drawing to a close, and the pluckers, bent under leaf-filled nets slung from their shoulders, were filing down the aisles between the rows of bushes, slowly making their way to the weighing shed. The afternoon had become colder and gloomier. Thickening mists obscured the summits of neighboring ridges. The wind was cutting. Smoke rose from a group of huts clustered together on the shallow slope of a nearby depression. A moorland bleakness overhung the scene. The pluckers — men, women, and children — crept like an army of subdued ghosts through the premature twilight, the sharp odor of the raw leaf they carried tanging the chill air. A muted murmur of conversation rose among them as they waited for the product of their day's labor to be weighed. All were equipped with shining aprons, reaching from neck to knee, made of vinyl.

"I supply the aprons myself," Mr. Palmer said. "They are very appreciative. It reduces the wear and tear on their clothing."

"They like the bright colors," Mrs. Palmer said. "They are very fond of bright colors."

The estate employed roughly two hundred people. Most of them had   24
been brought in from outside the district — or had migrated of their own accord in search of work. The local people were not particularly interested in agricultural labor of the type offered by the Palmers. Nairobi, less than a hundred miles away, was a powerful magnet.

"The local people have been spoiled," Mrs. Palmer said. "Many actually prefer to be beggars and prostitutes in Nairobi than to earn an honest living from the soil. They consider it to be beneath their dignity." She pursed her lips.

The pluckers smiled and saluted as they shuffled past with their loads. Mrs. Palmer's scarf snapped like a flag as she surveyed the beasts of burden who marched past her. They could, with luck, earn up to a pound a day.

"I know it sounds appallingly little by English standards," Mr. Palmer said. "But by *their* standards it's a good wage. *They* don't complain. *They* are grateful that they can actually work and earn something. It's only certain left-wing journalists looking for a sensational story who come here and weep crocodile tears on their behalf."

Mr. Palmer stooped, picked up a tea leaf from the ground, and stared   28
at it critically.

"These people," he went on, "are simple, hardworking folk. They're not spoiled . . ."

"Not as yet," Mrs. Palmer put in grimly. Her scarf fluttered and snapped.

"Their needs are basic," Mr. Palmer said. "They want to have food in their bellies, to be warm, to have a roof over their heads. *I* supply those basic needs. Many of them, you know, prefer to work for us whites than to work for their own people. Their own people often treat them like slaves. They don't pay them properly, they offer no medical facilities, they house them in atrocious conditions. Paternalism like mine has something to be said for it, don't you think?" He grinned at me.

He beckoned over a boy of about ten. "Have a look at this *toto*." He   32
squeezed the boy's arms and legs, lifted up his shirt and exhibited the well-fleshed diaphragm. "Six months ago Sammy was skeletal, covered with sores, had a bad cough. He's all right now, though. Aren't you, Sammy?" He chucked the boy under the chin. The boy, not knowing

what was happening to him, gazed at us with wild, frightened eyes. His mother watched from a distance, obviously pleased to see her son the focus of her master's attention.

"In the old days we used to have an estate shop," Mrs. Palmer said. "That way you made sure they got reasonably fed. Now they spend their money how and where they like." She laughed grimly. "Maize meal isn't good enough for them these days. They want rice."

"Rice is more nutritious than maize meal," Mr. Palmer said.

"But more expensive."

"It's their money."   36

Mrs. Palmer sighed. We returned to the house for lunch.

EXPLORATIONS

1. What is Mrs. Palmer's work, and what are its components? What does she perceive as the obstacles to her success? What is Mr. Palmer's work, and what are its components? What does he perceive as the obstacles to his success?

2. As tea planters the Palmers employ roughly two hundred people. What do Mrs. and Mr. Palmer think are the rewards and frustrations of their employees' jobs? What clues in his narrative suggest points on which Naipaul disagrees?

3. What are the sources of the Palmers' attitudes toward work? What are the sources of their employees' attitudes toward work? Look back at the biographical notes on Naipaul. In what ways is he qualified to write about both groups?

CONNECTIONS

1. Compare the Palmers' comments about Simon and their other black employees with Elliot Liebow's remarks about unskilled black workers in *Looking at Ourselves*. How do you think Liebow would reply to the Palmers? How do you think the Palmers would reply to Liebow?

2. In "Tradition and the African Writer" (p. 34), Ezekiel Mphahlele discusses the problems faced by black Africans whose country and culture had been "shanghaied into the history of the West." Which of these problems can you find evidence of in Naipaul's "The Palmers"?

3. Look back at "Entering the New World" (p. 47), by Shiva Naipaul's brother, V. S. Naipaul. What common ideas appear in both essays? Which of these ideas seem to reflect similarities between Kenya and the Ivory Coast, and which ones seem to reflect similar biases of the Naipauls?

4. What statements by Shiva Naipaul about Mr. and Mrs. Palmer indicate that they, like V. S. Naipaul in "Entering the New World" (p. 47), perceive the European "New World" in Africa as fragile and impermanent? What other evidence in "The Palmers" supports or conflicts with this idea?

ELABORATIONS

1. According to Naipaul, what is the attitude of black Kenyans toward their land? What is the Palmers' attitude toward the same land? Write an essay comparing and contrasting the ways these two groups think about land: What do they see when they look at it? What do they value most about it? How do they perceive their relationship to it? What are some likely reasons why many native Kenyans choose to leave their farms for Nairobi?

2. How would Naipaul's depiction of a Kenyan tea plantation be different if his information came from the employees instead of the owners? After rereading Elliot Liebow's remarks in *Looking at Ourselves* and Mphahlele's "Tradition and the African Writer" (p. 34), write an imaginary interview between Naipaul and one or more of the workers he mentions.

MAYA ANGELOU

Mary

At the time "Mary" took place, Maya Angelou was still going by her birth name, Marguerite Johnson. Born in St. Louis, Missouri, in 1928, by the age of sixteen she had survived rape, the breakup of her family, and unwed motherhood. (The rapist was her mother's friend Mr. Freeman, who was tried, convicted, and later found beaten to death — the sequence of events Angelou refers to in para. 21.) Support from her mother and her brother, Bailey, helped to keep her going. She later became a dancer, appeared in several plays (including a twenty-two-nation tour of *Porgy and Bess*), acted in the televised version of Alex Haley's *Roots,* and produced a series on Africa for the Public Broadcasting System. Angelou has been awarded three honorary doctorates and, at the request of Martin Luther King, Jr., served as a coordinator for the Southern Christian Leadership Conference. The author of five books of poetry, various songs and musical scores, and several plays and screenplays, she is best known for her five-volume autobiography. "Mary" comes from the first volume, *I Know Why the Caged Bird Sings* (1970), which recounts Angelou's childhood in Stamps, Arkansas.

Recently a white woman from Texas, who would quickly describe herself as a liberal, asked me about my hometown. When I told her that in Stamps my grandmother had owned the only Negro general merchandise store since the turn of the century, she exclaimed, "Why, you were a debutante." Ridiculous and even ludicrous. But Negro girls in small Southern towns, whether poverty-stricken or just munching along on a few of life's necessities, were given as extensive and irrelevant preparations for adulthood as rich white girls shown in magazines. Admittedly the training was not the same. While white girls learned to waltz and sit gracefully with a tea cup balanced on their knees, we were lagging behind, learning the mid-Victorian values with very little money to indulge them. (Come and see Edna Lomax spending the money she made picking cotton on five balls of ecru tatting thread. Her fingers are bound to snag the work and she'll have to repeat the stitches time and time again. But she knows that when she buys the thread.)

We were required to embroider and I had trunkfuls of colorful dish-towels, pillowcases, runners, and handkerchiefs to my credit. I mastered the art of crocheting and tatting, and there was a lifetime's supply of dainty doilies that would never be used in sacheted dresser drawers. It went without saying that all girls could iron and wash, but the finer touches around the home, like setting a table with real silver, baking roasts, and cooking vegetables without meat, had to be learned elsewhere. Usually at the source of those habits. During my tenth year, a white woman's kitchen became my finishing school.

Mrs. Viola Cullinan was a plump woman who lived in a three-bedroom house somewhere behind the post office. She was singularly unattractive until she smiled, and then the lines around her eyes and mouth which made her look perpetually dirty disappeared, and her face looked like the mask of an impish elf. She usually rested her smile until late afternoon when her women friends dropped in and Miss Glory, the cook, served them cold drinks on the closed-in porch.

The exactness of her house was inhuman. This glass went here and only here. That cup had its place and it was an act of impudent rebellion to place it anywhere else. At twelve o'clock the table was set. At 12:15 Mrs. Cullinan sat down to dinner (whether her husband had arrived or not). At 12:16 Miss Glory brought out the food. 4

It took me a week to learn the difference between a salad plate, a bread plate, and a dessert plate.

Mrs. Cullinan kept up the tradition of her wealthy parents. She was from Virginia. Miss Glory, who was a descendant of slaves that had worked for the Cullinans, told me her history. She had married beneath her (according to Miss Glory). Her husband's family hadn't had their money very long and what they had "didn't 'mount to much."

As ugly as she was, I thought privately, she was lucky to get a husband above or beneath her station. But Miss Glory wouldn't let me say a thing against her mistress. She was very patient with me, however, over the housework. She explained the dishware, silverware, and servants' bells.

The large round bowl in which soup was served wasn't a soup bowl, it was a tureen. There were goblets, sherbet glasses, ice-cream glasses, wine glasses, green glass coffee cups with matching saucers, and water glasses. I had a glass to drink from, and it sat with Miss Glory's on a separate shelf from the others. Soup spoons, gravy boat, butter knives, salad forks, and carving platter were additions to my vocabulary and in fact almost represented a new language. I was fascinated with the novelty, with the fluttering Mrs. Cullinan and her Alice-in-Wonderland house. 8

Her husband remains, in my memory, undefined. I lumped him with all the other white men that I had ever seen and tried not to see.

On our way home one evening, Miss Glory told me that Mrs. Cullinan couldn't have children. She said that she was too delicate-boned. It was hard to imagine bones at all under those layers of fat. Miss Glory went on to say that the doctor had taken out all her lady organs. I reasoned that a pig's organs included the lungs, heart, and liver, so if Mrs. Cullinan was walking around without those essentials, it explained why she drank alcohol out of unmarked bottles. She was keeping herself embalmed.

When I spoke to Bailey[1] about it, he agreed that I was right, but he also informed me that Mr. Cullinan had two daughters by a colored lady and that I knew them very well. He added that the girls were the spitting image of their father. I was unable to remember what he looked like, although I had just left him a few hours before, but I thought of the Coleman girls. They were very light-skinned and certainly didn't look very much like their mother (no one ever mentioned Mr. Coleman).

My pity for Mrs. Cullinan preceded me the next morning like the Cheshire cat's smile. Those girls, who could have been her daughters, were beautiful. They didn't have to straighten their hair. Even when they were caught in the rain, their braids still hung down straight like tamed snakes. Their mouths were pouty little cupid's bows. Mrs. Cullinan didn't know what she missed. Or maybe she did. Poor Mrs. Cullinan.

For weeks after, I arrived early, left late, and tried very hard to make up for her barrenness. If she had had her own children, she wouldn't have had to ask me to run a thousand errands from her back door to the back door of her friends. Poor old Mrs. Cullinan.

Then one evening Miss Glory told me to serve the ladies on the porch. After I set the tray down and turned toward the kitchen, one of the women asked, "What's your name, girl?" It was the speckled-faced one. Mrs. Cullinan said, "She doesn't talk much. Her name's Margaret."

"Is she dumb?"

"No. As I understand it, she can talk when she wants to but she's usually quiet as a little mouse. Aren't you, Margaret?"

I smiled at her. Poor thing. No organs and couldn't even pronounce my name correctly.

"She's a sweet little thing, though."

"Well, that may be, but the name's too long. I'd never bother myself. I'd call her Mary if I was you."

---

[1]The author's brother. — Ed.

I fumed into the kitchen. That horrible woman would never have the   20
chance to call me Mary because if I was starving I'd never work for her.
I decided I wouldn't pee on her if her heart was on fire. Giggles drifted
in off the porch and into Miss Glory's pots. I wondered what they could
be laughing about.

Whitefolks were so strange. Could they be talking about me? Everybody knew that they stuck together better than the Negroes did. It was
possible that Mrs. Cullinan had friends in St. Louis who heard about a
girl from Stamps being in court and wrote to tell her. Maybe she knew
about Mr. Freeman.

My lunch was in my mouth a second time and I went outside and
relieved myself on the bed of four-o'clocks. Miss Glory thought I might
be coming down with something and told me to go on home, that
Momma would give me some herb tea, and she'd explain to her mistress.

I realized how foolish I was being before I reached the pond. Of course
Mrs. Cullinan didn't know. Otherwise she wouldn't have given me the
two nice dresses that Momma cut down, and she certainly wouldn't have
called me a "sweet little thing." My stomach felt fine, and I didn't
mention anything to Momma.

That evening I decided to write a poem on being white, fat, old, and   24
without children. It was going to be a tragic ballad. I would have to
watch her carefully to capture the essence of her loneliness and pain.

The very next day, she called me by the wrong name. Miss Glory and
I were washing up the lunch dishes when Mrs. Cullinan came to the
doorway. "Mary?"

Miss Glory asked, "Who?"

Mrs. Cullinan, sagging a little, knew and I knew. "I want Mary to go
down to Mrs. Randall's and take her some soup. She's not been feeling
well for a few days."

Miss Glory's face was a wonder to see. "You mean Margaret, ma'am.   28
Her name's Margaret."

"That's too long. She's Mary from now on. Heat that soup from last
night and put it in the china tureen and, Mary, I want you to carry it
carefully."

Every person I knew had a hellish horror of being "called out of his
name." It was a dangerous practice to call a Negro anything that could
be loosely construed as insulting because of the centuries of their having
been called niggers, jigs, dinges, blackbirds, crows, boots, and spooks.

Miss Glory had a fleeting second of feeling sorry for me. Then as she handed me the hot tureen she said, "Don't mind, don't pay that no mind. Sticks and stones may break your bones, but words . . . You know, I been working for her for twenty years."

She held the back door open for me. "Twenty years. I wasn't much 32 older than you. My name used to be Hallelujah. That's what Ma named me, but my mistress give me 'Glory,' and it stuck. I likes it better too."

I was in the little path that ran behind the houses when Miss Glory shouted, "It's shorter too."

For a few seconds it was a tossup over whether I would laugh (imagine being named Hallelujah) or cry (imagine letting some white woman rename you for her convenience). My anger saved me from either outburst. I had to quit the job, but the problem was going to be how to do it. Momma wouldn't allow me to quit for just any reason.

"She's a peach. That woman is a real peach." Mrs. Randall's maid was talking as she took the soup from me, and I wondered what her name used to be and what she answered to now.

For a week I looked into Mrs. Cullinan's face as she called me Mary. 36 She ignored my coming late and leaving early. Miss Glory was a little annoyed because I had begun to leave egg yolk on the dishes and wasn't putting much heart in polishing the silver. I hoped that she would complain to our boss, but she didn't.

Then Bailey solved my dilemma. He had me describe the contents of the cupboard and the particular plates she liked best. Her favorite piece was a casserole shaped like a fish and the green glass coffee cups. I kept his instructions in mind, so on the next day when Miss Glory was hanging out clothes and I had again been told to serve the old biddies on the porch, I dropped the empty serving tray. When I heard Mrs. Cullinan scream, "Mary!" I picked up the casserole and two of the green glass cups in readiness. As she rounded the kitchen door I let them fall on the tiled floor.

I could never absolutely describe to Bailey what happened next, because each time I got to the part where she fell on the floor and screwed up her ugly face to cry, we burst out laughing. She actually wobbled around on the floor and picked up shards of the cups and cried, "Oh, Momma. Oh, dear Gawd. It's Momma's china from Virginia. Oh, Momma, I sorry."

Miss Glory came running in from the yard and the women from the porch crowded around. Miss Glory was almost as broken up as her mistress. "You mean to say she broke our Virginia dishes? What we gone do?"

Mrs. Cullinan cried louder, "That clumsy nigger. Clumsy little black   40
nigger."

Old speckled-face leaned down and asked, "Who did it, Viola? Was
it Mary? Who did it?"

Everything was happening so fast I can't remember whether her action
preceded her words, but I know that Mrs. Cullinan said, "Her name's
Margaret, goddamn it, her name's Margaret!" And she threw a wedge of
the broken plate at me. It could have been the hysteria which put her
aim off, but the flying crockery caught Miss Glory right over her ear and
she started screaming.

I left the front door wide open so all the neighbors could hear.

Mrs. Cullinan was right about one thing. My name wasn't Mary.   44

EXPLORATIONS

1. When Angelou first goes to work for Mrs. Cullinan, what is her attitude
   toward her employer? At what points does her attitude change, in what ways,
   and for what reasons?

2. What reason does Angelou give for a black person's horror of being "called
   out of his name" (para. 30)? Why does she find her change of name so
   offensive?

3. In paragraph 24, Angelou decides "to write a poem on being white, fat, old,
   and without children." Why do you think she wanted to do this? What
   personal goals does she seem to have achieved by writing about Mrs. Cullinan
   in her autobiography?

CONNECTIONS

1. In "Mary," as in Shiva Naipaul's "The Palmers," we see characters using their
   knowledge about other characters to assert a sort of secret superiority over
   them. What does Mary know about the Cullinans that makes her feel superior
   to them? What do the Palmers know about their workers that makes them
   feel superior?

2. What similar limitations confront Angelou in "Mary" and Mario Puzo in
   Looking at Ourselves? What qualities appear to have helped both authors
   conquer these limitations?

3. Reread paragraphs 19 and 20 of V. S. Naipaul's "Entering the New World"
   (p. 47). How does Naipaul explain the disorder he observed at the restaurant?
   After reading "Mary," what alternative explanation can you suggest?

ELABORATIONS

1. How old were you when you first worked for money? What do you remember of your feelings about the job, the people involved, and having an income? Write a narrative essay about your experience as an employee.

2. In paragraph 4 Angelou describes the "inhuman" exactness of Mrs. Cullinan's house: glasses precisely placed, meals precisely scheduled. Do you know anyone who is so demanding? Is there any aspect of your life — the way you arrange your desk, a recipe you prepare, specialized clothing you put on for some activity — that is so exact? Write a descriptive or process analysis essay on your experience with exactness.

R. K. NARAYAN

Trail of the Green Blazer

R. K. Narayan was born in Madras, India, in 1906. Best known for
his fiction, he has written fourteen novels, over two hundred short stories,
a memoir, travel books, three essay collections, and retellings of classic
Indian epics. In 1958 Narayan's novel *The Guide* received the National
Prize of the Indian Literary Academy, his country's highest literary honor;
it was later made into an American film. A frequent traveler, Narayan
has since 1959 lived on and off in New York City for months at a time.
In 1981 he was made an honorary member of the prestigious American
Academy and Institute of Arts and Letters. Now back at home in Mysore,
India, Narayan became a member of the Indian parliament in 1986.

The setting for "Trail of the Green Blazer," as for most of Narayan's
novels and stories, is the fictional town of Malgudi. Malgudi is said to
be a composite of Madras, the author's birthplace on India's southeast
coast, and Mysore, farther west, where he attended Maharaja's College
and has spent most of his life. Like William Faulkner's Yoknapatawpha
County, Narayan's Malgudi has been praised for the vivid sense of place
it conveys and the intimate details of its characters' daily life. Narayan
writes in English but not with a Western audience in mind; his work is
deeply and distinctively Indian.

(For background on India, see pp. 146, 262.)

The Green Blazer stood out prominently under the bright sun and
blue sky. In all that jostling crowd one could not help noticing it. Villagers
in shirts and turbans, townsmen in coats and caps, beggars bare-bodied
and women in multicolored saris were thronging the narrow passage
between the stalls and moving in great confused masses, but still the
Green Blazer could not be missed. The jabber and babble of the marketplace was there, as people harangued, disputed prices, haggled, or
greeted each other; over it all boomed the voice of a Bible-preacher, and
when he paused for breath, from another corner the loudspeaker of a
health van amplified on malaria and tuberculosis. Over and above it all
the Green Blazer seemed to cry out an invitation. Raju could not ignore
it. It was not in his nature to ignore such a persistent invitation. He kept
himself half-aloof from the crowd; he could not afford to remain completely aloof or keep himself in it too conspicuously. Wherever he might

be, he was harrowed by the fear of being spotted by a policeman; today he wore a loincloth and was bare-bodied, and had wound an enormous turban over his head, which overshadowed his face completely, and he hoped that he would be taken for a peasant from a village.

He sat on a stack of cast-off banana stalks beside a shop awning and watched the crowd. When he watched a crowd he did it with concentration. It was his professional occupation. Constitutionally he was an idler and had just the amount of energy to watch in a crowd and put his hand into another person's pocket. It was a gamble, of course. Sometimes he got nothing out of a venture, counting himself lucky if he came out with his fingers intact. Sometimes he picked up a fountain pen, and the "receiver" behind the Municipal Office would not offer even four annas for it, and there was always the danger of being traced through it. Raju promised himself that someday he would leave fountain pens alone; he wouldn't touch one even if it were presented to him on a plate; they were too much bother — inky, leaky, and next to worthless if one could believe what the receiver said about them. Watches were in the same category, too.

What Raju loved most was a nice, bulging purse. If he saw one he picked it up with the greatest deftness. He took the cash in it, flung it far away, and went home with the satisfaction that he had done his day's job well. He splashed a little water over his face and hair and tidied himself up before walking down the street again as a normal citizen. He bought sweets, books, and slates for his children, and occasionally a jacket piece for his wife, too. He was not always easy in mind about his wife. When he went home with too much cash, he had always to take care to hide it in an envelope and shove it under a roof tile. Otherwise she asked too many questions and made herself miserable. She liked to believe that he was reformed and earned the cash he showed her as commission; she never bothered to ask what the commissions were for: a commission seemed to her something absolute.

Raju jumped down from the banana stack and followed the Green   4
Blazer, always keeping himself three steps behind. It was a nicely cal-
culated distance, acquired by intuition and practice. The distance must not be so much as to obscure the movement of the other's hand to and from his purse, nor so close as to become a nuisance and create suspicion. It had to be finely balanced and calculated — the same sort of calculations

as carry a *shikari*[1] through his tracking of game and see him safely home again. Only this hunter's task was more complicated. The hunter in the forest could count his day a success if he laid his quarry flat; but here one had to extract the heart out of the quarry without injuring it.

Raju waited patiently, pretending to be examining some rolls of rush mat, while the Green Blazer spent a considerable length of time drinking a coconut at a nearby booth. It looked as though he would not move again at all. After sucking all the milk in the coconut, he seemed to wait interminably for the nut to be split and the soft white kernel scooped out with a knife. The sight of the white kernel scooped and disappearing into the other's mouth made Raju, too, crave for it. But he suppressed the thought: it would be inept to be spending one's time drinking and eating while one was professionally occupied; the other might slip away and be lost forever. . . . Raju saw the other take out his black purse and start a debate with the coconut seller over the price of coconuts. He had a thick, sawing voice which disconcerted Raju. It sounded like the growl of a tiger, but what jungle-hardened hunter ever took a step back because a tiger's growl sent his heart racing involuntarily! The way the other haggled didn't appeal to Raju either; it showed a mean and petty temperament . . . too much fondness for money. Those were the narrow-minded troublemakers who made endless fuss when a purse was lost. . . . The Green Blazer moved after all. He stopped before a stall flying colored balloons. He bought a balloon after an endless argument with the shop-man — a further demonstration of his meanness. He said, "This is for a motherless boy. I have promised it him. If it bursts or gets lost before I go home, he will cry all night, and I wouldn't like it at all."

Raju got his chance when the other passed through a narrow stile, where people were passing four-thick in order to see a wax model of Mahatma Gandhi reading a newspaper.

Fifteen minutes later Raju was examining the contents of the purse. He went away to a secluded spot, behind a disused well. Its crumbling parapet seemed to offer an ideal screen for his activities. The purse contained ten rupees in coins and twenty in currency notes and a few annas in nickel. Raju tucked the annas at his waist in his loincloth. "Must give them to some beggars," he reflected generously. There was a

---

[1]Professional hunter. — ED.

blind fellow yelling his life out at the entrance to the fair and nobody seemed to care. People seemed to have lost all sense of sympathy these days. The thirty rupees he bundled into a knot at the end of his turban and wrapped this again round his head. It would see him through the rest of the month. He could lead a clean life for at least a fortnight and take his wife and children to a picture.

Now the purse lay limp within the hollow of his hand. It was only left for him to fling it into the well and dust off his hand and then he might walk among princes with equal pride at heart. He peeped into the well. It had a little shallow water at the bottom. The purse might float, and a floating purse could cause the worst troubles on earth. He opened the flap of the purse in order to fill it up with pebbles before drowning it. Now, through the slit at its side, he saw a balloon folded and tucked away. "Oh, this he bought. . . ." He remembered the other's talk about the motherless child. "What a fool to keep this in the purse," Raju reflected. "It is the carelessness of parents that makes young ones suffer," he ruminated angrily. For a moment he paused over a picture of the growling father returning home and the motherless one waiting at the door for the promised balloon, and this growling man feeling for his purse . . . and, oh! it was too painful!

Raju almost sobbed at the thought of the disappointed child — the motherless boy. There was no one to comfort him. Perhaps this ruffian would beat him if he cried too long. The Green Blazer did not look like one who knew the language of children. Raju was filled with pity at the thought of the young child — perhaps of the same age as his second son. Suppose his wife were dead . . . (personally it might make things easier for him, he need not conceal his cash under the roof); he overcame this thought as an unworthy side issue. If his wife should die it would make him very sad indeed and tax all his ingenuity to keep his young ones quiet. . . . That motherless boy must have his balloon at any cost, Raju decided. But how? He peeped over the parapet across the intervening space at the far-off crowd. The balloon could not be handed back. The thing to do would be to put it back into the empty purse and slip it into the other's pocket.

The Green Blazer was watching the heckling that was going on as the Bible-preacher warmed up to his subject. A semicircle was asking, "Where is your God?" There was a hubbub. Raju sidled up to the Green Blazer. The purse with the balloon (only) tucked into it was in his palm. He'd slip it back into the other's pocket.

Raju realized his mistake in a moment. The Green Blazer caught hold of his arm and cried, "Pickpocket!" The hecklers lost interest in the Bible and turned their attention to Raju, who tried to look appropriately outraged. He cried, "Let me go." The other, without giving a clue to what he proposed, shot out his arm and hit him on the cheek. It almost blinded him. For a fraction of a second Raju lost his awareness of where and even who he was. When the dark mist lifted and he was able to regain his vision, the first figure he noticed in the foreground was the Green Blazer, looming, as it seemed, over the whole landscape. His arms were raised ready to strike again. Raju cowered at the sight. He said, "I . . . I was trying to put back your purse." The other gritted his teeth in fiendish merriment and crushed the bones of his arm. The crowd roared with laughter and badgered him. Somebody hit him again on the head.

Even before the Magistrate Raju kept saying, "I was only trying to put 12 back the purse." And everyone laughed. It became a stock joke in the police world. Raju's wife came to see him in jail and said, "You have brought shame on us," and wept.

Raju replied indignantly, "Why? I was only trying to put it back."

He served his term of eighteen months and came back into the world — not quite decided what he should do with himself. He told himself, "If ever I pick up something again, I shall make sure I don't have to put it back." For now he believed God had gifted the likes of him with only one-way deftness. Those fingers were not meant to put anything back.

EXPLORATIONS

1. Why is the ending of "Trail of the Green Blazer" ironic? What resolution for the future do Raju's wife and others want him to make after his experience with the Green Blazer? What conclusion does Raju draw instead, and why?

2. Look closely at the story's first paragraph. How does Narayan put us as readers in sympathy with Raju? What specific phrases or sentences suggest that the Green Blazer really is more at fault than Raju? How would the story's impact change if the Green Blazer were described as a person rather than a garment?

3. Elsewhere in the story, what specific actions on Raju's part, and what descriptive words on Narayan's part, show Raju as having admirable qualities? In what ways does the author depict his main character as a victim of circumstances? What are Raju's negative qualities? How would the story's effect be different if Raju were portrayed as purely admirable?

CONNECTIONS

1. Narayan, like Maya Angelou in "Mary," writes from the viewpoint of a character who sees himself or herself as more important than do the others in the story. What judgmental comments does the young Marguerite make about Mrs. Cullinan? What judgmental comments does Raju the pickpocket make about the Green Blazer? How do these comments affect your perception of their subjects and of the speakers?

2. Like Shiva Naipaul's "The Palmers," Narayan's "Trail of the Green Blazer" contrasts wealthy and poor characters. From whose point of view does Narayan tell his story? From whose point of view does Naipaul present the Palmers and their employees? Which characters in each narrative are most and least sympathetic, and why?

3. In *Looking at Ourselves*, Mario Puzo writes, "I wanted to be a killer hero in a worldwide war. . . . [Or] a footloose adventurer. Then I branched out and thought of being a great artist, and then, getting ever more sophisticated, a great criminal." How does Raju's vision of criminality as a profession differ from Puzo's?

4. Narayan's "Trail of the Green Blazer," like Gholam-Hossein Sa'edi's "The Game Is Over" (p. 164), shows a character brought to justice for doing wrong. In each story, why does the pivotal character commit the act that causes his downfall? What conflict exists in each story between justice and fairness?

ELABORATIONS

1. Narayan presents enough evidence on both sides to convince a jury that Raju is either a victim or a villain. What are the arguments for each view? Which position do you think is stronger? Choose a side, and write an essay that both makes your case and rebuts the opposing view.

2. "Trail of the Green Blazer" shares a central metaphor with Alberto Moravia's "The Chase" (p. 341): In each story, the main character sees himself as a hunter tracking a quarry. The contrast in these two authors' use of the same image shows how flexible the image is. What additional ways can you imagine using the hunting metaphor? Write a narrative essay about an adventure of your own which could be viewed as a hunt. Be sure to show, as Narayan and Moravia do, what this metaphor implies about the hunter, the quarry, and the social relationship between them.

DAVID ABRAM

Making Magic

Ecologist, writer, and free-lance magician David Abram was born on Long Island, New York, in 1957. A summa cum laude graduate of Wesleyan University in Connecticut, he is now a doctoral candidate in philosophy at the State University of New York at Stony Brook. Abram took up magic in high school and began performing professionally during his first year at college. In 1980 he was awarded a Watson Fellowship for a year's research among tribal healers in Indonesia, Nepal, and Sri Lanka. "Making Magic" grew out of that research; it was first published in *Parabola* in August 1982 and excerpted in the January–February 1988 *Utne Reader.* Abram's articles on ecological perception and magic have also appeared in *The Ecologist, Journal of Environmental Ethics, Appalachia,* and *Orion Nature Quarterly.* He has lectured extensively on the Gaia hypothesis, which holds that the earth's atmosphere is being modulated by all of the earth's organisms acting collectively. A resident of New Mexico, Abram is currently working on a book on perception and language with regard to the relation between human and nonhuman nature.

Indonesia, where the following adventures took place, is a republic comprising 13,500 islands south of the Philippines and north of Australia. Besides Bali, it includes Java, Sumatra, most of Borneo, and the western half of New Guinea. The islands' location made them attractive to European traders. First the Portuguese dominated, then the Dutch. In 1824 the British and Dutch split their holdings in the region, then known as the East Indies. The southern Dutch East Indies declared independence in 1945 as Indonesia, after being occupied by Japan through World War II. The northern British East Indies evolved into part of the Federation of Malaya, now Malaysia.

They told me I had powers.

Powers? I had been a magician for seven years, performing steadily back in the states, entertaining in clubs and restaurants throughout the country, yet I had never heard anyone mention powers. To be sure, once or twice a season I was rebuked by some spectator fresh out of Bible school for "doing the work of Satan," but the more customary refrain was: "How did you do that?" Every evening in the clubs: "How? How did *that* happen?" "C'mon, tell us — how does that work?"

"I don't know," I took to saying, mostly out of boredom, yet also because I felt there was a grain of truth in that statement, because there was some aspect of my sleight-of-hand tricks that mystified even me. It was not something I could experience when rehearsing alone, at home, or when practicing my sleights before a mirror. But when I would stand before my audience, letting my fingers run through one of their routines with some borrowed coins, and I'd see the spectators' eyes slowly widening with astonishment, well, there was something astonishing about that for me as well, although I was unable to say just what it was.

When I received a fellowship to support a year's research on the intertwining of magic and medicine in Asia, I thought I might have a chance to explore the secrets that lay hidden within my own magic, or at least to discern what mysteries my magic had in common with the magic used in traditional cultures not merely for entertainment, but for healing, fortification, and transformation. I was intending to use my skills as a Western sleight-of-hand magician to gain access to the native practitioners and their rituals — I would approach them not as an academic researcher, not as an anthropologist or sociologist, but as a magician in my own right, and in this manner would explore the relation between ritual and transformation from the inside.

As it turned out, this method worked well — at first almost too well, for the potency my magic tricks took on in rural Asia brought some alarming difficulties. In the interior of Sri Lanka, where I began my quest, I was rather too open with my skills; anxious to get a sense of the local attitude toward magic, I began performing on village street corners much as I had three years earlier while journeying as a street magician through Europe. But these were different streets, much more worn and dusty than those concrete thoroughfares, reeking with smells of incense and elephants, frequented as much by gods and demons as by the human inhabitants of the island. Less than a week after I began plucking handkerchiefs from the air, "the young magician from the West" was known throughout the country. Huge crowds followed me wherever I went, and I was constantly approached by people in the grip of disease, by the blind and crippled, all asking me to cure them with my powers. What a frightful, saddening position to be in! When, like a fool, I attempted to show that my magic feats were but illusions accomplished by dexterous manipulations, I only insulted these people — clearly, to them, I was using clumsy explanations to disguise and hide my real powers. I fled Sri Lanka after only three weeks, suffering from a severe case of ethical

4

paradox, determined to begin my work afresh in Indonesia, where I would above all keep my magic more to myself.

It was five months later — after carefully immersing myself in the Indonesian island universe, observing and recording the patterns of culture, while slowly, inadvertently, slipping into those patterns myself — that I first allowed myself a chance to explore the more unusual possibilities of my position. For five months I had been true to my resolve, keeping my magic much more "up my sleeve" than I had in Sri Lanka — waiting for just the right moment to make something impossible happen, and performing for only a few people at a time, perhaps in a tea stall or while sauntering past the rice paddies. In this manner I slowly and much more surely wove my way into the animist fabric of the society. I had the sense that I was becoming known in the region, but in a more subtle and curious manner than before — here and there I had begun to hear stories about a Westerner, glimpsed on the far side of the island, who actually had access to the invisible world, to the spirits.

Gradually I had been contacted by a number of *dukuns*, or sorcerers, often in some clandestine manner, through a child or a friend, and asked to visit them in their homes. The initial meetings had been strained, sometimes frightening, for these practitioners felt their status threatened by a stranger who could so easily produce shells from the air or make knives vanish between his hands. And I in return felt threatened by the resultant antagonism — I did not want these magicians to view me as their competitior, for I knew the incredible power of the imagination and had no wish to be the victim of any dark spells. (When I came down with a nightmarish case of malaria, I was sure, in my delirium, that I had brought it upon myself by offending a particular sorcerer.) As the months unfolded, I had learned not to shy away from these tensions, but to work with them. I had become adept at transforming the initial antagonism into some sort of mutual respect, at times into a real sense of camaraderie. I had lived with a sorcerer-healer in Java and traded magic with a *balian tapakan*, or spirit medium, in Bali, both of whom were convinced that my presence in their household enhanced their own access to the gods and accentuated their power as healers. But that is another story.

On a certain early monsoon day I sat in a rice stall in a small fishing village on the coast of Bali, shielding myself from the afternoon rain. Munching my rice, I stared out at a steamy, emerald landscape — with the rainy season finally breaking overhead, all the Balinese greens were beginning to leak into the air. Inside, the old woman was serving rice across the wooden slab of a counter to two solemn fishermen; in the corner of the hut three others were laughing and conversing in low Balinese. The downpour outside stopped abruptly; now other sounds — dogs fighting in the distance, someone singing.

I stood up to pay the woman, counting out the correct number of coins and reaching across to drop them into her hand. I opened my fingers — the coins were not there! The woman and I looked at each other, astonished. I turned my empty hands over several times, looked on the dirt floor behind me, then reached under my rice bowl and found the coins. Feigning relief, I took them up and reached across to hand them to the bewildered woman — except that the coins were missing once again when I opened my fist. By now the men in the corner had stopped talking and the two at the counter had paused in the middle of their meal, watching as I became more and more annoyed, searching the floor and the bench without finding my money. One of the fishermen suggested that I look under my bowl again. I lifted it up, but the coins were not there. Upset, I stared at the others. One of them backed slowly into the street. I shrugged my shoulders sadly at the woman, then caught sight of the two half-filled rice bowls resting in front of the other men at the counter. I motioned hesitantly for one of the fishermen to lift up his bowl. He looked around at the others, then gingerly raised one edge of the bowl — there they were! The coins glittered on the palmwood as the fishermen began shouting at each other, incredulous. The old woman was doubled over with laughter.

The man who had uncovered the coins stared at me long and hard. As the others drifted out onto the street, still shouting, this man shoved his rice aside, leaned over to me, and asked, in Indonesian, if I would be so kind as to accompany him to meet his family. Something urgent in his voice intrigued me; I nodded. He paid the old woman, who clapped me on the shoulder as we left, and led me down the street toward the beach. He turned off to the right before reaching the sand, and I followed him through the rice paddies, balancing like a tightrope-walker on one of the dikes that separate the flooded squares. To our left the village spread itself out along the shore: A young woman nursed an infant, smoke rose from cooking fires, three pigs rummaged through a pile of rags and wood. The man turned to the left between two paddies and led me through a makeshift gate into his family compound. Children were playing. He motioned me inside one of the two buildings — his brother lives in the other, he explained — where a young woman sat with a child on her lap. Before I could make a formal greeting, the fisherman pushed his wife and child out the door, slinging a blanket over the doorway and another over the window. He sat me down in the dark, offered a Javanese cigarette, lit one for himself, then sat down cross-legged on the floor next to me. He gripped my ankle as he began to explain his situation. He spoke quickly, in broken Indonesian, which was good, since I could never have followed his story had he spoken so quickly in Balinese.

Essentially what he had to say was this: that he was a poor and ignorant fisherman blessed with a loving wife and many children, and that despite his steady and enthusiastic propitiation of the local gods and ancestors, he had been unable to catch any fish for the last six months. This was especially upsetting since before that time he had been one of the most successful fishermen in the village. He said it was evident to everyone in the village that his present difficulties were the result of some left-handed magic; clearly a demon had been induced by some sorcery to take up residence in the hull of his fishing boat, and was now frightening the fish away from his nets. Furthermore, he knew that another fisherman in the village had secretly obtained a certain talisman from a priest, a magic shell that made this other man's boat fill up with fish whenever he took it out on the water. And so perhaps I, who obviously knew about such things and had some powers of my own, would be willing to work some special magic on *his* boat so that he could once again catch enough fish to feed his family.

Now, it was clear that this man was both honest and in earnest (his grip on my poor ankle had increased considerably), but I had been in this position before, and though less disconcerted by it than I had been five months earlier, I was still reluctant to play very deeply within the dream-space of a culture that was not my own. And so I explained to Gedé (one of his many names) that my magic was only good for things like making coins vanish or causing fruit to appear (I plucked a ripe banana out of the darkness, making him laugh), that my magic was useless when it came to really practical matters. Besides, I told him, I had never worked with fish, but was sure (since they could breathe underwater and all) that their own powers were even more potent than mine; if a demon was frightening them away, he or she was certainly beyond my influence. Gedé nodded in agreement, released my ankle, and changed the subject. After a few minutes he led me to the doorway and thanked me for coming.

I felt sure I had convinced him with my excuses. But perhaps I had failed to take into account the Balinese habit of self-effacement before

12

accepting praise (*Saya bodoh*, "I am stupid," any Balinese healer will reply when told that he or she is skillful), including, apparently, the praise and respect implied in being offered a difficult task. Unaware, I walked along the beach toward the little bamboo hut I had procured for the night. As the sun sank into the land, the moon rose from the ocean, pale white, nearly full. In the distance, between the rising and the lowering, sat the great volcano, silently looming on the horizon.

That night I had difficulty falling asleep. A weird symphony of chirping crickets accompanied the chorus of frogs gurgling in unison outside my hut. Sometimes this loud music stopped all at once — leaving only the faint lapping of waves and the afternoon rain dripping off the night leaves.

Toward midnight I was awakened by a persistent tapping at the window. I stumbled to my feet and lifted the thin slab of wood — there was Gedé, grinning nervously. He hissed that we must attempt the magic now, while the others were asleep. In an instant I understood the situation — that Gedé was not taking no for an answer, or rather that he had taken my refusal as an acceptance — and I found myself, oddly enough, giving in to the challenge this time without hesitation. Wrapping a sarong around myself, I recalled the dream from which Gedé's tapping had awakened me: I had been back in the states, performing strange, hypnotic magic for sea monsters in a nightclub that was actually an aquarium. Just before waking, I had heard one monster applauding; his clapping had become the tapping at my window. Now, looking around hastily for something to use, I grabbed an empty Coke bottle I had tossed in the corner, then, on an inspiration, dug in my backpack for some flashpaper I'd brought from the states. (Flashpaper, a common tool of the stage magician, is thin paper that has been soaked in a magnesium solution. When crumpled and ignited, it goes up in a sudden bright flash, leaving no ashes behind — wonderful stuff.) I shoved the flashpaper into a fold in my sarong and, gripping the Coke bottle, hurried outside where Gedé was fidgeting anxiously. When he saw me, he turned and led the way down to the beach.

We walked quickly along the water's edge to where the boats were resting on the sand, their long, painted hulls gleaming in the moonglow. As we walked, Gedé whispered to me that the fishermen don't go out fishing on nights when the moon is full or nearly full, since the fish can then see the nets. Only on such a night as this could we accomplish the magic in secret, while the other fishermen slept. He stopped before a sleek blue and white boat, somewhat longer than most of the others, and motioned for me to help him. We lifted the bamboo outriggers and slid

16

the craft into the dark water. I hopped back onto the beach and scooped my Coke bottle full of the black, volcanic sand, then waded back out and climbed into the boat with Gedé. Really a long dugout canoe with limbs — the two bamboo outriggers and a short, rough-hewn mast near the bow — it rested on the swells while Gedé unrolled a white triangle of sail and hoisted it from a beam on the mast. The breeze rose up and the boat glided silently into the night. Overhead, the moon drifted behind a cloud and set the whole cloud glowing. The volcano, luminous, watched and waited.

In the Balinese universe, the volcano provides a sort of gateway to and from the upper world, the world of the ancestors, of the gods. The sea, meanwhile, provides passage to the lower world of demons; these destructive forces are known to reside in the black depths of the waters that surround the island. Consequently, those islanders who live near the shore, and especially the fishermen who make their living on the water, are a highly nervous and wary bunch, and they partake even more than the average Balinese of the animistic rites and ceremonies of protection for which the island is famous. At this point in my journey I was only beginning to sense what I would later see clearly: that while the magicians of all traditional cultures are working fundamentally toward the same mystery, the magic of each culture takes its structure from the particular clues of the region, that is, from the particular powers of earth to be found only there — whether volcanoes, or wind, or ocean, or desert — for magic evolves from the land.

The wind shifted, became cooler. I moved close to where Gedé sat in the stern guiding the rudder, and asked him why it was so necessary for us to work in secret. "So other fishermen not jealous," he explained softly. He lit himself a cigarette. After some time I turned away from him and slipped a piece of flashpaper, crumpled, into the mouth of the Coke bottle. The beach was a thin silver line in the distance. I told Gedé that I thought we were out far enough for the magic to take effect, and he agreed. As I took down the sail, I wedged the rest of the flashpaper under a splinter near the top of the mast. Gedé heaved an anchor over the side, then settled back into the stern, watching me carefully.

How to improvise an exorcism? I leaned with my back against the mast, emptying my mind of thoughts, feeling the rock and sway of this tiny boat on the night waters. Small waves slapped against the hull, angrily at first, then softer, more playful, curious. Gradually something regular established itself — the swaying took on a rhythm, a steady rock and roll that grew in intensity as my body gave in to the dance. Phosphorescent algae glimmered like stars around me. The boat became a planet, and I leaned with my back against the axis of the world, a tree with roots in the ocean and branches in the sky, tilting, turning.

Without losing the rhythm, I began to move toward the rear of the   20
boat, keeping it rocking, swinging the bottle of black sand around myself in circles, from one hand to the other. When I reached Gedé I took the cigarette from his hand, puffed on it deeply once or twice, then touched the lit end to the mouth of the bottle. A white flash of fire exploded from the bottle with a "Whooshh," propelled by the pressure inside, a wild spirit lunging for air.

Gedé sat bolt upright, with his arms quivering, grasping the sides of the hull. I motioned for him to cup his hands, he did so, and I tipped the bottle down, pouring a small mound of spirit-sand onto his fingers. There were little platforms affixed symmetrically around the hull, platforms upon which Gedé, when fishing, would place his lanterns to coax the fish up from the depths. I moved around to each of them, nine in all, the cardinal points of this drifting planet, and carefully anointed each one with a mound of sand. I then sat down in the bottom of the carved-out hull and planted my hands against the wood, against the inside of that hollowed-out tree, waiting to make contact with whatever malevolent presence slumbered beneath the chiseled surface. I felt the need for a sound, for some chant to keep the rhythm, but I could think of nothing appropriate, until a bit of Jewish liturgy sprang to my lips from somewhere, perhaps from my own initiation at age thirteen. I sang softly. The planet heaved and creaked, the hollow tree rolled from side to side, the upright tree with roots in the sea swung like a pendulum against moon-edged clouds.

At some point the moon itself rolled out from a cloud pocket and the whole mood shifted — sharp shadows slid back and forth across the wood. Somewhere inside me another planet turned; I began to feel slightly sick. I stood up and began weaving from one side of the boat to the other, sweeping the mounds of sand off the platforms. When I came to the fisherman, I reached into the sky above him and produced another cigarette, already lit, from the dark. I felt a fever flushing my forehead and cheeks. I held the cigarette first to his mouth, then to my own, and we each took a puff on it. I held my breath, walked back rather dizzily, and blew a long line of smoke from the bottom to the top of the mast.

Then I touched the cigarette to the paper wedged in up among the invisible branches. A rush of flame shot into the sky. Instantly I felt better — the fever was gone, the turning stopped, the little boat rocked on the waves. I turned to Gedé and nodded. A wide grin broke across his face and he tossed the sand, still cupped in his hands, over his head into the water. We drew anchor, hoisted the sail, and tacked back to the village with Gedé singing gaily at the rudder.

I had to leave the coast the next day to begin work with a healer in   24
the interior, but I promised Gedé I would return in a month or so to check on the results of my impromptu exorcism.

Five weeks later I returned, with mounting trepidation, to the fishing village. I found Gedé waiting for me with open arms. I was introduced to his family, presented with gifts, and stuffed with food. The magic had been successful. The fishing business was thriving, as was apparent from the new gate and the new building Gedé had had built to house the family kitchen. After the meal Gedé took me aside to tell me of his new ideas, projects he could accomplish if only he had a little magic help. I backed off gracefully, paid my respects, and left the village, feeling elated and strange.

I am scribbling the last words of this story at a table in the small Vermont nightclub where I have been performing magic this winter. Tonight I was doing mostly card magic, with some handkerchiefs and coin stuff thrown in for good measure. Some hours ago a woman grabbed my arm. "How?" she gasped. "How did you do that?"

"I really don't know," I told her.

I think there's something honest in that.   28

EXPLORATIONS

1. What statements in Abram's essay suggest that he regards his magic as tricks and illusions? What statements suggests that he thinks there is more to it?

2. When Abram agrees to try to remove the spell from Gedé's boat, what are his hopes and expectations? What kinds of tactics does he use?

3. What role is played by descriptive and expository passages about the narrator's Balinese surroundings (see, for instance, paras. 14 and 17)? How would the essay's impact change without such passages?

CONNECTIONS

1. Abram, like R. K. Narayan in "Trail of the Green Blazer," shows a likable character holding beliefs with which most readers will not agree. What improbable ideas are expressed by Gedé in "Making Magic" and by Raju in "Trail of the Green Blazer"? How does the author make each character sympathetic in spite of his unsympathetic beliefs?

2. In Fred Moody's comments in *Looking at Ourselves*, what factors divide people's work from their nonworking lives? What factors create this division for the fisherman Gedé? How does Gedé's concept of work — and its role in his life — differ from Moody's?

3. According to the credo of the American Entrepreneurs' Association in *Looking at Ourselves*, is Abram an entrepreneur? How does his attitude toward his work differ from this credo?

ELABORATIONS

1. What similar goals appear to have motivated David Abram's trip to Southeast Asia and Mark Salzman's trip to China (see p. 235)? What similar discoveries emerge in "Making Magic" and "Gong Fu"? Write an argumentative or classification essay about what someone from the United States can learn from spending time in another country.

2. Many Americans define work as what goes on in their places of employment between 9:00 A.M. and 5:00 P.M. How does this definition differ from the fisherman Gedé's? What elements of each definition appear in Abram's biographical headnote and in "Making Magic"? Write a comparison-contrast or definition essay on the roles a person's work can play in his or her life.

JILL GAY

Patriotic Prostitutes

Jill Gay was born in New York in 1951 but grew up in Venezuela and Spain. She now lives in Maryland, near Washington, D.C., where she serves on the board of the Third World Women's Project at the Institute for Policy Studies. Gay spent 1971 in Israel, studied in Peru in 1972, graduated from Barnard College, and received her master's degree in international affairs from Columbia University in 1978. She has traveled through Western Europe, Latin America, Japan, and South Korea. The author of more than a dozen articles for various magazines, she has also coedited a book on Third World women. Most recently, Gay has worked as a consultant on women's health and development for the Pan American World Health Organization. Her recent writings on hunger for Bread for the World, a nonprofit organization, were published as part of a study on hunger in 1990. "Patriotic Prostitutes" is excerpted from an article that appeared in *The Progressive* (February 1985).

Gay quotes *World View 1984*: "Between 70 and 80 percent of male tourists who travel from Japan, the United States, Australia, and Western Europe to Asia do so solely for the purpose of sexual entertainment." When asked whether the situation had changed during the years since her article first appeared, Gay remarked that the statistics might have changed, but the situation remains almost the same. Women in the Philippines, Japan, and other Asian countries are becoming more active in trying to stop the sex trade, however. Of the roughly two dozen Asian countries, Gay focuses on three as providers of sex for hire: Thailand, the Philippines, and South Korea. All three are ancient nations with distinct ethnic and cultural heritages, altered dramatically by contact with the West.

Thailand lies between Burma and Laos on a peninsula across the Bay of Bengal from India. Inhabited for the last 20,000 years, it is the only Southeast Asian country never to have been taken over by a European power. King Mongkut and his son Chulalongkorn, who reigned from 1851 to 1910, modernized Thailand (then Siam); signed trade treaties with both Britain and France; ceded Laos and Cambodia to France; and hired the English teacher Anna Leonowens, from whose memoirs came the musical play *The King and I*. A coup in 1932 limited the monarchy and let in military control, which has persisted off and on to the present. Disrupted by Japanese occupation in World War II, surrounded by conflict in Vietnam, Laos, and Cambodia, inundated with foreign soldiers and refugees, Thailand has undergone more than two dozen coups in half a century.

Farther east is the Philippines, a republic of more than 7,000 islands extending northward from Malaysia and Indonesia off the coast of Vietnam. After Ferdinand Magellan brought the Philippines to Europe's attention in 1521, Spain took control of the archipelago, forcing a mass conversion to Roman Catholicism. Following the Spanish-American War of 1898, Spain ceded the islands to the United States, which proclaimed their independence on July 4, 1946. The present government is modeled on that of the United States; English as well as Pilipino are official languages. From 1965 to 1986 (and at the time this article first appeared) the Philippine president was Ferdinand Marcos, whose dictatorial regime had U.S. support until the assassination of opposition leader Benigno Aquino swept Aquino's widow, Corazón, into the presidency.

Due north of the Philippines is Korea, a peninsula jutting southward from China toward Japan. Annexed by Japan in 1910, Korea was divided after World War II into the northern, Soviet-controlled Democratic People's Republic of Korea and the southern, U.S.-controlled Republic of Korea. Although both powers soon withdrew, efforts at reunification failed. In 1950 North Korean troops invaded the South, pitting their Chinese backers against United Nations troops (mostly from the United States) who supported South Korea. The Korean War ended with an armistice in 1953. Currently two-thirds of the population lives in South Korea, which has been tightly controlled by its presidents since the republic was established in 1948.

Germany's Rosie Travel sells sex tours to Thailand. "Anything goes in this exotic country," says the company's brochure. "Especially when it comes to girls. Still, it appears to be a problem for visitors to Thailand to find the right places where they can indulge in unknown pleasures. . . . Rosie has done something about this. . . . You can book a trip to Thailand with erotic pleasures included in the price."

Japan Air Lines (JAL) is a little more subtle. "In order to embellish and relish better the nights of Korea," its brochure advises, "you must start above all else with a Kisaeng party." In South Korea, Kisaeng women were traditionally hired to sing and dance at parties; today, however, the word is synonymous with prostitute. "A night spent with a consummate Kisaeng girl dressed in a gorgeous Korean blouse and skirt is just perfect," continues the JAL pamphlet. Kisaeng parties, it adds, have "become one of the nation's most charming attractions."

"I felt I was picking out a slave girl at a slave market," says one Japanese tourist about his visit to Korea.

The international sex trade has reached shocking proportions. Between 4 70 and 80 percent of male tourists who travel from Japan, the United States, Australia, and Western Europe to Asia do so solely for the purpose of sexual entertainment, according to *World View 1984*, a French political almanac. The Thai police estimated in 1982 that there were 700,000 prostitutes in the country — about 10 percent of all Thai women between the ages of fifteen and thirty. A 1982 International Labor Organization (ILO) study found some 500,000 prostitutes in Bangkok alone. In the Philippines, an estimated 200,000 prostitutes operate; in South Korea, 260,000.

But far from being alarmed by these figures, leaders of the affected countries are spurring the trade along. "Within the next two years, we are going to need money," said Thailand's vice premier, talking to a meeting of provincial governors in 1980. "Therefore, I ask of all governors to consider the natural scenery in your provinces, together with some forms of entertainment that some of you might consider disgusting and shameful because they are forms of sexual entertainment that attract tourists.

"Such forms of entertainment should not be prohibited . . . because you are morally fastidious. . . . We must do this because we have to consider the jobs that will be created for the people."

In South Korea, the government sponsors an "orientation program" where prostitutes are issued identification cards that serve as hotel passes.

"You girls must take pride in your devotion to your country," the 8 women are told at the orientation sessions. "Your carnal conversations with foreign tourists do not prostitute either yourself or the nation, but express your heroic patriotism."

Though prostitution is called the world's oldest profession, the boom in Southeast Asia started with the U.S. presence in Vietnam. There were 20,000 prostitutes in Thailand in 1957; by 1964, after the United States established seven bases in the country, that number had skyrocketed to 400,000. Throughout the war, Bangkok was a favorite "rest-and-recreation" (R&R) spot for GIs. Similarly, the number of R&R centers in the Philippines increased from 20 to 600. And in South Vietnam itself, there were about 400,000 prostitutes at the height of the war — almost one for every GI.

"Saigon has become an American brothel," Senator J. William Fulbright noted. And the South Vietnamese government didn't seem to mind. "The Americans need girls; we need dollars," one official said. "Why should we refrain from the exchange? It's an inexhaustible source of U.S. dollars for the State."

When the American soldiers left in the mid-1970s, "the post-Vietnam slack was picked up by tourism," says an activist with Friends of Women, an organization based in Bangkok. The area around the U.S. military base at Subic Bay and the R&R center in Olongapo — both in the Philippines — are the largest bases for prostitution in Asia. But something more than the presence of soldiers accounts for the flourishing business.

"Sex tourism in the Philippines really took off during the period after 12 1972 when martial law was declared, and the government gave priority to export promotion," says Irene Santiago, a Filipina community organizer. "We needed a lot of dollars in order to pay off the foreign debt, so tourism was a major thrust for dollar earning. And with that, came the sex tourists — mainly from Japan." Currently, as the economy of the Philippines deteriorates, "the government feels there is a more urgent need to earn foreign exchange," adds Santiago, "so there's been a proliferation of prostitutes now."

The Manila Midtown Ramada Inn hands out a printed sheet "to our Japanese guests with ladies" that lists the charges for taking a woman to a room. One source reported in 1979 that the Manila Ramada made 40 percent of its income from extra fees for prostitutes.

In South Korea, massive investments have been made in resort areas for the sex trade, and the government is counting on billions of dollars in tourism revenues to help cover a foreign debt that exceeds $20 billion.

The sex trade has also figured in Thailand's economic development strategy, which calls for reducing investment in agriculture and aggressively pushing the export of goods produced in the cities. In a typical village in the north, as many as one-third of the families have no land, and three-quarters have less than the two acres needed for subsistence. Many send their daughters to Bangkok to work as prostitutes.

And some women opt for the profession because they don't care to 16 work in the hazardous export-oriented plants. "You get cancer working in factories, we get abortion and VD working as prostitutes," one woman says. Prostitution now vies with sugar as Thailand's second largest producer of foreign exchange.

Taew grew up as one of eight children in northern Thailand. Her two elder sisters worked as prostitutes to American GIs at the base at Udon. When the U.S. Air Force left in 1975, her sisters came back to farm the land. But the soil was too poor to support them, so they went back to work as prostitutes in the cities. Then they got married, and the family lost its major source of income.

So Taew was sent to Bangkok to find work. She made $1.50 a day mixing cement and steel, then $20 a month as a housemaid. Later she tried waitressing. Still struggling, she was finally persuaded to sell her virginity for $400, of which she received $100. Taew sent her earnings home so her family could build a well for drinking water.

After her parents kept writing letters asking for more money, Taew went back to work as a prostitute, frequenting the Grace Hotel.

The Grace Hotel does not employ prostitutes, but it makes its coffee 20
shop available as a marketplace. The owner charges an entrance fee of $2. Women who come to the Grace Hotel are usually on the way down in the market. They are not so attractive, having lost the sweet and innocent look, and are heavily made up. Men who come to the Grace Hotel are searching for specific styles of sex that they have difficulty finding elsewhere. They bargain. In the lounge of the hotel, men in their sixties can be seen propositioning girls in their teens.

Taew's story is not an aberration. Indeed, the ILO study found that of fifty prostitutes interviewed, all but four mail money home. Most sent one-third to one-half of their earnings, sums essential to their rural families' survival.

Pasuk Phongpaichit, author of the ILO study, says she first met a woman named Lek in a so-called massage parlor, which was actually a brothel. "She still had the look of a little girl, and her figure was not fully developed," recalls Phongpaichit. "When asked if she liked the job, she said she did not. She would like to go home."

But she couldn't go home. Lek's employer had lent her parents some money; it was up to Lek to work for the employer as repayment for the loan. She figured she would have to work 150 hours more, but then her parents took out another loan to pay for her grandparents' medical bills. Lek was their only source of income.

Many times, the prostitutes' earnings are meager. Airlines, travel agen- 24
cies, hotels, madams, pimps — all take a chunk of the prostitutes' earnings. Korea Church Women United estimates that prostitutes receive less than one-thirtieth of the fees their patrons pay.

But the hazards of the business are borne by the prostitutes alone. "After having my body ravaged by several customers in a row, I just get too tired to move my limbs," one prostitute says. "At times like this, a shot of heroin is needed. This enables me to handle five or six men in a single night. I can't help but take the drug in order to keep myself in working condition."

The United Nations Fund for Population Activities disclosed that out of 1,000 prostitutes studied in Thailand, one-quarter were regular users of drugs, particularly speed, barbiturates, and heroin; 41 percent of the prostitutes had venereal disease, and 19 percent had undergone abortions, which are prohibited by law in Thailand (and therefore often hazardous).

Suicides are not uncommon. One woman killed herself after observing her own naked body in a mirror. It was covered with scars inflicted by a man who used lit cigarettes. Another woman, as recounted in a Korean newspaper story a few years ago, tried unsuccessfully to escape, but failed.

"At one o'clock every night, a guard locked the door of my room and took away the key," the woman said. "In the daytime, a receptionist kept a constant watch over the entrance. Since all ground-floor windows were covered with iron grids, it was impossible to think of escaping through them. Even when I went to the bathhouse, someone was sent along to guard me." So she jumped out of a second-story window — and now is paralyzed from the waist down.

Women's groups around the world have begun to mobilize against the international big business of prostitution. In 1982, Dutch women held a protest at the Amsterdam airport near a departing plane to Bangkok, dubbed the "gonorrhea express." When the jet landed in Bangkok, it was greeted by another demonstration, held by Friends of Women and other Thai feminists.

In the Philippines as well, women have protested the sex trade. When then–Prime Minister Zenko Suzuki of Japan visited the Philippines in 1981, "the Japanese women's groups were able to link up with Philippine women's groups," recalls Irene Santiago. The protest was coordinated by the Filipina Organization, Third World Movement Against the Exploitation of Women, and it "really embarrassed the Prime Minister on his state visit," Santiago says. "They presented him with a letter of protest saying that this is a shame on the Japanese people, and that he should put a stop to the whole thing. That really got the attention of the press. And it actually stopped Japanese sex tours for a while."

Currently, the Catholic Women's League, other church groups, and even the mayor have been holding rallies against sex tourism in the Philippines town of Sebu, a new center of the trade.

Such demonstrations are essential if the sex trade is to come to a halt. But they are not likely to succeed unless there are more profound changes, both in the presence of the U.S. military and in the export-oriented development strategies of Asian countries that depend on foreign exchange — at the expense of their most impoverished women.

EXPLORATIONS

1. According to Gay, why do so many Asian women become prostitutes? What positive and negative factors keep women in the job once they start it?
2. What are the reasons for a government to encourage prostitution? How do the countries involved benefit from the sex trade? What reasons exist for these countries to discourage prostitution?
3. In countries that promote prostitution, how does the government encourage women to participate? In what ways do you think the government's encouragement helps to maintain the supply of prostitutes?

CONNECTIONS

1. Gay in "Patriotic Prostitutes" and David Abram in "Making Magic" present radically different pictures of life in Southeast Asia. What factors appear to be responsible for the difference?
2. What common ideas about work appear in Gay's "Patriotic Prostitutes" and R. K. Narayan's "Trail of the Green Blazer"? What is the relationship between morality and economics in each selection?
3. In Shiva Naipaul's "The Palmers," Mrs. Palmer says of the local workers: "Many actually prefer to be beggars and prostitutes in Nairobi than to earn an honest living from the soil." After reading "Patriotic Prostitutes," how do you think Gay would answer Mrs. Palmer?

ELABORATIONS

1. After seeing *Jaws*, in which a shark terrorizes a New England seaside town, Cuba's Premier Fidel Castro is said to have applauded the film's splendid socialist message: The town officials' refusal to close their beaches (said Castro) showed that capitalists value a chance to make money more than human life and safety. Is this true? Write an essay criticizing prostitution in Asia from a

socialist's point of view. Or write an essay from a capitalist's point of view rebutting the socialist argument.

2. In *Looking at Ourselves*, Elliot Liebow writes about unskilled workers and their middle-class critics. How does Liebow's analysis apply to the women in "Patriotic Prostitutes"? What problems do these women share with Fadik in Yashar Kemal's "A Dirty Story" (p. 371)? Write an essay on the clash between morality and practicality for people at the bottom of the economic ladder: What can and should they do for themselves? What can and should others (such as the government and private employers) do to help, deter, or punish them?

GEOFFREY MATTHEWS

"Good Sons" Who Kill

Colombia, the northwesternmost country in South America, is known in the United States for two of its biggest export crops: coffee and drugs. Colombian marijuana is legendary among U.S. users, but it is cocaine that has turned the country into a battleground. With strong political and economic encouragement from the United States, where tons of coca products are ultimately marketed, the Colombian government cracked down on the powerful Medellín cartel that controls the flow of coca plants from processing to distribution. The cartel struck back by assassinating judges who conducted trials on drug charges, political officials and candidates, and other figures involved in the drug war. This violent struggle forms the background for "'Good Sons' Who Kill," which originally appeared in the *Times* of London and was published in the United States by *World Press Review* in November 1989.

Geoffrey Matthews, a free-lance writer working for the *Times* of London, was living in Bogota, Colombia, until his death of a heart attack in early 1990. "'Good Sons' Who Kill" illustrates his interest in penetrating the surface of the news to reveal disturbing contradictions.

(For more background on Colombia, see p. 531.)

They come from Manrique, these youths who attend Mass regularly, venerate the local virgins, donate alms generously, and would never be caught naked on a mortuary slab — always an occupational hazard in their business — without silver chains bearing crucifix pendants around their necks. Their mothers insist they are "good sons" who take their family responsibilities seriously, an opinion confirmed by local priests.

Manrique is the oldest, toughest, most legendary working-class quarter of Medellín, Colombia's second city. In Latin American cities there is always a district like Manrique, marking a frontier between the haves and have-nots. Just north of the bustling city center, Manrique signals the demarcation line between the beauty and relative prosperity of what is still, miraculously, one of South America's most attractive, well-run provincial cities and a vast urban no man's land ranging from dangerous mean streets to shantytowns perched perilously on steep hillsides.

From Manrique has sprung a terrifying phenomenon variously known as the killing machines, guns for hire, contract-killers, or — in the trade's own jargon — "dispatchers" of "packages" to a "definitive goodbye." Medellín has the world's highest homicide rate: more than 4,000 murders last year in a population of 2.5 million.

This phenomenon was created by the Medellín drug cartel, said to   4 control about 80 percent of the world's cocaine business, in its war against the Colombian government. For the cartel, the hoodlums had several virtues: Their folk heroes were the top mafiosi; their services came cheap; and they were expendable. The first baby-faced assassins, a decade ago, were chosen for their almost Olympic abilities to shoot moving targets. Subsequent generations of gunmen rode on souped-up motorcycles, weaving their way through heavy traffic to shoot sitting targets.

The pinnacle of the assassin's profession is a call from the cocaine cartel, since the "package" will be important and surrounded by body-guards, the job dangerous, and the contract correspondingly high — worth several thousand "narco-dollars" if it can be pulled off. Such calls are likened to a lottery win, and assiduous competition makes the odds just as long. For regular income the killers are forced to accept more mundane assignments at bargain-basement prices. For about $150, a jealous husband can have his wife's lover rubbed out, or a "snake" (bad debtor) can be sent to the cemetery. The victim of an insult can take revenge for maybe $100. The gunmen are also in demand among street gangs vying for domination of the *basuco* market (the local variety of crack).

In a bizarre way, the rise of the teen-age gunmen is a new manifestation of the upward mobility for which the *paisas* — the people of Antioquia Province, whose capital is Medellín — have always been famed. The region is a fascinating mix of Spanish, Jewish, Catholic, and Protestant traditions. It was settled in the seventeenth century by Basques and by Spanish Jews who had been converted to Christianity. They intermarried and produced huge families.

But Antioquia also prides itself on being the most profoundly Roman Catholic region of Colombia. Three years ago, when Pope John Paul II visited Colombia, he was visibly moved by the warmth and religious fervor that greeted him in Medellín, vowing that if he ever had to relocate the Vatican, he would move it to that city.

Dedication to work and religious faith are the keys to the *paisa* char-   8 acter. They come together in what may be an apocryphal, though telling, story. A man marked for murder returned to his home in Medellín to find a gunman waiting for him. He begged for his life and offered money to dissuade the killer, all to no avail. Finally, resigned to his fate, he asked for a few moments to pray. The gunman withdrew to a respectful distance and, when the victim had finished, bade him the *definitivo adiós.*

After carrying out a lucrative contract, the killers often pay for a special Mass to give thanks at the same time the victim's funeral Mass is taking place elsewhere. "They find no contradiction between their beliefs and their activity, which they regard as a job and nothing more," says a local academic. Observers have noted the assassins' keen sense of commitment to their families. They buy expensive domestic appliances for their (usually single) mothers and subsidize their younger brothers' and sisters' education. They spurn brothels and pool halls, do not drink or use drugs, and keep in peak condition. Their career span is short, starting at fifteen, burnt-out — or dead — by twenty-five.

"You burn up a lot of adrenalin in this line of work," one young murderer told Elizabeth Mora, a sociologist. "It's a real son of a bitch to know that if you fail, you're the one who's going to end up dead." In some of the most notorious assassinations backed by the Medellín cartel, those who hired the killers murdered them, thus breaking the chain of intermediaries back to what under Colombian law are called the "intellectual authors" of the crime.

These violent young men are themselves children — or, more exactly, grandchildren — of violence. In the early 1950s, north Medellín mushroomed as peasants invaded the city to flee La Violencia, a sectarian conflict between liberals and conservatives in which an estimated 300,000 perished. Today in Manrique and northward, priests have noted with alarm that children play a new game of make-believe, pointing two fingers, revolver-style, and shouting: "Bang, bang, you're dead." Their role models are *los sicarios de sueldo* — the contract-killers.

EXPLORATIONS

1. For readers to appreciate Matthews's essay, they must share certain values and assumptions with the author. What are these values and assumptions?

2. What positive qualities does Matthews mention about Medellín and its people? How would the effect of his essay change if he mentioned only negative qualities?

3. How many sources of information does Matthews cite by name? How would the essay's impact change if more people were named or quoted or both? Why do you think Matthews uses so few direct quotations and citations?

CONNECTIONS

1. What cultural, economic, and personal characteristics do the contract killers in Matthews's "'Good Sons' Who Kill" share with the prostitutes in Jill Gay's "Patriotic Prostitutes"? What differences between these two groups seem to be significant?

2. Having read both Matthews's essay and Gay's, do you think Matthews has underestimated the inner conflict of "'good sons' who kill"? Which of his statements support the quoted comment that these young men "find no contradiction between their beliefs and their activity"? Which statements contradict this comment?

3. Look back at the interview with "Racketeer," a teenage Los Angeles gang member in *Looking at Ourselves* (p. 196). What are the similarities and differences between Racketeer's and the Colombian teenagers' reasons for, and responses to, killing people?

ELABORATIONS

1. Matthews's "'Good Sons' Who Kill," Gay's "Patriotic Prostitutes," and R. K. Narayan's "Trail of the Green Blazer" all show people making a living at some activity that conflicts with the rules of their culture. Write a cause-and-effect or argumentative essay examining some aspect of this conflict, such as the reasons for their choice, the price they pay for breaking the rules, or the validity of the rules.

2. Do people always act in accord with their beliefs? Think of a contradiction you have noticed between some person's or group's beliefs and actions: a religious sect that preaches universal love but practices discrimination, perhaps, or a vegetarian who wears fur and leather. Write an essay in which, as Matthews does, you describe the contradiction without openly judging it.

SATOSHI KAMATA

Six Months at Toyota

"Six Months at Toyota" comes from Satoshi Kamata's book *Japan in the Passing Lane*. Born in 1938, Kamata graduated from Waseda University in 1964. After working briefly for a trade paper in the steel industry and as an editor for a popular general magazine, he became a full-time free-lance reporter. He continues to write frequently about Japanese industry and labor.

The book's translator, Tatsuru Akimoto, writes: "The impetus for *Japan in the Passing Lane,* Kamata's third book, came in large part from conversations with a friend who had been a seasonal worker for several years at Honda manufacturing plants. . . . Kamata wanted to experience the situation firsthand and chose Toyota because he had heard that the working conditions there were much harsher than at other automobile plants in Japan. Kamata stayed at Toyota for the full term of his six-month contract, and the diary he kept there forms the basis of this book. Kamata was married, and while he worked at Toyota his wife and two small children lived at home a few hundred miles away." *Japan in the Passing Lane* was first published in Japan in 1973 and updated in 1980; it appeared in the United States in 1982.

(For more background on Japan, see p. 134.)

Monday, September 18

My first workday. Up at 5:00 A.M. It's still dark when I go out. The eastern mountains are glowing faintly, but I can still see the stars shining brightly in the sky. The street is lit by a few scattered lamps. It's a forty-minute walk to the factory. Unfortunately, the plant I have to work in is at the farthest corner of the factory compound. I can't find the canteen and miss breakfast.

I have really been fooled by the seeming slowness of the conveyor belt. No one can understand how it works without experiencing it. Almost as soon as I begin, I am dripping with sweat. Somehow, I learn the order of the work motions, but I'm totally unable to keep up with the speed of the line. My work gloves make it difficult to grab as many tiny bolts as I need, and how many precious seconds do I waste doing just that? I do my best, but I can barely finish one gear box out of three within the fixed length of time. If a different-model transmission comes along, it's simply beyond my capacity. Some skill is needed, and a new hand like me can't do it alone. I'm thirsty as hell, but workers can neither smoke nor drink water. Going to the toilet is out of the question. Who could have invented a system like this? It's designed to make workers do nothing *but* work and to prevent any kind of rest. Yet the man beside me the other day deftly handled his hammer, put the bolts into their grooves with both hands, and fastened them with a nut runner (a power screwdriver that can tighten six bolts simultaneously), seemingly with no difficulty.

The conveyor starts at 6:00 A.M. and doesn't stop until 11:00 A.M. One box of transmissions arrives on the conveyor belt every minute and twenty seconds with unerring precision. When the line stops at eleven o'clock, we tear off our gloves and leave our positions as quickly as we can. We wash our greasy hands and run to the toilet, then rush to the canteen about a hundred yards away where we wait in another line to get our food. After standing five hours, my legs are numb and stiff. My new safety shoes are so heavy that I feel I can barely move. I put my ticket into a box, take an aluminum tray, a pair of chopsticks, a plate of food, a tea cup, and a bowl of rice. I'm still unfamiliar with the routine and have a hard time finding a seat at one of the long tables. Finally, just as I'm settling down to eat, I have the sensation that the trays on the table are moving slowly sideways as if they're on a conveyor belt! At 11:45, the line starts again. There's not much time to rest since ten minutes before work starts we have to begin preparing a large enough supply of parts for the afternoon assemblage.

Above the line, a little to my right, there's a big electric display panel. Under the words "Transmission Assembly Conveyor," there are numbers from 1 to 15. When it is absolutely impossible to catch up with the conveyor, you have to push a button under the belt. This lights up your number in yellow on the board. To halt the line in an emergency, you have to push another button, which triggers a red light and stops the line. Although there are fifteen buttons on the line, there are now only eight workers. To increase production, Toyota decided to use two shifts starting this month. September is the beginning of the high-demand season, and I'm in the first group of seasonal workers hired under this new schedule.

The first shift ends at 2:15 P.M. Already, the man on the next shift is standing beside me, waiting for me to finish. As soon as I put my hammer down on the belt, he picks it up and begins precisely where I left off. A baton pass, and neatly done, too.

Still, it turns out I'm not finished! I have to spend thirty more minutes replenishing the supply parts for the afternoon shift. I also have to pick up the parts I've scattered on the floor. Damn! My legs ache the entire forty-minute walk back to the dorm. I'm bone tired. Is this the life for a worker in a great enterprise, a famous auto company, proud of being tops in Japan and the third in the world? Somehow I'll have to get used to it.

Tonight Kudo, who had left at eight in the morning, comes back a little after seven. He also had to work two hours overtime. For some reason, the lights in the dorms have gone out. It's really depressing to return to a dark room after walking all the way from the plant.

Kudo is lying spread-eagled on the mat floor. "I didn't quite expect the work to be so hard," he says. Still, he tells me somewhat proudly that he's made 400 pieces today. I don't know how many I made myself, or for that matter, don't really know what I was making. Exactly what part of the gear box were they? I was much too busy to look at the other guys' operations. I didn't even have time to look at my watch. After a while, I felt like I was making some part of a child's plastic toy. What was I really doing? The sign in my shop has a word for it — "Assembly"!

Tonight, I'm too tired to sleep and awfully nervous about having to get up early tomorrow. I get up and go out to buy a can of beer. A picture of Ken Takakura, a famous actor, smiles down at me from the vending machine. Even beer is sold by machines. . . .

Thursday, September 28

I went to take a bath downstairs this morning. When I came out, my wooden clogs were gone. You're not often robbed these days, even in public baths. When I went to the dining room, there was nothing left to eat. Here every day is a small war.

There is a Safety First meeting ten minutes before the shift begins. It's not fair for management to force a meeting on the workers during their off time, but no one protests.

There are some complaints among the workers. When the company declared an increase in output, it promised that ten workers from another plant would be sent here as reinforcements. In the end, only eight came.

The only way not to hold up the line was to offset the labor shortage by working overtime. Workers are angry.

"What we can't do, we can't do," one worker says. "The company should be satisfied."

"If we really care about Safety First," another says, "why don't they hire more workers? That's top priority."

But still, when the time comes, we all return to work without protest. By 10:00 P.M. everyone is exhausted. It is all I can do to keep my hands in motion on the line. But strangely, time passes and the line moves on, and somehow each day's work ends.

I'm responsible for assembling two kinds of truck transmissions, and   16
by now I can do about 90 percent of the required work. I'd give anything just to keep up with the murderous conveyor. I hate having to push the button to call the team chief and reveal my incompetence again and again.

Takeda, whose position is next to mine, helps me sometimes by rushing through his own work to give me a whole minute of his precious time. "Tell me how to do it and I'll help you. My job is simple. I can spare the minute."

I know he really can't spare the minute. Nobody on the line can afford the luxury of helping others. I am touched.

But there's another side to Takeda's generosity. He's dying from the monotony of his own work. I'm thankful for his help, of course, but Takeda also wants to try something new and strange, something that breaks the deadly boredom, the relentless repetition of the assembly line. There, where no amount of intelligence, creativity, or freedom is permitted, he can release some tension and refresh his energy by helping me, and that helps him get through the day.

Almost all the workers here are hardworking. In most factories, there   20
are those who work very hard and those who don't. But here, the conveyor-belt system makes everyone work at exactly the same pace. Even off the line, we all begin preparing parts even before our shift starts, time which is still our supper break, for without this preparation we'd never get the work done.

It is raining when work finishes. I am depressed, already worrying if I will make it through to next February, when my contract expires. Takeda asks Yoshizaki, who happens to live near my dorm, to give me a lift.

The joint at the base of my right third finger is numb. I can't bend it at all. . . .

Thursday, October 5

A meeting after work. Mostly, we talk about our section manager's new order to check the tightness of all six bolts in the transmission. It's impossible for us to add one more operation. We're already too pressed for time. The team chief tries to force it on us, using the oldest excuse in the world:

"It's an order from the section manager."   24

One worker answers coldly, "Well, if it's an order, it's an order. But the line's going to stop."

"I don't care. Let it stop."

"You say you don't care? But the people on the second shift will have to work overtime to make up for us."

Another worker exclaims, "They'll have to work until two or three   28 o'clock in the morning! That's impossible. What sort of people do the management think we are?"

Everybody starts complaining all at once. Finally, the general foreman, a stout man with a white cap, proposes a compromise: "Well, we'll try measuring at only one point. I'll ask the management about it."

"One place is plenty!" someone shouts in disgust.

Suddenly the section manager, who issued the order, comes in. He's still young, about forty. The general foreman tells us rather ceremoniously, "Please pay special attention to safety." Then he stands and leaves in spite of our anger. The meeting has "ended." We also stand and leave the narrow locker room. As we're filing out, someone tells the section manager, "You've got to think more about us," but the words no longer have an icy edge. They're more like a joke. Even the experienced workers are getting upset. I'm relieved to know that others are as discontented as I am. . . .

Thursday, January 11

When I went to work last night, I knew immediately something was   32 wrong. The team chief on the other shift stood there rather uneasily, and the workers who had just arrived surrounded him. I asked Miura, who works with me, if there had been an accident. He said that Kawamura, a seasonal worker, had been severely shocked. Kawamura is a young man from Hokkaido, where he worked as a carpenter. They carried him to the Toyota Hospital, and he'll probably be there for more than a week.

Before work started, the general foreman made one of his little speeches: "Kawamura's biorhythm chart shows that today is his worst day. Looks like the chart was right!"

The workers knew the real story. Going to get some parts he needed, Kawamura crossed over two small conveyor belts and touched a machine. But the machine (a parts feeder that fits washers in bolts) was so old that some of a 200-volt electric cord was frayed. And his gloves were wet. He received a severe shock and fell to the floor. He suffered a concussion and lost consciousness. Luckily the current passed through the base of his finger. If it had gone near his heart, he would have been killed instantly.

On the day of the accident, his team was short of workers, since two people hadn't showed up and one seasonal worker had quit. Superficially, the cause of the accident was that he took a shortcut to get the parts, but the real cause was the short circuit in the old machine, and also, the fact that there was no bridge over the line. But according to the general foreman (who's also a member of the union!), the problem was in the worker's biorhythm, and the key to safety is for all of us to be careful when our own biorhythms are bad.

This year's new slogan is written on the company's blackboard: "What-   36
ever you do, be prepared to take responsibility for it." . . .

Thursday, January 18

They say we made 425 boxes today. Though we have no time to count, our production has increased by 25 boxes a day. Soon we'll be making 450 boxes a day. When I get back tonight, I find Kudo still there.

"Aren't you going to work?"

"No, not today. Not tomorrow, either."

"Are you feeling bad?"   40

"I'm leaving. Today I fell on the floor unconscious," he says, looking at me weakly.

Last night he worked the night shift, but as soon as he started, he felt sick. He tried to keep on working. When he checked the clock, it was 12:50 A.M. Ten minutes to go until the break for the midnight meal. When he looked at the clock again, three minutes had passed. Seven more minutes, he thought, and then he fell on the floor. When he came to he was lying on a bench, covered with the coat he had just bought. Someone must have opened his locker and put it over him. The foreman, who was standing beside him, told him that right after he fell, they had carried him to the Toyota Hospital, just outside the factory grounds. They had given him an injection, and then he had been transferred to the infirmary inside the factory. It was already morning when he came to. Why hadn't they left him to sleep in a soft hospital bed?

When he was carried to the hospital again, Kudo told them about the traffic accident he'd had before. The general foreman told Kudo, "Once you fall, you can't work any more. I'll see that your account is settled. Rest well at home, and then come and see us again." That was all; he was fired.

"At least I'm glad I'm alive," Kudo adds. "Well, I won't worry. Anyway, they need someone at home to shovel the snow off the roof. It's only forty-six days till the end of my contract, though. Then I could have gotten my bonus." His voice becomes choked with emotion and he can't talk any more.

I recall how he worked from eight to eight, but he reported to the shop an hour early to prepare for work, wash parts, and melt wax. He wasn't paid for these jobs, but without doing them he wouldn't have been able to keep up with his work. He's a real craftsman. He wants to do his job well. Both of us just sit looking at each other for a while, and finally he speaks: "I'm feeling much better. I could go to work right now." . . .

Sunday, February 4

I rarely have time to sit and talk with the others in my team. But when we do talk over a glass of sake, they speak frankly of their discontent, even to a seasonal worker like me.

Worker A's story:

"Now the work is nearly three times tougher than when I came here six or seven years ago. Around 1965, they measured our work by stopwatch. Since then it's been getting tougher. But until a couple of years ago we still had enough workers, and the line used to stop ten minutes before finishing time. After the Tsutsumi plant was built in December 1970, everything really got worse. They changed from the daytime single shift to the two-consecutive-shift system, and now we've got day and night split shifts with time between shifts. And they keep speeding up the line. The faster the line gets, the harder we work to catch up, because we want to go home quickly. But when we finally get used to the speed, then they make it even faster. Right now it's a minute and fourteen seconds per unit, but I bet they'll speed it up. The new guys can't handle it any more. You read in the newspapers that Toyota workers are quick and active. We're not quick. We're forced to work quickly. It's the ones up there who benefit by exploiting us down here. I'm sure the section managers know very well how hard a time we're having. And the union, they're supported by our money, but they only work for the company. You can't expect anything from them because the leaders are all general foremen and foremen. They change every year, so nobody has enough time to get into the job seriously. If you complain to them, they just tell you to 'cooperate' and say, 'Unless you produce more your salary will not go up.'

"Two years ago we talked about ending overtime, but we realized that we couldn't make ends meet without it, so nothing changed. Personally, I enjoy physical labor. I like to work with my hands. But here, it's just too fast. I guess I can put up with the hard pace, but the trouble is I never know when I can go home. When I come home all I do is take a bath, have something to eat, and go to bed. I don't have more than an hour to talk with my wife. Nowadays I vomit whenever I'm not feeling well, and if I go see a doctor at Toyota Hospital, he just tells me to get back to work."

B's Story:

"You know Yamashita lost his finger, don't you? Or was that before you came? Anyway, during the break — we were on the second shift — the section manager came and made a speech on safety for about thirty minutes. So we were late for supper, and there were no noodles left at the canteen. We had some rice, but we all like to have a bowl of noodles at the end of the meal, you know. Afterwards we complained about this to the section manager. Then he took ten dollars out of his pocket and gave it to us. We handed it to our foreman, and he went out on his bicycle to buy some bread and ice cream. When he came back we stopped the line and sat around and ate. I was impressed. It was an amazing thing. I've decided to work for this section manager, and as long as he's here, I won't take any days off. I may be a fool, but I've never heard of anything like that happening at Toyota. Nobody would spend ten dollars out of his pocket for us. The section managers all think they have nothing to do with us.

"When I first came here the job was so tough I thought of quitting. I remember one morning I woke up and discovered I couldn't move my wrist. I wondered why I had to do work like this. And then I thought, once I've mastered the job it'll be a lot easier, and this idea kept me going. The people who stay here are the ones who have no other place to go and who like to endure pain. But in the end, we'll all be crushed by Toyota. There's hardly anyone at Toyota I can trust.

"The union? I hear they buy it off with women. I don't know if it's true or not, but I can't think of any other way. We all want to go home earlier. If you ask anybody, they'll say 'We don't want any more money, but let us go home without overtime.' When we come home late after overtime, we hardly have time to look at our wives, and they complain. That adds insult to injury. But they don't know what we go through. And I guess they'd better not find out. If they did, they'd tell us to quit. I don't want my wife to see what I'm doing here — it would make me feel even worse. I work for the sake of my children, and my only enjoyment here is having a good laugh over dumb jokes during the lunch break. Other than that, I don't have any hopes for this job.

"If you quit, Kamata, another guy'll take your place. With a new worker, the line'll stop again, and we won't be able to go home until we finish the day's quota. We'll be up shit creek."

Toyota's current slogan is "Toyota . . . Cars to Love, the World Over." On television, a charming film star, Sayuri Yoshinaga, smiles and says, "It's the car with distinction, the car for someone special." The people who buy the cars never realize that they were made, quite literally, over the dead and mutilated bodies of workers who were given no "distinction" at all. . . .

Thursday, February 15

I wake up around five this morning and hear the clatter of empty cans 56 echoing coldly on concrete as someone sorts them out of the trash cans. At 6:45 the sound of the morning chimes blares over the loudspeaker. Soon, I hear car engines warming up in the parking lot below my window. Then the clatter and hiss and banging of the heating system being turned on. Bright sunshine falls in through the cracks of my curtains. Fine weather. I couldn't sleep last night and stayed up until one. I was excited and nervous wondering if I could hold out one more day . . .

At the end of the morning meeting, the foreman orders me to stand beside him in the center of a circle and says, "Thank you very much for working with us for such a long time." He seems sincere. During the lunch break, as I walk to the canteen, a regular worker joins me.

"Finally finishing, aren't you?"

"Yeah, I'm getting out of this prison."

"Us regulars are condemned to life imprisonment, I guess," he says,   60
looking at the ground.

During the break, a guy I've never had a chance to talk to comes up
to me at the locker-room bench.

"You've only got three-and-a-half hours to go, haven't you? I wish I
did, too. I've got to stay here for life. And no matter how hard I try, I
doubt if I'll ever be able to wear a white general foreman's cap."

"Hey, you better not get too excited yet," someone else says. "I know
a guy, a seasonal, who drank the night he left and went walking with a
girl and got run over by a car."

"Maybe that was the best thing that could've happened," another guy   64
says. "Better to die happy than be killed little by little in this goddamn
factory."

Finally, it's time to go. Shimoyama, who works two positions ahead
of me on the line, keeps coming over to tease me.

"You'll be hit by the impactor at the last second," he says.

"Only thirty minutes left!"

At 4:27 the foreman comes over to take my place. He smiles and says   68
simply, "OK. That's all. You need time to change." Somehow, it is all
too simple. I feel strange, as if resigning means simply changing places
with somebody. I go around the line and say good-bye to everyone.
Shimoyama holds out his hand. Takeda says with a big smile, "Thanks
for everything." One worker says, "If you come back, you'd better get a
softer job in one of the subcontracting companies." The line doesn't let
us stop and talk. The team chief and the deputy section manager in the
office look at me as if I don't exist. I go to the personnel office to get my
pay and pick up some papers for unemployment insurance. My wages
for twelve days' work, including basic pay, overtime, night work, and
other fringe allowances together with the final bonus of $43, come to
$197.40. Net pay: $185.08. As he hands me the money the clerk says,
"Mr. Kamata, you earned it." He knows how it is. "Isn't there anyone
else finishing today?" I ask. "There was one in December." Only two
completed their contracts at the main plant — only Yamamoto and I.
Two! At first I can't believe it. After I get my money, I take a last slow
walk around the place. It all seems so simple and matter-of-fact, putting
an end to such hard work just like that. It isn't so much a feeling of
liberation as of weariness and emptiness. I have a dull pain in my right
wrist; my right fingers are stiff; my palms have shreds of metal in them;

my back is sore all over; I feel continually nauseated. These are the only things I can take with me.

I return to my room and find Hamada still in bed. I show him my pay slip and tell him how to read it. He looks at it closely and says, "I'll try hard to complete my contract." I go to the dormitory office and return my key, name tag, and bedding. The clerk glances at me, but doesn't say anything, not even thank you. I'm still nothing more to them than a thing. My neighbor Miyamoto drives me to the nearest train station. As soon as I sit down I'm overcome by fatigue, cold, and a deep desire to sleep. . . .

When I left Toyota in February 1973, assembly time at the Main Plant for transmissions was one minute and fourteen seconds. This had been shortened by six seconds in the six months since I had begun, while production had been increased by 100 to 415 units. Now, seven years later, the assembly time is forty-five seconds and the production is 690 units. This increase was achieved solely through accelerating the work pace. Knockdown part packing at the Takaoka plant needed sixty minutes for a set (which includes 20 cars) three years ago. Today it takes twelve minutes, and still the manpower has been reduced from 50 to 40. Before, workers stood in front of conveyors; now they rush around from one part to another, pushing mobile work desks with wheels.

At the assembly lines for passenger cars, parts have become larger and have increased in number, owing to exhaust-emission control. In addition, parts for various models come down the line all mixed together because of the simultaneous production of many models. Nevertheless, the speed of the conveyor belts only accelerates. The Tahara plant on the Chita Peninsula, which started its operation in January 1979, recently completed arrangements to produce 5000 small trucks and 5000 Corollas. To fill its manpower needs, many workers were taken from the other Toyota plants. Despite this loss, conveyor belts at each plant are running as if nothing had happened. Many workers have been moved onto the assembly line as "reinforcements." Workers are forced to work on Sundays and holidays. The reinforcement work and Sunday-holiday work are a lubricant without which the conveyors could not run.

At the management-union convention mentioned above, Executive 72 Director Yoshiaki Yamamoto said: "In this day and age of uncertainty and severe competition, we must and shall concentrate our production on popular models and adjust the imbalance of work loads among shops.

So please be cooperative in establishing flexible shop arrangements that will be able to respond quickly to requests for help."

Reinforcement work is feared by workers who have had no work experience on conveyor lines. Most workers begin losing weight within a few days. Even without the everyday work they're expected to do, inexperienced reinforcement workers would be exhausted by such difficult labor in a totally unfamiliar environment. A directive to management ("On Accepting Reinforcement Workers: Daily Guidance and Management") from the Takaoka plant personnel division shows that reinforcement workers have many complaints and dissatisfactions, more than half of which pertain to safety issues. But the guidance policy goes no farther than the following:

> Management personnel and the longtime workers in the shop should "say hello and a few words" to reinforcement workers at least once a day, and unit members should make an effort to create a congenial atmosphere so that the management and senior workers can easily "say hello and a few words." . . . It is not easy for reinforcement workers to speak out.

One evening, I met with workers from various plants. I wanted to know the facts behind Toyota's remarkable production records. What the workers counted on their fingers was the number of suicides — more than twenty in the past year. These were only cases that they remembered at that moment. They told me that in June there were three suicides within a couple of days. There was a twenty-seven-year-old worker at the Takaoka plant who reported to work and then disappeared; he had thrown himself into the sea. A team leader at the same plant drove his car into a reservoir. These were the only cases reported in the newspapers. The other cases were all related by those who had been close to the suicides. There are no statistics.

The number, they said, is particularly high at the Takaoka plant, whose products are popular and whose production cannot keep pace with demand. On June 28, a forty-five-year-old worker at the Tsutsumi plant hanged himself in his company-rented apartment. Around the same time, a Takaoka plant reinforcement worker from the Tsutsumi plant committed suicide in his dormitory by taking sleeping pills. He was depressed after having been blamed by the team leader for his tardiness and forced to "apologize to his fellow workers for the inconvenience he caused." Also around the same time, a team leader of the Maintenance Department in the Head Office hanged himself. A body found at the Takaoka plant dormitory was taken away by a member of the Security Division staff. Afterwards he complained that while playing pinball, he imagined he saw the suicide's face in the glass of the pinball machine. The workers who met with me that evening talked endlessly of similar cases. I had heard rumors of mentally disturbed workers and suicides many times while I worked at Toyota. But the rapid increase in their numbers is frightening.

EXPLORATIONS

1. What are the Toyota factory workers' general and specific complaints about their jobs? What are their sources of job satisfaction? If you were a manager at this plant, what change would be your top priority?

2. What passages on Kamata's first and last days at Toyota suggest that he viewed himself then more as a writer than as a factory worker? What passages in the rest of his narrative show him perceiving himself as a factory worker? How would his experience have been different if he had thought of himself as a writer throughout?

3. At several points Kamata quotes speeches by workers or managers. Why do you, or don't you, believe that these are exact quotations? How would the narrative's effect change if Kamata reported the gist of other people's comments instead of presenting them as dialogue?

CONNECTIONS

1. As reporters covering a line of work, how do Geoffrey Matthews in "'Good Sons' Who Kill" and Kamata in "Six Months at Toyota" differ in their approaches? their goals? their choice of emphasis?

2. At what points in Kamata's narrative and in Jill Gay's "Patriotic Prostitutes" do authorities appeal to workers' loyalty to persuade the workers to do something they would rather not? Do you think the authorities' appeals are justified in the prostitutes' case? in the factory workers' case? Why or why not?

3. "I think everybody ought to quit their job and do what they want to do," says Bill Talcott in *Looking at Ourselves*. What reasons do the Japanese Toyota workers give for not doing this? What other reasons does Kamata suggest, especially in his description of his last day on the job, for why quitting is difficult? To what extent do these same reasons apply to American workers?

ELABORATIONS

1. Imagine that you are an organizer who has come to the Toyota plant to help employees win better working conditions. Write a memo to the section manager describing the problems you think are most urgent, recommending changes, and making a case for the changes you suggest. (Take into account the management attitudes described by Kamata.)

2. Do you think American workers would put up with the conditions Kamata describes? What specific incidents in Kamata's account would draw a different response from Americans than they do from Japanese? Using "Six Months at Toyota," John David Morley's "Acquiring a Japanese Family" (p. 134), and Studs Terkel's and others' passages in *Looking at Ourselves* as references, write an essay comparing and contrasting the attitudes toward authority of American and Japanese workers. (You may also use excerpts from these selections as examples.)

HEDRICK SMITH

Skoro Budet — *It'll Be Here Soon*

Born in Scotland in 1933, Hedrick Smith graduated from Williams College in Massachusetts and studied at Balliol College at Oxford University on a Fulbright scholarship. Smith started his journalism career as a reporter for United Press International in Tennessee. Since 1962 he has worked for the *New York Times,* reporting from Saigon, Cairo, and Washington. From 1971 to 1974 he was *Times* bureau chief in Moscow; he prepared for the trip at Harvard University as a Neiman fellow. The author of several books and many magazine articles, Smith received the Pulitzer Prize for international reporting in 1974, two years after his work at the *Times* helped that paper win the Pulitzer Prize for public service. Since 1976 Smith has been chief *Times* Washington correspondent. He went on leave in 1985 to write *The Power Game: How Washington Works* (1988), an award-winning book that also became the basis for a 1989 PBS-TV special hosted by Smith. *"Skoro Budet — It'll Be Here Soon"* comes from his 1975 book *The Russians,* based on his years in the Soviet Union.

"Skoro Budet" paints a vivid picture of the problems President Mikhail Gorbachev has been attacking with his policy of perestroika (see p. 59). The "Plan" Smith refers to was a central component in the Soviets' pre-perestroika effort to modernize their economy, which was virtually feudal until this century. "It is the Five-Year Plans, launched in 1928 by Stalin to force the pace of industrialization, that are officially credited with multiplying Soviet output fiftyfold from 1913 to 1973 and building the backbone of the Soviet economy," writes Smith. "The Plan comes close to being the fundamental law of the land . . . treated with almost mystical veneration." Because most enterprises in the Soviet Union are state owned, the Plan was extremely comprehensive — as if the U.S. government set production goals for every corporation in the country. As Smith's essay illustrates, the Plan's advantages were more ideological than real. Gorbachev has been trying to replace its lumbering inefficiency with a less centralized, more market-oriented system — so far, with mixed success.

(For more background on the Soviet Union, see pp. 109, 301, and 507.)

"The tempo of work is different for each ten-day period of the month," said Rashid, a stocky, honey-colored factory foreman from Uzbekistan, who was explaining what work was like at the Tashkent Tractor Parts Factory. "Do you know the words — *spyachka, goryachka,* and *likhoradka?*"

Literally, I knew they meant something like hibernation, hot time, and feverish frenzy, but I did not immediately associate them with his factory, so I shook my head. Rashid smiled at my innocence and rubbed a calloused hand across his cheek.

"Those are the nicknames we give the 'decades,' the ten-day periods into which each month is divided," he said. "The first decade is the sleeper time, the second decade is for hot work, and the third decade is like fever." He paused to let me absorb that and went on. "The tempo of work also depends on payday. Normally, we have two paydays a month: one between the fifteenth and twentieth and the other, in the first days of the next month. Two or three days before payday, there is a preholiday feeling and no one is in the mood for working. And two or three days afterward, people are practically sick from drinking and they have to drink off their hangovers."

With variations and embellishments, it was a story repeated by others   4
including Yosif, a tall, slender, middle-aged engineer from a big city in southern Russia who chain-smoked as he talked about the plants where he had worked. To hear his description of Soviet factories that made air-conditioning and refrigeration units was to pass through a Soviet looking glass and to discover a world inside Soviet industry that seemed almost a travesty of the Command Economy imagined in the West to be functioning with monopolistic harmony and monolithic discipline.

"Storming" is what Rashid and Yosif were describing. It is a practice so endemic and essential to the Soviet system that Russians have coined the fancy word *shturmovshchina* to denote the entire national phenomenon of crash programs and the wildly erratic work rhythm of Soviet factories, large and small, civilian and military. Storming to fulfill the monthly, quarterly, or annual Plan turns every month into a sort of crazy industrial pregnancy, sluggish in gestation and frenzied at the finish.

"Usually, at the start of the month an enterprise is virtually paralyzed after the storming in the final days of the preceding month," Yosif explained. By his account, the work force was in a state of exhaustion not only because of drinking but because so many skilled workers had been pressed into long overtime shifts during the storming campaign. "A lot have to put in two shifts a day during storming," he said. "They work all day both Saturdays and Sundays, their normal days off. Management doesn't have the right [to pay them for overtime] because it has a ceiling on its payroll and financial inspection organs check on that. Sometimes if a worker is badly needed, he can get time-and-a-half or double time off to compensate for his overtime. But whether or not they get time off, workers have to put in those extra days [Black Saturdays, they are universally called] without extra pay. So usually there are a lot of workers off at the start of the month and the enterprise is in a state of paralysis."

"Plants couldn't operate at normal capacity anyway because they do not have a lot of the materials and components needed for operation," Yosif went on. "In spite of the Plan and seemingly definite delivery deadlines, suppliers don't fulfill the Plan or meet delivery schedules. So manufacturing plants cannot work rhythmically. Normally, not enough parts and components are available until about the tenth or twelfth of the month. Some items can be assembled almost completely, but they lack certain parts. A large number of items cannot be shipped out and accumulate in storerooms. They are held as late as the twentieth of the month because parts aren't ready or certain components are missing. Finally comes the third decade (twentieth to thirtieth). It's a good month if absolutely everything required is actually on hand by the twentieth. When everything has finally been received, the storming of the Plan can begin. Immediately work starts in many sections simultaneously."

Yosif spoke about it matter-of-factly, making clear this was a normal   8 state of affairs for Soviet industry, not some aberration peculiar to factories where he worked or to particular seasons of the year, though December, being the end of the year, is worse than other months.

"In other countries, production normally goes on throughout the month," Yosif observed, "but here, it can only begin on the fourteenth or twentieth when all materials have been received. So factories must fulfill about eighty percent of the Plan [quotas] in the last ten to fifteen days. No one cares any longer about quality. Volume is the main thing. Some workers are sent to finish the items that were partly assembled and kept in storerooms. Some of the production is no longer finished in factory conditions but often in the open air. Water, dirt, and dust can fall in the equipment which, of course, lowers its quality and cuts down its life span.

"The whole population knows all about this because everyone works," Yosif commented. "So normally, when someone buys a household appliance, he tries to buy one with a certificate saying that it was produced before the fifteenth of the month and not after the fifteenth. [Soviet goods carry tags with production dates.] If the item was made before the fifteenth, obviously it was not made in a rush and the customer thinks, 'maybe it will work.' If it was made after the fifteenth, there's a good chance it will stop working pretty quickly."

Other Russians with whom I talked were more flexible than Yosif who, as a technical man, may have had higher standards than most. They reckoned it was not too great a risk to buy something made as late as the twentieth. But no matter what the object, the candid advice of one middle-aged Moscow woman, echoed by others was: "Don't buy if it was made after the twentieth."

Her husband nodded in agreement and with a typical Russian laughter-   12
through-tears sense of humor launched into his favorite joke about storm-ing. It concerned a hapless Soviet worker who died and found himself in purgatory confronted by an official who addressed him in the stilted, condescending rhetoric of Soviet bureaucrats: "According to your moral qualities, you will not be permitted to enter heaven. Your papers are not in good enough order to be accepted. You may only enter hell. My duty is to warn you that there are two sections of hell — capitalist hell and socialist hell. You have a choice."

The worker inquired about the difference.

"In the capitalist hell, they will drive a nail into your butt every day all month long," the official said curtly.

"And does the same thing go on in the socialist hell, too?"

"The socialist hell is different, comrade," the functionary advised.   16
"There, the Devil gets drunk a lot and there is a chronic shortage of nails."

"Well, in that case," said the newcomer, brightening, "I'll take the socialist hell."

"All right, that is your choice," the official acknowledged, "but it is my duty to warn you that all the same they'll drive those thirty nails into your butt in the last five days of the month."

That irreverent view of the workings of the Soviet economy has the kind of insight into Russian reality that prompted Dostoyevski to describe his native land as a sublime, universal, ordered chaos. It is a far cry, however, from the picture that Western visitors derive from officially guided tours through spruced-up Soviet industrial installations, from the image of technological prowess given by live television coverage of the Soviet *Soyuz* spacecraft docking with an American *Apollo*, or from the impression projected to the world at large by the Kremlin's perennial boasting about overfulfilling its Five-Year Plans. . . .

The mechanistic Soviet Economic Plan seems to cut against the grain   20
of Russian nature. In the world at large, Russians have a reputation for discipline because of their seemingly docile obedience to authority. But

this is a discipline imposed from outside. Left to their own devices, Russians are generally an easygoing, disorderly, pleasantly disorganized, and not very efficient people. (Significantly, the Russian language had no word for efficiency and had to borrow one from English.) The typical Soviet office, often unseen by foreign visitors, is a supercrowded, disorderly muddle with a little propaganda corner and not enough desks to go around for everyone, I was told by Moscow friends. Factories through which I was taken were usually neat, though I was struck by the terrible din of machinery and by how few industrial safety signs there were. But Soviet friends insisted these were *pokazukha* factories, spruced up for show, and that the run-of-the-mill Soviet factory was "a bordello," as more than one put it.

Moreover, the foreigner can tour plenty of installations and stare at machinery without learning about "storming" or understanding that the Russian sense of time is at once enchantingly and frustratingly loose or nonexistent. It bears little relation to time in a commercial society. Most tourists learn to their consternation that just ordering dinner in a restaurant can require an hour or more. A one-hour press conference begins nearly an hour late and runs for two more; a short answer can take forty-five minutes; a ten-minute drop-in with friends invariably stretches to three or four hours; staying late, until 2:00 or 3:00 A.M., is one of the more attractive Russian vices; a week's job takes three weeks; elevators break down and stay out of order for a fortnight or more; other repair work consumes unpredictable gobs of time; construction timetables nationwide run years behind. Russians are genuinely put off by the impatience of Westerners, especially Americans, who go up the wall with frustration at the dawdling uncertainties of Russian life. The innocent Western visitor, assuming that the Soviet Union is an advanced society, is often bruised when he first bumps against the essentially underdeveloped tempo of most Soviet commerce. It takes a while to learn that *skoro budet*, literally, "It'll be here soon," is really *mañana*[1] stretched to eternity. For procrastination is built into the Russian temperament. Perhaps that's the main reason for constant propaganda hounding Russians to finish the Plan on time.

Although Russians are capable of great exertion if pressed to produce, sustained hard work is not a national characteristic. They do not have the work ethic of Americans, Germans, or Japanese. "Americans work

---

[1]Spanish for "tomorrow." — ED.

hard, put in long hours, get ahead, and also get ulcers," was the comment of a Soviet editor who admitted that he rarely strained on his job. "Russians don't work very hard or try very hard. And we live more relaxed lives." A schoolteacher told Ann that she considered her job the best part of her life "because no one pushes me there." Martic Martentz, an Armenian-American Communist who voluntarily returned from New York to try living in the Soviet Union, told me he was astonished at the Soviet image of Americans. "They think everyone [in America] is rich," he gasped. "They don't realize how hard people have to work in America."

A movie script writer suggested that one reason many Russians don't work harder is that generally it doesn't pay enough. If one doctor in a polyclinic gets a reputation for good, conscientious work, she winds up with extra patients and a lot of overtime work but she cannot be paid for overtime, the writer said, whereas those who get ahead are usually doctors who speak up in Party meetings and curry favor with Party officials. Another reason, Russian friends reminded me, is that the Soviet Union is still not as money oriented as Western societies. "Money alone is not enough, you have to have something to spend it on," remarked a young scientist. "Connections matter more than money. With connections you can find the deficit goods and spend the money. Without them, it's not worth the effort."

Playing hooky from work is a national pastime so common that Arkady 24 Raikin, the comedian, has gotten censors to approve several skits on that theme. In one, he plays an engineer who lolls all day on a bed the size of a putting green and rationalizes skipping work by recalling how little he does on the job. "I'm doing them a favor by staying away," he quips. In another, three men sneak out during working hours to the barbershop but get lousy service because the barbers themselves are trying to sneak away. One barber wants to buy oranges, another, to get some gadget repaired, and the third, to visit the dentist. The barbers return defeated, only to discover that the grocer, repairman, and dentist are the three customers sitting in their chairs. "That's just what happens," a Russian confessed to me during intermission. "My wife goes out shopping during working hours. It's the only way, because after work the crowds in the stores and the lines are simply terrible. Everybody does it." A linguist told me her friends would duck out of work just to pay social calls or see a movie.

If part-time hooky is a pervasive problem among white-collar workers, full-scale absenteeism among blue-collar workers reaches such disaster proportions, especially around paydays, that the Kremlin leadership and

Soviet press periodically inveigh against "slackers" and "bad labor discipline." The Moscow manager for a Western airline told me his Soviet ground crews were so unreliable that his Western technical chief had to check personally that fuel was available, ground service ready, and deicing and other equipment prepared for their incoming flights. On the days that their planes came in, the technical chief would pick up his Soviet mechanics and workmen at home to insure they would be on the job.

Soviet managers have a great deal of trouble disciplining factory workers not only because it is almost impossible to fire them but also because labor is generally short and a disgruntled worker knows he can quit and find another job easily. Theoretically, Soviet Marxism holds that workers are not alienated under socialism because they enjoy the full fruits of their labor, and Soviet propagandists seek to maintain this fiction. But occasional sociological studies and press items revealing that 2.8 million workers changed jobs in the Russian Republic alone in 1973 undercut that contention. Poor working conditions and lack of side benefits, such as housing, rather than pay are cited by workers as reasons for dissatisfaction. . . .

In an effort to increase output the Communist Party resorts to various moral inducements, from special awards to model workers, to "socialist competition" between work brigades or factories, to the perennial technique of "socialist obligations." Before every great holiday, work collectives across the country take upon themselves obligations to exceed their work norms. They solemnly pledge to implement Party decisions, to "increase their ideological level," and to raise their output. Steel mills promise to roll out 110 percent of their quota of steel, candy factories vow to produce a year's output of sweets in just eleven months, and libraries take an oath to insure that an unprecedented number of books by or about Lenin will be read in the next three months.

Another favorite gimmick of Soviet propagandists is the *vstrechny plan*,   28
literally, the Counter Plan, or the Plan the workers themselves put forward to meet, match, and exceed the official Plan fixed for them. Theoretically, it is spontaneously offered. But the entire ritual is widely viewed as such cynical humbug that factory workers have contrived their own raunchy put-down of the *vstrechny plan*. According to this joke, a factory worker arrives home late one evening and to protect himself from his wife's scolding, he explains that he was delayed by a long factory meeting on the *vstrechny plan*.

"What is this *vstrechny plan*?" asks his skeptical spouse.

"Well," he says, "it's as if I proposed that we screw twice tonight and you come back and propose we screw three times when both of us know damned well we couldn't do it more than once."

The two young Russians who told me this joke as we walked along a Moscow boulevard broke into loud guffaws and were disappointed that I was not similarly moved by their earthy humor. "At least you get the idea about the *vstrechny plan?*" one asked. I nodded.

EXPLORATIONS

1. What is storming, and when does it occur? According to Smith, what happens at a Soviet factory during each decade of the month?

2. What aspects of the Russian temperament does Smith believe help to explain workers' and consumers' acceptance of storming? What evidence does he give to support his theories, and how convincing is it?

3. At two points in "*Skoro Budet* — It'll Be Here Soon," Smith gives examples of Russian humor. What effect do these jokes have on the essay's interest level? What facts does each joke enable Smith to introduce or emphasize about Russian workers?

CONNECTIONS

1. Judging from Smith's description, what is the top-priority goal of Soviet factories? Judging from Satoshi Kamata's "Six Months at Toyota," what is the top-priority goal of Japanese factories? What secondary goals does each management group consider important and not so important?

2. How is the situation of the prostitutes described by Jill Gay in "Patriotic Prostitutes" similar to that of the factory workers described by Smith? What attitudes by government, and toward government, are noted by both Gay and Smith?

3. How do the Russians in "*Skoro Budet* — It'll Be Here Soon" describe American attitudes toward work? How do you think Bill Talcott, quoted by Studs Terkel in *Looking at Ourselves*, would agree and disagree? What does Smith see as the main contrasts in attitude between American and Soviet workers? Do you think Talcott would agree? Why or why not?

ELABORATIONS

1. The current Soviet leadership, headed by Mikhail Gorbachev, has been trying to raise the quality of Soviet-produced goods within the Communist framework. Based on *"Skoro Budet* — It'll Be Here Soon," what do you think are the main problems Gorbachev's administration must address? From your other reading in Part Five, Working, and from your own experience, what changes would you recommend in the way Soviet factories and workers were managed at the time of Smith's visit? Write an essay proposing your suggestions.

2. "Theoretically, Soviet Marxism holds that workers are not alienated under socialism because they enjoy the full fruits of their labor," writes Smith in paragraph 26. Theoretically, why does our American capitalist system claim to be the best one for workers? Using *"Skoro Budet* — It'll Be Here Soon," Kamata's "Six Months at Toyota," and *Looking at Ourselves* as sources, write an essay discussing the practical problems that get in the way of both the Communist and the capitalist ideals.

ROSARIO FERRÉ

Out of the Frying Pan

The daughter of a former governor of Puerto Rico, Rosario Ferré was born in Ponce in 1942. She received a bachelor's degree from Manhattanville College in New York, a master's from the University of Puerto Rico, and a doctorate in Spanish and Latin American literature from the University of Maryland. In the early 1970s she became editor of the magazine *Zona de carga*. The story she describes writing in the following essay — her first, *"La muñeca menor"* ("The Youngest Doll") was published there and later translated into English by Gregory Rabassa, who also translates most of the work of Gabriel García Márquez (see p. 531). "The Youngest Doll" has since appeared as the title piece of a 1990 short story collection. Ferré has published several other volumes of short stories, poems, essays, and children's stories, as well as two novels (*Maldito Amor*, "Damned Love," 1986, and *Sweet Diamond Dust*, 1988). She currently teaches literature at Johns Hopkins University. "Out of the Frying Pan" began as a talk given at several Latin American literary conferences. After appearing in Ferré's essay collection *Sitio a Eros* (1980), it was revised and translated from Spanish into English by Diana L. Vélez for the 1988 anthology *Lives on the Line: The Testimony of Contemporary Latin American Authors*, edited by Doris Meyer.

The Commonwealth of Puerto Rico (Estado Libre Asociado de Puerto Rico) is an island of just under 3,500 square miles lying between the Atlantic Ocean and the Caribbean Sea. Also known as Borinquen, Puerto Rico is the easternmost of the Greater Antilles, a group that includes Jamaica and Cuba. Nearly all of its 3.5 million people are Hispanic. The island was discovered in 1493 by Columbus; its Arawak Indian inhabitants called it Boriquen. In 1509 Ponce de León claimed it for Spain. After fighting off a series of British and Dutch attacks, the Spanish ceded Puerto Rico to the United States in 1898 as part of the settlement of the Spanish-American War. The island is now a self-governing part of the United States; residents cannot vote in national elections and do not pay income tax. Famous Puerto Ricans include the late cellist Pablo Casals and baseball player Roberto Clemente and the actors Raul Julia and Rita Moreno.

Throughout time, women narrators have written for many reasons: Emily Brontë wrote to prove the revolutionary nature of passion; Virginia Woolf wrote to exorcise her terror of madness and death; Joan Didion writes to discover what and how she thinks; Clarice Lispector discovered in her writing a reason to love and be loved.[1] In my case, writing is simultaneously a constructive and a destructive urge, a possibility for growth and change. I write to build myself word by word, to banish my terror of silence; I write as a speaking, human mask. With respect to words, I have much for which to be grateful. Words have allowed me to forge for myself a unique identity, one that owes its existence only to my efforts. For this reason, I place more trust in the words I use than perhaps I ever did in my natural mother. When all else fails, when life becomes an absurd theater, I know words are there, ready to return my confidence to me. This need to reconstruct which moves me to write is closely tied to my need for love: I write so as to reinvent myself, to convince myself that what I love will endure.

But my urge to write is also destructive, an attempt to annihilate myself and the world. Words are infinitely wise and, like all mothers, they know when to destroy what is worn out or corrupt so that life may be rebuilt on new foundations. To the degree that I take part in the corruption of the world, I turn my instrument against myself. I write because I am poorly adjusted to reality; because the deep disillusionment within me has given rise to a need to re-create life, to replace it with a more compassionate, tolerable reality. I carry within me a utopian person, a utopian world.

This destructive urge that moves me to write is tied to my need for hate, my need for vengeance. I write so as to avenge myself against reality and against myself; I write to give permanence to what hurts me and to what tempts me. I believe that deep wounds and harsh insults might someday release within me all the creative forces available to human expression, a belief that implies, after all, that I love the word passionately.

Now I would like to address these constructive and destructive forces   4
with relation to my work. The day I finally sat down at my typewriter to write my first story. I knew from experience how hard it was for a woman to obtain her own room with a lock on the door, as well as those metaphorical five hundred pounds a year that assure her independence. I had gotten divorced and had suffered many changes because of love, or because of what I had then thought was love: the renouncing of my own intellectual and spiritual space for the sake of the relationship with the one I loved. What made me turn against myself was the determination

---

[1]Emily Brontë (1818–1848), English novelist and poet. Virginia Woolf (1882–1941), English novelist and critic. Joan Didion (1934–), American novelist, essayist, journalist, and screenwriter. Clarice Lispector (1925–1977), Brazilian novelist, playwright, and journalist — ED.

to become the perfect wife. I wanted to be as they were telling me I should be, so I had ceased to exist; I had renounced my soul's private obligations. It has always seemed to me that living intensely was the most important of these obligations. I did not like the protected existence I had led until then in the sanctuary of my home, free from all danger but also from any responsibilities. I wanted to live, to enjoy firsthand knowledge, art, adventure, danger, without waiting for someone else to tell me about them. In fact, what I wanted was to dispel my fear of death. We all fear death, but I had a special terror of it, the terror of those who have not lived. Life tears us apart, making us become partners to its pleasures and terrors, yet in the end it consoles us; it teaches us to accept death as a necessary and natural end. But to see myself forced to face death without having known life — without passing through its apprenticeship — seemed to me unforgivable cruelty. I would tell myself that that was why children who die without having lived, without having to account for their own acts, all went to Limbo. I was convinced that Heaven was for the good, and Hell for the evil, for those men who had arduously earned either salvation or damnation. But in Limbo there were only women and children, unaware of how we had gotten there.

The day of my debut as a writer, I sat at my typewriter for a long time, mulling over these thoughts. Inevitably, writing my first story meant taking my first step toward Heaven or Hell, and that made me vacillate between a state of euphoria and a state of depression. It was as if I were about to be born, peering timidly through the doors of Limbo. If my voice rings false or my will fails me, I said to myself, all my sacrifices will have been in vain. I will have foolishly given up the protection that despite its disadvantages, at least allowed me to be a good wife and mother, and I will have justly fallen from the frying pan into the fire.

In those days, Virginia Woolf and Simone de Beauvoir[2] were my mentors; I wanted them to show me how to write well, or at least how not to write poorly. I would read everything they had written like a person who takes several spoonfuls of a health potion nightly before retiring. The potion would prevent death from a host of plagues and ills that had killed off the majority of women writers before them, as well as some of their contemporaries. I must admit that those readings didn't do much to strengthen my as yet newborn and fragile identity as a writer. My hand's instinctive reflex was still to hold the frying pan patiently over the fire — not to brandish my pen aggressively through the flames — and

---

[2]For more information on Simone de Beauvoir see p. 333. — Ed.

Simone and Virginia, while recognizing the achievements that women writers had attained up to that time, criticized them quite severely. Simone was of the opinion that women too frequently insisted on themes traditionally considered feminine, the preoccupation with love, for example, or the denunciation of training and customs that had irreparably limited their existence. Justifiable though these themes were, to reduce oneself to them meant that the capacity for freedom had not been adequately internalized. "Art, literature, and philosophy," Simone would say to me, "are attempts to base the world on a new human freedom, the freedom of the individual creator, and to achieve this goal a woman must, above all, assume the status of a being who already has freedom."

In her opinion, a woman should be constructive in her literature, not of interior realities, but of exterior realities, principally of those of a historical and social nature. For Simone, the intuitive capacity, the contact with irrational forces, the capacity for emotion, were all important talents, but they were also of secondary importance. "The functioning of the world, the order of political and social events which determine the course of our lives, are in the hands of those who make their decisions in the light of knowledge and reason," Simone would say to me, "and not in the light of intuition and emotion," and it was with those themes that women should henceforth occupy themselves in their literature.

Virginia Woolf, for her part, was obsessed with the need for an objectivity and distance which, she thought, had seldom been found in the writings of women. Of the writers of the past, Virginia excluded only Jane Austen and Emily Brontë, because only they had managed to write, like Shakespeare, "with a mind incandescent, unimpeded." "It is deadly for a writer to think about his or her gender," Virginia would say to me, and "it is deadly for a woman to register a complaint, however mild, to advocate a cause, however justifiably" — deadly then, to speak consciously as a woman. In Virginia's opinion, the books of a woman writer who doesn't free herself from rage will contain distortions, deviations. She will write with anger instead of with sensitivity. She will speak of herself, instead of about her characters. At war with her fate, how can she avoid dying young, frustrated, always at odds with the world? Clearly, for Virginia, women's literature should never be destructive or irate, but rather harmonious and translucid as was her own.

I had, then, chosen my subject — nothing less than the world — as well as my style — nothing less than an absolutely neutral and serene language, which could let the truth of the material emerge, exactly as Simone and Virginia had advised. Now I had only to find my starting point, that most personal window, from among the thouands that Henry

James says fiction possesses, through which I would gain access to my theme, the window to my story. I thought it best to select a historical anecdote, perhaps something related to how our Puerto Rican bourgeois culture changed from an agrarian one based on sugar cane and ruled by a rural oligarchy to an urban or industrial one ruled by a new professional class, an anecdote that would convey how this change brought about a shift in values at the turn of the century — the abandonment of the land and the replacement of a patriarchal code of behavior, based on exploitation but also on certain ethical principles and on Christian charity, with a new utilitarian code that came to us from the United States.

A story centered on this series of events seemed excellent to me in every way. There was no possibility whatever that I might be accused of useless constructions or destructions; there was nothing further from the boring feminine conflicts than that kind of plot. With the context of my plot finally chosen, I raised my hands to the typewriter, ready to begin writing. Under my fingers, ready to leap to the fore, trembled the twenty-six letters of the Latin alphabet, like the chords of a powerful instrument. An hour passed, two, then three, without a single idea crossing the frighteningly limpid horizon of my mind. There was so much information, so many writable events in that moment of our historical becoming, that I had not the faintest idea where to begin. Everything seemed worthy, not just of the clumsy and amateurish story I might write, but of a dozen novels yet to be written.

I decided to be patient and not to despair, to spend the whole night keeping vigil if necessary. Maturity is everything, I told myself, and this was, after all, my first story. If I concentrated hard enough, I would at last find the starting point of my story. It was dawn and a purple light washed over my study windows. Surrounded by full ashtrays and abandoned cups of cold coffee, I fell into a deep sleep, draped over my typewriter's silent keyboard.

Fortunately, I have since learned that the setbacks we must face don't matter, for life keeps right on living us. That night's defeat, after all, had nothing to do with my love for short stories. If I couldn't write stories I could at least listen to them, and in daily life I have always been an avid listener of stories. Verbal tales, the ones people tell me in the street, are the ones that always interest me the most, and I marvel at the fact that those who tell them tend to be unaware that what they are telling me is a story. Something like this took place a few days later, when I was invited to lunch at my aunt's house.

Sitting at the head of the table, dropping a slow spoonful of honey into her tea, my aunt began to tell a story while I listened. It had taken place at a sugarcane plantation some distance away, at the beginning of the century, she said, and its heroine was a distant cousin of hers who made dolls filled with honey. The strange woman had been the victim of her husband, a ne'er-do-well and a drunkard who had wasted away her fortune, kicked her out of the house, and taken up with another woman. My aunt's family, out of respect for the customs of the time, had offered her room and board, despite the fact that by that time the cane plantation on which they lived was on the verge of ruin. To reciprocate for their generosity she had dedicated herself to making honey-filled dolls for the girls in the family.

Soon after her arrival at the plantation, my aunt's cousin, who was still young and beautiful, had developed a strange ailment: her right leg began to swell with no apparent cause, and her relatives sent for the doctor from the nearby town so he could examine her. The doctor, an unscrupulous young man recently graduated from a university in the United States, made the young woman fall in love with him, then falsely diagnosed her ailment as being incurable. Applying plasters like a quack, he condemned her to live like an invalid in an armchair while he dispassionately relieved her of the little money the unfortunate woman had managed to save from her marriage. The doctor's behavior seemed reprehensible to me, of course, but what moved me most about the story were not his despicable acts but the absolute resignation with which, in the name of love, that woman had let herself be exploited for twenty years.

I am not going to repeat here the rest of the story my aunt told me that afternoon because it appears in "La muñeca menor," my first story. True, I didn't tell it with the words my aunt used, nor did I repeat her naive praises to a world fortunately gone by, a world in which day-laborers in the cane fields died of malnutrition while the daughters of plantation owners played with honey-filled dolls. But the story I listened to, in its broad outlines, fulfilled the requirements I had imposed on myself: it dealt with the ruin of one social class and its replacement by another, with the metamorphosis of a value system based on the concept of family into one based on profit and personal gain, a value system implanted among us by strangers from the United States.

The flame was lit. That very afternoon I locked myself in my study 16 and didn't stop until the spark that danced before my eyes stopped right at the heart of what I wanted to say. With my story finished, I leaned back in my chair to read the whole thing, sure of having written a story with an objective theme, a story absolutely free of feminine conflicts, a story with transcendence. Then I realized that all my care had been in vain. That strange relative, victim of a love that subjected her twice to exploitation by her loved one, had appropriated my story; she reigned over it like a tragic, implacable vestal. My theme, while framed in the historical and sociopolitical context I had outlined, was still love, complaint, and — oh! I had to admit it — even vengeance. The image of that woman, hovering for years on end at the edge of the cane field with her broken heart, had touched me deeply. It was she who had finally opened the window for me, the window that had been so hermetically sealed, the window to my story.

I had betrayed Simone, writing once again about the interior reality of women; and I had betrayed Virginia, letting myself get carried away by my anger, by the fury the story produced in me. I confess that I was on the verge of throwing my story into the trash so as to rid myself of the evidence that, in the opinion of my mentors, identified me with all the women writers past and present who had tragically wasted themselves. Luckily I didn't do it; I kept it in a desk drawer to await better times, to await a day when I would perhaps arrive at a better understanding of myself.

Ten years have passed since I wrote "La muñeca menor," and I have written many stories since then; I think now I can objectively analyze the lessons I learned that day with more maturity. I feel less guilt toward Simone and Virginia because I have discovered that, when one tries to write a story (or a poem or novel), stopping to listen to advice, even from those masters whom one most admires, almost always has negative consequences. Today I know from experience that it is no use to write by setting out beforehand to construct exterior realities or to deal with universal and objective themes if one doesn't first create one's own interior reality. It is no use to try to write in a neutral, harmonious, distant way if one doesn't first have the courage to destroy one's own interior reality. When writing about her characters, a writer is always writing about herself, or about possible versions of herself because, as with all human beings, no virtue or vice is alien to her.

By identifying with the strange relative from "La muñeca menor" I had made possible both processes. On the one hand I had reconstructed, in her misfortune, my own amorous misfortune; and on the other hand, by realizing where her weaknesses and failings were — her passivity, her acceptance, her terrifying resignation — I had destroyed her in my name. Although I may also have saved her. In subsequent stories, my heroines have managed to be braver, freer, more energetic and positive, perhaps because they were born from the ashes of "La muñeca menor." Her betrayal was, in any case, what brought about my fall from the frying pan into the fire of literature.

EXPLORATIONS

1. In paragraph 2 Ferré writes, "To the degree that I take part in the corruption of the world, I turn my instrument against myself." What do you think she means by this?
2. When Ferré started writing, what did she believe were her obligations to herself and to the world? How did her perception of her obligations change after she wrote *"La muñeca menor"*?
3. In her use of the metaphor "out of the frying pan and into the fire," what is Ferré defining as the frying pan and what is she defining as the fire?

CONNECTIONS

1. What statements by Ferré suggest agreement or disagreement with Alice Walker's passage in *Looking at Ourselves*?
2. What statements by Ferré seem to be making the same points as Vladimir Nabokov does in *Looking at Ourselves*?
3. Ferré cites Simone de Beauvoir as one of her literary mentors. What statements in Ferré's description of her life before she started writing are echoed by statements Beauvoir makes in "Woman as Other" (p. 333)?

ELABORATIONS

1. Ferré quotes Virginia Woolf in paragraph 8: "It is deadly for a writer to think about his or her gender." By the end of her essay, does Ferré agree? Do you think the joys and trials she associates with her work are shared only by women writers, or by people of both genders in a range of occupations? Write a profile of yourself in which you define yourself as a representative of your gender, your occupation, or both.
2. In paragraph 11, Ferré describes an experience most writers and would-be writers have shared, whether their goal is to produce a story or a term paper. Write a narrative essay about a false start or change in direction of your own, including — as Ferré does — the hopes and expectations you started with, and how your ideas had changed by the time you finished.

PABLO NERUDA

The Word

The Chilean writer Pablo Neruda is generally regarded as one of the foremost poets of our time. Born Ricardo Eliecer Neftalí Reyes y Basoalto in 1904, he died in 1973, two years after he won the Nobel Prize for literature. Recognition did not come easily. Neruda's early *Veinte poemas de amor y una canción desesperada* (1924, "Twenty Love Poems and a Song of Despair") was rejected by Chile's leading publisher as too blatantly erotic. The surreal *Residencia en la tierra* (1933, "Residence on Earth"), one of his most acclaimed works, is full of anguish and despair. In 1945 Neruda joined the Chilean Communist Party and was elected to the Senate. Shortly thereafter Communism was outlawed and Neruda's arrest was ordered. He fled to Mexico in 1948. There he wrote the poems that were published in 1950 as *Canto general* ("General Song"), a highly acclaimed examination of South America's cultural and political direction which was banned in Chile. Returning to his native country in 1952, Neruda published *Odas elementales* ("Elemental Odes") two years later, drawing critical fire for its poems' earthy simplicity. His last two books of poetry, *El mar y las campanas* (1973, "The Sea and the Bells") and *Jardín de invierno* (1974, "Winter Garden") show his awareness of his imminent death. "The Word" is excerpted from "My First Books" from *Memoirs* (1977) and was translated from the Spanish by Hardie St. Martin.

Chile is a long strip of seacoast that runs along western South America from Peru and Bolivia to the continent's southern tip. The Andes Mountains divide it on the east from Argentina. Spain took northern Chile from the native Incas in the mid-1500s; the southern Araucanian Indians held out for another three centuries. Chile won its independence in the early 1800s under José de San Martín and Bernardo O'Higgins, who became its first dictator. Following the military overthrow of Marxist President Salvador Allende Gossens in 1973, General Augusto Pinochet Ugarte headed a repressive right-wing government until his historic ouster by democratic elections sixteen years later.

. . . You can say anything you want, yessir, but it's the words that sing, they soar and descend . . . I bow to them . . . I love them, I cling to them, I run them down, I bite into them, I melt them down . . . I love words so much . . . The unexpected ones . . . The ones I wait for greedily or stalk until, suddenly, they drop . . . Vowels I love . . . They glitter like colored stones, they leap like silver fish, they are foam, thread, metal, dew . . . I run after certain words . . . They are so beautiful that I want to fit them all into my poem . . . I catch them in mid-flight, as they buzz past, I trap them, clean them, peel them, I set myself in front of the dish, they have a crystalline texture to me, vibrant, ivory, vegetable, oily, like fruit, like algae, like agates, like olives . . . And then I stir them, I shake them, I drink them, I gulp them down, I mash them, I garnish them, I let them go . . . I leave them in my poem like stalactites, like slivers of polished wood, like coals, pickings from a shipwreck, gifts from the waves . . . Everything exists in the word . . . An idea goes through a complete change because one word shifted its place, or because another settled down like a spoiled little thing inside a phrase that was not expecting her but obeys her . . . They have shadow, transparence, weight, feathers, hair, and everything they gathered from so much rolling down the river, from so much wandering from country to country, from being roots so long . . . They are very ancient and very new . . . They live in the bier, hidden away, and in the budding flower . . . What a great language I have, it's a fine language we inherited from the fierce conquistadors . . . They strode over the giant cordilleras, over the rugged Americas, hunting for potatoes, sausages, beans, black tobacco, gold, corn, fried eggs, with a voracious appetite not found in the world since then . . . They swallowed up everything, religions, pyramids, tribes, idolatries just like the ones they brought along in their huge sacks . . . Wherever they went, they razed the land . . . But words fell like pebbles out of the boots of the barbarians, out of their beards, their helmets, their horseshoes, luminous words that were left glittering here . . . our language. We came up losers . . . We came up winners . . . They carried off the gold and left us the gold . . . They carried everything off and left us everything . . . They left us the words.

EXPLORATIONS

1. The first part of Neruda's essay is in the first person. Identify at least four roles that he — the writer — plays in this section in relation to words.

2. What emotions toward words does Neruda express? Cite specific evidence for each.

3. What do you think Neruda means by "Vowels I love . . . They glitter like colored stones, they leap like silver fish, they are foam, thread, metal, dew . . ."?

CONNECTIONS

1. What points does Rosario Ferré make in "Out of the Frying Pan" that also appear, although in a different form, in "The Word"?

2. What statements can you find in Ezekiel Mphahlele's "Tradition and the African Writer" (p. 34) that echo ideas expressed by Neruda?

3. Look back at Octavio Paz's "Hygiene and Repression" (p. 9). What similarities do you notice between Paz's and Neruda's metaphorical use of food and eating?

ELABORATIONS

1. What are your favorite words? Write an essay about the beauties of words and parts of words in English. Include, as Neruda does, some reference to how we in the United States acquired our language (either English in general or American English in particular).

2. In the second half of his essay Neruda comments on the nature of conquest, mentioning some unexpected ways that conquerors affect the culture they take over (and are affected by it). Who are the "we" who came up losers and winners? Write an essay about a parallel "we" in the United States: native Americans affected by Europeans or their descendants, perhaps, or year-round residents affected by seasonal tourists, or neighborhood dwellers affected by development.

PART SIX

IDEOLOGY AND POLITICS

The Cost of Our Convictions

LOOKING AT OURSELVES

John Kenneth Galbraith, Vicki Williams, Lewis H. Lapham,
Tom Ashbrook, Ben H. Bagdikian, Annie Dillard

Hans Magnus Enzensberger, *Every Italian Is Privileged* (ITALY)

Janine Wedel, *Polish Line Committees* (POLAND)

Jane Kramer, *The Perils of Perestroika* (SOVIET UNION)

Václav Havel, *The Chance That Will Not Return*
(CZECHOSLOVAKIA)

Peter Schneider, *The End of the Wall* (GERMANY)

Gabriel García Márquez, *Death Constant Beyond Love*
(COLOMBIA)

Michele L. Norris, *A Child of Crack* (UNITED STATES)

Yoram Binur, *Palestinian Like Me* (ISRAEL)

Nadine Gordimer, *Africa Emergent* (SOUTH AFRICA)

Nelson Mandela, *The African National Congress*
(SOUTH AFRICA)

Colin Thubron, *At the Beijing Zoo* (CHINA)

THE FRAMERS OF THE U.S. CONSTITUTION, WRITHING FREE FROM ENG-land's colonial yoke, wrote a clear contract for their new republic. The people (defined then as male property owners) would elect a representative government whose job was to provide security, order, and coordination. The people in turn would abide by the rules their government made. To those of us who have grown up in the United States, such a social con-tract — yielding some personal freedom in return for protection — seems not only apt but natural. However, as recent world events have shown us, our system is in fact unusual, and much envied around the globe.

In *Looking at Ourselves*, we see pros and cons of living in the U.S. John Kenneth Galbraith warns of a switch in the relationship between our government and its military establishment. Vicki Williams complains about representatives who put words in her mouth. Lewis H. Lapham deplores the tendency among prosperous whites to link drugs, race, poverty, and crime. Returning from Asia, Tom Ashbrook is shocked by his homeland's sloppy complacency. Ben H. Bagdikian foresees a future in which a few corporations control world communications, and Annie Dillard compares American and Chinese definitions of "Mickey Mouse."

Across the Atlantic Ocean, German poet Hans Magnus Enzensberger muses about his favorite country in "Every Italian Is Privileged." Janine Wedel's "Polish Line Committees" describes a creative solution to the chronic shortages under Communism. Jane Kramer's "The Perils of Perestroika" traces those shortages to their source and considers why Soviet citizens have failed to rally behind Mikhail Gorbachev's plans for reform. In "The Chance That Will Not Return," Václav Havel, president of newly liberated Czechoslovakia, looks forward to a post–Cold War unity among the nations of Europe and the world. A pioneer of unification is Germany, where "The End of the Wall," Peter Schneider reports, means more than reopening the border between East and West Berlin.

The tangle of dreams, promises, and disillusion that constitutes politics is illuminated by Colombian novelist Gabriel García Márquez in his short story "Death Constant Beyond Love." In "A Child of Crack," Michele L. Norris reports on cocaine dealing and addiction in Prince George's County, Maryland. Israeli journalist Yoram Binur disguises himself as a Palestinian laborer in "Palestinian Like Me." Nadine Gor-dimer's short story "Africa Emergent" shows a group of black and white South Africans split by government-provoked suspicion. In "The African National Congress," South African leader Nelson Mandela responds to the white government's suspicions of black activists. Colin Thubron, in "At the Beijing Zoo," recalls a chance meeting with a former Chinese Red Guard which unfolds into a confession of violence and madness. ◈

LOOKING AT OURSELVES

1

In the United States, the first source of the military's power is the belief that all government instruments are subject to the democratic process. This belief is strong in our rhetoric; it is what our children are still taught in school. But it is, in fact, something that no fully informed citizen can believe. The modern military establishment extensively controls the democratic process. In the organization it possesses, the money it deploys, the captive politicians it commands, the scientific community it subsidizes, the military has become a force in its own right. It employs 4.5 million people and last year [1985] generated over $146 billion in business for private enterprise. The military now has in its embrace the civilian authority to which legally and constitutionally it is presumed to be subject.

– John Kenneth Galbraith
"The Military: A Loose Cannon?"

⬦–⬦–⬦–⬦

2

I consider myself the classic "poor overburdened taxpayer" that you hear so much about these days. I work for an electronics company and make $6.58 an hour which translates into $204 per week after deductions, $30.21 of which are federal withholding taxes. I have a husband, laid off, whose unemployment compensation has run out, and a thirteen-year-old son who thinks he should have a leather coat, a P. K. Ripper motocross bike, a Pioneer stereo, and an Asteroids game. It bothers me a lot that I can't afford to buy him any of these things. It also bothers me that I'm not sure how we're going to fill up the fuel tank often enough to stay warm this winter.

There is something else that bothers me, though not to the same extent as my son's unfulfilled desires or the ever-hungry fuel tank, and that is that every single politician and editorialist is positive he knows exactly what I think. Everyone seems to be wildly anxious to be my spokesman. Yet these people don't know a damn thing about how the "poor overburdened taxpayer" thinks or lives. I imagine it's been quite some time since most politicians or well-known journalists lived on $204 per week, though I've read plenty of complaints from congressmen about their meager salaries. One even said he had to sleep in his office because he couldn't afford to buy a house. Do you know how much pity I can spare for a senator who can't live on $60,000 a year?

I know I'm not as articulate as the people who write the editorials for newspapers and the speeches for politicians, but just once I'd like to have on the record the thoughts of an average taxpayer. I'm tired of these people putting their words in my mouth and their thoughts in my head.

One of the statements I read and hear most often is how fed up I'm supposed to be with the amount of my taxes that goes toward welfare, food stamps, programs for the elderly, subsidized school lunches, and other supportive social services. Wrong! What the people "up there" don't understand is that I identify with the beneficiaries of these programs much more than I do with the politicians and the media people. "There, but for the grace of God, go I." So far, I have never had to rely on welfare, free lunches, or Medicaid, but I very well might someday. When I was divorced, I could have qualified for welfare. Fortunately, I had parents who were in a position to help, but if I hadn't, you can believe I would have swallowed my pride rather than watch my son go hungry. People like me, who live only a hairbreadth from economic disaster, are glad those programs are out there, though we pray we'll never have to use them. We feel sympathy for the ones who do.

In 1977 my sister-in-law was abandoned by her husband. Her health did not permit her to work full-time, so she drew $194 per month from the welfare department to support herself and her child. I doubt that anyone can think she lived extravagantly on $194 per month.

I think it's possible that at least one of the very same politicians who are now complaining about welfare recipients might have taken a political junket during one of the months that my sister-in-law and her son lived on $194. Believe me, I resent that junket at my expense much, much more than I resent helping an ADC [Aid to Dependent Children] mother, or buying eyeglasses for an elderly person or free lunches for a ghetto child.

– Vicki Williams
"The View from $204 a Week"
Newsweek

3

The story of the drug war plays to the prejudices of an audience only too eager to believe the worst that can be said about people whom they would rather not know. Because most of the killing allied with the drug trade takes place in the inner cities, and because most of the people arrested for selling drugs prove to be either black or Hispanic, it becomes relatively easy for white people living in safe neighborhoods to blur the distinction between crime and race. Few of them have ever seen an addict or witnessed a drug deal, but the newspapers and television networks keep showing them photographs that convey the impression of a class war, and those among them who always worried about driving through Harlem (for fear of being seized by gangs of armed black men) or who always wished that they didn't feel quite so guilty about the socioeconomic distance between East 72nd Street and West 126th Street can comfort themselves, finally, at long last, and with a clear conscience, with the thought that poverty is another word for sin, that their BMW is a proof of their virtue, and that they or, more likely, their mothers were always right to fear the lower classes and the darker races.

As conditions in the slums deteriorate, which they inevitably must because the government subtracts money from the juvenile-justice and housing programs to finance its war on drugs, the slums come to look just the way they are supposed to look in the suburban imagination, confirming the fondest suspicions of the governing and possessing classes, justifying the further uses of force and repression. The people who pay the price for the official portrait turn out to be (wonder of wonders) not the members of the prosperous middle class — not the journalists or the academic theorists, not the politicians and government functionaries living behind hedges in Maryland and Virginia — but (mirabile dictu) the law-abiding residents of the inner cities living in the only neighborhoods that they can afford.

It is in the slums of New York that three people, on average, get killed every day — which, over the course of a year, adds up to a higher casualty rate than pertains in Gaza and the West Bank; it is in the slums that the drug trade recruits children to sell narcotics, which is not the result of indigenous villainy but of the nature of the law; it is in the slums that the drug trade has become the exemplary model of finance capitalism for children aspiring to the success of Donald Trump and Samuel Pierce; and it is in the slums that the police experiment with the practice of apartheid, obliging residents of housing projects to carry identity cards and summarily evicting the residents of apartment houses tainted by the presence of drug dealers.[1]

---

[1]The government's own statistics indicate that the middle classes no longer recognize the drug problem as one of their own. Doing lines of cocaine hasn't been hip for at least five years,

To the extent that the slums can be seen as the locus of the nation's wickedness (i.e., a desolate mise-en-scène not unlike the Evil Empire that Ronald Reagan found in the Soviet Union), the crimes allied with the drug traffic can be classified as somebody's else's moral problem rather than one's own social or political problem. The slums become foreign, alien nations on the other side of the economic and cultural frontiers. The deliberate confusion of geography with metaphysics turns out, again to nobody's surprise, to be wonderfully convenient for the sponsors of the war on drugs. The politicians get their names in the papers, the media have a story to tell, and the rest of us get off the hooks that otherwise might impale us on the questions of conscience or the obligation of higher taxes. In New York last week, I overheard a woman in an expensive restaurant say that she didn't understand why the government didn't arrange to put "arsenic or something" in a seized shipment of cocaine. If the government (or "the CIA or the FBI or whoever does that sort of thing") allowed the poisoned cocaine to find its way back onto the streets, then "pretty soon we'd be rid of the whole damn thing."

> – Lewis H. Lapham
> "A Political Opiate: The War on Drugs
> Is a Folly and a Menace"
> *Harper's Magazine*

4

What a country, my country, seen with a wary, Asia-fresh eye. It looks free, by all means — viscerally, unnervingly, exhilaratingly free. But to what end? It looks wealthy, by any measure, but drowsily, dangerously accustomed to its wealth and to its life on credit. It looks principled, in a noisy, faddish way, but afflicted with the crime, drugs, and alienation of moral decay.

For four years this time I had crisscrossed Asia out of Tokyo. It is a vast continent with great backwaters and problems of its own. But along the vigorous economic axis stretching from Japan to Singapore, it is hardheaded, dynamic, aggressive, and hungry. Most things work, and those that don't soon do. The region's cultures can seem, and often are,

---

and among college and high school students, the use of drugs has declined markedly over the same period of time. In fact, the number of current cocaine users has gone down from 5.8 million in 1985 to 2.9 million in 1988. A July [1989] poll conducted by the mayor's office in Washington, D.C., showed that the white residents in town worried more about potholes than about cocaine.

relative straitjackets demanding conformity and obedience. But a resident anywhere along Asia's industrialized spine soon develops a taste for precision, dependability, disciplined energy, and a certain high seriousness about the practical tasks, great and small, of life.

Ride the gleaming subway in Hong Kong. Feel the crisp concentration of a Singapore banker and his lowliest tellers, the fiery intensity of a Korean shipbuilding crew, the palpable dedication of a Yokohama schoolteacher. No one on cruise control. All alert, engaged, at grips with the importance of their roles and the gist of the national life they support. All infused with a powerful sense of forward motion, of purposefulness.

In just those terms, an American homecoming is a journey into shades of disarray. While veins of efficiency and competence feel ever-expanding in Asia, they appear to be contracting in the United States. Our cracked highways and rusting bridges seem physical reflections of falling standards of service, organization, simple care in the performance of jobs — of lost resolve.

How to judge? Trade figures? Foreign debt? Dire but dry. Atmospherics? Scary for a recent returnee. My brother-in-law sleeps with a large pistol in his nightstand and an alarm system that can track a burglar room by room. The news on arrival in America has the U.S. president turning to astrology, Los Angeles drivers taking potshots at one another on the freeway. American schoolchildren scoring at the bottom of the First World heap in key subjects. Drug lords reigning over urban fiefs. Alcoholics Anonymous and its ilk as a new religion. Wall Street sapping the economy it was intended to fuel. What is wrong with this picture?

True, the slippage is widely bemoaned. But to a returnee the more impressive point is the extent to which Americans have developed a tolerance for excess, ineptitude, and carelessness in the everyday business of life. To apply the sharper, more disciplined standards of contemporary Asia is to risk ostracism in the United States. Relax, man. Cool out. We don't want to hear about it.

If only it were a simple matter of life-style, the advice might have a certain charm. There is a beguiling aspect to a First World nation self-indulgently flirting with Third World standards, tempos, timetables — like seeing your father puttering around on vacation, or pampering yourself on a beach holiday.

But so much more is at stake here. In the realm of political ideals, of core values, America remains powerfully attractive to a returnee from Asia — that rare nation where individuals can assume individuality as a birthright, where diversity is, at least in principle, championed instead of smothered. Viewed against Asia's more restrictive norm, those American ideals have a sparkling, almost magical quality. But as the 1990s begin, one fears that critical links between industry and affluence, discipline and maintenance of national ideals, are slipping away.

Have we really reached a special plane of devotion to democracy, liberty, and civil rights? Or have we just been rich enough to pretend? We may soon have the chance to learn.

> — Tom Ashbrook
> "A View from the East"
> *Boston Globe*

5

In the 1960s, Marshall McLuhan promulgated the idea of a new "global village," a world knit together and transformed by television and other marvels of the electronic age. His popular book *Understanding Media* predicted that an information network would envelop the planet, spreading democracy and leading to "a Pentecostal condition of universal understanding and unity . . . a general cosmic consciousness." The global village is growing. *Glasnost* in the Soviet Union, stirrings in Eastern Europe, and demands for openness in China all respond in real measure to images of freedom and dignity transmitted by the penetrating networks foreseen by McLuhan.

But in recent years there have grown other networks designed to penetrate the world with messages far from the enlightenment and openness of "a general cosmic consciousness." A handful of mammoth private organizations have begun to dominate the world's mass media. Most of them confidently announce that by the 1990s, they — five to ten corporate giants — will control most of the world's important newspapers, magazines, books, broadcast stations, movies, recordings, and videocassettes. Moreover, each of these planetary corporations plans to gather under its control every step in the information process, from creation of "the product" to all the various means by which modern technology delivers media messages to the public. "The product" is news, information, ideas, entertainment, and popular culture; the public is the whole world.

This does not bode well for McLuhan's "universal understanding." The lords of the global village have their own political agenda. All resist economic changes that do not support their own financial interests. Together, they exert a homogenizing power over ideas, culture, and commerce that affects populations larger than any in history. Neither

Caesar nor Hitler, Franklin Roosevelt nor any Pope, has commanded as much power to shape the information on which so many people depend to make decisions about everything from whom to vote for to what to eat.

– Ben H. Bagdikian
"The Lords of the Global Village"
The Nation

6

It is a sunny September morning in Disneyland. Bands are playing; people are walking with their children and pushing empty strollers; couples are taking pictures. There is a good proportion of people, buildings, and trees.

The Chinese writers, the UCLA conference hosts, Allen Ginsberg, and I have all just seen a movie, *America the Beautiful*, put out by Bell Laboratories in the fifties. On seven big screens the movie showed highlights of U.S. tourism: the Liberty Bell, the Lincoln Memorial, the Rocky Mountains, Savannah, Big Sur. It also showed long, cheerfully filmed segments of U.S. militarism: tanks rolling on parade, soldiers firing salutes, cadets training with weapons at Annapolis and West Point — all to swelling music and rising choruses.

We have emerged, blinking, from this movie and entered the bright Disneyland streets. The Chinese writers seem content to be here. They are familiar with Disney paraphernalia. In China you can buy Donald Duck on pink thermos bottles, Mickey Mouse and Goofy on yellow cotton handkerchiefs. Filmed Disney cartoons are widely known.

A sophisticated and cosmopolitan Chinese writer named Liu Binyan is strolling down the street with Allen Ginsberg. At home in Beijing, Liu Binyan is a muckraking journalist. The target of his muckraking is corruption in high places; it is astonishing that he is free to travel. He is in the United States on a six months' visit. He speaks English, as well as Russian, Japanese, and Chinese.

Liu Binyan's upright, forceful carriage enhances the grandeur of his leonine head with its curved forehead, wide cheekbones, and strong jaw. He is young; he is at home in the world; his dark suit, remarkably, fits him. For twenty-two years in China he was not permitted to write; he worked at forced labor. Now he is in Disneyland.

Allen Ginsberg, beside Liu Binyan, is walking with his head down. He is sensibly dressed for a hot September day in a short-sleeved white shirt and green chinos. The spectacle of the movie we have just seen has made him gloomy. He says he considers all that military emphasis in the film to be Mickey Mouse.

Liu Binyan, walking so erectly in his fine suit, cocks an ear and says, "Mickey Mouse?"

"You know," Ginsberg says. He is preoccupied. "Mickey Mouse. With the ears?" He wags his fingers desolately over his head. "A little mouse?"

Liu Binyan stands on his dignity. "Yes," he says slowly, in his careful English, "I know Mickey Mouse. Yes. But the film?"

Ginsberg is emphatic. "That was a Mickey Mouse film."

It is all breaking down for Liu Binyan. He has probably seen dozens of Mickey Mouse films. Incredulity raises his voice: "The film we just saw was a Mickey Mouse film?"

Ginsberg, still shaking his head over the film, chooses another tack. "You know," he explains. "Hallucinatory. Delusional."

Liu Binyan slowly lights a cigarette and lets the subject go.[1]

> – Annie Dillard
> *Encounters with Chinese Writers*

---

[1]In 1987 Liu Binyan was expelled from the Communist Party and removed from his job. A visiting scholar at Trinity College in Connecticut in 1989–90, he continues to work for reform in China from abroad. — ED.

HANS MAGNUS ENZENSBERGER

Every Italian Is Privileged

Hans Magnus Enzensberger is widely regarded by Germans as their best living poet. In addition to dozens of volumes of poetry, he has published numerous essays, plays, and translations. Born in 1929 in Bavaria (later part of West Germany), Enzensberger was educated at the Universities of Erlangen, Hamburg, and Freiburg in Germany and the Sorbonne in Paris. His first two books of poetry, published in 1957 and 1960, made him famous as postwar Germany's "angry young man." A committed social critic, he has also worked as a literary consultant, translator, and teacher, resigning his fellowship at Wesleyan University in Connecticut in 1968 in protest against U.S. foreign policies. His play *Das Verhoer von Habana* (1970; *The Havana Inquiry,* 1974) dramatizes transcripts of hearings on President John F. Kennedy's abortive Bay of Pigs invasion of Cuba. Enzensberger's faith in social change, and in literature's power to bring it about, has tarnished over the years; his long poem *Der Untergang der Titanic* (1978; *The Sinking of the Titanic,* 1980) reflects his disillusion. "Every Italian Is Privileged," translated from the German by Martin Chalmers, comes from an essay in *Granta 26* (Spring 1989) and is part of Enzensberger's book *Europe, Europe* (1990).

Luigi Barzini wrote in *The Italians:* "People still come [to Italy] as they came for centuries because they are attracted by a certain quality in Italian life. . . . It somehow quickens their blood." Coupled with Italy's age-old attraction for artists and tourists is a postwar economic boom which has drawn immigrants from all around the Mediterranean. Like the United States, today's Italy is a multicultural society. In this nation of entrepreneurs, a hefty chunk of the economy — perhaps 20 percent — operates outside the official structure. One element is a system of political parties which supply their members with work and contacts. Another is the Mafia, which the social research institute Censis calls Italy's most important private industry. Its estimated annual income of $75 billion comes largely from drugs. Along with growing prejudice against foreigners, gypsies, homosexuals, and drug addicts, Italy now has the world's highest per capita heroin addiction. In spite of these problems, Italy continues to rank among the best places in the world to live.

(For more background on Italy, see p. 341.)

Customs declaration. I was relieved when the bill of lading came. The house I had found in the Alban Hills was no noble villa, but my family was small and it would do very well for a year. The lease had been signed;

I had been initiated into the secrets of the *carta bollata* (the taxable paper on which Italian legal documents are drawn up); the notary had explained to me the contract's more obscure clauses. Only one small detail was left: my baggage had to be brought through customs.

One morning I went to the appropriate government office, located in an old, seedy, barracks-like building on the outskirts of Rome. I let the taxi driver wait, because I thought it was all a mere formality — no merchandise, no valuables, just a few boxes with household goods, clothes, books. I spent three days of my life in this barracks — in a labyrinth of storerooms, offices, corridors, antechambers, and counters — unbelieving at first, then outraged, and finally embittered and de-moralized. All around me everything was running like clockwork. Brisk, business-like but mysterious people with thick gold watches hurried past me, laughing and exchanging greetings and jokes with the officials. Countless cups of coffee were being drunk. I was the only person who had to wander from one counter to the next with my forms (five copies of each), with duty stamps, clearance vouchers, receipts, and certificates. I pleaded my case a dozen times, was forced to wait, was put off with fine words, was sent from pillar to post, and was ignored.

On the evening of the third day I received my possessions with a stony expression. There were no fewer than thirty-eight rubber stamps on my bill of lading and my customs declaration. I had fought doggedly and resentfully for each one. That was more than twenty years ago, but even today I'm gripped by an unreasoning repugnance when I catch sight of an Italian customs official.

Of course, I learned long ago that this absurd adventure was my own   4
fault. If I tell my Roman friends about it, they listen with amusement but also with admiration and alarm in their laughter. What? You went there yourself? Alone? They treat me as if I had crossed the Alps on foot. I had broken the basic rules; I had behaved like an American from the Midwest preparing to set up a vegetable stall in the middle of Nepal. I had no idea that if a customs official tried to live off his salary he would be virtually condemned to death by starvation, and that by trying to deal with things on my own I was behaving in a dangerous way. An Italian would never conceive of going through customs by himself. Today I also know who the brisk creatures were who whisked past me in the halls of the customs house. They were the *galoppini*, the professional interme-diaries and agents. Pay them and all thirty-eight rubber stamps can be effortlessly mustered in half an hour. Everything works out, everyone makes some money, everyone benefits.

The broad road and the narrow. A foreigner will never understand all the subtleties, but the principle is clear: the direct route is not the direct route. There is no point, under any circumstances, appealing to rights common to everyone. It is more important to acquire a favor, an obligation, or a privilege that then demands a deviation, a recommendation, a middleman.

A world of fabulous richness opens up, inexhaustible in its variety. We meet the fireman who always has a ticket for the sold-out performances at La Scala; the neighbor who, a friend of the janitor's daughter, can find out in advance the test questions for the high-school graduation certificate; the Mafia boss who has a teleprinter brought into his cell; the male nurse who obtains a *turno* for a patient — the numbered slip that allows him to attend a clinic for which others have been queuing since six in the morning; the industrialist's wife who hasn't a clue how to mail a registered letter or renew a driving license, because a crowd of *galoppini* — her husband's secretaries — relieve her of every conceivable errand; and the ironing lady who brings a chicken for this same woman, her employer, because her nephew is a dermatologist to whom the ironing lady now looks to cure her breast cancer (not his specialty), because she is frightened that the obscure, nameless machinery of medicine will kill her . . .

Yet everything has its price. It will take the outsider years to learn the rules of the game. It is easy enough to understand the 50,000-lira note (about $46) placed between the pages of the passport, but what about the visiting card with a couple of friendly, vague lines written to the bursar? The visitor from the north who cries "Bribery!" makes it too easy for himself. He lacks a feel for suggestion, an ear for words left unspoken. His brutal simplifications don't do justice to the diversity and elegance of the system.

What, for example, is the significance of the flowers, strawberries, embroidered napkins, and cakes — a whole tableful of offerings — that the wife of a personnel manager, who has moved from Milan to Naples, finds outside her front door the day after her arrival? Who laid all this out? What is the point of this display?

"If you eat even a single cherry from this cake," she explained to me, "then you're in their hands. You've concluded an agreement that lasts a lifetime. Not one but three, four, five large families will demand that you get them work, get them into college, get them pensions. What could I do? I had no choice but to go out on to the balcony and proclaim loudly that I didn't need anything, didn't want anything, couldn't accept anything."

I have no ready answer to the question of how the unwritten laws of Italy relate to the written ones. The country's legal traditions are impressive, its laws numerous, and its hair-splitting achievements legendary. There is no shortage of standards, but they are so diverse, complicated, and contradictory that only someone tired of life could dream of observing them all. Their strict application would instantly paralyze Italy. You would have to use a magnifying glass to find an Italian citizen living by the book. Anyone who tried to go by the rules, whether applying for a building license, seeking a residence permit, or trying to exchange currency, would suffocate under a paper mountain of files and official documents.

Extras. Every Italian, even the poorest wretch, is privileged. Nobody is a nobody. An observer might conclude that often these privileges exist only in the imagination — but they are the essence of life. A logician might object that a society consisting exclusively of the advantaged, in which each person is "doing better" than everyone else, is an impossibility. But the Italians have made this miracle — somewhat akin to the Indian rope trick or squaring the circle — come to pass.

Five long-distance lorry drivers stand at a bar in Andria, and each one asks for a coffee: one wants it *molto stretto* (extra strong), another *macchiato* (with just a dash of milk), the next one *con latte caldo* (with warm milk), his colleague asks for *cappuccino*, but the last one calls triumphantly through the bar: "*Un espresso doppio con latte aparte!*" (a double espresso with the milk on the side). He's known in every truck-stop from Verona to Brindisi, and no barkeeper would dare deny him his desire. He's not average, he's special. The round of privileges begins harmlessly but it continues endlessly.

An extremist. He says: "We hate equality. We despise it. We only like distinctions. Communism in Italy is a joke. Even the word "comrade" is hyperbole. We aren't a collective: we're an accumulation of free individuals. We loathe anonymity. No one feels responsible for the "whole," everyone looks out for himself, for his clan, his clique, his gang. Of course, that means we feel contempt for our neighbors; we dump our garbage on other people's doorsteps. There were two murders in our town this summer because noise had become unbearable in the heat. One was right next door. For nights on end the whole street couldn't sleep, so one guy drew his gun and shot another who was making a racket. That's normal. No one has a conscience about anything. We have left-wing rhetoric but no social super-ego. We don't need any good shepherds, pastors, or wardens. Too bad for you, you'll say. Maybe you're right. But I also think there's something healthy in all of this."

Attempts at explanation, hypotheses, excuses. It's an old story, a very old story. It's a consequence of the late unification of Italy. It's related to the fact that the state always appeared as an occupying power, so the people resisted it. It's the Mediterranean character, like the Spanish or the Levantine or the Greek. It's a matter of capitalist attitudes, remnants of feudalism. It's a rejection of the "naked cash nexus" Marx talks about, of the impersonal power of money that forces an empty and faceless equality on people. It's due to the traditional structure of the family, as it fought for survival in agrarian conditions. It's a sign of our backwardness . . .

No, someone says, it's none of these things. I'll tell you what's to blame: particularism, localism. There are no Italians in Italy, only natives and newcomers. As in art history, everyone defines himself by where he was born: *il Parmegiano, il Veronese, il Perugino.* And that's how it stays. The man from Turin remains the man from Turin, even if he has been living in Cagliari for a generation. That explains why he's so down-to-earth and meticulous and why he understands nothing about Sardinia. The poor soul doesn't have a clue! The Milanese woman born in Giglio has to invite, put up, and protect anyone who comes from Giglio, even if she left the island forty years ago, even if she returns only at Easter to visit her aged mother. Giglio will always be her capital, her metropolis. On the other hand, she can't be held responsible for Milan. Her distinction is to have come into the world in this spot and nowhere else. One may admire other villages, regions, countries, continents — but envy? Or even love? Never! So every Italian town is the best, with perhaps one exception, on which everyone agrees. The exception, and I don't know why, is Rovigo. ("Oh, you're from Rovigo? What a shame.")

An extremist (continued). He says: "Where does your equality get you? Of all the slogans of 1789,[1] it's the emptiest. Your equality is a phantom. It has never come remotely close to being realized. Or do you think there's anything in the so-called socialist countries deserving of the name? What's the situation at home, in the decent, well-protected, orderly   16

---

[1]The slogans of the 1789 French Revolution were "Liberty, Equality, Fraternity." (see p. 16). — ED.

north? Is there no selfishness, no muddle, no nepotism, no corruption, no privilege?

"I know your objection. You'll fall back on the formal equality of citizens and praise it to the skies. Equality before the law; the fact that even the rich pay taxes; the conviction that you have certain rights, just like everyone else, to which you are entitled without a letter of recommendation, without patronage, without a *galoppino*, 'without respect of person.' Maybe you will extol the joys of anonymity, the impersonal exchange of services, commodities, ideas, jobs, and administrative documents. You'll tell me that alienation is a pleasure, that inconspicuousness is a release, that you live in the best of all possible worlds — a social machine that functions smoothly.

"To me you're like millionaires who don't want to admit they're millionaires, who travel second-class and run around in shabby jackets, enjoying their privileges in secret because they're ashamed of them. When it's a matter of life and death, then everybody, even in Frankfurt and Stockholm, wants the best doctor and the most expensive private hospital — but discreetly, of course. The radical English trade union boss sends his children to the public school whose abolition he champions. The truth is, you can't bear the truth! Your social-democratic utopias, your Swedish dream in which naked power dresses up in angelic white, are bleak and dreary."

The potentates. No important figure in Italy can be accused of resorting to such disguise. Power, the ultimate privilege, isn't hidden. Invoked and exhibited, displayed and admired, it's an inexhaustible topic of conversation. Its transformation, its nuances, and it vicissitudes are discussed with passion. No one is interested in structural, impersonal, or distant forms of the exercise of power. Power is experienced as real, and taken seriously, only when embodied in a person or encountered face to face. One can — one wants to — touch it; something of its *mana*, its electricity, is transferred to anyone who comes in contact with it. It's the most widely used aphrodisiac. In the word *potenza* the political significance merges with the sexual. A famous Sicilian saying expresses this duality with matchless precision: "*Commandare e meglio di fottere*" (Ruling is better than fucking).

The dream. I'm sitting on a high, old-fashioned, black-leather barber's   20
chair, which is being cranked further and further back till I'm almost lying horizontal. In the tall, peeling mirrors I see only familiar faces —

the men from the village, sitting on a long wooden bench and waiting: the tobacconist, the priest, the wine-grower, the man from the petrol station. They talk, they leaf through the newspaper, they smoke. Outside, dogs doze on the piazza in the midday heat. The barber, a toothless old man, has just lathered me. The clock on the wall says a minute before noon.

Then the door opens and a bald little gentleman enters. A freshly and carefully pressed brown suit, medal ribbons in his buttonhole, a watch-chain, pointed shoes brilliantly polished. He stands still and looks around. All conversation ceases. The barber rushes over to the new customer and greets him with enthusiasm. Astonished, I watch as the tobacconist takes his hat, the priest helps him off with his jacket, and the petrol station attendant hands him his newspaper. The fat man doesn't say a word. He only runs his long, pink tongue over his lips and solemnly sits down on the chair beside me. He's quickly rubbed with eau-de-Cologne, tucked up in hot and cold cloths, massaged, powdered, combed. No one bothers about me; I feel the soap slowly drying on my cheeks. I'd like to stand up and protest, but I can't rise from my chair. It's hot. I hear the scraping of the blade, the smacking of fingers on the fat man's skin. A long time passes. Then the fat man jumps up and everyone thanks him. He doesn't leave a tip; in fact, he doesn't pay at all, but the barber's apprentice kisses his hand. I stare at him with utter loathing because I've realized at last who this is before me — this puffed-up zero, this fat little man, is "power."

Hardly has the door closed behind him than they all laugh and slap their thighs, pick up newspapers, and light their cigarettes again. "And why doesn't he pay?" I ask. "Why doesn't he wait until it's his turn, like everyone else?"

The apprentice looks at me with astonishment. "But he comes here every day at twelve on the dot for his shave," says the old barber.

"Why do you put up with it?" I cry angrily.　　24

"It's none of your business," says the tobacconist.

"We'll do what we like," says the priest.

"Damn foreigner," mutters the petrol station attendant.

I jump up and run out of the shop. Suddenly I'm standing in the　28 middle of the street in Milan, opposite San Babila, with the village barber's white bib around my neck. Traffic racing past. A little boy points at me; others turn around and laugh. There's still soap on my face. . . .

Typically Italian. Which is it, then? The opera or the Mafia? A *cappuccino* or bribery? Macchiavelli or Missoni? Whenever anyone says that something or other is "typically Italian," I want to jump up with impatience, overturn my chair, and run out of the room. Could anything be more barren than the study of "national psychology," that moldy garbage heap of stereotypes, prejudices, and accepted ideas? And yet it is impossible to dislodge these traditional garden gnomes with their naively painted faces: the taciturn Scandinavian, blonder than straw; the obstinate German, beer stein in hand; the red-faced, garrulous Irishman, always smelling of whiskey; and, of course, the Italian with his mustache, forever sensual but regrettably unreliable, brilliant but lazy, passionate but scheming . . .

The notion of the typical also seems to be indispensable for home consumption, for the elevated purpose of self-criticism — a genre to which Italian authors have made outstanding contributions. In Alberto Arbasino's furious diatribe *Un paese senza*, one can read: "It must be recognized that regardless of every kind of survey technique, behavioral pattern, or grid, an ancient, archetypal, and cunning meanness predominates in the behavior of the Italian . . . The anomalies, monstrosities, madness, and outrageous crimes of contemporary Italy — yes, even the 'typically Italian' horror stories — can hardly be said to be anomalous, monstrous, or shocking when considered in their 'normal' context." How did Arbasino's countrymen respond to these 350 pages of merciless abuse? They elected the author to Parliament three years later!

But the unsuspecting foreigners, on the other hand! As long as a handbag isn't actually snatched or a car broken into, their enthusiasm remains unbounded. Take Gisela G., for example, an unemployed teacher from Munster in Westphalia. She has retired to taste the joys of solitude, i.e., to the obligatory farmhouse in Tuscany. A couple of drop-outs from Dusseldorf — former marketing experts — have built an extension on to the nineteenth-century villa on the hill. A commune of hippies from Berlin is living in the old school building amid empty wine bottles and dirty dishes. A mysteriously named "Study Group for Trans-personal Therapy" has installed itself a few doors down; for a weekend fee of 600 marks [$465], tired branch managers and sportswriters can re-arm themselves for the struggle for survival in Frankfurt. And a Swiss photographer is said recently to have bought the manor on the other side of the river.

Anyway, Gisela G. writes to me (and I have no idea how to reply):   32

Dear M.,

I feel sorry for you! I don't know [how] you can bear to go on living in those "well-ordered" German surroundings. I've been unable to cope with them for a long time now. In the north we're constantly being terrorized — by money, by technology, by discipline. Too much property, too many neuroses. Life here is simpler, more natural, more human, not so anonymous and cold — and not just because of the climate. I look after the garden, I meet the people from the village on the piazza . . . I'm simply happier here.

Good for you, dear Gisela! Best of luck. It's just that your ingenuous letter is completely plagiarized, a compendium of platitudes that have figured in European literature for 200 years . . . Your Tuscan idyll is nothing but a feeble recapitulation. A great love for Italy was first kindled in the sensitive natures of certain visitors in the middle of the eighteenth century. Since then it's become the basis of a billion-dollar industry. It has remained an unrequited love from the start. No Italian would dream of moving voluntarily to Munster in Westphalia or to Trelleborg or the Hook of Holland without a compelling practical reason.

At home, dear Gisela, you were always getting worked up about acid rain and the arms race — but in Tuscany you wear rose-colored glasses. Or haven't you noticed that the Italians don't give a damn about the environment and think pacifism is a fad? You complain about the wealth and greed of the north — but what would you do if the monthly check from the cold north stopped coming and you had to earn a living in Poggibonsi? The local people are friendly as long as you can pay. They tolerate you, just as the whole country accepts the permanent invasion from the north, and I admire their patience. I don't find it surprising that they pluck you clean as a Christmas goose, charmingly, ruthlessly, and with an irony that escapes you entirely.

In fact, I understand you all too well, because I share your stubborn love of Italy. We can't survive without this refuge. It's our favorite projection, our drive-in movie theater, our all-purpose Arcadia. Now, as 200 years ago, we can compensate for our defects here, load up with illusions, and dig among the ruins of an ancient, half-forgotten utopia.

Have it your own way. But why must this love be so ignorant, stupid, and narrow-minded? Why does Gisela so persistently overlook everything in Italy that cries to heaven? If she came home to cool, boring Munster-land and found conditions there like those in Mestre or Avellino, she would be outraged by so much cruelty, harshness, and indifference to others.

Every doting love has its reverse side. Tourism can't exist without a double standard. When the visitor from the north has spent his last lira and returned to the German, Belgian, or Swedish autumn, doesn't he after all heave a secret sigh of relief because everything in the north — the central heating, the state, the telephone — works so well? Then when he opens his newspaper and reads the latest horror stories from Italy (chaos, Camorra, corruption) he leans back and thinks, *It can't happen here.* And this pious belief is the final proof that he hasn't understood anything.

EXPLORATIONS

1. According to Enzensberger, what are the main advantages of a social system in which every individual is special? What are its main disadvantages?

2. Where in this essay does Enzensberger make his point by using rhetorical questions? — that is, questions to which he already knows the answers? What is the effect of this device?

3. Enzensberger's last sentence is "And this pious belief is the final proof that he hasn't understood anything." What does he mean by this? What has "the visitor from the north" failed to understand?

CONNECTIONS

1. What characteristics does Italy, as described by Enzensberger, share with the United States as described by Tom Ashbrook in *Looking at Ourselves?* How do these two authors react differently to the problems of the countries they are writing about, and why?

2. Do the Italians described by Enzensberger have more in common with the Russians described by Hedrick Smith in *"Skoro Budet — It'll Be Here Soon"* (p. 461) or with the Japanese described by Satoshi Kamata in "Six Months at Toyota" (p. 447)? What shared qualities can you identify? What are some possible reasons for the similarity?

3. Look back at Ezekiel Mphahlele's "Tradition and the African Writer" (p. 34). How does Mphahlele report being unreasonably treated by authorities? How do he and Enzensberger differ in their reactions to such treatment? What do you think are the reasons for the difference?

ELABORATIONS

1. "The category of the *Other* is as primordial as consciousness itself," writes Simone de Beauvoir in "Woman as Other" (p. 333). "To the native of a country all who inhabit other countries are 'foreigners.' " What qualities does Enzensberger, a German, attribute to Italians which lump them together as "other"? How does he respond to being treated as "other" by Italians? What points does he make about "otherness" in his closing comments to and about his countrywoman Gisela G.? Write a definition or classification essay on the ways that Beauvoir's concept of Other appears in "Every Italian Is Privileged."

2. What ways have individuals in the United States found to make ourselves feel set apart and special? Are we more inclined to distinguish ourselves, as Enzensberger says the Italians do, or to merge inconspicuously with the group? Write an argumentative essay answering these questions, supporting your views with specific examples.

JANINE WEDEL

Polish Line Committees

Originally from Newton, Kansas, Janine Wedel [b. 1957] has traveled
and lived in Poland since 1977. She studied at Bethel College and Indiana
University, receiving her Ph.D. in social anthropology from the University
of California at Berkeley. A Fulbright scholar, Wedel has published
articles in the United States, Western Europe, and Poland. In addition
to living with Polish families around the country, she toured as a singer
with a Polish country music group. "Polish Line Committees" is from
her book *The Private Poland* (1986), based on her experiences and
research there.

The Poland described by Wedel was a Soviet satellite, annexed by the
USSR after being occupied by Germany during World War II. Domination, however, did not quell the Poles' sense of national (and European)
identity. In the decades after the war, strict Stalinism gradually yielded
more freedom to Polish Communists and to the Roman Catholic church.
In 1979 Pope John Paul II made a historic visit to his Polish homeland.
The next year the illegal union Solidarity organized shipyard strikes and
won concessions, including legalization, most of which were reversed by
the declaration of martial law in December 1981. Fear of a Soviet crackdown kept the government antagonistic to Solidarity and its leader, Lech
Walesa, as the union continued to press for change and protested the
jailing of Czech dissident Václav Havel (see p. 517). Solidarity's persis-
tence won the 1983 Nobel Peace Prize for Walesa and forced the government to agree to hold elections. When the 1980s ended, so did Communist rule in Poland. General Wojciech Jaruzelski remained as
president; but the country's real head was Solidarity prime minister
Tadeusz Mazowiecki. Besides inaugurating a new democratic political system, Mazowiecki has moved Poland rapidly toward a free-market economy. Although the process has brought currency devaluation, inflation,
unemployment, and other painful changes, it has already alleviated many
of the shortages that led to such tactics as refrigerator line committees.

Exchange in Poland is generally based on individual problem-solving
strategies. A striking exception to the purely individual approach is the refrigerator "line committee," an ad hoc organization of individuals who have
one thing in common — a hope to buy refrigerators and other goods.
Since demand for refrigerators far exceeds supply, consumers are not

likely to be successful by simply arriving at a store and standing in line for a refrigerator, unless they have an unofficial exchange relationship with the store management or access to unofficial information about delivery schedules. Consumers without such privileges would have to maintain their place in line twenty-four hours a day for however long it might take for their turn to arrive — often weeks. Given these conditions, line committees have spontaneously arisen, organized and controlled solely by people who wish to buy refrigerators.

In order to get a refrigerator for the apartment he will inherit from his great aunt when she dies, Paweł voluntarily took part in a line committee.

Paweł heard about the line committee through acquaintances, so one   4
day he simply went to the refrigerator store. People connected with the line committee congregated outside to conduct unofficial business. The main activity was the control of a list of names of individuals who wanted to buy refrigerators. The list was made up of people in the order in which they had arrived at the state store. An average list might consist of 300 names; Paweł was number 440 when he signed up.

Deliveries of refrigerators to state stores are sporadic and no information on inventories or delivery schedules is publicly available. Deliveries take place from several times a week to once in six weeks. Anywhere from five to sixty refrigerators may be delivered in a given shipment.

Controlling the list requires time and cooperation from everyone whose name appears on it. Twice each day, at 10:00 A.M. and at 9:00 P.M. at Paweł's store, the roll call of all the names on the list is read off. This is called "verifying the list." People whose names appear on the list of the line committee choose the person who will read off the list for each roll call. This is usually the person who is first on the list at the moment. Of course, as soon as that person succeeds in buying his refrigerator, he is no longer on the list or a participant in the line committee.

If Paweł is unable to be present for a particular roll call, he sends a friend or family member to say, "I am here" when his name is read off. For, if no one were to speak for Paweł, his name would be automatically crossed off the list and added to the end. Missing only one roll call would cause him to lose his place.

But the line committee's work involves more than controlling the list.   8
Even though a delivery of refrigerators arrives only every two weeks on the average, eighteen people must stand guard in front of the refrigerator store round the clock. Vigilant groups are necessary to protect the integrity of the list by preventing people from barging into the store. Store managers do not honor the list.

So, in addition to roll call twice a day, Paweł has obligatory guard duty for three hours, roughly every third day. Though no information is officially available, individuals participating in the line committee do their best to find out when deliveries will arrive. They do this by developing relationships with clerks or with the store manager, who is sometimes tipped off about when deliveries will be made or how many refrigerators are scheduled to arrive. In exchange for information on delivery schedules and inventories, people connected with the line committee may tip the clerks or manager by doing favors or giving gifts such as flowers.

But the line committee is rarely privy to information that is completely reliable, and so the store must be guarded from potential line jumpers. Round the clock, day after day, people on the committee's list take turns at guard duty. Paweł was on the list for four weeks, appearing for roll call and assuming guard duty, before there were any actual deliveries of refrigerators.

Any information about timing and number of refrigerators is of vital importance, for, when an individual is in the first sixty on the list, he is wise to stay after morning roll call in case a delivery materializes that day.

If a delivery materializes, those who have numbers one through about   12 sixty are allowed by the others on the line committee to go into the store when sales begin, in the order they appear on the list. If only twenty or thirty refrigerators are delivered, the remaining thirty or forty people will move up in the line and have more likelihood of success when the next delivery is made, perhaps in days or weeks.

Line committees have been formed not only among prospective refrigerator buyers. They also conserve time for and improve the success of prospective washing machine, sewing machine, and other household appliance consumers. Line committees tend to be found in conjunction with the purchase of commodities that are unevenly distributed and in scarce supply.

EXPLORATIONS

1. Who organizes and runs line committees in Poland? What economic conditions brought these committees into existence? What social conditions make them practical?

2. At the time Wedel wrote this essay, Poland had a mixed economy consisting of some centralized, state-controlled businesses and some private enterprises. In what way(s) do line committees represent the socialist side of Poland, with its emphasis on state control? In what way(s) do they represent the country's capitalist or private-enterprise side?

3. How would the impact of Wedel's account of line committees change without Paweł as a central character? What facts about line committees would Wedel probably have been unable to learn except through a friend like Paweł?

CONNECTIONS

1. What similarities do you notice in the coping strategies of the Poles described by Wedel and the Italians described by Hans Magnus Enzensberger in "Every Italian Is Privileged"? What fundamental differences in attitude separate these two societies?

2. What attitudes do the Poles in Wedel's essay share with Vicki Williams in *Looking at Ourselves*? What customs do we have in the United States that serve a purpose similar to that of refrigerator line committees?

3. How did Poland at the time of Wedel's visit resemble the Soviet Union as described by Hedrick Smith in "*Skoro Budet* — It'll Be Here Soon" and Carola Hansson and Karin Lidén in "Liza and Family" (p. 109)? Taking into account that Wedel describes only a small segment of Polish life, what differences do you notice from the Soviet Union?

ELABORATIONS

1. As archaeologists or art historians sometimes use an object to illustrate the culture that made it, so do writers. What can we learn about state-controlled manufacturing and distribution of consumer goods by studying a refrigerator? Based on Wedel's "Polish Line Committees" and Hedrick Smith's "*Skoro Budet* — It'll Be Here Soon" (p. 461), write an essay describing the life cycle of a refrigerator in a pre-glasnost Soviet-bloc country, from the day its com-

ponents began to arrive at the manufacturing plant to the day it broke down in someone's home.

2. Why do you think the Solidarity movement began in Poland, where citizens already had some freedom to take part in private enterprise, instead of in the Soviet Union or some other more rigidly socialist state? Referring to your reading elsewhere in this book on the Soviet Union and other countries, write an argumentative or comparison-contrast essay suggesting some reasons that Poles united behind a labor union and the idea of drastic political change a decade before these ideas took hold in the Soviet Union.

JANE KRAMER

The Perils of Perestroika

Jane Kramer is best known as the European reporter for *The New Yorker* magazine, for which she has written since leaving *The Village Voice* in 1963. She and her husband, writer Vincent Crapanzano, live in New York and Paris. Kramer was born in Providence, Rhode Island, in 1938; she received her bachelor's degree from Vassar College and her master's from Columbia University. Her 1966 TV documentary "This Is Edward Steichen" won an Emmy Award; *Mademoiselle* magazine named her woman of the year in 1968. A member of the Council on Foreign Relations, the Journalists' Human Rights Committee, and the Environmental Defense Fund, she has also served as a consultant to the German Marshall Fund. Her books offer unusual and often ironic perspectives on human experience: *Honor to the Bride* (1970) shows an Arab family fighting to reestablish their kidnapped daughter's virginity and hence her bride-price; *The Last Cowboy* (1982) follows a Texas ranch hand who has modeled himself on western movie heroes. "The Perils of Perestroika" comes from her "Letter from Europe" in the March 12, 1990 issue of *The New Yorker*.

About the Soviet Union's history Kramer writes: "The Russian empire has always been policed by bureaucrats. . . . Five hundred years after the Moscow conquests began in earnest there is still no reason for the Soviet Union to call itself a country — no national dream, no shared "history," no identity that people can agree on to make them responsible to one another." As *perestroika*[1] loosens their bonds to the central, Russian-dominated government in Moscow, the Soviet Union's fourteen other republics have been flaunting their individuality. The Baltic republics of Estonia, Latvia, and Lithuania "can point to moments, at least, when they were free, and Lithuania, for one, ruled a medieval empire that cut a swath through Russia from the Baltic to the Black Sea," notes Kramer. South of Lithuania, at the eastern edge of Europe, are Byelorussia (White Russia), the Ukraine, and Moldavia. Across the Black Sea, Russia is linked to Islamic Turkey and Iran by Georgia, Azerbaijan, and Armenia. Besides having little in common with the Baltic and European border states, this region has long been divided by its own ethnic enmities. So have the Asian republics, east across the Caspian Sea:

---

[1]One of Gorbachev's pivotal policies, this "restructuring" involves rethinking and reorganizing the USSR's inefficient, state-run economy (see "The US and the USSR," p. 51). — ED.

Kazakhstan, Uzbekistan, Turkmenistan, Tadzhikistan, and Kirghizia. Ironically, as these nationalities assert themselves, a parallel call for separatism has arisen within Russia, encouraged by Russian president Boris Yeltsin (see para. 3).

(For more background on the Soviet Union, see pp. 109, 301, and 461.)

There is virtually nothing to buy in the Soviet Union. Russian industry has been accountable to the Party and to its quotas but not to its products, and the result is that the foreign businessmen coming to the country now come as salesmen, or as developers, or to buy something promising that they can straighten out and sell back, or to recycle the rubles they have made selling something else. They come to a never-never land of consumers waiting for something — anything — to appear and for the chance to buy it. Right now there are twelve hundred foreign firms with joint-venture contracts in the Soviet Union (although the newspapers say that fewer than fifty of them are actually in business). The best newspaper in Estonia, *Edasi*, is going into partnership with the Tartu town council and a Swiss fast-food company that wants to make a market in hamburgers and hot dogs. Robert Maxwell is printing the English-language edition of *Moscow News*. The Red Apple people are going to build Moscow supermarkets. Sheraton is building hotels. McDonald's is building restaurants. The first of twenty McDonald's restaurants opened a month ago, in Pushkin Square (it has nine hundred seats, in the tradition of the KGB cafeterias), after a year when there was talk of trouble and everybody had his own McDonald's-in-Moscow story to explain it. At one point, the rumor, which McDonald's denied, was that the project was foundering because McDonald's had made a deal with the Russians to unload its rubles by buying Russian pickles for its restaurants in Europe, and the Russians had kept on making test pickles "in the Russian way," and had refused to change their recipe, and the only thing that would save the Moscow McDonald's was a compromise that involved McDonald's using its rubles to buy Russian hamburger buns.

Mainly, what the Soviets have to offer here *is* rubles. Their only surplus is their own money. It is not worth anything outside the country, and Gorbachev devalued it for tourists by 90 percent this winter to end the fiction that it was worth something *inside* the country. (Before the devaluation, a dollar bought 60 kopecks on the official exchange and 10 rubles on the black market, which is the market everyone who comes to

Russia uses.) But there has been so little to buy for so long, so little on the store shelves, so little coming out of the state farms and factories, that even the poorest intellectuals — an academic with no Party honorariums starts out at 120 rubles a month, which is half a factory worker's starting salary — have rubles in the tea tin. There is rarely tea in the tea tin. Tea is rationed now in the Soviet Union, along with sugar and salt, and even soap. The shortages are chronic. They used to be most severe in what is properly Russia, but now there is rationing in Georgia (where the people brag about hoarding for themselves, like a big family) and in the Baltics (where the Estonians brag about having a Protestant work ethic, and the Lithuanians and the Latvians about having a Catholic work ethic), and even in the cities of Central Asia, where the commissars rule like pashas, and are rich with drug money. Ordinary medicine is so scarce that it is hard to find a pharmacy open in the Soviet Union, and the hospitals are so short of antibiotics that surgery is often the only available treatment. Some hospitals cannot even get sterilizers. People with access to the West buy their own examining instruments abroad and bring them, sterilized, to the doctor, and every mother who can get hold of a syringe keeps one at home, in case her children need shots. Foreigners who live in the Soviet Union routinely bring in cigarettes and Scotch and instant coffee for their friends (in most of the country Marlboros are an acknowledged form of currency), but usually what their friends want most is medicine, any medicine — aspirin, cough syrup, penicillin. Important Party people have always had their own hospitals, where the medicine was fresh and the equipment was Western — the way they have always had hard currency stores and, like the foreigners, charge accounts with Stockmann's, the Finnish provisioner that ships in meat and milk and vegetables, and just about anything else you want, twice a week to Leningrad and Moscow. In most of Russia, it is impossible to get fresh, pasteurized milk for your children or, say, lettuce for yourself.

The reformers — in the local political shorthand, Gorbachev's people are the reformers or the liberals or the moderates, [Boris] Yeltsin's people are the radicals or the democrats or the insurgents, and Yegor Ligachev's people are the conservatives — say that the shortages today represent a kind of attrition, the end of a long line that never led anywhere but failure. They are certainly not celebrating *glasnost* and *perestroika* anymore. No one talks about celebrating. People in Moscow talk instead about their "post-*perestroika* depression." (A doctor I know, who practices acupuncture at one of the Moscow hospitals, says that her patients complain about post-*perestroika* depression the way they used to complain about "Russian soul-sickness.") They say that the excitement foreigners feel in Moscow is the foreigners' own excitement — that it it easy to get excited about *perestroika* when you are eating prosciutto sandwiches and drinking a Montepulciano *riserva* in an hard-currency bar run by an Italian franchise and staffed by friendly and efficient German waiters — and masks the fact that nothing Russian is working in the USSR, that life for most Russians isn't getting better. The *apparatchiks*[2] blame Gorbachev for the chaos of *perestroika*, and the radicals blame Gorbachev for the shortcomings of *perestroika*, and Gorbachev's people say that their enemies are sabotaging *perestroika*, inciting strikes and holding back production, and, in a way, all of them are right. But there is not much that Gorbachev can do alone, and not much that Russia seems willing to do to help him. The real sabotage is a kind of endemic indifference and contempt.

Contempt is one of the givens of Soviet life. People accept it, and, to   4
the extent they do, it makes the problems of a bankrupt political system or a bankrupt economy look relatively easy to solve — even when . . . there is no consensus on basic political and social values, and no democratic mechanism for establishing economic ones. When you travel in Russia, on a plane with cramped seats and filthy toilets and angry attendants and prison fare consisting of pink sugared water in dirty brown plastic cups and chicken necks and chunks of stale bread in paper bags that are held together by rusty staples, you learn something about the kind of contempt the Soviet state has had for its citizens, and its citizens have had for one another, and about the damage this contempt has done and the "soul-sickness" it has inevitably produced. You learn, sadly, that the crisis is only peripherally about shortages, or about nationalities, or even about the sacrifices made for too long by too many people to Communism's domestic and imperial adventures. The country is as labor-intensive as a Hong Kong sweatshop. (Russians like to say that the definition of a job is five people not doing the work of one.) Whatever the other shortages, there is no shortage of people who could wash a plastic cup or put the bread away in a breadbox, or, for that matter, design a pretty pair of shoes instead of an ugly pair, or paint the waiting room at the hospital, or boil the forceps and syringes, or fix the elevator in a housing project full of babushkas[3] who can't make it up the stairs.

---

[2]Members of the Communist Party bureaucracy. — ED.
[3]Grandmothers, elderly women. — ED.

But when the job counts, even Russians want foreigners. A couple of years ago, a group of American developers went into business with one of the construction companies of the Moscow City Council. They financed themselves by selling long-term prepaid hard-currency leases to foreign companies that needed Moscow offices and housing, and then they and their Russian partners, who have 35,000 local workers on the payroll, hired a construction crew of Yugoslavs and Italians. (For a year, the only change in crew came when the Italian workers brought in Portuguese helpers.) It may have been taken for granted that no foreigner would buy a long lease in a building that Russian workers were putting up, because the Russians were bound to cheat on time and materials, and the workmanship was bound to be terrible — and, besides, the reputation of the Moscow City Council was at stake. In the end, the directors pulled out the Portuguese and put in Soviet labor.

Russia has always been a country of cruel bluff and impulsive, extravagant, fatal gestures — a candy-cane Kremlin thrown up among the raw-wood slums and open sewers of Ivan's Moscow, or a Pushkin card game where champagne and ruin are passed around on the same silver platter, or a feast in Chekhov where the vodka flows and the caviar keeps coming and the drunk dancing bear attacks the guests, and the host weeps because the guests complain.[4] The great public spaces that were a Soviet specialty were displays, really — variations on the old Potemkin-village theme. Stalin's famous subway stations, with their shining tiles and socialist murals and crystal chandeliers, still lead into dangerous, deteriorated neighborhoods. His sweeping parks have grass where no one is allowed to play. His "people's" restaurants hold thousands, but the food is so grim and the service so insulting that "the people" eat fast, looking at their plates, as if they were on lunch shift at a labor camp, and leave as soon as they can get the bill. A welcoming place is almost by definition someplace out of sight, someplace private and unobserved. . . .

People seem to survive by turning in on themselves, turning invisible, hoping that no one will notice them as they endure the intimacies of going to work or getting the marketing done or doing business. They do not expect anything very pleasant from their dealings with each other. They joke about it sometimes. They say that, after all, Russians are peasants, and peasants are pigheaded and distrustful, childish in their

---

[4]Ivan IV, sixteenth-century czar known as Ivan the Terrible. Alexander Pushkin, early nineteenth-century poet, dramatist, and short story writer. Anton Chekhov, late nineteenth-century dramatist and short story writer. — ED.

resentments and quite irrationally abusive — that this is why the waiter locks the door of the restaurant when he sees you coming down the street, and the salesgirl picks up a magazine when you approach her counter, and the train station closes when you are trying to buy a ticket. "We're peasants," your Russian friend will say, and shrug, and look a little sheepish — and laugh. It is the national explanation and, in a way, the national absolution, a sworn statement of helplessness by people who have been so damaged by their own history that they are tempted to use what liberty they have now not for ordering their public lives and commitments but for claiming the privileges of the nomenklatura for themselves.

Gorbachev's "Russian" problem is that for millions of Russians democracy does not mean working harder, or even working together. It certainly does not mean sacrifice. Sacrifice is what Russians had to do for Stalin, and for Khrushchev, and for Brezhnev, and, with some logic, they say that the end of Stalinism means the end of sacrificing. It means that anyone with the wit to arrange it can take a van and "borrow" plates or chairs or punch bowls from the Hermitage for his daughter's wedding, the way only the Party bosses used to, or can smuggle in English sports jackets and American cigarettes and West German stereos or deal in favors like Paris travel vouchers and foreign-currency accounts and dachas in the country, and that it is up to the new, free Soviet state to guarantee, if not provide, protection. In a way, it means institutionalizing the lawlessness that was here before, sharing the opportunities for exploitation and the corruption — which is why Andrei Sakharov[5] talked so much about the urgency of making laws and writing a proper constitution. Sakharov believed that until Russia came under the rule of law, "reform" was simply an extended concept of lawlessness.

Right now, there are 3 million people working in what Russians call   8
the cooperative sector. "Cooperative," in Russia, is another way of saying "private." It means an entrepreneurial adventure in goods or marketing or services, and has nothing to do with the great cooperative movements of the 1920s — which is to say with workers owning their farms and factories together and sharing profits. A cooperative today works this way:

---

[5]Andrei Dmitrievich Sakharov (1921–1989) was a Russian theoretical physicist who helped develop the first Soviet hydrogen bomb. He later became an outspoken political dissident, criticizing his government for the lack of legality and democracy in the Soviet Union. In 1975 he was awarded the Nobel Peace Prize for his work in human rights. — ED.

three or four or a dozen people get together and decide, say, to produce T-shirts. They cut in the appropriate apparatchik and register as a cooperative, and the apparatchik sees to it that they get their knitting machines and cotton before the state T-shirt factories get theirs, and that a flat or a studio becomes "available" for their factory, and then they hire workers for often pitiful salaries and sell the T-shirts to GUM for twice the usual state T-shirt price, or privately for five or ten times that price, and people pay. People pay because the cooperative's T-shirts come in nice colors (and shrink in the first wash), whereas the state's T-shirt come in one ugly color (and shrink in the first wash). They know they are being taken — in Moscow, people who own cooperatives have been making as much as 2,000 or 3,000 rubles a day — but at least they end up with T-shirts they wish would last. When you ask Moscovites about cooperatives, they sometimes talk about T-shirts, and they sometimes talk about veal. They say that it costs 4 rubles to produce a pound of veal, and that the state sells veal for 2 rubles a pound and bankrupts itself, the cooperatives sell veal for 6 rubles a pound and bankrupt their customers — and no one seems to have thought of selling veal for anything near the 4 rubles it is worth.

There are all kinds of cooperatives in Moscow: doctors' cooperatives, so that the doctor who gave you a cursory examination at the state hospital can make a proper diagnosis at home; lawyers' cooperatives, so that you will not lose your case with a state lawyer languidly defending you; grocery cooperatives, so that you can find fresh beets and string beans at the end of the line when you do your marketing; agricultural cooperatives, so that the local Party bosses can get free string beans for themselves; restaurant cooperatives, where you pay with a hard-currency credit card and drink the Georgian wine that never sees the inside of a state liquor store or a state restaurant; secretaries' cooperatives and translators' cooperatives and interpreters' cooperatives for the foreigners who have come to do business in the new Russia and can pay for their services in what the secretaries and translators and interpreters refer to nicely as "golden rubles," which is another way of saying dollars. Sometimes it seems as if the only people in Moscow who have not started cooperatives are the people who have always operated on their own — the taxi-drivers who demand 5 dollars and a pack of Marlboros to drive you around the corner to your next appointment, and expect to settle for 2 dollars or the cigarettes (and still get rich on what they make from the 2 dollars or the cigarettes on the black market), or the babushkas who line up at the state vodka stores at eleven in the morning, when the stores open, and wait in line all afternoon, and then, at six, sell their places to thirsty men coming off the afternoon factory shifts.

Most Russians have had their first legal experience of "the market" with one of these makeshift, middleman experiments in supply and demand. But the practice is old. The Party has always done business by selling favors — for complicity, if not for cash — and so has the Soviet underworld, which is an ethnic hodgepodge of a protection racket that everyone calls the Mafia to glamorize it. In fact, there is a Central Asian Mafia (which deals in drugs and arms, and is said to encourage a lot of the ethnic violence in Central Asia, so that it can arrange to keep the peace in exchange for a measure of immunity from Moscow). There is an Azerbaijani Mafia and a Georgian Mafia and an Armenian Mafia and a Jewish Mafia and, of course, a Russian Mafia. Russian Jews who are trying to emigrate now because of anti-Semitism — there have been mornings when five thousand Jews line up outside the American Embassy, on Tchaikovsky Street, to wait for visa applications — say that most of the Jews who got out before them had to do business with the various Mafias, and put money in the right Party pockets, to purchase the favor of emigration permits in return.

Russians have grown up with these ironies of citizenship. They were given the West as an enemy by policemen and politicians whose own great privilege was access to the enemy's goods and the enemy's money, and often their only reward for complicity or for silence was the chance to flee to the enemy's country. At the worst of the Cold War, the most desirable piece of paper in Moscow was a dollar bill, and the national fantasy was an hour with a shopping cart in one of the dollar shops where the important Cold Warriors bought their Scotch and their stereos, and nobody bothered to explain to ordinary Russians why the enemy was so desirable. Russians who were paid abroad — musicians on tour, say, or writers with royalties — put their hard currency either in foreign banks, where they could never get at it, or in special Soviet banks that kept as much as 90 percent of it for "taxes" and occasionally released the 10 percent that was left for officially approved foreign travel. (Hard currency buys a seat on Aeroflot that most Russians would have to wait a year for.) The Party used that currency to import luxuries for itself. Everyone knew it. Everyone knew that the measure of success for a Communist was his power to beat the system, to corrupt the system — ultimately, to ignore the system. It is not surprising that that kind of power became the measure for ordinary Russians, too, or that Russian workers, caught in the system still, are sullen and suspicious and unproductive, or that they keep to themselves and rarely smile at a stranger or do a favor for anyone who is not a relative, or that they are impatient and indignant when foreigners come and seek them out and start talking to them about George Bush's faults or Margaret Thatcher's problems — about social cost and social conflict and how nothing at home is perfect. A lot of Russian workers think that George Bush is perfect. They thought that Ronald Reagan was perfect. They know that American Presidents are "for" the market, which to their mind means "for" everybody making money and having nice clothes and taking foreign vacations (though they would never spend a vacation visiting other people's factories). The irony escapes them, but after forty-five years of Cold War most Russians love America and their idea of America. They would be startled to learn that people in countries like Czechoslovakia want to be "European," and to keep America out of their affairs. In America, everyone is an apparatchik, and can hold up his neighbor for as much as "the market" will bear.

EXPLORATIONS

1. What Soviet biases or assumptions about the United States does Kramer mention which you and most other U.S. residents do not share?

2. What appear to be the main reasons for the "post-*perestroika* depression" Kramer describes in paragraph 3?

3. "Russia has always been a country of cruel bluff," writes Kramer in paragraph 5. What examples does she give to support this statement?

CONNECTIONS

1. What similarities and differences in attitude do you notice between the Poles described by Janine Wedel in "Polish Line Committees" and the Soviets described here by Kramer? What are some likely reasons for the differences?

2. In what ways does the Soviet Union depicted by Kramer resemble the United States depicted by Tom Ashbrook in *Looking at Ourselves*? What common causes appear to underlie problems in both countries? What problems do you think have different causes in each country?

3. What explanations does Kramer suggest for practices mentioned by Hedrick

Smith in *"Skoro Budet — It'll Be Here Soon"* (p. 461)? What changes, if any, appear to have taken place in Soviet attitudes during the fifteen years between Smith's essay and Kramer's?

4. Compare the Soviet view of President Gorbachev, summarized in Kramer's paragraph 3, with the American view expressed by Joyce Carol Oates in "Meeting the Gorbachevs" (p. 66). What are some likely reasons why the grass looks greener on the other side of the fence?

ELABORATIONS

1. Reread Mikhail Gorbachev's "The US and the USSR" (p. 59) and Joyce Carol Oates's "Meeting the Gorbachevs" (p. 66). Write an essay either defining perestroika as seen by Gorbachev, the Soviet people, and American observers or describing the United States and its people as viewed by Gorbachev and the Soviets. (You may refer also to Francine du Plessix Gray's "Sex Roles in the Soviet Union," p. 301).

2. Write an essay comparing and contrasting the Russian concept of government — its purposes, its functions, the role it plays in citizens' lives — with your concept of government as an American. In addition to Kramer's "The Perils of Perestroika," refer to Gorbachev's "The US and the USSR" (p. 59), Oates's "Meeting the Gorbachevs" (p. 66), Carola Hansson and Karin Lidén's "Liza and Family" (p. 109), and Hedrick Smith's *"Skoro Budet* — It'll Be Here Soon" (p. 461).

VÁCLAV HAVEL

The Chance That Will Not Return

Václav Havel's roundabout route to the presidency of Czechoslovakia might be a plot for one of his plays. The fifty-four-year-old writer was born in Prague, the son of a wealthy entrepreneur. When the Communists took power in 1948, Havel's family's assets were seized. He was barred from attending college. Instead he held menial jobs, attended night school, and read and wrote whenever he could. In the late 1950s he became a stagehand for an avant-garde theater troupe and began writing plays with a political slant. *The Garden Party* (1963) was a hit in Prague, followed by *The Memorandum* (1965), a satiric look at power struggles in a state-run company whose employees are forced to learn an artificial language. Havel came to New York in 1968 for *The Memorandum*'s U.S. opening. Three months after his return home, Czechoslovakia was overrun by Soviet tanks, and his plays were banned. Although assigned to work in a brewery, Havel and his wife, Olga, managed to keep their comfortable apartment and country home.

In 1977 Havel helped found the human rights organization Charter 77. He was jailed for four months, and two years later sent to prison for four years. Despite ill health, he refused to request a pardon or leave the country. He continued to write plays, which were produced in New York, and letters to his wife, which became the book *Letters to Olga* (1983). Sentenced to another prison term in February 1989, he was released four months later after a deluge of protests from fellow artists. In November his political group Civic Forum spearheaded the "velvet revolution" that toppled the Communist government. Less than a year after being a prisoner of the state, Václav Havel was unanimously elected its president.

Czechoslovakia, part of the oft-disputed corridor between East and West, borders Hungary, Austria, Germany, Poland, and the Ukraine (USSR). Prague, its capital, was the cultural center of Central Europe in the fourteenth century. In 1918 Bohemia and Moravia (formerly part of the Holy Roman Empire) united with Slovakia as the Republic of Czechoslovakia. Twenty years later British Prime Minister Neville Chamberlain, with the acquiescence of France, signed an agreement allowing German Führer Adolf Hitler to annex part of Czechoslovakia in return for a guarantee of peace. But World War II was not to be averted: Six months later Hitler dissolved the Czechoslovak republic and coopted Bohemia and Moravia. In 1944 Soviet leader Joseph Stalin's troops entered eastern

Czechoslovakia, and in 1948 the Communists took full control of the government. Twenty years later came the famous "Prague Spring," when Slovak Alexander Dubcek replaced the country's Stalinist head and pledged democratic and economic reforms. This window of hope lasted only seven months before Soviet and Warsaw Pact armies once again invaded Czechoslovakia and installed a new puppet regime. Repression continued through the 1970s and 1980s, tightening at each sign of resistance, until an incident of police brutality in November 1989 sparked a popular uprising that forced the Communist government to yield power in democratic elections to Civic Forum.

"The Chance That Will Not Return" comes from *U.S. News & World Report,* February 26, 1990. The European unity to which Havel refers is a long-range plan by the European Community — currently Belgium, Denmark, France, Germany, Greece, Ireland, Italy, Luxembourg, the Netherlands, Portugal, Spain, and the United Kingdom — to move toward economic and political union; for more details, see p. 690.

All continents are equally old. Yet people speak of Europe as "the old continent." It is because Europe has been the cradle of a civilization that has shaped the history of the world for the last 2,000 years. The spiritual impulses of Antiquity, Judaism and Christianity, merged into a force that has forged the world as we know it. European civilization discovered, explored, conquered, and dominated other continents, other civilizations. It has brought European thinking, enterprise, and inventions to the remotest corners of the earth. It has also brought war, misery, and endless suffering to millions of people in less fortunate countries. In this century in particular, Europe became the center of mercilessly competing ideologies and of two world wars that cost tens of millions of European lives and other millions elsewhere.

Still, Europe's power and its ability to project its civilization and strength have diminished. It no longer has the power to dominate other continents, other cultures. New centers of power and thought have emerged. Europe has aged; it has become old in another sense of the word.

In yet another sense, Europe is a continent that does not exist. For more than forty years, there has been not one Europe, but at least two. One is the Europe of the West, the land of democracies and relative prosperity. The other is the Europe of the East, of totalitarianism until recently unchallenged, the Europe that has finally awakened.

Western Europe was often taken to stand for the whole of the conti-   4
nent, while obituaries were periodically pronounced over the East. Eastern Europe, or at least the people who lived in it, felt equally European
and watched with envy and despair the luckier half that seemed to be
floating away all the time. The dividing line became a gap which threatened to widen into an abyss.

But Europe has been divided in yet another sense. The dividing line
in my country did not run between the Communists and the rest of the
people, it ran between what is good and bad in the heart of each man.
So, too, the dividing line in Europe did not run only between the East
and the West, but through the heart of the continent.

Materialism may have failed as an ideology in the East, but it has
certainly triumphed as a matter of practice in the West. In exchange for
the prospect of prosperity and security, many Europeans became all too
willing to forget about the bigger Europe of spiritual values, humanistic
ideals, and intellectual integrity. A strange sort of newspeak developed in
which "noninterference" stood for indifference and "détente" for appeasement.

Then the tide turned, and the concept that turned it was the old
European (and American) concept of human rights. Perhaps a political
invention in the beginning, designed to win concessions from the other
side, it soon evolved into something vitally important and real for the
people east of the dividing line.

In less than fifteen years, this simple concept of human rights came   8
close to accomplishing what the theories of "containment," "deter-
rence,"and "mutual assured destruction" could not. Let us note that
unlike these concepts, backed by the most impressive collection of hard-
ware that Man has ever assembled, this was a concept purely spiritual.
With the moral rather than tangible support of other Europeans (and
Americans and Canadians), this concept of human rights paved the way
for the enormous changes in Eastern Europe that we have recently
witnessed.

These changes, and the steps toward integration in the West, now
offer Europe a chance to become a whole after forty years of dual existence
(or nonexistence). And for the first time in its history, the old continent
has a chance to do so not through war, but through a consensus of its
nations and people. Such chances do not occur twice.

Europeans in the West have made clear their intention to overcome
national, political, and geographical barriers, and to enter the next mil-

lennium as a single community. Europeans in the East have made equally clear their interest in joining this community of free nations.

What kind of place could or should the new Europe be? What principles would hold this community together and what could it contribute to the rest of the world?

The spirit of history moves in mysterious ways, and it is hardly possible   12 to pose a definite answer to these questions. But perhaps it is possible to glimpse in the mist of the unknown an outline of the place the Europe could become.

First of all, because Europe is as much an idea as a place, it would have to remain bigger than a sum of its parts. Any concept of a new Europe will have to deal with the existence of the United States and the Soviet Union, and not only for political reasons.

The United States, though completely outside Europe, is not entirely non-European. It was born out of Europe in a rebellion against it. The Soviet Union, though not completely inside Europe, has gravitated toward Europe for centuries, without ever taking the final step. In this century, the U.S. and the Soviet Union fought a war against a totalitarian ideology that threatened to undermine the very idea of Europe. Then, they almost fought each other over another incarnation of totalitarianism. If that had happened, the battlefield almost certainly would have been Europe once again. Thus both the Americans and the Russians, though in different degrees, may lay claims on the loyalty of Europeans. And both, fighting as they have for control of the continent, have earned different measures of distrust from Europeans.

If Europe becomes whole, it will have no need for guardians or protectors. But there should always be a place in Europe for the United States, the strongest democracy in the world. And there should be a place in Europe for a truly democratic Soviet Union. The histories and destinies of Europeans, Russians, and Americans are interlinked in countless ways.

Germany, the country that started the last world war, has paid for that   16 with its identity. As Europe has embarked on a search for a new identity of its own, the reunification of Germany is apparently drawing near. With the last of the Nazi war criminals dead or dying, the Germans are certainly entitled to a fresh start if that is their will. Just let us not forget that it was not the changes in Germany that brought about the changes in Europe, it was the other way around.

The process of European integration should not stop at the reunification of Germany; it should go on. Only then will Europe be a safe place for Germany. Only then will Germany be a safe place for Europe.

How can we, the people of the East, the prodigal sons and daughters of Europe, help to make this vision reality, and what, if anything, can we contribute to it?

The answers must lie in our unique, if unpleasant, experience of the last forty-plus years in the equally unique, and more pleasant, experience of our awakening.

As people who have suffered or who saw other people suffer the   20
consequences of totalitarian rule, we may have developed a heightened sensitivity to the symptoms of totalitarian thinking in ourselves and in others.

As people only recently released from bondage, we may have developed an empathy with all people who have not been so lucky. We may remember that oppression and poverty in countries of the Third World (which is really third to nothing) all too often have grown from a legacy left them by us, Europeans. We may remind Europe of this and urge that the debt be repaid.

As people who were finally liberated not by any outside force, but by an upswelling of millions of individual human wills, we can remind Europe of its own legacy, of the importance of individual responsibility for the fate of the community, and thus repay it for the concept of human rights it has given us. In fact, individual rights together with individual responsibility for the common good may constitute the very idea of Europe we are looking for.

As countries that were often divided and turned against one another to crush the aspirations for freedom and European identity in other nations, we can try to make our way back in a dignified and coordinated manner rather than trampling one another in a rush to outrun the others. We can show that Europe can be integrated by first integrating a small part of it.

And finally, as people who achieved change in a peaceful, nonviolent   24
manner, we can advocate the values of nonviolence and tolerance not only as a possible, but perhaps as the only way of achieving social change. Today, we who were terrorized for so long in the surreal world of real socialism know with something approaching certainty that terror does not work and that nonviolence does.

So what kind of place will Europe be? When all is said, it will not become an Orwellian superpower, it will not become a fortress. It will be a smaller but perhaps a nicer place. Yet it will be big enough to be a home not only for James Joyce and Marcel Proust but also for Franz Kafka, Fyodor Dostoevsky, and William Faulkner.[1]

We hope that it will become a community of many different but equal people who will share individual responsibility for the welfare of the community, and who will show empathy and tolerance to all other communities.

Europe is "the old continent." Its qualities, then, should be the qualities of many, though not all, older people: wisdom, tolerance, and understanding.

EXPLORATIONS

1. What relationship does Havel seem to want between Czechoslovakia and the Europe of the future? In his view, what can Eastern Europe gain from unity with the West? What can Western Europe gain from unity with the East?

2. In paragraph 14 Havel writes that the United States and Soviet Union "fought a war against a totalitarian ideology" and later "almost fought each other over another incarnation of totalitarianism." What were these two instances of totalitarianism?

3. Also in paragraph 14, Havel writes, "Both the Americans and the Russians, though in different degrees, may lay claims on the loyalty of Europeans." What are the bases for each country's claims? What clues indicate which country Havel believes is more entitled to Europeans' loyalty?

4. What are Havel's probable reasons for asserting in paragraph 17 that only when Europe is more fully integrated will it be a safe place for Germany, and vice versa?

---

[1]James Joyce (1882–1941), an Irish writer; Marcel Proust (1871–1922), a French writer; Franz Kafka (1883–1924), a German writer born in Prague; Fyodor Dostoevsky (1821–1881), a Russian writer; William Faulkner (1897–1962), an American writer from the South.—ED.

CONNECTIONS

1. In paragraph 11 of "The Perils of Perestroika," what attitude toward the United States and toward Europe does Jane Kramer ascribe to the people of Czechoslovakia? What remarks by Havel suggest that he would agree or disagree with Kramer's statement?

2. What role does Havel see military power as having played in recent European history? Do you think he would agree with John Kenneth Galbraith's comments in *Looking at Ourselves*? What relationship does Havel's view of world military establishments have to the title and thesis of his essay?

3. In paragraph 21 Havel writes, "Oppression and poverty in countries of the Third World . . . all too often have grown from a legacy left them by us, Europeans." Identify at least two other selections you have read in this book that contain evidence supporting his statement. What is that evidence?

ELABORATIONS

1. What is Havel's concept of Europe? Using his essay and others in this book as resources, write a definition or process analysis essay describing Europe as a geographic, political, and cultural force in the world.

2. In paragraphs 6–10, Havel writes about ideas and attitudes that have underlain European history in the twentieth century. On the basis of the headnote preceding this selection, and the headnotes preceding Janine Wedel's "Polish Line Committees," Jane Kramer's "The Perils of Perestroika," and Milovan Djilas's "Ideas Against Torture" (p. 652), write an essay combining Havel's comments with a description of the historic events and changes they refer to.

PETER SCHNEIDER

The End of the Wall

Born in 1940, Peter Schneider was part of the postwar German generation who entered politics on the antiauthoritarian wave of the late 1960s. He has lived in West Berlin since 1961 — the year East Germany built a wall across the city to prevent any more of its citizens from joining the 3 million who had already gone west. A political journalist and essayist, Schneider has published feature stories in *The New York Times Magazine, Harper's,* and elsewhere on issues of German identity. He is the author of a novel, *The Wall Jumper* (1984), and the screenplay for the film *Knife in the Head* (1979). "The End of the Wall" comes from "Concrete and Irony," translated by Elliott Rabin, in *Harper's,* April 1990.

The Allies (the United States, the United Kingdom, France, and the Soviet Union) defeated the Axis powers (Germany, Italy, and Japan) and ended World War II in 1945. German Führer Adolf Hitler committed suicide a month before his nation's surrender ended the Nazi (National Socialist Party) conquest of Europe and slaughter of millions of Jews and others. The Allies — recalling such horrors as the concentration camps in which Nazi victims were imprisoned and killed, and Kristallnacht ("crystal night") in 1938, when Nazis rioted all over Germany, burning synagogues, destroying Jewish shops and homes, and persecuting the Jews — divided Germany into four zones of control. In 1949 the American, British, and French zones together became the Federal Republic of Germany (West Germany), while the Soviet zone became the German Democratic Republic (East Germany). West Germany included West Berlin, a section of the nation's former capital islanded inside East Germany (and still joined like a Siamese twin to the East German capital, East Berlin).

When West Germany joined the European Defense Community in 1952, the East German government declared a 3-mile prohibited zone along their common border and cut Berlin's telephone system in two. Nine years later East Germany built the Berlin Wall, a massive structure of concrete, barbed wire, and guard posts, to keep East Germans from fleeing to West Berlin. The West German economy was booming, however, and efforts to emigrate continued. As the Soviet Union's grip on Eastern Europe loosened in 1989, nearby countries provided a more roundabout escape route from East to West Germany. Finally, on November 9, the East German government announced it would open (and later tear down) the Berlin Wall. Schneider, who was visiting the German department at Dartmouth College in New Hampshire, writes, "I returned to Berlin in December and, of course, began asking everyone I met about his or her experiences on the already famous day." Soon afterward, both Germanies began planning for full reunification of their country, to take place as soon as possible.

Great events change one's feelings. One should take the time to name them properly. What Berliners on both sides of the Wall felt on November 9, and have continued to feel in the months since, cannot be reduced to the common denominator of "Germany." These feelings were simultaneously more modest and more generous than some new nationalist feeling. A wall knocked down after three decades is a powerful metaphor.

Among the grotesque miscalculations of the architects of the East German state, is there any greater than the decision to protect the "socialist fatherland" by constructing an edifice that couldn't help but evoke a yearning for freedom in men and women everywhere? With the construction of the Wall, the East German Communists instantly made the problem of the division of Germany into an issue for all humanity and provided the then-not-so-warmly-loved Germans — the Wall went up sixteen short years after the war — with some emotional sympathy they otherwise would not have been granted.

I saw the events of November 9 courtesy of Tom Brokaw and NBC — not much in the way of insights, but great camera angles. News items from Germany on American TV are normally over in seconds, but on this particular evening, the shots of Berliners dancing on the Wall were long and varied. These pictures brought about, I think, in the autumn days that followed, a historical caesura: They suddenly, positively, and decisively changed the American image of the Germans. Yes, the West German "economic miracle" brought a kind of bloodless respect, but by its very nature — *economic* news — it could never seriously overcome the black-and-white pictures of the Nazis extending their arms to greet Hitler. Perhaps November 9 was the first time since the war that the Germans encountered American — even worldwide — affection. Germans like myself who saw TV footage overseas gained the impression that the new pictures from Berlin had, for the first time, the power of an emotional counterweight. The hated Nazi German and the tedious, if possibly respected, economic-miracle German were joined in the minds of foreigners by the warm, sympathetic German!

Germans should not be deceived, however: this new international sympathy for Germany runs only so deep. The German crimes remain vivid, if not always to Germans themselves. At the official celebrations that followed the spontaneous festivities of November 9, no German politician dared to make clear that the Wall was not a "tragedy" but a direct result of a world war contrived by the Germans. And just after November 9, T-shirts with the inscription NOVEMBER 9 — I WAS THERE! were sold at a kiosk in the Potsdamerplatz. Only Richard Chaim Schneider, a son of Holocaust survivors, was struck by how much amnesia was required to purchase the new feeling of exaltation. "The sight of these souvenir articles took my breath away," he wrote in the December 29 *Die Zeit.* "What was this? did the Germans suddenly want to own up to the fact that they were there?

At that time, on November 9, 1938?

On the so-called Kristallnacht?"

Scene in West Berlin disco, December 1989:

"Give me the key!"

"You have your own!"

"But it's my apartment."

"So starting today, should I sleep in the East?"

"What do I care? I simply don't want somebody coming to my pad at the drop of a hat!"

The opening of the Wall was a catastrophe for many who had tied their fortunes to the durability of this structure. The West Berlin woman demanding her key back is no longer so enamored of her East Berlin lover now that he can come over and see her anytime. And it can get even more complicated: West Berlin Romeos, including not a few Turks, maintained, along with their marriages in the West, romantic attachments in the East, the discreet existence of which the Wall quietly guarded. On the long night of November 9, and into the gray morning of November 10, many mistresses — some with kids in tow — stood before this or that door in the West, uninvited. With freedom comes responsibility.

But for the most part, upon my return to Berlin, I found the city startlingly unchanged. The stories about West Berliners doing their weekend shopping by noon on Thursday? A fairy tale. That West Berlin, because of the East German throngs, was suffering an easternlike shortage of goods? Not true either, not yet anyway.

Only in front of cheap grocery stores, electronics shops, and the post offices (where every East German was handed one hundred marks by the government — Western pocket money) did I discover the notorious lines. What I did notice was price gouging: in the Wilmersdorf shopping quarter, a pedestrian mall whose shops cater to the not-so-well-to-do, many things suddenly cost more, much more — radios, cameras, ski jackets, and, of course, blue jeans.

The recommendation in *Der Spiegel* of the East German author Heiner Müller to his fellow countrymen — that they should clean out West Berlin's KaDeWe department store instead of pressing their noses against shop windows — seemed to have been heeded. A new announcement over the loudspeakers at the big Hertie store warned, "Pay attention to your handbags!" The West Berlin police announced that the number of robberies doubled in the last two weeks of November.

Upon my first step across the border in December, I peeked into the customs booths and was struck by how the photos of Erich Honecker had been taken down so quickly. You could *see* the blank rectangles, the clean, unfaded paint long hidden — Honecker had run East Germany for a long time. I asked a border agent, "When had the president been taken down?"

"Two days after his resignation."   16

"And who will take that place next?"

He shrugged his shoulders and grinned. "Who indeed?"

It can be said without exaggeration: the new friendliness, the looseness of the border agents, is almost eerie. I still have the harsh tone in my ear; I continue to wait for that inexorable gaze pinned to the bridge of my nose that used to last for several minutes. This particular guard winked me through, joked around, asked me, sounding truly interested, when I would come again! Had it all been just a bad dream? Can people so quickly unlearn habits ingrained over decades? When the Wall fell, what must have gone on in the heads of these people for whom it provided not only work but power?

"What did you do on November 9?" I asked.   20

"I went to station headquarters. We had to get ready for all the turmoil!"

I took out my papers. "Did you enjoy it? You personally?"

"Everything's okay now, yes? Have a good trip back!"

Why did I hope that he would refuse to answer at all, rather than   24
make this friendly small talk?

What I could have gathered from any map of the city I discover first
by walking around. The Potsdamerplatz (West Berlin), which I have
known for years, leads directly through a hole in the Wall into Leipziger-
strasse (East Berlin), which I have also known for years. Through the
Brandenburg Gate, which used to symbolize the end of the West, one
arrives at Berlin Middle, at Pariserplatz; and just beyond that is Unter
den Linden. In Berlin, what for the past four weeks had been called
"madness," "crazy," "unbelievable" in truth is the most normal thing:
After all, what could be more normal than for people to be able to walk
from one end of a street to the other? Having grown accustomed to an
insane situation, we experience the normalization as something completely crazy.

A sense that things were crazy . . . but no sense, oddly, of happiness,
defiance, triumph — no trace of euphoria, even of the Germanically
moderate and inhibited kind. Wasn't this the first successful and, moreover, peaceful revolution ever in Germany? Walking in East Berlin, I
felt as if nothing had happened.

The four East Berlin construction workers I met in the Sports Corner,
a bar in Prenzlauer Berg, were, by four in the afternoon, pretty drunk.
It took them a while to warm up to me. "Wall up, Wall down. What is
really going to change for us?" one of them said. "Business is so washed
out that everyone from the West would have to invest themselves to
death. From floor to roof, we are going to have to start our business from
scratch before we are going to move forward." . . .

In the junk market at Potsdamerplatz, I asked a Turkish man what the   28
opening of the Wall meant to him. "Wonderful!" he said. "I rejoiced!"
And for himself? Wouldn't he face increasing competition? "Wonderful.
No problem!"

I felt that I was caught in an old leftist role — that, for the sake of my
own worldview, I was asking people about problems that they didn't have.
Only when he brought the table I had bought from him back to my
house did I learn that a customer like me receives different answers before
the sale than after. He didn't want to intimidate a potential German
buyer with candid information.

"Frankly, we're all afraid," he said, after I'd made him a cup of
espresso. "Today at noon they punctured all four tires of the car belonging

to the Polish man two stalls down. As we were trying to patch up the car, two other Poles came by who had had the same thing happen to them. Until now, we Turks have fared better. We've been living here for thirty years, we know the language and don't constantly walk around with the city map in front of our noses. But how much longer will it last?"

"I was three years old when I came here, and I grew up here," his wife, who had come along, said. "I am not German, but I am also not a foreigner. What kind of country is this, in which even after thirty years one is still treated like a foreigner? The only thing that distinguishes me from a German is that I do not look like a German. What's so terrible about that?"

In the West German media for some time now there has been a 32 discussion about the model of a "multicultural" society. I think that the Germans from East Germany have good reasons, entirely their own, for participating in this discussion. For Germans in the East and the West are also, after forty years, different *culturally*. After the first thrill of unity, it will become clear that, on either side of the Wall, not only two states but two societies have developed. It is not yet apparent which differences will vanish overnight and which will prove to be resilient. For now, one thing is clear: a unity that would try to iron smooth all differences is one that not just our neighbors need to fear.

EXPLORATIONS

1. Judging from Schneider's essay, what appear to be the main hopes and concerns about a united Germany on the part of East Germans? West Germans?

2. Adolf Hitler's Nazi (National Socialist) Party preached the racial superiority of Germans, as the non-German "guest workers" in Schneider's paragraphs 28–32 are aware. How does their knowledge of German history evidently affect these workers' reaction to the fall of the wall and the prospect of German reunification?

3. What international attitudes toward Germans does Schneider mention? What other attitudes toward German reunification have you read about in countries that fought or were conquered by German armies in World War II?

CONNECTIONS

1. What common ideas about Europe's history and its failure appear in Schneider's essay and in Václav Havel's "The Chance That Will Not Return"? How is Germany's relationship with the United States different from Czechoslovakia's?

2. After reading "The End of the Wall," what predictions can you make about the reactions of the Poles in Janine Wedel's "Polish Line Committees" as their country moves from Soviet domination and a mostly centralized economy to a democratic government and a market-based economy?

3. "Walking in East Berlin, I felt as if nothing had happened," writers Schneider in paragraph 26. Based on what you have read elsewhere in this book about Communist societies, why do you think East Germans in "The End of the Wall" are more reticent than the West Germans?

ELABORATIONS

1. Based on "The End of the Wall" and other selections in this book, write a comparison-contrast essay on the changes in Germany's role in Europe and the Soviet Union's role in Europe from World War II to the present.

2. "I saw the events of November 9 courtesy of Tom Brokaw and NBC," writes Schneider in paragraph 3. How has television affected your experience of world events? What are the pros and cons of being able to watch history long distance as it happens? Write an essay analyzing the impact of TV news on those who watch it and on those who make history.

GABRIEL GARCÍA MÁRQUEZ

Death Constant Beyond Love

"It bothers me that the people of the United States have appropriated the word *America* as if *they* were the only Americans," Gabriel García Márquez told an interviewer shortly before he won the 1982 Nobel Prize for literature. A devotee of North American fiction, García Márquez was for a time prevented from entering the United States because he had worked for the Cuban news agency in New York in 1961. His old friendship with Fidel Castro, he says, is based on a shared love of literature and fish recipes. Born in the Caribbean coastal village of Aracataca, Colombia, in 1928, García Márquez grew up listening to his grandfather's tales of war and politics and his grandmother's stories of the supernatural. Out of this mix came the town of Macondo, the setting for much of his fiction, akin to William Faulkner's Yoknapatawpha County and R. K. Narayan's Indian village of Malgudi (see p. 419). García Márquez studied at the University of Bogotá in Colombia's capital; he left to be a journalist, traveling to other parts of South America, the United States, and Europe, and began writing short stories. Recognition came with his 1961 novella *El coronel no tiene quien le escriba* (*No One Writes to the Colonel,* 1968), during a general flowering of Latin American literature referred to as "El Boom." But it was *Cien años de soledad* (1967; *One Hundred Years of Solitude,* 1970) that made him famous, selling more than 10 million copies in more than thirty languages. García Márquez's fusion of naturalism and fantasy has given him a central place in the genre known as magic realism. Among his other novels are *Crónica de una muerte anunciada* (1981; *Chronicle of a Death Foretold,* 1982), which won the Nobel Prize; *El amor en los tiempos del cólera* (1985; *Love in the Time of Cholera,* 1988); and *General en su Laberingo* (1989; *The General in His Labyrinth,* 1990); a novel about South American liberator Simón Bolívar which sold 700,000 copies within two weeks of its March 1989 publication in Bogotá. The following story, "Death Constant Beyond Love," reached the United States in 1978 as part of the collection *Innocent Erendira and Other Stories,* translated from the Spanish by Gregory Rabassa.

The Panama-Colombia border is where Central and South America meet. Colombia thus is the only South American country with both a Caribbean and a Pacific coast. Like Panama, Venezuela, and Ecuador, it was ruled by Spain as part of New Granada from the 1500s until independence in 1819. (Venezuela and Ecuador broke away ten years later; Panama followed in 1903.) The national language is Spanish, and 97 percent of Colombians are Roman Catholic. Ethnically a majority are mestizos (mixed Spanish and Indian blood). One of the continent's longest-lived democracies, Colombia continues to be plagued by economic and social problems, most notably the war between the government and the drug cartels.

(For more background on Colombia, see p. 443.)

Senator Onésimo Sánchez had six months and eleven days to go before his death when he found the woman of his life. He met her in Rosal del Virrey, an illusory village which by night was the furtive wharf for smugglers' ships, and on the other hand, in broad daylight looked like the most useless inlet on the desert, facing a sea that was arid and without direction and so far from everything no one would have suspected that someone capable of changing the destiny of anyone lived there. Even its name was a kind of joke, because the only rose in that village was being worn by Senator Onésimo Sánchez himself on the same afternoon when he met Laura Farina.

It was an unavoidable stop in the electoral campaign he made every four years. The carnival wagons had arrived in the morning. Then came the trucks with the rented Indians who were carried into the towns in order to enlarge the crowds at public ceremonies. A short time before eleven o'clock, along with the music and rockets and jeeps of the retinue, the ministerial automobile, the color of strawberry soda, arrived. Senator Onésimo Sánchez was placid and weatherless inside the air-conditioned car, but as soon as he opened the door he was shaken by a gust of fire and his shirt of pure silk was soaked in a kind of light-colored soup and he felt many years older and more alone than ever. In real life he had just turned forty-two, had been graduated from Göttingen with honors as a metallurgical engineer, and was an avid reader, although without much reward, of badly translated Latin classics. He was married to a radiant German woman who had given him five children and they were all happy in their home, he the happiest of all until they told him, three months before, that he would be dead forever by next Christmas.

While the preparations for the public rally were being completed, the senator managed to have an hour alone in the house they had set aside for him to rest in. Before he lay down he put in a glass of drinking water the rose he had kept alive all across the desert, lunched on the diet cereals that he took with him so as to avoid the repeated portions of fried goat that were waiting for him during the rest of the day, and he took several analgesic pills before the time prescribed so that he would have the remedy ahead of the pain. Then he put the electric fan close to the hammock and stretched out naked for fifteen minutes in the shadow of the rose, making a great effort at mental distraction so as not to think about death while he dozed. Except for the doctors, no one knew that he had been sentenced to a fixed term, for he had decided to endure his secret all alone, with no change in his life, not because of pride but out of shame.

He felt in full control of his will when he appeared in public again at   4
three in the afternoon, rested and clean, wearing a pair of coarse linen slacks and a floral shirt, and with his soul sustained by the antipain pills. Nevertheless, the erosion of death was much more pernicious than he had supposed, for as he went up onto the platform he felt a strange disdain for those who were fighting for the good luck to shake his hand, and he didn't feel sorry as he had at other times for the groups of barefoot Indians who could scarcely bear the hot saltpeter coals of the sterile little square. He silenced the applause with a wave of his hand, almost with rage, and he began to speak without gestures, his eyes fixed on the sea, which was sighing with heat. His measured, deep voice had the quality of calm water, but the speech that had been memorized and ground out so many times had not occurred to him in the nature of telling the truth, but, rather, as the opposite of a fatalistic pronouncement by Marcus Aurelius in the fourth book of his *Meditations*.

"We are here for the purpose of defeating nature," he began, against all his convictions. "We will no longer be foundlings in our own country, orphans of God in a realm of thirst and bad climate, exiles in our own land. We will be different people, ladies and gentlemen, we will be a great and happy people."

There was a pattern to his circus. As he spoke his aides threw clusters of paper birds into the air and the artificial creatures took on life, flew about the platform of planks, and went out to sea. At the same time, other men took some prop trees with felt leaves out of the wagons and planted them in the saltpeter soil behind the crowd. They finished by setting up a cardboard facade with make-believe houses of red brick that had glass windows, and with it they covered the miserable real-life shacks.

The senator prolonged his speech with two quotations in Latin in order to give the farce more time. He promised rain-making machines, portable breeders for table animals, the oils of happiness which would make vegetables grow in the saltpeter and clumps of pansies in the window boxes. When he saw that his fictional world was all set up, he pointed to it. "That's the way it will be for us, ladies and gentlemen," he shouted. "Look! That's the way it will be for us."

The audience turned around. An ocean liner made of painted paper   8 was passing behind the houses and it was taller than the tallest houses in the artificial city. Only the senator himself noticed that since it had been set up and taken down and carried from one place to another the super-imposed cardboard town had been eaten away by the terrible climate and that it was almost as poor and dusty as Rosal del Virrey.

For the first time in twelve years, Nelson Farina didn't go to greet the senator. He listened to the speech from his hammock amidst the remains of his siesta, under the cool bower of a house of unplaned boards which he had built with the same pharmacist's hands with which he had drawn and quartered his first wife. He had escaped from Devil's Island and appeared in Rosal del Virrey on a ship loaded with innocent macaws, with a beautiful and blasphemous black woman he had found in Para-maribo and by whom he had a daughter. The woman died of natural causes a short while later and she didn't suffer the fate of the other, whose pieces had fertilized her own cauliflower patch, but was buried whole and with her Dutch name in the local cemetery. The daughter had inherited her color and her figure along with her father's yellow and astonished eyes, and he had good reason to imagine that he was rearing the most beautiful woman in the world.

Ever since he had met Senator Onésimo Sánchez during his first electoral campaign, Nelson Farina had begged for his help in getting a false identity card which would place him beyond the reach of the law. The senator, in a friendly but firm way, had refused. Nelson Farina never gave up, and for several years, every time he found the chance, he would repeat his request with a different recourse. But this time he stayed in his hammock, condemned to rot alive in that burning den of buccaneers. When he heard the final applause, he lifted his head, and looking over the boards of the fence, he saw the back side of the farce: the props for the buildings, the framework of the trees, the hidden illusionists who were pushing the ocean liner along. He spat with rancor.

"*Merde*," he said. "*C'est le Blacamán de la politique.*"[1]

After the speech, as was customary, the senator took a walk through   12 the streets of the town in the midst of the music and the rockets and was

---

[1]"Shit. . . . It's the Blacamán of politics." In Márquez's story "Blacamán the Good Vendor of Miracles," two magicians (one a huckster and one a miracle worker) share the name Blacamán. — ED.

besieged by the townspeople, who told him their troubles. The senator listened to them good-naturedly and he always found some way to console everybody without having to do them any difficult favors. A woman up on the roof of a house with her six youngest children managed to make herself heard over the uproar and the fireworks.

"I'm not asking for much, Senator," she said. "Just a donkey to haul water from Hanged Man's Well."

The senator noticed the six thin children. "What became of your husband?" he asked.

"He went to find his fortune on the island of Aruba," the woman answered good-humoredly, "and what he found was a foreign woman, the kind that put diamonds on their teeth."

The answer brought on a roar of laughter.   16

"All right," the senator decided, "you'll get your donkey."

A short while later an aide of his brought a good pack donkey to the woman's house and on the rump it had a campaign slogan written in indelible paint so that no one would ever forget that it was a gift from the senator.

Along the short stretch of street he made other, smaller gestures, and he even gave a spoonful of medicine to a sick man who had had his bed brought to the door of his house so he could see him pass. At the last corner, through the boards of the fence, he saw Nelson Farina in his hammock, looking ashen and gloomy, but nonetheless the senator greeted him, with no show of affection.

"Hello, how are you?"   20

Nelson Farina turned in his hammock and soaked him in the sad amber of his look.

"*Moi, vous savez*,"[2] he said.

His daughter came out into the yard when she heard the greeting. She was wearing a cheap, faded Guajiro Indian robe, her head was decorated with colored bows, and her face was painted as protection against the sun, but even in that state of disrepair it was possible to imagine that there had never been another so beautiful in the whole world. The senator was left breathless. "I'll be damned!" he breathed in surprise. "The Lord does the craziest things!"

That night Nelson Farina dressed his daughter up in her best clothes 24
and sent her to the senator. Two guards armed with rifles who were nodding from the heat in the borrowed house ordered her to wait on the only chair in the vestibule.

---

[2]"Me, you know." — ED.

The senator was in the next room meeting with the important people of Rosal del Virrey, whom he had gathered together in order to sing for them the truths he had left out of his speeches. They looked so much like all the ones he always met in all the towns in the desert that even the senator himself was sick and tired of that perpetual nightly session. His shirt was soaked with sweat and he was trying to dry it on his body with the hot breeze from an electric fan that was buzzing like a horsefly in the heavy heat of the room.

"We, of course, can't eat paper birds," he said. "You and I know that the day there are trees and flowers in this heap of goat dung, the day there are shad instead of worms in the water holes, that day neither you nor I will have anything to do here, do I make myself clear?"

No one answered. While he was speaking, the senator had torn a sheet off the calendar and fashioned a paper butterfly out of it with his hands. He tossed it with no particular aim into the air current coming from the fan and the butterfly flew about the room and then went out through the half-open door. The senator went on speaking with a control aided by the complicity of death.

"Therefore," he said, "I don't have to repeat to you what you already   28
know too well: that my reelection is a better piece of business for you than it is for me, because I'm fed up with stagnant water and Indian sweat, while you people, on the other hand, make your living from it."

Laura Farina saw the paper butterfly come out. Only she saw it because the guards in the vestibule had fallen asleep on the steps, hugging their rifles. After a few turns, the large lithographed butterfly unfolded completely, flattened against the wall, and remained stuck there. Laura Farina tried to pull it off with her nails. One of the guards, who woke up with the applause from the next room, noticed her vain attempt.

"It won't come off," he said sleepily. "It's painted on the wall."

Laura Farina sat down again when the men began to come out of the meeting. The senator stood in the doorway of the room with his hand on the latch, and he only noticed Laura Farina when the vestibule was empty.

"What are you doing here?"   32

"*C'est de la part de mon père,*"[3] she said.

The senator understood. He scrutinized the sleeping guards, then he

---

[3]"It's on behalf of my father." — ED.

scrutinized Laura Farina, whose unusual beauty was even more demanding than his pain, and he resolved then that death had made his decision for him.

"Come in," he told her.

Laura Farina was struck dumb standing in the doorway to the room: 36 thousands of bank notes were floating in the air, flapping like the butterfly. But the senator turned off the fan and the bills were left without air and alighted on the objects in the room.

"You see," he said, smiling, "even shit can fly."

Laura Farina sat down on a schoolboy's stool. Her skin was smooth and firm, with the same color and the same solar density as crude oil, her hair was the mane of a young mare, and her huge eyes were brighter than the light. The senator followed the thread of her look and finally found the rose, which had been tarnished by the saltpeter.

"It's a rose," he said.

"Yes," she said with a trace of perplexity. "I learned what they were 40 in Riohacha."

The senator sat down on an army cot, talking about roses as he unbuttoned his shirt. On the side where he imagined his heart to be inside his chest he had a corsair's tattoo of a heart pierced by an arrow. He threw the soaked shirt to the floor and asked Laura Farina to help him off with his boots.

She knelt down facing the cot. The senator continued to scrutinize her, thoughtfully, and while she was untying the laces he wondered which one of them would end up with the bad luck of that encounter.

"You're just a child," he said.

"Don't you believe it," she said. "I'll be nineteen in April."   44

The senator became interested.

"What day?"

"The eleventh," she said.

The senator felt better. "We're both Aries," he said. And smiling, he 48 added:

"It's the sign of solitude."

Laura Farina wasn't paying attention because she didn't know what to do with the boots. The senator, for his part, didn't know what to do with Laura Farina, because he wasn't used to sudden love affairs and, besides, he knew that the one at hand had its origins in indignity. Just to have some time to think, he held Laura Farina tightly between his knees, embraced her about the waist, and lay down on his back on the cot.

Then he realized that she was naked under her dress, for her body gave off the dark fragrance of an animal of the woods, but her heart was frightened and her skin disturbed by a glacial sweat.

"No one loves us," he sighed.

Laura Farina tried to say something, but there was only enough air   52
for her to breathe. He laid her down beside him to help her, he put out the light and the room was in the shadow of the rose. She abandoned herself to the mercies of her fate. The senator caressed her slowly, seeking her with his hand, barely touching her, but where he expected to find her, he came across something iron that was in the way.

"What have you got there?"

"A padlock," she said.

"What in hell!" the senator said furiously and asked what he knew only too well. "Where's the key?"

Laura Farina gave a breath of relief.   56

"My papa has it," she answered. "He told me to tell you to send one of your people to get it and to send along with him a written promise that you'll straighten out his situation."

The senator grew tense. "Frog bastard," he murmured indignantly. Then he closed his eyes in order to relax and he met himself in the darkness. *Remember,* he remembered, *that whether it's you or someone else, it won't be long before you'll be dead and it won't be long before your name won't even be left.*

He waited for the shudder to pass.

"Tell me one thing," he asked then. "What have you heard about   60
me?"

"Do you want the honest-to-God truth?"

"The honest-to-God truth."

"Well," Laura Farina ventured, "they say you're worse than the rest because you're different."

The senator didn't get upset. He remained silent for a long time with   64
his eyes closed, and when he opened them again he seemed to have returned from his most hidden instincts.

"Oh, what the hell," he decided. "Tell your son of a bitch of a father that I'll straighten out his situation."

"If you want, I can go get the key myself," Laura Farina said.

The senator held her back.

"Forget about the key," he said, "and sleep awhile with me. It's good   68
to be with someone when you're so alone."

Then she laid his head on her shoulder with her eyes fixed on the rose.

The senator held her about the waist, sank his face into woods-animal armpit, and gave in to terror. Six months and eleven days later he would die in that same position, debased and repudiated because of the public scandal with Laura Farina and weeping with rage at dying without her.

EXPLORATIONS

1. How is the title "Death Constant Beyond Love" appropriate to this story's plot? What does the title mean in relation to the story's underlying theme?

2. How does Senator Onésimo Sánchez define his job to the ordinary people of Rosal del Virrey? How does he define it to the town's important people? How do you think he defines it to himself?

3. The author tells us that Senator Onésimo Sánchez "had decided to endure his secret all alone, with no change in his life, not because of pride but out of shame" (para. 3). What reasons does Sánchez have to be proud? What reasons does he have to be ashamed? How does his pride contribute to his shame?

4. García Márquez starts a pattern of ironically juxtaposed opposites with his title, which reverses the common expression "love constant beyond death." What pair of opposites appears in the story's first sentence? What further pairs appear in the opening paragraph? What roles do these juxtaposed opposites play in the rest of the story?

CONNECTIONS

1. In "Death Constant Beyond Love," Senator Sánchez tells his backers that if he ever kept his promises to improve the local people's lives, "that day neither you nor I will have anything to do here" (para. 26). In Peter Schneider's "The End of the Wall," what government and other jobholders in Berlin do you think will have nothing to do without the wall?

2. What common ideas about political power appear in "Death Constant Beyond Love" and Jane Kramer's "The Perils of Perestroika"? What characters hold these ideas in each selection?

3. Looking back at Jill Gay's "Patriotic Prostitutes" (p. 435), what attitude(s) do you think Nelson Farina shares with the Asian governments that encourage prostitution? What attitude(s) does Laura Farina share with the prostitutes? What clues in the story suggest García Márquez's feelings about these attitudes?

4. Raju in R. K. Narayan's "Trail of the Green Blazer" (p. 419) succeeds as a criminal but fails when he yields to a noble impulse. In what sense is this also true of Senator Sánchez? What are the significant differences in these two characters' fates? What contrast in the two stories' themes is reflected by those differences?

ELABORATIONS

1. García Márquez has been hailed for his masterful fusion of realism with myth and fantasy, as well as for the political implications of his work. To analyze his writing is probably a task beyond the most ambitious critic, but we can gain some appreciation of his art by looking closely at his craft. What, for instance, are the functions of flying paper in "Death Constant Beyond Love"? Write an essay describing and explaining García Márquez's uses of this phenomenon.

2. "No one loves us," sighs Senator Sánchez to Laura Farina (para. 51). What does he mean? Is he correct? Why or why not? Write an essay on the role and significance of love in "Death Constant Beyond Love."

MICHELE L. NORRIS

A Child of Crack

Journalist Michele L. Norris was born in 1961 and grew up in Minneapolis. After starting as a biomedical engineering major at the University of Wisconsin, she switched to journalism at the University of Minnesota, where she won a minority scholarship from CBS affiliate WCCO-TV. Norris wrote for the student newspaper and worked as a dispatcher for WCCO. A 1985 summer internship at the *Los Angeles Times* turned into a two-year job, after which Norris was hired by the *Chicago Tribune*. There she worked both as a general assignment reporter and with a seven-member investigative team which won four awards for a series of articles on Chicago's schools. "I really like covering education," says Norris, "because it's a window for examining larger issues in society." She joined the *Washington Post* in 1988 and was assigned to report on education in Prince George's County, Maryland, just outside the District of Columbia. "A Child of Crack" is excerpted from her 1989 series of stories on Dooney Waters, which won her a Livingston Award, the Federal Bar Association's Media Award, and a second-place Feature Writing Award from the Maryland/Washington, D.C./Delaware Press Association.

The story of Dooney Waters may have a happy ending. In May 1989 his father took Dooney to live with him; and as Norris's articles ran over the summer his mother, Addie, entered a rehabilitation program. In September 1989 President Bush mentioned the boy in an antidrug speech. Dooney moved in with a friend to stay in school in Prince George's County; when last heard from, he was wearing clean clothes, slept on Batman sheets, had gained ten pounds, was receiving counseling, and had just made the honor roll at school.

Dooney Waters, a thickset six-year-old missing two front teeth, sat hunched over a notebook, drawing a family portrait.

First he sketched a stick-figure woman smoking a pipe twice her size. A coil of smoke rose from the pipe, which held a white square he called a "rock." Above that, he drew a picture of himself, another stick figure with tears falling from its face.

"Drugs have wrecked my mother," Dooney said as he doodled. "Drugs have wrecked a lot of mothers and fathers and children and babies. If I don't be careful, drugs are going to wreck me too."

His was a graphic rendering of the life of a child growing up in what   4
police and social workers have identified as a crack house, an apartment
in Washington Heights, a federally subsidized complex in Landover,
Maryland, where people congregated to buy and use drugs. Dooney's life
was punctuated by days when he hid behind his bed to eat sandwiches
sent by teachers who knew he would get nothing else. Nights when
Dooney wet his bed because people were "yelling and doing drugs and
stuff." And weeks in which he barely saw his thirty-two-year-old mother,
who spent most of her time searching for drugs.

Addie Lorraine Waters, who described herself as a "slave to cocaine,"
said she let drug dealers use her apartment in exchange for the steady
support of her habit. The arrangement turned Dooney's home into a
modern-day opium den where pipes, spoons, and needles were in supply
like ketchup and mustard at a fast-food restaurant. . . .

Addie's apartment was on Capital View Drive, site of more than a
dozen slayings last year. Yet, the locks were removed from the front door
to allow an unyielding tide of addicts and dealers to flow in and out.
Children, particularly toddlers, often peered inside to ask: "Is my mommy
here?"

While he was living in the crack house, Dooney was burned when a
woman tossed boiling water at his mother's face in a drug dispute, and
his right palm was singed when his thirteen-year-old half brother handed
him a soft drink can that had been used to heat crack cocaine on the
stove.

Teachers say that Dooney often begged to be taken to their homes,   8
once asking it he could stay overnight in his classroom. "I'll sleep on the
floor," Dooney told an instructor in Greenbelt Center Elementary
School's after-school counseling and tutorial program. "Please don't make
me go home. I don't want to go back there."

Dooney was painfully shy or exhaustively outgoing, depending largely
on whether he was at home or in school — the one place where he
could relax. In class, he played practical jokes on friends and passed out
kisses and hugs to teachers. But his mood darkened when he boarded a
bus for home.

The violence that surrounded Dooney at home was, in most cases, a
byproduct of the bustling drug trade. Washington Heights was host to
one of the largest open-air drug markets in Prince George's County,
Maryland, until a series of police raids last winter drove the problem
indoors.

On Saturday, April 29, Dooney was sitting in the living room near his mother when a fifteen-year-old drug dealer burst in and tossed a pan of boiling water, a weapon that anybody with a stove could afford. Dooney, his mother, and two neighbors recalled that the dealer then plopped down on a sofa and watched as Dooney's weeping mother soothed the burns on her shoulder and neck. Dooney also was at home when another adolescent enforcer leaned through an open window on Sunday, May 14 and pitched a blend of bleach and boiling water in the face of nineteen-year-old Clifford E. Bernard, a regular in the apartment, for ignoring a $150 debt.

"People around here don't play when you owe them money," said 12 Sherry Brown, twenty-five, a friend of Addie Waters who frequented the apartment. Brown said she smokes crack every day and has given birth to two crack-addicted babies in the past three years. "These young boys around here will burn you in a minute if you so much as look at them the wrong way," she said. "I'm telling you sure as I'm sitting here, crack has made people crazy."

Almost everyone was welcome at "Addie's place." Her patrons included some unlikely characters, but as one said, "Addie don't turn nobody away." Not the fifteen-year-old who in May burned her furniture and clothing intentionally with a miniature blow torch. Not even the twenty-one-year-old man who "accidentally" shot her thirteen-year-old son, Frank Russell West, five inches above the heart last Dec. 16. Police ascribed the shooting to a "drug deal gone bad."

Dooney was sleeping when Russell, shot in the left shoulder, stumbled back into the apartment. Dooney will not talk about the night his half brother was shot except to say, "Russell was shot 'cause of drugs."

Waters did not press charges against Edward "June" Powell, the man police charged with shooting Russell. Powell, whose trial has been continued because he did not have an attorney, is out on bail. "He didn't mean to do it," said Waters, who referred to Powell as a close friend of the family. "It was an accident. He meant to kill someone else." . . .

Dooney's mother and others who congregated in her apartment were 16 bound by a common desperation for drugs. The majority, in their late twenties or early thirties, described themselves as "recreational" drug users until they tried the highly addictive crack. Many said they had swapped welfare checks, food stamps, furniture, and sexual favors to support their craving for crack. They had lost jobs, spouses, homes, and self-respect. Nearly all were in danger of losing children, too.

The Prince George's County Department of Social Services was in-

vestigating charges of parental neglect against many of the people who
frequented Waters's apartment. But they rarely took the county's investigations seriously. Some would joke about timid caseworkers who were
too "yellow" to visit Washington Heights or would pass around letters in
which officials threatened to remove children from their custody. The
problem, as in Dooney's case, was that the county's threats lacked teeth.
Caseworkers were usually so overloaded that they rarely had time to bring
cases to court, even after they had corroborated charges of abuse and
neglect.

Prince George's County police said they knew about Waters's operation
but never found enough drugs in the apartment to charge her or others.
"The problem is that drugs don't last long up there," said Officer Alex
Bailey, who patrols the Washington Heights neighborhood. "They use
them up as soon as they arrive."

Such explanations seemed lost on Dooney.

"Everybody knows about the drugs at my house," he said with a matter-   20
of-fact tone not common to a first-grader. "The police know, too, but
they don't do nothing about it. Don't nobody do nothing about it," he
said.

Police did raid Dooney's apartment on Saturday, May 13, after they
were called there by neighbor who complained about noise. "They were
looking for the drugs," Dooney said two days later, as his eyes grew full
of tears. "They took all the clothes out of my mother's closets. They
threw it all on my mother. They called my mother names."

Dooney also said he was afraid of the police, and when asked why, he
inquired, "How do you spell the word 'shoot'?" Supplied with a notebook
and pen, he wrote the word slowly in large, shaky letters and then
repeatedly punched the pen into the paper to form a circle of black marks.
Pausing a minute, he drew a person holding a pipe, a smiling face atop
a body with a circle in her belly. "That's my mother." Dooney said,
pointing to the figure's face. He moved his finger toward the circle. "And
that's a bullet hole."

Around the apartment, Dooney was constantly on guard, watchful for
signs of a ruckus or a raid. "Don't stand too close," he told a visitor
standing near the front door, warning that the lockless door was often
kicked open.

Since kindergarten, Dooney has pulled himself out of bed almost every   24
school morning without the help of adults or alarm clocks, said his
mother, who boasted about his independence. Asked how he got himself

up in the morning, Dooney tapped a finger to his foreheard and said, "My brain wakes me up. I get up when it gets light outside."

Dooney rarely bathed or brushed his hair before he went to school while he was living with his mother. The bathroom was inoperable during the period that a *Washington Post* reporter and photographer regularly visited. The toilet overflowed with human waste. Stagnant water stood in the bathtub. There was no soap, no shampoo, no toilet paper or toothpaste.

When Dooney did wash, he used a yellow dishpan that doubled as a washtub for rinsing out his clothes. Without a working toilet in the apartment, Dooney went across the hall when he needed to use the bathroom. If he couldn't wait, or if the neighbors weren't home, Dooney went outside in the bushes or urinated in the bathtub. He reasoned that this was the root of his bed-wetting. "I didn't want to get up to go to the bathroom, and now I pee in my bed every night," he said. . . .

Dooney's mother moved to Washington Heights in 1977, a time when the complex advertised "luxury apartments." During Dooney's preschool years, Waters says, the complex was "a nice, clean place full of working class folks." Even then, marijuana, speed, powder cocaine, and other drugs circulated through the community.

But the introduction of crack swept in a new era. Nothing before it   28
had spawned so rapid and so wrenching an addiction.

Not all Washington Heights residents are involved in the drug trade. Many families take pains to shield themselves and their children from drugs and violence. But the vast numbers that started using crack tell similar tales about addictions that rapidly exceeded their incomes.

Three years ago, Dooney's father worked as an electrician's apprentice. His mother was a typist for the Prince George's County Board of Education and took night courses in interior design at a nearby community college.

"We had two incomes, two kids, all the things that you dream about in a marriage," Waters said. "There was always food in the refrigerator and money in the bank. We did drugs then, but only at night and on weekends."

Dooney's parents were introduced to crack shortly after their separa-   32
tion, and their drug use became less recreational. Dooney's father said he became a small-time drug dealer to support his crack habit and spent six months in jail in 1988 for selling drugs. Dooney's mother said she

traded away most of the family belongings — and all of her sons' toys — to buy drugs.

Waters, who has no criminal record, said she lost her job with the Armed Forces Benefit and Relief Association in the District of Columbia a few months after she was hired last year because she kept falling asleep on the job after smoking crack all night. With an abundance of time and a circle of drug-addicted neighbors, Waters's occasional crack use became an insatiable ache. She said she began selling crack to support her mounting habit by buying one large rock, smoking some, and selling the rest at a profit. By her account, the addiction quickly outgrew her drug-dealing income, and she began to let people smoke or sell drugs in her apartment on the condition that they shared their bounty with her.

At that point, Dooney's apartment became a crack house. "All of a sudden, they just set up shop," his mother said. "I told people never to keep more than $100 worth in my house. Smoking is one thing but for the police to walk up in your house and have people selling, that's two charges."

The children's lives declined in step with their parents. Dooney's thirteen-year-old half brother dropped out of the seventh grade last fall and has been arrested six times in two years on charges ranging from jumping trains to stealing cars.

Both of Waters's sons begged her to seek help. In the last three years, 36 addiction had whittled her body from a size 16 to a size 5. Her eyes were sunken, underlined by tufts of purplish skin. Her complexion, which she said was once "the envy" of her three sisters, was lifeless, almost like vinyl.

Pictures in a blue photo album she kept in her living room show a more attractive Addie L. Waters — a buxom woman with radiant eyes, bright red lipstick, and a voluminous hairdo. Dooney paged through the photo album one afternoon and said, "My mother used to be pretty."

Dooney comes from a family with a legacy of addiction. His mother said she bought her first bag of drugs, a $5 sack of marijuana, from her alcoholic father in the late seventies. Dooney's father said he started smoking marijuana in high school and moved on to using PCP, speed, and powder cocaine.

Dooney's father says he smoked his first hit of crack about two years ago, when a girlfriend encouraged him to try the drug. Dooney's mother also tried crack for the first time with a lover, a boyfriend who said it "was the best high around."

When she first started smoking crack, Waters said, she would lock   40
herself in the bathroom to hide from her two sons. The charade didn't
last long. One evening Russell threw open the bathroom door and discovered his mother with a plastic pipe in her mouth.

"I tried to hide it and he saw me," says Waters, who went on to
describe how Russell, then in the fifth grade, slapped her several times
and flushed the drugs down the toilet. "By him seeing me, it really
affected me," Waters says. "I left it alone for about an hour."

Eventually she says, Russell's reactions became less extreme, and he
got involved with the drug trade himself by selling soap chips on the
street to unsuspecting buyers.

In early interviews, Waters called herself a good parent, a claim her
two sons disputed. During the two months a reporter and photographer
visited the apartment, Waters never checked Dooney's homework after
school and in interviews couldn't remember his teachers' names.

Over time, Waters backed away from her earlier descriptions of herself.   44
"I can't be the kind of mother I should be when I'm smoking crack," she
said. "If I could do it all over again I would not do drugs."

Waters will take the blame for Russell, but she maintained that it
would not be her fault if Dooney started using or selling drugs.

"If he does, it won't be because of me," Waters said. "I learned with
Russell so I tell [Dooney] not to smoke or sell drugs. It's my fault that
I'm doing it but I think [Dooney] knows better. I tell him all the time
that he don't want to live like me."

Waters said that Dooney had seen her smoke crack "hundreds" of
times. "He would always tell me, 'Mommy, say no to drugs' and I would
say, 'Okay, baby.'" She eventually stopped trying to hide her crack habit
from Dooney.

Crack became such a part of Dooney's life that he could list the steps   48
for cooking it before he could tie his shoelaces. Perhaps that's why he
sometimes scoffed at school programs designed to teach pupils to "just
say no" to drugs.

"The Drug Avengers ain't real," he said, referring to an educational
cartoon in which a band of superheroes prevents children from buying
and using drugs. "They couldn't stop my mother from doing drugs."

"You have to ask yourself, 'What am I telling a child when I say to
him that drugs are bad and yet everyone he knows is using drugs
regularly?'" says John Van Schoonhoven, principal of Greenbelt Center.
"It worries me that perhaps we aren't reaching these children and teaching

them that they don't have to get involved with drugs, even though almost everyone they know already has." . . .

To help Dooney and others like him, teachers are being called on increasingly to attend to physical and emotional needs that are ignored in the pupils' homes.

"You do more parenting than teaching nowadays," says Wendy Gea-   52
gan, an instructional aide who tutors children with learning problems at Greenbelt Center. "It's all so different now. We have always had to help children with their problems, but these kids want to be held. They want to be mothered. They need affection. They need their emotions soothed." . . .

Dooney's teachers began to suspect that his mother had a drug problem shortly after he entered kindergarten.

"It was rather sudden," said Janet Pelkey, Dooney's kindergarten teacher. "He wasn't bathed. He became very angry and started striking out. He started gobbling down food whenever he got it, even candy and snacks in the classroom. It was obvious that something was going on at home."

School officials said they could not reach Dooney's mother by phone and no one answered the door during several home visits. The school-community link is difficult to maintain for many pupils from Washington Heights because they are bused to the school for desegregation purposes. Many families in Washington Heights do not own cars, making it difficult to visit a school that took three bus transfers to reach. Conversely, teachers say they are afraid to visit Washington Heights, particularly during the winter, when daylight is scarce. So teachers had little or no contact with the parents of pupils with the most turbulent home lives.

Concerned about his emotional problems, Dooney's kindergarten   56
teacher placed him in the "transitional first grade," a class for students with academic problems that set them a few steps behind other children their age.

Dooney's condition worsened when he entered first grade last September, teachers said. He was given to fits of screaming and crying and came to school wearing torn and filthy clothes. "It was almost like he was shellshocked when he came to school . . . ," Field said. "He is such a sad little boy. He walks around with his head down and he's always sucking his little thumb."

"When I discovered what he was going through at home, I thought, 'My goodness, it's amazing that he even gets to school,'" Field said.

His mood swung like a pendulum. "Sometimes he comes in and he is just starving for affection," said Susan Bennett, an instructional assistant. "He clings to his teacher like he is afraid to let go. . . . Or sometimes when he comes to school he is angry. You brush by him and he is ready to attack."

Dooney entered first grade lacking several basic skills children normally   60
master before leaving kindergarten. Teachers say he had a difficult time distinguishing among colors and could not count past ten. But Dooney's academic skills improved in classes that provided special equipment and individual tutoring. By the end of the year, his test scores put him in line with others his age, though he still had trouble tying his shoes and telling time.

Acting on the advice of teachers, the Prince George's County Department of Child Protective Services investigated Dooney's mother in April 1988.

"Based on the provided investigative information, the allegations of neglect have been indicated," child protective services worker Conchita A. Woods wrote in a letter to Waters dated April 24, 1989, a year after the investigation began. But a caseworker said that it would be "months, maybe even years" before they could seek to remove Dooney from his mother's custody.

Russell Brown, the investigator, said he had about twenty cases on his desk just like Waters's.

"We have a lot of cases that are much worse than that," Brown said.   64
"There's probably not a whole lot I can do" for Dooney. Brown said that he does not have time to go through the arduous process of taking a child from a parent unless there is imminent danger.

"It's up to you guys to help this little boy because we just don't have the manpower to do it," Brown told Dooney's teachers over lunch on April 27. . . .

At the principal's urging, Prince George's school and government officials created a pilot after-school program that offers tutoring, counseling, and drug education for students at Greenbelt Center. Equally important, it shields them from neighborhood violence for a few extra hours. Although its primary function is to help children with drug-related trauma, the program also provides academic enrichment and free day care for other students. From 3:00 to 6:30 P.M., children get help with homework, counseling, playtime, and a snack — the last meal of the day for many of them.

School officials around the country say such programs may be the vanguard of school reform as more children enter schools with a crush of physical and emotional problems that detract from standard academic work.

"It's become apparent that schools cannot do all that they are supposed to be doing in a six-hour day," says Nancy Kochuk, a spokeswoman for the National Education Association. "The schools are basically set up as an industrial model. It's like a factory line. That doesn't seem to serve our society very well anymore when we are dealing with children with such intense and overwhelming problems." . . .   68

Last spring Dooney said he hated drugs and what they have done to his life. Yet he seemed to view the drug trade as an inevitable calling in the way that some children look at the steel mills and coal mines in which their forebears worked.

Asked if he would sell or use drugs when he grows up, Dooney shook his head violently and wrinkled his nose in disgust. But the expression faded, and Dooney looked at the floor: "I don't want to sell drugs, but I will probably have to."

EXPLORATIONS

1. What specific information about crack does Norris include in her essay? What does she evidently assume her audience already knows about the drug?

2. How do Norris's use of quotations and other interview data, and her paragraphing, show that "A Child of Crack" was written as a news feature? If she were to rewrite it as an expository essay, what kinds of changes would she need to make?

3. How are Dooney Waters's life and family affected by the police? his school? other social and governmental agencies? the news media?

CONNECTIONS

1. In Gabriel García Márquez's short story "Death Constant Beyond Love," love redeems the impotence of political power, but death is stronger than both. What nonfictional examples of these ideas appear in "A Child of Crack"?

2. Jane Kramer writers in "The Perils of Perestroika": "Everyone knew that the measure of success for a Communist was his power to beat the system, to corrupt the system — ultimately, to ignore the system. . . . That kind of power became the measure for ordinary Russians, too." What evidence in "A

Child of Crack" suggests that these statements also hold for people inside and outside the system in the United States?

3. In *Looking at Ourselves*, Lewis H. Lapham writes about the tendency "for white people living in safe neighborhoods to blur the distinction between crime and race." What examples can you find in "A Child of Crack" of this and other points made by Lapham? What evidence, if any, contradicts Lapham's ideas?

ELABORATIONS

1. In Geoffrey Matthews's "'Good Sons' Who Kill" (p. 443), the drug trade is the indirect reason that people who consider themselves devout and moral commit immoral acts. How do drugs and drug money exert similar effects in Dooney Waters's neighborhood? Write a classification or cause-and-effect essay on the attractive and the destructive impact of crack cocaine in Colombia and in Prince George's County, Maryland.

2. Drug use in the United States takes an enormous toll on our economic and human resources, in terms of business productivity, AIDS, and the quality of life, to name just three examples. The government's war on drugs is aimed at all aspects of the problem: discouraging or destroying the crop at its source; preventing it from crossing the U.S. border; educating citizens on the dangers of drugs; seizing drugs inside this country; arresting dealers and users; and treating addicts. Our failure to win the war has led some critics to recommend the death penalty for drug dealers, while others advocate legalizing drugs to separate use from crime. What do you think the U.S. government should do about drugs? Drawing on "A Child of Crack," Lewis H. Lapham's observations in *Looking at Ourselves*, and Matthews's "'Good Sons' Who Kill" (p. 443), as well as any other information you wish to use, write an argumentative essay presenting the drug policy you believe is most likely to work.

YORAM BINUR

Palestinian Like Me

At 33, Israeli journalist Yoram Binur was fluent in Arabic and knowl-edgeable about Palestine. He had lived in the Arab city of Ramallah while serving as a lieutenant in the Israeli Defense Forces' elite Para-chutists' Unit in 1976. Binur began writing for the Jerusalem weekly newspaper *Kol Ha'ir* in 1983 and soon was assigned to cover the Arab beat, where his familiarity with Arab speech, clothing, gestures, and mannerisms increased. He decided to make bold use of his skills. A committed Zionist, for six months he posed as an Arab laborer in Jeru-salem and Tel Aviv. Living as part of a despised minority group showed him an unexpectedly dark side of these familiar cities, as he became the victim of prejudice, discrimination, and sometimes violence from his own people. Out of Binur's experiences came his book *My Enemy, My Self* (1989), from which "Palestinian Like Me" was excerpted in *New Age Journal* (May/June 1989) and reprinted in the *Utne Reader* (Sept./Oct. 1989). Yoram Binur continues to live and work in Jerusalem.

After World War I, victorious Britain and France divided up the Middle Eastern remnants of Turkey's Ottoman Empire. France was to control Syria and Lebanon, while Britain continued to dominate Egypt, Iraq, the newly created Transjordan, and Palestine (the southeastern Mediterranean coast). Their plans to make these territories independent were hampered in Palestine by the struggle for dominance between its Arab and Jewish populations. With World War II, and the Nazi slaughter of Jews, the need for an official Jewish homeland became urgent. After the war, Britain turned Palestine over to the United Nations, which in 1948 voted to create the state of Israel. The angry Arabs denied Israel's right to exist. Tensions flared in 1967 into the Six Day War, which ended with Israel not only intact but in control of the rest of Palestine, previously managed by Syria, Jordan, and Egypt (see p. 86). A new attack on Israel by Syria and Egypt in 1973 brought the United States into the picture as a mediator. An Arab summit conference the next year recognized the Palestine Liberation Organization (PLO) under Yasir Arafat as the sole legitimate representative of the Palestinian people — that is, the Arab Palestinians living in the West Bank and Gaza Strip, now occupied by Israel. Israel's refusal to negotiate with the PLO and its policy of building settlements in the occupied territories have increased Arab resentment, Palestinian resistance, and Israeli reprisals. It was in that climate of hostility, repression, and terrorism that Yoram Binur launched the experiment he describes in "Palestinian Like Me." His essay continues into the *intifada,* an uprising of Palestinians inside and outside Israeli-run refugee camps against the troops whom they regard as an army of occupation (see paras. 44–45). The Israeli government treated the grass-roots violence of the intifada as a terrorist campaign. However, the hundreds of Palestinian casualties focused worldwide attention on the PLO's demand for an independent Palestinian state.

(For more background on Palestine and Israel, see pp. 86 and 618. For more background on the Arab countries, see pp. 23 and 348.)

In 1984, I began work as a reporter for the local weekly newspaper in Jerusalem, *Kol Ha'ir* ("The Voice of the City"). I took the Arab beat, covering not only East Jerusalem but also most of the West Bank and occasionally the Gaza Strip as well. My close daily interaction with Arabs from the occupied territories considerably improved my command of spoken Arabic as well as my knowledge of Arab manners and gestures.

I first became aware of the degree to which I had absorbed Palestinian culture when I traveled to Nablus with Danny Rubinstein, a seasoned reporter from the newspaper *Davar,* to interview a relative of Abu Nidal, the notorious Palestinian terrorist leader. During our conversation, I learned that the interviewee thought I was Rubinstein's Arab guide. On other occasions, too, Arabs from the occupied territories mistook me for a compatriot.

This misapprehension, together with the fact that news items on the West Bank tended to be rather dull and routine at the time, led me to suggest to my editor a different approach to my reporting. My idea was to offer a fresh perspective on Israeli Jews' relationship with the Palestinians by posing as a Palestinian in a variety of settings and recording my feelings, as well as the reactions of people toward me.

After I'd established an identity and made my preparations, I discussed 4 my plan with Feisal Al Husseini, one of the most important Arab leaders in the occupied territories (who had recently spent nine months under administrative detention). Husseini explained the risk I was running: if the Arabs I contacted suspected me of being an undercover agent working for the Shin Beth (the Israeli secret service, now known as Shabak), my life would be in danger. Husseini gave me a letter in which he asked that I be given all possible assistance so that I might carry out my journalistic mission without hindrance. In view of his uncontested leadership among the people of the occupied territories, the letter would serve as a sort of insurance policy. It could save my life in a tight spot — provided I had time enough to whip it out.

And so, over a period of six months, I lived more or less continuously as an Arab, generally seeking to involve myself in situations that were typical for the average Palestinian living under Israeli military rule. I stayed in cities and in refugee camps. I worked in restaurants and garages. I lodged with Arab laborers. I even, in my guise as an Arab, had a relationship with a Jewish Israeli woman and volunteered on a kibbutz.

Posing as a Palestinian Arab enabled me to see the conflict in a different perspective and to experience it with a greater intensity. To state that Arabs are discriminated against in the Jewish state of Israel is hardly an earthshaking revelation. But posing as a Palestinian, I was able to understand, for the first time, what it means for a man to feel afraid and insecure inside his own home when a military patrol passes outside his window. I had heard Palestinians tell of such things many times, and I had always regarded it as an exaggerated example used to embellish their arguments against the occupation. But when I was myself gripped by that paralyzing fear, when I felt it in my guts, I grasped a dimension of their lives in a way that I never really could have as an Israeli journalist, however understanding I might be of the Palestinian situation. It wasn't a question of discovering new facts, but of discovering what it meant to *feel* the facts.

Among my first jobs was a stint as a restaurant worker at Hatuki ("The Parrot"), a small Tel Aviv pub. A family atmosphere prevailed there, but, needless to say, I wasn't really a part of the family. I was a servant. Everyone ordered me around: "I see our Arab is a little idle, so let him take out the glasses and wash them over again." Once, when Osnat, a young waitress, had some friends visiting, I overhead one of them ask about "her" Arab worker. I also clearly heard her answer: "This Arab, I swear — with just a little improvement he could be a Jew."

One night at Hatuki, all the feelings of frustration and humiliation   8
that I was to experience as an Arab worker were brought home. The owner's sister, Michal, and her boyfriend came in the kitchen around two in the morning, when most of the customers had already gone. I was in the kitchen washing dishes. Laughing excitedly, they pushed their way into the kitchen — which had hardly enough room for one person to move around in — and squeezed themselves into a small corner

between me and the refrigerator and proceeded to kiss each other passionately.

Suddenly, a sort of trembling came over me. I realized that they had not meant to put on a peep show for my enjoyment. The two of them were not the least bit concerned about what I saw or felt, even when they began practically screwing under my nose. For them I simply didn't exist. I was invisible, a nonentity! It is difficult to describe the extreme humiliation I felt. Looking back, I think it was the most degrading moment of my entire posing adventure.

I stuck with my awful job at Hatuki more out of inertia than by virtue of any strength of will. In the meantime, I moved in with a group of Arabs, residents of the Israeli town of Um El Fahem. Since they were citizens of Israel, they were not living in the city illegally, and the flat was rented for them by the restaurant at which they all worked.

On my first night there, I dined with my roommates. They had brought a bag from their restaurant containing some pita bread and various salads. When we ran out of pita and were still hungry, Abu Kasem, the eldest of the group, took a few shekels out of his pocket and turned to the youngest. "Hussein," he requested, "go to the bakery and get some more pita." Hussein checked his shirt pocket to confirm that his ID card was in place and asked Kasem whether there were any police detectives about. Kasem assured him that the coast was clear, and Hussein left.

It was around seven in the evening, an hour when innocent pedestrians   12 aren't ordinarily arrested in the streets, and I professed astonishment at their caution. "What? You have an Israeli ID, don't you?"

"What do you know?" replied Kasem. "In the West Bank, you call us 'Jews,' but for the cops here we're 100 percent Arabs, and it's bad news when they get their hands on us.

"Our land has all been appropriated by the Jews," he continued, "so there's nothing to cultivate. There aren't any factories, and there are no other jobs, so we depend completely on the Jews for work."

Hussein — who had by then returned with the pita — joined in, pointing out that the Arabs from the occupied territories are not the only ones who suffer. "At the restaurant they were looking for someone educated to sit by the cash register. I brought in my cousin, who is studying computers at Tel Aviv University. When they saw he was an Arab, they said they didn't need anyone any more, and a few days later they brought in a Jewish guy who had hardly finished elementary school."

The television set was on and the news broadcast had begun. A report   16 of a terrorist attack on a Jewish synagogue in Istanbul was accompanied by harrowing images of the victims being taken away for burial. Just then, Hussein took a phone call. After a few seconds, he pounded violently on the table in front of him. "What do you want from me? What do you *suppose* I think about it?!" he shouted, and slammed down the receiver. A few minutes later he calmed down sufficiently to tell us what the argument had been about. "That was my Jewish girlfriend. She saw the news and called to ask me what I thought about the [Palestinian] organizations' attacking a synagogue in Istanbul and killing the Jewish worshipers. I'm fed up with having to justify myself every time something like that happens. They demand constantly that you prove you aren't a terrorist and want you to apologize for everything that happens in the world."

That was the sort of bitterness I would be exposed to throughout my project. Another such incident occurred at the small home of Abd Al Karim Lubad, with whom I stayed for a couple of weeks while visiting Jebalya, one of the largest refugee camps in the area that was occupied by Israel in 1967. Several of my host's friends had stopped by; one of them was telling us about his experience working among the Jews:

"Once I was picking fruit on some farm near Ashkelon. We worked like donkeys from morning to evening and slept in a stinking, run-down shed in the orchard. After a week, payday came around, and that night the boss brought in some thugs armed with guns who beat us and chased us, yelling, 'You're all terrorists!' We had to get out of there, and a whole week of hard work went to hell. We didn't get a shekel."

Lubad, my host, erupted. "Those Zionists are getting money from America all the time. Like a flock of sheep, they just stand with mouths open and ask for more. And they're always talking about what Hitler did to them in Europe. I don't believe that Hitler killed the Jews, they just killed each other."

His wicked assertion made my blood boil. The young Palestinians in whose company I found myself were intellectuals who knew — or should have known — the truth about the Holocaust. But because so much of their pent-up anger and frustration had resulted from their growing up in a refugee camp, it would have been hard for me to protest against the hatred they felt toward anything that even faintly smacked of Zionism.   20

In October 1986, I ventured to a large right-wing Israeli demonstration in support of "Jewish Underground" members who had been imprisoned for terrorist acts — bombings, shootings, murder, and more — against

Palestinians living on the West Bank. The demonstration took place in the square opposite the main synagogue in Jerusalem, less than a mile away from the Arab section of the city. Most of the men were bearded and wore knitted skullcaps, a style that Israelis instantly identify with a form of religious nationalism tinged with a messianic streak. Some of the men were also armed. Many of the demonstrators were waving small replicas of the Israeli flag.

The event was a show of strength for Israel's radical right wing, and my presence there, in my Arab outfit, was an extreme form of provocation. I pushed my way through the crowd and began listening to the speeches about the "beloved sons who were not guilty of any wrongdoing." The prevailing sentiment was that to spray a college campus with bullets and to freely fling hand grenades at students did not constitute a criminal offense so long as the victims were Arabs. Nor was it considered a crime to plant bombs in the cars of public servants, or to demolish buses loaded with peaceful civilians, if those being blown to pieces were Arabs.

Suddenly a hand grabbed hold of my arm and viciously yanked me backward. Turning, I found myself confronting a very red, bearded face that was contorted with hatred. The face rapidly fired questions at me in English: "Who are you? What are you doing here? Where are you from?"

"This is a public place and it is my right to be here," I protested feebly. 24

Under the circumstances, I could hardly have chosen a less effective argument. Some members of the crowd seemed convinced that this time they had a bona fide terrorist on their hands. Curses, kicks, and blows rained down on me. Curious newcomers, inquiring what it was all about, received this illuminating explanation: "There's an Arab here!" A voice in the mob cried out, "Get out of here! You have nothing to do with us!" I undoubtedly would have complied with this helpful suggestion if only I could have freed myself from the tight group in which I was being held. And so the hysterical shouting went on: "We've caught an Arab, call the police! Quick!"

A path opened up in the crowd as people moved aside to let a policeman through. Without wasting words, he led me away. As we left, we were joined by two of my captor's colleagues, young border policemen like himself. Together we crossed the street and headed toward a very dark and narrow alley. These cops have a devilish knack for finding — conveniently close to the commotion — the kind of dark and isolated corner that perfectly suits their purposes.

"Stand up straight!" I was ordered, and a direct punch in the stomach immediately followed. It was powerful enough to make me double up in pain — in violation of the instruction I'd just been given. A second policeman countered the effect of the blow by shoving a crooked finger under my chin, like a hook, and abruptly pulling me back to an upright position. They announced their next decision: "All right! Now we'll take out everything he's got in his stinking pockets." All they found was a keffiyeh (the traditional Arab headdress), a bunch of keys, and a wallet.

They returned the keys and the wallet to me, but one of them wound   28
the red keffiyeh (the color favored by many Palestinian leftists) tightly around his hand, as if underscoring the point that I wasn't going to get it back soon. "Now take out your ID."

I was released with another blow, this time to the back of my neck. I hastily drew my Israeli ID from my wallet and fearfully handed it over. I knew that this humiliating experience could continue for hours. The policeman examining my document whistled in surprise. "We've caught a big fish here! He's got a false ID. I'm taking him over to the patrol car, and you" — he turned to his subordinates — "keep very close watch from behind so he doesn't escape."

The two policemen obediently positioned themselves behind me while the one in charge escorted me, steering me by the arm. "Come on, you bastard. We're taking you to our superior now; then you're going for a ride to detention, and on the way we'll take care of you in such a way that you'll never forget it as long as you live."

The blows that were urging me to move along ceased abruptly the moment we reached the brightly lit street. I was taken to a border-police jeep that was parked across from the demonstration. A giant of an officer, well over six feet tall, accepted my ID and keffiyeh with as much satisfaction as if he'd just been presented with a firearm taken from a captured terrorist. Then he instructed me to wait a short distance from the jeep while he spoke into his walkie-talkie. He reported that an extremely suspicious ID had been found on the person of an Arab who was just apprehended at the demonstration, where he had been loitering with no apparent purpose.

Soon, the walkie-talkie barked back instructions concerning my ID: it   32
seemed that the police computer had a file on me. The officer wasn't able to hide his frustration as he gave me the welcome news, "I'm giving you three minutes to get out of here, and don't you dare enter the area of the demonstration or you'll be arrested."

This time I had no intention of compromising. "I have a right to be at the demonstration," I insisted.

"All right," the officer conceded, "but without that red keffiyeh. If I see you with the keffiyeh, I'm arresting you on the spot." Of course, there was no legal basis for this demand, either. His job, as a policeman, was to protect me even if I went in there with a dozen keffiyehs, but I had no strength for further arguments.

I returned to the demonstration, which was about to end. The flags were raised up high and the crowd began to sing "Hatikva"; they must have felt that invoking the Israeli national anthem was an appropriate gesture in support of Jewish terrorists. They stood motionless as they sang, but I couldn't remain still and moved restlessly about. Even though I was an Israeli Jew, their *tikva* ("hope") was certainly not mine.

Before one can speak of the *intifada*, as the Palestinians call the current 36 uprising, one must first understand how the Palestinians have coped with life under the Israeli occupation up to this point. The key concept in this respect is *sumud*, which means "sticking with it," "staying put," "holding fast" to one's objectives and to the land — in a word, survival. Sumud is an attitude, a philosophy, and a way of life. It maintains that one must carry on in a normal and undisturbed fashion, as much as possible. Compared with organized civil disobedience, or passive resistance as preached by Gandhi, sumud is a more basic form of resistance growing out of the idea that merely to exist, to survive, and to remain on one's land is an act of defiance — especially when deportation is the one thing Palestinians fear most.

Although sumud is essentially passive by nature, it has a more active aspect, consisting of gestures that underscore the difference between surviving under difficult conditions and accepting them. During the course of my project, I was several times presented with examples of this active sumud. On one occasion, I met a Palestinian youth whom I shall call Abed, who told me about his version of sumud. "Despite the fact that I am a university graduate," he said, "I can't find work in my profession, so I earn my living as a construction worker."

"Where do you work?" I asked.

"In Beit El, up there." He pointed at the hill that overlooked the refugee camp. On the hillside, one could see scattered houses with the European-style, slanted red-tile roofs that are characteristic of the Jewish settlements in the West Bank. "That means you not only work for the Jewish, but you work for the worst of them, for the settlers," I said, in an admonishing tone of voice.

Abed exchanged glances with his friends — as if to ask them whether 40 to include me in their little secret — and replied, "True, we work for the settlers. The money we earn allows us to live here, to be *samidin* (practitioners of sumud), but that isn't all. For us, in this camp, sumud isn't just bringing home money and buying a sack of rice and a few bags of sugar. When I work at the settlement I take advantage of every opportunity to fight them."

"What can you do as a simple laborer?"

"Quite a bit. First of all, after I lay tiles in the bathroom or kitchen of an Israeli settler, when the tiles are all in place and the cement has already dried, I take a hammer and break a few. When we finish installing sewage pipes, and the Jewish subcontractor has checked to see that everything is all right, then I stuff a sackful of cement into the pipe. As soon as water runs through that pipe the cement gets hard as a rock, and the sewage system becomes blocked."

Two older men who were sitting at a table near ours joined in the conversation. Abu Adnan and Abu Ibrahim represented a generation of Palestinians that is haunted by the stinging defeat of 1948, at which time the Arabs either fled — leaving behind their villages and land — or were forcibly deported. But the younger generation, which is more active in resisting the occupation, owes its nationalistic education and inspiration to these elders. The elders are the ones who nurtured and sustained the Palestinian's identification with the villages of their origin. When asked where they are from, even youngsters who have never known an existence other than in the miserable shanties of a refugee camp can proudly name the place of their family's origin — which is often a village that ceased to exist long before they were born.

The intifada, which means "the shaking" (in the sense of shaking 44 oneself free or awake), began with demonstrations in the Jebalya refugee camp on December 8, 1987, spread quickly to other camps, and continues to this day. There have been hundreds of deaths and casualties, mostly among Palestinians.

The intifada, in my opinion, can be understood as the anguished cry of a minority trying to call attention to the discrimination that is being practiced against it, as much as a demand for national liberation. But Israeli officials prefer to speak of "violent disturbances of order," or just plain riots.

About three weeks after the intifada broke out, I visited the Shati refugee camp near Gaza. Shati is a miserable place to live even in ordinary times; now the chaos was unprecedented. The sewer had run over, flooding entire streets. Large garbage cans were being used as road barriers, and the sand in the alleys was covered with a black layer of

burned rubber, the residue of all the tires that had blazed there over the
past three months. Children, rulers of the intifada, could be found at all
points along the perimeter of the camp, armed with improvised slingshots
and creating an atmosphere of apocalypse and anarchy.

We went over to the Shifa hospital, which was located near the camp.
There we visited, among others, Muhriz Hamuda Al Nimnin, a young
victim of the recent violence. His brother, who was at his bedside, said,
"If they had done it to me it would at least have made some sense,
because I throw rocks and Molotov cocktails. But Muhriz is a sick person
who never participated in a demonstration." He then told us as much of
the story as he knew.

People in the camp had seen Muhriz being arrested by the soldiers   48
who manned a lookout post. Eighteen days after his arrest, he was found
unconscious in front of the entrance to the Shifa hospital. In addition to
the usual injuries inflicted by the Israeli troops — broken arms and legs
— Muhriz had been hit on the head. He was now a vegetable, incapable
of speaking, unable to tell what had happened. The palms of his hands
and his fingers were badly burned, as though he had been forced to grasp
a red-hot metal object.

I asked Muhriz's brother if he was sure that it was the soldiers who
had inflicted these injuries. He replied that there were witnesses who had
seen Muhriz being beaten by soldiers when he was arrested, "but not in
such a way." The brother spread out the contents of a sack that had been
found next to Muhriz at the gate of the hospital. In it were the clothes
that the victim had apparently worn throughout the period of his absence.

To my dismay, I discovered a damning piece of evidence among the
foul-smelling rags: a strip of flannel cloth of the kind used in the army
for wiping weapons clean of grime and oil. The rag was tied in the shape
of a loop the size of a man's head. Since soldiers commonly use these
strips of cloth for blindfolding suspects, the chances seemed good that
the criminal act of sadism committed against Muhriz had indeed been
carried out by members of the Israeli Defense Forces.

For twenty years the Palestinians have lived among us. During the
day we have been the employers who profited by their labor and exploited
them for all they are worth; in the afternoon we have been the police; in
the evening we have been the soldiers at the roadblock on the way home;
and at night we have been the security forces who entered their homes
and arrested them. The young Palestinians work in Tel Aviv, Jerusalem,
and other Israeli cities. They identify with the values of Israeli society at

least as much as they do with their traditional backgrounds. They get a whiff of the democratic privileges that Israeli citizens enjoy, but they cannot share in them. The young man who spends his work week among a people living under democratic rule returns to his home, which is only an hour away but which has (in effect, if not officially) been under curfew for twenty years. Any Arab who walks in the streets at a late hour can expect to be detained and questioned about his actions, even during periods of relative calm. He sees and recognizes the value of freedom but is accorded the kind of treatment that characterizes the most backward dictatorial regimes. How can he be anything but frustrated?

In the end, the impressions I was left with formed a depressing picture   52 of fear and mistrust on both sides. The Palestinians, employed as a cheap labor force, are excluded from Israeli society, whereas Israeli Jews are satisfied to rule without the least curiosity about how the other side lives. My conclusion is that a continuation of Israel's military presence in the West Bank and Gaza Strip threatens to change Israel into a place that many people, including myself, will find unlivable. I am tired of witnessing the disastrous results of the occupation every day. And I am frightened that many more people, on both sides, may be doomed to suffer bloodshed and destruction.

EXPLORATIONS

1. What did Binur hope to accomplish when he started posing as an Arab? What surprises did his project bring him? How does he change from the beginning to the end of this essay?

2. What are the similarities between *sumud* (para. 36) and the *intifada* (paras. 44–45)? What are the differences?

3. What does Binur gain by reporting as a Jew and an Arab at the same time? How would the impact of his essay change if he wrote from an objective third-person viewpoint instead of a subjective first-person viewpoint?

CONNECTIONS

1. What do the children in the Shati refugee camp (para. 46) have in common with the urban American slum children described by Michele L. Norris in "A Child of Crack" and by Lewis H. Lapham in *Looking at Ourselves*? Why do you think children are "rulers of the intifada"? What important role(s) do children play in the U.S. drug trade, and why?

2. Look back at Naila Minai's "Women in Islam" (p. 348) and Cherry Lindholm and Charles Lindholm's "Life Behind the Veil" (p. 359). What examples in those essays suggest that women in Islamic countries practice tactics much like the Palestinian sumud (see Binur's para. 36)? What circumstances seem to foster such tactics?

3. What similarities do you notice between the jobs held by Arabs in Binur's essay and the job Maya Angelou holds in a white Arkansas household in "Mary" (p. 412)? What similar actions do the Arab workers and Angelou take against their employers, and why?

ELABORATIONS

1. Write an essay about some aspect of the nature (geographic, political, religious, economic) or history or both of the Arab-Jewish conflict in the Middle East. Use as sources Binur's essay, Bruno Bettelheim's "Why Kibbutzim?" (p. 86), Amos Oz's "If There Is Justice" (p. 618), Edward T. Hall's "Proxemics in the Arab World" (p. 23), Minai's "Women in Early Islam" (p. 348), and the headnotes preceding these selections.

2. In "Tradition and the African Writer," (p. 34), Ezekiel Mphahlele talks about black Africans' second-class status in their own countries. Write an essay comparing and contrasting that experience with the Palestinian's experience described by Binur.

NADINE GORDIMER

Africa Emergent

Born in South Africa in 1923 and educated there, Nadine Gordimer is an outspoken civil libertarian who believes that change in her country's policies is best spurred from within. Her writing — much of it focusing on the impact of apartheid on South Africans — is renowned around the world. "I think when you're born white in South Africa, you're peeling like an onion," she has said. "You're sloughing off all the conditioning that you've had since you were a child." Gordimer's novels, short stories, and essays have won her numerous awards and honorary degrees. She has contributed to many American magazines, including *The New Yorker, Harper's, The Atlantic Monthly,* and *The New York Review of Books,* as well as taught creative writing at Columbia University's Graduate School of the Arts. In 1978 she was elected an honorary member of the American Academy and Institute of Arts and Letters, whose citation read: "The brilliance with which she renders her varied characters has opened her country to passionate understandings which most of us have no other access to." Gordimer currently lives with her family in Johannesburg. She has published nine novels, including *The Conservationist* (1974), *July's People* (1981), and *A Sport of Nature* (1987), as well as several volumes of short stories. "Africa Emergent" comes from her 1971 collection *Livingstone's Companions.*

(For background on South Africa, see pp. 34 and 578.)

He's in prison now, so I'm not going to mention his name. It mightn't be a good thing, you understand. — Perhaps you think you understand too well; but don't be quick to jump to conclusions from five or six thousand miles away: if you lived here, you'd understand something else — friends know that shows of loyalty are all right for children holding hands in the school playground; for us they're luxuries, not important and maybe dangerous. If I said, I was a friend of so-and-so, black man awaiting trial for treason, what good would it do him? And, who knows, it might draw just that decisive bit more attention to me. *He'd* be the first to agree.

Not that one feels that if they haven't got enough in my dossier already, this would make any difference; and not that he really was such a friend. But that's something else you won't understand: everything is ambiguous, here. We hardly know, by now, what we can do and what we can't do; it's difficult to say, goaded in on oneself by laws and doubts and rebellion and caution and — not least — self-disgust, what is or is not a friendship. I'm talking about black-and-white, of course. If you stay with it, boy, on the white side in the country clubs and garden suburbs if you're white, and on the black side in the locations and beer halls if you're black, none of this applies, and you can go all the way to your segregated cemetery in peace. But neither he nor I did.

I began mixing with blacks out of what is known as an outraged sense of justice, plus strong curiosity, when I was a student. There were two ways — one was through the white students' voluntary service organization, a kibbutz-type junket where white boys and girls went into rural areas and camped while they built school classrooms for African children. A few coloured and African students from their segregated universities used to come along, too, and there was the novelty, not without value, of dossing down alongside them at night, although we knew we were likely to be harboring Special Branch spies among our willing workers, and we dared not make a pass at the coloured or black girls. The other way — less hard on the hands — was to go drinking with the jazz musicians and journalists, painters and would-be poets and actors who gravitated towards whites partly because such people naturally feel they can make free of the world, and partly because they found an encouragement and appreciation there that was sweet to them. I tried the VSO briefly, but the other way suited me better; anyway, I didn't see why I should help this Government by doing the work it ought to be doing for the welfare of black children.

I'm an architect and the way I was usefully drawn into the black scene   4 was literally that: I designed sets for a mixed colour drama group got together by a white director. Perhaps there's no urban human group as intimate, in the end, as a company of this kind, and the colour problem made us even closer. I don't mean what *you* mean, the how-do-I-feel-about-that-black-skin stuff; I mean the daily exasperation of getting round, or over, or on top of the colour bar laws that plagued our productions and our lives. We had to remember to write out "passes" at night, so that our actors could get home without being arrested for being out after the curfew for blacks, we had to spend hours at the Bantu Affairs Department trying to arrange local residence permits for actors who were being "endorsed out" of town back to the villages to which, "ethnically," apparently, they belonged although they'd never set eyes on them, and we had to decide which of us could play the sycophant well enough to persuade the Bantu Commissioner to allow the show to go on the road from one Group Area, designated by colour, to another, or to talk some town clerk into getting his council to agree to the use of a "white" public hall by a mixed cast. The black actors' lives were in our hands, because they were black and we were white, and could, must, intercede for them. Don't think this made everything love and light between us; in fact it caused endless huffs and rows. A white woman who'd worked like a slave acting as PRO-cum-wardrobe-mistress hasn't spoken to me for years because I made her lend her little car to one of the chaps who'd worked until after the last train went back to the location, and then he kept it the whole weekend and she couldn't get hold of him because, of course, location houses rarely have telephones and once a black man has disappeared among those warrens you won't find him till he chooses to surface in the white town again. And when this one did surface, he was biting, to me, about white bitches' "patronage" of people they secretly still thought of as "boys." Yet our arguments, resentments, and misunderstandings were not only as much part of the intimacy of this group as the good times, the parties, and the lovemaking we had, but were more — the defining part, because we'd got close enough to admit argument, resentment, and misunderstanding between us.

He was one of this little crowd, for a time. He was a dispatch clerk and then a "manager" and chucker-out at a black dance club. In his spare time he took a small part in our productions now and then, and made himself generally handy; in the end it was discovered that what he really was good at was front-of-house arrangements. His tubby charm (he was a large young man and a cheerful dresser) was just the right thing to deal with the unexpected moods of our location audiences when we went on tour — sometimes they came stiffly encased in their churchgoing best and seemed to feel it was vulgar to laugh or respond to what was going on, on stage; in other places they rushed the doors, tried to get in without paying, and were dominated by a *tsotsi*, street urchin, element who didn't want to hear anything but themselves. He was the particular friend — the other, passive half — of a particular friend of mine, Elias Nkomo.

And here I stop short. How shall I talk about Elias? I've never even learnt, in five years, how to think about him.

Elias was a sculptor. He had one of those jobs — messenger "boy" or some such — that literate young black men can aspire to in a small gold-mining and industrial town outside Johannesburg. Somebody said he was talented, somebody sent him to me — at the beginning, the way for every black man to find himself seems inescapably to lead through a white man. Again, how can I say what his work was like? He came by train to the black people's section of Johannesburg central station, carrying a bulky object wrapped in that morning's newspaper. He was slight, roundheaded, tiny-eared, dunly dressed, and with a frown of effort between his eyes, but his face unfolded to a wide, apologetic yet confident smile when he realized that the white man in a waiting car must be me — the meeting had been arranged. I took him back to my "place" (he always called people's homes that) and he unwrapped the newspaper. What was there was nothing like the clumps of diorite or sandstone you have seen in galleries in New York, London, or Johannesburg marked "Africa Emergent," "Spirit of the Ancestors." What was there was a goat, or a goatlike creature, in the way that a centaur is a horselike, manlike creature, carved out of streaky knotted wood. It was delightful (I wanted to put out my hand to touch it), it was moving in its somehow concretized diachrony, beast-man, coarse wood–fine workmanship, and there was also something exposed about it (one would withdraw the hand, after all). I asked him whether he knew Picasso's goats? He had heard of Picasso but never seen any of his work. I showed him a photograph of the famous bronze goat in Picasso's own house; thereafter all his beasts had sex organs as joyful as Picasso's goat's udder, but that was the only "influence" that ever took, with him. As I say, a white man always intercedes in some way, with a man like Elias; mine was to keep him from those art-loving ladies with galleries who wanted to promote him, and those white painters and sculptors who were willing to have him work under their tutelage. I gave him an old garage (well, that means I took my car out of it) and left him alone, with plenty of chunks of wood.

But Elias didn't like the loneliness of work. That garage never became 8 his "place." Perhaps when you've lived in an overcrowded yard all your life the counterstimulus of distraction becomes necessary to create a tension of concentration. No — well all I really mean is that he liked company. At first he came only at weekends, and then, as he began to sell some of his work, he gave up the messenger job and moved in more or less permanently — we fixed up the "place" together, putting in a ceiling and connecting water and so on. It was illegal for him to live there in a white suburb, of course, but such laws breed complementary evasions in people like Elias and me and the white building inspector didn't turn a hair of suspicion when I said that I was converting the garage as a flat for my wife's mother. It was better for Elias once he'd moved in; there was always some friend of his sharing his bed, not to mention the girls who did; sometimes the girls were shy little things

almost of the kitchen maid variety, who called my wife "madam" when
they happened to bump into her, crossing the garden, sometimes they
were the bewigged and painted actresses from the group who sat smoking
and gossiping with my wife while she fed the baby.

And *he* was there more often than anyone — the plump and cheerful
front-of-house manager; he was married, but as happens with our sex,
an old friendship was a more important factor in his life than a wife and
kids — if that's a characteristic of black men, then I must be black under
the skin, myself. Elias had become very involved in the theater group,
anyway, like *him*; Elias made some beautiful *papier-mâché* gods for a
play by a Nigerian that we did — "spirits of the ancestors" at once amusing
and frightening — and once when we needed a singer he surprisingly
turned out to have a voice that could phrase a madrigal as easily as
whatever the forerunner of Soul was called — I forget now, but it blared
hour after hour from the garage when he was working. Elias seemed to
like best to work when the other one was around; *he* would sit with his
fat boy's legs rolled out before him, flexing his toes in his fashionable
shoes, dusting down the lapels of the latest thing in jackets, as he changed
the records and kept up a monologue contentedly punctuated by those
soft growls and sighs of agreement, those sudden squeezes of almost silent
laughter — responses possible only in an African language — that came
from Elias as he chiseled and chipped. For they spoke in their own
tongue, and I have never known what it was they talked about.

In spite of my efforts to let him alone, inevitably Elias was "taken up"
(hadn't I started the process myself, with that garage?) and a gallery
announced itself his agent. He walked about at the opening of his one-
man show in a purple turtlenecked sweater I think his best friend must
have made him buy, laughing a little, softly, at himself, more embarrassed
than pleased. An art critic wrote about his transcendental values and
plastic modality, and he said, "Christ, man, does he dig it or doesn't he?"
while we toasted his success in brandy chased with beer — brandy isn't
a rich man's sip in South Africa, it's made here and it's what people use
to get drunk on. He earned quite a bit of money that year. Then the
gallery owner and the art critic forgot him in the discovery of yet another
interpreter of the African soul, and he was poor again, but he had
acquired a patroness who, although she lived far away, did not forget
him. She was, as you might have thought, an American lady, very old
and wealthy according to South African legend but probably simply a
middle-aged widow with comfortable stock holdings and a desire to get
in on the cultural ground floor of some form of art collecting not yet

overcrowded. She had bought some of his work while a tourist in Johannesburg. Perhaps she did have academic connections with the art world; in any case, it was she who got a foundation to offer Elias Nkomo a scholarship to study in America.

I could understand that he wanted to go simply in order to go: to see the world outside. But I couldn't believe that at this stage he wanted or could make use of formal art school disciplines. As I said to him at the time, I'm only an architect, but I've had experience of the academic and even, God help us, the frenziedly nonacademic approach in the best schools, and it's not for people who have, to fall back on the jargon, found themselves.

I remember he said, smiling, "You think I've found myself?"   12

And I said, "But you've never been lost, man. That very first goat wrapped in newspaper was your goat."

But later, when he was refused a passport and the issue of his going abroad was much on our minds, we talked again. He wanted to go because he felt he needed some kind of general education, general cultural background that he'd missed, in his six years at the location school. "Since I've been at your place, I've been reading a lot of your books. And man, I know nothing. I'm as ignorant as that kid of yours there in the pram. Right, I've picked up a bit of politics, a few art terms here and there — I can wag my head and say 'plastic values' all right, eh? But man, what do I know about life? What do I know about how it all works? How do I know *how* I do the work I do? Why we live and die? — If I carry on here I might as well be carving walking sticks," he added. I knew what he meant: there are old men, all over Africa, who make a living squatting at a decent distance from tourist hotels, carving fancy walking sticks from local wood; only one step in sophistication below the "Africa Emergent" school of sculptors so rapturously acclaimed by gallery owners. We both laughed at this, and following the line of thought suggested to me by his question to himself: "How do I know how I do the work I do?" — although in me it was a different line of thought from his — I asked him whether in fact there was any sort of traditional skill in his family? As I imagined, there was not — he was an urban slum kid, brought up opposite a municipal beer hall among paraffin-tin utensils and abandoned motorcar bodies which, perhaps curiously, had failed to bring out a Duchamp in him but from which, on the contrary, he had sprung, full-blown, as a classical expressionist. Although there were no rural walking-stick carvers in his ancestry, he did tell me something I had no idea would have been part of the experience of a location childhood

— he had been sent, in his teens, to a tribal initiation school in the bush, and been circumcised according to rite. He described the experience vividly.

Once all attempts to get him a passport had failed, Elias's desire to go to America became something else, of course: an obsessive resentment against confinement itself. Inevitably, he was given no reason for the refusal. The official answer was the usual one — that it was "not in the public interest" to reveal the reason for such things. Was it because "they" had got to know he was "living like a white man"? (Theory put to me by one of the black actors in the group.) Was it because a critic had dutifully described his work as expressive of the "agony of the emergent African soul"? Nobody knew. Nobody ever knows. It is enough to be black; blacks are meant to stay put, in their own ethnically apportioned streets in their own segregated areas, in those parts of South Africa where the government says they belong. Yet — the whole way our lives are maneuvered, as I say, is an unanswered question — Elias's best friend suddenly got a passport. I hadn't even realized that *he* had been offered a scholarship or a study grant or something, too; *he* was invited to go to New York to study production and the latest acting techniques (it was the time of the Method rather than Grotowski). And *he* got a passport, "first try" as Elias said with ungrudging pleasure and admiration; when someone black got a passport, then, there was a collective sense of pleasure in having outwitted we didn't quite know what. So they went together, *he* on his passport, and Elias Nkomo on an exit permit.

An exit permit is a one-way ticket, anyway. When you are granted 16 one at your request but at the government's pleasure, you sign an undertaking that you will never return to South Africa or its mandatory territory, South West Africa. You pledge this with signature and thumbprint. Elias Nkomo never came back. At first he wrote (and he wrote quite often) enthusiastically about the world outside that he had gained, and he seemed to be enjoying some kind of small vogue, not so much as a sculptor as a genuine, real live African Negro who was sophisticated enough to be asked to comment on this and that: the beauty of American women, life in Harlem or Watts, Black Power as seen through the eyes, etc. He sent cuttings from *Ebony* and even from the *New York Times Magazine*. He said that a girl at *Life* was trying to get them to run a piece on his work; his work? — well, he hadn't settled down to anything new, yet, but the art center was a really swinging place, Christ, the things people were doing, there! There were silences, naturally; we forgot about him and he forgot about us for weeks on end. Then the local papers picked up the sort of news they are alert to from all over the world. Elias Nkomo had spoken at an antiapartheid rally. Elias Nkomo, in West African robes, was on the platform with Stokely Carmichael. "Well, why not? He hasn't got to worry about keeping his hands clean for the time when he comes back home, has he?" — My wife was bitter in his defense. Yes, but I was wondering about his work — "Will they leave him alone to work?" I didn't write to him, but it was as if my silence were read by him: a few months later I received a cutting from some university art magazine devoting a number to Africa, and there was a photograph of one of Elias's wood sculptures, with his handwriting along the margin of the page — *I know you don't think much of people who don't turn out new stuff but some people here seem to think this old thing of mine is good.* It was the sort of wry remark that, spoken aloud to me in the room, would have made us both laugh. I smiled, and meant to write. But within two weeks Elias was dead. He drowned himself early one morning in the river of the New England town where the art school was.

It was like the refusal of the passport; none of us knew why. In the usual arrogance one has in the face of such happenings, I even felt guilty about the letter. Perhaps, if one were thousands of miles from one's own "place," in some sort of a bad way, just a small thing like a letter, a word of encouragement from someone who had hurt by being rather niggardly with encouragement in the past . . . ? And what pathetic arrogance, at that! As if the wisp of a letter, written by someone between other preoccupations, and in substance an encouraging lie (how splendid that your old work is receiving recognition in some piddling little magazine) could be anything round which the hand of a man going down for the second time might close. Because before Elias went under in that river he must have been deep in forlorn horrors about which I knew nothing, nothing. When people commit suicide they do so apparently out of some sudden self-knowledge that those of us, the living, do not have the will to acquire. That's what's meant by despair, isn't it — what they have come to know? And that's what one means when one says in extenuation of oneself, *I knew so little about him, really.* I knew Elias only in the self that he had presented at my "place"; why, how out of place it had been, once, when he happened to mention that as a boy he had spent weeks in the bush with his circumcision group! Of course we — his friends — decided out of the facts we knew and our political and personal attitudes, why he had died: and perhaps it is true that he was sick to death, in the real sense of the phrase that has been forgotten, sick unto death with homesickness for the native land that had shut him out forever and that he was forced to conjure up for himself in the parody of "native" dress that had nothing to do with his part of the continent, and the shame that a new kind of black platform-solidarity forced him to feel for his old dependence, in South Africa, on the friendship of white people. It was the South African government who killed him, it was culture shock — but perhaps neither our political bitterness nor our glibness with fashionable phrases can come near what combination of forces, within and without, led him to the fatal baptism of that early morning. *It is not in the private interest that this should be revealed.* Elias never came home. That's all.

But his best friend did, towards the end of that year. *He* came to see me after he had been in the country some weeks — I'd heard he was back. The theater group had broken up; it seemed to be that, chiefly, he'd come to talk to me about: he wanted to know if there was any money left in the kitty for him to start up a small theatrical venture of his own, he was eager to use the know-how (his phrase) he'd learned in the States. He was really plump now and he wore the most extraordinary clothes. A Liberace jacket. Plastic boots. An Afro wig that looked as if it had been made out of a bit of karakul from South West Africa. I teased him about it — we were at least good enough friends for that — asking him if he'd really been with the guerrillas instead of Off Broadway? (There was a trial on at home, at the time, of South African political refugees who had tried to "infiltrate" through South West Africa.) And felt slightly ashamed of my patronage of his taste when he said with such good humor, "It's just a fun thing, man, isn't it great?" I was too cowardly to bring the talk round to the point: Elias. And when it couldn't be avoided I said the usual platitudes and he shook his head at them — "Hell, man," and we fell silent. Then he told me that that was how he had got back — because Elias was dead, on the unused portion of Elias's air ticket. *His* study grant hadn't included travel expenses and he'd had to pay his own way over. So he'd had only a one-way ticket, but Elias's scholarship had included a return fare to the student's place of origin. It had been difficult to get the airline to agree to the transfer; he'd had to go to the scholarship foundation people, but they'd been very decent about fixing it for him.

He had told me all this so guilelessly that I was one of the people who became angrily indignant when the rumor began to go around that he was a police agent: who else would have the cold nerve to come back on a dead man's ticket, a dead man who couldn't ever have used that portion of the ticket himself, because he had taken an exit permit? And who

could believe the story, anyway? Obviously, *he* had to find some way of
explaining why he, a black man like any other, could travel freely back
and forth between South Africa and other countries. He had a passport,
hadn't he? Well, there you were. Why should *he* get a passport? What
black man these days had a passport?

Yes, I was angry, and defended him, by proof of the innocence of the   20
very naïveté with which — a black man, yes, and therefore used to the
necessity of salvaging from disaster all his life, unable to afford the nice
squeamishness of white men's delicacy — he took over Elias's air ticket
because he was alive and needed it, as he might have taken up Elias's
coat against the cold. I refused to avoid him, the way some members of
the remnant of our group made it clear they did now, and I remained
stony-faced outside the complicity of those knowing half-smiles that accompanied the mention of his name. We had never been close friends,
of course; but he would turn up from time to time. He could not find
theatrical work and had a job as a traveling salesman in the locations.
He took to bringing three or four small boys along when he visited us;
they were very subdued and whisperingly well-behaved and well-dressed
in miniature suits — our barefoot children stared at them in awe. They
were his children plus the children of the family he was living with, we
gathered. He and I talked mostly about his difficulties — his old car was
unreliable, his wife had left him, his commissions were low, and he
could have taken up an offer to join a Chicago repertory company if he
could have raised the fare to go back to America — while my wife fed
ice cream and cake to the silent children, or my children dutifully placed
them one by one on the garden swing. We had begun to be able to talk
about Elias's death. He had told me how, in the weeks before he died,
Elias would get the wrong way on the moving stairway going down in
the subway in New York and keep walking, walking up. "I thought he
was foolin' around, man, you know? Jus' climbin' those stairs and goin'
noplace?"

He clung nostalgically to the American idiom; no African talks about
"noplace" when he means "nowhere." But he had abandoned the Afro
wig and when we got talking about Elias he would hold his big, well-
shaped head with its fine, shaven covering of his own wool propped
between his hands as if in an effort to think more clearly about something
that would never come clear; I felt suddenly at one with him in that
gesture, and would say, "Go on." He would remember another example
of how Elias had been "acting funny" before he died. It was on one of
those afternoon visits that he said, "And I don't think I ever told you

about the business with the students at the college? How that last weekend
— before he did it, I mean — he went around and invited everybody to
a party, I dunno, a kind of feast he said it was. Some of them said he
said a barbecue — you know what that is, same as a *braaivleis*, eh? But
one of the others told me afterwards that he'd told them he was going to
give them a real African feast, he was going to show them how the
country people do it here at home when somebody gets married or there's
a funeral or so. He wanted to know where he could buy a goat."

"A goat?"

"That's right. A live goat. He wanted to kill and roast a goat for them,
on the campus."

It was round about this time that *he* asked me for a loan. I think that 24
was behind the idea of bringing those pretty, dressed-up children along
with him when he visited; he wanted firmly to set the background of his
obligations and responsibilities before touching me for money. It was
rather a substantial sum, for someone of my resources. But he couldn't
carry on his job without a new car, and he'd just got the opportunity to
acquire a really good secondhand buy. I gave him the money in spite of
— because of, perhaps — new rumors that were going around then that,
in a police raid on the house of the family with whom he had been
living, every adult except himself who was present on that night had been
arrested on the charge of attending a meeting of a banned political
organization. His friends were acquitted on the charge simply through
the defense lawyer's skill at showing the agent provocateur, on whose
evidence the charge was based, to be an unreliable witness — that is to
say, a liar. But the friends were promptly served with personal banning
orders, anyway, which meant among other things that their movements
were restricted and they were not allowed to attend gatherings.

He was the only one who remained, significantly, it seemed impossible
to ignore, free. And yet his friends let him stay on in the house; it was a
mystery to us whites — and some blacks, too. But then so much becomes
a mystery where trust becomes a commodity on sale to the police.
Whatever my little show of defiance over the loan, during the last year
or two we have reached the stage where if a man is black, literate, has
"political" friends and white friends, *and* a passport, he must be considered a police spy. I was sick with myself — that was why I gave him the
money — but I believed it, too. There's only one way for a man like
that to prove himself, so far as we're concerned: he must be in prison.

Well, *he* was at large. A little subdued over the fate of his friends,
about which he talked guilelessly as he had about the appropriation of

Elias's air ticket, harassed as usual about money, poor devil, but generally
cheerful. Yet our friendship, that really had begun to become one since
Elias's death, waned rapidly. It was the money that did it. Of course; he
was afraid I'd ask him to begin paying back and so he stopped coming to
my "place," he stopped the visits with the beautifully dressed and well-
behaved black infants. I received a typed letter from him, once, solemnly
thanking me for my kind cooperation and, etc., as if I were some business
firm, and assuring me that in a few months he hoped to be in a position,
etc. I scrawled a note in reply, saying of course I darned well hoped he
was going to pay the money he owed, sometime, but why, for God's
sake, in the meantime, did this mean we had to carry on as if we'd
quarreled? Damn it all, he didn't have to treat me as if I had some nasty
disease, just because of a few rands.

But I didn't see him again. I've become too busy with my own work
— the building boom of the last few years, you know; I've had the
contract for several shopping malls, and a big cultural center — to do
any work for the old theater group in its sporadic comings-to-life. I don't
think he had much to do with it anymore, either; I heard he was doing
quite well as a salesman and was thinking of marrying again. There was
even a — yet another — rumor, that he was actually building a house
in Dube, which is the nearest to a solid, bourgeois suburb a black can
get in these black dormitories outside the white man's city, if you can be
considered to be a bourgeois without having freehold. I didn't need the
money, by then, but you know how it is with money — I felt faintly
resentful about the debt anyway, because it looked as if now *he* could
have paid it back just as well as *I* could say I didn't need it. As for the
friendship; he'd shown me the worth of that. It's become something the
white man must buy just as he must buy the cooperation of police stool
pigeons. Elias has been dead five years; we live in our situation as of
now, as the legal phrase goes; one falls back on legal phrases as other
forms of expression become too risky.

And then, two hundred and seventy-seven days ago, there was a new   28
rumor, and this time it was confirmed, this time it was no rumor. *He*
was fetched from his room one night and imprisoned. That's perfectly
legal, here; it's the hundred-and-eighty-day Detention Act. At least, because he was something of a personality, with many friends and contacts
in particular among both black and white journalists, the fact has become
public. If people are humble, or of no particular interest to the small
world of white liberals, they are sometimes in detention for many months
before this is known outside the eyewitness of whoever happened to be

standing by, in house or street, when they were taken away by the police. But at least we all know where *he* is: in prison. They say that charges of treason are being prepared against him and various others who were detained at the same time, and still others who have been detained for even longer — three hundred and seventy-one days, three hundred and ten days — the figures, once finally released, are always as precise as this — and that soon, soon they will be brought to trial for whatever it is that we do not know they have done, for when people are imprisoned under the Detention Act no one is told why and there are no charges. There are suppositions among us, of course. Was he a double agent, as it were, using his laissez-passer as a police spy in order to further his real work as an underground African nationalist? Was he just unlucky in his choice of friends? Did he suffer from a dangerous sense of loyalty in place of any strong convictions of his own? Was it all due to some personal, unguessed-at bond it's none of our business to speculate about? Heaven knows — those police spy rumors aside — nobody could have looked more unlikely to be a political activist than that cheerful young man, second-string, always ready to jump up and turn over the record, fond of Liberace jackets and aspiring to play LeRoi Jones Off Broadway.

But as I say, we know where he is now; inside. In solitary most of the time — they say, those who've also been inside. Two hundred and seventy-seven days he's been there.

And so we white friends can purge ourselves of the shame of rumors. We can be pure again. We are satisfied at last. He's in prison. He's proved himself, hasn't he?

EXPLORATIONS

1. What facts does Gordimer tell us about her story's narrator? about the man referred to as *he*? How does her depiction of the two main protagonists bear out the narrator's comment in the second paragraph that "everything is ambiguous, here"?

2. What impression of South Africa is created by Gordimer's first sentence? by her first two paragraphs? How would the story's impact change if she omitted these two paragraphs?

3. What conflict(s) does the sculptor Elias embody or represent? What facets of the two protagonists are brought out by their involvement with Elias?

4. What laws and rules are mentioned in "Africa Emergent"? Who evidently made these laws? How are they enforced? How would the story's impact change if government officials made personal appearances in it?

CONNECTIONS

1. What problems and responses do the Palestinians in Yoram Binur's "Palestinian Like Me" share with the black South Africans in Gordimer's "Africa Emergent"? How are these two groups' problems and responses different?

2. Which of Lewis H. Lapham's comments in *Looking at Ourselves* appear to apply to the South African whites and to the racial situation in Gordimer's story? How are racial attitudes different in South Africa and the United States?

3. Look back at Ezekiel Mphahlele's "Tradition and the African Writer" (p. 34). What comments by Mphahlele are exemplified by Elias Nkomo? Having read Mphahlele's essay, why do you think Elias committed suicide?

4. "Africa Emergent," Mphahlele's "Tradition and the African Writer" (p. 34), V. S. Naipaul's "Entering the New World" (p. 47), and Wole Soyinka's "Nigerian Childhood" (p. 154) all depict Africans living in former European colonies. According to these writers, what qualities make up a traditional African consciousness or character? What qualities were brought into Africa by European colonizers?

ELABORATIONS

1. "Everything is ambiguous, here," writes Gordimer in her second paragraph. How might the events she narrates in "Africa Emergent" look different to different observers? Write a synopsis of these events from the viewpoint of a South African official reporting to a superior. Then summarize the same events from the viewpoint of a Western journalist hoping to sell the story to a magazine or newspaper.

2. What is the literal meaning of Gordimer's title, "Africa Emergent"? On the basis of the other African writing you have read, particularly Mphahlele's "Tradition and the African Writer" (p. 34), write an essay explaining the title's deeper meaning.

NELSON MANDELA

The African National Congress

In February 1990 the world celebrated Nelson Mandela's release from South African prison after twenty-seven years. Now a leader of the African National Congress (ANC), Mandela was born in 1918 to one of the royal families of the Transkei, the eldest son of a Tembu chief. He ran away to Johannesburg to escape an arranged tribal marriage; there he studied arts by correspondence and law at the University of Witwatersrand. With his law partner, Oliver Tambo, Mandela became active in the then illegal ANC, whose mission Tambo has described as "the African struggle against the most powerful adversary in Africa: a highly industrialized, well-armed State manned by a fanatical group of White men determined to defend their privilege and their prejudice, and aided by the complicity of American, British, West German, and Japanese investment in the most profitable system of oppression on the continent."

When an all-white referendum voted to declare South Africa a Nationalist Republic in 1961 (see p. 34), Mandela called a general strike to dramatize black opposition. He left his home, family, and office to live as a political outlaw, nicknamed "the Black Pimpernel." In 1962 he was betrayed by an informer, arrested, tried, and sentenced to three years in prison for leading the strike and for leaving the country illegally. From his cell he became a defendant in the notorious Rivonia Trial, accused of sabotage and conspiracy to overthrow the government by force. Mandela and six codefendants were sentenced to life in prison.

The growing worldwide human rights movement (see p. 519) increased international pressure on the South African government, which made such concessions as allowing Asians and Coloureds (but not blacks) to vote and repealing laws banning interracial marriage. The slow pace and limited scope of change fueled protest inside and outside South Africa, some of it violent, to the point that the government barred foreign news media from covering disruption. Popular pressure in the United States led many organizations to divest their holdings of stock in South African companies. After years of worldwide economic and political protest, President P. W. Botha was replaced by the more liberal F. W. De Klerk. Within months De Klerk met with Mandela in prison, unbanned the ANC and the Communist Party, desegregated beaches, limited detention without trial, lifted restrictions on the media, dismantled the repressive state security management system, and released seven other jailed ANC leaders before freeing Mandela.

The struggle for full political rights for black South Africans is far from over, however. Besides opposition from conservative whites, including the neo-Nazi Afrikaner Resistance Movement (AWB), the ANC has been contending with the Zulu Inkatha, supporters of kwaZulu Chief Minister Mangosuthu Gatsha Buthelezi, who favor a traditional self-governing tribal structure. "The African National Congress" is an excerpt from Mandela's testimony at the Rivonia Trial, reprinted in his 1965 book *No Easy Walk to Freedom.*

(For more background on South Africa, see p. 34.)

The ideological creed of the ANC is, and always has been, the creed of African Nationalism. It is not the concept of African Nationalism expressed in the cry, "Drive the White man into the sea." The African Nationalism for which the ANC stands is the concept of freedom and fulfillment for the African people in their own land. The most important political document ever adopted by the ANC is the "Freedom Charter." It is by no means a blueprint for a socialist state. It calls for redistribution, but not nationalization, of land; it provides for nationalization of mines, banks, and monopoly industry, because big monopolies are owned by one race only, and without such nationalization racial domination would be perpetuated despite the spread of political power. . . . In this respect the ANC's policy corresponds with the old policy of the present Nationalist Party which, for many years, had as part of its program the nationalization of the gold mines which, at that time, were controlled by foreign capital. Under the Freedom Charter, nationalization would take place in an economy based on private enterprise. The realization of the Freedom Charter would open up fresh fields for a prosperous African population of all classes, including the middle class. The ANC has never at any period in its history advocated a revolutionary change in the economic structure of the country, nor has it, to the best of my recollection, ever condemned capitalist society.

As far as the Communist Party is concerned, and if I understand its policy correctly, it stands for the establishment of a State based on the principles of Marxism. Although it is prepared to work for the Freedom Charter, as a short-term solution to the problems created by White supremacy, it regards the Freedom Charter as the beginning, and not the end, of its program.

The ANC, unlike the Communist Party, admitted Africans only as members. Its chief goal was, and is, for the African people to win unity and full political rights. The Communist Party's main aim, on the other hand, was to remove the capitalists and to replace them with a working-class government. The Communist Party sought to emphasize class dis-

tinctions whilst the ANC seeks to harmonize them. This is a vital distinction.

It is true that there has often been close cooperation between the ANC   4
and the Communist Party. But cooperation is merely proof of a common
goal — in this case the removal of White supremacy — and is not proof
of a complete community of interests.

The history of the world is full of similar examples. Perhaps the most
striking illustration is to be found in the cooperation between Great
Britain, the United States of America, and the Soviet Union in the fight
against Hitler. Nobody but Hitler would have dared to suggest that such
cooperation turned Churchill or Roosevelt into communists or communist tools, or that Britain and America were working to bring about a
communist world. . . .

I believe that communists have always played an active role in the
fight by colonial countries for their freedom, because the short-term
objects of communism would always correspond with the long-term
objects of freedom movements. Thus communists have played an important role in the freedom struggles fought in countries such as Malaya,
Algeria, and Indonesia, yet none of these States today are communist
countries. Similarly in the underground resistance movements which
sprung up in Europe during the last World War, communists played an
important role. . . .

I joined the ANC in 1944, and in my younger days I held the view
that the policy of admitting communists to the ANC, and the close
cooperation which existed at times on specific issues between the ANC
and the Communist Party, would lead to a watering down of the concept
of African Nationalism. At that stage I was a member of the African
National Congress Youth League, and was one of a group which moved
for the expulsion of communists from the ANC. This proposal was heavily
defeated. Amongst those who voted against the proposal were some of
the most conservative sections of African political opinion. They defended
the policy on the ground that from its inception the ANC was formed
and built up, not as a political party with one school of political thought,
but as a Parliament of the African people, accommodating people of
various political convictions, all united by the common goal of national
liberation. I was eventually won over to this point of view and I have
upheld it ever since.

It is perhaps difficult for White South Africans, with an ingrained   8
prejudice against communism, to understand why experienced African
politicians so readily accept communists as their friends. But to us the

reason is obvious. Theoretical differences amongst those fighting against oppression is a luxury we cannot afford at this stage. What is more, for many decades communists were the only political group in South Africa who were prepared to treat Africans as human beings and their equals; who were prepared to eat with us, talk with us, live with us, and work with us. They were the only political group which was prepared to work with the Africans for the attainment of political rights and a stake in society. Because of this, there are many Africans who, today, tend to equate freedom with communism. They are supported in this belief by a legislature which brands all exponents of democratic government and African freedom as communists and bans many of them (who are communists) under the Suppression of Communism Act. Although I have never been a member of the Communist Party, I myself have been named under that pernicious Act because of the role I played in the Defiance Campaign. I have also been banned and imprisoned under that Act.

It is not only in internal politics that we count communists as amongst those who support our cause. In the international field, communist countries have always come to our aid. In the United Nations and other Councils of the world the communist *bloc* has supported the Afro-Asian struggle against colonialism and often seems to be more sympathetic to our plight than some of the Western powers. Although there is a universal condemnation of apartheid, the communist *bloc* speaks out against it with a louder voice than most of the White world. In these circumstances, it would take a brash young politician, such as I was in 1949, to proclaim that the communists are our enemies.

EXPLORATIONS

1. Mandela's argument in "The African National Congress" obviously is a rebuttal of accusations by the government which has put him on trial. What seems to be the central accusation, and what is the government implying by it?

2. What positive statements does Mandela make about what the ANC is and does? What fears on the part of his accusers (and the South African whites they represent) does he address?

3. Where in this essay does Mandela use the rhetorical strategy of comparison and contrast? How does he support his central argument concerning the Communist Party without accepting the government's position on that organization?

4. When Mandela made his speech to the court, what do you think were his hopes and fears for his personal future and that of the ANC? What appear to have been his top priorities?

CONNECTIONS

1. What attitudes about their homeland and its people do Mandela and Nadine Gordimer share? What role does Gordimer show black South Africans playing in "Africa Emergent"? What role does Mandela show black South Africans playing in "The African National Congress"? Why are these two writers' emphases different?

2. What similarities can you find between Mandela's goals, as expressed in "The African National Congress," and Václav Havel's goals, as expressed in "The Chance That Will Not Return"? How does each writer use world history to support his argument?

3. Look back at Shiva Naipaul's "The Palmers" (p. 405). How do you think Mandela would react to the Palmers' relationship with their employees? How do you think the Palmers would react to the goals of the ANC, as expressed by Mandela, and why?

ELABORATIONS

1. What audience is Mandela addressing in "The African National Congress," and how does he want his argument to affect their emotions? their actions? What audience is Gordimer addressing in "Africa Emergent," and how does she want her argument to affect their emotions? their actions? What goals do both writers have in common? Write an essay comparing and contrasting Mandela's and Gordimer's aims, their strategies, and their depiction of South African blacks.

2. Based on Ezekiel Mphahlele's "Tradition and the African Writer" (p. 34), V. S. Naipaul's "Entering the New World" (p. 47), Wole Soyinka's "Nigerian Childhood" (p. 154), Shiva Naipaul's "The Palmers" (p. 405), Gordimer's "Africa Emergent," and Mandela's "The African National Congress," write an essay on the problems faced by blacks, whites, and the country as a whole when control of a former European colony is returned to its native African inhabitants.

COLIN THUBRON

At the Beijing Zoo

The opening of China to foreign visitors in the 1980s was irresistible to Colin Thubron. Born in London in 1939, he has written several travel books based on journeys through Damascus, Cyprus, and western Russia. Thubron, a fellow of the British Royal Society of Literature, learned Mandarin for his trip to China. He crisscrossed the country by foot, bicycle, and train in a 10,000-mile trek that took him from Beijing to Tibet, from the Burma border to the Gobi Desert. Along the way he visited a marriage bureau, toured underground nuclear shelters, and conversed with Chinese from all walks of life. "It was like discovering a new room in a house in which you'd lived all your life," he recalls. The result of his travels was his book *Behind the Wall* (1987), from which "At the Beijing Zoo" is taken. Thubron also has published three novels, the most recent being *Falling* (1989). He currently lives in London.

The period recalled by the man with whom Thubron spoke at the Beijing Zoo was a chilling time in Chinese history. In 1949 Communists led by Mao Zedong took control of China and began restructuring its economy on the Soviet model: Private property was turned over to collectives, and central planning replaced markets. Throughout Chairman Mao's regime, the priorities of the state (which supposedly meant the people) outweighed those of individuals. The Hundred Flowers Movement of 1957 quickly boomeranged into the Anti-Rightist Movement (see p. 93). The following year Mao launched the Great Leap Forward, in which hundreds of millions of people were put to work on large industrial projects and over 40 million starved to death. In 1966 began the Cultural Revolution, which glorified workers, peasants, and soldiers and purged "bourgeois" intellectuals and officials — including Deng Xiaoping, who would later become Mao's successor. As Thubron reports in this essay, millions of bright young Chinese were exiled to remote rural areas to be reformed by hard work and "struggle" (criticism). The Cultural Revolution ended in 1976, following protests, Mao's death, and the failure of the Gang of Four to sustain it (see p. 235).

(For more background on China, see pp. 93 and 656.)

In the zoo everything unusual seemed to be asleep. A herd of square-lipped rhinoceroses had foundered like battleships into the dust, and three pandas lay on iron benches in the sun, their fur discolored and their arms wrapped over their faces. The visitors tried to goad the animals into action, but the sour-faced gorillas only went on chewing at their grasses; the big cats yawned as if reality stopped at their bars; and the Yangtze alligators focused on nothing through burnt-out eyes.

But the place of people's greatest fascination was the aquarium. In these dark corridors, hung with their illumined panels, the crowds banked six deep to investigate the goofy-faced paradise fish or watch the *Santamariae* fluttering across their tank in a silver diagonal of sparks.

I was looking for creatures special to China: the white-lipped deer, the wild Tibetan donkey, golden-hair monkeys. I found the deer swatting insects out of their eyes with casual rotations of their ears. Their white lips lent them a painted calm and seemed faintly to smile. But the golden-haired monkey turned out to be a recluse. A man was standing at its cage with his small daughter, shouting for it to emerge from its hutch. But nothing happened. We joined our voices in a comical request to it — first courteous, then cajoling, finally rude. But it turned away in its shelter, so that we glimpsed only a moody, black-streaked back and disconsolate ears.

The man was humorously disappointed. He had spent years in the wilds of the northern provinces, he said, and had never spotted a monkey — and now here he was, within shouting distance of one, and it wouldn't even look round.   4

Some reticent difference of dress or manner distinguished him (I never defined it) and he was tall for a Chinese, gangling even.

There were greenish-furred apes in the north, I'd heard, which looked as if they were covered in lichen. Had he never glimpsed those?

"I don't remember any wildlife at all." His hands dropped to his daughter's, as if they were about to go, but instead he leant back against the cage. We were alone. "Up there in Shanxi province the peasants have stripped all the trees, they're so poor. They kill and eat anything that moves. There's scarcely even wood for building materials." His lips enacted the tasting of something bitter, and this fleeting expression all at once seemed natural to him, and his suavity just a temporary concession. He asked suddenly: "Why are you speaking Mandarin? Are you a teacher?"

"No. I'm just . . . interested." I was uneasily aware of the monkey   8
stirring in its shelter behind us. The man smiled.

"Out there in the northwest life is much harder," he went on. "You can't imagine. So little food, fuel. And terrible winters. I remember seeing ancestral tablets reused as timber in the walls. The ancestor cult had been banned by then — so there they were, just stuffed into the walls like bricks."

"Really forgotten?"

"Well, not really. They stayed in the peasants' memories even if they weren't on their altars" — he tapped with his fingertips at his forehead — "and as soon as new policies came in they started returning. Not the old tablets, I mean, those were burnt or lost. But the peasants made new ones. It was all in their minds, you see. It never left."

I asked: "Do you come from the northwest?" But I had guessed, already, that he did not, and why he'd been there. He was in his mid-thirties, the age of China's lost generation: 17 million youths exiled to the country.

"No."

I blundered on: "Were you away long then? I mean during the" — I hoisted the name gingerly — "Cultural Revolution."

"I had seven years. I was young then. I should have been able to bear it." Between one sentence and another the urbane veneer had slipped from his face. Its flesh had stiffened. He said incongruously: "I see you're interested in our history." That turned my questions — and his experiences — impersonal. "I was sixteen when I was banished. I lived with another youth — an ex–Red Guard like me — in a peasant's two-room cottage. We took over one room while the farmer and his four children moved into the other. Half theirs was occupied by a brick bed heated from beneath, where they all slept. That was all there was. With a pig-sty and a closet for night-soil in the courtyard. That was us." By now he was speaking with slight theatricality. "But of course the peasants didn't welcome us. We were just extra mouths to feed. We knew nothing about farming. Some years the family came near starvation and the man thought of selling one of his daughters — the sickly one. Quite a few from our village were sold off like that, as cheap future brides. That way a peasant could get a bride for 1,000 yuan, perhaps, instead of paying 2,000. They were sold off while they were still young."

I glanced down at his daughter. Her face held an empty clarity. She was tying her hair-ribbon. "How young?"

"I can't remember. One was eight, I think, another only five." They went to distant villages, he said, these brides for £200 [$560]. It was better then being killed in infancy. "I heard of them being killed in other villages. It was quite common. The peasants would just drop them in the water and drown them." His lean hands lobbed an imaginary baby into a pool: his gestures had grown constricted, filled with histrionic

12

16

revulsion. "You see, they don't think. They just drop it in. They just say 'It's a girl! It's worthless!' Girls are not *descendants*, you understand. They're not viewed that way. It's boys who continue our line."

He stopped, as if at some ghastly logic in the thing. His little girl's hand was still in his, but she was gazing behind us, waiting for the monkey to emerge.

"What do the other villagers say about it?" I asked.

"They probably say nothing. They understand. They're peasants too, after all. They don't denounce them. Only if officials hear, then the man will go to prison." 20

"And the woman?"

"The woman maybe not. It's the men who get the long sentences. Five years for a man — one for a woman! Perhaps, I don't know." He glanced up suddenly — like someone just waking. A few people were walking near us. "You're interested in Chinese animals? I'll find a takin for you. . . . "

His smile relaxed him into somebody else again, somebody pleasant, studiously courteous. We ambled away up a slope to a new line of enclosures. Half unconsciously, perhaps, he had chosen somewhere lonely. His daughter ran ahead of us to find the takin (whatever that was) while I asked him tentatively about the Red Guards. The year 1966, when they were unleashed upon the country, still touched me with a faint, naïve regret. I remembered Mao Zedong's belief that the Chinese were a blank sheet of paper on which could be written a poem of creative and unending revolution.

But men turned out to be different, of course. Between 1966 and 1968 24 China sank into a terrified collective madness. Nobody was safe. Officials, doctors, teachers, scientists — all the élite of the professions and the arts, anybody tinged with privilege or the West (and millions who weren't) — were ritually humiliated, ingeniously tortured, exiled, beaten to death. In the peculiarly Chinese "struggle sessions," the victim was subjected to a remorseless psychological and physical battering by hundreds of jeering co-workers over days or weeks, his every word contradicted, his past shredded by accusation, his will broken, until he had groaned out confession. A hysterical xenophobia reigned. Cultural life was laid waste. Variety and beauty in themselves became criminal. Even pet cats and dogs were slaughtered (producing a plague of rats). Ornamental trees and flower-beds were dug up. Stamp-collecting, chess, keeping goldfish — nothing was innocent.

The man had the feeling that he had been somebody else at that time.

"Yet I remember it very distinctly. Everything. We only had one idea then. Whatever Chairman Mao said was right, God-given. Our heads were empty. Perhaps we had gone mad. We didn't think at all." He was staring into vacant cages. "And now it seems like a nightmare."

I didn't answer, because I didn't really understand. He was deeply bewildered at his own past. Once authority had sanctioned violence, no monitor inside him had called a halt. Such a pattern, I realized, ran far back in China's history: a recurring cycle of constraint broken by sudden ungovernable savagery.

And what had he done?

As he spoke about it, the tension crawled back into his voice. But instead of silencing him, it seemed to be this which made him speak — a tension created simply by recollection, by reentering a past in which (he now felt) he had been a sleepwalker, another man.

"I was at high school then, when some of us attacked our teacher. Those whose work he'd criticized were out for revenge, of course, and others joined in, but not me. They starved him of food and water, then 'struggled' him for being a revisionist until he confessed." The essence was to humiliate, to break a man's image and remake his thoughts — or to create the illusion of this. "But he didn't die. For years he was forced to clean out the school lavatories. His hair was shaved in a criss-cross pattern over his skull, so that he was made to look ridiculous, terrible." He added in the same tone: "He's principal of the school now. I go to see him sometimes."

"Did people believe their own confessions?" I had no idea of the answer.

"No, not often, no. This is a very old and complex thing. Perhaps a few of the academic ones thought they'd had wrong ideas. But mostly people just accepted criticism and bent." He leaned forward and cupped his hands pathetically in front of his face as if to drink from them, then gazed up with beseeching eyes — a picture of supplicating helplessness. "This confessing is our custom, you know. You choke down what you really feel." Now he curled a finger down his neck as if swallowing pain, swallowing until it nestled deep inside. He made the whole rigmarole of confession seem like a perverted charade, at once sophisticated and tribal — and as I looked at him I had the confused idea that the breathy cabaret of his talk belonged to the same order: an archaic theater of signs.

"And this is the takin." We had reached an enclosure labeled *Budorcas Taxicolor,* and there it stood. "I believe it's exclusive to China," he said. With its droll, equine head, it did indeed look like the member of some old and exclusive club, possibly China. A drizzle of tufts fell from its chin, and it was crowned by a pair of short, useless horns, set between its ears like a little anvil. The girl was trying to feed it sweets.

The man ignored it. "I've never talked to my teacher about these things. And he's never asked me. It's difficult."

Why then, I wondered, could he talk to me? But perhaps a foreigner, with his outlandish rules and values, didn't count.

Then some violence of nerves erupted in the man again. "That year we beat up several people in the street," he said. "If our leaders said 'He's a reactionary! Beat him!,' we beat him." His lips squirmed back from his teeth and he lifted his interlaced hands and chopped the air with an imaginary club. "We didn't know — we didn't ask — why this or that man was bad. People said hit him, so you hit him. It was simple. It wasn't even personal." He was reenacting the past with an odd fear, yet without a trace of guilt. In his own eyes he was no more to blame than the splinter of a bomb which somebody else — the guilty one — had exploded. I was reminded of what anthropologists said about "guilt cultures" and "shame cultures": that a "guilt culture" is characterized by an internalized sense of sin, whereas a "shame culture" stresses only outward social values, and that once these are gone, all is havoc. Next year, doubtless, the theories would be different. But this man would be the same, enigmatic even to himself.

I found it hard to meet his gaze. I kept my eyes on the outlandish 36 face of *Budorcas taxicolor*. Its presence was ludicrous, reassuring. The man went on: "We found a porter who had been reading novels with a love interest. I don't mean porn. Just a personal story. This was decadent. We beat him unconscious, and burnt the books. Then he died."

I looked at him in astonishment, mesmerized, for some reason, by his immaculately pressed trousers. Once the armor of social constraint had been stripped from him, the person inside had been exposed as a baby: conscienceless. Was that China, I wondered bleakly, or just him? Or perhaps it was no longer him. In any case, where was that feeling of pity which Mencius[1] said was common to all men?

"We were just the tools of the others," he said. "We were children. We didn't know a thing." Yet his face was a rack of bones and tightened skin.

A little later he walked off with his daughter's hand in his, and I was left gazing at the calm herbivorous[2] movements of the takin.

---

[1]Fourth-century B.C.E. Chinese philosopher. — ED.
[2]Plant-eating. — ED.

EXPLORATIONS

1. The Chinese man whom Thubron meets at the zoo recalls the violence he and other young people committed during the Cultural Revolution. What possible explanations for this behavior emerge from Thubron's essay?

2. What role do *Budorcas taxicolor* and other animals play in this essay? How would the impact of Thubron's narrative change if he took out the zoo setting? if he left out the Chinese man's daughter?

3. In paragraph 35 Thubron writes about "guilt cultures" and "shame cultures." To which does the Chinese man seem to belong? What qualities of Chinese culture put it in that category?

4. Thubron's essay contains a series of examples of inhumanity. What are these examples? In what kind of order are they arranged, with what effect?

CONNECTIONS

1. In paragraphs 23–24 Thubron writes: "I remembered Mao Zedong's belief that the Chinese were a blank sheet of paper on which could be written a poem of creative and unending revolution. But men turned out to be different, of course." According to Nelson Mandela in "The African National Congress" and Nadine Gordimer in "Africa Emergent," what kind of text has the South African government tried to write on its people? How have South Africans proved themselves not to be a blank sheet of paper?

2. In retrospect, notes Thubron, China seems to have sunk between 1966 and 1968 "into a terrified collective madness" (para. 24). What two instances in Peter Schneider's "The End of the Wall" show Germans having accommodated to a situation which afterward they realized was madness?

3. How do the structure and goals of Annie Dillard's passage in *Looking at Ourselves* resemble the structure and goals of "At the Beijing Zoo"?

4. Look back at Liang Heng and Judith Shapiro's "Chairman Mao's Good Little Boy" (p. 93). What similar experiences and emotions are recalled by Thubron's Chinese friend and by Liang? What are some probable reasons that Liang left China, while the other man (like most Chinese) remained?

ELABORATIONS

1. How drastically will an individual violate his or her personal moral standards when pressed by the group? What factors encourage or discourage such violations? On the basis of Thubron's essay and other selections you have read, write a classification or comparison-contrast essay addressing these questions.

2. What shameful or heroic acts have you committed in the past which make you feel, as Thubron's Chinese friend does, that you were someone else at the time? Write a narrative essay describing such an experience from your point of view then and now.

PART SEVEN

WITNESSES TO WAR

Soldiers and Survivors

LOOKING AT OURSELVES

Harry S Truman, Omar Bradley, Dwight D. Eisenhower, William
H. Sullivan, Mark Baker, George Gilder, Barbara Ehrenreich,
William Broyles, Jr.

Czeslaw Milosz, *American Ignorance of War* (POLAND)

Roger Rosenblatt, *Children of Cambodia* (CAMBODIA)

Amos Oz, *If There Is Justice* (ISRAEL)

The New Yorker, The Price of the Panama Invasion
(UNITED STATES)

Shelley Saywell, *Women Warriors of El Salvador* (EL SALVADOR)

Milovan Djilas, *Ideas Against Torture* (YUGOSLAVIA)

John Simpson, *Tiananmen Square* (CHINA)

Jon Lee Anderson and Scott Anderson, *The Troubles*
(NORTHERN IRELAND)

Rian Malan, *Msinga* (SOUTH AFRICA)

Chinua Achebe, *Civil Peace* (NIGERIA)

WHAT DOES *WAR* MEAN IN THE UNITED STATES AS WE NEAR THE CLOSE of the twentieth century? Modern communications technology enables us to watch combat around the world on nightly television, where one country looks much like another and news clips are only a bit less thrilling than feature films. Meanwhile, modern military technology enables ragged guerrillas to launch missiles from the backs of camels. We see war; perhaps we discuss it or deplore it or send money to its refugees; but do we believe it's real?

Looking at Ourselves opens with a journal entry by President Harry S Truman written shortly before he ordered the first atomic bomb dropped on a Japanese city. General Omar Bradley hails the team spirit of our military forces, and President Dwight D. Eisenhower warns about the growing military-industrial complex. William H. Sullivan, retired from the U.S. Foreign Service, recalls a 1962 war game with the Joint Chiefs of Staff. Mark Baker interviews a nurse who patched up casualties in Vietnam; economist George Gilder argues that, in one sense, the United States won that war. Barbara Ehrenreich describes the "Warrior Caste," who seek in each war the seeds of the next. Finally, William Broyles, Jr., wonders why he and other veterans remember wartime with such nostalgia.

"Are Americans *really* stupid?" ask postwar Eastern Europeans, as Polish writer Czeslaw Milosz reports in "American Ignorance of War." Roger Rosenblatt visits a Thai camp for Khmer refugees to interview "Children of Cambodia," whose concept of revenge is as unique as their ancient culture. Amos Oz follows an Israeli soldier home on leave in the short story "If There Is Justice." "The Price of the Panama Invasion," from *The New Yorker*, suggests that the United States and Latin America scored the fall of dictator Manuel Noriega quite differently. Canadian Shelley Saywell, in "Women Warriors of El Salvador," talks with two resistance fighters who give a passionate account of their country's guerrilla revolution. Milovan Djilas offers advice to potential torture victims in "Ideas Against Torture," based on his own experience in Yugoslavia.

John Simpson of the BBC writes in "Tiananmen Square" of being present on the fateful June night when the Chinese army turned tanks and guns on thousands of peaceful demonstrators. In Northern Ireland, Jon Lee Anderson and Scott Anderson interview pro-British Loyalists and pro-Irish Republicans about the war of nerves, pipe bombs, and kneecappings known as "The Troubles." South African Rian Malan shares the perplexity of a local policeman over endless tribal warfare in "Msinga." Chinua Achebe's short story "Civil Peace" shows a Nigerian family facing a new round of challenges in the wake of Biafra's failed attempt at secession.   ◈

LOOKING AT OURSELVES

1

July 18, '45

Ate breakfast with nephew Harry, a sergeant in the Field Artillery. He is a good soldier and a nice boy. They took him off Queen Elizabeth at Glasco [Glasgow] and flew him here. Sending him home Friday. Went to lunch with P.M. [British Prime Minister Winston Churchill] at 1:30 walked around to British Hqtrs. Met at the gate by Mr. Churchill. Guard of honor drawn up. Fine body of men Scottish Guards. Band played Star Spangled Banner. Inspected Guard and went in for lunch. P.M. and I ate alone. Discussed Manhattan[1] (it is a success). Decided to tell Stalin about it. Stalin had told P.M. of telegram from Jap Emperor asking for peace. Stalin also read his answer to me. It was satisfactory. Believe Japs will fold up before Russia comes in.

I am sure they will when Manhattan appears over their homeland.

– President Harry S Truman
Personal journal

2

Our military forces are one team — in the game to win regardless of who carries the ball. This is no time for "fancy dans" who won't hit the line with all they have on every play, unless they can call the signals. Each player on this team — whether he shines in the spotlight of the backfield or eats dirt in the line — must be an All-American.

– General Omar Bradley
Testimony to the Committee on Armed Forces,
House of Representatives
October 19, 1949

3

This conjunction of an immense military establishment and a large arms industry is new in the American experience. . . . In the councils of government, we must guard against the acquisition of unwarranted

---

[1]The Manhattan Project, code name for the creation of the first atomic bomb, which Truman ordered U.S. forces to drop on the Japanese city of Hiroshima less than a month after this journal entry. The USSR had agreed to enter the war on the Allied side on August 15. — ED.

influence, whether sought or unsought, by the military-industrial complex. The potential for the disastrous rise of misplaced power exists and will persist.

> – President Dwight D. Eisenhower
> Farewell Radio and Television Address
> to the American People
> January 17, 1961

4

My first serious involvement with Vietnam was in the form of a weeklong war game organized by the Joint Chiefs of Staff in 1962. In order to ensure maximum objectivity, the Chiefs had engaged the Rand Corporation to draw up the rules of the game and to act as a control team. The opposing red and blue teams were to represent all factions that would presumably be involved if the United States were to expand its role in Vietnam. The game would be played as a command post exercise; its point was to project how the Vietnam situation might unfold over a span of about ten years given certain assumptions that would be introduced into the proceedings from a script prepared by the control team. In principle, those assumptions were neutral, and their effect on the outcome of the game would be determined by the way in which the red and blue teams reacted to them.

The opposing teams were divided into two echelons. The senior group functioned on the policy level and met only sporadically during the game. The other group operated at the action level and was in session eight hours a day. The blue team's policy chief was John McCone, head of the CIA, and its action chief was an Air Force general. The red team's policy chief was General Maxwell Taylor, former chief of staff of the Army, who was then senior military adviser to President Kennedy; I was head of the red action team. On my action team there was a Marine Corps general, colonels from the Army and Air Force, a Navy captain, some senior intelligence officers, and civilians from relevant government departments and agencies.

Taylor instructed me to play the game according to the rules of guerrilla warfare, accept heavy casualties, exploit propaganda opportunities, and brazenly disregard the truth. He particularly wanted our action group to play upon any weaknesses we could find in the traditional military doctrines of our opponents as well as in the civil processes of a democracy. He took some relish in casting himself as Ho Chi Minh and encouraged me to think of myself as General Giap, the case-hardened commander of North Vietnam's troops. We launched the game with zeal.

By the end of the week — a point that represented the winter of 1972 — the game had played itself out. The red (North Vietnamese) forces were everywhere on the map on Indochina. We had overrun most of Laos and we controlled the countryside of South Vietnam and the cordillera extending into Cambodia. We had suffered severe casualties, but our structure was still intact and we had solid support from the Soviet Union and China. We had extended and demoralized the forces of South Vietnam. Most important, 500,000 American troops had been bogged down in the quagmire of Indochina and a large portion of the U.S. Navy and Air Force had become involved. We had caused great U.S. expenditures on this feckless enterprise and had provoked great agitation and unrest in the American population, especially on university campuses. Moreover, we had all but isolated the United States in the United Nations and in world public opinion and we had driven the U.S. Congress to the brink of revolt over the seemingly endless war.

John McCone concluded that his organization ought to call it quits and cut its losses. The experience of playing that game made him a dove on Vietnam. He felt that its projections were accurate and that the shadows they cast should be heeded.

Other participants drew different conclusions. Some Air Force officers felt that the control team was unrealistic in its scoring of certain actions. . . . I specifically remember their cry of foul when my guerrillas were able to blow up a large number of U.S. aircraft at Bien Hoa airfield. I remember this so clearly because when I looked out the window of my airplane in November 1964 as I was leaving Vietnam to return to Washington to be sworn in as ambassador to Laos, I saw black smoke billowing from the airport at Bien Hoa, where a guerrilla attack had succeeded in blowing up fuel, ammunition, and a number of U.S. aircraft.

– William H. Sullivan
"Vietnam Portents"
Harper's

5

I never saw so many guys cry as I did while I was in Vietnam. Some of those corpsmen and men from the field amazed me with how gentle they were with their buddies. One of the big fears the guys had was of dying alone. A lot of guys came into the hospital really badly hurt and they did die, but their buddies stayed with them.

"Don't leave me, please don't leave me." And they didn't.

About the time I'd get fed up with being there, I'd walk into the ward and see a paraplegic who could still use his arms, feeding the guy next to him who had been blinded. I'd think to myself, "You may hate it here and you may feel like shit and look like hell and think you just can't stand another day, but at least you're not one of these guys. If that boy with no legs can get over to feed his blind friend, you can do what *you* have to do."

I went over to Vietnam thinking Army doctors were hard-asses. It's just not so. We had a Vietnamese girl on the ward. She was the same age as I was — twenty-one. She was cleaning the barracks. They used to clean the floors with kerosene or something to get the wax off. Some smart guy flipped a match on the floor while she was down there scrubbing it. *Whoosh*, she was gone in a puff of smoke.

The surgeon taking care of her was named Paul. When he got to her, she was 100 percent second- and third-degree burns. Plus she had inhaled a lot of smoke. Usually these people are going to die, so you let them. The thing was, she was still conscious and talking, and her kidneys were still working. So he had to try and save her. He started an IV on her and she came up to my ward.

Burn victims shed the inside of their lungs. It's like getting sunburned on the inside and peeling. She would cough up her lungs and she'd be bleeding and slowly choking to death. She could speak English. She would hold on to Paul and beg him not to let her die.

It was getting to the point that she was really bad and he had to make a decision. Either you trach her, so that you can clean her out and let her breathe, or you just let her die. Paul said, "I've got to think about it. I'm going to leave the ward for a while. I'll be back in an hour."

An hour went by and he didn't come back. Another hour went by and he didn't show. Finally, I went looking for him. He was in this place that was our library — it was about the size of a walk-in closet. He was in there crying his eyes out. He said, "What am I going to do? I never should have started that IV on her. I never should have put that catheter in her. But she was alive when she came in and I had to do something. I can't trach her. She'll live six weeks and then she'll die horribly. What am I going to do with her? What am I going to do?"

He didn't do anything. He was going to let her die. We had to go over and change the dressings on her. He didn't want to do it any more than I did. But he helped me. The whole time she just cried and begged him not to let her die. But it was inevitable; she was gone in another day or so.

The doctors used to help us with the dressing changes quite a bit, because they knew how ugly they were. You've got a guy and you've got to change his whole body when you change the dressing. You have to give the guy morphine just to take the edge off, because he's so badly injured. The doctors felt bad for us. There were days when there wasn't a dry eye in the house, what with the patients screaming and us crying, trying to get the job done.

> – A nurse, quoted by Mark Baker
> *Nam: The Vietnam War in the Words*
> *of the Men and Women Who Fought*
> *There*

<><><><><>

6

If we consider the economic consequences of Vietnam, I think we'll see that there's a real sense in which the United States won the Vietnam War. At least we won the one prize that was worth anything — the boat people [Southeast Asian refugees]. The boat people are now key figures in the high-tech companies in Silicon Valley and across the country, and are thus contributing substantially to American economic growth. . . .

There was economic devastation for several years because of Vietnam. But as soon as the war was over, as soon as tax rates were cut, the United States began to demonstrate that it could again dominate the world economically — which is the way that counts.

Indeed, perhaps the most harmful consequence of Vietnam was that it helped reinforce the fallacy of geopolitics — the idea that the cold war is about real estate, that it really makes a difference to America's power that the Russians control Afghanistan or Angola or Ethiopia, all those pathetic countries you can't even visit without getting sick.

> – George Gilder
> in "What Are the Consequences of Vietnam?"
> *Harper's*

<><><><><>

7

What defines the Warrior Caste, and sets it apart from the mass of average military men, is a love of war that knows no bounds, accepts no peace, and always seeks, in the ashes of the last battle, the sparks that might ignite the next. For [Lieutenant Colonel Oliver] North and many of his key collaborators, the sequence was Vietnam, then Nicaragua, with detours into war-torn Angola and prerevolutionary Iran. The end of one war demanded the creation of the next. . . .

My guess is that the historical "success" of the Warrior Caste rests on the fact that it is, in more than one sense, self-propagating. First, in a geographical sense: the existence of a warrior elite in City-State 1 called forth its creation in City-State 2 — otherwise the latter was likely to be reduced to rubble and the memories of slaves. Natural selection, as it has operated in human history, favors not only the clever but the murderous.

Second, and quite apart from ordinary biology, the Warrior Caste has the ability to reproduce itself from one generation to the next. Only women can produce children, of course; but — more to the point — only wars can produce *warriors*. One war leads to the next, in part because each war incubates the warriors who will fight the next, or, I should say, *create*, the next. The First World War engendered the warrior elite that ushered in the Third Reich, and hence the Second World War. And Vietnam created men like Oliver North, who, through subterfuge and stealth, nourished the fledgling war in Central America. . . .

The men of the true warrior elite in the United States today (and no doubt in the Soviet Union as well) wear tailored suits, kiss their wives good-bye in the morning, and spend their days at desks, plotting covert actions, megadeaths, and "low-intensity" interventions. They are peaceable, even genial, fellows, like the President himself. But still I would say, to the extent that they hoard the resources of the nation for the purposes of destruction, they live for war.

> – Barbara Ehrenreich
> "Iranscam: The Real Meaning
> of Oliver North"
> *Ms.*

8

Ask me, ask any man who has been to war about his experience, and chances are we'll say we don't want to talk about it — implying that we hated it so much, it was so terrible, that we would rather leave it buried. And it is no mystery why men hate war. War is ugly, horrible, evil, and it is reasonable for men to hate all that. But I believe that most men who have been to war would have to admit, if they are honest, that somewhere inside themselves they loved it too, loved it as much as anything that has happened to them before or since. And how do you explain that to your wife, your children, your parents, or your friends?

That's why men in their sixties and seventies sit in their dens and recreation rooms around America and know that nothing in their life will equal the day they parachuted into St.-Lô or charged the bunker on Okinawa. That's why veterans' reunions are invariably filled with boozy awkwardness, forced camaraderie ending in sadness and tears: you are together again, these are the men who were your brothers, but it's not the same, can never be the same. That's why when we returned from Vietnam we moped around, listless, not interested in anything or anyone. Something had gone out of our lives forever, and our behavior on returning was inexplicable except as the behavior of men who had lost a great — perhaps the great — love of their lives, and had no way to tell anyone about it.

In part we couldn't describe our feelings because the language failed us: the civilian-issue adjectives and nouns, verbs and adverbs, seemed made for a different universe. There were no metaphors that connected the war to everyday life. But we were also mute, I suspect, out of shame. Nothing in the way we are raised admits the possibility of loving war. It is at best a necessary-evil, a patriotic duty to be discharged and then put behind us. To love war is to mock the very values we supposedly fight for. It is to be insensitive, reactionary, a brute.

But it may be more dangerous, both for men and nations, to suppress the reasons men love war than to admit them. In *Apocalypse Now*, Robert Duvall, playing a brigade commander, surveys a particularly horrific combat scene and says, with great sadness, "You know, someday this war's gonna be over." He is clearly meant to be a psychopath, decorating enemy bodies with playing cards, riding to war with Wagner blaring. We laugh at him — Hey! nobody's like that! And last year [1984] in Grenada American boys charged into battle playing Wagner, a new generation aping the movies of Vietnam the way we aped the movies of World War II, learning nothing, remembering nothing.

Alfred Kazin wrote that war is the enduring condition of twentieth-century man. He was only partly right. War is the enduring condition of man, period. Men have gone to war over everything from Helen of Troy to Jenkins's ear. Two million Frenchmen and Englishmen died in muddy trenches in World War I because a student shot an archduke. The truth is, the reasons don't matter. There is a reason for every war and a war for every reason.

For centuries men have hoped that with history would come progress, and with progress, peace. But progress has simply given man the means to make war even more horrible; no wars in our savage past can begin to match the brutality of the wars spawned in this century, in the beautifully ordered, civilized landscape of Europe, where everyone is literate and classical music plays in every village café. War is not an aberration; it is part of the family, the crazy uncle we try — in vain — to keep locked in the basement.

– William Broyles, Jr.
"Why Men Love War"
Esquire

CZESLAW MILOSZ

American Ignorance of War

Czeslaw Milosz (pronounced Ches-law Mee-losh) has been called Poland's greatest living poet. Ironically, his work was refused publication in Poland from 1936 until 1980, when he won the Nobel Prize for literature. Milosz was born in 1911 in Lithuania, a small Baltic country historically controlled by Poland or the Soviet Union (see p. 507). He began writing poetry and became active in leftist politics while studying law at the University of Vilnius. After Germany invaded Poland in 1939, he wrote, edited, and translated for the Polish resistance in Warsaw. In 1946 he entered the diplomatic service of Poland's new Communist government and was stationed at the Polish embassy in Washington until 1950. After a year as first secretary for cultural affairs in Paris, Milosz broke with the Warsaw government, feeling too restricted as a writer by its regimentation of cultural life. He now lives in Berkeley, California, where he continues to write both poetry and prose. "American Ignorance of War," translated from the Polish by Jane Zielonko, comes from Milosz's first American publication, *The Captive Mind* (1953), which examines life under totalitarianism and explains why he defected. Written soon after World War II, the essay appeared more than thirty-five years before the "people's democracies" of Eastern Europe began freeing themselves from Soviet domination (see pp. 517 and 524).

(For more background on Poland, see p. 502.)

"Are Americans *really* stupid?" I was asked in Warsaw. In the voice of the man who posed the question, there was despair, as well as the hope that I would contradict him. This question reveals the attitude of the average person in the people's democracies toward the West: it is despair mixed with a residue of hope.

During the last few years, the West has given these people a number of reasons to despair politically. In the case of the intellectual, other, more complicated reasons come into play. Before the countries of Central and Eastern Europe entered the sphere of the Imperium,[1] they lived through the Second World War. That war was much more devastating there than in the countries of Western Europe. It destroyed not only

---

[1]Empire; that is, the Soviet Union. — ED.

their economies, but also a great many values which had seemed till then unshakable.

Man tends to regard the order he lives in as *natural*. The houses he passes on his way to work seem more like rocks rising out of the earth than like products of human hands. He considers the work he does in his office or factory as essential to the harmonious functioning of the world. The clothes he wears are exactly what they should be, and he laughs at the idea that he might equally well be wearing a Roman toga or medieval armor. He respects and envies a minister of state or a bank director, and regards the possession of a considerable amount of money as the main guarantee of peace and security. He cannot believe that one day a rider may appear on a street he knows well, where cats sleep and children play, and start catching passersby with his lasso. He is accustomed to satisfying those of his physiological needs which are considered private as discreetly as possible, without realizing that such a pattern of behavior is not common to all human societies. In a word, he behaves a little like Charlie Chaplin in *The Gold Rush*, bustling about in a shack poised precariously on the edge of a cliff.

His first stroll along a street littered with glass from bomb-shattered windows shakes his faith in the "naturalness" of his world. The wind scatters papers from hastily evacuated offices, papers labeled "Confidential" or "Top Secret" that evoke visions of safes, keys, conferences, couriers, and secretaries. Now the wind blows them through the street for anyone to read; yet no one does, for each man is more urgently concerned with finding a loaf of bread. Strangely enough, the world goes on even though the offices and secret files have lost all meaning. Farther down the street, he stops before a house split in half by a bomb, the privacy of people's homes — the family smells, the warmth of the beehive life, the furniture preserving the memory of loves and hatreds — cut open to public view. The house itself, no longer a rock, but a scaffolding of plaster, concrete, and brick; and on the third floor, a solitary white bathtub, rain-rinsed of all recollection of those who once bathed in it. Its formerly influential and respected owners, now destitute, walk the fields in search of stray potatoes. Thus overnight money loses its value and becomes a meaningless mass of printed paper. His walk takes him past a little boy poking a stick into a heap of smoking ruins and whistling a song about the great leader who will preserve the nation against all enemies. The song remains, but the leader of yesterday is already part of an extinct past.

He finds he acquires new habits quickly. Once, had he stumbled upon a corpse on the street, he would have called the police. A crowd would have gathered, and much talk and comment would have ensued. Now he knows he must avoid the dark body lying in the gutter, and refrain from asking unnecessary questions. The man who fired the gun must have had his reasons; he might well have been executing an Underground sentence.

Nor is the average European accustomed to thinking of his native city as divided into segregated living areas, but a single decree can force him to this new pattern of life and thought. Quarter A may suddenly be designated for one race; B, for a second; C, for a third. As the resettlement deadline approaches, the streets become filled with long lines of wagons, carts, wheelbarrows, and people carrying bundles, beds, chests, caldrons, and bird cages. When all the moves are effected, 2,000 people may find themselves in a building that once housed 200, but each man is at last in the proper area. Then high walls are erected around quarter C, and daily a given lot of men, women, and children are loaded into wagons that take them off to specially constructed factories where they are scientifically slaughtered and their bodies burned.

And even the rider with the lasso appears, in the form of a military van waiting at the corner of a street. A man passing that corner meets a leveled rifle, raises his hands, is pushed into the van, and from that moment is lost to his family and friends. He may be sent to a concentration camp, or he may face a firing squad, his lips sealed with plaster lest he cry out against the state; but, in any case, he serves as a warning to his fellow men. Perhaps one might escape such a fate by remaining at home. But the father of a family must go out in order to provide bread and soup for his wife and children; and every night they worry about whether or not he will return. Since these conditions last for years, everyone gradually comes to look upon the city as a jungle, and upon the fate of twentieth-century man as identical with that of a caveman living in the midst of powerful monsters.

It was once thought obvious that a man bears the same name and 8 surname throughout his entire life; now it proves wiser for many reasons to change them and to memorize a new and fabricated biography. As a result, the records of the civilian state become completely confused. Everyone ceases to care about formalities, so that marriage, for example, comes to mean little more than living together.

Respectable citizens used to regard banditry as a crime. Today, bank robbers are heroes because the money they steal is destined for the Underground. Usually they are young boys, mothers' boys, but their appearance is deceiving. The killing of a man presents no great moral problem to them.

The nearness of death destroys shame. Men and women change as soon as they know that the date of their execution has been fixed by a fat little man with shiny boots and a riding crop. They copulate in public, on the small bit of ground surrounded by barbed wire — their last home on earth. Boys and girls in their teens, about to go off to the barricades to fight against tanks with pistols and bottles of gasoline, want to enjoy their youth and lose their respect for standards of decency.

Which world is "natural"? That which existed before, or the world of war? Both are natural, if both are within the realm of one's experience. All the concepts men live by are a product of the historic formation in which they find themselves. Fluidity and constant change are the characteristics of phenomena. And man is so plastic a being that one can even conceive of the day when a thoroughly self-respecting citizen will crawl on all fours, sporting a tail of brightly colored feathers as a sign of conformity to the order he lives in.

The man of the East cannot take Americans seriously because they 12 have never undergone the experiences that teach men how relative their judgments and thinking habits are. Their resultant lack of imagination is appalling. Because they were born and raised in a given social order and in a given system of values, they believe that any other order must be "unnatural," and that it cannot last because it is incompatible with human nature. But even they may one day know fire, hunger, and the sword. In all probability this is what will occur; for it is hard to believe that when one half of the world is living through terrible disasters, the other half can continue a nineteenth-century mode of life, learning about the distress of its distant fellow men only from movies and newspapers. Recent examples teach us that this cannot be. An inhabitant of Warsaw or Budapest once looked at newsreels of bombed Spain or burning Shanghai, but in the end he learned how these and many other catastrophes appear in actuality. He read gloomy tales of the NKVD[2] until one day he found he himself had to deal with it. *If something exists in one place, it will exist everywhere.* This is the conclusion he draws from his observations, and so he has no particular faith in the momentary prosperity of America. He suspects that the years 1933–1945 in Europe[3] prefigure what will occur elsewhere. A hard school, where ignorance was punished not by

---

[2]The Soviet secret police, 1935–1943. — ED.
[3]Hitler's takeover of Germany through World War II. — ED.

bad marks but by death, has taught him to think sociologically and historically. But it has not freed him from irrational feelings. He is apt to believe in theories that foresee violent changes in the countries of the West, for he finds it unjust that they should escape the hardships he had to undergo.

EXPLORATIONS

1. Why does Milosz's questioner wonder in the opening sentence, "Are Americans *really* stupid?" What is Milosz's answer?

2. What comments in Milosz's essay suggest why, thirty-five years later, the "people's democracies" finally rebelled against their repressive postwar governments? What comments reflect a fatalistic sense that rebellion was hopeless? What combination of events mentioned in paragraph 2 explains that sense of fatalism?

3. How would the impact of Milosz's observations change if he presented them in a historical or argumentative essay instead of in narrative form? What concepts and comments in "American Ignorance of War" struck you most forcefully, and why?

CONNECTIONS

1. What statements by Milosz are supported by President Harry S Truman's comments in *Looking at Ourselves*? How did Truman's experience of World War II affect Milosz's experience?

2. Milosz writes about the dramatic change during wartime in what people perceive as "natural." What incidents and comments in the nurse's story quoted by Mark Baker in *Looking at Ourselves* show that Milosz's observations were true for Americans in Vietnam?

3. In paragraph 1 Milosz describes Eastern Europeans' attitude toward the West after World War II as "despair mixed with a residue of hope." What evidence of this attitude appears in Václav Havel's "The Chance That Will Not Return" (p. 517)? in Peter Schneider's "The End of the Wall" (p. 524)?

ELABORATIONS

1. When he wrote this essay some forty years ago, what did Milosz predict would happen in the West? What were the grounds for his prediction? How have the problems Milosz mentions produced different results from the ones he anticipated? Write a cause-and-effect essay answering these questions by examining the course of events in Poland, or Eastern Europe in general, from World War II to the present.

2. How would your life change if the United States went to war tomorrow? Imagine your school or town under attack by a foreign power. Write a letter to a friend or family member describing, as Milosz does, what you observe around you and how you respond to it.

ROGER ROSENBLATT

Children of Cambodia

Journalist and essayist Roger Rosenblatt was born in 1940 in New York, where he now lives with his family. His book *Children of War* (1983), in which "Children of Cambodia" appears, took him to Thailand, Hong Kong, Israel, Lebanon, Greece, and Northern Ireland. In addition to winning the 1984 Robert F. Kennedy Book Award, *Children of War* was nominated for the 1983 National Book Critics Circle Award. Rosenblatt studied at New York University and Harvard University; he taught English and American literature at Harvard from 1963 to 1973 and was a Fulbright scholar in 1965–66. For two years he served as director of education at the National Endowment for the Humanities in Washington, D.C. He has served variously as a staff writer, literary editor, and essayist for the *New Republic,* the *Washington Post, Time* magazine, *U.S. News & World Report, Life* magazine, and public television's "MacNeil/Lehrer NewsHour," commenting on events from presidential politics to whale watching.

Cambodia first came to the attention of many Americans during the Vietnam War, when U.S. troops — supporting democratic South Vietnam — crossed its border to pursue Communist Vietcong guerrillas. As Rosenblatt notes, enmities in the region go back many centuries: the Khmer dominated the peninsula that now comprises Thailand, Laos, Cambodia, and Vietnam from the ninth to thirteenth centuries, losing its east and west coasts finally to invading Siamese and Vietnamese. France took control of most of the region in the mid-1800s. Prince Norodom Sihanouk ruled Cambodia from 1941 through its independence from France in 1953 until pro–United States Lon Nol seized power in 1970. After American troops left Vietnam in the early 1970s, the Communist Khmer Rouge ousted the Lon Nol government. Then commenced the brutal regime of Pol Pot, who forced people out of the cities and towns to clear jungle and forest, and slaughtered not only his opponents but intellectuals and anyone else not aligned with his ideology. Over a million Cambodians were killed or died of hardship. Four years later, just as the United States recognized the Khmer Rouge government, Vietnam invaded Cambodia and forced Pol Pot and his troops into the jungles, setting up an austere Communist regime. Vietnam withdrew its troops in 1989 from the People's Republic of Kampuchea, a move that revitalized the unlikely alliance among the Khmer Rouge, supported by China, and two non-Communist groups: the Khmer People's National

Liberation Front and the former national army of Prince Sihanouk. Despite the Khmer Rouge's murderous past and Communist credentials, the United States for years supported this alliance as opponents of the Vietnamese.

(For more background on Cambodia and Vietnam, see p. 435.)

The road to Khao I Dang is a looping highway extending from Bangkok east southeast 150 miles to the Thai-Cambodian border. . . .

Socua assumes the task of telling me about the region. Socua is herself Khmer. She prefers the term *Khmer* to *Cambodian,* as do her countrymen, yet they also prefer *Cambodia* to *Kampuchea,* since that is the name Pol Pot gave the country after his takeover in April 1975. Wherever possible, they seek to draw a distinction between the peaceful, dignified people once known as the Khmer and the murderers who called themselves the Khmer Rouge. Socua is in her midtwenties, self-confident, attractive, her black hair cut short like a flapper's. A refugee herself, she lived and studied in San Francisco, and only recently came to Thailand to work with other refugees. Because of the war between the Khmer Rouge and the invading Vietnamese, travel to her homeland is impossible. She tells me that most of the people in Khao I Dang would also prefer to return home rather than be dispersed abroad.

For the present hope of returning is out of the question. The Vietnamese and Khmer Rouge are stalking each other in the jungles, leaving the innocent majority of Khmer terrorized, helpless, and starving. The Thais, suffused with traditional hatred of the Vietnamese and with traditional contempt for the Khmer, sell weapons to the Khmer Rouge. These are largely U.S. weapons. I discover that my country is in the idiotic and shameful position of recognizing the Khmer Rouge in the UN, arming them in the jungles, and accepting their victims as refugees. As a sidelight to the Cambodian war, the Thai government does nothing to restrain the Thai pirates from raping and slaughtering the Vietnamese boat people, including children, whose junks stray into Thai waters. Later in Hong Kong I read of a thirteen-year-old Vietnamese girl raped over and again by Thai pirates who passed her around. In seven days aboard the West German rescue ship she did not smile once. The nurses wept when they first saw her.

On a map one can see how close these now famous nations are —   4 Thailand, Laos, Vietnam, Cambodia — pressed together as tightly as

four midwestern American states. The Thais first won independence from
the Khmer in 1238. It has taken awhile to hone these enmities. . . .

Many of the houses rest on stilts here. Socua tells me that in Cambodia
the height of one's house signifies how rich and important he is. The
height of a house is often increased by piling roof upon roof. "If one
wishes to determine how powerful you are, he will not ask directly, which
would be rude. He will ask instead how many roofs your house has." At
least that was so when Cambodia still had gradations of self-esteem. That
is gone now, Socua says. War has changed her people. A country known
for centuries for docility, gentleness, and pride — "known mainly for
smiling" — is ravaged now, the people shaken, their former values ruined
and cast away. "Still, you will see vestiges of the old dignity in Khao I
Dang. Whenever parents want to discipline their children, all they do is
remind them: 'You are Khmer. Behave like Khmer.'" From a very early
age, Socua says, the children are taught to honor, in this order, the land, the
nation, their dead ancestors, their parents, their village, including their
friends. "They continue to do so, even in a place like Khao I Dang." . . .

In the middle of the morning on October 13, we arrive in Khao I
Dang, swarmed immediately by small girls calling "Buy, please, buy,"
and selling wooden birds on wooden perches. Socua guides us through
the children. She points to a huddle of Khmer adults waiting by the gate
to be moved in trucks to other camps. Their faces are lifeless. At its
largest Khao I Dang held over 120,000 refugees. That population is
reduced to 40,000 now, a number that sounds more manageable, given
the small-town size of the camp, about seventy square acres. Behind the
neat rows of straw-roofed huts rises the mountain Khao I Dang, or
"spotted bitch mountain" or simply "spotted mountain"; evidently it translates both ways. Socua leads Matthew and me along Phnom Penh Road,
a mud path named to recall the homeland of the Khmer. Their camp
looks like an ancient village to me. Women in *sampots* skitter by with
naked babies riding on their hips. Monks in yellow gowns sit cross-legged
on long bamboo tables, their shaved heads lowered in contemplation.
We arrive on a holiday, the last days of the Buddhist Lent. Everyone
smiles at us openly, the children tagging along. Some are in tatters. I
find them astonishingly beautiful.

"They think you'll take them home with you," says Socua. "Take care
to say nothing that would indicate you might."

Neil Boothby greets us at the Children's Center, a long, dirt-floor hut   8
the size of a mess hall in an army camp. We wired Neil from Bangkok
to say why we were coming. He has already engaged an interpreter for

us. Socua is thus free to work elsewhere in the camp. She will arrange a dance performance by the children later in the day. Our interpreter, Khav Yuom, called Yuom, is a man so small and fresh-faced he could pass for a child himself. In fact, I take him for a teenager until I look at him more earnestly. Yuom is in his midtwenties. Partly because he looks like a boy, he not only managed to escape from the Khmer Rouge himself but to smuggle his wife and mother out of the country as well. He goes to get Ty Kim Seng, a ten-year-old who also escaped Pol Pot's soldiers and who arrived at Khao I Dang about a year ago. Ty Kim Seng is one of several children Neil has lined up for me to meet. . . .

"He always talked fairly freely, even when he first came to the camp and looked like this." Neil slides a sheet of paper toward me across the kitchen table where we sit. It is a crayon drawing of a bright orange skeletal figure with a grim mouth in an open frown. Round teardrops fall from the skeleton's eyes. Ty Kim Seng drew this picture shortly after he arrived at Khao I Dang. It refers to the time when the boy was eight and was forced to join one of the mobile work teams instituted by Pol Pot for the Khmer children's "education and well-being." When Ty Kim Seng first walked down into Khao I Dang, he was nearly dead from malnutrition.

No longer, Ty Kim Seng enters the hut alongside Yuom and greets me with a *wai*, a small bow of homage in which one's hands are pressed together as if in prayer and raised to one's face, the fingertips stopping at about eye level. I return the gesture, asking Yuom with my eyes if I have done the *wai* correctly. I soon realize he would never risk discourtesy by telling me if I erred. Yuom and Ty Kim Seng take the bench on the opposite side of the kitchen table, and we begin to talk above the squeals of the children outside the hut. The boy is visible to the middle of his chest. He wears a white sport shirt. His face is bright brown, his head held in balance by a pair of ears a bit too large for the rest. The effect is scholarly, not comical. . . . I ask a few introductory questions to which at first he gives only brief answers.

"Are your parents living?"

"No. They are dead." 12

"What work did they do in Cambodia?"

"My father was a doctor. My mother did housework."

"Would you also like to be a doctor someday?"

"No. I would like to be an airplane pilot." He tells me that once in 16 1974 he flew in an airplane from his village to Phnom Penh.

"Was it exciting?"

"It was wonderful." He smiles at last.

In fact, I had not needed to ask him if his parents were living. Neil gave me Ty Kim Seng's background earlier while we waited for the boy. Ty Kim Seng's father was shot to death by a Pol Pot firing squad, for no reason other than that he was a doctor. The policies of the Khmer Rouge included the execution of all Cambodian intellectuals. The definition of a Cambodian intellectual was quite flexible. It included dancers, artists, the readers of books. Under Pol Pot it was a capital offense to wear eyeglasses, which signified one might be able to read. At the age of five Ty Kim Seng watched his father being taken away in a helicopter. A few days later the body of his father was returned to his village, also by helicopter. For a long while in Khao I Dang, Ty Kim Seng only drew pictures of helicopters.

His mother died of starvation a few years later. By then, Ty Kim Seng belonged to the mobile work team and he no longer lived at home. His mother remained in their village, in which nearly everyone was starving. Much of the country was starving. Ty Kim Seng received word that his mother was very weak, and he managed to be taken to her. The night before she died he came to her bedside and saw how swollen she was, how weak her voice, with what difficulty she was breathing. The woman held her son's hand and told him that very soon now he was going to be an orphan, that he would have to be strong and look out for himself.

Then her eyes focused more clearly for a moment, and she said to her son: "Always remember your father's and mother's blood. It is calling out in revenge for you." She then told him to leave her room and to try to sleep.

At the time, Ty Kim Seng was keeping a diary, on which he would rely as a source of solace. He described this diary to Neil, but he had lost it by the time he came to Khao I Dang. In it he would begin his entries, "Dear Friend, I turn to you in my hour of sorrow and trouble." On the night his mother spoke to him he could not sleep, and he wrote in his diary how helpless and frightened he felt. In the morning his mother was dead. He knelt at her bed and he prayed. Then he walked to the house of a neighbor and asked that man to bury his mother beside his father in the village cemetery. Ty Kim Seng brought a shirt with him as payment for this service.

The neighbor and his wife carried Ty Kim Seng's mother in their arms to the burial ground, the boy walking several paces behind them. Ty Kim Seng was himself quite weak and thin. The neighbors buried his mother, burned incense, and departed. Then the boy knelt by the grave

and burned three incense sticks of his own. Finally, he took a handful
of dirt from each of his parents' graves, poured it together in his hands,
and beseeched his dead parents to look after him. Afterward, he returned
to the mobile team.

"Do you feel your parents' spirit inside you now?"   24

"Yes, it talks to me. It tells me that I must gain knowledge and get a
job." He says that knowledge makes people good.

"Does your spirit tell you to take revenge?"

"Yes," solemnly.

"So, will you go back to Cambodia one day and fight the Khmer   28
Rouge?"

"No. That is not what I mean by revenge. To me revenge means that
I must make the most of my life."

I place before him one of the other pictures he drew when he arrived
at Khao I Dang, one that Neil showed me before, along with the skeleton
drawing. "What is happening here, Ty Kim Seng?"

The drawing is of three boys, stick figures, standing to the side of
several gravestones at night. The background consists of a large mountain
with a leering yellow moon resting on its peak. Perched on a tree is an
oversized owl, whose song, says Ty Kim Seng, is mournful.

"One day I left my mobile team to go find food for myself, to look for   32
yams. I was very hungry. I met two boys, and together we came upon a
mass grave of thirty bodies. They were piled up and rotting. The Khmer
Rouge soldiers found me. I lied and told them I had gone for firewood.
But they punished me. They bound my hands to a bamboo stick behind
my back. I was tied up without food for several days."

He is asked what it is that makes a man strong. He tells me, "a spirit."
Is there a spirit within him? "Yes. I talk to my spirit. I tell my spirit that
I must study diligently and work in order to find a home in America. Or
perhaps in France." Yuom explains that France is much on Ty Kim
Seng's mind these days, because he has recently learned that his older
brother lives there. The boy hopes to join his brother in France eventually, though for the present that is unlikely. The refugee allotments for
all countries are quite low now.

"Is the spirit that makes you strong that of your mother and father?"

"Yes. My spirit told me how to find my way to the border when I
escaped from the mobile team." Neil told me that before making his way
to Thailand, the boy walked more than sixty miles to Phnom Penh,
hoping for news of his brother. I see him doing so as he talks, traveling
mainly at night to avoid detection, the small face alert in the dark. I ask

him if he believes his spirit will always guide him toward the right destinations. He says yes, definitely. "One day it will lead me home."

Presenting his drawing of the orange skeleton, I ask if he would explain 36 it too. "I drew this after the death of my mother," he says softly. "I ate leaves then. That is why there is a tree in the picture."

"If you drew yourself today, would the picture be different?"

"Yes, very different." He looks happier. "Here I have food. And there would be a smile on my face."

"Would you do a self-portrait for me now?" Unhesitating, he moves to a long worktable under a window at the far end of the hut. An elder provides him with paper and crayons, and he works in silence. The noise of the other children has abated momentarily, the only sound being an occasional squawk of a late-rising rooster. Soon the boy returns and presents me with his drawing, which is not a self-portrait at all, but a bright blue airplane with green doors, green engines, and a red nose and tail.

"But where are *you*, Ty Kim Seng?"   40

"I am the pilot!" He points himself out enthusiastically. "We are flying to France!"

Yuom brings a second child to the table. I am beginning to feel like a village official, a census taker. At the window beside me, a square hole in the wall, little faces pop up and down, vivid with curiosity. Nop Narith performs the *wai*. He is Ty Kim Seng's size and age, has shaggy black hair and great buck teeth that gleam in a smile. He holds his left arm below the table. Nop Narith had polio when he was younger, and the arm is withered. Both his parents are dead.

"When the soldiers came to my house, they took our whole family away. Me they took to a mobile team. I never saw my parents again. But I have a photograph of my father. My father was worried that I could not take care of myself. Yet I feel guarded by his spirit. I dreamed that I saw him, and he promised that his spirit would protect me. In the dream he told me to gain knowledge and to take revenge on his killers."

I ask him what is the happiest time he has known. The Lon Nol 44 regime, he says, because that is when his family prospered. Lon Nol deposed Norodom Sihanouk and was himself overthrown by the Khmer Rouge. "We had air conditioning then." I ask what to him is the most important thing in the world. He answers, "Diamonds and gold."

"Which would you rather have, a peaceful time or diamonds and gold?"

"Peace is worth more than gold," he says.

"Your father's spirit told you to gain knowledge. Does knowledge lead to peace?" He says that it does. "Your father's spirit also told you to seek revenge against Pol Pot's soldiers. Is it your plan to do that?" Again he says yes.

"What do you mean by revenge?"   48

The boy responds at once: "Revenge is to make a bad man better than before."

Two more children come to talk with me, and they, like Ty Kim Seng and Nop Narith, define revenge either as self-improvement or as working to instill virtue in others. I wish to ask Neil about this. When I considered the subject of revenge in Athens, I only noted its absence in the children I had met up to that point. I was defining vengeance conventionally. It did not occur to me that the idea could ever be applied in such a way as to make it an instrument of beneficence or generosity. Was this something cultural, I wondered. Something derived from Khmer history or from Buddhist doctrine? The Theravada version of Buddhism practiced by the Khmer centers on the Four Noble Truths, which define wisdom as abjuring worldly desires. Perhaps so worldly a desire as revenge would be thought to impede salvation. . . .

A twelve-year-old girl, Meng Mom, approaches the table next. She is puffy-cheeked and very shy. She toys with her purple sleeve throughout our conversation and only smiles and looks straight at me when I mention that her gold circular earrings are becoming. No other subject I introduce elicits a response. She will not speak of her father, who is long missing, or of life under Pol Pot. She will not make small talk. Yuom tries his utmost to encourage her. Still, nothing. Then once again I bring up the problematical question: "Meng Mom, why do men make wars?"

Suddenly she blurts out, "There are lot of bad men in the world."   52

"How does someone manage to remain good if so many men are bad?"

"Good must fight the bad."

"Can good and bad exist in the same person?"

"No. Not together. They are in separate places. The good must beat   56
the bad." All this is said quite rapidly. Then she is silent again.

I begin to suspect that the intensity with which the children contemplate the idea of good and evil residing in the same person has some connection with their unorthodox views of revenge as charity. That morning one of the other children I spoke with, Gnem Thy Rak, a boy of sixteen, told of watching a Khmer Rouge soldier cut a man's throat in the jungle. When I asked what it is that makes someone do so dreadful a thing, he like the other children responded that some people are born with a good spirit inside them, some with a bad one, and that these two warring spirits cannot coexist in the same person. He added further that there are many more bad spirits than good ones in Cambodia these days. To the question, then, of how the good may ever prevail, he replied, "The good spirit must revenge the bad spirit," meaning, I gathered, that while good and evil are discrete qualities, it is still possible for virtue to triumph by exerting its influence on the corrupted spirit.

The idea is admirable but illogical. If the world is divided between the predetermined good and the predetermined wicked, then how would either be susceptible to change by the other? Would it not have been simpler for these children to allow that good and evil do exist in some proportions in everyone and that the problem of mastery is a continuous struggle? In order to answer that with a sure "yes," one would have to appreciate the depth and extent of the evil these children have witnessed and experienced. And clearly, some of the things perpetrated by the Pol Pot regime were so far beyond the imagination that the idea of a good spirit coexisting with that degree of evil must have seemed intolerable. Was it possible, then, that the children made their neat division of the spirits because they felt that no people who behaved like the Khmer Rouge could conceivably have any goodness in them?

Still, that would not account for the deep anxiety in their eyes and voices as they confronted this issue. What might explain it, however, was their knowledge that those who were carrying on the acts of murder and torture were neither strangers nor foreign invaders but were their own people, their neighbors, perhaps their relatives. This odd fact pertained in Northern Ireland and in the Middle East as well, but the depth and extent of destruction in those places was nothing like Cambodia. The term *genocide* has been used carelessly and indiscriminately since 1945, but what Pol Pot did was genocide, tens of thousands killed in a sweep. Some now call it "autogenocide." The killers and the victims were one people: the same skin, the same hands. How does one explain such a thing to the satisfaction of one's conscience except to contend that some people must be born with one spirit, and some with another? To believe otherwise would be to suggest that Ty Kim Seng's father had in himself the capacity to be his own executioner, that Ty Kim Seng and Nep Phem and Meng Mom had that same capacity. It was a terrible thing to concede.

Could their idea of revenge thus be a way of dealing with the fear of evil in themselves? If they could see how dangerous a good and gentle people can become, was it not possible that the only form of revenge to which they might be susceptible would be the reassertion of greater 60 goodness and mercy? Revenge, conventionally defined, cannot be taken against oneself. If hate destroys the hater, it does so doubly when the enemy is within. "Revenge is to make a bad man better than before," said Nop Narith. What the children meant by revenge might be that revenge is a self-healing act, a purification into compassion and wisdom, as Buddhism itself prescribes. Revenge is to be taken against fate, against a whole world of incomprehensible evil. Living well, in a moral sense, is the best revenge. Logical or not, such a thought was at least a way of avoiding the essential nightmare that each of us is his own beast in the jungle.

EXPLORATIONS

1. How do Rosenblatt's young Cambodian interviewees define "revenge"? What explanation does Rosenblatt suggest for their unusual views?

2. What happened to Ty Kim Seng and Nop Narith after Pol Pot's soldiers took over their villages? What happened to their parents? How did Ty Kim Seng get to Khao I Dang?

3. What aspects of Cambodian culture make this an unlikely country for war and genocide? What factors in the region's history make the war there not so surprising?

CONNECTIONS

1. Rosenblatt writes: "I discover that my country is in the idiotic and shameful position of recognizing the Khmer Rouge in the UN, arming them in the jungles, and accepting their victims as refugees" (para. 3). What explanation do you think Czeslaw Milosz would suggest for this tragic dilemma? What recommendations might he make to the individuals responsible for American policy in Southeast Asia at the time of Rosenblatt's comment?

2. Rosenblatt narrates his visit to Khao I Dang in the present tense, whereas the nurse quoted by Mark Baker in *Looking at Ourselves* narrates her tour in Vietnam in the past tense. How do these strategies create different effects? What techniques do both narrators use to make their stories vivid?

3. Examine George Gilder's suggestion in *Looking at Ourselves* that the United States in a sense won the war in Vietnam. How do you think Rosenblatt would reply to Gilder? Which writer's viewpoint is closer to your own, and why?

ELABORATIONS

1. The passages by William Broyles, Jr., and Barbara Ehrenreich in *Looking at Ourselves* contrast sharply with the views about violence expressed by the children Rosenblatt interviews. What do you think are the reasons for the difference? What conclusions do you draw about people's (or men's) innate love of war? Write an argumentative essay answering these questions and supporting your position.

2. "Living well is the best revenge" is a common remark in the United States. What does it mean in American conversations and advertising? What does it mean in Rosenblatt's paragraph 60? Write a comparison-contrast essay on the concepts and values reflected by this expression in the United States and in Cambodia.

AMOS OZ

If There Is Justice

Born Amos Klausner in Jerusalem in 1939, Amos Oz belongs to the first generation of Israeli writers who are sabras (native born). His grandfather had fled anti-Semitism in Russia and Poland to help build an ideal Jewish state in Palestine. As a schoolchild Oz filled sandbags after the British departure in 1948. Four years later, as the fledgling state of Israel struggled to accommodate over a million refugees, Oz's mother committed suicide. Her son cast off his father's scholarly right-wing Zionism to become a peasant-soldier on Kibbutz Hulda, midway between Jerusalem (then half in Israel and half in Jordan) and Tel Aviv to the north. There Oz took his new last name, which means "strength" in Hebrew; worked in the cotton fields; studied socialism; and eventually was sent to Hebrew University in Jerusalem for his bachelor's degree. On his return he adopted the routine he still follows: teaching in the high school, doing assigned chores, and writing stories and novels involving kibbutz life and ideals. Except for fellowships at Oxford and Hebrew universities, and a lecture tour of U.S. campuses, Oz, who has won several international literary awards, continues to live with his wife and three children at Kibbutz Hulda.

"If There Is Justice" was translated from the Hebrew by Nicholas de Lange with assistance from the author. It comes from Oz's novel *Elsewhere, Perhaps,* which was published in Israel shortly before the Six Day War in 1967. Oz served with Israeli armored divisions in that war, which ended in Israel's almost doubling its roughly 8,000-square-mile territory by occupying Syria's Golan Heights to the north, Jordan's West Bank to the east (including Jerusalem), and the Gaza Strip, formerly administered by Egypt, to the southeast. The conflict between Jews and Arabs in this region is more than 3,000 years old (human habitation dates back at least 100,000 years), and it has shaped not only Oz's writing but his homeland.

(For more background on Israel, see p. 86 and 552.)

Rami Rimon came home for the weekend on leave.

His face was thinner. His skin had shrunk a little. His jaws seemed more prominent. The lines on his face were sharper. His mother's face struggling to get out. Fine creases ringed his mouth. The sun had etched wrinkles round his eyes. Twin furrows ran from his nose to the corners of his mouth.

He was wearing an impeccable greenish uniform, with his beret tucked in his pocket. His stout boots were shod with steel at toe and heel. His sleeves were rolled up to reveal hairy forearms, and his hands were covered with little scars. He was conscious of his manly appearance as he strode slowly across the yard with an air of studied indifference. The men and women he met greeted him warmly. He responded with an offhand nod. There were traces of gun grease under his fingernails, and his left elbow was dressed with a grubby bandage.

When the first tumult of hugs and kisses, received by Rami with a   4
wavering smile, had died down, Fruma said:

"Well, you won't believe it, but I was just thinking of you the moment before you turned up. Mother's intuition."

Rami thought there was nothing strange in that. He had said in his letter that he would come on Friday afternoon, and she knew perfectly well what time the bus came. As he spoke, he put down his shabby kit bag, pulled his shirt outside his trousers, lit a cigarette, and laid a heavy hand on Fruma's shoulder.

"It's good to see you, Mom. I wanted to tell you that I'm really glad to see you again."

Fruma glanced at his dusty boots and said: 8

"You've lost so much weight."

Rami drew on his cigarette and asked about her health.

"Come inside and have a shower before dinner. You're all sweaty. Would you like a cold drink first? No. A warm drink would be better for you. Wait, though, the first thing is to take you along to the surgery. I want the nurse to have a look at your elbow."

Rami started to explain about the wound. It happened during a bayonet   12
practice; the clumsy oaf of a section commander . . . but Fruma did not let him finish the story.

"There you go dropping your ash on the floor. I've just washed it in your honor. There are four ashtrays in the house, and you . . ."

Rami sat down in his filthy clothes on the clean white bedspread and kicked off his boots. Fruma rushed to fetch her husband's old slippers. Her eyes were dry, but she tried to turn her face away from her son to hide the look he disliked so much. Rami, however, pretended not to have seen that strained look, as of a dam about to burst. He lay back on the bed, looked up at the ceiling, drew the ashtray that Fruma had put in his hand closer to him, and blew out a puff of smoke.

"The day before yesterday we crossed a river on a rope bridge. Two ropes stretched one above the other, one to walk on and the other to hold. With all our stuff on our backs, spade, blankets, gun, ammunition, the lot. Now, who do you suppose it was who lost his balance and fell in the water? The section commander! We all . . ."

Fruma eyed her son and exclaimed: 16

"You've lost at least ten pounds. Have you had any lunch? Where? No, you haven't. I'll dash across to the hall and get you something to eat. Just a snack — I'll make you a proper meal when you've had a rest. How about some raw carrot? It's very good for you. Are you sure? I can't force you. All right, then, have a shower and go to sleep. You can eat when you wake up. But perhaps I'd better take you to the surgery right away. Wait a minute. Here's a nice glass of orange juice. Don't argue, drink it."

"I jumped in the water and fished him out," Rami continued. "Then I had to dive in again to look for his rifle. Poor wretch! It was hilarious. It wasn't his first accident, though. Once, on an exercise . . ."

"You need some new socks. They're all falling apart," Fruma remarked as she pulled his dirty laundry out of the kit bag.

"Once, on an exercise, he fired his submachine gun by accident.   20 Nearly killed the battalion commander. He's the clumsiest fool you can imagine. You can tell what he's like from his name. He's called Zalman Zulman. I've written a song about him, and we sing it all day long. Listen."

"But they don't feed you there. And you didn't write every other day, as you promised. But I saw in the letter box that you wrote to Noga Harish. That's life. Your mother works her fingers to the bone, and some child comes and collects the honey. It doesn't matter now. There's something I must know: did she answer your letter? No? Just as I thought. You don't know what she's like. It was just as well you ditched her. Everybody knows what she is. The mistress of a man who's old enough to be her grandfather. It's disgusting. Disgusting. Have you got enough razor blades? It's disgusting, I tell you."

"Is it true they're starting to work the Camel's Field? That's going to cause a flare-up, all right. Provided, of course, the powers that be don't get cold feet. You know, Jewish sentimentality and all that. My buddies say . . ."

"Go and have a shower. The water's just right now. No, I heard every word. Test me. 'Jewish sentimentality.' There aren't many boys of your age with such an independent way of thinking. After your shower you can have a nap. Meanwhile, I'll ask the nurse to come here. That wound looks very nasty. You've got to have it seen to."

"By the way, Mom, did you just say that she . . ."   24
"Yes, son?"
"All right. Never mind. It doesn't matter now."
"Tell me, tell me what you need. I'm not tired. I can do anything
you want me to."
"No, thanks, I don't need anything. I just wanted to say something,   28
but it's not important. It's irrelevant. I've forgotten. Stop running around.
I can't bear it. We'll talk this evening. Meanwhile, you must have a rest,
too."
"Me! I'll rest in my grave. I don't need to rest. I'm not tired. When
you were a baby, you had something wrong with your ears. A chronic
infection. There weren't any antibiotics then. You cried all night, night
after night. You were in pain. And you've always been a sensitive boy. I
rocked your cradle all night, night after night, and sang you songs. One
does everything for children, without counting the cost. You won't repay
me. You'll repay it to your own children. I won't be here any more, but
you'll be a good father, because you're so sensitive. You don't think about
rest when you're doing something for your children. How old were you
then? You've forgotten all about it. It was the time when Yoash started
going to school, so it must have been when you were eighteen months
old. You were always a delicate child. Here am I rambling on, and you
need to sleep. Go to sleep now."
"By the way, Mom, if you're going to the surgery could you bring me
some corn ointment. You won't forget, will you?"

At five o'clock Rami woke up, put on a clean white shirt and gray
trousers, quietly helped himself to a snack, and then went to the basketball
field. On the way he met Einav, limping awkwardly. She asked how he
was. He said he was fine. She asked if it was a hard life. He said he was
ready to face any hardship. She asked if his mother was pleased with him
and answered her own question:
"Of course Fruma's pleased with you. You're so bronzed and hand-   32
some."
The field was floodlit, but the light was not noticeable in the bright
twilight. The only living souls there were Oren's gang. Rami put his
hands in his pockets and stood for a while without doing or saying
anything. The Sabbath will go by. Empty. Without anything happening.
With mother. Sticky. What do I need? A cigarette. That thin boy playing
by himself over there in the corner is called Ido Zohar. Once I caught

him sitting in the common room at night writing a poem. What was I saying? A cigarette.

Rami put the cigarette to his mouth and two planes roared by, shattering the Sabbatical calm, hidden in the twilight glow. The dying sun struck sparks off their fuselage. The metal shone back dazzlingly. In a flash Rami realized that they were not our planes. They had the enemy's markings on their wings. An excited shout burst from his throat.

"Theirs!"

Instinctively he looked down, just long enough to hear Oren's confused   36 cry, but by the time he looked up again the drama was almost over. The enemy planes had turned tail and were fleeing from other planes that were approaching powerfully from the southwest, evidently trying to block their escape. Instantly, dark shapes fell through the air toward the orchards to the north. Both planes had jettisoned the spare fuel tanks fixed to their wings to speed their flight. Rami clenched his fists and growled through his teeth, "Let them have it." Before he had finished there was an answering burst of gunfire. Lightning flashed. After what seemed a long interval, there came a dull roll of thunder. The fate of the raid was settled in an instant. The enemy planes disappeared over the mountains, one of them trailing a cloud of white smoke mixed with gray. Their pursuers paused, circled the valley twice like angry hounds, then vanished into the darkening sky.

Oren shouted jubilantly:

"We hit one! We smashed one! We brought one down!"

And Rami Rimon, like a child, not like a soldier, hugged Oren Geva and exclaimed:

"I hope they burn! I hope they burn to death!"   40

He pounded Oren's ribs exultantly with his fists until Oren drew away groaning with pain. Rami was seized by demented joy.

His joy accompanied him to the dining hall, where a spirit of noisy excitement reigned. He made his way among the tables to where Noga Harish stood in her best dress, looking at the notice board. He put his hands on her shoulders and whispered in her ear:

"Well, silly girl, did you see or didn't you?"

Noga turned to face him with a condescending smile.   44

"Good Sabbath, Rami. You're very brown. It suits you. You look happy."

"I . . . I saw it all. From beginning to end. I was up at the basketball field. Suddenly I heard a noise to the east, and I realized at once that . . ."

"You're like my little brother. You're cute. You're happy."

These remarks encouraged Rami. He spoke up boldly: 48

"Shall we go outside? Will you come outside with me?"

Noga thought for a moment. Then she smiled inwardly, with her eyes, not with her mouth.

"Why not?" she said.

"Come on then," said Rami, and took hold of her arm. Almost at   52 once he let it go.

When they were outside the dining hall, Noga said:

"Where shall we go?"

Strangely enough, at that moment Noga remembered something she had forgotten: Rami's full name was Avraham. Avraham Rominov.

"Anywhere," Rami said. "Let's go."   56

Noga suggested they sit down on the yellow bench, facing the door of the dining hall. Rami was embarrassed. People would see them there, he said. And stare at them. And talk.

Noga smiled again, and again she asked calmly, "Why not?"

Rami could find no answer to her question. He crossed his legs, took a cigarette out of his shirt pocket, tapped it three times on his matchbox, stuck in in the corner of his mouth, struck a match, shielded the flame with both hands even though there was no wind, inhaled deeply with half-closed eyes, blew out a long stream of smoke, and when all this was done, lowered his eyes to the ground once more. Finally, he gave her a sidelong glance and began:

"Well? What have you got to say for yourself?"   60

Noga replied that she hadn't been going to say anything. On the contrary, she thought it was he who was going to do the talking.

"Oh, nothing special. Just . . . What do you expect me to do?" he suddenly burst out violently. "Spend the whole evening, the whole Sabbath, my whole leave with my mother, like some mother's darling?"

"Why not? She's missed you badly."

"Why not? Because . . . All right. I can see I bore you. Don't think   64 I can't live without you. I can get on quite well without you. Do you think I can't?"

Noga said she was sure he could manage perfectly well without her.

They fell silent.

Hasia Ramigolski and Esther Klieger-Isarov came toward them, chatting in Yiddish and laughing. When they caught sight of Noga and Rami their conversation stopped dead. As they walked past, Hasia said:

"Good evening. Shabbat Shalom." She dwelt suggestively on the stressed syllables.

Rami grunted, but Noga smiled and said gently:

"A very good evening to you both."

Rami said nothing for a while. Then he murmured:

"Well?"

"I'm listening."

"I hear they're going to start working on the hill," Rami said. "There's going to be trouble."

"It's so pointless."

Rami quickly changed the subject. He told the story of his section commander who had fallen in the water trying to demonstrate how to cross a river on a rope bridge. He went on to say that it wasn't the poor fool's first accident. "Once, on an exercise, he accidently fired his submachine gun and nearly killed the battalion commander. You can tell what he's like from his name. He's called Zalman Zulman, of all things. I've written a rhyme about him:

> "Zalman Zulman's full of fun,
> Always letting off his gun.
> Zalman Zulman lost his grip,
> Took an unexpected dip.
> Zalman Zulman . . ."

"Just a minute. Does he play an instrument?"

"Who?"

"Zalman. The man you were talking about. What's the matter with your elbow?"

"What's that got to do with it?" Rami asked indignantly.

"With what?"

"With what we were talking about."

"You were telling me about someone called Zalman. I asked if he played an instrument. You haven't answered my question."

"But I don't see what . . ."

"You're very brown. It suits you."

"It's hardly surprising. We train all day in the sun. Of course we get brown. Listen: we went on a fifty-mile route march, with all the kit, gun, pack, spade, and all at the trot. Eight of the people in my squad . . ."

"Chilly, don't you think?"

". . . collapsed on the way. And we had to carry them on stretchers. 88
I . . ."

"I'm cold. Couldn't you finish the story tomorrow? If you don't mind
terribly."

"What's the matter?" Rami considered, and then asked thickly, "What's
up? Is somebody waiting for you? Are you rushing off to . . . to keep an
appointment?"

"Yes, I've got to take my father his dinner. He isn't well."

"What, again?" Rami asked absently. Noga explained that he had a 92
pain in his chest and the doctor had ordered him to go to bed.

"Next week he's got to go and have an examination. That's all. Shall
we meet here again tomorrow afternoon?"

Rami did not answer. He lit another cigarette and threw the lighted
match away behind the bench. Noga said good night and started to go.
Then she stopped, turned, and said:

"Don't smoke too much."

At that moment five steps separated them. Rami asked irritably why 96
she should care whether he smoked a lot or a little. Noga ignored his
question and said:

"You're very brown. It suits you. Good night."

Rami said nothing. He sat alone on the bench until the dancing
started in the square, as it did every Friday night at a quarter past nine.

When it was over, shortly before midnight, he set off for his mother's
room. He changed his course, however, because he met Dafna Isarov,
who asked him if he was going home to bed already, and Rami thought
he detected a sneer in her voice. So he turned off the path. His feet
guided him toward the cow shed, where he had worked before he was
called up. And as he walked he talked to himself.

This could never have happened to Yoash. It's happened to me, 100
though. Women understand only one language, brute force. But, as
mother said, I was always a delicate child. Hell. Now they're laughing.
Everybody wants something bad to happen to someone else so as to make
life more interesting. It's like that everywhere; it's like that on the kibbutz
and it's even like that in the army. You're a child you're a child you're
a child. You're like my little brother. Maybe being brown does suit me,
but it hasn't got me anywhere. She didn't insult me for once. She didn't
even call me a horse. What did she do to me tonight, how did she make
fun of me? My Rami is a delicate, sensitive boy. I wish I could die.
That'd show them. I can bend this sprinkler with my bare hands. That'll

drive Theodor Herzl Goldring mad. I've got stronger hands than Yoash. If only he weren't dead, I'd show him. Where am I going? Walking around like some Jack looking for his Jill. Leaping on the mountains, skipping in the hills, as that filthy old lecher would say. People like that ought to be put down. Like Arabs. Punch him in the face, he raises his hands to protect himself, you hit him in the stomach and give him a kick for good measure. All over. Here we are at the cow shed. Hey, Titan, good bull. Are you awake? Bulls sleep standing up because they can't lie down because of the iron ring. If they come to slaughter you, Titan, don't let them. Don't give in. Show your mettle. Don't be a ghetto bull. Give them a *corrida*. We mustn't give in without a struggle. We must be strong and quick and light and violent like a jet fighter. Swoop and dart and turn and soar like a knife flashing through the sky like a fighter. A fighter is such a powerful thing. I could have been a pilot, but Mother.

Strange that the moon is shining. The moon does strange things. Changes things strangely. Changes the colors of things. Silver. My Rami is a delicate sensitive child Rami writes poems like Izo Zohar he loves nature hell he loves plants and animals hope they burn to death. Her father has a pain in his chest. It's because of old Berger. Dirty old man. Her father taught us a poem by Bialik once, called "The Slaughter," where it says that there is no justice in this world. It's true. It's a ghetto poem, but it's true. He's lived his life, he's got grown-up children, he's found his niche. Why did he steal her from me? What have I done to him? And she said I was brown and handsome. If I'm brown and handsome, and he's old and fat, then why.

When I die, she'll know. It'll shatter her. The moon colors everything white. Silver. Listen, Noga, listen. I've also got a pain in my chest, I'm also in pain, so why don't you. I make fun of Zalman Zulman, she makes fun of me, they all make fun of me. It shows there isn't any justice in the world, only slaughter, Titan, worse than anything the Devil could invent. That's from the same poem. The man who's being slaughtered starts thinking about justice. The man who's slaughtering him thinks only about violence. My mistake was not to use force on her. Why, Titan, why didn't I use force, do you know why? I'll tell you. Because my Rami is a delicate boy curse them he loves nature hope they burn he loves plants and animals fithy whores. That sounds like planes overhead. It's after midnight. I love these planes, roaring along without lights. There's going to be a big war. I'll die. Then they'll know.

The fish ponds. A light in Grisha's hut. A pressure lamp. I can hear

Grisha's voice. In the boat. Shouting to his fishermen. He's been in three wars and he's come out alive.

Maybe Dafna, his daughter. Ridiculous. They'd laugh. What's in this 104 filthy shed? Barrels. Sacks of fish food. The fishermen's supper. If they find me here. Grisha's belt. A pistol. It's a revolver. Fancy leaving a revolver in an empty shed. They'll be coming back to eat soon. They'll laugh, they'll laugh. They'll say I went for a walk to look for inspiration. I know how it works. It has a revolving drum with six chambers. You put a bullet in each chamber. After each shot the drum revolves and brings another bullet in line with the barrel. That's how the revolver works. Now let's see how Rami Rimon works. A trial. Without a judge. I'm the judge. Now let's begin.

Rami takes a bullet out of the leather holster, a yellow metal case containing a little brown metal projectile. First of all, he puts the bullet in his mouth. A sharp, metallic taste. Then he puts the bullet in one of the chambers. He spins the drum without looking, because luck must be blind. He puts the gun to his temple. The chances are five to one. He squeezes the trigger. A dry thud. Rami inserts a second bullet. Spins the blind drum. Four to two. Gun to temple. Squeezes. Dry thud. Maybe I'm being silly. We'll soon know, Judge. I'm not trying to kill myself. It's only an experiment. Up to five. A delicate sensitive child couldn't do this. A third bullet. Blind spin. Cold damp hand. I've touched something damp. If I can do this, I'm not a delicate sensitive child. Up to five. Gun to temple. Squeeze the trigger. Dry thud. I'm past halfway. Two more tries. Fourth bullet. Now the odds are against me. Now comes the test. Watch carefully, Judge. Spin. Slowly. The drum, slowly. Without looking. Slowly. Temple. You're crazy. But you're no coward. Slowly squeeze. It's cold here.

Now the fifth. Last one. Like an injection. Delicate sensitive child's trembling. Why? Nothing will happen because nothing's happened so far, even though according to the odds I should have died with the fourth bullet. Don't tremble, dear little delicate child who cried all night with earache, don't tremble, think of Grisha Isarov who's come out of three wars alive. Yoash wouldn't have trembled, because he was Yoash. Little ghetto boy, with a little cap and a gray coat and side curls. I want to know how many I. Not to kill myself. Four. That's enough. Madness to go on. No, we said five — five let it be. Don't change your mind, coward, don't lie, you said five, not four. Five let it be. Put the gun to your temple. Now squeeze, horse, squeeze, you're a ghetto child, you're a little boy, you're my little brother, squeeze. Wait a moment. I'm allowed

628 Witnesses to War

think first. Suppose I die here. She'll know. She'll know I wasn't

to think first. Suppose I die here. She'll know. She'll know I wasn't joking. But they'll say "broken heart" they'll say "unrequited love" they'll say "emotional crisis." Sticky, very sticky. Hell. Squeeze. You won't feel a thing. A bullet in the brain is instant death. No time for pain. And afterward? Like plunging through the sky. An invisible fighter. It doesn't hurt. Perhaps I've already pressed the trigger and died perhaps when you die nothing changes. Other people see a corpse blood bones and you carry on as usual. I can try again. If I press the trigger, it's a sign I'm still alive. Afterward everything will be black and warm. When you die it's warm even though the body gets cold. Warm and safe like under a blanket in winter. And quiet. Squeeze. You've got a chance. Like when we used to play dice when I was little and sometimes I wanted very badly to throw a six and I threw a six. Now I want very badly to press the trigger but my finger won't press. Trembling. Careful you don't press it accidentally. Everything is different when the moon shines yellow. Can hear Grisha cursing next week we're going to the firing range that'll be interesting I'll be top of the class I'm an excellent shot now count up to three and shoot. Eyes open. No. Eyes closed. No. One, two, th- no. Up to ten. One, two, three, four, five, six, seven, eight, nine, t-.

But Rami Rimon did not try his luck the fifth time. He put down the revolver and went out into the fields and wandered about till his feet guided him back to the cow shed. Grisha won't notice. And if he does, he'll have a shock. I forgot to check the most important thing. I didn't look inside the gun to see what would have happened if I'd pressed the fifth time. Better not to know. Some things are better left undone.

A new thought occurred to Rami. It soothed him like a gentle caress. 108 Not all men are born to be heroes. Maybe I wasn't born to be a hero. But in every man there's something special, something that isn't in other men. In my nature, for instance, there's a certain sensitivity. A capacity to suffer and feel pain. Perhaps I was born to be an artist, or even a doctor. Some women go for doctors and others go for artists. Men aren't all cast in the same mold. It's true. I'm not Yoash. But Yoash wasn't me. I've got some things he didn't have. A painter, perhaps.

It'll be morning soon. Planes in the sky. Sad Zalman Zulman's full of fun, always letting off his gun. Zalman Zulman lost his grip, took an unexpected dip. Zalman Zulman, whore like me, looking for justice in the w.c. Zalman Zulman go to bed, time to rest your weary head.

I composed the poem. I can abolish it. It's an abolished poem.

EXPLORATIONS

1. Who is Yoash? What can you tell about him from the story? What is his current significance to Rami? to Fruma?

2. How does Rami feel about his mother's view of him as a "delicate sensitive child"? What kind of person does he want to be, and what kind of person does he think he is?

3. How has Rami's self-image — the qualities he sees as desirable and undesirable in himself — evidently been affected by his role as a soldier? by living in a close-knit, war-oriented community?

4. What does Rami learn from his game of Russian roulette? Why does he start it? Why does he stop?

CONNECTIONS

1. Oz in "If There Is Justice," Roger Rosenblatt in "Children of Cambodia," and Czeslaw Milosz in "American Ignorance of War" all focus in different ways on the jolting contrast between war and normal, everyday existence. What techniques or images does each writer use most effectively to show that contrast?

2. Which characters in "If There Is Justice" are oblivious to the military life from which Rami has just returned? What comments by Rami (and by Oz about Rami) echo comments by Milosz in "American Ignorance of War"?

3. Which of William Broyles, Jr.'s, comments about war in *Looking at Ourselves* also describe the views of Rami in "If There Is Justice"?

ELABORATIONS

1. Write an essay explaining Oz's story title, "If There Is Justice." What theme(s) does the title reflect? How do specific incidents, such as Rami's game of Russian roulette, exemplify or illuminate the story's larger theme(s)?

2. In "Why Kibbutzim?" (p. 86), Bruno Bettelheim discusses how and why the kibbutzniks' child-rearing system evolved. In "If There Is Justice," Oz focuses on a young man whose home is a kibbutz. Based on Bettelheim's essay and Oz's story, write an essay evaluating the advantages and disadvantages of the kibbutz way of life compared with a more traditional social structure.

The Price of the Panama Invasion

Panama, the southeasternmost country of Central America, is a curved neck of land linking Costa Rica and Colombia. It offers the narrowest crossing for voyagers between the Atlantic (Caribbean) and Pacific sides of the Americas. Until the mid-1800s, any U.S. traveler to the Mexican territories on the continent's west coast typically sailed around the tip of South America. The discovery of gold near San Francisco in 1848 encouraged U.S. interests to build a railway across Panama — then part of New Granada (see p. 531). A riot among the natives after it was finished was quickly put down: The United States had paid for the railway and meant to keep it. In the 1880s, when French efforts to build a canal across Panama foundered, the United States maneuvered Panama's independence from Colombia and took over the project. Panama granted the United States jurisdiction over the canal zone, a privilege zealously guarded until President Jimmy Carter agreed to return control of it to the Panamanians as of 1997. Soon after Ronald Reagan replaced Carter, General Manuel Noriega became Panama's real ruler behind a figurehead president. "The Price of the Panama Invasion" describes the transformation of Noriega's image from CIA informer and U.S. ally to enemy. After Noriega forced his president into exile and took power openly, U.S. President George Bush tried a range of legal means to remove him. Failing, Bush sent U.S. troops to occupy Panama in December 1989 and bring back Noriega on drug charges.

The following essay appeared as an unsigned editorial in the "Talk of the Town" section of *The New Yorker* on January 8, 1990.

Last December 21st [1989], as the United States invasion of Panama entered its second day, *El Diario–La Prensa*, a New York Spanish-language daily, carried a front-page photograph — under the headline "THE PRICE OF THE INVASION" — of eight bodies on the floor of a Panama City morgue. An article said that the hospitals were in "chaos." One hospital administrator reported, fourteen hours into the invasion, that he had so far taken in fifty bodies, forty-three of them civilian. The same day as the *El Diario* story, the *New York Times* carried a front-page news analysis concluding that George Bush had completed "a presidential initiation rite" and had moved into the ranks of "American leaders" who "since World War II have felt a need to demonstrate their willingness to shed blood to protect or advance . . . the national interest." The *Times* said that Bush had thereby erased his image of indecisiveness, and shown himself "a man capable of bold action." That night, on ABC's "Prime Time Live," Colonel Ron Sconyers, the spokesman for the Pentagon's Southern Command, said, "If you have to fight and shed a little blood for democracy . . . it's great." Arthur Davis, the United States ambassador to Panama, said that the costs of the invasion were justified, because it had "restored dignity to the United States."

On the fourth day of the invasion, Geoffrey Garin, a Democratic consultant, told the *Times* that "Panama was not as clean for George Bush as Grenada was for Ronald Reagan" — a reference not to the Panamanian and American dead but to the fact that General Manuel Noriega was still at large. Once Noriega sought refuge in the Vatican Embassy, even small tactical reservations began to fade from the Washington discussion.

In Latin America, by contrast, outrage was nearly universal, and was especially strong among those governments which Washington had long counted as its friends. Argentina decried the invasion as "a clear violation of the internationally enshrined principles of non-intervention." Peru noted that it had been a longtime critic of "the dictatorial regime of General Noriega," but nevertheless recalled its ambassador from Washington, on the ground that the invasion "constitutes an outrage against Latin America" and "evidences the most grotesque practices of imperialism."

In Washington, however, little attention was paid to the fact that an   4 invasion ostensibly mounted — as Dan Rather announced on CBS — "to restore democracy to Panama" was being overwhelmingly condemned by the hemisphere's democratic governments. Guillermo Endara, the man whom Washington installed as Panama's new president, was the apparent winner of the elections there last May, but there is reason to wonder what fate will befall him if he should decide in the future to steer a course independent of Washington's desires. The United States, after all, had helped overthrow elected presidents in Guatemala (1954), the Dominican Republic (1963), Brazil (1964), El Salvador (1972), Chile (1973), and Panama itself (1941), and is currently trying to do so in Nicaragua.[1] In 1984, the United States recognized a fraudulent Pana-

---

[1]This piece was written before the 1990 elections in Nicaragua. On February 25, Violeta Chamorro, a candidate supported by the Bush administration, defeated the incumbent Sandi-

manian election (so described in cables from the United States Embassy in Panama) and sent Secretary of State George Shultz to attend the inauguration of Noriega's handpicked candidate.

That, of course, was when Noriega was still working for the United States. He had been recruited by the CIA in the late nineteen-sixties, while he was a junior officer, and eventually he collected an annual CIA stipend of 200,000 dollars. And in 1983, with full United States support, he became Panama's de-facto ruler. Although the 1977 Torrijos-Carter Canal Treaties specified that American forces in Panama could be used only to defend the canal, Noriega in the early nineteen-eighties helped the United States turn Panama into an intelligence, training, resupply, and weapons base for the Reagan Administration's campaigns in Nicaragua and El Salvador. Along the way, he collected a sheaf of letters from the United States Drug Enforcement Administration thanking him for help in the fight against marijuana and cocaine. At no point was Noriega's relationship with our government impeded by the fact that Noriega was a drug trafficker himself. In 1976, after two drug-enforcement officials had gone as far as to recommend that Noriega be assassinated to stop his drug dealing, George Bush, who was then the director of the CIA, met with Noriega personally and took no action to remove him from its rolls. In 1983, after Noriega had joined forces with the Medellín cocaine cartel and Bush had become vice-president and the coordinator of the Reagan drug war, Bush and Noriega met again, and Noriega's CIA contract continued undisturbed.

President Bush justified the invasion as an effort "to combat drug trafficking," yet the cartel had shifted its business to other intermediaries after Noriega was indicted, in Miami, in 1988. The indictment followed a falling out with the United States which began in 1987, for reasons that are still unclear but apparently involved a cooling of Noriega's support for the Contras.

The President also said that the invasion was necessary "to safeguard the lives of Americans," citing the killing of an American soldier at a Panama military checkpoint. But the preinvasion events claimed one American life, and the invasion itself claimed two dozen. Moreover, at least one American soldier is killed every month in some incident at one of our outposts around the world — often in an allied country — and the United States does not send in the Marines.

---

nista president, Daniel Ortega, making U.S. attempts to overthrow Ortega by some other means unnecessary. — ED.

As the troops poured into Panama City, Dan Rather denounced No-   8
riega as being "at the top of the list of the world's drug thieves and scums."
Peter Jennings called him "one of the more odious creatures with whom
the United States has had a relationship." Yet the uncomfortable truth is
that, with the exception of Costa Rica (which does not have an army),
Noriega's Panama had for years been the least violent and repressive
member of Washington's Central American team. According to Amnesty
International, Americas Watch, and the Organization of American
States, Noriega's forces had been responsible for perhaps a dozen political
killings from 1983 until the coup attempt last fall. In Honduras in the
early eighties, just one military unit, the CIA-backed Battalion 3–16, was
implicated in at least 142 death-squad murders. The Nicaraguan Contras
have murdered thousands, and more than 70,000 civilians have perished
at the hands of the American-trained Salvadoran Army since 1979. And
in Guatemala, where in 1954 the CIA overthrew a democracy and put
the military in power, the army, funded and trained by Washington, has
wiped out 662 rural villages, and killed more than 100,000 civilians since
1978.

In 1927, Robert Olds, an under-secretary of state, explained a United
States invasion of Nicaragua (the last of four) by writing that "Central
America has always understood that governments which we recognize
and support stay in power, while those which we do not recognize and
support fall." With the crucial — and, for the Reagan and Bush Administrations, maddening — exception of Nicaragua, that principle has held
true to this day. General Noriega lived off the CIA payroll for twenty
years but thought that he could somehow survive when Washington told
him it was time to go. What Noriega did not reckon on was the price
that our government was willing to pay — a price consisting of Panamanian lives and ruined Panamanian property, and of American lives as
well — in return for the restoration of American "dignity," and proof
that a maligned American president was really a bold man after all.

EXPLORATIONS

1. What is the price of the Panama invasion, according to *The New Yorker* essay, and who pays it? What is the thesis of this essay? Does the author agree or disagree with the comments by the U.S. media quoted in paragraphs 1–2? How can you tell?

2. What did President Bush hope to achieve by sending U.S. troops to remove Manuel Noriega from power in Panama? What positive and negative results did the invasion actually achieve?

3. What are the main sources of evidence in this essay? Which sources does the author treat as most believable? least believable?

4. What positive and negative statements about Noriega does the author make or quote in this essay? Judging from his actions, what other qualities can you deduce that Noriega has?

CONNECTIONS

1. How would you summarize the view of military action expressed by the U.S. media in "The Price of the Panama Invasion"? What passages in Amos Oz's "If There Is Justice" indicate that the story's characters share or do not share this view?

2. Paragraph 1 of *The New Yorker* essay contains several statements about why the Panama invasion was important. What observations in *Looking at Ourselves* echo these judgments or suggest reasons for them?

3. Look back at Peter Schneider's "The End of the Wall" (p. 524). What role do the U.S. media, especially television, play in that essay and in "The Price of the Panama Invasion"?

ELABORATIONS

1. The Bush administration did not call its military actions in Panama an invasion; it used less violent terms, such as "intervention." Go through "The Price of the Panama Invasion" and find as many words and phrases as you can that are value laden — that is, that express a judgment by the author. Write an essay about the U.S. military action in Panama that takes the opposite position from *The New Yorker* piece, describing the same people and events but using different terms.

2. The United States has been accused of increasing its efforts to influence foreign events, especially in the Americas, at the same time the Soviet Union is reducing its intervention in other countries. Is this true? True or not, is it a good or bad policy? Why? Write an argumentative essay stating and defending your position on some aspect of this issue.

SHELLEY SAYWELL

Women Warriors of El Salvador

Shelley Saywell was born in Ottawa, Canada, and now lives with her husband in Toronto. She is a television researcher and producer whose credits include *The Ten Thousand Day War,* an acclaimed documentary series about the war in Vietnam. Saywell works for the Canadian Broadcasting Company, where she was senior producer and writer for the series *Going Great.* "Women Warriors of El Salvador" comes from her book *Women in War* (1985); to research it she traveled to Britain, France, the United States, Italy, and the Soviet Union.

Saywell interviewed the women she calls Ileana and Maria in Toronto, where they had been sent to recuperate from imprisonment, torture, and their husbands' deaths. Saywell writes: "Both women are twenty-five years old, both are mothers, and both have spent the past decade fighting for the revolutionary forces in El Salvador." She describes Ileana as "the more political" of the two: "She is a small woman with large dark eyes and a soft voice. She wears no makeup, and nondescript clothes." Maria, who speaks no English, "wears makeup and colorful clothes. She looks small and fragile. . . . Still a devout Catholic, Maria believes that revolution in El Salvador has little to do with Marxism. 'There are Marxists and socialists fighting,' she concedes, 'but there are also many of us who believe in democracy. We have united because revolution is the only way to end the tyranny.'"

The Republic of El Salvador is a nation the size of Massachusetts, south of Guatemala and Honduras in Central America. Its capital is San Salvador. Like the rest of the region, El Salvador was controlled for centuries by Spain, from which it became independent in 1821. Saywell writes: "The war in El Salvador is a passionate subject, going back a hundred years to the 1880s, when the government decreed laws that recognized only private property, thereby effectively destroying the traditional communal landownership of the peasants. . . . Today the rich largely control the government and an economy that is described by experts as the most inegalitarian in that part of the world."

Inequality persists since President José Napoleón Duarte died and Alfredo Cristiani of the right-wing Arena party was elected in 1989. El Salvador has no working criminal justice system; half its people are unemployed or underemployed; few rural dwellers can get clean drinking water; poverty, malnutrition, and disease are widespread. Although death-squad murders have decreased somewhat, the war between government and guerrillas — which has killed over 70,000 people — continues.

Ten years ago Ileana was a fifteen-year-old high school student in San Salvador, a deeply religious Catholic, reared in a middle-class home, who liked rock-and-roll, boys, and nice clothes. Today she is a committed revolutionary, living underground, rotating between the city and the countryside where she carries out organizational work and participates in armed actions against the government.

"I believe now that armed confrontation is the only way for El Salvador, even if it is the most painful way, because all the political expressions of the people have been suppressed, all the peaceful means of protest have been attacked, and even our archbishop was killed for his views. What other way is there to change things? The only way left is to pick up our guns and fight for a better life."

After eighteen months of safety and rest in Canada, her choice to return was in many ways more difficult than her decision to become a revolutionary in the first place, because now she knows all too well what being there means. "It frightens me," she said before leaving, "because here I've grown used to being safe, and I've lost many of the instinctive defense habits I once had in El Salvador, the things that I used to do automatically to keep safe. Here you can walk down the street day or night, sit in a restaurant, talk about politics, and your life is not endangered. I feel that I need more preparation, that I'm no longer ready to face the confrontation. I have to find the strength to leave my daughter, knowing I might not return, and then both her parents will be dead."

She looks at me with wide eyes but speaks with the hardened resolve 4 of a veteran revolutionary who has robbed banks, kidnapped men, and killed. She has done these things because "I believe that only revolution can bring about the changes we need in our country."

The guerrilla war in El Salvador has veteran Vietnam correspondents shivering with déjà vu in the tropical jungle. American involvement continues to escalate in the region, and there is equal evidence of aid and military advisers from the Socialist bloc.[1] Families are divided; sons and daughters fight each other. The television images are hardly distinguishable from the scenes the world watched not so long ago from Southeast Asia. But comparisons with Vietnam serve only to remind us

---

[1]As East-West tensions have decreased, these policies have undergone reexamination. Until 1990, only five countries received more annual aid from the Bush administration than tiny El Salvador; in that year, responding to the 1989 murder of six Jesuit priests, apparently by government soldiers, Congress voted a significant decrease in aid. — ED.

that protracted civil wars become part of wider geopolitical cold war — and that millions of people die.

Ileana's father was a politician and businessman throughout his active life. His beliefs were to greatly influence the fate of his family and the choices made by his children. "He was involved in the struggle in his time," she says. "As a politician he saw too clearly the poverty and desperation of most of the people of El Salvador. He spoke up about it and was imprisoned and 'disappeared' several times. Finally he was exiled from the country. El Salvadorans have been opposing the regime for decades. In 1932 the peasants rebelled against their low wages and loss of employment. Thirty thousand were massacred by the military and landowners. Because of my father's activities in the 1950s, we went to live in Guatemala for a while. Ever since I was a child we have lived in fear of what was going to happen to us. After we returned from Guatemala my father decided not to get involved in politics anymore. He could not take imprisonment or torture at his age. When we kids became active he told us to be careful. He is scared for us, but he supports us."

Ileana's mother was never really involved: "She really didn't understand anything, even after all those years with my father. Now they are separated, but even when she was with him she didn't understand. Still, she is very good-hearted and always helps us when we need her."

There had always been revolutionary currents, predominantly stem- 8 ming from the middle class. The seeds of the present state of civil war were sown in 1970 when university students and professors began to protest against the excesses and corruption of the government, including nepotism, electoral frauds, payoffs by the rich for legislation of benefit to them, and suppression by threats, torture, and murder of opposition politicians and clergy.

In a country where the vast majority of the population is Catholic, priests and nuns working among the lower class also became opponents of the regime. They began to organize Christian-based rural communities that were in effect communes where peasants could collectively manage such needs as medical services and education. It was through church groups that Ileana and Maria became involved in their war.

Ileana remembers: "I was religious then, at fifteen. I belonged to a Church group and did social work in the community. It was at that time that many of the priests began to preach that our rulers were not good. The Church became more and more involved in the problems of the people — not spiritually, but in day-to-day life — and then they began to talk about it."

It was 1975 when Maria, also fifteen, joined a Church group in the town of Aguilares. "My father was from the lower middle class," she says. "He works as the overseer of a manor, and so from childhood I lived on manors and saw how the peasants lived, the kind of work they were subjected to and the problems they had just to feed their large families. I started studying in the nearby town of Aguilares, and that is when I first came into contact with Father Rutilio Grande."

Grande, a Salvadoran Jesuit, had arrived in Aguilares in 1972. In the rich, sugar-growing regions outside the town the peasants were unable to get more than three or four months' labor each year, backbreaking work that helped provide the average annual income per family of seven hundred dollars. The rampant malnutrition of their children affected him deeply. He and three other priests began organizing rural communities and preached that "they must not live in conditions of such tremendous inequality that the very Fatherhood of God is denied." During the next four years Father Rutilio led peasants in several strikes and sit-ins at the haciendas in the vicinity.

Maria remembers the effect Grande had on the people: "He told us that in the Bible it says that people must not be exploited, people must not be oppressed. A hacienda in the area was an example of the way people lived. The peasants who worked there during harvest season were starving to death, and the rich widow who owned the estate would not allow most of it to be cultivated because she wanted it to be a memorial to her dead husband. The peasants had no running water, no electricity in their one-room huts. They had no education for their children, no medical care. Father Rutilio and three co-workers visited the widow and suggested an agreement for sharecropping in which the peasants would pay her for the use of her land. She refused, and so we organized a takeover of the hacienda. About two hundred peasants simply squatted on her land. We put up armed sentinels at different points, and we were prepared to confront the authorities." Maria was armed. Asked about weapons training, she said she had already been taught to shoot by her father, for recreation and hunting on the hacienda. Her parents believed her still a student who dutifully came home on weekends. But she had quit school and devoted all her time to the cause.

It was May 1975. The peasants remained on the estate for three months. They had begun to cultivate the land when the area was surrounded and attacked by the Security Forces in the middle of the night. "One of our sentinels had fallen asleep on guard," says Maria. "The troops were already inside the estate when our second sentry gave us the

12

warning. We had prepared for this and had our escape routes planned. Each of us who was armed was responsible for leading out a small group of peasants — about fourteen or fifteen people. Others were assigned to cover our retreat. About fifteen minutes after we heard the warning, helicopters came and began dropping barrels of flaming gasoline on us. Our plastic, plywood shacks caught fire immediately. A lot of people were badly burned. We walked . . . ran, through the night. We had to cross a river. One of the women was in labor. She gave birth during the night." Maria led her group to a prearranged location where they met up with the others the next day. The peasants were told to disperse and remain silent about their involvement in the takeover.

Asked if they weren't expecting that kind of reaction to the illegal takeover of the hacienda, Maria said, "We were of course expecting the authorities to come and make us leave. What we didn't expect was that the army would attack us in the middle of the night with helicopters and flaming gasoline. I was very scared after that backlash, but my older brother, who was also involved, said to me, 'Sure you can stay home and Daddy will pay for your studies. You'll have something to eat. But what about the other people?'"

Father Rutilio Grande continued his work among the peasants. He   16 organized literacy classes in which Maria and other young students helped teach the children. But the local landowners had by now had enough of the priests in Aguilares who, they said, "were instigating class warfare," and the members of the Christian movement realized that there would be further violence.

"We were given training, told what to do if we were captured and questioned, how to respond, to make up a story quickly. They taught us how to deal with many problems. Throughout the rest of 1975 we led demonstrations in Aguilares. We went to the high schools and got more students involved."

In the capital, San Salvador, dissent was brewing in schools and universities. In July 1975 the army attacked a student demonstration protesting the government expenditure of three million dollars to host a Miss Universe Pageant. The army blocked off the streets to those trying to escape and opened fire on the crowds. Twelve students were killed, eighty wounded, and twenty-four "disappeared." Ileana: "It was a peaceful demonstration, and they attacked us with tanks! People were screaming, in complete panic. It was terrifying. We joined together with other protest groups and decided on a joint action. Several days later we took over one of the cathedrals of San Salvador. We did it to denounce the army and what it had done at the demonstration. We asked the government to state who was responsible for the killing, and that the chief of police and the army be forced to resign.

"The one thing we did succeed in was getting attention, letting people know the truth. Because all the newspapers are controlled by the rich people, when things like that happened they would write a lot of lies. For example, if the army killed one hundred people, they would write that three people died in a crossfire between guerrillas and the army.

"This joint action was important because it brought several groups   20 together — peasants, students, teachers, labor unions, and people from the ghettos. We discussed a revolution which would change the whole basis of society. We had learned that it was impossible to achieve reforms in the existing government. They would never change. By 1975 we were thinking of armed revolution. Several political groups formed armed sections and began taking armed actions against the government. They began in the cities, and then more and more grew in the countryside. I left the Church group. It was good, but I didn't think it was doing enough. That is when I joined the Revolutionary Popular Front."

By the end of that year there were many groups of opposition to the government, several with their own guerrilla armies. Eventually the left wing and liberals united and formed the Democratic Revolutionary Front (FDR) whose military arm was the Farabundo Marti Front for National Liberation (FMLN), named after the most famous communist leader of the 1932 peasant rebellion. . . .

In 1976, at sixteen years of age, Maria married one of the *compañeros* ("comrades-in-arms") with whom she had participated in several actions. She says she married so young because of the situation in her family home. "I had not been able to discuss anything with my parents. I couldn't tell them what I was doing, thinking, or feeling. I was completely absorbed in the revolution and often endangered, and yet I went home on weekends and pretended to be a meek, obedient little school girl. Getting married was my freedom from this double life." She adds, "My husband was a few years older than me, and it was an intense relationship: we believed in the same things and took the same risks."

Shortly thereafter Maria had her first baby, a daughter. Asked if be-coming a mother had led her to consider leaving the movement, to avoid the risks, she said no. "Having a child reinforced my commitment. As a mother I felt even more strongly about helping to create a new society for our children to grow up in." But only fifteen days after the baby was born, she and her husband were arrested in Aguilares. "We were caught spraying slogans on a wall. I was not mistreated, just interrogated. They asked my why I was doing this, who my family was. I told them my uncle was a colonel in the Security Forces and hoped that would carry some weight. After two weeks they released us.

"After we were released from jail we stayed in Aguilares for two more   24
months. Then Father Rutilio told us we should relocate and begin living underground. The police had our number, they were watching us, so we moved to another district and went 'underground.'"

Ileana was also married that year, to a man she had met in the cathedral takeover in August 1975. He had subsequently joined the guerrillas. "For the first four months we lived separately. Then the organization authorized us to live together, but we were told to be careful because it would be dangerous for us to be identified together. That is because he was a known guerrilla, while I was still working in the open. I was only home one or two days a week. The rest of the time I was in the countryside. It was a difficult period. I felt as though I didn't have any home. I was always traveling from one place to another, sleeping here and there, and worrying about my husband while we were apart."

In a political climate where ten thousand people became *desaparecidos*, or "disappeared," each year, working underground in the city created enormous stress. Maria says: "It was very tense. We constantly had to change our names and identities. We were always on the move. Sometimes I would forget what name I had used with different people. I would run into someone and not know how to respond, desperately trying to remember what I had told them about myself. But the nature of our work gave me energy. I found it so rewarding. I got used to the pressure."

Maria's work was still with Christian groups. "We had contacts in different parishes with different priests and we would join them in their discussion groups. We worked in their parishes in the shantytowns or slums. We discussed ways of helping the poor. We related the Bible to the reality in which we were living. We helped the poor with their sick children, and even with their household chores." In 1977, she and her husband left this work and joined the People's Army. The move was a personal reaction to the assassination of Father Rutilio Grande on 12 March 1977. He was gunned down as he drove to Sunday mass.

That year the military government of Colonel Arturo Molina had   28
launched an all-out campaign to terrorize and kill parish priests and nuns. Anonymous pamphlets dropped into the street blamed the war on

"Marxist priests." The slogan ran, "Be a patriot! Kill a priest!" When
Rutilio Grande was killed, the newly appointed Archbishop Romero, a
man noted for his moderation, openly condemned the Molina government. Molina had come to power in 1972 in a particularly scandalous
election. Though his opponent, Napoleón Duarte, was ahead at the polls
by two to one, Molina's well-placed supporters in the previous administration stopped all election broadcasts and finally pronounced the colonel
president. The Christian Democrats were outraged by the flagrant fraud.
Molina's answer was to have Duarte arrested, imprisoned, and tortured,
although he was released when international pressure was brought to
bear.

A month before his death Grande had told a crowd, "Nowadays it is
dangerous and practically illegal to be an authentic Christian in Latin
America. I greatly fear that very soon the Bible and the Gospel will not
be allowed within the confines of our country. Only the bindings will
arrive, nothing else, because all the pages are subversive — they are
against sin." Despite a government-declared state of siege, over a hundred
thousand people risked their lives to attend Grande's funeral at a San
Salvador cathedral. Eight bishops, Archbishop Romero, and four
hundred priests held mass for the slain father.

For Maria, who had known and loved the priest, it was a deep personal
loss. It seemed that the last vestiges of humanity had been swept away,
and in their place the war became uglier and uglier. That year when
President Molina retired, his minister of defense, General Carlos Hum-
berto Romero, was "elected" president in his place. The priest-killing
campaign continued. Priests were found decapitated, disfigured by battery
acid, and otherwise mutilated. In Aguilares the army launched an attack
in which several more Jesuits were murdered, and code-named it Operation Rutilio.

"Things really heated up," recalls Ileana. "Women in large numbers
began to join the revolutionary movement. I think they found this final
obscenity impossible to condone or ignore. . . . We had some problems
with chauvinism in the beginning. The men didn't want us to join, or
they wanted us to stay in subservient roles. But soon they realized the
importance of having as many people fighting as possible, and they
changed a bit. I think it actually helped make male-female relationships
more equal." . . .

Maria and her husband were asked to open a supermarket in San
Salvador that would serve as a cover for shipping supplies to the guerrillas.
"We lived over the store — my husband, our two daughters, and two of

my husband's sisters. Our house became a meeting place and the kids used to help camouflage it. When we were having a meeting one of us would go out and play with the kids on the street in front of the houses, making sure the coast was clear. We all carried guns for personal protection. We knew if we were searched by the authorities we would be killed. I used to carry a huge bag with all this kids' stuff in it — talcum powder, diapers, baby bottles. I hid my gun and pamphlets underneath. Sometimes I would even put my gun in my baby's diapers. The soldiers never thought of checking in the baby's diapers.

"The supermarket was a good front. We had a delivery van and I used to deliver goods to the groups in the countryside. I took them everything — shoes, beans, and Kotex. Kotex was used for dressing wounds because if we took real bandages it would be too obvious. . . ."

In July 1979 the Sandinista revolution in neighboring Nicaragua succeeded in overthrowing dictator Anastasio Somoza. "When we saw them succeed," says Ileana, "it gave us hope. I really didn't believe they could succeed so quickly. We thought if they can do it, we can too. But on the other hand, the United States learned a lot from the Nicaraguan revolution. Now they are applying that knowledge to El Salvador, giving enormous aid to the government for the military. They began sending in military advisers."

In Washington the Carter administration was sore on the point of human rights abuses, perpetrated by the Romero regime in San Salvador, which were making it increasingly difficult to get military aid bills through Congress. Washington needed a more moderate government in El Salvador. On 15 October 1979 a military-civilian junta overthrew the ruling regime in a brief coup d'état. The junta was comprised of younger, more moderate officers, and a number of representatives of opposition parties were appointed to the cabinet. The new government immediately began land reforms designed to restore land to the peasants. The reforms were ill-fated from the start. Army troops sent to redistribute parcels of land took over haciendas, helped themselves to the goods, then systematically murdered peasants who came to claim their new plots. Payoffs and threats protected the estates of the richest families.

One by one the more moderate civilian politicians were forced out of 36 office by the military leaders who controlled the army. One such politician, Hector Dada Hirezi, wrote in his letter of resignation: "The facts are indisputable proof of the conclusion. We have been unable to stop the repression, and those who commit acts of repression in defiance of the junta's authority remain unpunished; the promised dialogue with the popular organizations has not come about; the possibilities of generating reforms supported by the people have retreated beyond our grasp."

Six months after the new junta took power, the archbishop of San Salvador, Archbishop Oscar Amulfo Romero y Galdames, was assassinated as he gave mass. *Time* and *Newsweek* magazines recounted the carnage that followed when thousands of people attended his funeral and army troops opened fire into the crowds. Three weeks after the archbishop's assassination the United States government committed another $5.7 million in military aid to the ruling junta. By this time it was estimated that in the country of five million people, two thousand people a week were dying in the war.

Ileana was caught in 1980. She says, "I can't tell you everything, but I was at the house of one of our *compañeros* for a meeting. The army found out about us and came and surrounded the house. We heard the trucks and jeeps pull up, and out stormed dozens of soldiers with machine guns. We considered holding them off and trying to escape, but when we realized we were surrounded we surrendered. They arrested everyone in the house.

"I was taken to the National Guard's secret jail, where they interrogate political prisoners, and kept there for one week. I was raped repeatedly and tortured with electric shocks. I was three months pregnant, but thank God it didn't show. I knew if they found out it would be worse. They would have tried to hurt the baby, to abort it or something. They would have asked me who the father was. They continually threatened to kill me and my family. Sometimes I had to answer them, but I would just tell them things that they already knew, like where I had studied. Other times I would make up stories. I always thought about what I was saying and tried not to endanger the others.

"They didn't treat me better because I was a woman. To them there was no difference. I think for women it was worse. They thought we were worthless, so they wanted to defile us. I was constantly pawed, threatened with rape or raped. They were pigs." She pauses, then adds, "I know this sounds hard to believe. I was very lucky because many, many people never get out of those clandestine jails. I tried to keep myself together by telling myself how many others were in the same situation I was in. It made me stronger. When I was being tortured I kept thinking of my friends who had gone through this, as an example to keep me brave. I kept thinking that they had held out in even worse situations. . . .

"My husband didn't know I had been arrested until I was sentenced and sent to the penal institution. Of course he couldn't come to see me. But it was a regular prison run by the Ministry of Justice, so I had visitors every Sunday. My family came and brought me some things — milk, because I was pregnant. I was kept there for four months."

On 5 March 1980 Napoleón Duarte, the Christian Democrat who had run against Colonel Arturo Molina in 1972, been arrested and later exiled, agreed to head the eroding junta. Those who considered Duarte a moderate could not understand why he chose to become a part of the corrupt and brutal government, but those who knew him well have said that his tremendous ego eventually dictated his quest for leadership, even at the helm of a mutinous group of military leaders.

One of Duarte's first public statements was that "the Security Forces had been trained for fifty years to do things 'the other way.'" He said it would take "time to change things." He refused to negotiate with the FMLN despite the fact that Mexico, several European governments, and many Salvadoran clergy recommended that he do so. Instead, he declared the country in a state of siege.

By 1980 the revolutionary forces had greatly expanded and were said   44 to have gained widespread public support. They claimed in that year that 40 percent of their leadership were women, and women were increasingly adopting military roles in the war. A women's military school was opened, offering a twenty-day training course to all women between sixteen and twenty-two years of age. At least two all-women battalions were formed, and Maria fought with one of them for a few months in the guerrilla-controlled zones of the countryside. . . .

The women taught Maria many new maneuvers. "For example, how to cross a river using ropes. We would throw the ropes like lassos, and swing ourselves across the river holding the rope with one arm and our grenades and weapons with the other. We covered each other as we made our way. We left these ropes on the trees and periodically went to check to make sure they were not rotting and the knots were still secure. Work was the same as in the mixed guerrilla groups," she says. "But when the enemy was killed or ambushed by the women's battalions they found it more demoralizing. They consider women worthless.

"We used this to our advantage. Whenever we successfully killed a number of army troops we always put out communiqués saying that we were responsible. We wanted to rub it in.

"I found that the all-women battalion was even more disciplined than the mixed units. For example, if we were given an order not to smoke all day because we were staked out somewhere, we wouldn't. If it had been men, someone would have found a way to sneak a cigarette. Women were more punctual about meeting times and places, too."

Maria says that despite their youth most of the women combatants   48 had children, who were left in care of their families or friends. "Women still did most things during their pregnancies," she says. "It was just for a short time after the baby was born that they couldn't do all the things they normally did." She shows an easy acceptance of motherhood, at any age or in any circumstances, that "is prevalent in El Salvador. It just doesn't seem onerous to us to have babies. We don't wait for the right time and place." Despite the availability of birth control, both Maria and Ileana said that most women wanted to become pregnant because it was psychologically uplifting to give birth when so much death was going on around them.

Ileana had been released from jail and had given birth to a daughter. Six months later her husband was killed. "They came at five in the morning to murder him," she says. "That is when the death squads operate. Dawn is the most terrifying time for all of us. We would lie awake and half expect to hear the loud knocks and yells at the door. I hid myself and the baby while he went to hold them off. They took him away and shot him. Members of the organization came for me and took me to a safe place. I stayed in El Salvador for seven more months before they got me out to Canada."

The FMLN planned to instigate a general offensive in January 1981 for which Maria and her husband had been training in the countryside's "liberated zones." They were told to return to the city in December 1980 to help coordinate the uprising there. On the first of December four American Catholic nuns were assassinated by members of the government forces. American President Jimmy Carter condemned the murders and ordered all military and economic aid to the junta suspended. Five weeks later, on 3 January 1981, two American economic aid consultants with the American Institute for Free Labor Development (AIRFLD) were shot to death in a hotel coffee shop, presumably by government enforcers of the agrarian "reform" program: the Americans had been privy to information that exposed corruption within the program. Washington leaders were outraged at the excesses, which were causing an uproar at home and making it increasingly difficult to get public support for American aid to the regime.

On 10 January Maria and her husband waited at home for their final orders. The next day guerrillas overran a classical music radio station and broadcast an appeal to the people of the country to rise up in a general insurrection.

A number of guerrilla units operating in the capital launched hit-and-run attacks against police and military targets. Maria was assigned to a unit attacking the air force base. "The base is located a little way from the center of the city. We were to go in and plant the explosives, liquidate the guards, and get as many of their munitions as we could. I was in charge of distributing arms to different groups after we got hold of them.

"The offensive began at seven o'clock in the evening, when there would be a minimum of patrol cars, and the majority of people would be at home. That way there would be fewer civilian casualties. We managed to attack the air base and get the weapons. But we were identified. They saw our car and the license plate number. We returned home and hid the armaments in the back room."

The general insurrection had failed. The army had mobilized within the capital and imposed martial law and a dusk-to-dawn curfew. The FMLN had poorly coordinated their own forces and had counted, unrealistically it seemed, on the majority of the people in the city to rise up. In the countryside guerrilla gains were substantial, but in the cities the uprising was a failure.

The following morning the army surrounded Maria's home. "We heard their tanks and trucks and patrol cars surrounding the house. The trucks were full of soldiers. There were six adults and six children there, and we were all captured.

"I was taken to a cell where I was raped and beaten. For a few days they kept me inside a gas drum, and when they took me out for interrogation I would be tied hands and feet on metal bars, suspended horizontally with bags of sand on my stomach and then beaten. They used psychological torture as well. They would bring in my children, point pistols at their heads, and ask me to talk. . . . I would make up things to trick them for a while.

"I was being kept at the National Police headquarters. In the beginning they said that they had documents to back up all their accusations. They told me they had spoken to my parents and that my parents had told them to kill me, had said bitter things about me, that I was a terrorist and should be killed.

"I was given electrical shocks, attached to all parts of my body. I was raped many times. I had tried to prepare psychologically for this. I had answers ready for them, a lot of garbage that they already knew or that was fabricated."

After two and a half months at the National Guard headquarters she was removed to Ilopango Prison for women political prisoners. Her children were allowed into the custody of relatives, her husband imprisoned elsewhere. The cell at Ilopango was her world for the next two years, during which time she participated in three hunger strikes that badly affected her health. The electric shocks had caused partial paralysis in her legs, which she is only now recovering from.

"Our capture was broadcast on the Liberation Radio, a station run by   60 the FMLN. The archbishop, the Red Cross, and Amnesty International began to lobby for our release. Because of the six children who had been taken at the same time there was a lot of across-the-board-pressure on the government not to let us 'disappear' — not to kill us. That is the only reason I am still alive. In April 1983 I was released from prison. My husband was already dead — he was killed at some point during those two years. I left my children with my relatives and came to Canada. I was sent here by the FMLN to recuperate, basically. This is a recovery period."

Since Maria has been in Canada, the civil war has escalated in El Salvador. The Reagan administration continues to pour large amounts of military aid into the country despite continued pressure and documentation, by human rights organizations, of the junta's atrocities. The killings continue, indiscriminately; laborers, priests and nuns, students, suspected leftists, and even foreign journalists are targets. The majority of the killing is attributed to the right-wing death squads operating for Napoleón Duarte's government. . . . As one foreign journalist wrote: "The government's stand — and Duarte's — is that the guerrillas must lay down their guns and join an electoral process set up by the government. For the guerrilla movement, the problem with this stance is that it may mean both literal and figurative suicide. Literal because leftists could not campaign in El Salvador without getting murdered. . . . The left could never afford to lose an election, and the U.S. government would never allow it to win."[2]

The FMLN has moved noticeably further to the left and undoubtedly receives financial support from the Socialist bloc. One American jour-

---

[2]The Bush administration in the United States and the Cristiani government in El Salvador continued the policies of their predecessors into the 1990s. — ED.

nalist who traveled deep into guerrilla zones recently was asked by local villagers if he was the guerrillas' Russian adviser. It is apparent that despite the many political beliefs that united to form the FMLN, it has now turned for help to those who are sympathetic — typically the Socialist countries. Once again a civil war fought only because of brutal internal oppression has become a battleground for the superpowers. Still, women like Ileana and Maria remain convinced that the only way to effect change in their country is to fight.

"It is such a strange state of consciousness to leave that reality and come to this one," says Maria. "I don't think I have really adapted at all. There are always reminders. I am never without the presence of El Salvador. If I am eating a good meal, I think about those who don't have enough to eat there, people so poor that they eat roots and weeds. I think of my children every minute. It has not been a tranquil time here, either. . . ."

"It is an area of strategic importance to the United States," Ileana told me before she returned, "so they continue to support the government and ignore the human rights abuses. I think the war will continue for a long time. Mothers are fighting, kids are fighting, priests and nuns are fighting or helping us to fight. We won't give up. We have tried to negotiate, but it never works. It is not to their advantage to come to an agreement with us. They have all the power and all the wealth, so why should they? They just go on suppressing the movement and increasing their military strength." . . .

Maria: "We are willing to die to change the basis of our society, to feed and educate our children, to end the murders, the terror, and the oppression. You might not understand that, here. But there, it is another reality."

EXPLORATIONS

1. How did Maria and Ileana first become involved in the war? What was the focus of their early efforts on behalf of their fellow Salvadorans?

2. What incident pushed each woman out of peaceful social activism into acceptance of armed confrontation? What subsequent actions by the government persuaded Ileana, and Maria, that revolution is the only way to achieve reforms?

3. What reasons does Maria give for marrying at age sixteen? What other factors

appear to have influenced her and Ileana to marry within a year of becoming involved in the war? What positive and negative effects have their marriages had on their work in the movement?

CONNECTIONS

1. What common U.S. goals and policies appear in both "Women Warriors of El Salvador" and "The Price of the Panama Invasion"? In each essay, who are the chief opponents of the United States' policy? Do these critics also oppose the United States' goals?

2. Like Roger Rosenblatt, Saywell based her account of a foreign war on interviews. How are the two writers' purposes similar? How is their use of interview material different? How would the impact of "Women Warriors of El Salvador" change if Saywell chose a format like Rosenblatt's?

3. "Both Maria and Ileana said that most women wanted to become pregnant," reports Saywell in paragraph 48, "because it was psychologically uplifting to give birth when so much death was going on around them." How are Salvadoran attitudes toward childbearing and child care in a war zone, as described by these women, different from those in the early kibbutzim described by Bruno Bettelheim (p. 86)?

ELABORATIONS

1. In "The Price of the Panama Invasion," paragraph 1, the author quotes statements about American (that is, U.S.) leaders' willingness to "shed a little blood for democracy." According to Saywell, how is this policy being applied in El Salvador? Do you think U.S. military aid to our embattled allies in Central America and elsewhere proves that Czeslaw Milosz is wrong about Americans' ignorance of war? Why or why not? Using Saywell's and other essays in this book as sources, write a cause-and-effect or argumentative essay responding to Milosz's suggestion in paragraph 12 of "American Ignorance of War" that people in the United States are naively optimistic because they have never experienced war.

2. Should the United States allow women to take part in combat? For that matter, should the U.S. armed forces have let women join at all? Write a definition or classification essay indicating what roles you think are appropriate for women in the military, using "Women Warriors of El Salvador" and the comments in *Looking at Ourselves* as sources.

MILOVAN DJILAS

Ideas Against Torture

Milovan Djilas was born in the small Eastern European kingdom of Montenegro (now part of Yugoslavia) in 1911. At eighteen he went to the University of Belgrade in Yugoslavia's capital, where he won recognition for his poems, short stories, and revolutionary activities. Joining the then illegal Communist Party in 1932, he was arrested, imprisoned, and released; he became a partisan leader, a general, and finally one of the four chiefs of the Communist Yugoslav government until the Central Committee expelled him in 1954. Over the twenty years following, Djilas was continually in and out of prison for writings critical of Marshal Tito's bureaucracy and Communism in general. After a brief trip to this country and Great Britain in 1968, Djilas and his wife were refused passports, so they have remained in Belgrade. A translator as well as a writer of fiction, nonfiction, biography, and poetry, Djilas was among the first to contend that nationalism among its member states would eventually fragment the Soviet Union (and also Yugoslavia). "Ideas Against Torture" comes from his book *Of Prisons and Ideas* (1986), translated from the Serbo-Croatian by Michael Boro Petrovich.

The Socialist Federal Republic of Yugoslavia was created after World War II when the partisan fighter Josip Broz, known as Marshal Tito, executed his main competitor and established himself at the head of a Communist government. Yugoslavia, which lies north of Greece, south of Austria and Hungary, and across the water from Italy, comprises several former provinces of the Austro-Hungarian Empire plus the state of Montenegro. Unified as Yugoslavia after the empire's collapse following World War I, it was invaded by Germany in 1941. Both the Soviet Union and Great Britain supported Marshal Tito, and Tito maintained ties with Western as well as Eastern Europe when he became president. He died in 1980; for the next decade the Party leadership and presidency rotated among the heads of Yugoslavia's member republics and provinces, but the political change sweeping Eastern Europe in 1989 and 1990 affected Yugoslavia as well. As we go to press, free elections are planned to choose members for a representative government.

A fighting man possessed of faith in an idea need not fear, and has no reason to fear, prison, torture, or even death. He will survive. He will live on in the lives of his comrades, in the life of the idea. Nevertheless, he will be all the more confident and able to bear torture all the more easily if he is familiar with certain "weak points" innate to the act itself and those who practice it.

First, no torture has ever been devised that a victim dedicated to an idea and ready to die for it cannot withstand. Torturers are seldom possessed of a particularly inventive imagination in devising their terrors. Most frequently they find it easiest to follow long-trodden paths and make use of those tried and true methods handed down from the past. They rely on ready-made instruments: whips, truncheons, sandbags, needles, castor oil, electric currents, and the like. It is common, of course, especially where torture is not standard procedure, for the police to use whatever instruments may be at hand — pencils (for jabbing between fingers), drawers (for crushing hands), chairs (for jamming bodies against walls), and, most frequently, to be sure, the most direct, handiest instrument of all, their fists.

Second, the victim will often be more terrified by his imagination of the event than by the event itself. This being so, he should exert every effort not to think about torture or any of its particular methods. Such efforts, alas, are all too frequently less powerful than the imagination, which, since it secretly nurtures the will to live, cannot be completely suppressed. If the victim is lucky enough to be put in a cell with other prisoners, he will have a chance to talk, to swap stories, to while away the time in idle games and so keep his wilder flights of fancy under control. But if he is alone in a cell, he must fill his time as best he can — by cleaning the cell, by taking care of his personal hygiene, and the like. For it is time that is the intractable sworn enemy of the prisoner. And though time in a single cell — even without books, without pen and paper, without anything of one's own — passes faster than it does in a common jail pen, it is more deadly because of its killing monotony.

In the period before torture, as well as between bouts, it is the very   4 uneventfulness of time that fires the imagination and intensifies torment into seemingly unbearable pain. Consequently, one must learn to stifle the imagination from the start, to trick it and to master it. As soon as one's feelings give signs of taking over, one must force oneself to think of something else and to think of it constantly, persistently, all the time. Occupy your mind so that it doesn't occupy you. It will finally submit. It is not separate from the will, however limitless and unrestricted in its choice of subject it may seem to be. And even in the most difficult, most adverse circumstances, even if both hands and feet are shackled and one is exposed all night to the cries of tortured victims and the curses of guards, one must make one's mind concentrate on insignificant concrete things — spots on the ceiling, say — with a steady stare, until one's surroundings and all their details utterly vanish.

Third, all individual acts of torture have their limits, just as our bodies have limits of endurance. When the infliction of pain reaches the outer limits, the body and spirit protect themselves by lapsing into unconsciousness. In those moments of unconsciousness even torments become sweet, turning into the most subtle, spiritual joys imaginable. This is the beginning of the victory over torturers and tortures alike.

Fourth, one should never be afraid of dying while being tortured. In any case, there would be no point to it. Most torturers employed by the police are careful and experienced. The sadists are much rarer than rebels against authority and potential political criminals believe. Brutality, violence, and self-assertion are part and parcel of a policeman's profession, qualities which in time become habit, an adjunct of the personality. Such qualities do not necessarily take over the personality to such a degree that it gives in to murderous passions and mindless caprice. This restraint is particularly true of the political police, for they are controlled by political leaders as well as by their own politically disciplined organization. As a rule, political police do not kill or even torture if they are not ordered to do so and if such practices do not conform to the policy of the dictator and the oligarchy. The police — the political police in particular — are generally intelligent, experienced, and moderate, even in the practice of torture. It is virtually by sheer chance that a prisoner dies while undergoing torture, unless specific orders have been given to deal with him without regard for his life. And no one anywhere can ever be made safe from accidental death.

EXPLORATIONS

1. What does Djilas cite as the greatest dangers to a torture victim? What does he cite as a potential victim's greatest fears? What does he mean in paragraph 2 by "withstand" torture?

2. Djilas writes mostly in the third person, referring to "the victim" and "one." How would his essay's impact change if he had written it in the first person, about his own experience, or in the second person, giving advice? What does he gain (and lose) by using a matter-of-fact rather than a dramatic tone?

3. What is the meaning of Djilas's title, "Ideas Against Torture"?

CONNECTIONS

1. In what ways do Ileana and Maria in Shelley Saywell's "Women Warriors of El Salvador" follow Djilas's advice? What tactics do they use to resist torture besides the ones he mentions?

2. Czeslaw Milosz writes in "American Ignorance of War" that Americans take their war-free existence for granted and that "their resultant lack of imagination is appalling." What does Djilas say about imagination? Do you think he would agree with Milosz's essay? Why or why not?

3. Djilas suggests that torture is easier to bear if one is prepared for it. What aspects of Mark Baker's account in *Looking at Ourselves* suggest that Americans who found the Vietnam War unbearable might have stood the strain better if they had been better prepared? What kinds of preparation might have helped?

ELABORATIONS

1. Aside from personal revenge, what factors and forces can persuade one individual to do serious harm to another? Reread Colin Thubron's "At the Beijing Zoo" (p. 583), Geoffrey Matthews's "'Good Sons' Who Kill" (p. 443), and the comments by "Racketeer" in *Looking at Ourselves* in Part Three (p. 191). Write a classification or cause-and-effect essay in which you identify and explain the reasons why an otherwise decent person beats, tortures, or kills someone who is not a personal enemy.

2. Is there an idea you are dedicated enough to withstand torture for? to die for? to kill for? Suppose you were kidnapped by terrorists and held hostage as a privileged citizen of the exploitive imperialist United States. Write a process analysis essay, like Djilas's, giving a step-by-step description of how you would respond to your captors' demands and abuse. Use the essays in this book and your imagination as sources.

JOHN SIMPSON

Tiananmen Square

John Cody Fidler-Simpson was born in 1944 and educated at St. Paul's School and Magdalene College, Cambridge University. Since 1982 he has been foreign affairs editor of BBC (British Broadcasting Company) Television News. He joined the BBC as a radio news reporter in 1970. From there he traveled, becoming first the network's Dublin correspondent, then their Common Market correspondent in Brussels, and then their Southern Africa correspondent in Johannesburg. Simpson has written articles for *World Monitor* and other publications; a book, *Inside Iran* (1988), on life under the Ayatollah Khomeini's regime; and two novels, *Moscow Requiem* (1981) and *A Fine and Private Place* (1983). "Tiananmen Square" comes from *Granta 28* (Autumn 1989).

The events that would culminate in the Tiananmen Square confrontation described by Simpson began in April 1989. The death of Hu Yaobang, a former general secretary ousted for sympathizing with the protests of Chinese students, brought thousands of mourners to the Square. The gathering turned into a demonstration in favor of faster-paced and wider-ranging reforms in China's government. The pro-democracy movement gained strength over the next seven weeks, condemning government corruption, calling on Deng and Prime Minister Li Peng to resign, embarrassing the Chinese leadership when Soviet President Mikhail Gorbachev paid a state visit, and erecting in the square a 33-foot plaster and plastic foam Goddess of Democracy which resembled the Statue of Liberty. Over the opposition of Zhao Ziyang, the moderate head of the Communist Party, the leadership declared martial law on May 20. Deng and his colleagues began efforts to purge Zhao (that is, to remove him from power); and on June 4, troops attacked demonstrators who remained in and around Tiananmen Square. Hundreds, perhaps thousands, were killed. Exactly what happened may never be known (some observers have disputed parts of Simpson's account) because the Chinese government immediately began censoring news reports, redefining the pro-democracy forces as "counterrevolutionaries" (that is, traitors), imprisoning or executing the movement's leaders, and rewriting history to both understate the violence and deflect blame for it. The head of the Thirty-eighth Army (see para. 5) reportedly was sentenced to ten years in prison for refusing to use military force against the demonstrators. Since June 1989, Chinese authorities have tried to prevent any recurrence or even remembrance of the protests in Tiananmen Square.

(For more background on China, see pp. 93, 235, and 583.)

It was humid and airless, and the streets around our hotel were empty. We had set out for Tiananmen Square: a big, conspicuous European television team — reporter, producer, cameraman, sound-recordist, translator, lighting man, complete with gear. A cyclist rode past, shouting and pointing. What it meant we couldn't tell. Then we came upon a line of soldiers. Some of them had bleeding faces; one cradled a broken arm. They were walking slowly, limping. There had been a battle somewhere, but we couldn't tell where.

When we reached Changan Avenue, the main east-west thoroughfare, it was as full of people as in the days of the great demonstrations — a human river. We followed the flow of it to the Gate of Heavenly Peace, under the bland, moonlike portrait of Chairman Mao. There were hundreds of small groups, each concentrated around someone who was haranguing or lecturing the others, using the familiar, heavy public gestures of the Chinese. Other groups had formed around radios tuned to foreign stations. People were moving from group to group, pushing in, crushing round a speaker, arguing, moving on, passing along any new information.

For the most part these were not students. They were from the factories, and the red cloths tied around their heads made them look aggressive, even piratical. Trucks started arriving from the outskirts of the city, full of more young workers, waving the banners of their factories, singing, chanting, looking forward to trouble.

People were shouting: there was a battle going on between tanks and the crowd, somewhere to the east of the city center. Details differed, and I had trouble finding out what was being said: I watched the animated faces, everyone pushing closer to each new source of information, pulling at each other's sleeves or shoulders. Tanks and armored personnel carriers, they were saying, were heading towards the Square. They were coming from two directions, east and west. The crowds that gathered couldn't stop them.

"It's a different army. It's not the Thirty-eighth!" The man who said this was screaming it, clutching at our translator, holding on to him, trying to make him understand the significance of it. "It is *not* the Thirty-eighth!" It had been the Thirty-eighth Army that had tried to recapture the city twice before. The soldiers had been unarmed: the commander, the father of a student in the Square, had ordered that operations be carried out peacefully.

We pushed our way towards the Square where, despite the rumors and the panic, we saw something very different: several thousand people standing in silence, motionless, listening to a large loudspeaker, bolted to a street lamp:

> Go home and save your life. You will fail. You are not behaving in the correct Chinese manner. This is not the West, it is China. You should behave like a good Chinese. Go home and save your life. Go home and save your life.

The voice was expressionless, epicene, metallic, like that of a hypnotist. I looked at the silent, serious faces, illuminated by the orange light of the street lamps, studying the loudspeaker. Even the small children, brought there with the rest of the family, stared intently. The order was repeated again and again. It was a voice the people of China had been listening to for forty years, and continued listening to even now. But now no one did what the hypnotist said. No one moved.

And then, suddenly, everything changed: the loudspeaker's spell was broken by shouts that the army was coming. There was the sound of a violent scraping, and across the Avenue I saw people pulling at the railings that ran along the roadway and dragging them across the pavement to build a barricade. Everyone moved quickly, a crowd suddenly animated, its actions fast and decisive, sometimes brutal. They blocked off Changan Avenue and the Square itself, and we began filming — flooding the sweating enthusiasts with our camera-light. People danced around us, flaunting their weaponry: coshes, knives, crude spears, bricks. A boy rushed up to our camera and opened his shabby green wind-cheater like a black marketeer to reveal a row of Coca-Cola bottles strapped to his waist, filled with petrol and plugged with rags. He laughed, and mimed the action of pulling out each bottle and throwing it. I asked him his age. He was sixteen. Why was he against the government? He couldn't answer. He gripped another of his Molotov cocktails, laughing all the time.

That the army was coming was no longer rumor but fact and our translator heard that it would move in at one o'clock. It was half-past midnight. In the distance, above the noise of the crowd, I thought I could hear the sound of guns. I wanted to find a vantage point from which we could film, without being spotted by the army. But the tension that was bonding members of the crowd together did not have the same effect on the members of our small team. It was hot and noisy. We argued. We started shouting, and I headed off on my own.

I pushed through the crowds, immediately feeling better for being on my own. There were very few foreign journalists left in the Square by now, and I felt especially conspicuous. But I also felt good. People grabbed my hand, thanking me for being with them. I gave them a V for Victory sign and was applauded by everyone around me. It was hard to define the mood. There was still a spirit of celebration, that they were out on the streets, defying the government, but the spirit was also giving way to a terrible foreboding. There was also something else. Something I hadn't seen before: a reckless ferocity of purpose.

I crossed back into the main part of Tiananmen Square, the village of student tents. There were sticks and cardboard and broken glass underfoot. The smells were familiar and strong — wood-smoke, urine, and heavy disinfectant. A couple clung to each other, her head on his shoulder. I passed in front of them, but they didn't raise their eyes. A student asked me to sign his T-shirt, a craze from earlier days. He had thick glasses and a bad complexion, and he spoke English. "It will be dangerous tonight," he said. "We are all very afraid here."

I finished signing his shirt, at the back below the collar. He grabbed my hand and shook it excitedly. His grip was bony and clammy. I asked him what he thought would happen.

"We will all die."   12

He straightened up and shook my hand again, and slipped away between the tents.

The camp was dark. There were a few students left; most of them had gathered in the center of the Square, around the Monument to the People's Heroes. I could hear their speeches and the occasional burst of singing — the Internationale,[1] as always. Here, though, it was quiet. This was where the students had chosen to build their statue of the Goddess of Democracy, with her sightless eyes, her torch held in both hands. The symbol of all our aspirations, one of the student leaders called her: the fruit of our struggle. To me, she looked very fragile.

The speeches and the songs continued in the distance. Then suddenly they stopped. There was a violent grinding and a squealing sound — the familiar sound of an armored personnel carrier. I heard screaming, and behind me, in the Avenue, everyone started running. When I finally spotted the vehicle, I could see that it was making its way with speed down the side of the Square. It seemed uncertain of its direction — one

---

[1]Communist anthem. — ED.

moment driving straight for the Square, and then stopping, turning, stopping again, as if looking for a way to escape. There was a sudden angry roar, and I know it was because the vehicle had crushed someone under its tracks. It then turned in my direction — it was pointed at me — and I felt a different kind of panic. The action was starting and I was separated from my colleagues: it is an article of faith to stay with your camera crew in times of danger.

The vehicle carried on, careering back and forth. It must have knocked   16
down six or seven people. By now it was on fire, having been hit repeatedly by Molotov cocktails. Somehow, though, it escaped and headed off to the west.

Then a second armored personnel carrier came along Changan Avenue, alone and unsupported like the first. This time everyone turned and ran hard towards the vehicle, knowing that they, with their numbers and their petrol bombs, had the power to knock it out. They screamed with anger and hate as the vehicle swung randomly in different directions, threatening to knock people down as it made its way through the Square. The Molotov cocktails arched above our heads, spinning over and over, exploding on the thin shell of armor that protected the men inside. Still the vehicle carried on, zigzagging, crossing the Avenue, trying to find a way through the barricade. A pause, and it charged, head-on, straight into a block of concrete — and then stuck, its engine whirring wildly. A terrible shout of triumph came from the crowd: primitive and dark, its prey finally caught. The smell of petrol and burning metal and sweat was in the air, intoxicating and violent. Everyone around me was pushing and fighting to get to the vehicle. At first I resisted; then, close beside it, I saw the light of a camera, just where the crowd was starting to swarm. There were only three cameramen still filming in the entire Square, and I knew that my colleague was the only one crazy enough to be that close. Now I was the one fighting, struggling to get through the crowd, pulling people back, pushing them out of my path, swearing, a big brutal Englishman stronger than any of them. I tore one man's shirt and punched another in the back. All around me the men seemed to be yelling at the sky, their faces lit up; the vehicle had caught fire. A man — his torso bare — climbed up the side of the vehicle and stood on top of it, his arms raised in victory, the noise of the mob welling up around him. They knew they had the vehicle's crew trapped inside. Someone started beating at the armored glass with an iron bar.

I reached the cameraman and pulled hard at his arm to get his attention. He scarcely noticed me, amid the buffeting and the noise and the violence, and carried on filming. He and his sound recordist and the Chinese lighting man were a few feet from the vehicle: close enough to be killed if it exploded or if the soldiers came out shooting. But I couldn't make them step back, and so we stayed there, the four of us, the heat beating against our faces as people continued to pour petrol on the bonnet and roof and smashed at the doors and the armored glass. What was it like inside? I imagined the soldiers half-crazed with the noise and the heat and the fear of being burned alive.

The screaming around me rose even louder: the handle of the door at the rear of the vehicle had turned a little, and the door began to open. A soldier pushed the barrel of a gun out, but it was snatched from his hands, and then everyone started grabbing his arms, pulling and wrenching until finally he came free, and then he was gone: I saw the arms of the mob, flailing, raised above their heads as they fought to get their blows in. He was dead within seconds, and his body was dragged away in triumph. A second soldier showed his head through the door and was then immediately pulled out by his hair and ears and the skin on his face. This soldier I could see: his eyes were rolling, and his mouth was open, and he was covered with blood where the skin had been ripped off. Only his eyes remained — white and clear — but then someone was trying to get them as well, and someone else began beating his skull until the skull came apart, and there was blood all over the ground, and his brains, and still they kept on beating and beating what was left.

Then the horrible sight passed away, and the ground was wet where 20 he had been.

There was a third soldier inside. I could see his face in the light of the flames, and some of the crowd could too. They pulled him out, screaming, wild at having missed killing the other soldiers. It was his blood they wanted, I was certain, it was to feel the blood running over their hands. Their mouths were open and panting, like dogs, and their eyes were expressionless. They were shouting, the Chinese lighting man told me afterwards, that the soldier they were about to kill wasn't human, that he was just a thing, an object, which had to be destroyed. And all the time the noise and the heat and the stench of oil burning on hot metal beat at us, overwhelming our senses, deadening them.

Just as the third soldier was lifted out of the vehicle, almost fainting, an articulated bus rushed towards us stopping, with great skill, so that its rear door opened just beside the group with the soldier. The students had heard what was happening, and a group had raced the bus over to save whomever they could. The mob did not want to give up its prize. The students tried to drag the soldier on board, and the crowd held on to him, pulling him back. By some mischance the bus door started closing and it seemed that he must be killed.

I had seen people die in front of me before. But I had never seen three people die, one after the other, in this way. Once again the members of the crowd closed around the soldier, their arms raised over their heads to beat him to death. The bus and the safety it promised were so close. It seemed to me then that I couldn't look on any longer, a passive observer, watching another man's skin torn away or his head broken open, and do nothing. I saw the soldier's face, expressing only horror and pain as he sank under the blows of the people around him, and I started to move forward. The ferocity of the crowd had entered me, but I felt it was the crowd that was the animal, that it wasn't properly human. The soldier had sunk down to the ground, and a man was trying to break his skull with a half-brick, bringing it down with full force. I screamed obscenities at the man — stupid obscenities, as no one except my colleagues could have understood them — and threw myself at him, catching him with his arm up, poised for another blow. He looked at me blankly, and his thin arm went limp in my grasp. I stopped shouting. He relaxed his grip on the brick, and I threw it under the bus. It felt wet. A little room had been created around the soldier, and the student who had tried to rescue him before could now get to him. The rest of the mob hadn't given up, but the students were able to pull the soldier away and get him on to the bus by the other door. He was safe.

The vehicle burned for a long time, its driver and the man beside him burning with it. The flames lit up the Square and reflected on the face of the Monument where the students had taken their stand. The crowd in Changan Avenue had been sated. The loudspeakers had stopped telling people to save their lives. There was silence. 24

The students sang the Internationale. It would be for the last time, and it sounded weak and faint in the vastness of the Square. Many were crying. No doubt some students joined in the attacks on the army, but those in the Square kept to their principle of nonviolence. Although the army suffered the first casualties, it was the students who would be the martyrs that night.

My colleagues and I wanted to save our pictures in case we were arrested, and I told the others that we should go back to the Beijing Hotel and come out again later. I now feel guilty about the decision; it was wrong: we ought to have stayed in the Square, even though the other camera crews had already left and it might have cost us our lives. Someone should have been there when the massacre took place, filming what happened, showing the courage of the students as they were surrounded by tanks and the army advancing, firing as it went.

Instead, we took up our position on the fourteenth floor of the Beijing Hotel. From there, everything seemed gray and distant. We saw most of what happened, but we were separated from the fear and the noise and the stench of it. We saw the troops pouring out of the Gate of Heavenly Peace, bayonets fixed, shooting first into the air and then straight ahead of them. They looked like automata, with their rounded dark helmets. We filmed them charging across and clearing the northern end of the Square, where I had signed the student's T-shirt. We filmed the tanks as they drove over the tents where some of the students had taken refuge, among them, perhaps, the young couple I had seen sitting silently, their arms around each other. Dozens of people seem to have died in that way, and those who saw it said they could hear the screams of the people inside the tents over the noise of the tanks. We filmed as the lights in the Square were switched off at 4:00 A.M. They were switched on again forty minutes later, when the troops and the tanks moved towards the Monument itself, shooting first in the air and then, again, directly at the students themselves, so that the steps of the Monument and the heroic reliefs which decorated it were smashed by bullets.

Once or twice, we were ourselves shot at, and during the night the security police sent men to our room to arrest us: but I shouted at them in English, and they went away, uncertain of the extent of their powers. Below us, people still gathered in the Avenue, shouting their defiance at the troops who were massed at the farther end. Every now and then the crack of a rifle would bring down another demonstrator, and the body would be rescued by a trishaw driver or the crew of an ambulance. Below us, the best and noblest political protest since Czechoslovakia in 1968[2] was being crushed as we watched. I knelt on the balcony, beside the cameraman and a Chinese woman, one of the student leaders.

She had taken refuge in our room because we were foreigners. I shouted at her to go back inside, but she refused, turning her head from me so that I wouldn't see she was crying, her hands clenched tight enough to hurt, intent on watching the rape of her country and the movement she and her friends had built up in the course of twenty-two

28

---

[2]The famous "Prague Spring"; see page (517). — ED.

days. I had seen the river of protest running along Changan Avenue in that time; I had seen a million people in the streets, demanding a way of life that was better than rule by corruption and secret police. I recalled the lines of the T'ang dynasty poet Li Po, that if you cut water with a sword you merely made it run faster. But the river of change had been dammed, and below me, in the Avenue where it had run, people were dying. Beside me, the cameraman spotted something and started filming. Down in the Square, in the early light, the soldiers were busy unrolling something and lifting it up. Soon a great curtain of black cloth covered the entrance to Tiananmen Square. What was happening there was hidden from us.

EXPLORATIONS

1. What different Chinese population segments does Simpson notice in Tiananmen Square? Which group started the protests? Which group attacks the armored personnel carriers? Which group evidently suffers the heaviest casualties?

2. What do you think the voice on the loudspeaker means by "This is not the West, it is China" (para. 6)?

3. In paragraph 27 Simpson describes troops charging across the same parts of the square where earlier (paras. 10–13) he had peaceful encounters with students. What are the effects of his using the same setting for two contrasting incidents?

4. At three points in his essay Simpson writes a one-sentence paragraph. What are these sentences? How would their impact be different if Simpson made them part of longer paragraphs?

CONNECTIONS

1. In "Ideas Against Torture," Milovan Djilas writes, "As a rule, political police do not kill or even torture if they are not ordered to do so and if such practices do not conform to the policy of the dictator and the oligarchy." When the Chinese in Tiananmen Square discover that the approaching army is not the unarmed Thirty-eighth, what do they conclude about Deng Xiaoping's policy toward their peaceful protest? How does their conclusion affect their reaction to vehicles and soldiers entering the square?

2. What similar behavior by the Chinese is described in "Tiananmen Square"

and in Colin Thubron's "At the Beijing Zoo" (p. 583). How does each essay's Western author react to that behavior, and what explanation does he propose for it?

3. In "Gong Fu" (p. 235), what evidence does Mark Salzman see of a Chinese belief that to achieve great things one must be willing to suffer? What evidence of that belief appears among the protesters in "Tiananmen Square"? among the Chinese authorities?

ELABORATIONS

1. Simpson describes in paragraph 23 his switch from being a recorder of the violence in Tiananmen Square to being a participant in it. Some observers believe that members of the media should never intervene in events they cover; others believe that, as human beings, media people sometimes have an obligation to intervene. Which is your position, and why? Write an essay arguing in favor of your viewpoint, using this and other selections as sources.

2. Are governments in the United States "soft on crime"? Would our streets be safer, our population better behaved, our society saner and happier, if our law enforcement policies were more like those of the Chinese? Reread Thubron's "At the Beijing Zoo" (p. 583); Lewis H. Lapham's "Racketeer" passage in *Looking at Ourselves*, (p. 484); Liang Heng and Judith Shapiro's "Chairman Mao's Good Little Boy" (p. 93); and James Fallows's "A Few Pointers" (p. 52). Write an essay comparing and contrasting attitudes toward law enforcement in China and the United States, or describing the ways Chinese citizens learn socially acceptable behavior from infancy through adulthood.

JON LEE ANDERSON AND
SCOTT ANDERSON

The Troubles

Jon Lee Anderson and Scott Anderson are brothers who joined forces to research and write *War Zones: Voices from the World's Killing Grounds* (1988), from which "The Troubles" is taken. They had previously published *Inside the League* (1986), "an exposé of how terrorists, Nazis, and Latin American death squads have infiltrated the World Anti-Communist League." Jon Lee Anderson previously had worked for syndicated columnist Jack Anderson (no relation) and lived in El Salvador, where he reported for *Time* magazine. He has since gone on to research a book on Israeli military involvement in Central America. Scott Anderson, a free-lance writer based in Spain, coauthored *Mega Tips*. He is currently working on several screenplays and a novel.

The Andersons chose to write about The Troubles in Northern Ireland as "the only Anglo-Saxon conflict taking place in the world." Protestants from Scotland began emigrating to Ireland in the 1600s, soon after England conquered the island, and displacing Gaelic-speaking Catholics in the northern counties known as Ulster (see p. 201). The Irish Republican Army (IRA) formed in 1919 to drive the British out. When Ireland became a dominion two years later and then a republic, Britain responded to the fears of the Ulster Protestants by keeping control of Northern Ireland. Catholic resentment simmered until the 1960s, flaring in 1968–69 into demonstrations against housing, voting, and employment discrimination. As the outlawed IRA reemerged as a militant force, Protestant paramilitary groups formed to oppose it. In 1972 Britain suspended Northern Ireland's parliament and reimposed direct rule. After thirteen more years of turmoil, including a 1981 hunger strike that left ten Republicans dead, Britain agreed over Loyalist protests to give the Republic of Ireland a voice in governing Northern Ireland. Today The Troubles continue. The conflict, write the Andersons, "is political in that the Catholic minority wants political equality in a system that they have been historically shut out of by the Protestant majority. It is territorial in that the Catholic Republicans want nothing less than the merger of Ulster with the Irish Republic, while the Protestant Loyalists want to maintain their links to Great Britain. And it is religious in that virtually all Catholics are Republicans and virtually all Protestants are Loyalists. But perhaps, most of all, it is tribal, and the bloodletting a ritual of rehearsed animosity."

Since The Troubles began in earnest in 1969, over 230 policemen of the Royal Ulster Constabulary (RUC) have been killed and nearly 6,000 have been injured. Overwhelmingly Protestant, RUC police, both on and off duty, are considered legitimate "targets of war" by the Provisional IRA and the Irish National Liberation Army (INLA). Since the 1985 signing of the Anglo-Irish Agreement, the Constabulary has also come under attack from angered Loyalist militants who have burned out the homes of scores of RUC officers.

For these reasons, policemen are not allowed to be photographed, and any interviews are conducted anonymously. The following interview is with a senior police official who works at the fortresslike RUC headquarters in East Belfast. At the time of the interview, the Provisional IRA had just extended its "target list" for assassination to include anyone entering or leaving an RUC installation.

Recently a group of Republicans went to a guy's house and asked for a lad by name. They were armed with staves and hurley sticks. Fortunately for him, he wasn't there, because the IRA are judge, jury, and executioner. He had been remanded to us for some petty crime. Their objective in being there was to break that fellow's bones; the second thing they'd do is to blow your kneecaps. Third place is you don't get any warning and you're taken in a car to an isolated area and shot in the head.

It's not a religious war at all. It's a situation created by the paramilitaries 4 trying to take power and bring communities into conflict with each other, create economic instability and mayhem and to bring down law and order. And it's a helluva long way off, the day before the paramilitaries are extinct.

As a policeman, you just have to be careful where you travel and when you travel. You don't just jump out of your Land Rover and try to catch some young guy throwing stones. You have always the possibility that there could be a sniper attack, because they have employed children in the past to be at the forefront, while behind there's a sniper.

Also, they'll find a sweet jar and fill it with petrol and they'll drop it out of a window when they see a Land Rover. Your engine stalls, and inside it's an oven. If you bail out, you're almost bound to be dead; there's almost always a sniper there. You don't get out.

The threats have been there for quite a number of years. Many policemen have been killed. What happens is that a lot of these police are also farmers . . . so, on their way home, they are killed, attacked from a ditch, or whatever. We've had them where a farmer is walking into a field and they'll have a booby-trapped mine. It is a very nasty situation, because when a policeman is on duty, he knows he's safe enough, but naturally the situation at his home is on his mind — his wife has to go shop, the kids have to go to school, and often, his family is ostracized in the community.

But if one were to give up hope, it's a lost cause. We will continue to be a police force and carry out law and order. Everyone is entitled to the benefit of the law, but it needs the assistance of the community and political entities. There is a vacuum at the moment, but we must carry on.

The RUC is standing right in the middle between both communities and holding this country together to enable the politicians to get together to solve the problems of the society. Whenever both sides are getting at you, like now, it's an indication that you're doing something right.

Emma Groves sits in the austere living room of her middle-class home on Andersontown Road, her golden retriever sprawled at her feet. Dressed in a black skirt and a frilly, high-necked white blouse, the sixty-five-year-old woman speaks in a soft Irish brogue, occasionally overpowered by the sounds of commotion in other rooms of the house where grandchildren play. Her eyes are hidden behind oversized dark glasses.

My children were very angry and very bitter when I was shot. But I talked to them and told them not to try to do anything, because . . . I mean, it wouldn't help me. It wouldn't help anybody if one of my children had gone out to shoot a British soldier.

I've lived a long time, and I was born in Northern Ireland. There has always been a struggle, all my life. I mean, the struggle has never stopped. It has just come to a head since 1969, but all durin' my lifetime, we had troubles, in the thirties when I was a teenager, and we had troubles in the forties. And then, of course, in the fifties . . . Do you know what I mean?

It developed into a bigger struggle. How would you describe it, the struggle at the minute? It has involved more people, but it has always been there. You know, people have never stopped fightin' for their freedom. Every generation, men have died on hunger strike. Men have spent long terms of imprisonment because they felt an injustice was being done on their country and an injustice is still bein' done. So, the fact that I was shot is all part of the struggle.

They were always raiding yer house, especially if you was a mother of boys. But on that particular morning, the British Army had just left my home when someone mentioned that a young man two doors from me had been arrested. And I ran down to see what help I could do, because his wee wife was in a very bad state and the children were all cryin'. So I tried to comfort her and made her some tea and helped her to dress the children and, just then, someone shouted, "Here are the paratroopers in."

So I went to the door, and they definitely were in, with a lot of aggression, because they had guns drawn. So they told everybody to get into their own homes, which I had to do; I had to leave the wee woman and her children and go back into my own home. And we were all put under house arrest, which meant there was a soldier put in every doorway to make sure no one got in or out.

Now, we were all lookin' out of our windows, which was all we could do, and the British Army, the paratroopers, were in the street. And they were arrestin' young boys and men, and it was — some were in their bare feet and some had just pulled on their shirts and trousers — and it was very, very frustratin' to watch, and you felt so helpless just lookin' out the window and there wasn't anything you could do. You didn't know whether to scream or cry or what to do. It was a terrible situation. So I said to one of my teenage daughters, "Would you please put on a record and boost up our morale," because, as I say, it was very frustratin' to have to watch what was happenin' in the streets.

The last thing I ever saw was one young man havin' his head beat up [on the side of] a Saracen [armored personnel carrier]. The record was only playin' minutes when a paratrooper stepped right in front of my window and fired directly into my face.

Now, all my children were present when that happened. So you can imagine what a horrible experience it was for my husband and my children to see me, because my face was a mass of blood. And I was taken to the hospital and was told a week later by Mother Teresa of Calcutta, who was in the north of Ireland at that particular time tryin' to help the situation — and none of my family were brave enough to tell me or had the courage to tell me that I would never see again — so Mother Teresa come to my bedside and told me that I would never see again.

And I just wanted to die. 'Cause when you've been the mother of eleven children and a very active woman . . . you know, even thinkin' about it now, like . . . 'twas a terrible shock to be told that you would

never ever see again. So when I was taken out of hopsital I just wanted
to die . . . just . . . I nearly did die . . . just took to me own room and
I had to take one o' me teenaged daughters out o' work and look after
the house and look after the children. I just couldn't cope with the whole
thing. As I say, I just wanted to die. But as time went on and the children
were depressed, my husband was depressed and . . . no family life and
— it was so sad, because, previously to me being shot, we had been a
very, very happy family and there was always plenty o' laughter and all
in the house — so I just, one morning, decided that I would just have
to come to terms with what happened, for the sake o' me children.
Which I did do. I taught meself to do me own washin', taught meself to
do me own ironing, and taught meself to clean me own house, and then,
eventually, took over the runnin' of the house.

Lookin' back on it, it was a terrible, terrible time of my life. And the   20
one thing that still makes me very angry — because I've learned to live
with the fact that I'll never see again; my children are all married and
doin' well — is the injustice, 'cause the mornin' that that soldier fired
that bullet into my living room, his commandin' officer knew who he
was, his comrades knew who he was, because he was the only soldier
who fired a shot that morning. And still I couldn't get him into the
courts. I tried very, very hard to have that soldier brought to justice but
I never succeeded. See, there isn't any justice here.

I have not bitterness against the soldier that shot me; I have a bitterness
against the state who put him there, the system who allowed him to get
away with it.

*The blinding of Emma Groves played a prominent role in the campaign
to end the use of rubber bullets by the security forces. The rubber bullet
had first been introduced for use in riot situations in the belief that it
would provide a nonlethal method for crowd control, but before it was
withdrawn in 1975, it had caused three deaths. Its replacement, the plastic
bullet, was hailed as a safer and more accurate alternative but, since its
introduction, it has caused at least sixteen deaths. Emma Groves is now
active in the campaign to ban the plastic bullet. . . .*

*"Betty" is a thirty-one-year-old Catholic divorcee and mother of two
children living in a strongly Republican West Belfast district. She works
sixteen hours a week for a small Falls Road business and receives twenty-
two pounds ($32) a week in government financial assistance. A bright,*

vivacious woman, her nerves seem frayed and her fingers tremble as she chain-smokes Silk Cut cigarettes in the kitchen of her small rowhouse.

I was out in a drinking club one night and I was sitting with my sister 　24
and her husband, who's English, and we were just sitting there having a drink and there was a band playing. And the lights went out and the group stopped playing and we were told to keep still and nobody to leave the hall. And we saw all these masked men coming inside with balaclavas. We were absolutely terrified. Everybody froze. We've got about a hundred people in the hall; it was a social night. We didn't know what was happening. Everybody I was sitting with, every fella I was sitting with, drained. Pure white! Everybody thought, "They're coming for me," you know the way people think?

My poor brother-in-law happened to be at the top of the hall to talk with someone and, him being English, these guys went straight up to where he was and he thought, "My God, I'm English; they're coming for me!"

But it was the fella sitting beside Nigel.

All I seen was, "Stand up! You, stand up! Put your hands on your head!" And this guy stood up and put his hands on his head. His face was pure white! And they frog-marched him out. And I'm going, "My God, this is awful!"

You know, people don't like witnessing that, no matter how bad the 　28
person is and what he's done. Because you know what's going to happen to him when they get him outside. They break his legs and arms with hurley sticks.

And we were going, "Oh God, we come out to enjoy ourselves, not to witness this. Things are bad enough. You try to escape the tensions of the house and to come out to relax, and you see this?" Which is really upsetting.

And my sister said to me, "If I hear any gunfire, I'm going home." We were so upset. And I read about it in the paper the next morning and they had broken nearly every bone in his body.

But anyway, the lights went back on, the music started again, and everybody resumed drinking. Fellas were going, "God, I thought they were coming for me, because you know, they looked so menacing with those cudgels and balaclavas."

And we're still talking about it when the lights went out again and the 　32
man who was responsible for the hall said, "Ladies and gentlemen, the

club has now been surrounded by the RUC, and we advise all patrons to leave now in case of a disturbance."

I thought — I mean, I am paranoid anyway at the best of times, and this country has really made me totally paranoid — "Oh, by God, the RUC is going to come in and fire rubber bullets, shoot in here." That's the way you're geared to think here. You really don't trust anybody.

It was really terrible. It was my birthday, actually. I went out to celebrate my birthday, and that's how it ended up. A totally bad night.

The Troubles have made me really paranoid. I really hate . . . the thing I really fear is sectarian murder. It really terrifies me. Just people getting murdered. Because I've known people that got murdered. Went out to drink and were found next morning, hooded, shot through the head, their hands behind their back. I mean, when sectarian murders start up it's awful, because when you're walking down the road at night in the dark, I'm really scared when cars slow down, you know, in case they're going to try to pull you in or shoot you. I've got this fear all the time. I actually left Belfast when I was eighteen because I couldn't stick it anymore. I went to live in Dublin.

This is such a backward place. I find it hard to understand. I mean,   36 we pick up a paper and find out a Catholic has been mutilated and badly tortured just because he's a Catholic. Only certain people can do this. They must have this really intense hatred of Catholics to be able to do anything like that. I don't think the Catholic community is capable of being that vicious.

Protestant people have a deep fear of losing. They've a lot to lose — let's face it — if this did become a united Ireland. They own the best land. For hundreds and hundreds of years, all the best farming land is owned by Protestants. They've got the best jobs, so they have a helluva lot to lose. And that's why they can be vicious.

People years ago used to hide it all from their children. You weren't allowed to mention Protestants or Catholics. If someone said Protestant, you'd go, "Where did you hear that? What's a Protestant?" But now, I want my children . . . I mean, I — they can't understand, they think — My two children went with my mother last Sunday down to the big march for the ninth of August. Well, there were colorful bands and everything, and my children said to my mother, "Granny, are they the Protestants?" They still don't really understand.

They have a fear of soldiers and big armored cars, because they have seen rioting on television. But they think the police are doing it to the people; they don't understand that they're fighting back, that the people are retaliating with bricks and bottles. They think it's the soldiers, and they're wary of them.

My daughter was lost one time about two years ago, and I couldn't   40
see her and I couldn't think straight, all these masses of people in the town. I mean, you could tell on my face, I just couldn't think of where she'd gone. You know, you think someone's snatched her. . . .

This woman seen my face; I looked so really anxious. She said, "Have you lost a little girl?" and I said, "Yes." She said, "She's up there; a policeman has her." And I thought, thank God the policeman has her. And here he was carrying her and she was trying to get away from him and he said to me, "She wouldn't tell me her name." And I says to her, "My little one, why did you not tell the policeman your name?" She said, "I thought he was going to shoot me with a plastic bullet." She was only three or four. And that there brought it home to me; it's a terrible situation that we're living in here.

I just feel that I'm a puppet in between all these politicians, organizations. I am completely disillusioned with the whole thing, to be quite honest. I haven't got faith in their word. That's the way I think, and that's why I don't like living in Belfast anymore. I hate it, absolutely hate it. How can people be so stupid?

About eleven years ago, I lived in London; (laughs) this sounds like a fairy story! I was in a restaurant on Carnaby Street and an Arab came in. I didn't know he was very wealthy at the time.

And he couldn't speak good English and he asked could I order him   44
a meal, and I ordered for him what I was eating. And he was very grateful, and he asked would I go out with him. But I was a bit wary, and I said, "No; I'm going back to Belfast shortly; there would be no point." And he asked for my address in Belfast, and I give it to him and he sent a postcard from Italy.

I was feeling a bit depressed here about the beginning of last year, and I discovered the postcard and I said, "I think I'll write this guy and see if he's still alive" — I mean, this was after eleven, twelve years.

I was sitting here one night and the phone rang and he phoned me from Saudi Arabia! I have been keeping in contact with him ever since, and he said to me on the phone last week — I wrote and I told him about Belfast, about the lack of employment and what it was like — and he phoned me back and he says, "How's Belfast? Is it cold there?", and I says, "It's absolutely freezing!"

He said to me at one stage on the phone, "Betty (imitates his accent), is there anything you want! Is there anything you need?" And I thought,

"My God (laughs), I could use a lot of things," but I didn't say it — put him off!

But he said to me — he must be a bit stupid, you know — "You want   48 to come to Arabia, I find you work. What would you like to work?" (laughs)

I don't know, and people keep saying to me, "God that's your meal ticket out of here!" This is the way you come to think, you know? So I think to meself, "God, I'm gonna stick with this guy. He might get me out of here."

But it really is strange, and I think, wouldn't it be wonderful and . . . Oh, I don't know . . . I'm just waiting for another letter.

I mean, am I going to die in this place?

EXPLORATIONS

1. What does each of the three people interviewed by the Andersons believe the conflict in Northern Ireland is about? Cite statements by the RUC policeman, Emma Groves, and "Betty" regarding the nature or purpose or both of The Troubles.

2. What is each interviewee's greatest personal concern about The Troubles? What emotions does each person express about her or his greatest concern?

3. Who are the "good guys" and "bad guys" in The Troubles from the viewpoint of the RUC policeman? from the viewpoint of Emma Groves? from the viewpoint of "Betty"? What role does each of them see himself or herself playing in the conflict?

CONNECTIONS

1. What violent acts committed by the Republicans and Loyalists in "The Troubles" are similar to acts committed by the Chinese protesters and soldiers in John Simpson's "Tiananmen Square"? What purposes and attitudes do the Irish share with the Chinese? What are some possible reasons for the parallels?

2. Like Maria and Ileana in Shelley Saywell's "Women Warriors of El Salvador," the RUC policman, Emma Groves, and "Betty" are all parents. How do their children influence their beliefs and actions? How are their children used as weapons by their opponents?

3. Having read "The Troubles," look back at Nik Cohn's "Delinquent in Derry" (p. 201). At what points and in what ways did The Troubles shape or affect Cohn's boyhood?

ELABORATIONS

1. Using these three interviews as sources, write an expository essay on The Troubles comparing and contrasting the IRA/Republican/Catholic and the RUC/Loyalist/Protestant goals and policies.

2. In *Looking at Ourselves*, Barbara Ehrenreich describes a type of man who lives for war, "accepts no peace, and always seeks, in the ashes of the last battle, the sparks that might ignite the next." How does her definition of the "Warrior Caste" apply to the Irish combatants in "The Troubles"? or the Chinese in Simpson's "Tiananmen Square"? or the Salvadorans in Saywell's "Women Warriors of El Salvador"? Write an essay defining the "Warrior Caste" as it appears in one or all of these societies.

3. Go through each interview in "The Troubles" and list the speaker's positive and negative opinions about the IRA/Republicans/Catholics and the RUC/Loyalists/Protestants. Who is the most biased? Who tries the hardest to be fair? Choosing one interviewee as your subject, write an essay evaluating her or his position on the basis of your judgment and statements made by the other two.

RIAN MALAN

Msinga

A member of a powerful South African Boer family that included a prime minister, the chief architect of apartheid, and the current defense minister, Rian Malan was born into a privileged but troubled world. When he was growing up in the white suburbs, Malan says terror had a black face — was in every rattle of the window. In 1977 he escaped this South Africa and the draft and came to America. Living as an exile and a nomad for eight years, he worked as a journalist for the *LA Weekly, Los Angeles Herald Examiner,* and *Esquire* magazine. He returned to South Africa because he missed the "battle against the howling moral head winds." There he encountered the bloody opposition to President Botha's reforms that had affected Asians and Coloureds but excluded blacks. Thousands were killed and thousands more wounded. Malan, once a crime reporter in Johannesburg, turned his investigation inward to write *My Traitor's Heart* (1989). This autobiographical book explores the contradictions and anguish a white man experiences in a black land. Malan now lives in Los Angeles, where he continues to write. "Msinga" was originally published in *Granta: New World* (Winter 1989).

Msinga lies north of the Indian Ocean port of Durban in eastern South Africa. It is part of a coastal plain settled more than a thousand years ago by Zulus from central Africa.

(For more background on South Africa, see pp. 34 and 578.)

Msinga is . . . Oh, God, how do I explain Msinga? Msinga is wild and yet it is not leaping with buck and lions. There is probably not a single antelope left alive in the entire valley. The district is criss-crossed by tar roads and power lines, packed with tin-roofed shanties and mud huts. It is a place of head-spinning contrasts. In Msinga, you see black men driving goats and black men driving BMWs. You see Zulu women going down on all fours at the feet of nondescript old men in ill-fitting three-piece suits; they are tribal chiefs or headmen and must be shown respect. You see bare-breasted Zulu maidens with shaved heads and bodies draped with beads. They seem to have stepped out of *National Geographic*, but if you look closer you see that they're wearing Day-Glo leg-warmers and running shoes. You see men in traditional dress carrying briefcases through the bush, and school-uniformed teenagers dancing through the wastelands with ghetto-blasters on their shoulders. So Msinga isn't quaint and it's not storybook Africa. It is a sprawling rural slum, infested with dope-smugglers, gun-runners, and bandits. It is the Iron Age shat squalling and sullen into the twentieth century. Its people look broken as they eat the dust of your passing car, but in their hearts they are proud and untamed and utterly ungovernable by anyone.

It's easy to blame the apartheid regime for Msinga's misery, but Nelson Mandela or Fidel Castro might not have done any better. The district capital, Tugela Ferry, is an indescribably forlorn and dusty little hamlet on the banks of the Tugela River. From its rooftops, you look out over a broad flood-plain. A network of gravity canals comes snaking out down the distant hills and fans out across the plain. These canals draw irrigation water from the Tugela eight miles upstream, carry it across the plain, past the town, and finally return it to the river — unused. There are hundreds of hectares of rich, irrigable land there, enough land to render Msinga agriculturally self-sufficient if it were farmed intensively. But much of it isn't farmed at all. It has lain fallow almost constantly since 1928, its ownership a matter of dispute between subtribes of the Zulu nation. A Thembu who sinks a plowshare into that plain will surely be killed by the Mabaso, and vice versa.

Even the kwaZulu government, a neutral party, cannot use this land. A few years ago, the government assumed direct control of part of the irrigation scheme and invited tribesmen to farm it under government supervision. An official involved in the project was assassinated. After that, kwaZula formed a cash-crop consortium with some white farmers and planted strawberries on the disputed land. When the first crop was ripe, someone opened the gates and drove hundreds of cattle and donkeys into the strawberry fields. The consortium disintegrated. The government gave up. The land lay fallow and the people of Msinga stayed hungry.

So the Thembu and Mabaso are hostile towards one another, but that is only the first order of battle in Msinga. The Zulu nation consists of 250 such subtribes, seven of which call Msinga home. Those seven subtribes are in turn divided into dozens of subgroups called *isigodi*, each 3,000 to 5,000 strong. An *isigodi* is a neighborhood, for lack of a better word. This hill is Mashunka, the valley beyond Ngubo. The land to this side of that dry watercourse is Ndlela; the land beyond is Mhlangaan. It takes a Msinga man to know the borders between these *isigodi*, and the consequences that await if he crosses them in wartime. There is nothing to distinguish the people on one side from those on the other. They speak the same language, belong to the same nation, suffer the same deprivations. And yet, every now and then, they fight bloody wars against one another.

Why? It's hard to say. There are several theories, but in the end I preferred the word of an old white policeman who said he didn't really know.

Warrant-Officer Jurgen Freese was a crusty old militarist who lived in a firearm-squad camp on the outskirts of Tugela Ferry. His superiors posted him to Msinga in 1956 and he'd been there ever since. In 1956, there were few roads in Msinga and police still patrolled the valley on horseback. The district was administered by old Africa hands, portly colonials with handlebar mustaches, pith helmets, and hides blackened by decades in the sun. The whites played tennis on an old clay court, swam in a pool, and sipped pink gins at sunset on the verandas of quaint colonial bungalows. Tugela Ferry was a lost outpost of the dying British Empire.

Jurgen Freese's mission in Msinga was to stamp out the gun trade and combat "faction fighting," the official term for Msinga's fratricidal wars. In the 1950s, Msinga's wars were honorable, manly affairs, fought under the sun on open plains by half-naked warriors. The death toll was light, and the whole thing was over quickly, usually in a single day. If a man fell in battle, every warrior in the opposing *impi* would stab a blade into his corpse, a traditional Zulu battle ritual.

Such killings were not regarded as murder by the white authorities. They were treated as tribal offenses and tried under African law. Whenever someone died in a faction fight, Freese would mount his horse and visit the chief in whose territory the killing had taken place. He would say: "Listen, you fellows know you're not supposed to do this. Now I want the names of those involved." The chief and his headmen would confer with the warring parties. Some warriors were appointed to be the accused, others to give evidence. Such decisions were based less on guilt than on a man's ability to pay a fine. On the appointed day, all the warriors would appear before the white magistrate in the courthouse at Tugela Ferry. Everyone understood that the trial was essentially a farce, a ritual designed to preserve the white man's face and honor. The witnesses told a yarn, the accused tried to look contrite, the magistrate handed down a few two-pound fines, and it was all over.

In the early days, Freese's firearm squad seized the occasional sidearm or hunting rifle, but Msinga's wars were mostly fought with spears and homemade blunderbusses crafted from spare parts and plumbing supplies. As Msinga's migrant laborers were integrated into the white cash economy, however, more and more guns started coming into the district. Battles fought with guns fell outside the legal definition of faction fighting, so warriors who took part in them were charged with murder and tried under white law. "I suppose the change was well meant," said Freese, "but I don't know that it was a good thing." Once white law started superseding traditional Zulu law, there was virtually no law in Msinga at all.

Msinga's warriors saw little wrong in these killings, you see. They saw no reason why a man who slew an enemy in honorable battle should be taken away and hanged by the white man, so they stopped cooperating with the police. It became hard to find witnesses. Freese's cozy arrangement with the chiefs gave way to elaborate trials in white courts, where white judges followed white evidentiary rules and white lawyers found it easy to confuse and discredit illiterate witnesses. The state case inevitably fell apart in a welter of contradictions and the accused went unpunished in those rare cases where they were charged at all.

It was hard to say how many murderers there were in Msinga, or how many victims they had claimed, because nobody was really counting. Suffice to say Msinga's murder rate was ten to twenty times higher than New York's and its conviction rate so low that it was impossible to measure. It was once the practice to post photographs of executed killers on the wall of Tugela Ferry's courthouse. To the best of anyone's recollection, the last time this happened was in 1964.

In the seventies, Msinga's warfare underwent a further evolution, 12 driven this time by soaring sales of the district's chief cash crop, marijuana. Msinga suddenly had money with which to cut big deals on the underground arms market. It was illegal for South African blacks to own guns, but Msinga scoffed at the white man's laws. The latest South African automatic rifles were going into use in Msinga before the South African Defence Force got to test them in combat in Angola. Soviet AK-47s smuggled into the country by brave revolutionaries were sold for beer money on the black market and wound up in the hands of rival factions in the hills above Tugela Ferry.

Msinga's armies dressed to kill in army-surplus combat fatigues and carried deadly modern weaponry, but their campaigns remained curiously archaic. Leaders sought strategic advantage in witchcraft and most soldiers' marksmanship was erratic. They were reluctant to squint down the sights of a rifle in the heat of battle, believing that the spirit of a warrior who died with closed eyes was likely to remain trapped inside his body. So they shot from the hip instead. In 1978, the Sithole hired a white mercenary sharpshooter to aid them in a war against the Zwane and a great slaughter ensued. The sharpshooter decimated the front ranks of the Zwane army, which broke and ran. At day's end, there were fifty-six bodies strewn across the plain. Such battles were rare, though. Msinga's wars were mostly furtive hit-and-run affairs. Combatants were ambushed on lonely footpaths, shot in their huts at night, pulled off buses at roadblocks and executed. Wars that were once over in a day now dragged on for months or even years, unreported even in the South African press. There was always fighting in Msinga, and always had been. In 1978, black officials of the kwaZulu government took over the district's administration and most whites left Tugela Ferry. The tennis-court disappeared under weeds and the swimming pool was filled with rubble. Only Jurgen Freese stayed on, alone in his Quonset hut on the river bank, with flies buzzing around his head and sweat trickling down his back. His job was impossible. For every gun his squad seized, another came in and there were more corpses to account for. In the end, Msinga turned the man into a Graham Greene character. There was a time when he spent most of his day on his back in his hut, contemplating hell through the bottom of a brandy bottle.

After twenty-seven years in purgatory, Freese retired to the suburbs and quit drinking. Msinga was an intoxicant in its own right, though. He found it hard to readjust to normal life and the South African Police found it equally hard to do without him. And so, when the force asked, Freese returned to Msinga to resume his weary struggle. I found him sitting behind a desk in a prefabricated hut, surrounded by squawking radios and maps festooned with colored pins and pennants, each marking the site of a trouble-spot. Over a cup of tea, he told me that he had learned a great deal about Msinga in thirty years — enough to know that he knew virtually nothing. "You will never find out why a war starts," he said, "and once it has started, you will never stop it."

I asked why, and the old policeman shrugged. "The Zulu is a brave man," he said. "You and I would not go into something looking to be killed, but a Zulu will, if honor demands it. To him, death is of no particular concern. An ox is killed; it's eaten. A man gets killed, and his brothers look after his wives and children. That's it. It's no big thing. If we go out to stop a war, the men know we are coming. They watch us with binoculars watching them with binoculars. So we see no guns, but they're there, hidden within a few hundred feet. They are waiting for us to pass. Once we're gone, they collect the guns and start fighting again. We have postponed some wars by arriving, but we've never stopped one. Not ever yet."

When war was brewing, the police were tipped off by a spy in the 16 dusty post office across the river. The spy knew trouble was coming when women started drifting in to send telegrams to their husbands, fathers, and brothers in the cities. All the telegrams contained a similar message: "There has been a death in the family. Come home."

Those who did not answer this veiled call to arms were expected to make cash contributions to their faction's war effort, but most men came home. You could not avoid war by staying in Soweto, Kimberley, or Pretoria. Disputes rooted in Msinga's dusty hills often bore bloody blossoms in distant white cities. In 1983 in Soweto, one such battle claimed forty-two lives, but slaughter on that scale was unique. Msinga men were more often hunted down singly by hit squads from a rival *isigodi* and killed quietly in their migrant-worker barracks. There was no escape.

So most men came home, dug up their guns, slung greatcoats over their shoulders, and headed for the hills, where they lived for the duration. They slept in the open, in the high ravines, plagued by ticks and heat in summer, freezing cold in winter. There was no respite. The war dragged on until enough blood had been shed to satisfy honor. Then the dead were buried but never forgotten. In two years, or five, or ten, the war would flare up again.

That's Msinga; that's the way it is. If you asked Msinga's warriors why they fight, they say that someone stabbed someone else's father at a beer-drink in Kimberley in 1965 and that the insult must be avenged. White academics, on the other hand, advance a theory that revolves around apartheid-induced land hunger and frustration. In Msinga, life is an appallingly grim business. Most people are hungry most of the time. There are no pipes, so women have to carry water on their heads from distant springs and streams. Even firewood is a luxury. In 1975, there was only one school in Msinga and one high-school graduate. Eighty-three percent of the populace was illiterate. Msinga's population density is 101 per square kilometer, versus 14 per square kilometer in white South Africa. About 80 percent of Msinga's people have too little land from which to feed themselves.

It makes complete sense that anyone trapped in such a shithole should 20 want to take up arms and fight. All that's odd about Msinga's wars is that Zulus kill one another, instead of joining forces and wiping out the whites across the border.

EXPLORATIONS

1. How and why did the availability of modern guns change the nature of tribal warfare in Msinga?

2. What possible causes does Malan give for the continual fighting in Msinga? If you had the authority and the budget to make changes in the region, what steps would you try to stop the warfare?

3. What sources of information for this essay does Malan identify? What other sources does he appear to have used?

CONNECTIONS

1. What similarities do you notice between the tribal warfare in Msinga and the fighting in Northern Ireland as described by Jon Lee Anderson and Scott Anderson in "The Troubles"? What are the main differences? Which conflict has more chance of being brought to an end, and why?

2. According to Malan, how do Zulu warriors define revenge? According to Roger Rosenblatt in "Children of Cambodia," how do the Khmer define revenge? What attitudes and experiences do you think may account for the difference?

3. Reread Nelson Mandela's "The African National Congress" (p. 578). What advice would you expect Mandela to give the people of Msinga?

ELABORATIONS

1. "Msinga," Mandela's "The African National Congress" (p. 578), Nadine Gordimer's "Africa Emergent" (p. 564), and Ezekiel Mphahlele's "Tradition and the African Writer" (p. 34) all focus on current problems arising from a colonial past. After reading the Andersons' "The Troubles" and other selections in Part Seven, what do you think are the key factors behind the present conflicts in South Africa? How important is race, for instance, in comparison with religion, social customs, and cultural values? Write a cause-and-effect or argumentative essay analyzing the reasons for the violent mistrust between groups in South Africa today.

2. In *Looking at Ourselves*, President Harry S Truman notes that he expects Japan to surrender even before the Soviet Union joins the Allies in Asia near the end of World War II. Given that expectation, why do you think Truman dropped the atomic bomb on Hiroshima shortly before the USSR entered the

war? Malan states that "faction fighting" in Msinga was brief and produced few casualties until the 1970s. Why do you think the warring tribes put their new income into high-powered modern weapons? In each case, what was state-of-the-art military technology intended to accomplish? What were its actual results? Write a comparison-contrast or cause-and-effect essay answering these questions.

CHINUA ACHEBE

Civil Peace

One of the foremost contemporary African writers, Chinua Achebe was born in Ogidi, Nigeria, in 1930. After receiving his bachelor's degree from University College in Ibadan, he went to work for the Nigerian Broadcasting Company as a producer and later director. Meanwhile, he published the widely acclaimed *Things Fall Apart* (1959). The novel depicts Achebe's Ibo (or Igbo) tribe in the late 1880s, just before Nigeria — a center for Portuguese and British slave traders since the 1500s — became a British colony. His next novel, *No Longer at Ease,* examines the clash between an Ibo upbringing and a Western education and life-style; it appeared in 1960, the year Nigeria became an independent entity within the British Commonwealth. Achebe turned to writing essays and poetry and joined the University of Nigeria, Nsukka, as a senior research fellow in 1966. The following year Eastern Nigeria, his tribal homeland, proclaimed itself the Republic of Biafra. Civil war followed, with casualties of over a million — including many Biafrans (mostly Ibos) who starved despite international relief efforts. In 1970 the secessionists capitulated. Achebe, who had been active on Biafra's side, began editing *Okike: An African Journal of New Writing* the next year. "Civil Peace" takes place during that postwar period; it first appeared in *Okike 2.* Since then Achebe has taught at the universities of Massachusetts and Connecticut; published essays, poetry, stories, and children's literature; and won a number of international awards and honorary degrees. His long-awaited fifth novel, *Anthills of the Savannah,* appeared in 1987.

(For more background on Nigeria, see p. 154.)

Jonathan Iwegbu counted himself extraordinarily lucky. "Happy survival!" meant so much more to him than just a current fashion of greeting old friends in the first hazy days of peace. It went deep to his heart. He had come out of the war with five inestimable blessings — his head, his wife Maria's head, and the heads of three out of their four children. As a bonus he also had his old bicycle — a miracle too but naturally not to be compared to the safety of five human heads.

The bicycle had a little history of its own. One day at the height of the war it was commandeered "for urgent military action." Hard as its loss would have been to him he would still have let it go without a thought had he not had some doubts about the genuineness of the officer.

It wasn't his disreputable rags, nor the toes peeping out of one blue and one brown canvas shoe, nor yet the two stars of his rank done obviously in a hurry in biro [ballpoint] that troubled Jonathan; many good and heroic soldiers looked the same or worse. It was rather a certain lack of grip and firmness in his manner. So Jonathan, suspecting he might be amenable to influence, rummaged in his raffia bag and produced the two pounds with which he had been going to buy firewood which his wife, Maria, retailed to camp officials for extra stockfish and cornmeal, and got his bicycle back. That night he buried it in the little clearing in the bush where the dead of the camp, including his own youngest son, were buried. When he dug it up again a year later after the surrender all it needed was a little palm-oil greasing. "Nothing puzzles God," he said in wonder.

He put it to immediate use as a taxi and accumulated a small pile of Biafran money ferrying camp officials and their families across the four-mile stretch to the nearest tarred road. His standard charge per trip was six pounds and those who had the money were only glad to be rid of some of it in this way. At the end of a fortnight he had made a small fortune of one hundred and fifteen pounds.

Then he made the journey to Enugu and found another miracle   4
waiting for him. It was unbelievable. He rubbed his eyes and looked again and it was still standing there before him. But, needless to say, even that monumental blessing must be accounted also totally inferior to the five heads in the family. This newest miracle was his little house in Ogui Overside. Indeed nothing puzzles God! Only two houses away a huge concrete edifice some wealthy contractor had put up just before the war was a mountain of rubble. And here was Jonathan's little zinc house of no regrets built with mud blocks quite intact! Of course the doors and windows were missing and five sheets off the roof. But what was that? And anyhow he had returned to Enugu early enough to pick up bits of old zinc and wood and soggy sheets of cardboard lying around the neighborhood before thousands more came out of their forest holes looking for the same things. He got a destitute carpenter with one old hammer, a blunt plane, and a few bent and rusty nails in his tool bag to turn this assortment of wood, paper, and metal into door and window shutters for five Nigerian shillings or fifty Biafran pounds. He paid the pounds, and moved in with his overjoyed family carrying five heads on their shoulders.

His children picked mangoes near the military cemetery and sold them to soldiers' wives for a few pennies — real pennies this time — and his wife started making breakfast akara balls for neighbors in a hurry to start life again. With his family earnings he took his bicycle to the villages around and bought fresh palm wine which he mixed generously in his rooms with the water which had recently started running again in the public tap down the road, and opened up a bar for soldiers and other lucky people with good money.

At first he went daily, then every other day, and finally once a week, to the offices of the Coal Corporation where he used to be a miner, to find out what was what. The only thing he did find out in the end was that that little house of his was even a greater blessing than he had thought. Some of his fellow ex-miners who had nowhere to return at the end of the day's waiting just slept outside the doors of the offices and cooked what meal they could scrounge together in Bournvita tins. As the weeks lengthened and still nobody could say what was what Jonathan discontinued his weekly visits altogether and faced his palm-wine bar.

But nothing puzzles God. Came the day of the windfall when after five days of endless scuffles in queues and counterqueues in the sun outside the Treasury he had twenty pounds counted into his palms as ex-gratia award for the rebel money he had turned in. It was like Christmas for him and for many others like him when the payments began. They called it (since few could manage its proper official name) *egg-rasher.*

As soon as the pound notes were placed in his palm Jonathan simply   8
closed it tight over them and buried fist and money inside his trouser pocket. He had to be extra careful because he had seen a man a couple of days earlier collapse into near-madness in an instant before that oceanic crowd because no sooner had he got his twenty pounds than some heartless ruffian picked it off him. Though it was not right that a man in such an extremity of agony should be blamed yet many in the queues that day were able to remark quietly at the victim's carelessness, especially after he pulled out the innards of his pocket and revealed a hole in it big enough to pass a thief's head. But of course he had insisted that the money had been in the other pocket, pulling it out too to show its comparative wholeness. So one had to be careful.

Jonathan soon transferred the money to his left hand and pocket so as to leave his right free for shaking hands should the need arise, though by fixing his gaze at such an elevation as to miss all approaching human faces he made sure that the need did not arise, until he got home.

He was normally a heavy sleeper but that night he heard all the neighborhood noises die down one after another. Even the night watchman who knocked the hour on some metal somewhere in the distance had fallen silent after knocking one o'clock. That must have been the last thought in Jonathan's mind before he was finally carried away himself. He couldn't have been gone for long, though, when he was violently awakened again.

"Who is knocking?" whispered his wife lying beside him on the floor.

"I don't know," he whispered back breathlessly.   12

The second time the knocking came it was so loud and imperious that the rickety old door could have fallen down.

"Who is knocking?" he asked them, his voice parched and trembling.

"Na tief-man and him people," came the cool reply. "Make you hopen de door." This was followed by the heaviest knocking of all.

Maria was the first to raise the alarm, then he followed and all their   16
children.

"*Police-o! Thieves-o! Neighbors-o! Police-o! We are lost! We are dead! Neighbors, are you asleep? Wake up! Police-o!*"

"You done finish?" asked the voice outside. "Make we help you small. Oya, everybody!"

"*Police-o! Tief-man-so! Neighbors-o! we done loss-o! Police-o! . . .*"

There were at least five other voices besides the leader's.   20

Jonathan and his family were now completely paralyzed by terror. Maria and the children sobbed inaudibly like lost souls. Jonathan groaned continuously.

The silence that followed the thieves' alarm vibrated horribly. Jonathan all but begged their leader to speak again and be done with it.

"My frien," said he at long last, "we don try our best for call dem but I tink say dem all done sleep-o . . . So wetin we go do now? Sometaim you wan call soja? Or you wan make we call dem for you? Soja better pass police. No be so?"

"Na so!" replied his men. Jonathan thought he heard even more voices   24
now than before and groaned heavily. His legs were sagging under him and his throat felt like sandpaper.

"My frien, why you no de talk again. I de ask you say you wan make we call soja?"

"No."

"Awrighto. Now make we talk business. We no be bad tief. We no like for make trouble. Trouble done finish. War done finish and all the katakata wey de for inside. No Civil War again. This time na Civil Peace. No be so?"

"Na so!" answered the horrible chorus.   28

"What do you want from me? I am a poor man. Everything I had went with this war. Why do you come to me? You know people who have money. We . . ."

"Awright! We know say you no get plenty money. But we sef no get even anini. So derefore make you open dis window and give us one hundred pound and we go commot. Orderwise we de come for inside now to show you guitar-boy like dis . . ."

A volley of automatic fire rang through the sky. Maria and the children began to weep aloud again.

"Ah, missisi de cry again. No need for dat. We done talk say we na   32 good tief. We just take our small money and go nwayorly. No molest. Abi we de molest?"

"At all!" sang the chorus.

"My friends," began Jonathan hoarsely. "I hear what you say and I thank you. If I had one hundred pounds . . ."

"Lookia my frien, no be play we come play for your house. If we make mistake and step for inside you no go like am-o. So derefore . . ."

"To God who made me; if you come inside and find one hundred   36 pounds, take and shoot me and shoot my wife and children. I swear to God. The only money I have in this life is this twenty-pounds *egg-rasher* they gave me today . . ."

"OK. Time de go. Make you open dis window and bring the twenty pound. We go manage am like dat."

There were now loud murmurs of dissent among the chorus: "Na lie de man de lie; e get plenty money . . . Make we go inside and search properly well . . . Wetin be twenty pound? . . ."

"Shurrup!" rang the leader's voice like a lone shot in the sky and silenced the murmuring at once. "Are you dere? Bring the money quick!"

"I am coming," said Jonathan fumbling in the darkness with the key   40 of the small wooden box he kept by his side on the mat.

At the first sign of light as neighbors and others assembled to commiserate with him he was already strapping his five-gallon demijohn to his bicycle carrier and his wife, sweating in the open fire, was turning over akara balls in a wide clay bowl of boiling oil. In the corner his eldest son was rinsing out dregs of yesterday's palm wine from old beer bottles.

"I count it as nothing," he told his sympathizers, his eyes on the rope he was trying. "What is *egg-rasher*? Did I depend on it last week? Or is it greater than other things that went with the war? I say, let *egg-rasher* perish in the flames! Let it go where everything else has gone. Nothing puzzles God."

EXPLORATIONS

1. Why does Jonathan Iwegbu count himself extraordinarily lucky? What does his definition of luck say about the condition of other Biafrans? Who seems to have come out on top in this war, and who has come out on the bottom?

2. What has been the war's effect on currency? What kind of money is most plentiful in Biafra? What kind is most valuable?

3. Where does the name *egg-rasher* come from? How does Iwegbu's *egg-rasher* embody the theme of "Civil Peace"? Why is this an appropriate title for the story, and for the situation in Biafra when the story takes place?

CONNECTIONS

1. What attitude toward the war around them is shared by Jonathan Iwegbu in "Civil Peace" and Jurgen Freese in Rian Malan's "Msinga"? What experience do these characters have in common that shapes their attitude?

2. "Which world is 'natural'?" asks Czeslaw Milosz. "That which existed before, or the world of war?" Look closely at Milosz's examples of how war changes human perceptions, and at Achebe's examples. What changes noted in "American Ignorance of War" are illustrated in "Civil Peace"?

3. Wole Soyinka's "Nigerian Childhood" (p. 154) is a vivid example of the blend of Western and African traditions described by Ezekiel Mphahlele in "Tradition and the African Writer" (p. 34). How does Achebe — also writing about Nigeria — portray that dual heritage? What items in "Civil Peace" represent native African tradition? What items represent British colonial tradition?

ELABORATIONS

1. What does Jonathan Iwegbu mean by "Nothing puzzles God"? Write an essay explaining this expression's significance in "Civil Peace" by examining the specific contexts in which Iwegbu uses it, as well as the story as a whole.

2. The saying "Necessity is the mother of invention" is amply borne out during a war. Using "Civil Peace," Shelley Saywell's "Women Warriors of El Salvador," and other selections from Part Seven as sources, write an essay illustrating human ingenuity under wartime and postwar stress.

APPENDIX

The European Community (EC)
The North Atlantic Treaty Organization (NATO)
The Warsaw Pact

EUROPEAN COMMUNITY

The European Community (EC) is the collective name for the older European Economic Community (Common Market), European Coal and Steel Community, and European Atomic Energy Community. The EC comprises Belgium, Denmark, France, Germany, Greece, Ireland, Italy, Luxembourg, the Netherlands, Portugal, Spain, and the United Kingdom. Some sixty nations in Africa, the Caribbean, and the Pacific are affiliated with the EC, and other nations that consider themselves part of Europe, such as Turkey and the Eastern Bloc, have indicated a desire to join. Begun as a regional economic alliance, the EC now represents a long-range plan for member nations to move toward economic and political unity. Acting cooperatively has decreased friction and red tape within Europe and increased members' political and economic clout in relation to other nations and alliances. To gain these advantages, member countries have had to yield some individual sovereignty and in several cases ally themselves with ancient rivals.

The EC was born in 1952, when Belgium, France, Italy, Luxembourg, the Netherlands, and West Germany established the European Coal and Steel Community to pool their coal and steel resources in a single market. This organization expanded six years later into the European Economic Community and the European Atomic Energy Community, extending these nations' common market to include all their economic activities. In 1973 the United Kingdom, Ireland, and Denmark joined, followed in 1981 by Greece and in 1986 by Spain and Portugal. With German reunification in 1990, East as well as West Germany became part of the EC. Meanwhile, in 1979, the first European Parliament was elected by direct vote in member countries — a revolutionary move for nations that had jealously preserved their individuality for centuries. That same year the European Monetary System was established for stable currency exchange.

The EC (although not its individual member countries) is currently governed by its own democratic institutions. A seventeen-member commission proposes policies and legislation and monitors compliance with EC decisions. A Council of Ministers from each member country enacts legislation. The 518-member European Parliament works cooperatively with these two groups. A Court of Justice adjudicates disputes. An Economic and Social Committee supplies proposals and policy advice. A Court of Auditors reviews spending.

In 1992 the EC plans an ambitious merger of members' economies into a single market, having a common currency and abolishing national borders, within which people, goods, capital, and services can circulate freely.

NORTH ATLANTIC-TREATY ORGANIZATION

The North Atlantic Treaty Organization (NATO) was created after World War II as an alliance to prevent or, if necessary, defend against future armed conflict. NATO's original members were the United States and Canada, Iceland, Norway, Denmark, the United Kingdom, Portugal, France, Belgium, the Netherlands, Luxembourg, and Italy. Since its founding in 1949, Greece, Turkey, West Germany, and Spain have also joined. NATO's members agreed to resolve disputes peacefully, to develop their resources to resist armed attack, to regard an attack on one as an attack on all, and to fight back if necessary. In 1967, after France withdrew from NATO's military affairs, the organization's headquarters was moved from Paris to Brussels. Greece withdrew in 1974 over a dispute with Turkey but rejoined in 1980. When Germany reunified in 1990, East Germany — formerly part of the Warsaw Pact — joined West Germany as a NATO member. With the end of the Cold War, NATO is expected to shift its emphasis from military to other arenas.

WARSAW PACT

The Warsaw Pact was the Eastern Bloc's answer to NATO. Created in 1955 as a mutual defense alliance with headquarters in Moscow, the Warsaw Pact by the mid-1980s included the Soviet Union, Bulgaria, Czechoslovakia, East Germany, Hungary, Poland, and Romania. As members began moving out of the Soviet orbit and the Cold War thawed, the Warsaw Pact lost East Germany and showed signs of becoming obsolete.

Milovan Djilas, English translation copyright © 1986 by Harcourt Brace Jovanovich, Inc., reprinted by permission of the publisher.

Gayle Early, "The Hazards of Being Male," excerpted with permission from the *Chico News & Review* (July 11, 1985).

Barbara Ehrenreich, from "Iranscam: The Real Meaning of Oliver North," *Ms.* Magazine, May 1987. Reprinted by permission of the author.

Hans Magnus Enzensberger, from *Europe, Europe* by Hans Magnus Enzensberger. English translation copyright © 1988 by Random House, Inc. Reprinted by permission of Pantheon Books, a division of Random House, Inc.

James Fallows, "A Few Pointers," by James Fallows, In *The Atlantic Monthly*, November 1989. Reprinted by permission.

Rosario Ferré, "The Writer's Kitchen," from *Lives on the Line: The Testimony of Contemporary Latin American Authors*, edited by Doris Meyer. Copyright © 1988 by The Regents of the University of California. Used by permission.

Gabriel García Márquez, "Death Constant Beyond Love" from *Collected Stories* by Gabriel García Márquez, translated by Gregory Rabassa. English language translation copyright © 1978 by Harper & Row, Publishers, Inc. Reprinted by permission of HarperCollins, Publishers.

Jill Gay, from "The Patriotic Prostitute." Reprinted by permission from *The Progressive*, 409 East Main Street, Madison, WI 53703.

George Gilder, "What Are the Consequences of Vietnam?" Copyright © 1985 by *Harper's Magazine*. All rights reserved. Reprinted from the April issue by special permission.

Ellen Goodman, "Family," from *Close to Home*. Copyright © 1979 by The Washington Post Company. Reprinted by permission of Simon & Schuster, Inc.

Mikhail Gorbachev, excerpt from *Perestroika* by Mikhail Gorbachev. Copyright © 1987 by Mikhail Gorbachev. Reprinted by permission of HarperCollins, Publishers.

Nadine Gordimer, from *Livingston's Companions* by Nadine Gordimer. Copyright © 1971 by Nadine Gordimer. Reprinted by permission of Viking Penguin, a division of Penguin Books USA, Inc.

Francine du Plessix Gray, excerpts from *Soviet Women: Walking the Tightrope* by Francine du Plessix Gray, copyright © 1990 by Francine du Plessix Gray. Used by permission of Doubleday, a division of Bantam Doubleday Dell Publishing Group, Inc.

Amy Gross, from "The Appeal of the Androgynous Man." Courtesy *Mademoiselle*. Copyright © 1976 by The Condé Nast Publications.

Gyanranjan, "Our Side of the Fence and Theirs," from *Modern Hindu Short Stories*, edited by Gordon Roadarmel, pp. 139–145. Copyright © 1972 The Regents of the University of California. Used by permission.

Edward T. Hall, excerpts from *The Hidden Dimension* by Edward T. Hall, copyright © 1966, 1982 by Edward T. Hall. Used by permission of Doubleday, a division of Bantam Doubleday Dell Publishing Group, Inc.

Carola Hansson and Karin Lidén, Text Copyright © 1983 by Random House, Inc. Reprinted from *Moscow Women: Thirteen Interviews* by Carola Hansson and Karin Lidén by permission of Pantheon Books, a division of Random House, Inc.

Paul Harrison, "The Westernization of the World," from *Inside the Third World*. Reprinted by permission of the author.

Václav Havel, "The Chance That Will Not Return." Copyright ©, February 26, 1990, *U.S. News & World Report*. Used with permission.

Liliana Heker, "The Stolen Party." Copyright © 1982 by Liliana Heker. Translation copyright © 1985 by Alberto Manguel. Reprinted from *Other Fires: Short Fiction by Latin American Women* by Alberto Manguel by permission of Clarkson N. Potter, Inc., and the copyright holder.

Arlie Hochschild with Anne Machung, from *Second Shift* by Arlie Hochschild with Anne

Machung. Copyright © 1989 by Arlie Hochschild. Reprinted by permission of Viking Penguin, a division of Penguin Books USA, Inc.

Langston Hughes, "Salvation" from *The Big Sea* by Langston Hughes. Copyright © 1940 by Langston Hughes. Renewal copyright © 1968 by Arna Bontemps and George Houston Bass. Reprinted by permission of Hill & Wang, a division of Farrar, Straus and Giroux, Inc.

Joe Kane, from "Star Wars." *Ms.* Magazine, Sept. 1985. Reprinted by permission of the author.

Yashar Kemal, "A Dirty Story," from *Anatolian Tales*. Reprinted by permission of the publisher, Collins Harvill.

Carol Kleiman, from "My Home Isn't Broken—It Works." *Ms.* Magazine, November 1984. Reprinted by permission of the author.

Jane Kramer, from "The Perils of Perestroika," *The New Yorker*, March 12, 1990, pp. 82–86. Copyright © 1990 by Jane Kramer. First published by *The New Yorker*.

Lewis Lapham, "A Political Opiate." Copyright © 1989 by *Harper's Magazine*. All rights reserved. Reprinted from the December issue by special permission.

Liang Heng and Judith Shapiro, from *Son of the Revolution* by Liang Heng and Judith Shapiro. Copyright © 1983 by Liang Heng and Judith Shapiro. Reprinted by permission of Alfred A. Knopf, Inc.

Elliot Liebow, from *Tally's Corner: A Study of Negro Streetcorner Men* by Elliot Liebow. Copyright © 1967 by Little, Brown and Company (Inc).

Cherry Lindholm and Charles Lindholm, "Life Behind the Veil," as published in *Science Digest*, Summer 1980. Reprinted by permission of the authors.

Sophronia Liu, "So Tsi-fai." Originally appeared in *Hurricane Alice*, Vol. 2, No. 4 (Fall 1986). Copyright © 1986 by Sophronia Liu. Reprinted by permission of the author.

Rian Malan, from the book *My Traitor's Heart*, copyright © 1990 by Rian Malan. Used by permission of Atlantic Monthly Press.

Nelson Mandela, from *No Easy Walk to Freedom*, published by Heinemann International Publishers Ltd. Reprinted by permission.

Geoffrey Matthews, " 'Good Sons' Who Kill," *The Times*, London, November 1989, © Times Newspapers Ltd. 1989. Reprinted by permission.

Ved Mehta, reprinted from *The Ledge Between the Streams* by Ved Mehta, by permission of W. W. Norton & Company, Inc. Copyright © 1982, 1983, 1984 by Ved Mehta.

Czeslaw Milosz, Copyright 1951, 1953 by Czeslaw Milosz. Reprinted by permission of Alfred A. Knopf, Inc.

Naila Minai, "Women in Early Islam," from *Women in Islam*. Seaview Books, 1981.

Alberto Moravia, "The Chase" from *Command and I Will Obey You* by Alberto Moravia. English translation copyright © 1969 by Martin Secker & Warburg Limited. Reprinted by permission of Farrar, Straus and Giroux, Inc.

John David Morley, from the book, *Pictures from the Water Trade: Adventures of a Westerner in Japan* by John David Morley. Copyright © 1985 by John David Morley. Used by permission of Atlantic Monthly Press.

Ezekiel Mphahlele, "African Literature: What Tradition?" retitled "Tradition and the African Writer" from *Voices in the Whirlwind and Other Essays* by Ezekiel Mphahlele. Copyright © 1972 by Ezekiel Mphahlele. Reprinted by permission of Hill & Wang, a division of Farrar, Straus and Giroux, Inc.

Vladimir Nabokov, excerpt from "Good Writers and Good Readers" in *Lectures on Literature*. Copyright © 1980 by the Estate of Vladimir Nabokov; reprinted by permission of Harcourt Brace Jovanovich, Inc.

Shiva Naipaul, "The Palmers," from *North of South: An African Journey*. Copyright © 1979 by Shiva Naipaul. Reprinted by permission of Simon & Schuster, Inc.

V. S. Naipaul, from *Finding the Center: Two Narratives* by V. S. Naipaul. Copyright © 1984 by V. S. Naipaul. reprinted by permission of Alfred A. Knopf, Inc., and Aitken & Stone Ltd.

R. K. Narayan, from *Malgudi Days* by R. K. Narayan. Copyright © 1972, 1975, 1978, 1980, 1981, 1982 by R. K. Narayan. Reprinted by permission of Viking Penguin, a division of Penguin Books USA, Inc.

Pablo Neruda, excerpt from "Lost in the City" from *Memoirs* by Pablo Neruda, translated by Hardie St. Martin. Translation copyright © 1976, 1977 by Farrar, Straus and Giroux, Inc. Reprinted by permission of Farrar, Straus and Giroux, Inc.

Michele L. Norris, from "Growing Up in a World of Crack—Dooney Water's life was a struggle to survive," *The Washington Post National Weekly Edition*, September 11–17, 1989, p. 6. Reprinted by permission.

"Notes and Comments" from The Talk of the Town section of *The New Yorker*, January 8, 1990. Reprinted by permission; © 1990 The New Yorker Magazine, Inc.

Michael Novak, "The Family out of Favor," by Michael Novak. Copyright © 1976 by *Harper's Magazine*. All rights reserved. Reprinted from the April issue by special permission.

Joyce Carol Oates, from "Meeting the Gorbachevs," by Joyce Carol Oates. Reprinted by permission of the author and Blanche C. Gregory, Inc., Agent. Copyright © 1988 by The Ontario Review Press, Inc.

Amos Oz, "If There Is Justice" from *Elsewhere, Perhaps* by Amos Oz. Copyright © 1966 by Sifriat Poalim; English translation copyright © 1973 by Harcourt Brace Jovanovich, Inc. Reprinted by permission of Harcourt Brace Jovanovich, Inc.

Octavio Paz, "Hygiene and Repression," from "At Table and in Bed" in *Convergences: Essays on Art and Literature*, copyright © 1984, 1983 by Octavio Paz; copyright © 1984, 1983, 1979 by Editorial Seix Barral, S. A.; copyright © 1973 by Editorial Joaquin Mortiz, S. A.; English translation copyright © 1987 by Harcourt Brace Jovanovich, Inc.; reprinted by permission of Harcourt Brace Jovanovich, Inc.

Clara Piriz, "Marriage by Pros and Cons" by Clara Piriz, translated by Regina M. Kreger, from *You Can't Drown the Fire: Latin American Women Writing in Exile*, copyright © 1988 by Alicia Partnoy. Cleis Press, 1988. Used by permission.

Ishmael Reed, reprinted with permission of Atheneum Publishers, an imprint of Macmillan Publishing Company, from *Writin' Is Fightin'* by Ishmael Reed. Copyright © 1988 Ishmael Reed.

Richard Rodriguez, from *Hunger of Memory* by Richard Rodriguez. Copyright © 1982 by Richard Rodriguez. Reprinted by permission of David R. Godine, Publisher.

Richard Rodriguez, "Proofs." Reprinted by permission of Georges Borchardt, Inc., for the author. Copyright © 1989 by Richard Rodriguez.

Anne Roiphe, "Confessions of a Female Chauvinist Sow" by Anne Roiphe. First published in *New Yorker Magazine*. Copyright © 1972, by Anne Roiphe. Reprinted by permission of Brandt & Brandt Literary Agents, Inc.

Roger Rosenblatt, excerpts from *Children of War* by Roger Rosenblatt, copyright © 1983 by Roger Rosenblatt. Used by permission of Doubleday, a division of Bantam Doubleday Dell Publishing Group, Inc.

Gholam-Hossein Sa'edi, from *Dandil: Stories from Iranian Life*. Copyright © 1981 by Gholam-Hossein Sa'edi. Reprinted by permission of Random House, Inc.

Gholamhosein Saedi, "The Game is Over," translated by Robert A. Campbell. Copyright © 1978 by Robert A. Campbell and Gholamhosein Saedi. From *New Writing from the Middle East*, edited by Leo Hamalian and John D. Yohannan. New American Library, 1978.

Ghulamhusayn Sa'idi, "The Game Is Up," translated by Minoo S. Southgate, reprinted by permission of Three Continents Press of Washington, D.C., from its *Modern Persian Short Stories*, © 1980 by Minoo Southgate.

Mark Salzman, from *Iron and Silk* by Mark Salzman. Copyright © 1986 by Mark Salzman. Reprinted by permission of Random House, Inc.

Scott Russell Sanders, excerpt from "Looking at Women," © 1989 by Scott Russell Sanders. First published in *The Georgia Review* (Spring 1989), © 1989 by The University of Georgia. Reprinted by permission of the author and *The Georgia Review.*

Shelley Saywell, from *Women in War* by Shelley Saywell. Copyright © Shelley Saywell, 1985. Reprinted by permission of Penguin Books Canada Limited.

Peter Schneider, excerpt from "Concrete and Irony." Copyright © 1990 by Peter Schneider. Reprinted by permission of Hill and Wang, a division of Farrar, Straus and Giroux, Inc.

Jean Seligman, from "Variations on a Theme," by Jean Seligman, *Newsweek*, Special Issue, Winter/Spring 1990, p. 38. Used by permission.

Gail Sheehy, from *Passages: Predictable Crises of Adult Life* by Gail Sheehy. Copyright © 1974, 1976 by Gail Sheehy. Reprinted by permission of the publisher, Dutton, an imprint of New American Library, a division of Penguin Books USA, Inc.

Marjorie Shostak, "Nisa's Marriage," excerpted by permission of the author and publishers from *Nisa: The Life and Words of a !Kung Woman.* Cambridge, Massachusetts: Harvard University Press. Copyright © 1981 by Marjorie Shostak.

Leslie Silko, "Yellow Woman," by Leslie Silko from *The Man to Send Rain Clouds,* edited by Kenneth Rosen, copyright © 1969 by Leslie Chapman. Used by permission of Leslie Silko.

Olga Silverstein, "The Good Mother: An Interview with Olga Silverstein," *Vogue*, June 1987. Courtesy Vogue. Copyright © 1987 by The Condé Nast Publications, Inc.

John Simpson, "Tiananmen Square." This piece was first published in *Granta 28,* Autumn 1989. Copyright © 1989 by John Simpson. Reprinted by permission.

Hedrick Smith, from *The Russians* by Hedrick Smith. Copyright © 1976 by Hedrick Smith. Reprinted by permission of Times Books, a division of Random House, Inc.

Wole Soyinka, from *Aké: The Years of Childhood* by Wole Soyinka. Copyright © 1982 by Wole Soyinka. Reprinted by permission of Random House, Inc.

Gloria Steinem, from *Outrageous Acts and Everyday Rebellions* by Gloria Steinem. Copyright © 1984 by East Toledo Productions, Inc. Reprinted by permission of Henry Holt and Company, Inc.

William H. Sullivan, from "Vietnam Portents" from *Obbligato, 1939–1979, Notes on a Foreign Service Career,* by William H. Sullivan, reprinted by permission of W. W. Norton & Company, Inc. Copyright © 1984 by William H. Sullivan.

Amy Tan, reprinted by permission of The Putnam Publishing Group from *The Joy Luck Club* by Amy Tan. Copyright © 1989 by Amy Tan.

Studs Terkel, from *Working: People Talk About What They Do All Day and How They Feel About What They Do* by Studs Terkel. Copyright © 1972, 1974 by Studs Terkel. Reprinted by permission of Pantheon Books, a division of Random House, Inc.

Colin Thubron, from *Behind the Wall: A Journey Through China,* copyright © 1987 by Colin Thubron. Used by permission of Atlantic Monthly Press and William Heinemann Ltd.

John Updike, from *Trust Me* by John Updike. Copyright © 1987 by John Updike. Reprinted by permission of Alfred A. Knopf, Inc.

Mario Vargas Llosa, "On Sunday" from *The Cups and Other Stories.* English translation copyright © 1979 by Harper & Row Publishers, Inc. Reprinted by permission of Farrar, Straus and Giroux, Inc., and the translator.

Claudia Wallis, from "The Child-Care Dilemma," by Claudia Wallis. Copyright © 1987 Time Inc. Reprinted by permission.

Janine Wedel, from *Private Poland* by Janine Wedel. Copyright © 1986 by Janine Wedel. Reprinted with the permission of Facts on File, Inc., New York.

Rose Weitz, "What Price Independence? Social Reactions to Lesbians, Spinsters, Widows, and Nuns," from *Women: A Feminist Perspective,* Third Edition, edited by Jo Freeman. Copyright © 1984 by Mayfield Publishing Company. Used by permission.

Vicki Williams, from "The View from $204 a Week," as published in *Newsweek*, January 18, 1982. Reprinted by permission of the author.

GEOGRAPHICAL INDEX

AFRICA

Botswana: Nisa's Marriage (Marjorie Shostak), 272
Ivory Coast: Entering the New World (V. S. Naipaul), 47
Kenya: The Palmers (Shiva Naipaul), 405
Nigeria: Civil Peace (Chinua Achebe), 684; Nigerian Childhood (Wole Soyinka), 154
South Africa: Africa Emergent (Nadine Gordimer), 564; The African National Congress (Nelson Mandela), 578; Msinga (Rian Malan), 676; Tradition and the African Writer (Ezekiel Mphahlele), 34

ASIA

Asia (general): A Few Pointers (James Fallows), 52
Bali: Making Magic (David Abram), 425
Cambodia: Children of Cambodia (Roger Rosenblatt), 607
China: At the Beijing Zoo (Colin Thubron), 583; Chairman Mao's Good Little Boy (Liang Heng and Judith Shapiro), 93; A Few Pointers (James Fallows), 52; Gong Fu (Mark Salzman), 235; Tiananmen Square (John Simpson), 656
Hong Kong: So Tsi-fai (Sophronia Liu), 218
India: Our Side of the Fence and Theirs (Gyanranjan), 146; Pom's Engagement (Ved Mehta), 262; Trail of the Green Blazer (R. K. Narayan), 419
Indonesia: Making Magic (David Abram), 425
Japan: Acquiring a Japanese Family (John David Morley), 134; A Few Pointers (James Fallows), 52; Six Months at Toyota (Satoshi Kamata), 447
Philippines: Patriotic Prostitutes (Jill Gay), 435
South Korea: A Few Pointers (James Fallows), 52; Patriotic Prostitutes (Jill Gay), 435
Soviet Union: Liza and Family (Carola Hansson and Karin Lidén), 109; Meeting the Gorbachevs (Joyce Carol Oates), 66; The Perils of Perestroika (Jane Kramer), 507; Sex Roles in the Soviet Union (Francine du Plessix Gray), 301; *Skoro Budet* — It'll Be Here Soon (Hedrick Smith), 461; The US and the USSR (Mikhail Gorbachev), 59

INDEX OF
AUTHORS AND TITLES

SOVIET UNION

IRELAND
GERMANY   POLAND
FRANCE   CZECHOSLOVAKIA
         YUGOSLAVIA
ITALY   TURKEY
         ISRAEL   IRAN   PAKISTAN   CHINA   SOUTH KOREA
                   SAUDI ARABIA   INDIA   LAOS   TAIWAN
                                                    HONG KONG
         NIGERIA   THAILAND   VIETNAM
                                          CAMBODIA
IVORY COAST   SINGAPORE
              KENYA   INDONESIA
                        INDIAN OCEAN   BALI

ATLANTIC

OCEAN
              BOTSWANA
              SOUTH AFRICA

In the interest of visual clarity and simplicity, only countries treated in the selections are labeled on this map.